1,001 ACT® Practice Questions

for dummies®
A Wiley Brand

by Lisa Zimmer Hatch, MA
and Scott A. Hatch, JD

1,001 ACT® Practice Questions For Dummies®

Published by: **John Wiley & Sons, Inc.,** 111 River Street, Hoboken, NJ 07030-5774, www.wiley.com

For general information on our other products and services, please contact our Customer Care Department within the U.S. at 877-762-2974, outside the U.S. at 317-572-3993, or fax 317-572-4002. For technical support, please visit https://hub.wiley.com/community/support/dummies.

Wiley publishes in a variety of print and electronic formats and by print-on-demand. Some material included with standard print versions of this book may not be included in e-books or in print-on-demand. If this book refers to media such as a CD or DVD that is not included in the version you purchased, you may download this material at http://booksupport.wiley.com. For more information about Wiley products, visit www.wiley.com.

Library of Congress Control Number: 2016950158

ISBN 978-1-119-27543-5 (pbk); ISBN 978-1-119-27544-2 (ebk); ISBN 978-1-119-27545-9 (ebk)

Manufactured in the United States of America

10 9 8 7 6 5 4 3 2 1

Contents at a Glance

Table of Contents

Introduction

Welcome to *1,001 ACT Practice Questions For Dummies*. Don't take the book title personally. We certainly aren't suggesting you're a dummy. In fact, we're celebrating your overwhelmingly sage foresight in purchasing this valuable text! Putting in the time and dedication to practice for the ACT is a very wise decision indeed.

Along with your GPA and the rigor of your high school curriculum, your ACT score is a very important factor in getting into college and getting money to pay for your education. Improving your score by just a couple of points can mean gaining thousands of dollars in scholarships and financial aid. With that in mind, don't waste any time. Get practicing already!

What You'll Find

One of the best ways to maximize your exam performance (and elevate the quality of your free time, of course) is to continually expose yourself to questions that mimic the ones you'll encounter on the ACT. The practice problems in this book are divided into five chapters that correspond to the five sections on the test: English, math, reading, science, and the optional writing. We've constructed the questions to closely resemble the actual test in both format and level of difficulty so you know what to expect when you plop yourself down in front of the proctor on test day.

If you miss a question or just make a good guess, be sure to examine the answer explanations for tips on how to master your approach next time. Heck! Check out the explanations for those questions you answer correctly. Often, we reveal not only how to answer the problem but how to answer it most efficiently.

Be proactive. This book contains hundreds of questions, so after you've taken a bunch of tests and evaluated your performance, review the questions you miss and form your own explanations for why the credited answer is better than yours. Then check our explanations for confirmation. Apply your discoveries to more practice problems.

You can benefit from this book all by itself, but it's even better when you pair it with the in-depth reviews and strategies available in latest edition of *ACT For Dummies* (Wiley). Either way, this book helps you solidify your approach and confidence in all subject areas.

How This Book Is Organized

The first half of this workbook contains the practice English, math, reading, science, and writing questions. You find the answers and explanations in the second half of the book.

When you open your test booklet on exam day, the first test you see is the English. Five scintillating passages await. Each presents around 15 questions for a total of 75 questions. To maintain the pace required by the ACT, plan to spend no more than 9 minutes answering the questions for one passage. The English questions may be classified in one of two main categories: grammar and usage and rhetorical skills (a fancy way of saying knowing what makes for good writing):

- **Grammar and usage:** Included grammar concepts are punctuation, proper pronoun use, parts of speech, subject and verb agreement, verb tense, parallel structure, possessive forms, and the correct positioning of describing elements. The ACT tests your knowledge of hard and fast rules. "Controversial" grammar issues, such as whether you place a comma before the *and* at the end of the series, won't be tested.
- **Rhetorical skills:** In addition to grammar and usage, the ACT also determines what you know about the practices of good writing. Questions regarding rhetorical skills test your awareness of the need to eliminate redundant and irrelevant information, choose precise words and phrasings, include specific detail rather than general statements, make smooth transitions between ideas, and organize sentences and paragraphs logically.

The many math questions in the book represent the range of topics and difficulty in the 60 questions ACT math test. Formatted as word problems or straightforward expressions, these questions provide you with practice in the following subtopics:

- **Pre-algebra and elementary algebra:** These questions are based on core arithmetic and algebra concepts, including number definitions, absolute values, decimals, fractions, ratios, proportions, operations, solving equations, variables, inequalities, factoring, and quadratic equations. You can also expect to see both basic and advanced statistics problems involving average, median, probability, combinations, and permutations.
- **Plane geometry and trigonometry:** The ACT presents problems regarding the rules and formulas surrounding basic 2D and 3D shapes, such as angles, triangles, circles, squares, and regular solids. Also included are questions that test your knowledge of trigonometric ratios and identities.
- **Intermediate algebra and coordinate geometry:** These questions test a variety of concepts: functions, linear equations, graphing functions and shapes on the coordinate plane, vectors, unit circle, periodic functions, logarithms, imaginary numbers, and other advanced topics covered in algebra II and pre-calculus classes.

The ACT tests your reading ability through a set of four passages: fiction, social science, humanities, and natural science. Each passage contains 10 questions that should be answered in less than 9 minutes. One of the passages in each section is actually a set of two passages on a similar topic; a few questions require to you to compare the ideas in both.

The passages in the science section primarily test your ability to carefully examine and apply data conveyed in tables and graphs and evaluate experimental procedure and the reasons for a study's set up. The ACT presents you with six science passages per test and allows you roughly six minutes per passage. Although almost all you need to know comes straight from the passages, a few questions require you to rely on basic vocabulary and concepts you picked up in middle school science and freshman biology.

The ACT gives you the option of writing a 40-minute essay. "If it's optional, why do it?" you ask? Many colleges require the essay part, so if you're applying to one of those colleges, taking the writing test is *not* optional. For your writing pleasure, the ACT describes a current issue, gives you three perspectives on the issue, and asks you to create a persuasive essay that advances your position. Included in our answer explanations for the writing questions in this book are sample essays of varying proficiency to show you examples of how your response may be scored. Your writing test score ranges between 2 and 12 and is never averaged into your composite score.

Beyond the Book

Your purchase of this book gives you so much more than a thousand (and one) problems to work on to improve your ACT performance. It also comes with a free, one-year subscription to hundreds of practice questions online. Not only can you access this digital content anytime you want, on whichever device is available to you, but you can also track your progress and view personalized reports that show you which concepts you need to study the most.

What you'll find online

The online practice that comes free with this book offers you the same questions and answers that are available here. Of course, the real beauty of the online problems is your ability to customize your practice. In other words, you get to choose the types of problems and the number of problems you want to tackle. The online program tracks how many questions you answer correctly versus incorrectly so you can get an immediate sense of which topics need more of your attention.

This product also comes with an online Cheat Sheet that helps you increase your odds of performing well on the ACT. To get the Cheat Sheet, go to `www.dummies.com` and type 1,001 ACT Practice Questions For Dummies cheat sheet in the search box. (No access code required. You can benefit from this info before you even register.)

How to register

To gain access to practice online, all you have to do is register. Just follow these simple steps:

1. **Find your PIN access code:**
   - **Print-book users:** If you purchased a print copy of this book, turn to the inside front cover of the book to find your access code.
   - **E-book users:** If you purchased this book as an e-book, you can get your access code by registering your e-book at `www.dummies.com/go/getaccess`. Go to this website, find your book and click it, and answer the security questions to verify your purchase. You'll receive an email with your access code.
2. **Go to `Dummies.com` and click *Activate Now.***
3. **Find your product (*1,001 ACT Practice Questions For Dummies*) and then follow the on-screen prompts to activate your PIN.**

Now you're ready to go! You can come back to the program as often as you want — simply log in with the username and password you created during your initial login. No need to enter the access code a second time.

TIP

For Technical Support, please visit http://wiley.custhelp.com or call Wiley at 1-800-762-2974 (U.S.) or +1-317-572-3994 (international).

Where to Go for Additional Help

The solutions to the practice problems in this book are meant to walk you through how to get the right answers; they're not meant to teach the material. If certain concepts are unfamiliar to you, you can find help at www.dummies.com. Just type "ACT" into the search box to turn up a wealth of ACT-related information.

If you need more detailed instruction, check out *ACT For Dummies*, 6th Edition, written by none other than the humble authors of this practice text.

1 The Questions

IN THIS PART . . .

Work through grammar and writing questions.

Practice basic math, algebra, geometry, algebra II, pre-calculus, and statistics problems.

Read passages and answer reading comprehension questions.

Tackle science questions related to biology, chemistry, and physics.

Answer practice essay questions.

Chapter 1

The English Test

Brush off your grammar rules and scrutinize your writing skills. About an equal number of the 75 English test questions test your knowledge of both. The ACT presents five passages with about 15 questions each for you to examine within a total limit of 45 minutes. The passages cover a range of topics and tones to allow you to evaluate all kinds of writing forms.

The Problems You'll Work On

When working through the questions in this chapter, be prepared to do the following:

- » Pick apart underlined portions to determine whether they're presented properly or need a change.
- » Decide when you need to insert a comma, semicolon, colon, or dash — and when you don't.
- » Choose the right words for the context and clarity of the sentence.
- » Organize words, sentences, and paragraphs in the most logical manner.
- » Determine the purpose and relevance of ideas in an essay.
- » Discover the relationship between ideas to create the most accurate transitions.

What to Watch Out For

Trap answers include the following:

- » Phrasings that seem correct until you read them within the context of the entire sentence
- » Misused alternatives to proper phrasing, such improperly using *effect* instead of *affect* or *it's* instead of *its*
- » Options that entice you by duplicating language in the question instead of providing the specifically requested construction

Public Relations for Nonprofits

Questions 1–15 are based on the following information.

(adapted from *The Public Relations Handbook for Nonprofits*, by Art Feinglass, Wiley, 2005)

A obvious, (1) goal of public relations campaigns are (2) to stand out from the crowd. And when it comes to nonprofits, there is always a crowd.

People in the nonprofit world (3) often don't like to think of theirselves (4) as being in competition in the way that businesses are. But the competition is there just the same, and ferocious (5).

No matter what your organization's (6) field of activity — health care, community service, education, the arts, environmental protection, promotion of cultural activities, historical preservation, or any other worthwhile cause (7) — you are, in affect, in competition (8) with all the other organizations that specialize in the same area. And not only are you competing with your sister's organizations, (9) you are also in de facto competition with organizations that operate in other areas. Despite the focus of your efforts, the odds are that you and your competitors are reaching out to many of the same people.

The reality is that people usually don't support just one organization. (10) More typically, they support concerns ranging from the local to the global. It is not unusual for one person to support his local library and homeless shelter and symphony orchestra (11) while being involved with organizations that protect whales in the Pacific, support medical research in the Amazon, or providing care for orphans in Africa. (12) And then there is your organization who is trying (13) desperately to be heard above the clamor. That one individual may receive letters, appeals, and newsletters from literally dozens of organizations, all asking for backing and support (14). Therefore, one obvious job that your public relations efforts should accomplish is to help your organization stand out from the background noise by making a personal connection. In more hard-nosed terms; public relations (15) can be a tool to help you beat the competition.

1.

(A) NO CHANGE
(B) One obvious
(C) A obvious
(D) One, obvious

2.

(A) NO CHANGE
(B) campaign are
(C) campaigns is
(D) campaign is

3.

(A) NO CHANGE
(B) Those people in the nonprofit world
(C) A person in the nonprofit world
(D) In the nonprofit world there are people

4.

(A) NO CHANGE
(B) themselves
(C) himself
(D) themself

5.

(A) NO CHANGE
(B) and its ferocious
(C) and it can be ferocious
(D) the competition is ferocious

6.

(A) NO CHANGE
(B) organizations
(C) organizations'
(D) organization is

7. The best placement in the sentence for the underlined portion would be:

(A) where it is now

(B) after *field*

(C) after *No matter what*

(D) after *organizations*

8.

(A) NO CHANGE

(B) are, in effect, in competition

(C) are in affect in competition

(D) are in effect, in competition

9.

(A) NO CHANGE

(B) sisters' organizations,

(C) sister's organization's

(D) sister organizations,

10. If the writer were to delete the preceding sentence, the passage would primarily lose:

(A) an insignificant detail.

(B) a point that contradicts statements made earlier in the passage.

(C) a necessary transition between the third and fourth paragraphs.

(D) a concise summary of the author's knowledge of nonprofits.

11.

(A) NO CHANGE

(B) library, homeless shelter, and symphony orchestra

(C) library, homeless shelter, and, symphony orchestra

(D) library and homeless shelter, symphony orchestra

12.

(A) NO CHANGE

(B) organizations that protect whales in the Pacific or support medical research in the Amazon; caring for orphans in Africa.

(C) organizations that protect whales, in the Pacific, supporting medical research in the Amazon or caring for orphans in Africa.

(D) organizations that protect whales in the Pacific, support medical research in the Amazon, or care for orphans in Africa.

13.

(A) NO CHANGE

(B) organization, trying

(C) organization who are

(D) organization trying though it may

14.

(A) NO CHANGE

(B) support

(C) backing up and support

(D) support to back them up

15.

(A) NO CHANGE

(B) hard-nosed terms: public relations

(C) hard-nosed terms public relations,

(D) hard-nosed terms, public relations

West African Dances

Questions 16–30 are based on the following information.

[1] Rather than through the media and peers, [2] in West Africa, [3] social patterns and values as well as the tools needed to help people work, mature, and praise members of the community [4] are taught through dances. (16) The power of dance provides for the sense (17) of belonging and solidarity that brings people together no matter there

(18) age or the status they hold in the community. In the West African county of Guinea, there are many rhythms each (19) comes from different parts of it's (20) eight regions. A few of these Guinean rhythms include Kuku; Yole; Sonsorne; and Sinte. (21) (22)

Kuku comes from the forest part of Beyla. Located (23) in the region of Nzerekore, and is performed by the Koninkey, Manian, and Maokaethnic groups. It is mostly common (24) played at festivals, including the full moon celebration, and is one of the most popular West African rhythms. It is a celebration dance known as a womens (25) dance and is performed in a circle. The rhythm, traditionally played with sticks on Krins which are hollowed wood logs, (26) was originally played when the women would come back from fishing. The women used a variety of tools to make their fishing trips more efficient. (27) The dance of the Kuku embodies the people who perform it. The rhythm of Yole comes from Sierra Leone near the Guinean border, from the Temne people. (28) The Yole is the traditional mask dance and is danced by young and old at nearly all (29) festive occasions.

16. Given proper capitalization of the first word and the appropriate punctuation, which of the following arrangements of the designated parts of the sentence makes this sentence most logical?

(A) NO CHANGE
(B) 2, 3, 4, 1
(C) 2, 4, 1, 3
(D) 1, 4, 2, 3

17.

(A) NO CHANGE
(B) provides that the sense
(C) provides a sense
(D) provide the sense

18.

(A) NO CHANGE
(B) they're
(C) they are
(D) their

19.

(A) NO CHANGE
(B) rhythms. Each
(C) rhythms, each
(D) rhythms and each

20.

(A) NO CHANGE
(B) its
(C) it is
(D) it has

21.

(A) NO CHANGE
(B) Kuku and Yole, Sonsorne and Sinte.
(C) Kuku, Yole, Sonsorne, and Sinte.
(D) Kuku, Yole, Sonsorne, Sinte.

22. Assuming that all are true, which of the following additions to the preceding sentence (replacing *Sinte*) would be most relevant?

(A) Sinte, and each one has a distinctive beat.
(B) Sinte, words that sound unfamiliar to people in North America.
(C) Sinte, beats that originate in different regions of West Africa.
(D) Sinte. I like some of these rhythms better than others.

23.

(A) NO CHANGE
(B) Beyla, located
(C) Beyla; located
(D) Beyla, and located

24.

(A) NO CHANGE
(B) mostly commonly
(C) most common
(D) most commonly

25.

(A) NO CHANGE
(B) women
(C) women's
(D) womans'

26.

(A) NO CHANGE
(B) Krins, that have been hollowed logs,
(C) Krins that have been created from hollowing out wooden logs,
(D) hollowed logs called Krins,

27. The author is considering removing the preceding sentence from the essay. Should the author make this deletion?

(A) No, because the sentence contains information about fishing traditions that relate directly to understanding how Kuku is performed.
(B) No, because without the inclusion of the sentence, the reader would not know that the women use tools to fish.
(C) Yes, because the sentence does not provide information that is relevant to understanding how Kuku is performed.
(D) Yes, because the sentence provides details that contradict information that the author presents earlier in the essay.

28.

(A) NO CHANGE
(B) The Guinean border is near Sierra Leone, which is where the rhythm of Yole comes from, from the Temne people.
(C) From the Temne people, the rhythm of Yole comes from Sierra Leone near the Guinean border.
(D) The rhythm of Yole comes from the Temne people, who live in Sierra Leone near the Guinean border.

29.

(A) NO CHANGE
(B) most nearly all
(C) most all
(D) each and every one of the

Question 30 asks about the preceding passage as a whole.

30. Suppose the author's intention was to write a brief essay describing some West African dances and summarizing their significance to the current culture. Would this passage fulfill the author's intent?

(A) No, because the author does not provide any details about the origins of some of the dances.
(B) No, because the author describes some of the dances, but he does not summarize how they are significant.
(C) Yes, because the essay presents the benefits of the dances and gives some details about the way some of them are performed.
(D) Yes, because it compares the way people danced in earlier times to the way that people dance in modern day.

Reflections on Toothpaste Considerations

Questions 31–45 are based on the following information.

<u>Shopping for groceries, the one area</u> (31) that <u>in an irrational way</u> (32) overwhelms me is the toothpaste aisle. Every brand claims to do the same thing with the only variation being a slight taste difference or maybe a promise of <u>"fresh breath strips" inside.</u> (33)

[1] In order to avoid anxiety in the grocery store, <u>I will have</u> (34) stuck to the same tube since high school. [2] Recently, however, I've noticed that the <u>whitening affect</u> (35) it claims to have may actually

just be their (36) to compete with the other brands that surround it in the store. [3] Due to the fact that sorority recruitment is in two weeks, I've wanted to brighten my smile, but like most college students, I don't have the $60 to spend on whitening strips. [4] When I saw a commercial for a new line of whitening toothpaste and mouthwash, I immediately thought about making the switch. (37)

I trust whitening strips because I've used them in the passed but (38) even more convincing was the commercial, which featured a person who was in a similar situation to the won (39) I was in. It showed a woman who (40) needed her teeth to be whiter in 14 days but at the same time didn't want (41) to give up the things in her daily lifestyle that make teeth yellow as coffee and blueberries, (42) two things that I consume daily. (43)

If I can get the same whitening effect with an inexpensive mouthwash and toothpaste combination that I can with a $60 whitening strip product and still be able to consume what I do regularly, the switch from my old standby, which has been having no whitening effect (44), seems like something I should've done a long time ago. I look to my next trip to the toothpaste aisle with eager anticipation.

31.

(A) NO CHANGE
(B) When I grocery shop, the one area
(C) Grocery shopping, the one area
(D) Shopping for groceries, the main area

32.

(A) NO CHANGE
(B) irrationalness
(C) irrational
(D) irrationally

33.

(A) NO CHANGE
(B) fresh breath strips inside?
(C) "fresh, breath strips" inside.
(D) "fresh breath strips," inside.

34.

(A) NO CHANGE
(B) I had
(C) I should have
(D) I've

35.

(A) NO CHANGE
(B) whitening effect
(C) whitening's affect
(D) whitening affects

36.

(A) NO CHANGE
(B) they're
(C) there
(D) they are

37. Which of the following sequences of sentences makes this paragraph most logical?

(A) NO CHANGE
(B) 2, 1, 3, 4
(C) 3, 2, 1, 4
(D) 3, 4, 2, 1

38.

(A) NO CHANGE
(B) passed, but
(C) past, but
(D) past but

39.

(A) NO CHANGE
(B) one
(C) won,
(D) one,

40.

(A) NO CHANGE
(B) women who
(C) women whom
(D) woman whom

41.

(A) NO CHANGE

(B) days, but at the same time didn't want

(C) days but at the same time, didn't want

(D) days but, at the same time didn't want

42.

(A) NO CHANGE

(B) teeth yellow, such as coffee and blueberries,

(C) teeth yellow, as coffee and blueberries,

(D) teeth yellow; like coffee and blueberries,

43. At this point in the essay, the author is contemplating including a list of other foods and liquids that stain teeth. Would that addition to the paragraph be appropriate?

(A) Yes, because the essay is about ways to whiten teeth, and a list of items that stain teeth would provide readers with the knowledge of what to avoid.

(B) Yes, because the addition of the list would provide interesting detail that would help the reader better understand the author's personality.

(C) No, because the list would interrupt the flow of the author's story.

(D) No, because, although the list would provide relevant information, this information would be more appropriately placed in the final paragraph of the essay.

44. Given that all of the choices are true, which provides information that most logically completes the point of the paragraph?

(A) NO CHANGE

(B) which seems to be working just fine

(C) which tastes like blueberries

(D) which I've used for most of my life

Question 45 asks about the preceding passage as a whole.

45. Suppose the author wrote this essay in response to a writing assignment that asked for an analysis of the particular conditions that influence consumers to change toothpaste brands. Would this response successfully fulfill the assignment?

(A) Yes, because the essay gives descriptive detail of a particular time when the author changed toothpaste brands.

(B) Yes, because the essay shows that the quality of a particular toothpaste brand's whitening effect is what inspires consumers to choose that brand.

(C) No, because the essay does not specify the name of the brand of toothpaste she decides to switch to.

(D) No, because the essay is a personal account rather than an analysis.

A Study of Soap Operas

Questions 46–60 are based on the following information.

[1] Soap operas have become <u>the modern, day melodrama</u>. (46) [2] Characters are classified <u>as good guys, or bad guys,</u> (47) and the bad guys are always trying to find some way to make the lives of the good guys miserable. [3] Soap operas sets are <u>boring and bland,</u> (48) and directors tend to rely on the close up to convey characterization. [4] The shot closes in on the bad character displaying an evil and calculating expression as she informs the good character that she is going to ruin her life. [5] The camera then captures the <u>worried and helpless</u> (49) expression of the potentially ruined good girl. [6] Most actors confirm that they would rather play bad characters than <u>good, but</u> (50) it is more fun to give evil expressions <u>then helpless ones.</u> (51) (52)

There seems to be <u>those</u> (53) for <u>every scene, for instance,</u> (54) whenever two lovers embrace in reconciliation, the camera closes in on the face of one of them to show the worry and doubt that character has about the stability of the reconciliation. <u>The camera pulling away,</u> (55) the audience can view the results of very little rehearsal. Actors appear wooden and posed in full length. <u>As</u> (56) there seems to be stock facial expressions, there also appears to be stock physical poses. Exasperated <u>characters breathing deeply and heaving their shoulders</u> (57) up and <u>down.</u> Pleading characters <u>embrace</u> (58) their ground and lift their hands in supplication. (<u>59</u>) The only overt physical demonstrations of <u>emotion is</u> (60) raging lunges and passionate embraces.

46.

(A) NO CHANGE
(B) todays melodrama
(C) the modern-day melodrama
(D) the modern, day, melodrama

47.

(A) NO CHANGE
(B) good guys. Or, bad guys
(C) good guys or bad guys
(D) good guys or bad guys,

48.

(A) NO CHANGE
(B) bland,
(C) boring and uninteresting,
(D) boring

49.

(A) NO CHANGE
(B) worried, helpless,
(C) worried,
(D) worried and helpless,

50. Which of the following choices provides the most logical transition between the ideas in the sentence?

(A) NO CHANGE
(B) good; therefore,
(C) good;
(D) good; however,

51.

(A) NO CHANGE
(B) then it is to give a helpless one.
(C) than those that look helpless.
(D) than helpless ones.

52. What is the most logical position for the preceding sentence?

(A) Where it is now
(B) After Sentence 1
(C) After Sentence 3
(D) After Sentence 4

53.

(A) NO CHANGE
(B) them
(C) stock expressions
(D) some of those

54.

(A) NO CHANGE
(B) every scene; for instance,
(C) every scene: for instance
(D) every scene, for instance

55.

(A) NO CHANGE
(B) Pulling away, the camera reveals
(C) When the camera pulls away,
(D) Because the camera pulls away,

56. Which of the following alternatives to the underlined word would be LEAST appropriate?

(A) Whereas

(B) While

(C) At the same time as

(D) Just as

57.

(A) NO CHANGE

(B) characters breathe deeply and heave their shoulders

(C) characters that breathe deeply and heave their shoulders

(D) characters, which breathing deeply and heaving their shoulders,

58.

(A) NO CHANGE

(B) defend

(C) hold

(D) clutch

59. The author is considering revising the paragraph by deleting the preceding two sentences because he thinks they may be irrelevant. If the author makes this deletion the paragraph will primarily lose:

(A) interesting but irrelevant details about the kinds of facial expressions soap opera characters make.

(B) examples of the common types of poses soap opera characters strike to portray emotions.

(C) examples of the rare instances of overt physical demonstrations of emotion portrayed in soap operas.

(D) important details about the kinds of poses the audience sees in camera close ups of soap opera characters.

60.

(A) NO CHANGE

(B) emotion are

(C) emotion has been

(D) emotion had been

Why Study Philosophy?

Questions 60–75 are based on the following information.

In an essay entitled Philosophy: Who needs it? (61), Ayn Rand explains that philosophy answers three questions; (62) Where am I, how do I know, and what do I do. These questions are also (63) the three branches of philosophy, metaphysics, epistemology, and ethics. (64) The answers to these questions determine how we live our lives and arguably make up the most essential (65) elements of human survival. Other philosophers go along (66) and explain that we need to understand philosophy or we will end up like ancient cave dwellers' (67) without an understanding of how the world works.

Many people avoiding philosophy (68) for several main reasons. The first reason why (69) some choose to avoid studying philosophy is because they fear change and don't want to leave there (70) comfort zones. Philosophy is a very deep process of thinking (71) and some decide they don't want to discover new ideas because they will go against their prior knowledge and make them leave a level of comfort that they are not willing to let go. (72)

The second reason people do not want to study philosophy is because of the feeling of insignificance they can feel (73) when they explore the vast world of philosophy. Philosophy studies everything that has to do with human life and the human mindset, and this (74) can sometimes leave one with a sense of insignificance. The third reason that some may choose to avoid philosophy is because they feel that they will lose control over their lives. When studying philosophy, some theories (75) suggest that what humans perceive as the world is really just made up in their minds. This concept leaves some people feeling as though they have no true sense of reality and therefore no control over their lives.

61.

(A) NO CHANGE

(B) "Philosophy: Who Needs It?"

(C) "Philosophy: Who Needs It"?

(D) Philosophy: Who Needs It?

62.

(A) NO CHANGE
(B) questions
(C) questions, such as,
(D) questions:

63.

(A) NO CHANGE
(B) also are
(C) also correspond to
(D) also represent

64.

(A) NO CHANGE
(B) philosophy being metaphysics, epistemology, and ethics.
(C) philosophy, metaphysics; epistemology; ethics.
(D) philosophy, which are metaphysics, epistemology, and ethics.

65.

(A) NO CHANGE
(B) and arguably, make up the most essential
(C) and, arguably, make up the more essential
(D) and, arguably comprise the most essential

66. Which of the following choices provides the best alternative to the underlined words?

(A) get along
(B) concur
(C) disagree
(D) acquiesce

67.

(A) NO CHANGE
(B) cave dweller's
(C) cave's dwellers
(D) cave dwellers

68.

(A) NO CHANGE
(B) people who are avoiding philosophy
(C) people have avoided the study of philosophy
(D) people avoiding philosophy study

69.

(A) NO CHANGE
(B) reason for which
(C) reason which
(D) reason

70.

(A) NO CHANGE
(B) their
(C) they're
(D) them, the

71.

(A) NO CHANGE
(B) Philosophy has been a very deep process of thought,
(C) Philosophy requires a deep thought process,
(D) Philosophy requires you to think deeply,

72. Which of the following would NOT be a suitable replacement for the underlined text?

(A) make them leave their comfort zone.
(B) create discomfort.
(C) force them to step outside their comfort zone.
(D) make them leave a level of discomfort for which they are unprepared.

73.

(A) NO CHANGE
(B) the feeling of insignificance they experience
(C) the feeling of insignificance they're feeling
(D) the feeling of insignificance experienced

74.

(A) NO CHANGE
(B) it
(C) this breadth
(D) they

75.

(A) NO CHANGE
(B) Philosophy provides theories that some
(C) When studying philosophy, some
(D) Some philosophical theories

Planning for Human Error

Questions 76–90 are based on the following information.

(adapted from Contingency Planning and Disaster Recovery: A Small Business Guide, by Donna R. Childs and Stefan Dietrich, Wiley)

[1] Human error is by far, (76) the most commonly frequent (77) cause of business disasters. [2] By definition, human errors are unintentional, and (78) because they occur randomly, we hope that the overall impact on your business operations will be negligible. [3] Each of us have had (79) the experience of developing a new document by revising an older document or by using a template. [4] The same is true when we reorganize our files to reduce the clutter we made in the last month and unintentionally delete a whole folder of important documents. (80) [5] When we finish our work, hit (81) the "save" button, and immediately realize that we have just written over with new text an old document that we will need again in the future.

Unfortunately, there is no simple single, solution. (82) We have to expect that human errors will be made, and we must be able to protect our businesses from ourselves' (83) to the extent possible. I often notice that managers hope that they're (84) employees will be careful with important files, and when they inadvertently delete a file they (85) hope a backup file exists. I usually suggest keeping track of these events. If you do so, you will begin (86) to realize that these errors occur with greater frequency than you thought. Another drive is enthusiastically used for backing up data and then forgotten after a few weeks passed. (87) And (88) the corrective action taken is most often less than satisfactory.

In fact, we have observed with frequency that the loss of a file is either not even realized or simply never reported, until someone runs, nervous, through (89) the company asking if anyone still has a copy of a particular file.

76.

(A) NO CHANGE
(B) human error is, by far,
(C) human error by far
(D) By far, human error, is

77.

(A) NO CHANGE
(B) most frequent
(C) most frequently common
(D) most common and most frequent

78.

(A) NO CHANGE
(B) unintentional and,
(C) unintentional and
(D) unintentional, but

79.

(A) NO CHANGE
(B) Each of us have
(C) Each of us has had
(D) Each of us had

80. The best placement for this sentence would be:

(A) where it is now
(B) after sentence 1
(C) after sentence 2
(D) after sentence 5

81.

(A) NO CHANGE
(B) our work hit
(C) our work, we hit
(D) our work I hit

82.

(A) NO CHANGE
(B) simple, single, solution
(C) single simple, solution
(D) single simple solution

83.

(A) NO CHANGE
(B) itself
(C) ourselves
(D) themselves

84.

(A) NO CHANGE
(B) their
(C) there
(D) they are

85.

(A) NO CHANGE
(B) when, inadvertently, they delete a file, managers
(C) when employees inadvertently delete a file they
(D) when employees inadvertently delete a file, managers

86.

(A) NO CHANGE
(B) If you do so you'll begin
(C) If you do, so you will begin
(D) If you'll do so, begin

87.

(A) NO CHANGE
(B) a few weeks have passed
(C) a few weeks have past
(D) few weeks have passed

88. Which of the following alternatives to the underlined portion is most acceptable?

(A) While
(B) But
(C) Therefore,
(D) OMIT the underlined portion and capitalize *The*.

89.

(A) NO CHANGE
(B) runs nervous through
(C) running nervously through
(D) runs nervously through

Question 90 asks about the preceding passage as a whole.

90. A business owner is looking for an article that explains how businesses can avoid costly employee mistakes. Would this passage be appropriate for that purpose?

(A) Yes, because the passage gives examples of common office errors.
(B) Yes, because the passage offers a simple solution to correcting human errors.
(C) No, because the passage does not specifically address the kinds of errors employees make.
(D) No, because although it describes the types of human errors that occur in the office environment, the passage does not provide an explanation of how to avoid them.

Is Deviant Behavior Learned?

Questions 91–105 are based on the following information.

Aleister Crowley was born on <u>October 12, 1875</u> (91) and from birth he <u>marked himself already for deviant behavior</u> (92). He was born with a swastika-shaped <u>birthmark,</u> (93) and in many ways this birthmark shaped the rest of his life. Born into a Protestant family, his dad was an influential preacher. (94) Crowley came to despise the Christian religion, and his mother named him "The Beast." (95) At a later age, turning (96) to the occult and practice of black magic. Crowley experimented with it (97) and continued a life of deviant behavior, acting violent, and was devoted to the powers of darkness throughout his life. (98) Crowley perfectly exemplifies the fact that it may be nature not nurture that determines one's bent (99).

[1] Crowley has had many followers since his death, but none of them were born with the cruel mindset that Crowley was born with. (100) [2] Some philosophers and psychologists try to argue that its (101) in fact nurture that determines if a person is evil (102). [3] When you consider the case of Crowley, however (103), it is hard to argue that he was nurtured to be the demon that he was. [104] [4] The nature theory explains why identical twins, raised under different conditions (105) grow up to have very similar personalities instead of different personalities as the nurture theory would suggest.

91.

(A) NO CHANGE

(B) October 12, 1875,

(C) October 12, 1875

(D) October, 12, 1875

92.

(A) NO CHANGE

(B) he was marked for behavior that was deviant already

(C) he, marked already for deviance

(D) he was already marked for deviance

93.

(A) NO CHANGE

(B) birthmark;

(C) birthmark:

(D) birthmark —

94.

(A) NO CHANGE

(B) Crowley was born into a Protestant family; his father was an influential preacher.

(C) Born into a Protestant family, Crowley's father was an influential preacher.

(D) Being born into a Protestant family, an influential preacher was his dad.

95. The author is considering deleting the underlined portion from the sentence. If the author were to delete this clause, the essay would primarily lose:

(A) a minor detail about Crowley's family life.

(B) an explanation of why Crowley rejected Christianity.

(C) an additional detail that supports the author's point that Crowley engaged in deviant behavior from an early age.

(D) a necessary transition that links a major point the author makes in the first few sentences to a contrasting point at the end of the paragraph.

96.

(A) NO CHANGE

(B) he turned

(C) was turning

(D) he had been turning

97.

(A) NO CHANGE

(B) them all

(C) it all

(D) the supernatural

98.

(A) NO CHANGE

(B) a life of deviant behavior, acting violently, and was devoted to the powers of darkness throughout his life

(C) a life of deviant behavior, violent actions, and devotion to the powers of darkness

(D) a life of deviant behavior, acting violently and devoted to the powers of darkness

99.

(A) NO CHANGE

(B) ones bent

(C) their bent

(D) the way that one bends

100. Upon reviewing this sentence, the author is considering moving it to another place in the paragraph. The most logical position for this sentence would be:

(A) where it is now

(B) before sentence 3

(C) after sentence 3

(D) after sentence 4

101.

(A) NO CHANGE

(B) it is

(C) it has

(D) it's

102.

(A) NO CHANGE

(B) if a person is evil or not

(C) whether a person's evil or not

(D) whether a person is evil

103. Which of the following choices would be the LEAST acceptable alternative to the underlined word given the context of the sentence?

(A) but

(B) though

(C) in contrast

(D) on the other hand

104. Which of the following sentences if added here would provide the best transition to the next sentence and remain consistent with the main idea of the passage?

(A) Some of Crowley's followers hold to the nature theory while others accept the nurture theory.

(B) The nature theory provides a different philosophy from the nurture theory.

(C) Had Crowley been a twin, that twin could have had a completely different personality from his.

(D) A better explanation for Crowley's personality would be the nature theory.

105.

(A) NO CHANGE

(B) twins who are raised under different conditions

(C) twins, raised under conditions that are different,

(D) twins who, raised under the different conditions,

The Legend of the Five Suns

Questions 106–120 are based on the following information.

The Mexica people's history of constant migration and destruction of community <u>are communicated</u> (106) in the Legend of the Five Suns. "The Codex of Chimalpopoca," <u>which has been translated by John</u>

Bierhorst, (107) documents this legend about what happened to the Mexica people as a result of the five suns.

The first sun was known as Four Water and was supposedly the tale of how the gods created humans, yet its ending (108) a flood where the survivors turned into fish. The second sun, Four Jaguar, (109) ended when the sun fell to the earth and set it ablaze. Like the second sun, (110) the third sun, known as Four Rain, also ended in a blaze, when it and gravel, (111) rained down from the sky and ignited the land. The remaining people turned into birds. Four Winds, the fourth sun, existing as it did (112) under the rule of Quetzalcoatl and ended with a hurricane that blew the people off the face of the earth. Those who survived were changed into monkeys and scattered throughout (113) the forests and mountains. The fifth sun is known as Four Movement, and it is supposed to end in earthquakes. (114)

Although the story of the five suns' is just (115) a legend; it has helped (116) show the origins of the Mexica people's struggle to keep a community together despite disaster and death. Disasters did not occur exactly like the ones described in the Legend of the Five Suns, but (117) native people experienced similar disasters when marauders annihilated several city states, crushing their communities, taking away their beliefs, and wiping out their histories. (118) For example, the Tolltecs disbanded in 1064 under the leadership of Huemac due to the fact that (119) the city of Tollan fell. The people wandered for seven years, which caused the city to fall apart and (120) resulted in the dispersal of the people throughout the continent.

106.

(A) NO CHANGE
(B) are told
(C) is communicated
(D) have been conveyed

107. If the author deleted the underlined clause and comma that precedes it, the reader would primarily lose:

(A) specific documentation of the source of the author's materials.
(B) an important transition between the purpose of the legend and the information it contains.
(C) a relevant detail that helps the reader gain an understanding of the origins of the legend.
(D) insight into why the legend was documented in "The Codex of Chimalpopoca."

108.

(A) NO CHANGE
(B) humans, yet its ending with
(C) humans yet ending with
(D) humans, yet it ended with

109.

(A) NO CHANGE
(B) sun Four Jaguars
(C) sun called Four Jaguars,
(D) sun, with a name of Four Jaguars

110.

(A) NO CHANGE
(B) As the second sun,
(C) As for the second sun,
(D) Like the second sun did

111.

(A) NO CHANGE
(B) they and gravel
(C) it, and gravel,
(D) fire and gravel

112.

(A) NO CHANGE
(B) existing
(C) existed
(D) as it did exist

113.

(A) NO CHANGE
(B) within
(C) by
(D) between

114. The author is considering adding the following sentence to beginning of this paragraph:

The people who lived by the Legend of the Five Suns had very little hope.

Given the subject matter of the information in the rest of the paragraph, would this sentence be a relevant first sentence to the paragraph?

(A) Yes, because it lets the reader know that there were people who lived by the Legend of the Five Suns.
(B) Yes, because it provides a helpful introduction that ties together the subsequent descriptions of the five suns.
(C) No, because it conveys a negative tone that is not consistent with the rest of the paragraph.
(D) No, because it does not provide a relevant transition between this paragraph and the one that precedes it.

115.

(A) NO CHANGE
(B) suns are just
(C) sun's only
(D) suns is just

116.

(A) NO CHANGE
(B) legend. It helps
(C) legend it helps out to
(D) legend, it helps

117. If the writer were to delete the underlined portion and capitalize "native" to begin the sentence, the essay would primarily lose:

(A) an insignificant detail.
(B) information that clarifies the difference between myth and what really happened to the Mexica people.
(C) evidence of the author's extensive knowledge about each of the stories of the five suns.
(D) descriptive detail that links the Legend of the Five Suns to the concept of Armageddon.

118.

(A) NO CHANGE
(B) when several city-states were annihilated, their communities were crushed, their beliefs were taken from them, and their history was wiped out
(C) when several city-states were annihilated, crushing their communities, their beliefs were taken from them, and wiping out their history
(D) when marauders destroyed several city-states by crushing their communities, their beliefs taken from them, and their history wiped out

119.

(A) NO CHANGE
(B) because
(C) owing to the fact that
(D) due to

120.

(A) NO CHANGE
(B) which, causing the city to fall apart,
(C) which
(D) OMIT the underlined portion.

Acting for Television

Questions 121–135 are based on the following information.

At first, acting for television seems to be similar to acting on the big screen. Although (121) there are similarities between the two, such as the use of a camera to capture the performance, (122) television acting is different from that of motion pictures in its resources and purpose. Acting for television tends to be (123) more superficial then (124) acting on the big screen.

To begin with, (125) television as a medium is more limited than motion pictures. As compared to the big screen, television generally requires significantly fewer (126) preparation time for each episode; less taped footage to draw from; and less time to edit the final product. (127) Characters, therefore, may be more one-dimensional and lack depth (128). (129)

Deviations from the script may be more common and even acceptable on television. The time constraints for filming a motion picture, on the other hand (130), are generally not as severe, and big screen actors can rehearse and film their presentations for a much longer period of time. Giving them (131) a better opportunity to develop their characters' reactions to the particular circumstances presented in the film.

Time and budget restraints also effect (132) the amount of taped footage in television. Therefore, television actors do not have the luxury of providing a variety (133) of takes. Unless there are blatant errors in a scene, the actors' first performance for the camera will be there final one (134).

121.

(A) NO CHANGE

(B) However, although

(C) But,

(D) Likewise,

122.

(A) NO CHANGE

(B) two like the use of a camera to capture the performance

(C) two, like the use of a camera to capture the performance

(D) two; such as the use of a camera for performance capture,

123. Which of the following alternatives to the underlined portion would *not* be acceptable?

(A) can be

(B) is likely

(C) leans toward being

(D) has a tendency toward

124.

(A) NO CHANGE

(B) as

(C) than

(D) as is

125. If the author deletes the underlined portion, the sentence will primarily lose:

(A) a beginning phrase that introduces the sentence but does not add vital information.

(B) an essential transition without which the preceding paragraph does not flow to the second paragraph.

(C) the first designation of a numbered list.

(D) an example of how television acting differs from movie acting.

126.

(A) NO CHANGE
(B) significant fewer
(C) significantly less
(D) less significance in

127.

(A) NO CHANGE
(B) for each episode, which means there is less taped footage to draw from and less time to edit the final product.
(C) for each episode, less taped footage to draw from, and less time to edit the final product.
(D) for each episode: fewer taped footage to draw from and fewer time to edit the final product.

128.

(A) NO CHANGE
(B) be more one-dimensional than and lack as much depth
(C) be one-dimensional and more
(D) lack depth

129. At this point, the author is considering adding the following sentence:

Actors exhibit much more spontaneity, too.

Would this addition be appropriate?

(A) Yes, because the sentence adds another reason that television actors are different, and a writer should include as many supporting examples as possible.
(B) Yes, because it provides a necessary transition to the next paragraph.
(C) No, because the sentence presents a positive difference about television actors, and the rest of the passage focuses on only the negative aspects of television acting.
(D) No, because the sentence contains comparison language but doesn't provide a specific comparison.

130. Which of the following alternatives to the underlined portion would be LEAST acceptable?

(A) conversely
(B) in other words
(C) in contrast
(D) on the contrary

131.

(A) NO CHANGE
(B) This giving them
(C) Providing them
(D) This gives them

132.

(A) NO CHANGE
(B) effect, too,
(C) also affect
(D) are also affecting

133.

(A) NO CHANGE
(B) diverse variety
(C) small variety
(D) various diversity

134.

(A) NO CHANGE
(B) they're final one
(C) his final act.
(D) their last

Question 135 asks about the preceding passage as a whole.

135. Given that the author intended to write an essay that contrasts television acting with movie acting, did the passage fulfill this goal?

(A) Yes, because the passage states that television acting is different from movie acting and then provides specific ways that the two types of acting differ.

(B) Yes, because the passage points out that despite their differences, television acting and movie acting are really quite similar.

(C) No, because the passage focuses on only the differences between acting for television and acting in movies.

(D) No, because the author does not provide specific examples of television and movie actors to support the points made in the passage.

Greek Tragedy

Questions 136–150 are based on the following information.

[1]

[1] Greek drama evolved during the fifth century B.C. from the public performance of narrative lyrics. [2] Three dramatists (136) dominated the fifth-century Athenian stage, they were (137) Aeschylus, Sophocles, and Euripides. (138) [3] Actors dressed in masks and platform shoes accompanied by a chorus, (139) performed the plays for large audiences using mostly dialogue rather than action to tell the story. (140)

[2]

Their tragedies chronicled the inevitable (141) movement of a tragic hero from good fortune to destruction usually due to (142) a flaw in the hero's character. The tragedies focused on human's (143) inability to control their own fates. Attempts by the hero to change fate usually result (144) in increased suffering. (145)

[3]

Sophocles' *Oedipus Tyrannus* is a classic example of the tragic dilemma. Oedipus, through a series of deceits and mistaken identities, learning (146) that he cannot escape the prophecy that he would murder his father. He accepts his role in the situation (147), which leaves the chorus to lament about the cruelty and inevitability of fate.

[4]

The tragedies of Euripides, who was Sophocles' contemporary, are different, however (148). Euripides, one of the great Greek dramatists of the fifth century B.C., (149) was the first to express some of his ideas about man through the principal actors. In so doing, he made his characters more human, made them feel and think more like men, and showed how love and passion influenced the course of men's lives. Rather that emphasizing one tragic flaw and the inevitability of fate, Euripides' *Alcestis* focuses on friendship and its ability to affect the course of fate.

136.

(A) NO CHANGE
(B) 3 dramatists
(C) Three dramatists'
(D) 3 dramatist's

137.

(A) NO CHANGE
(B) stage, being
(C) stage:
(D) stage. They

138. The author is considering adding this sentence:

Greek dramatists created great works in other centuries, too.

Would this addition be appropriate given the primary topic of the paragraph?

(A) Yes, because the paragraph is about Greek dramatists.

(B) Yes, because the sentence provides additional information about Greek dramatists that improves the readers understanding of how influential Greek drama was in early times.

(C) No, because the paragraph is about dramatists from all cultures and the sentence only mentions Greek dramatists.

(D) No, because the paragraph is specifically about fifth-century Greek drama.

139.

(A) NO CHANGE

(B) Actors, dressed in platform shoes and they have masks on and are accompanied by a chorus,

(C) Actors, dressed in masks, platform shoes, and accompanied by a chorus,

(D) Actors, accompanied by a chorus and dressed in masks and platform shoes,

140. Upon reviewing the previous paragraph, the author is considering changing the order of the sentences. Which ordering of the sentences would be the most logical?

(A) NO CHANGE

(B) 1, 3, 2

(C) 2, 1, 3

(D) 3, 1, 2

141. Which of the following would be the LEAST acceptable substitute for the underlined word given the context of the paragraph?

(A) unavoidable

(B) usual

(C) inescapable

(D) certain

142.

(A) NO CHANGE

(B) because of the fact that there is

(C) due

(D) since there is

143.

(A) NO CHANGE

(B) humans'

(C) human

(D) humanity

144.

(A) NO CHANGE

(B) results

(C) resulted

(D) had resulted

145. Given that the following choices are true, which would most effectively lead the reader from the information in the previous paragraph to the description that follows in the third paragraph?

(A) NO CHANGE

(B) All three Greek dramatists wrote plays that provide classic examples of the tragic hero.

(C) Like those by the other two dramatists, Sophocles wrote tragedies that focused on heroes who could not control their own fates.

(D) Sophocles wrote a tragedy about one of those heroes, called *Oedipus Tyrannus*.

146.

(A) NO CHANGE

(B) ascertains

(C) making the discovery

(D) stumbles upon

147. Given that the following choices are true, which one states the most logical cause for the action described in the clause that follows the underlined portion?

(A) NO CHANGE

(B) He learns that his attempts to escape his fate serve to worsen his destruction.

(C) The members of his family point out that Oedipus's pride contributed to his destruction.

(D) Only Oedipus has the power to undo the destruction that has taken place.

148.

(A) NO CHANGE

(B) therefore

(C) mostly

(D) supposedly

149. The author is considering removing the underlined portion and omitting the comma after *Euripides*. The primary effect of this change would be that the

(A) reader would be confused about the identity of Euripides

(B) flow of the last paragraph would be interrupted

(C) sentence would be punctuated incorrectly

(D) passage would avoid stating an unnecessary redundancy

Question 150 asks about the preceding passage as a whole.

150. The most logical arrangement of the paragraphs in this passage would be

(A) as it is now

(B) 4, 3, 2, 1

(C) 2, 1, 3, 4

(D) 1, 2, 4, 3

Wonderful Wokamama

Questions 151–165 are based on the following information.

From the first day we arrived in London, and on, (151) all I heard about was a casual restaurant called Wokamama. I eventually got around to trying it, and I was in love. From the relaxed atmosphere to the amazing, and unique (152) Asian fusion cuisine, it quickly became my number one place to get a delicious meal. I consumed a variety of dishes; sumptuous sushi, (153) aromatic noodle bowls, and crunchy spring rolls were among my favorites. (154)

London had many other great restaurants, but I didn't have time to visit them all. (155) When in Amsterdam, they had (156) a place with a similar concept to Wokamama; yet, offered a (157) create-your-own Asian noodle bowl, called Wok the Walk (158). This establishment had a fast food style set up that made it easy to take it (159) home or eat there. Like Wokamama, Wok the Walk had tasty, delicious (160) food, and I was pretty bummed that I arrived back in the States and then found out there had been one pretty close by me in (161) London the entire time. Guess it made me realize that even if I had grown up in London, I would have always been discovering new restaurants no matter how much I explored.

Back in the States, due to a lack of good Asian restaurants, (162) I realize that likely the closest I can get to Wokamama is (163) Panda Panda in the mall. I used to like Panda Panda, but now that I have experienced a true melting pot of cultures like that in London, this "foreign" cuisine just doesn't taste right. However, (164) I learned that Wok the Walk and Wokamama exist in the United States on the east coast and are expanding. Soon, these excellent establishments will reach the west coast so those of us who live east of the Mississippi have an opportunity to expand our experience of Asian cuisine. (165)

151.

(A) NO CHANGE
(B) and continuing on,
(C) including the days ever after in the future,
(D) OMIT the underlined portion.

152.

(A) NO CHANGE
(B) amazing and unique
(C) amazing and, unique
(D) amazing, and unique,

153.

(A) NO CHANGE
(B) dishes, sumptuous sushi,
(C) dishes sumptuous sushi,
(D) dishes, which were sumptuous sushi,

154. If the writer were to delete the preceding sentence, the paragraph would essentially lose:

(A) more specific details about the restaurant's offerings.
(B) an explanation of why Wokamama became the writer's favorite restaurant.
(C) insight into how frequently the writer patronized the restaurant.
(D) a list of the types of food a visitor to London may expect to find in its top restaurants.

155. Which of these sentences provides the best transition from the first paragraph to the information that follows:

(A) NO CHANGE
(B) Although I ate at other Asian restaurants in Europe, none was as satisfying as Wokamama.
(C) I later learned that Wokamama had locations in the United States.
(D) My travels provided other encounters with Asian fusion.

156.

(A) NO CHANGE
(B) When in Amsterdam, it had
(C) When I went to Amsterdam, they had
(D) In Amsterdam, I found a place that

157.

(A) NO CHANGE
(B) Wokamama, which offered a
(C) Wokamama, but mostly offered a
(D) Wokamama was more of a

158. Based on information in the paragraph, the best location in the sentence for the underlined part is:

(A) where it is now.
(B) after *place*.
(C) after *concept*.
(D) after *Wokamama*.

159.

(A) NO CHANGE
(B) them
(C) meals
(D) it all

160.

(A) NO CHANGE
(B) tasty and delicious
(C) delectably tasty
(D) tasty

161.

(A) NO CHANGE
(B) when I discovered after I arrived back in the States that one had been pretty close to me in
(C) that I discovered one pretty close by me after I arrived back to the States in
(D) when one pretty close to me was discovered not until after arriving back in the States from

162.

(A) NO CHANGE
(B) States due to a lack of good Asian restaurants
(C) States due to a lack, of good Asian restaurants,
(D) States, due to a lack of good, Asian, restaurants,

163.

(A) NO CHANGE
(B) was
(C) would have been
(D) had been

164.

(A) NO CHANGE
(B) Consequently,
(C) On the other hand,
(D) Happily,

165. Suppose the writer had intended to create an essay that explores the role that food plays in helping a person from one country appreciate the culture of a foreign country. Would this essay accomplish that goal?

(A) Yes, because the essay gives examples of foreign food that she likes better than food from her native country.
(B) Yes, because the passage indicates that the writer gained a better appreciation for London culture by eating in its various restaurants.
(C) No, because although the writer explores her developing appreciation for London cuisine, it doesn't provide examples of her appreciation for other cultures.
(D) No, because the essay doesn't directly relate appreciation of foreign food to appreciation of foreign cultures.

Seeking Partners for Greater Competitive Advantage

Questions 166–180 are based on the following information.

(adapted from *Adapt or Die: Transforming Your Supply Chain into Adaptive Business Network*, by Claus Heinrich, Wiley)

[1]

Few businesses truly exist in isolation. No matter the strength, the power, and market force a company can bring to <u>bear, it</u> (166) always has suppliers and customers. [A] To flourish in <u>todays rapid-paced</u> (167) business landscape, companies need to work <u>quicker and more effectively</u> (168) to form partnerships with multiple customers and suppliers. (<u>169</u>)

[2]

Partnerships present the opportunity to quickly gain access to a technology or product, develop a broader mix of products and services, and achieving (170) the nimbleness (171) required to adapt to rapidly changing market conditions. In today's fast-moving economy, if companies don't form effective partnerships, they're not just marginalized — (172) they're eliminated. Yet, with all the potential partnerships offer to enhance a companys' (173) competitiveness, businesses continue to either resist partnerships in general or form partnerships that are limited in scope. (174) [B]

[3]

First, many companies view themselves as isolated entities. They're focused on performing better, more cheaply, and faster within their own walls. Just like two divisions within a corporation, (175) a company that fails to integrate it's (176) business processes and share information with its partners will not be able to work with those partners efficiently. Suppliers can't effectively manage their inventory when they have no information about demand for the finished product. Similarly, suppliers (177) can't respond quickly to changes in customer demand when it takes weeks or months to learn about these changes. [C] These are just some of the issues companies could address by working closer (178) with their trading partners.

[4]

Second, until recently, the technology has not existed to allow companies to form flexible, low-cost relationships with partners. Over the past few decades, larger companies have began (179) communicating electronically through direct links with their suppliers, but these linkages remain expensive to install and maintain. [D] In addition to its expense, this technology doesn't provide the flexibility needed to change suppliers if they are later deemed ineffective or if market conditions change. [180]

166.

(A) NO CHANGE
(B) bear; it
(C) bear: it
(D) bear, and

167.

(A) NO CHANGE
(B) today's rapid-paced
(C) today's rapid-paced,
(D) todays' rapid-paced,

168.

(A) NO CHANGE
(B) more quicker and effective
(C) quickly and effectively
(D) quick and effective

169. The writer is considering adding the following statement to the end of this paragraph:

Businesses should also invest dollars in and devote time to research and development.

Should the writer add the statement here?

(A) Yes, because it summarizes the paragraph's main point by providing another way businesses can flourish.
(B) Yes, because it shows that owning a business requires a large number of resources.
(C) No, because it interrupts the transition between this paragraph and the one that follows.
(D) No, because providing ways to make businesses more successful is inconsistent with the rest of the essay.

170.

(A) NO CHANGE
(B) are achieving
(C) achieved
(D) achieve

171. Which of the choices provides a state most consistent with the requirement mentioned in the rest of the sentence?

(A) NO CHANGE
(B) caution
(C) evolvement
(D) accomplishment

172.

(A) NO CHANGE
(B) marginalized, they're
(C) marginalized, their
(D) marginalized they're

173.

(A) NO CHANGE
(B) companies
(C) company's
(D) companies'

174. Which of the following statements provides the best transition from this paragraph to the rest of the essay?

(A) NO CHANGE
(B) Businesses have at their disposal two ways to overcome their resistance to forming partnerships.
(C) The isolation created when businesses fail to join forces with other may be devastating.
(D) Businesses are best served when they approach forming alliances with caution.

175.

(A) NO CHANGE
(B) Just like two divisions of a corporation,
(C) Just like a corporation that lacks communication between its divisions,
(D) Just as a corporation with two divisions,

176.

(A) NO CHANGE
(B) its
(C) their
(D) its'

177. Which of the following alternatives to the underlined portion is LEAST acceptable?

(A) And
(B) Consequently,
(C) Additionally,
(D) Likewise,

178.

(A) NO CHANGE
(B) in a much closer manner
(C) more close
(D) more closely

179.

(A) NO CHANGE
(B) begun
(C) had begun
(D) have begun

Question 180 asks about the passage as a whole.

180. The writer wants to add the following sentence to the essay:

But not every company has partners.

The most logical placement for this sentence is:

(A) point A in paragraph 1.
(B) point B in paragraph 2.
(C) point C in paragraph 3.
(D) point D in paragraph 4.

The Rise of Feudalism

Questions 181–195 are based on the following information.

Rome began to fall. Barbarian raiders pillaged and raided (181) Roman cities. Forced to pull back, the Roman army were losing (182) many battles against several Barbarian tribes. It took time, but (183) the formerly strong, unbeatable Roman Empire gradually disintegrated.

As one Barbarian tribe, the Visigoths, who was led by a warrior king named Alaric, marching toward Rome. the inhabitants (184) were quaking with fear. The Senate tried to pay off the Visigoths. Therefore, (185) on the fourth of August in 410 AD, Rome was defeated (186) in a six-day rampage, and no mercy was given.

Without the authority and stability, the Roman Empire had supplied, (187) confusion and instability (188) broke out among common people and farmers. They gravitated to rural estates and away from urban cities, which were targeted by Barbarian raids. Wealth began to shift from money to land because land, not money, produced food.

Estate owners, the nobility, took over Roman government, and they provided protection from raiders to farmers in trade for (189) their farm land and labor. This was the beginning of the age of Feudalism, a hierarchical pyramid where all members knew their place. (190)

Medieval kings were at the very top of the feudal pyramid and lived lives of complete luxury, with every other level of the system supplying them with everything they needed and more. They ate gourmet meals with many fantastically plated courses and were entertained by minstrels and jokers who kept them entranced. They showed off extravagantly and wore fancy clothes and jewelry. Some kings had several majestic castles with beautiful keeps and thick, strong, siege-proof, curtain walls (191) surrounding their kingdoms. These (192) often were fitted with the latest luxuries and included a nearby cathedral or abbey, which were led (193) by an abbot.

The king was the leader of a kingdom, sometimes an entire country, and this title brought many duties. One of the most important was to create laws for his country to keep order and prevent chaos. The king had to protect his land and its inhabitants against any attackers that could take over and plunder his kingdom. In addition to fortifying his kingdom against attackers, the king had to keep peace with the nobles on his land. These things could lead to a successful kingdom. (195)

181.

(A) NO CHANGE

(B) pillaged by looting and stealing from

(C) pillaged loot from

(D) pillaged

182.

(A) NO CHANGE

(B) lost

(C) have lost

(D) losing

183.

(A) NO CHANGE

(B) time and

(C) time, however,

(D) time: but

184.

(A) NO CHANGE

(B) Alaric, march toward Rome,

(C) Alaric marched toward Rome. The inhabitants

(D) Alaric, marched toward Rome, the inhabitants

185.

(A) NO CHANGE
(B) Consequently,
(C) However,
(D) Additionally,

186. Of the following alternatives to the underlined portion, which is the LEAST acceptable?

(A) conquered
(B) taken over
(C) subdued
(D) rebuffed

187.

(A) NO CHANGE
(B) stability the Roman Empire had supplied,
(C) stability, supplied by the Roman Empire,
(D) stability supplied by the Roman Empire

188.

(A) NO CHANGE
(B) unstableness
(C) disarray
(D) OMIT the underlined portion.

189.

(A) NO CHANGE
(B) to trade from
(C) as trade with
(D) by trading with

190. At this point in the essay, the writer is considering adding the following sentence:

This system was structured like a pyramid with the king or very powerful lord on top.

Should the writer make this addition here?

(A) No, because the sentence offers irrelevant information that distracts the reader from the main idea of the essay.
(B) No, because the addition provides details that are already stated elsewhere in the essay.
(C) Yes, because without the addition, the reader would not be aware that kings occupied the highest position in the feudal system.
(D) Yes, because the addition provides details that help the reader envision the pyramid structure introduced in the preceding sentence.

191.

(A) NO CHANGE
(B) keeps, and thick, strong, siege-proof curtain walls
(C) keeps and thick, strong, siege-proof curtain walls
(D) keeps, and thick, strong, siege-proof, curtain walls

192.

(A) NO CHANGE
(B) They
(C) These bastions
(D) It

193.

(A) NO CHANGE
(B) abbey which was led
(C) abbey, which was led,
(D) led

194. Of the following alternatives to the underlined portion, which is the LEAST acceptable?

(A) Though he fortified his kingdom against attackers,

(B) Additionally,

(C) Also,

(D) As well as fortifying his kingdom against attackers,

195. Which of the following choices best summarizes the final paragraph in keeping with the purpose of the passage as a whole?

(A) NO CHANGE

(B) The successful accomplishment of these goals resulted in a feudalistic system that lasted for centuries.

(C) The other members of the feudalistic society had their own duties to fulfill.

(D) Kings who fulfilled their responsibilities were rewarded by the Roman government.

Earning a Nursing Associate Degree

Questions 196–211 are based on the following information.

[1]

After securing a high school diploma, earning an associate degree is the path many students choose to follow. (196) This degree, which is an internationally acknowledged academic achievement earned by students who participate in about two years of close study of a particular topic, field, or industry has become (197) increasingly popular. One of the most sought after degree paths is that of a nurse, and many people find that a nursing associate degree is a great way to find entry-level work within the medical profession.

[2]

The program itself (198) may vary considerably regarding (199) factors, such as where the nursing program is offered and whether it is taken full or part-time, However, the curriculum studied in these programs is often similar. (200) Some nursing programs also emphasize a particular aspect of the medical practice, such as pediatric nursing or obstetric nursing, while others offer a broader and comprehensive (201) discussion of medical topics.

[3]

Once a graduate is armed with an associate degree, he or she is (202) generally prepared to enter the nursing profession or health care field in some capacity. Many graduates of nursing associate degree programs find gainful employment within doctor's offices, hospitals, rehabilitation clinics, and other (203) clinical settings. While (204) some graduates choose to work on the administrative side of things. (205) Some nursing professionals may decide to return to a more advanced nursing program with the goal of furthering their (206) education, career opportunities, and earning potential.

[4]

The nursing field is desirable for many people, part (207) of the attraction is that the industry is poised for long-term growth. As long as populations continue to age, the need for nurses continue (208) to grow. Pursuing an associate degree offers a great way to train to become a nurse, a career with global opportunities. (209) (210) (211)

196.

(A) NO CHANGE

(B) an associate degree is chosen by many students.

(C) many students choose to earn an associate degree.

(D) the path many choose to follow is earning an associate degree.

197.

(A) NO CHANGE
(B) industry, has become
(C) industry, becoming
(D) industry, and has become

198.

(A) NO CHANGE
(B) program, itself
(C) program, itself,
(D) program itself,

199. After rereading this paragraph, the writer wishes to add a word that will clarify the types of factors described in last part of the sentence. Which of the choices best accomplishes the writer's goal?

(A) intangible
(B) crucial
(C) administrative
(D) content-based

200. The writer is considering adding the following true statement here:

Common areas and subjects of study often include anatomy, chemistry, biology, pharmacology, and nutrition.

Should the writer make this addition?

(A) Yes, because the statement provides more detailed information to support the sentence that precedes it.
(B) Yes, because without the sentence, the reader would not know that different programs share common courses of study.
(C) No, because the statement contains unnecessary details that interrupt the paragraph's flow of ideas.
(D) No, because the paragraph focuses on how programs are different rather than how they are the same.

201.

(A) NO CHANGE
(B) broader and more comprehensive
(C) comprehensive
(D) broader, all-encompassing

202.

(A) NO CHANGE
(B) they are
(C) it is
(D) which is

203. If the writer were to delete the underlined portion, the paragraph would essentially lose:

(A) detailed descriptions of the kinds of employment opportunities available to nurses.
(B) more specific information about the types of possible working environments for nurses.
(C) a logical transition from the types of careers available to associate degree holders as compared to those available to those who complete more advanced programs.
(D) an explanation of why a nursing career is desirable.

204.

(A) NO CHANGE
(B) Although
(C) Whenever
(D) OMIT the underlined portion and capitalize *some*.

205.

(A) NO CHANGE
(B) side.
(C) side, which is an option.
(D) end of things.

206.

(A) NO CHANGE

(B) there

(C) they're

(D) an

207.

(A) NO CHANGE

(B) people; part

(C) people part

(D) people, who are part

208.

(A) NO CHANGE

(B) have continued

(C) continues

(D) are continuing

209.

(A) NO CHANGE

(B) a global career with world-wide opportunities.

(C) a global career with opportunities that are available around the world

(D) a career that has opportunities that span the globe.

Questions 210–211 ask about the preceding passage as a whole.

210. For the sake of logic and cohesion, paragraph 2 should be placed:

(A) where it is now.

(B) before paragraph 1.

(C) after paragraph 3.

(D) after paragraph 2.

211. Suppose the writer had intended to create an essay that compares the opportunities available from obtaining an associate degree with those available from holding more advanced degrees. Would this essay accomplish that goal?

(A) Yes, because the essay gives specific examples of one career opportunity available by obtaining an associate degree.

(B) Yes, because the essay discusses a career for which one may prepare by obtaining an associate degree or a more advanced degree.

(C) No, because the essay compares the opportunities available for those with an associate degree with those with advanced degrees but only for nursing and not for other vocations.

(D) No, because although the essay mentions that nurses may pursue advanced degrees, it does not explain how the resulting opportunities differ from those available to holders of an associate degree.

Environmental Disturbances

Questions 212–225 are based on the following information.

(adapted from *Environmental Science For Dummies*, by Alecia M. Spooner, Wiley)

[1]

Disturbances can change the structure of plant communities in several different ways, including knocking down trees or removing plants and animals from large parts of an environment. Although your instinct may tell <u>you</u> (212) to protect communities from such disruptive events, scientists have found that some communities actually prefer to be disturbed every now and then.

[2]

Even without humans or other animals, plant communities often have to deal with unexpected changes, such as floods, fires, and windstorms. (213) These events that disrupt the community are called (214) disturbances.

[3]

Take for example the ponderosa pine tree forests in the western U.S. Under natural conditions, these forests experience common (215) relatively small fires that burn away the low-growing plants and grasses, but only (216) gently burn the bark of the trees, leaving them to recover and continue growing. The U.S. Forest Service's efforts to reduce and diminish (217) forest fires interrupted this natural cycle of disturbance. As a result, instead of an occasional small fire, when fires did occur in these forests, they grew to a much larger size and caused a lot more damage — (218) destroying every tree in their path. The buildup of low-growing plants and small trees gave fuel to the fires, making them strong enough for more than 200 years to destroy pine trees that had weathered smaller fires. (219)

[4]

Scientists have since realized that fire is a welcome occasional disturbance in these communities. In fact, some species are considered disturbance-adapted species because they have adapted and evolved (220) to depend on the occasional community disturbance. In the case of the lodgepole pine, however, (221) the trees need fire in order to open its (222) pine cones and release seeds.

[5]

[1] When any type of disturbance disrupts a community, the organisms in the community must respond quickly and effectively if they want to survive. [2] This ability to respond quickly (in other words, to bounce back) from a disturbance is called resilience. [3] The resilience of a specific community often depends on the complexity and structure of that community. [4] The more diverse a community is, the more easily it can respond quickly to a disturbance. [5] For example, a community, with a high degree of diversity (223) has many species available to refill the ecological niches left empty after a disturbance. (224) (225)

212.

(A) NO CHANGE

(B) one

(C) them

(D) people

213. If the writer were to delete the underlined part and adjust the punctuation, the sentence would primarily lose:

(A) information that explains why plant communities have to code with unforeseen circumstances.

(B) specific types of natural disturbances.

(C) examples of disasters caused by humans and other animals.

(D) a list of ways that communities may protect themselves from unexpected events.

214.

(A) NO CHANGE

(B) has been called

(C) are calling

(D) were called

215. Given that all choices are true, which provides the clearest representation of the occurrence frequency of the small forest fires?

(A) NO CHANGE

(B) a high frequency of

(C) quinquennial

(D) numerous

216.

(A) NO CHANGE

(B) grasses but only

(C) grasses, only

(D) grasses but they only

217.

(A) NO CHANGE

(B) reduce

(C) lessen the occurrences of

(D) diminish down to nothing

218.

(A) NO CHANGE

(B) damage

(C) damage;

(D) damaging and

219. The best location for the underlined phrase in the sentence is:

(A) where it is now.

(B) after *pine trees.*

(C) after *destroy.*

(D) after *fires.*

220.

(A) NO CHANGE

(B) adapt and evolve

(C) have evolved

(D) adapted and evolved

221.

(A) NO CHANGE

(B) therefore,

(C) consequently,

(D) for example,

222.

(A) NO CHANGE

(B) its

(C) they're

(D) it's

223.

(A) NO CHANGE

(B) a community with a high degree of diversity

(C) a community with a high degree, of diversity,

(D) a community with a high degree of diversity,

224. For the sake of logic and coherence of the paragraph, sentence 3 should be placed:

(A) where it is now.

(B) before sentence 1.

(C) after sentence 4.

(D) after sentence 5.

Question 225 asks about the passage as a whole.

225. For the sake of logic and cohesion, paragraph 2 should be placed:

(A) where it is now.

(B) before paragraph 1.

(C) after paragraph 3.

(D) after paragraph 4.

Flu Care Packages

Questions 226–240 are based on the following information.

[1]

On average about 15 percent of people in the United States get the flu each year, and more than 200,000 people are hospitalized from flu-related complications. [A] Because stress (226) can make flu symptoms worse, and flu season peaks right around the most stressful time in a college student's life, (227) December during finals. Although many students will be lucky enough to avoid the flu this year, others, possibly your friends and family members, will not. (228) With flu season quickly approaching, how will you and your readers cheer up your loved ones when they have the flu this year without putting yourself at risk of receiving this nasty (229) virus?

[2]

According to *Forbes Magazine*, one remedy for the flu is eating oats. [B] However, (230) when people have the flu, they hardly have enough energy to get up and make themselves oatmeal or even purchase superfoods like oats to help them get better.

Being sick is never fun, and as your college readers know (231) receiving just about anything from a loved one when they're (232) sick means the world. With this knowledge, (233) many Madison businesses are using this information to cater to the needs of suffering students this flu season through care package delivery programs. [C] These local Madison businesses, such as Fresh Baked and Spruce Confections, allow you to design the combination of goodies you want to include, compose a specialized note with what you want to say to your sick loved one, and provide delivery of the treats. (234) It also helps that both of these businesses offer numerous items with oats, to further promote a speedy recovery. (235)

[3]

There are many college students that have shared (236) their flu season stories with us and (237) will be available to share heartwarming stories about how much receiving one of these care packages meant. [D] We will also introduce you to the owners of the two bakeries so they can explain what makes these care packages so beneficial, as well as how they came (238) up with such a unique idea. (239)

226.

(A) NO CHANGE
(B) If stress
(C) While stress
(D) Stress

227.

(A) NO CHANGE
(B) college's students life,
(C) college students' life,
(D) college student's life

228. The writer is considering deleting the underlined part of the preceding sentence. Should the part be kept or deleted?

(A) Kept, because it provides a helpful transition to an idea in the following sentence.
(B) Kept, because without it the reader would not know that many people suffer from the flu.
(C) Deleted, because it contains a reference to *you* than is inconsistent with the rest of the passage.
(D) Deleted, because it repeats information previously stated in the passage.

229. Which of the following choices is the LEAST acceptable alternative to the underlined word?

(A) horrible
(B) loathsome
(C) vile
(D) raunchy

230.

(A) NO CHANGE
(B) Similarly,
(C) Likewise,
(D) Consequently,

231.

(A) NO CHANGE
(B) know,
(C) know;
(D) know:

232.

(A) NO CHANGE
(B) their
(C) it is
(D) one is

233.

(A) NO CHANGE

(B) Knowing this,

(C) Having this knowledge available to them,

(D) OMIT the underlined portion and capitalize *many*.

234.

(A) NO CHANGE

(B) include and compose a specialized note to your sick loved one, and they

(C) include, compose a specialized note with what you want to say to your sick loved one, and they

(D) include and compose a specialized note to your sick loved one, providing

235.

(A) NO CHANGE

(B) businesses, offer numerous items with oats, to further promote a speedy recovery

(C) businesses offer numerous items with oats to further promote a speedy recovery

(D) businesses offer numerous items with oats to further promote, a speedy recovery

236.

(A) NO CHANGE

(B) There exist many college students who have shared

(C) Many college students have shared

(D) There are many students who are in college that have shared

237.

(A) NO CHANGE

(B) us, and

(C) us; and

(D) us but

238.

(A) NO CHANGE

(B) come

(C) had came

(D) has come

Questions 239–240 ask about the passage as a whole.

239. The writer wants to add the following sentence to the passage:

Since last year's outbreak, the flu is on the minds of many people, especially frequent readers of your articles and blogs about staying healthy.

Which of the following is the best placement for the sentence in the passage?

(A) Point A in paragraph 1

(B) Point B in paragraph 2

(C) Point C in paragraph 2

(D) Point D in paragraph 3

240. Suppose the writer's goal was to persuade other writers to promote a particular service. Would this essay accomplish this goal?

(A) Yes, because the essay discusses the benefits of eating oats.

(B) Yes, because the essay directs information about care packages toward blog writers.

(C) No, because the essay is primarily directed toward parents rather than writers.

(D) No, because the essay promotes a particular lifestyle instead of a service.

Planning Your Wedding

Questions 241–255 are based on the following information.

Congrats on finding that person with <u>whom</u> (241) you want to spend the rest of your life! Now that you've said "I will," <u>its</u> (242) time to start thinking dresses, dates, and details. [A] If you don't have a year or two to carefully plan every last detail, don't <u>stress —</u> (243) many couples find that they can design dream weddings in only about six months with <u>minimal stress and anxiety.</u> (244) While <u>it</u> (245) may force you to be more flexible when it comes to selecting dates, vendors, and venues, you should otherwise experience very little trouble designing a day you will remember forever, as long as you draft a <u>schedule, and stick</u> (246) to it.

[1] Arguably, <u>one of the biggest</u> (247) decisions you'll have to make, at least at the beginning of the wedding-planning process, involves setting a budget. [2] You may have heard the phrase "budget drives strategy," and <u>this rule rings true for</u> (248) wedding planning. [3] Once you settle on a number, you will have a far better idea of how many people you can invite, how far you'd like to travel, if at all, and so on. [B] [4] With the budget taken care of, it's time to concentrate on the nitty-gritty details. [5] Wedding dresses take a notoriously long time to be altered in most cases (the same goes for <u>bridesmaid's dresses</u> (249) and tuxedos), so you may want to place <u>this</u> (250) toward the top of your to-do list. [6] You may also benefit financially from booking your honeymoon as far in advance as possible. [C] (<u>251</u>)

Once you have worked your way through the details, it is time to start thinking of the <u>things</u> (252) you've likely overlooked. Did you <u>send save-the-dates, or at least, invitations,</u> (253) in a timely manner? Is your photographer booked, and your vows written? Make a list and check it <u>carefully — twice, because</u> (254) you want nothing left to chance when it comes to your big day. [D](<u>255</u>)

241.

(A) NO CHANGE

(B) who

(C) which

(D) OMIT the underlined word.

242.

(A) NO CHANGE

(B) it's

(C) it

(D) its'

243.

(A) NO CHANGE

(B) stress

(C) stress,

(D) stress, so

244.

(A) NO CHANGE

(B) a minimum of stress and anxiety.

(C) minimal anxiety.

(D) a minimum of stress.

245.

(A) NO CHANGE

(B) they

(C) its

(D) a shortened timeline

246.

(A) NO CHANGE

(B) schedule and, stick

(C) schedule and stick

(D) schedule, stick

247.

(A) NO CHANGE

(B) one of the most biggest

(C) the biggest

(D) the most big

248. Which of the choices best references the quote provided in the first part of the sentence and remains consistent with the following sentence?

(A) NO CHANGE

(B) this maxim applies to

(C) this proverb relates to

(D) following this cliché ruins

249.

(A) NO CHANGE

(B) bridesmaids' dresses

(C) bridesmaid dresses

(D) dresses for bridesmaids'

250.

(A) NO CHANGE

(B) alterations

(C) these

(D) that

251. After reading this paragraph, the writer decides to break it into two. The best place to begin the new paragraph is after sentence:

(A) 3, because this sentence completes the discussion of the topic discussed in the first three sentences before a new topic is introduced in the last sentences.

(B) 3, because this sentence is the last to mention the necessity of a budget.

(C) 4, because this sentence provides information that summarizes the importance of the budget and sets up the next paragraph about alterations.

(D) 4, because this sentence emphasizes the importance of a budget before the essay talks about wedding details in the next paragraph.

252.

(A) NO CHANGE

(B) details

(C) tasks

(D) stuff

253.

(A) NO CHANGE

(B) send save-the-dates or at least invitations,

(C) send save-the-dates, or, at least, invitations

(D) send save-the-dates or, at least, invitations

254.

(A) NO CHANGE

(B) carefully — twice — because

(C) carefully, twice — because

(D) carefully twice because,

Question 255 asks about the preceding passage as a whole.

255. The writer wants to add the following sentence to the essay:

So it's wise to start looking into your dream destination sooner than later.

The best placement for this addition would be:

(A) point A.

(B) point B.

(C) point C.

(D) point D.

Early History of Electricity Markets

Questions 256–270 are based on the following information.

(adapted from *Electricity Markets: Pricing, Structures and Economics*, by Chris Harris, Wiley)

[1]

In the late 19th century, the economic model in the industrial nations for new infrastructure development such as railways and canals was a mixture of private and municipal development, a time in which electricity supply could be said to have become an industry. (256) Governments imposed a series of laws and rulings that first increased the standardization and coordination and then expanding (257) the degree of public ownership and control where national interests dictated that it should. Then, as much as now, the organizational structure of the ESI was strongly shaped (258) by the prevailing political paradigm. Closely following attempts to standardize were attempts to regulate. Therefore, (259) in 1898 Samuel Insull in the USA who tried to impose regulation over "debilitating competition" and New York and Wisconsin that initiated (260) state regulation of utilities in 1907, while England took a more liberal view and allowed a "rabble of small inefficient electrical undertakings with which parliament had unwisely saddled the country."

[2]

[A] In the early days, electricity usage was largely for municipal installations <u>such as lighthouses and street lighting</u> (261). [B] In truth, the product sold was light rather than electricity. [C] The provision of the service used a levy, and <u>the municipality contracted directly with utilities with names, such as Illinois Power and Light, which raised debt and equity from private investors.</u> (262) [D] [263]

[3]

With the rapid arrival of new utilities providing light and power and light to <u>an increasing number</u> (264) of buildings, the need for greater coordination became apparent, and legislation was set up to systematize the procedure for setting up public supplies. Then national grids <u>being</u> (265) set up by statute. For example, <u>in the U.K. in the 1926 Electricity Supply Act, the General Electricity Board was created</u> (266) and the National Grid <u>begun</u> (267) development and construction. Between 1920 and 1950, most houses in <u>Europe, and</u> [267] America became connected to the networks. [269] [270]

256.

(A) NO CHANGE

(B) The economic model in the industrial nations for new infrastructure development such as railways and canals was a mixture of private and municipal development in the 19th century, a time in which electricity supply could be said to have become an industry.

(C) The economic model in the industrial nations in the 19th century for new infrastructure development such as railways and canals was a mixture of private and municipal development, a time in which electricity supply could be said to have become an industry.

(D) Being a mixture of private and municipal development in the 19th century, there was an economic model in the industrial nations for new infrastructure development such as railways and canals, a time in which electricity supply could be said to have become an industry.

257.

(A) NO CHANGE

(B) then expand

(C) expanding then

(D) then expanded

258.

(A) NO CHANGE

(B) Then as much as now, the organizational structure of the ESI was strongly shaped,

(C) Then, as much as now, the organizational structure, of the ESI, was strongly shaped

(D) Then as much as now the organizational structure of the ESI was strongly shaped,

259.

(A) NO CHANGE
(B) For example,
(C) Likewise,
(D) Also,

260.

(A) NO CHANGE
(B) initiating
(C) initiated
(D) who initiated

261. If the writer were to delete the underlined information, the paragraph would primarily lose:

(A) details about the types of electricity available in the early days.
(B) examples of the types of entities that required electricity.
(C) an explanation of the difference between light products and electricity products.
(D) irrelevant information about early sources of light.

262.

(A) NO CHANGE
(B) the municipality contracted directly with utilities with names, such as Illinois Power and Light which raised debt, and equity from private investors.
(C) the municipality contracted directly with utilities, with names such as Illinois Power and Light, which raised debt and equity from private investors.
(D) the municipality contracted directly with utilities with names such as Illinois Power and Light that raised debt and equity from private investors.

263. The writer wants to add the following sentence to this paragraph:

The earliest installations were a matter of civic pride.

The most logical placement for this sentence is at:

(A) point A.
(B) point B.
(C) point C.
(D) point D.

264.

(A) NO CHANGE
(B) a greater amount
(C) an increasing amount
(D) an increasingly number

265.

(A) NO CHANGE
(B) were
(C) have been
(D) are

266.

(A) NO CHANGE
(B) under the 1926 Electricity Supply Act, the U.K. created the General Electricity Board,
(C) in the U.K., under the 1926 Electricity Supply Act, the General Electricity Board was created,
(D) created by the 1926 Electricity Supply Act in the U.K. was the General Electricity Board

267.

(A) NO CHANGE
(B) begins
(C) has begun
(D) began

268.

(A) NO CHANGE

(B) Europe and,

(C) Europe and

(D) Europe, and,

Questions 269–270 ask about the preceding passage as a whole.

269. Which of the following orderings of the paragraphs is most logical?

(A) NO CHANGE

(B) 1, 3, 2

(C) 2, 1, 3

(D) 2, 3, 1

270. Suppose the writer wanted to write an essay that documents a complete history of electricity markets in England and the United States. Would this essay accomplish that goal?

(A) Yes, because it mentions regulation of utilities in 1907 England.

(B) Yes, because the essay covers electricity products during two different centuries.

(C) No, because the essay covers the rise of electricity markets in earlier centuries but not in current markets.

(D) No, because the essay does not specifically reference electricity markets in the United States.

When You Leave Your Vehicle

Questions 271–285 are based on the following information.

Whether you are a "snowbird," or (271) simply someone who splits his or her (272) time among several addresses, you may find yourself leaving your vehicle unattended for extended periods of time. Even cars that don't move too often are in need of a little TLC now and then, however, so (273) read on for a look at how to keep it (274) safe and sound — even when you're not around.

Though it may sound as if it would be wasteful (275) to wash that car right before you leave town, doing so is actually a smart move. Water spots, bird droppings, and dried mud or dirt (276) can damage your car's paint job if they are left on a vehicle for an extended period, but (277) washing (and, ideally, waxing) your vehicle carefully before you leave will help prevent this harm. (278)

You should also think twice about leaving your vehicle parked on the street outside (279) for multiple reasons. Criminals and critters being (280) just a few of things you may have to worry about (281) in your absence. For example, (282) rain and snow can do a number on the overall condition of your car. Your best bet is to keep the car inside a garage, but if you're forced to park it on street, be sure to protect it with a weather-resistant cover.

In addition to washing your car, its (283) smart to fill it with oil and gas before embarking on any type of long-term absence. When a less-than-full gas tank sits for a long time, it may (284) absorb moisture, which may cause damage. Engine oil, too, can prove dangerously (285) to your car if it's left to sit without being changed for an extended period of time. Take these minor precautions prior to traveling, and you'll enhance the chances your car will be road-ready upon your return.

271.

(A) NO CHANGE

(B) "snowbird" or,

(C) "snowbird" or

(D) "snowbird," or,

272.

(A) NO CHANGE

(B) they're

(C) its

(D) your

273.

(A) NO CHANGE
(B) then; however so
(C) then: however, so
(D) then however so,

274.

(A) NO CHANGE
(B) yours
(C) its
(D) it all

275.

(A) NO CHANGE
(B) as though it would be wasteful
(C) like it's wasteful
(D) wasteful

276. The writer wants to show the variety of grimy substances that can harm car finishes. Which choice best accomplishes this goal?

(A) NO CHANGE
(B) Grimy substances from air and land
(C) A wide variety of dirty elements
(D) There is no end to the substances that

277. Which of the following choices is the LEAST acceptable alternative to the underlined part?

(A) time; however,
(B) period; though,
(C) time; nonetheless,
(D) period, for

278. At this point in the essay, the writer is considering adding the following sentence:

Grimy substances from the air and ground can also damage the paint on your home.

Should the writer make this addition here?

(A) Yes, because the sentence relates to the paragraph's main point about the damage caused by dirt.
(B) Yes, because without it the reader would not know that houses also need protection from the elements.
(C) No, because the sentence introduces a new dilemma that is unrelated to the essay's main idea.
(D) No, because the essay fails to state how homeowners can prevent the elements from damaging paint on their homes.

279.

(A) NO CHANGE
(B) outdoors
(C) out-of-doors
(D) OMIT the underlined part.

280.

(A) NO CHANGE
(B) creating
(C) are
(D) were being

281.

(A) NO CHANGE
(B) from
(C) on
(D) by

282.

(A) NO CHANGE
(B) Accordingly,
(C) On the other hand,
(D) Furthermore,

283.

(A) NO CHANGE
(B) it's
(C) its'
(D) you're

284.

(A) NO CHANGE
(B) could
(C) could have
(D) should

285.

(A) NO CHANGE
(B) dangerous
(C) to be dangerously
(D) danger

The Link Between Substance Abuse and Assault

Questions 286–300 are based on the following information.

[1]

Common knowledge indicates that alcohol and drug use and abuse is (286) prevalent in today's society. Different perceptions regarding (287) what constitutes the difference between use and abuse. What some may see as a casual night of drinking, (288) or needing to drink to fit in, has many consequences and for some may lead to a substance dependency. The use of alcohol and drugs has shown to have a negative affect (289) on the human body, whether by (290) impairing one's judgment, a coping device, (291) or further promoting aggressive behavior, and causing people to do things (292) they would not likely do otherwise. Much research has been done to study the role that alcohol and drug use has in cases of sexual abuse and assault, both for the victim and the abuser. However, it is too simplistic to say the consumption of drugs and alcohol are the cause of sexual assault and sexual abuse.

[2]

The idea of alcohol consumption's being a social reality surrounding (293) us given the media and personal daily experience. This common exposure seems to make alcohol and drug use common (294) and therefore acceptable. Antonia Abbey's research cites a study conducted by Kilpatrick and colleagues that reveals that alcohol is the drug of choice, and more than 95 percent of victims who were impaired reported that they had consumed alcohol. (295)

[3]

Numerous cases of sexual assault and abuse have been dismissed because one or both parties involved had been drinking. Excusing cases involving alcohol suggests that society sees it as more acceptable for someone to force sexual acts on one who is impaired. However, according to Bedard-Gilligan and her colleague's (296) research, in many cases when alcohol is involved, the assaults, "were more severe in terms of injuries, and the use of force." The fact that research showed that assaults were more violent when alcohol was involved (297) poses a major problem if the "I was drunk" excuse is used to minimize the responsibility for sexual assault.

[4]

Societal influence also plays a major role in the relationship between alcohol use and the steps that lead to sexual assault or abuse. The desire to use alcohol and drugs is often promoted by the influence of others around one is using them as well (298). As explained by Michele Berdard-Gilligan and several colleagues, using alcohol as a form of "liquid courage" may lead to increased intoxicated risk-taking, which may put victims in situations where they are more likely to experience an assault. (299) The need to use alcohol to feel more comfortable in a social setting may more likely result in the occurrence of some form of assault. (300)

286.

(A) NO CHANGE

(B) were

(C) has been

(D) are

287.

(A) NO CHANGE

(B) exist regarding

(C) regards

(D) regarded

288.

(A) NO CHANGE

(B) drinking

(C) drinking;

(D) drinking:

289.

(A) NO CHANGE

(B) effect

(C) affectation

(D) effectuation

290.

(A) NO CHANGE

(B) as

(C) on

(D) for

291.

(A) NO CHANGE

(B) judgment, coping device,

(C) judgment by a coping device,

(D) judgment, becoming a coping device,

292. The writer wants to convey the danger of substance abuse. Which of the choices best accomplishes this goal?

(A) NO CHANGE

(B) commit acts

(C) engage in risky behaviors

(D) perform activities

293.

(A) NO CHANGE

(B) surrounds

(C) had surrounded

(D) surrounded

294.

(A) NO CHANGE

(B) familiar

(C) day-to-day

(D) useless

295. The writer is considering deleting the underlined sentence. Should the sentence be kept or deleted?

(A) Kept, because the sentence cites statistical data, and statistics are always relevant.

(B) Kept, because the sentence provides clear support for the premise that daily exposure to media has made alcohol use more common.

(C) Deleted, because the statistics presented are not directly relevant to the statements made in the first sentences of the paragraph.

(D) Deleted, because although the statistical data in the sentence supports the main topic of the paragraph, it does not pertain to the main idea of the passage.

296.

(A) NO CHANGE

(B) colleagues

(C) colleagues'

(D) colleague

297.

(A) NO CHANGE

(B) research shows that assaults were more violent when alcohol was involved

(C) research shows that assaults are more violent when alcohol was involved

(D) research shows that assaults are more violent when alcohol is involved

298.

(A) NO CHANGE

(B) others that surround one

(C) all of the others that are around you

(D) others

299.

(A) NO CHANGE

(B) risk-taking, which may put victims in situations, where they are more likely to experience an assault.

(C) risk-taking, which may put victims, in situations where they are more likely to experience an assault.

(D) risk-taking which may put victims in situations, where they are more likely to experience an assault.

Question 300 asks about the preceding passage as a whole.

300. Which of the following provides the most logical placement of paragraph 4?

(A) where it is now

(B) before paragraph 1

(C) before paragraph 2

(D) before paragraph 3

Chapter 2

The Math Test

The longest section of the ACT is the 60-minute math test. With a total of 60 questions, you have about a minute to answer each question, an objective that's more easily achieved on the easier questions at the beginning and more difficult for the more complex questions at the end.

The ACT allows you use a calculator throughout the section, but you may not need it much. Keep a constant eye on your answer possibilities and eliminate those that don't make sense. Often, you'll find you don't have to complete your calculations to arrive at the correct answer.

The Problems You'll Work On

When working through the questions in this chapter, be prepared to answer questions on these topics:

- **Basic math,** including fractions, decimals, percentages, exponents, ratios, and proportions
- **Algebra,** including linear equations, coordinate geometry, and quadratic equations
- **Geometry,** including knowing definitions and formulas for working with two and three-dimensional shapes
- **Algebra II and pre-calculus,** including functions, trigonometry, logarithms, and vectors
- **Probability and statistics,** including average, median, probability, combinations, and permutations

What to Watch Out For

To increase your accuracy and improve time management, avoid these snags:

- Making mistakes in simple math, such as improperly subtracting negative numbers
- Spending more than a couple of minutes on any one problem instead of marking time-consuming questions and returning to them later
- Failing to review key formulas and concepts from all math areas
- Engaging in complex calculations when you can instead apply time-saving strategies such as trying answer choices and plugging in values for variables

301. What is the least common denominator of these fractions: $\frac{2}{7}, \frac{4}{15}, \frac{1}{2}$?

(A) 10

(B) 21

(C) 45

(D) 60

(E) 210

302. Jenny's rectangular bedroom has an area of 120 square feet. One contractor calculates the cost to wallpaper her bedroom using the formula of $0.80A + 100d$, where A is the area of the room and d is the number of days required to apply wallpaper to the room. How much will Jenny pay this contractor to apply wallpaper to her bedroom if it takes 4 days to complete the project?

(A) 96

(B) 180

(C) 496

(D) 800

(E) 960

303. For what value(s) of x is $(x+5)(x-1)=0$ true?

(A) 5 and −1

(B) −5 and 1

(C) 5 only

(D) −5 only

(E) −1 only

304. Which is the median of −3, 18, −4, $\frac{1}{2}$, 11.

(A) −3

(B) 18

(C) −4

(D) $\frac{1}{2}$

(E) 11

305. A store owner wants to make a 35% profit on the sale of her shovels. If the store owner purchased each shovel for $16, at what price per shovel will she have to sell the item to achieve the desired profit?

(A) $20.00

(B) $21.60

(C) $22.00

(D) $25.60

(E) $32.60

306. A fencepost that measures exactly $1\frac{2}{3}$ yards long is cut into three pieces. The first piece measures 30 inches. The second piece measures 15 inches. How long is the third piece?

(A) 15 inches

(B) 14 inches

(C) $10\frac{1}{3}$ inches

(D) 13 inches

(E) $13\frac{1}{3}$ inches

307. Three friends, Ben, Keisha, and Stanley, earned an average of $40,000 each for their work on a political campaign. Their total earnings were exactly 60% of the total earnings of everyone who worked on the campaign. How much were the total earnings of all of the campaign workers?

(A) $400,000

(B) $350,000

(C) $200,000

(D) $140,000

(E) $60,000

308. Given that $(a+7)(a-4)=0$, which of the following is a true statement?

(A) a could be +7 or +4

(B) a could be −7 or −4

(C) a could be +7 or 4

(D) a could be −7 or +4

(E) a could be 0

309. A telemarketer makes 75 calls a day for 5 days. In order to average 100 calls per day for 10 days, how many calls must the telemarketer make in the following 5 days?

(A) 1,200

(B) 1,075

(C) 1,000

(D) 625

(E) 375

310. If two of the angles in a triangle are acute, which of the following is a true statement regarding the other angle in the triangle?

(A) The third angle must measure twice the measure of the smallest angle.

(B) The third angle must measure 90 degrees.

(C) The angle must be obtuse.

(D) The angle must also be acute.

(E) The angle may be acute, obtuse, or right.

311. Which of the following is a factor of $a^2 - 14a - 15$?

(A) $a + 5$

(B) $a + 3$

(C) $a - 1$

(D) $a - 3$

(E) $a - 15$

312. A biker cycles nonstop for 3 hours and 20 minutes and travels for 8 miles. The formula for finding distance (d) is $d = rt$ where t stands for the time and r is the miles per hour (mph). At what rate does the biker cycle?

(A) 2 mph

(B) $2\frac{1}{10}$ mph

(C) $2\frac{1}{2}$ mph

(D) $2\frac{2}{5}$ mph

(E) 3 mph

313. In a classroom of children, every child has either blue, brown, or green eyes. The probability of randomly selecting a child with green eyes is $\frac{1}{8}$. The probability of randomly selecting a child with brown eyes is $\frac{1}{4}$. If 15 children have blue eyes, how many children are in the classroom?

(A) 12

(B) 15

(C) 24

(D) 30

(E) 120

314. If a is five greater than b, and the sum of a and b is −15, then $b^2 =$

(A) 100

(B) 64

(C) 25

(D) 20

(E) 0

315. Tina is building a border for her rectangular garden. Before she buys supplies, she needs to find the perimeter of her garden boundaries. She measures the length to be 4.5 feet and the width to be 5 feet. What is the perimeter in feet of Tina's garden?

(A) 9.5

(B) 19

(C) 22.5

(D) 45

(E) 90

316. If $5p - 2p = 7p + 2p - 24$, then $p =$

(A) 1

(B) 12

(C) −4

(D) 4

(E) 0

317. If lines l and m are parallel, what is the degree measurement of $x+y$?

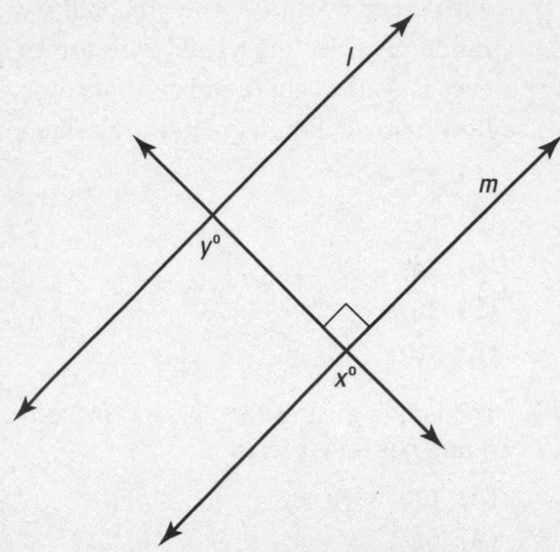

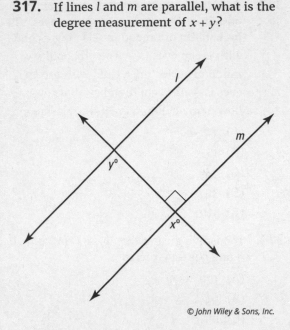

© John Wiley & Sons, Inc.

(A) 45
(B) 90
(C) 180
(D) 270
(E) 360

318. Jordy earns a 4% commission on every magazine subscription he sells. If he sells $1,354 in magazine subscriptions, how much does he earn?

(A) $5.47
(B) $54.16
(C) $140.82
(D) $541.60
(E) $1,408.16

319. Which of the following orders these numbers from greatest to least: 0.02, $\frac{1}{8}$, $\frac{3}{7}$?

(A) $\frac{2}{7} > \frac{1}{8} > 0.02$
(B) $\frac{2}{7} > 0.02 > \frac{1}{8}$
(C) $\frac{1}{8} > \frac{2}{7} > 0.02$
(D) $0.02 < \frac{1}{8} < \frac{2}{7}$
(E) $\frac{2}{7} < \frac{1}{8} < 0.02$

320. If $7x+10=31$, then $4x=$

(A) 3
(B) 4
(C) 12
(D) 16
(E) 28

321. What is the value of $x-y+z$ given that $x=3$, $y=-2$, and $z=-1$?

(A) −4
(B) −1
(C) 0
(D) 1
(E) 4

322. If $y=2$, then $(y-4)(y+2)=?$

(A) −24
(B) −8
(C) 2
(D) 8
(E) 24

323. Justin tried to compute his average score out of 8 tests. He mistakenly divided the correct sum of all of his test scores by 7 and got an average of 96. What is Justin's actual average test score?

(A) 76
(B) 80
(C) 84
(D) 106
(E) 672

324. The value of $3-0.5$ is how many times the value of $1-0.5$?

(A) 2
(B) 4.5
(C) 5
(D) 5.5
(E) 6

325. If $\left(\frac{3}{4}+2\right)(7-5)=0$ and $y \neq 5$ then y = ?

(A) $-\frac{3}{2}$

(B) $-\frac{2}{3}$

(C) $\frac{2}{3}$

(D) $\frac{3}{2}$

(E) 6

326. Bridget is putting carpet in her bedroom that covers the entire floor. If carpeting costs $5 per square foot, how much will Bridget spend on the carpet if her room is 10 feet by 16 feet?

(A) $800

(B) $550

(C) $255

(D) $130

(E) $120

327. If Emilio will be 35 years old in 6 years, how old was he *x* years ago?

(A) $41-x$

(B) $x-41$

(C) $35-x$

(D) $x-39$

(E) $29-x$

328. If $3a+2>14$, then a^2 must be

(A) equal to 9

(B) equal to 16

(C) less than 16

(D) less than 9

(E) greater than 16

329. After a hockey game, Bernie checks his body and finds that he has three bruises for every five cuts. Which of the following could be the total number of bruises and cuts on Bernie's body?

(A) 53

(B) 45

(C) 35

(D) 33

(E) 32

330. In which of the following pairs are the two numbers reciprocals of one another?

I. $\frac{1}{15}$ and $-\frac{1}{15}$

II. $\sqrt{2}$ and $\frac{\sqrt{2}}{2}$

III. 4 and $\frac{1}{4}$

(A) I only

(B) III only

(C) I and II

(D) II and III

(E) I and III

331. If $3x^3=4$, then $4\left(3x^3\right)^3$ is equal to

(A) 16

(B) 32

(C) 64

(D) 256

(E) 1,024

332. Given that $3x+2=14$, what is the value of $(x-1)^3$?

(A) 1

(B) 9

(C) 27

(D) 63

(E) 81

333. The hypotenuse of a right triangle measures 35 centimeters long. One of the legs measures 21 centimeters in length. What is the length in centimeters of the other leg?

(A) 4

(B) 15

(C) 28

(D) 42

(E) 49

334. What is the slope of the line given by the equation $3x=30-5y$?

(A) 5

(B) 3

(C) $\frac{3}{5}$

(D) $-\frac{3}{5}$

(E) -3

335. From a box containing 52 rectangular cards individually colored red, blue, white, and green, Julian randomly pulls one card at a time. The box originally held 13 red cards, 12 blue cards, 14 white cards, and 13 green cards. Julian pulls a white card, a blue card, and a green card from the box and places the cards on the table in front of him. What is the probability that the next card he pulls from the box will be green?

(A) $\frac{12}{49}$

(B) $\frac{1}{49}$

(C) $\frac{13}{52}$

(D) $\frac{3}{13}$

(E) $\frac{7}{26}$

336. A particular city bus makes the same route throughout the downtown area many times each day. If this city bus traveled 1,525 miles last week, approximately how many miles did it travel on average for each day of the full week?

(A) 173

(B) 200

(C) 218

(D) 242

(E) 300

337. Given that 6% of $(a+b)=12\%$ of b, which of the following must be true?

(A) $a<b$

(B) $a>b$

(C) $a=b$

(D) $a+b=0$

(E) $a<0$ and $b<0$

338. If x is an integer between 5 and 12, which of the following could be a true statement?

(A) $x^2=25$

(B) $\sqrt{x}=4$

(C) $2x=10.5$

(D) $\frac{1}{3}x=24.5$

(E) $4x=36$

339. A square has side lengths that measure 8 units. If that square and an isosceles right triangle have equal areas, then the side length of one of the legs of that triangle measures which of the following units?

(A) $4\sqrt{2}$

(B) $8\sqrt{2}$

(C) $4\sqrt{3}$

(D) $8\sqrt{3}$

(E) $12\sqrt{3}$

340. The sides of a triangle measure 10, 24, and 26. What is the degree measure of the angle formed by the sides measuring 10 and 24?

(A) 15

(B) 30

(C) 45

(D) 60

(E) 90

341. Nine friends intend to buy leather jackets at $299 each. The jackets cost $3,336 per dozen if bought in a full dozen batch. If those friends can convince three additional people to purchase jackets, how much would each of the jacket purchasers save on the price of the jacket?

(A) $13.00

(B) $14.23

(C) $15.00

(D) $20.75

(E) $21.00

342. Claude was y years old n years ago. How many years old will he be in terms of y in 15 years?

(A) $y+n+15$

(B) $yn+15$

(C) $y-n+15$

(D) $yn-15$

(E) $y-n-15$

343. $\left(2x^3y^4\right)^2\left(3xy^2\right)^2 =$

(A) $36x^8y^{12}$

(B) $36x^{12}y^{32}$

(C) $6x^{12}y^{32}$

(D) $6x^4y^6$

(E) $5x^{12}y^{32}$

344. A blueprint is to be an exact plan of a house's main bedroom on a reduced scale. If the main bedroom on the blueprint measures 18 inches long by 24 inches wide, the homeowner's bedroom of 15 feet long is how many feet wide?

(A) 24

(B) 22

(C) 20

(D) 12

(E) 10

345. What is the sum of the interior angle measures of a regular figure with five sides?

(A) 900

(B) 720

(C) 540

(D) 360

(E) 300

346. A circle with a radius of 12 inches has $\frac{3}{4}$ the area of a circle with a radius of how many inches?

(A) $4\sqrt{3}$

(B) 8

(C) 13

(D) $8\sqrt{3}$

(E) $64\sqrt{3}$

347. At Make-Your-Own-Burrito Restaurant, there are 4 stations of the burrito assembly line. The first station provides you with your choice of either flour or corn tortillas. From the second, you choose steak, chicken, pork, or guacamole. The options at the third station are either black beans or pinto beans. From the fourth station, you pick any one salsa. You can pick only one item from each station. If there are 48 different burrito possibilities, from how many different salsas can you choose?

(A) 2

(B) 3

(C) 4

(D) 5

(E) 6

348. In ΔABC, the measures of $\angle A$ and $\angle B$ total less than $< 48°$. Which of the following must be the measure of $\angle C$?

(A) $> 132°$

(B) $\geq 132°$

(C) $132°$

(D) $< 132°$

(E) $\leq 132°$

349. A decorator uses graph paper to plan the furniture layout for a large office. Each square box on the graph paper measures $\frac{1}{4}$ inch $\times$ $\frac{1}{4}$ inch. If each box represents 1 square foot of office space, how many inches on the graph represent a 30-foot wall in the office?

(A) 120

(B) 30

(C) 10

(D) 7.5

(E) 4

350. Denny receives a gross wage of $10.50 for every hour he works in a regular 40-hour work week. For every hour over 40 hours that Denny works in one week, he receives 1.5 times his hourly wage. In a given week, Denny works 54 hours. What were Denny's total gross earnings for that week?

(A) $220.50

(B) $420.00

(C) $567.00

(D) $588.00

(E) $640.50

351. The cost of a tablet increased 25% from 2014 to 2015. In 2016, the cost of the tablet was $\frac{1}{4}$ less than its 2014 cost. By what percentage did the cost of the tablet decrease from 2015 to 2016?

(A) 5%

(B) 25%

(C) 40%

(D) 50%

(E) 75%

352. A festival is visited one day by at total of 2,000 German tourists, 3,200 American tourists, 1,400 Mexican tourists, 1,770 French tourists, 2,400 Japanese tourists, and 1,030 tourists from other countries. If a circle graph were made representing the various countries represented by the total number of tourists, the central angle created by the segment representing the French would measure how many degrees?

(A) 360°

(B) 270°

(C) 54°

(D) 45°

(E) 15°

353. When asked how many years she had worked at her job, Leah responded, "Take the square root of 605, add it to the square of 5, and take 25 percent of the resulting sum." Which of the following expresses Leah's years on the job (L)?

(A) $L=\sqrt{(630)25}$

(B) $L=0.25\left(\sqrt{630}\right)$

(C) $L=0.25\left(\sqrt{605}\right)25$

(D) $L=0.25+\sqrt{605}+25$

(E) $L=0.25\left(\sqrt{625}+25\right)$

354. $(x+y+4)(x+y-4)=?$

(A) x^2+y^2-16

(B) x^2+y^2+16

(C) $(x+y)^2+8(x+y)-16$

(D) $(x+y)^2+8(x-y)-16$

(E) $(x+y)^2-16$

355. A statistician for a baseball team calculated that the average batting-average for the 9 starters is 0.252, and the average batting-average for the 11 reserves is 0.225. What is the average batting-average for the whole team?

(A) 0.23625

(B) 0.23715

(C) 0.23850

(D) 0.23050

(E) 0.24020

356. What are all values for z for which $|z-4|<5$?

(A) $0<z<8$

(B) $-1<z<9$

(C) $0\le z\le 8$

(D) $z<9$

(E) $z>9$

357. When $\overline{OA}$ is rotated counterclockwise 29° about point O, $\overline{OA}$ and $\overline{OB}$ will form a straight line. What is the measure of $\angle AOB$ before this rotation?

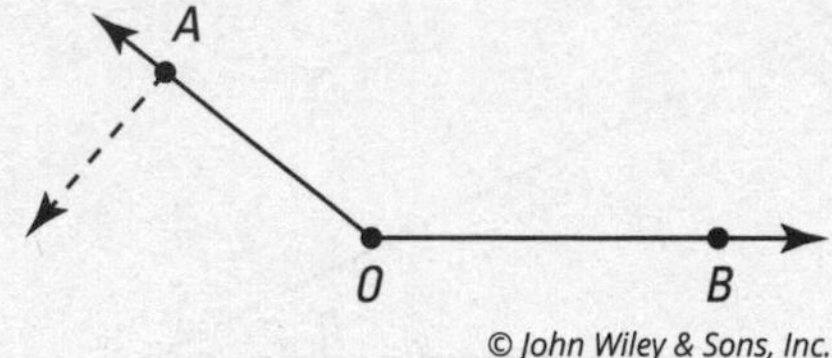

(A) 90°
(B) 119°
(C) 151°
(D) 180°
(E) 209°

358. If $10x^4 = 5$, then $5\left(10x^4\right)^2 =$?

(A) 5
(B) 25
(C) 125
(D) 625
(E) 3125

359. Line l has a positive slope and a positive x-intercept. Line m is parallel to l and has a positive y-intercept. The x-intercept of m must be

(A) positive and less than the x-intercept of l
(B) positive and greater than the x-intercept of l
(C) negative and less than the x-intercept of l
(D) negative and greater than the x-intercept of l
(E) zero

360. In the figure below, the product of the three numbers in the horizontal row equals the sum of the three numbers in the vertical column. What is the value of $x + y$?

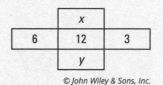

	x	
6	12	3
	y	

(A) 12
(B) 24
(C) 114
(D) 204
(E) 216

361. On her annual road trip to visit her family, Traci stopped to rest after she traveled $\frac{1}{3}$ of the total distance. She stopped again after she traveled $\frac{1}{4}$ of the distance remaining between her first stop and her family's home. She then drove the remaining 200 miles and arrived safely at her destination. What was the total distance, in miles, Traci traveled from her starting point to her family's home?

(A) 250
(B) 30
(C) 30
(D) 40
(E) 550

362. In the triangle in the figure below, what is a in terms of b?

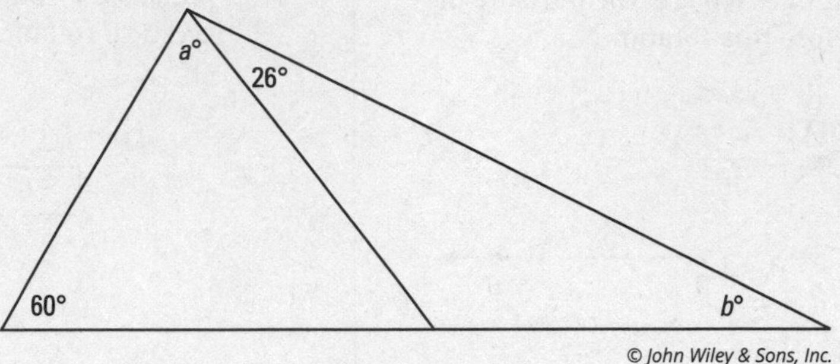

(A) $b+94$
(B) $94-b$
(C) $b-94$
(D) $70-b$
(E) $70+b$

363. The circle in the figure has a center C and a chord EF of length 15 units. What is the length in units of radius r?

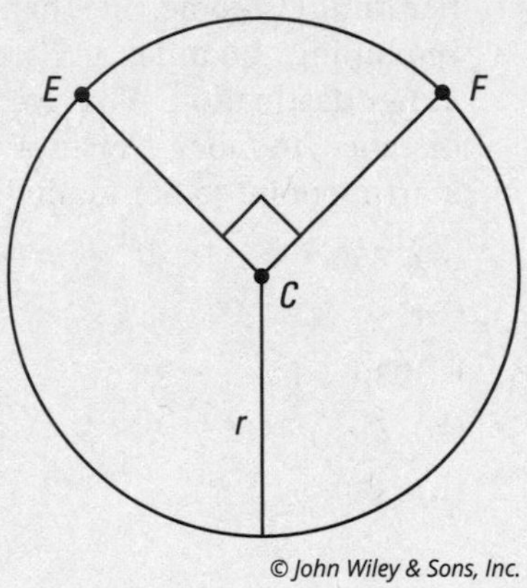

(A) $\sqrt{2}$
(B) $\sqrt{15}$
(C) 5
(D) 15
(E) $\frac{15\sqrt{2}}{2}$

364. If $f(x)=\frac{1}{1.5x}$ for $x > 0$, then $f(0.25) = ?$

(A) $\frac{1}{4}$
(B) $\frac{3}{8}$
(C) $\frac{5}{8}$
(D) $\frac{8}{5}$
(E) $\frac{8}{3}$

Questions 365–367 are based on the following information.

In the standard coordinate plane below, line l bisects the angle formed by the x- and y-axes and line m is perpendicular to the x-axis. Point C is the center of the circle. $\overline{CA}$ measures 2 units and is a radius of the circle.

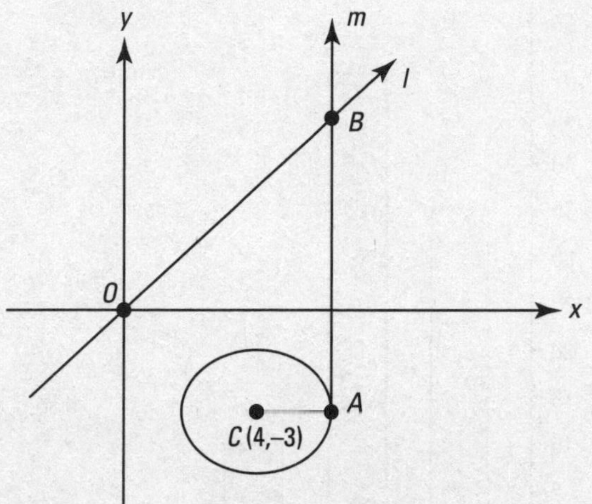

© John Wiley & Sons, Inc.

365. What is the measurement in degrees of the angle formed by line l and the y-axis?

(A) 15

(B) 30

(C) 45

(D) 60

(E) 90

366. What is the measurement in units of $\overline{OB}$?

(A) $12\sqrt{2}$

(B) $6\sqrt{2}$

(C) 6

(D) $4\sqrt{2}$

(E) 4

367. If the circle is reflected across line l, what would be the coordinates of the reflection of point A?

(A) $(-4, 3)$

(B) $(-3, 4)$

(C) $(-6, 3)$

(D) $(-5, 4)$

(E) $(-2, 2)$

368. A probability and statistics class conducted a die-rolling experiment. Each trial of the experiment consisted of rolling a single, fair, six-sided die six times and counting the number of 3s that resulted from each roll. The class recorded the results for 100 trials in the graph. In approximately what percent of trials did the class roll 3s more than two times?

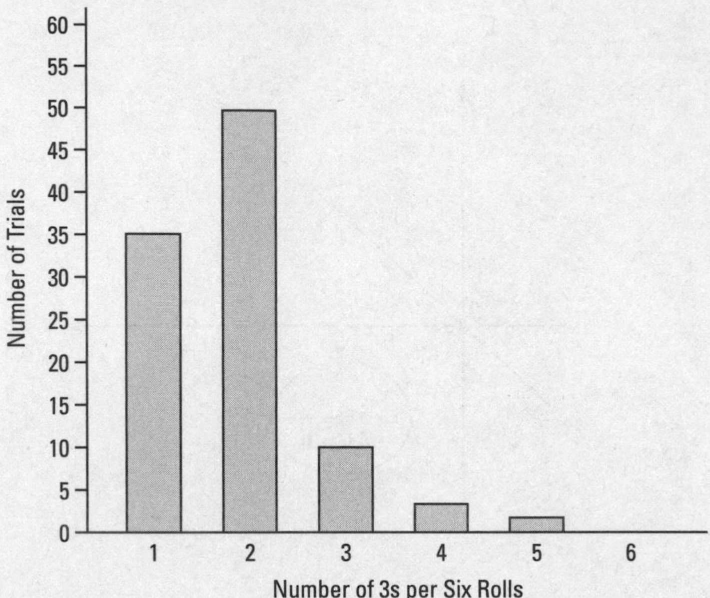

(A) 3%

(B) 5%

(C) 10%

(D) 15%

(E) 85%

369. Which of the following choices represents the correct sum and product of the roots of the equation $x^2 + 2x - 15 = 0$?

(A) Sum: −2 Product: −15

(B) Sum: −2 Product: 15

(C) Sum: 2 Product: −15

(D) Sum: 2 Product: 15

(E) Sum: −8 Product: 15

370. Individually, Jan, Steve, and Jack can complete a certain job in 3, 4, and 5 hours, respectively. What is the lowest fraction of the job that can be done in 1 hour by 2 of the three working together at their respective rates?

(A) $\frac{1}{3}$

(B) $\frac{9}{20}$

(C) $\frac{8}{15}$

(D) $\frac{7}{12}$

(E) $\frac{2}{3}$

371. If the perimeter of a rectangular swimming pool is 40 feet and its area is 75 square feet, what is the length in feet of each of the shorter sides of the swimming pool?

(A) 5

(B) 10

(C) 15

(D) 20

(E) 25

372. If basis points are defined so that 5 percent is equal to 100 basis points, then 7.5 percent is how many basis points greater than 5.5 percent?

(A) .04

(B) 40

(C) 400

(D) 4,000

(E) 40,000

373. If $y = 2$, then $(y-4)(y+2) = ?$.

(A) −24

(B) −8

(C) 2

(D) 8

(E) 24

374. In the figure, $\triangle CDE$ is equilateral, and $CE \parallel BF \parallel AG$. What is the perimeter of $\triangle ADG$?

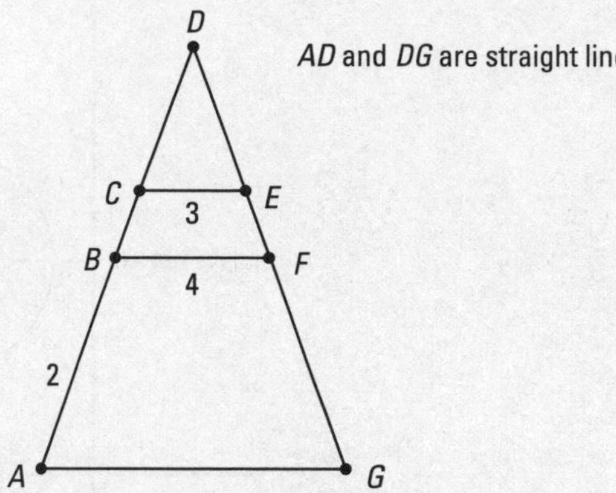

Note: Figure not drawn to scale.

(A) 9

(B) 12

(C) 15

(D) 18

(E) 21

375. In the figure, $\overline{AC}$ is parallel to the x-axis and $AC \parallel BD$. Point O is the center of the circle. What are the coordinates of point C?

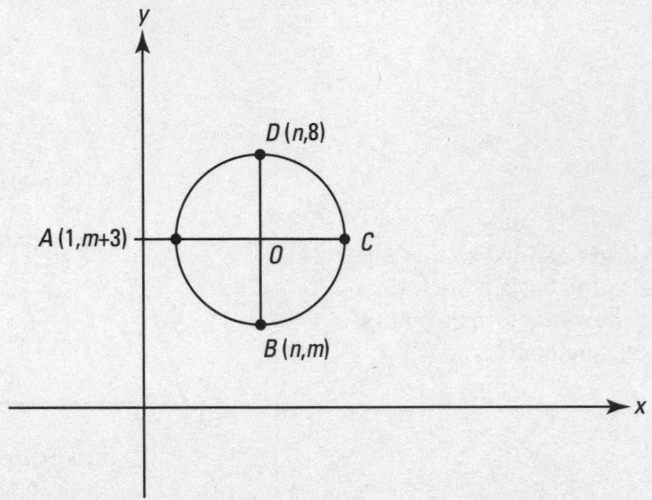

(A) (7, 4)

(B) (6, 5)

(C) (7, 5)

(D) (8, 5)

(E) (9, 4)

376. Chris lives in Omaha, Nebraska. He works in regional sales and has to travel throughout the week to meet with clients. The graph shows the distance that Chris's car is away from his home over a period of time in a given week. Which of the following situations best fits the information recorded in the graph?

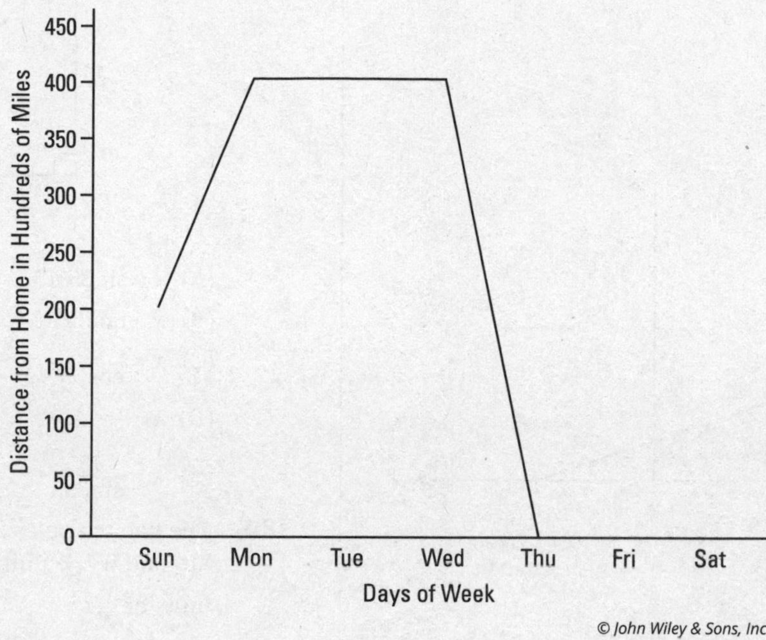

(A) Chris leaves one of his clients, drives to another client, stays there a few days, and then returns home.

(B) Chris leaves one of his clients, drives to another client, and then drives back home.

(C) Chris leaves one of his clients, drives back home, stays for a few days, and then drives to another client.

(D) Chris leaves home, drives to a client, stays there a few days, and then drives to another client.

(E) Chris leaves home, drives to a client, stays there a few days, and then drives home.

377. In the rectangular coordinate system in the figure below, the shaded region is bound by straight lines. Which of the following is NOT an equation of one of the boundary lines?

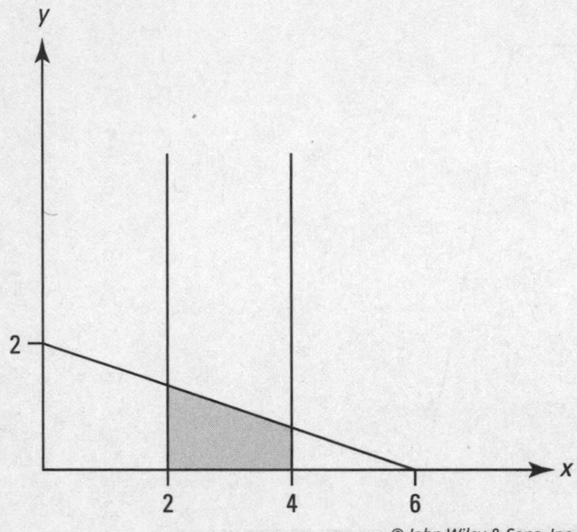

© John Wiley & Sons, Inc.

(A) $x = 2$

(B) $y = 0$

(C) $x = 4$

(D) $x + 2y = 6$

(E) $x + 3y = 6$

378. If the number of airline tickets sold per week (t) varies with the price (p) in dollars, according to the equation $t = 1000 - 2p$, what would be the total weekly revenue from the sale of airline tickets with a price of $200?

(A) $600

(B) $1,000

(C) $1,400

(D) $120,000

(E) $280,000

379. If $\Theta = 35°$ in the triangle, what is the value of x?

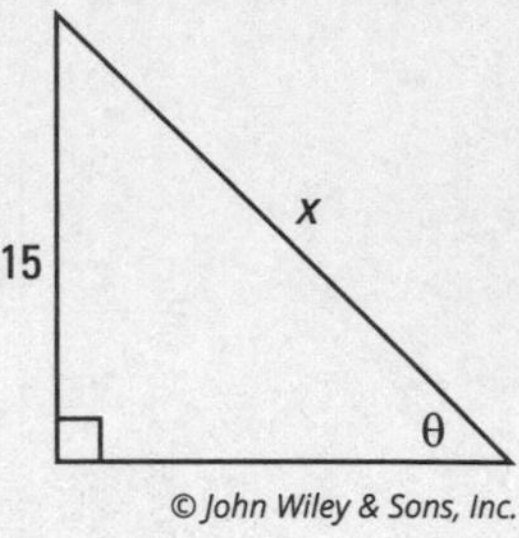

© John Wiley & Sons, Inc.

(A) $x = \sin 35° 15$

(B) $x = \tan 35° 15$

(C) $x = \dfrac{15}{\cos 35°}$

(D) $x = \dfrac{15}{\tan 35°}$

(E) $x = \dfrac{15}{\sin 35°}$

380. The two triangles in the figure are similar, and $W = 6$ units. What is the value in units of $\frac{Y}{X}$?

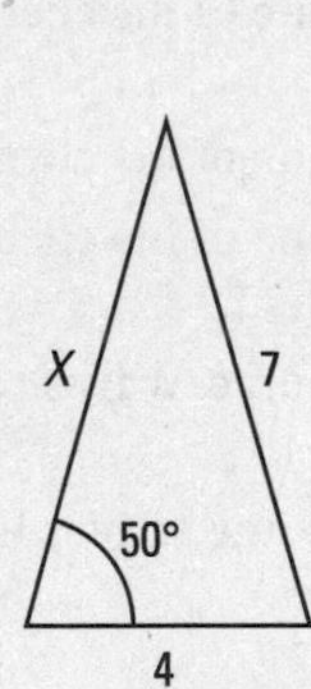

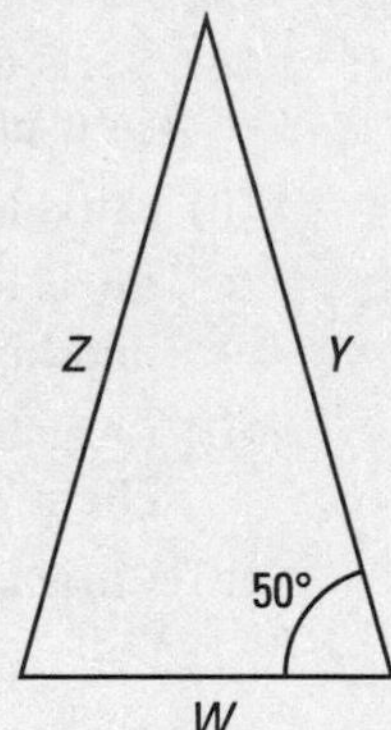

© John Wiley & Sons, Inc.

(A) $\frac{2}{3}$

(B) $\frac{4}{7}$

(C) $\frac{6}{7}$

(D) $\frac{3}{2}$

(E) $\frac{7}{4}$

Questions 381–383 are based on the following chart.

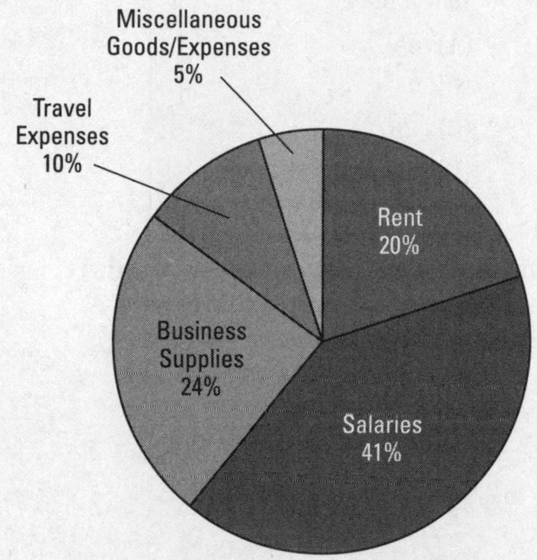

381. Welch Inc recorded its expenses for the month on this pie chart. What fraction of expenses does the company spend on rent?

(A) $\frac{2}{5}$

(B) $\frac{1}{2}$

(C) $\frac{1}{5}$

(D) $\frac{3}{4}$

(E) 20

382. If monthly expenses at Welch Inc total \$45,000, what does the company spend each month on salaries and rent?

(A) \$9,000

(B) \$17,550

(C) \$18,450

(D) \$27,450

(E) \$29,250

383. The owners want to reduce total monthly expenses from \$45,000 to \$40,000 per month. They cannot reduce their rent and salaries expenses, so they must reduce what they spend for travel, business supplies, and miscellaneous goods to meet their goal. Under the new reduced spending policy, Welch Inc. would spend a total of \$10,125 on business supplies and miscellaneous goods. Approximately what percentage of total expenses would Welch Inc. spend on travel under the reduced spending policy?

(A) 5%

(B) 6%

(C) 10%

(D) 25%

(E) Cannot be determined

384. In rectangle *ABCD*, what are coordinates of vertex *D*?

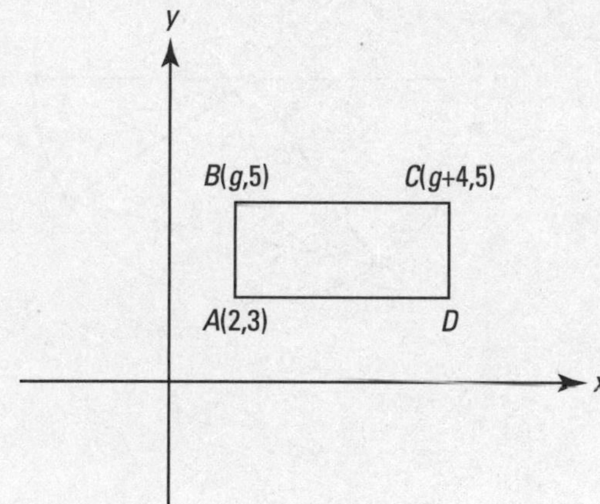

(A) (6, 3)

(B) (9, 5)

(C) (3, 6)

(D) (8, 3)

(E) (6, 5)

385. License plate designations in Tinytown consist of three characters. The first is either the letter M or F depending on the gender of the car's owner, the second is a single digit between 0 and 9, and the last is a single letter of the entire alphabet from A to Z. How many license plate designations are possible?

(A) 38

(B) 468

(C) 520

(D) 780

(E) 6,760

386. The circle in the figure has a center *C* and a radius of 5. What is the length of chord *EF*?

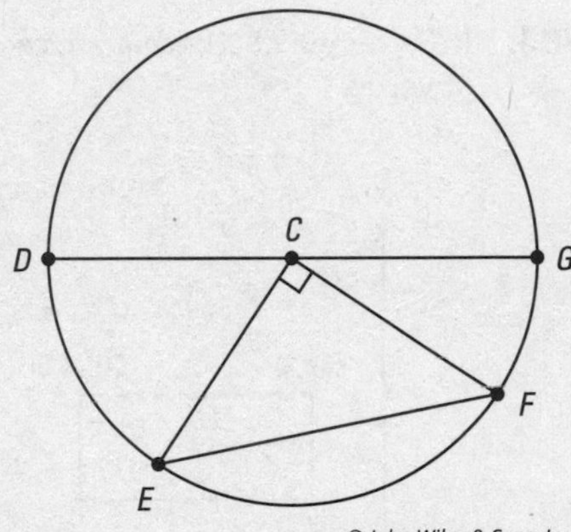

© John Wiley & Sons, Inc.

(A) 5

(B) $5\sqrt{2}$

(C) 10

(D) $10\sqrt{2}$

(E) 50

387. If $f(x)=\frac{1}{x^2}$ for $x>0$, then $f(0.5)=$

(A) $\frac{1}{4}$

(B) $\frac{1}{2}$

(C) 1

(D) 2

(E) 4

388. Larry, Greg, and Ralph raise dogs. Larry's Labradors has two-thirds as many dogs as Greg's Goldens, which has three-fourths as many dogs as Ralph's Retrievers. If Larry has 50 dogs, how many dogs does Ralph have?

(A) 25

(B) 75

(C) 100

(D) 125

(E) 150

389. How many multiples of 3 are there between 15 and 81, inclusive?

(A) 22

(B) 23

(C) 24

(D) 25

(E) 26

390. If 80 percent of a rectangular park is covered by a rectangular football field that is 120 yards by 50 yards, what is the area of the park in square yards?

(A) 4,800

(B) 6,000

(C) 7,200

(D) 7,500

(E) 10,000

391. How many minutes does it take to travel 140 miles at 200 miles per hour?

(A) $\frac{7}{10}$

(B) $1\frac{3}{10}$

(C) 14

(D) 21

(E) 42

392. If $35^c = 5^2 \times 7^2$, what is the value of *c*?

(A) 2

(B) 4

(C) 8

(D) 16

(E) 32

393. If Dora is 3 times as old as she was 6 years ago, how old is Dora now?

(A) 3

(B) 9

(C) 18

(D) 27

(E) Cannot be determined

394. Which of the following is a solution to the equation $x^2 - 49x = 0$?

(A) 98

(B) 49

(C) 24.5

(D) 7

(E) −7

395. What is the value of $\dfrac{2}{\left(\frac{4r}{6}\right)}$ when $r \neq 0$?

(A) $\frac{1}{12r}$

(B) $\frac{1}{3r}$

(C) $\frac{4r}{3}$

(D) $\frac{3}{r}$

(E) $6r$

396. At what point does $3x - 5y = 15$ intersect the y-axis of the coordinate plane?

(A) (−3, 0)

(B) (0, 3)

(C) (0, −3)

(D) (5, 0)

(E) (0, 5)

397. A professional women's basketball team conducted a free-throw shooting experiment. Each trial of the experiment consisted of each member of the team taking turns shooting 10 free throws and counting the number of made baskets that resulted. The results for 50 trials were recorded in the chart below. Approximately what percent of the trials had 7 or more made baskets?

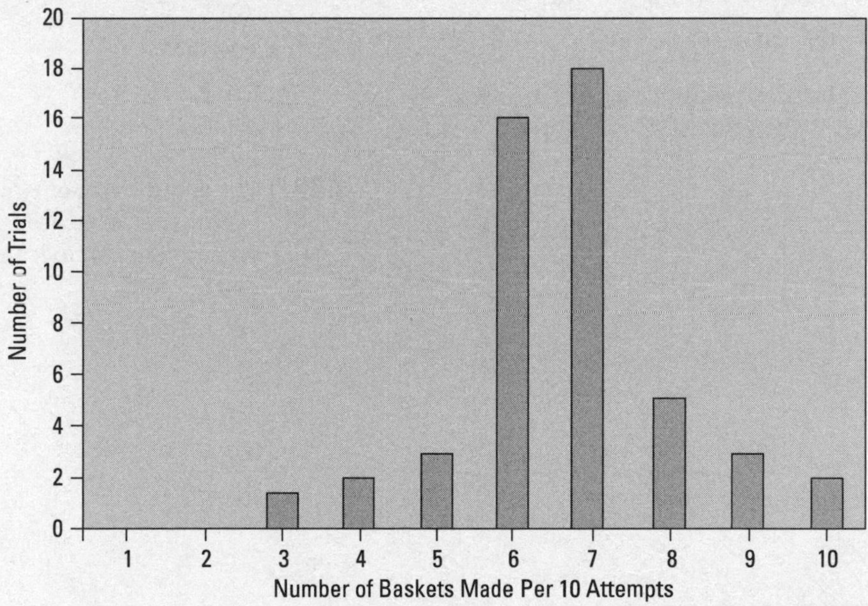

© John Wiley & Sons, Inc.

(A) 20%

(B) 28%

(C) 50%

(D) 56%

(E) 88%

398. In the figure, the following is true about value of the degree measurement of angles a and b: $70 < a + b < 150$. Which of the following describes all possible values in degrees of $c + d$?

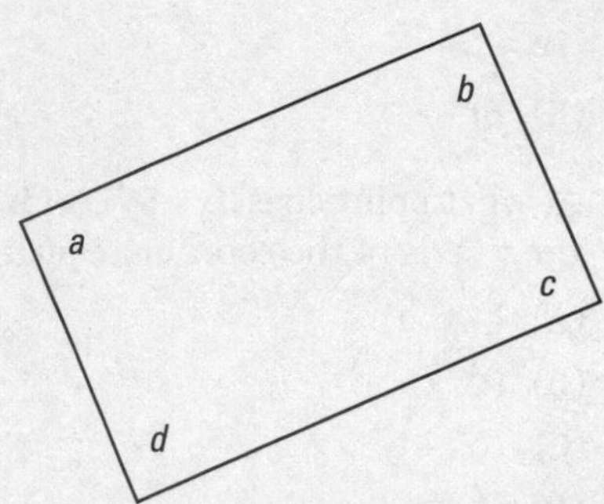

Note: Figure not drawn to scale.

© John Wiley & Sons, Inc.

(A) $210 < c + d < 290$

(B) $30 < c + d < 110$

(C) $120 < c + d < 200$

(D) $390 < c + d < 470$

(E) $570 < c + d < 650$

399. For the triangle in the figure, if $\Theta = 36°$, what is the value of x?

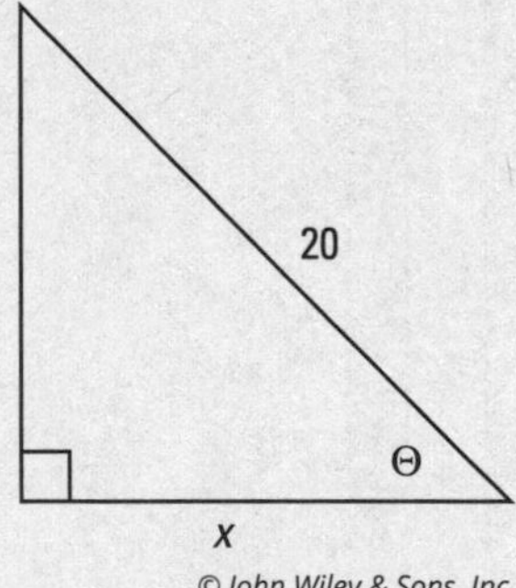

© John Wiley & Sons, Inc.

(A) 720

(B) $\dfrac{\cos 36°}{20}$

(C) $\dfrac{20}{\cos 36°}$

(D) $\cos 36° \times 20$

(E) 0

400. If x is an integer and $x^2 - 1 \leq 15$, what is the smallest value of x?

(A) −16

(B) −5

(C) −4

(D) 0

(E) 4

401. The radius of the circle in the figure is 5 inches, and $\angle ROS$ measures 6°. What is the length in inches of the minor arc RS?

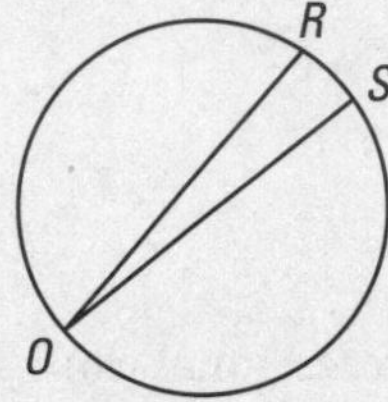

© John Wiley & Sons, Inc.

(A) $\frac{1}{3}\pi$

(B) π

(C) 3π

(D) 4π

(E) 12

402. The coordinates of two points on the coordinate plane are (9, 4) and (8, 6). What is the distance in units between the two points?

(A) $\sqrt{29}$

(B) 5

(C) 4

(D) $\sqrt{7}$

(E) $\sqrt{5}$

403. The members of set A are {5, 10, 15, 20}, the members of set B are {2, 4, 6, 8, 10}, and the members of set C consist of the union of set A and set B. What is the average of the members of set C?

(A) 5

(B) 7

(C) 8.75

(D) 8.99

(E) 10

404. If 3 pounds of dried cherries that cost x dollars per pound are mixed with 4 pounds of dried apple chips that cost y dollars per pound, what is the cost, in dollars, per pound of the mixture?

(A) $3x+4y$

(B) $\frac{3x+4y}{x+y}$

(C) $\frac{3x+4y}{xy}$

(D) $\frac{3x+4y}{12}$

(E) $\frac{3x+4y}{7}$

405. On the number line in the figure below, the segment from 0 to 1 has been divided into fourths, as indicated by the large tick marks, and also into fifths, as indicated by the small tick marks. What is the least possible distance between any of the two tick marks?

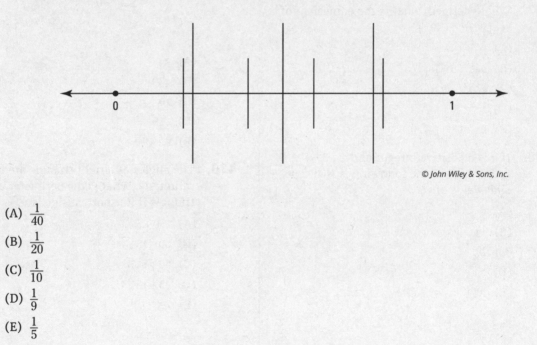

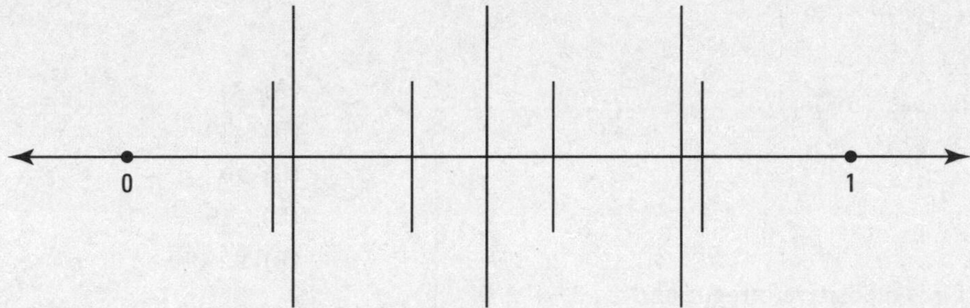

© John Wiley & Sons, Inc.

(A) $\frac{1}{40}$

(B) $\frac{1}{20}$

(C) $\frac{1}{10}$

(D) $\frac{1}{9}$

(E) $\frac{1}{5}$

406. A man threw a baseball from the top of a skyscraper at a height of 1,454 feet. The height of the baseball after the man threw it is a function of the time that has expired from the time he threw it. If t represents the time, in seconds, that has expired since the man threw the ball and $h(t)$ represents the height, in feet, of the baseball, then $h(t) = 1{,}454 - 16t^2 + 8t + 4$. What is the closest approximation to the height, in feet, of the height of the baseball at 2 seconds?

(A) 450

(B) 727

(C) 1,410

(D) 1,454

(E) 1,538

407. Where defined, what is the equivalent of $\sec(3\Theta)\cos(3\Theta)$?

(A) 0

(B) $\sec^2(3\Theta)$

(C) $\cos^2(3\Theta)$

(D) 1

(E) $2\sin(3\Theta)$

408. If n is a positive integer and $x + 3 = 4^n$, then which of the following is NOT a possible value of x?

(A) 1

(B) 13

(C) 45

(D) 61

(E) 253

409. The cube in the figure has an edge length of 3 inches. What is the distance in inches from vertex E to point G on $\overline{FH}$ if point G is one-third of the way between points F and H on $\overline{FH}$?

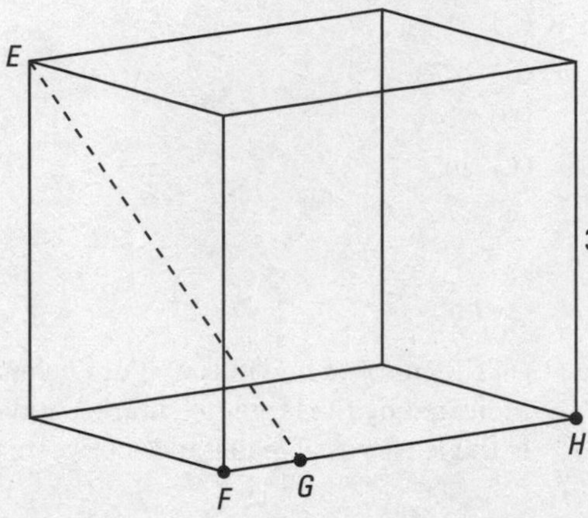

(A) 3

(B) $\sqrt{10}$

(C) 10

(D) $\sqrt{19}$

(E) $9 + \sqrt{10}$

410. The angles of a right triangle are in the ratio 1:2:3. What is the perimeter of the triangle if its shortest side is 15?

(A) $150 + 5\sqrt{3}$

(B) $60 + 15\sqrt{3}$

(C) $60 + 5\sqrt{3}$

(D) $45 + 15\sqrt{3}$

(E) 45

411. Which of the following changes must be made to $\overline{DF}$ to make the equation $\sin x = \sin y$ true?

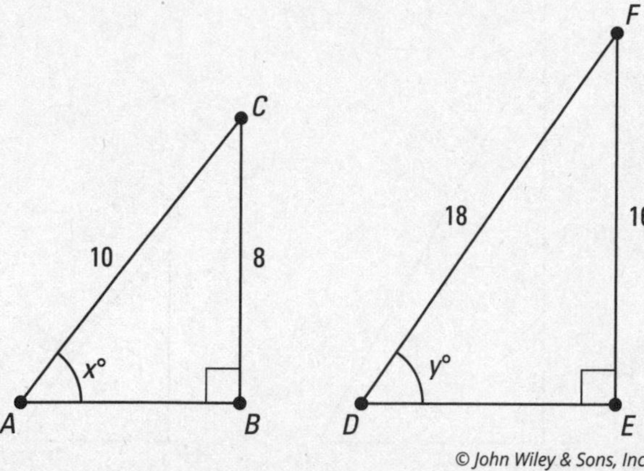

© John Wiley & Sons, Inc.

(A) Increase its length by 3 units

(B) Increase its length by 2 units

(C) Increase its length by 1 units

(D) Decrease its length by 1 units

(E) Decrease its length by 2 units

412. For all x and y, $\left(3x^2y + xy^2 - 4\right) - \left(2x^2y - 2xy^2 + 3\right) =$

(A) $x^2 - x - 1$

(B) $x^2y - xy^2 - 1$

(C) $x^2y + 3xy^2 - 7$

(D) $5x^2 - xy^2 - 7$

(E) $xy^2 + 3x^2y^2 + 1$

413. Line segment *XY* has endpoints with the coordinates (−4, 6) and (2, 6), what are the coordinates of its midpoint?

(A) (−1, 6)

(B) (0, 0)

(C) (1, 6)

(D) (3, 0)

(E) (3, 6)

414. A candy and nut company sells a bag of candy that contains a mixture of just lollypops and chocolate bars. The ratio of lollypops to chocolate bars in the bag is 3:5, and the difference between the number of lollypops and the number of chocolate bars is 18. What is the total number of candies in the bag?

(A) 90

(B) 72

(C) 40

(D) 27

(E) 24

415. Given that x is an integer, for what value of x is $x + \frac{4}{5}x > 16$ and $x + 4 < 16$?

(A) 7

(B) 8

(C) 10

(D) 12

(E) 13

416. One fourth of the product of 8 and 3 is four less than 2*x*. What is *x*?

(A) 8

(B) 7

(C) 5

(D) $\frac{3}{2}$

(E) 1

417. Jenny's lucky number is 12. On any simultaneous roll of two six-sided regular dice, what is the probability that she will roll her lucky number?

(A) $\frac{1}{2}$

(B) $\frac{1}{3}$

(C) $\frac{1}{6}$

(D) $\frac{1}{12}$

(E) $\frac{1}{36}$

418. Isosceles right triangle *ABC* has a perimeter of $16+8\sqrt{2}$. What is its area?

(A) $256\sqrt{2}$

(B) 256

(C) $64\sqrt{2}$

(D) 64

(E) 32

419. Priya wants to buy a new litter box that has the same volume as her old one. Her former rectangular litter box measured 12×24 inches on the base and was 4 inches tall. If her new rectangular litter box has a base with a length and width that are exactly 50 percent longer than the corresponding length and width of the base of the former litter box, to the nearest tenth of an inch approximately how many inches tall will the new litter box be?

(A) 1.7

(B) 2

(C) 2.9

(D) 3.0

(E) 4.1

420. Triangles *ABC* and *DEF* are similar figures. The area of $\triangle ABC$ is $50\sqrt{3}$ square units. What is the perimeter of triangle *DEF*?

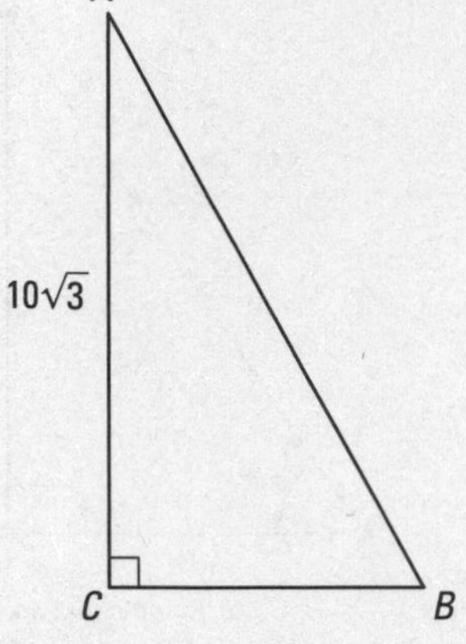

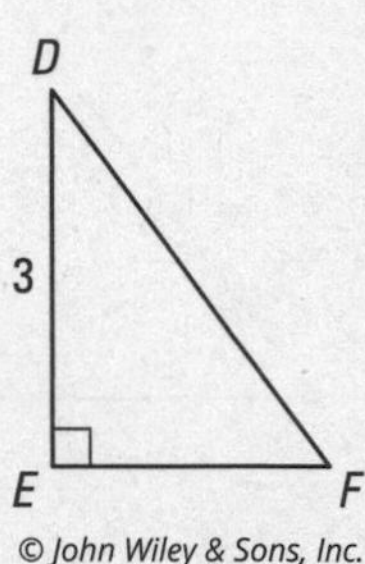

© John Wiley & Sons, Inc.

(A) $9+3\sqrt{3}$

(B) $12\sqrt{3}$

(C) $30+10\sqrt{3}$

(D) $50\sqrt{3}$

(E) $100\sqrt{3}$

421. Which of the following values is NOT an irrational number?

(A) $\sqrt{2}$

(B) $\sqrt{8}$

(C) π

(D) $\sqrt{13}$

(E) $\frac{\sqrt{256}}{\sqrt{4}}$

422. Given that $-|3-3a|=-12$, which of the following could be *a*?

(A) 5

(B) 4

(C) 3

(D) 2

(E) 1

423. Triangle *ABC* is an equilateral triangle with an area of 16. Triangle *DEF* is an isosceles right triangle with an area of 32. Which of the following represents the ratio of the sum of the interior angles in triangle *ABC* to the sum of the interior angles in *DEF*?

(A) 4:1

(B) 3:1

(C) 2:1

(D) 1:1

(E) 1:2

424. Matt bought six toy cars costing *x* cents each. He gave the clerk *y* quarters. In terms of *x* and *y*, how much change should Matt receive?

(A) $y-6x$

(B) $25y+6x$

(C) $25y-6x$

(D) $6x-y$

(E) $\frac{6x}{25y}$

425. Arc *AB* measures 17 centimeters. What is the circumference of Circle *O* in centimeters?

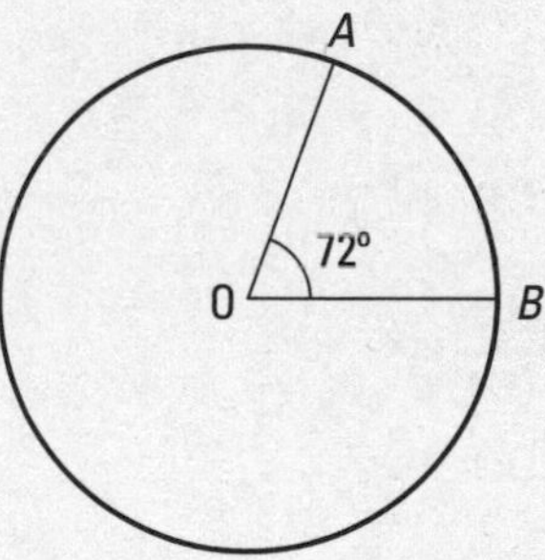

© John Wiley & Sons, Inc.

(A) 17π

(B) $\frac{85}{\pi}$

(C) 34π

(D) 85

(E) 85π

426. Debbie starts at point *A*, walks 39 yards due north, and stops. Jaspar starts at the same point *A*, walks due east for a distance, and stops. The shortest distance between Debbie and Jaspar is 65 yards. How many yards did Jaspar walk?

(A) 52

(B) $\sqrt{5,746}$

(C) 78

(D) 104

(E) $65\sqrt{3}$

427. What point on the graph of $x^2-y=6$ has an *x*-coordinate of 2?

(A) (−2, 2)

(B) $\left(2,\sqrt{2}\right)$

(C) (2, 6)

(D) (2, −2)

(E) (2, 12)

428. In the standard *xy*-coordinate plane, what is the slope of the line that is perpendicular to the line $5y-12x=35$?

(A) $-\frac{5}{12}$

(B) $-\frac{12}{5}$

(C) $\frac{5}{12}$

(D) $\frac{7}{5}$

(E) $\frac{12}{5}$

429. What is the fourth term of the geometric sequence whose second term is −6 and whose fifth term is 0.75?

(A) −3

(B) −1.5

(C) −0.5

(D) 1.5

(E) 3

430. A merry-go-round ride at the local amusement park has a radius of 30 feet. The ride moves at a constant speed and completes 5 rotations in 1 minute. How many degrees does the ride rotate in 10 seconds?

(A) 12°

(B) 180°

(C) 300°

(D) 330°

(E) 360°

431. For what value of a would this system of equations have an infinite number of solutions?

$$2x+3y=12$$
$$8x+12y=4a$$

(A) 3

(B) 6

(C) 12

(D) 48

(E) 60

432. Given that $x=3$ when $y=18$ for the proportion $\frac{x}{27}=\frac{k}{y}$, what is x when $y=6$?

(A) 2

(B) 3

(C) $\frac{27}{6}$

(D) 6

(E) 9

433. An equilateral triangle has an altitude of 5 units. What is the perimeter of the triangle?

(A) 5

(B) $10\sqrt{3}$

(C) 30

(D) $20\sqrt{3}$

(E) Cannot be determined

434. An automatic water system fills a city water tank one-quarter full in one hour. Each hour thereafter the system fills the tank with water at the same rate. After how many hours is the pool $\frac{3}{4}$ full?

(A) 12

(B) 9

(C) 4

(D) 3.4

(E) 3

435. If doughnuts cost n dollars per dozen, which of the following expresses the cost of t doughnuts?

(A) $\frac{t}{12n}$ dollars

(B) $12+\frac{t}{n}$dollars

(C) $12+\frac{n}{t}$ dollars

(D) $\frac{12t}{n}$ dollars

(E) 12nt dollars

436. Mickey can process 600 mailings in $2\frac{1}{2}$ hours. Ferah can process 200 mailing in 45 minutes. If Ferah works for exactly $4\frac{1}{2}$ hours and finishes the same number of mailings as Mickey, how many hours did Mickey work?

(A) 5

(B) $4\frac{1}{2}$

(C) $4\frac{1}{4}$

(D) 4

(E) $3\frac{3}{5}$

437. The cost of a lawnmower increases 50% from May to June, deceases 20% from June to July, and decreases another 30% from July to August. The cost of the lawnmower in August is what percent of the cost of the lawnmower in May?

(A) 110%

(B) 100%

(C) 90%

(D) 84%

(E) 61%

438. For what value of a would this system of equations have an infinite number of solutions?

$$x + 2y = 15$$
$$2x + 3a = 4y$$

(A) 5

(B) 10

(C) 15

(D) 30

(E) 45

439. A biker travels for 300π yards. In that distance, the bike's front tire revolves exactly 15 times. What is the radius of the bike's front tire.

(A) 30π

(B) 10π

(C) 25

(D) 20

(E) 10

440. The product of any two prime numbers could NOT be

(A) prime

(B) composite

(C) rational

(D) odd

(E) even

441. The figure shows a circle inscribed in a square. One side of the square measures 16 units. What is the area of the shaded portion of the figure?

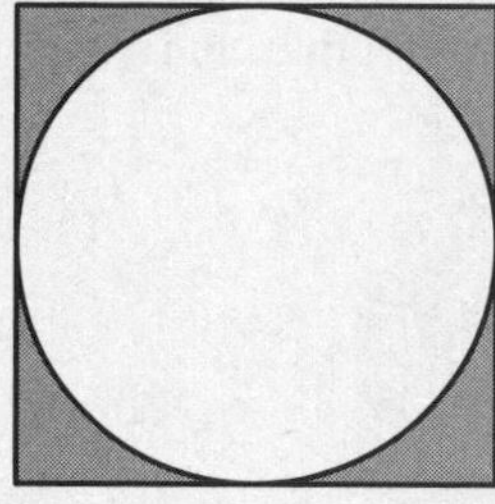

(A) 256π

(B) 192π

(C) $256 - 64\pi$

(D) $64 - 16\pi$

(E) $16 - 8\pi$

442. On the xy-coordinate plane, a circle with the equation $x^2 + y^2 = 49$ has point on the circumference with an x-coordinate of -2. The y-coordinate of this point could be which of the following?

(A) -2

(B) 0

(C) $\sqrt{45}$

(D) 7

(E) 49

443. $(a+3)^2 + (a-2)^2 =$

(A) $2a^2 + 10a + 5$

(B) $2a^2 + 2a + 13$

(C) $2a^2 - 2a - 4$

(D) $a^2 + 2a + 13$

(E) $a^2 - 2a - 13$

444. A jar is filled with 30 blue marbles, 50 green marbles, and 25 red marbles. A shopper randomly selects 1 blue marble, 2 green marbles, and 2 red marbles from the jar and places them in a bag. What is the probability of the shopper selecting a green marble from those remaining in the jar?

(A) $\frac{1}{7}$

(B) $\frac{23}{105}$

(C) $\frac{28}{105}$

(D) $\frac{16}{35}$

(E) $\frac{23}{50}$

445. In the right triangle below, what is the value of tan 30°?

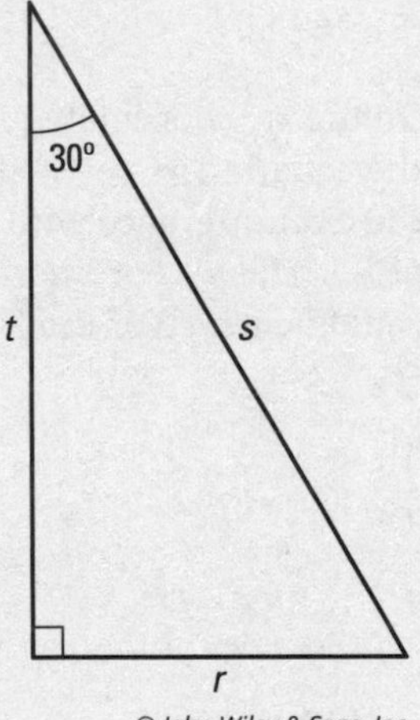

© John Wiley & Sons, Inc.

(A) $\frac{r}{s}$

(B) $\frac{r}{t}$

(C) $\frac{t}{s}$

(D) $\frac{t}{r}$

(E) $\frac{s}{r}$

446. Which of the following is best expressed by the figure below?

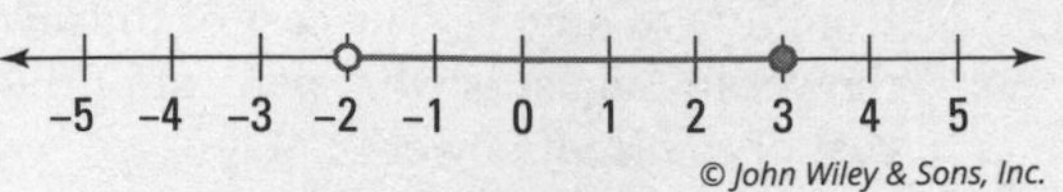

© John Wiley & Sons, Inc.

(A) $x > -2$

(B) $x < -2$

(C) $-2 \le x < 3$

(D) $-2 < x \le 3$

(E) $-2 \le x \le 3$

447. If $2ay - \frac{5b}{c} = 2ax$, then $y - x =$

(A) $-\frac{5b}{4ac}$

(B) $-\frac{5b}{c} + \frac{1}{2a}$

(C) $\frac{5b}{6c} - 2a$

(D) $\frac{5b}{2ac}$

(E) $\frac{5c}{b} + 2a$

448. For all $a \ne 0$ and $b \ne 0$, what is the slope of the line passing through $(-a, b)$ and $(a, -b)$?

(A) 0

(B) 1

(C) $\frac{a}{b}$

(D) $\frac{b}{a}$

(E) $-\frac{b}{a}$

449. Two light beams designated *A* and *B* emanate from a lighthouse. The ray of light from Beam *A* is parallel to the straight concrete slab at the base of the lighthouse. The left side of the slab forms a right angle with the straight side of the lighthouse as shown in the figure. The distance from the base of the lighthouse to Beam *A* is 72 feet. The ray of light from Beam B forms a 68° with Beam A. What is the length of Beam *B* from the point where it emanates from the lighthouse to the point where it meets the concrete slab?

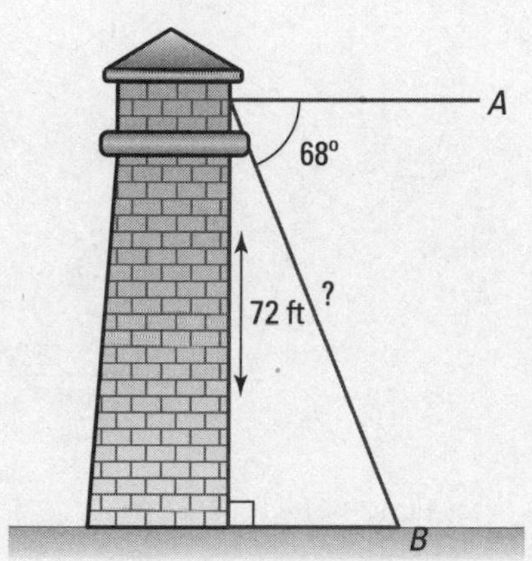

© John Wiley & Sons, Inc.

(A) $\dfrac{72}{\cos 22°}$

(B) $\dfrac{7}{\tan 22°}$

(C) $\dfrac{\cos 68°}{72}$

(D) $72 \tan 68°$

(E) $72 \sin 68°$

450. On the *xy*-coordinate plane, a line has endpoints (3, 4) and (−8, −7). What is the distance of the line between its endpoints?

(A) 11

(B) $\sqrt{142}$

(C) $\sqrt{165}$

(D) 34

(E) 142

451. Which of the following is equivalent to $\dfrac{\sin^2\theta + \cos^2\theta}{\sec^2\theta}$?

(A) $\dfrac{1}{\cos^2\theta}$

(B) $\sin^2\theta$

(C) $\tan^2\theta$

(D) $\dfrac{1}{\sec^2\theta}$

(E) $\sin^2\theta + 1$

452. On average, a machine and a half can produce a widget and a half in 36 hours. How many widgets can three machines give on average in 72 hours? (All machines produce widgets at the same rate.)

(A) 3

(B) 4

(C) 5

(D) 6

(E) 7

453. As shown in the figure, a handyman leans a 16-foot ladder from the ground to the bottom of a roof to clean debris from some gutters. The bottom of the ladder forms a 56° angle with the ground. What is distance from the ground to the top of the ladder?

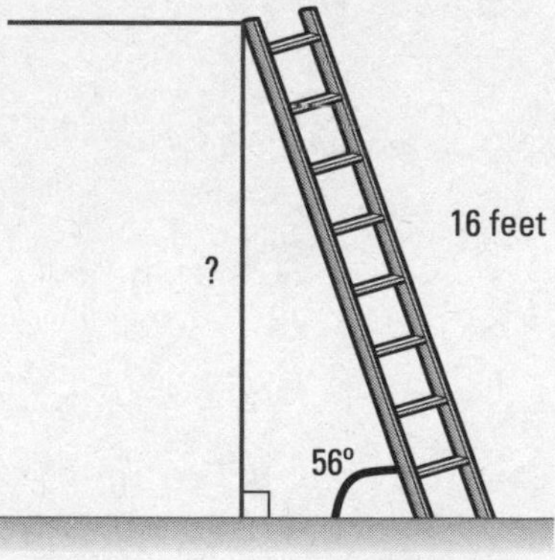

© John Wiley & Sons, Inc.

(A) $\dfrac{16}{\cos 56°}$

(B) $\dfrac{16}{\sin 56°}$

(C) $16 \sin 56°$

(D) $16 \cos 56°$

(E) $16 \tan 56°$

454. If $0 < \theta < \pi$ and $\tan\theta = \frac{3}{4}$, what are all possible values of $\cos\theta$?

(A) $-\frac{4}{5}$ and $\frac{4}{5}$

(B) $\frac{3}{5}$ only

(C) $\frac{5}{4}$ and $-\frac{5}{4}$

(D) $\frac{4}{3}$ and $-\frac{4}{3}$

(E) $\frac{4}{5}$ only

455. At the end of 2010, four pairs of red wolves, an endangered species, were reintroduced to the wild on the Alligator River National Wildlife Refuge in North Carolina. If the population of red wolves in the refuge increased at the rate of 12 percent each year, how many more red wolves existed in the refuge at the end of 2014 than were introduced in 2010?

(A) 2

(B) 4

(C) 6

(D) 10

(E) 12

456. $\dfrac{a}{\left(\frac{1}{b} - \frac{1}{c}\right)} =$

(A) 0

(B) $-abc$

(C) $ab - ac$

(D) $\dfrac{abc}{b-c}$

(E) $\dfrac{ac-ab}{bc}$

457. In the pentagon, $160 < r + s < 240$, which of the following describes all possible values of $t + u + v$?

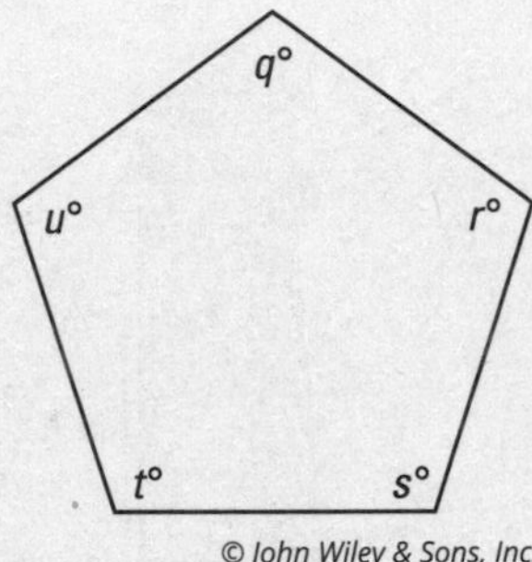

(A) $120 < t + u + v < 300$

(B) $300 < t + u + v < 380$

(C) $480 < t + u + v < 560$

(D) $660 < t + u + v < 740$

(E) $840 < t + u + v < 920$

458. The figure shows a sequential arrangement of squares that are formed according to a pattern. Each arrangement after the first is generated by adding one row and one column to the number of rows and columns in the previous arrangement. If this pattern continues, which of the following gives the number of squares in the *n*th arrangement?

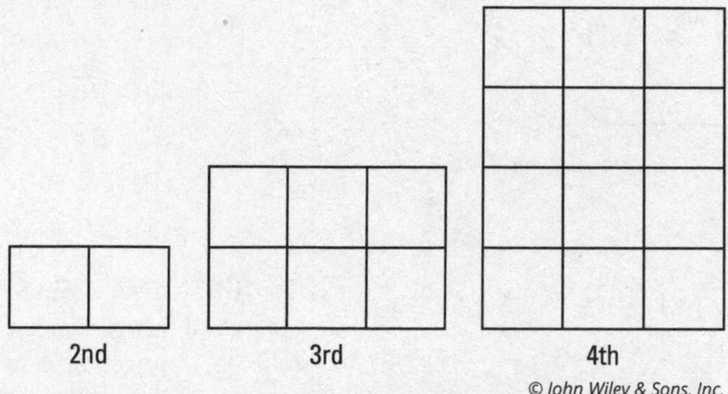

(A) $2n$

(B) $2n^2$

(C) $n(n-1)$

(D) $n(n+1)$

(E) $2(2n-1)$

459. In the standard *xy*-coordinate plane, Point *C* has coordinates (2, −1), Point *A* has coordinates (1, −1), and Point *B* has the coordinates (−1, 0). The three points can be connected to form line segments. Which of the following represents the lengths of the segments from least to greatest?

(A) $\overline{AB}, \overline{CB}, \overline{CA}$

(B) $\overline{AB}, \overline{CA}, \overline{CB}$

(C) $\overline{CA}, \overline{CB}, \overline{AB}$

(D) $\overline{CA}, \overline{AB}, \overline{CB}$

(E) $\overline{CB}, \overline{CA}, \overline{AB}$

460. Points *A*, *B*, and *C* lie on a circle. The center of the circle is the midpoint of $\overline{AC}$. If the length of $\overline{AB}$ is 3 cm and the length of $\overline{BC}$ is 4 cm, the radius of the circle in cm measures

(A) $2\frac{1}{2}$

(B) $2\sqrt{2}$

(C) 3

(D) $4\frac{1}{2}$

(E) 5

461. What is the area in square units of the parallelogram with vertices E, F, G, and H?

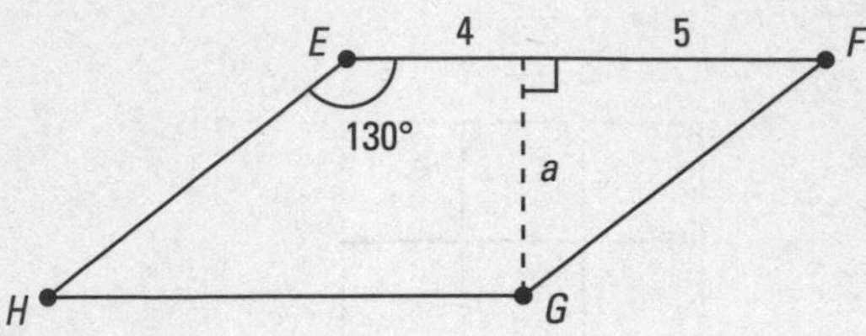

(A) 60

(B) $18(10\tan 50°)$

(C) $45\cos 40°$

(D) $9\times\frac{5}{\sin 40°}$

(E) $45\tan 50°$

462. What is the maximum number of $1\frac{3}{4}$ foot lengths of wood that can be cut from 4 pieces of wood that are 12 feet in length?

(A) 6

(B) 7

(C) 21

(D) 24

(E) 27

463. Two positive integers q and r satisfy the relationship $q\Diamond r$ if and only if $q=r^3$. If s, t, and u satisfy the relations $s\Diamond t$ and $t\Diamond u$, what is the value of s in terms of u?

(A) $s=u^0$

(B) $s=u$

(C) $s=u^6$

(D) $s=u^9$

(E) $s=u^{27}$

464. The line with the equation $y=4$ is graphed on the same xy-coordinate plane as the circle with center (2, 3). If the circle and line intersect at the point where the x-coordinate is 5, what is the radius of the circle?

(A) $2\sqrt{2}$

(B) $\sqrt{10}$

(C) $\sqrt{11}$

(D) 8

(E) 10

465. A local diner prepares orange juice beverage every morning by adding orange juice concentrate to water. The owner has determined that the best beverage mix results when 27 percent of the orange juice beverage is made up of orange juice concentrate. How many liters of water to the nearest full liter should be added to 3 liters of concentrate to create the optimum mixture of orange juice beverage?

(A) 8

(B) 11

(C) 14

(D) 17

(E) 20

466. The figure shows a right circular cylinder with points C and O at the centers of its bases. $\overline{XY}$ measures 8 units and is a diameter of one of the bases. If $\triangle XYO$ is equilateral, what is the measure of the triangle's area in square units?

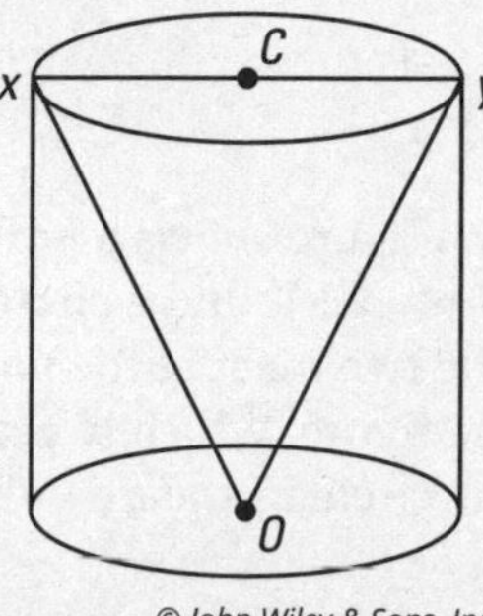

© John Wiley & Sons, Inc.

(A) 4

(B) $4\sqrt{3}$

(C) 8

(D) $16+8\sqrt{3}$

(E) $16\sqrt{3}$

467. a, b, and c are nonzero real numbers, and $a^5b^4c^3 = \frac{a^5b^2}{ab^{-2}c^{-4}}$. What is the expression $a^5b^4c^3$ in its simplest form?

(A) b^4c^8

(B) $\frac{b^4}{c^2}$

(C) $\frac{c^8}{b^{16}}$

(D) $\frac{b^4}{c^3}$

(E) c

468. What is the value of $\left[\cos^2\Theta+6-\left(-\sin^2\Theta+2\right)\right]^2$?

(A) $\cos^2\Theta-\sin^2\Theta+4$

(B) $\cos^2\Theta-\sin^2\Theta+8$

(C) 0

(D) 25

(E) 81

469. The table in the figure below shows the amount of waste material in pounds thrown away by each of five different families in a single year and the amount of waste material in pounds recycled by each of the five families in that same year. According to the table, which family had the highest ratio of waste material recycled to waste material thrown away?

Family	*Waste Material Thrown Away*	*Waste Material Recycled*
A	100	30
B	50	22
C	20	7
D	55	30
E	10	4

© John Wiley & Sons, Inc.

(A) Family A

(B) Family B

(C) Family C

(D) Family D

(E) Family E

470. The graph of $\begin{Bmatrix} x = 4r - 2 \\ y = -3r + 1 \end{Bmatrix}$ is a straight line with an x-intercept of

(A) $-\frac{2}{3}$

(B) $-\frac{1}{2}$

(C) 1

(D) $\frac{1}{2}$

(E) $\frac{2}{3}$

471. The figure shows a cube with an edge length that measures 6 centimeters and a circle, with center C, inscribed in one of the bases of the cube. What is the area, in square centimeters, of $\triangle ABC$?

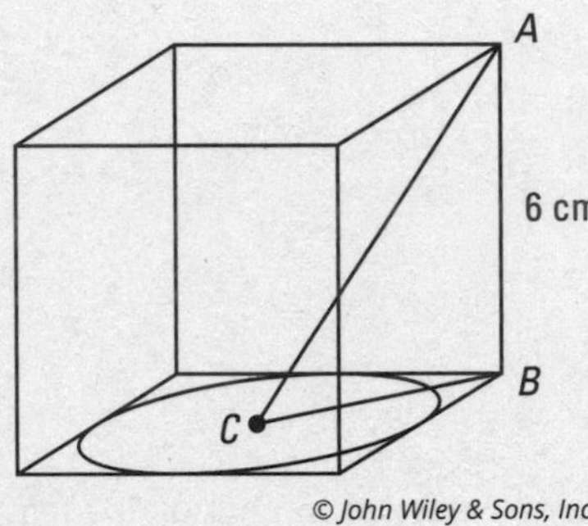

© John Wiley & Sons, Inc.

(A) $3\sqrt{2}$

(B) 4.5

(C) $\frac{9\sqrt{2}}{2}$

(D) $9\sqrt{2}$

(E) $18\sqrt{2}$

472. If $3^x = 4^y$ and $5^y = 6^z$, then $\frac{x}{z} =$

(A) $\frac{\log 3 \log 5}{\log 4 \log 6}$

(B) $\frac{\log 4 \log 6}{\log 3 \log 5}$

(C) 1

(D) $\log 4 \log 6 + \log 3 \log 5$

(E) $\log 3 \log 4 \log 5$

473. If $2 + \frac{3}{a} = 4 + 5a$ and $a > 0$, then which is the solution for a?

(A) $\frac{3}{7}$

(B) $\frac{1}{2}$

(C) $\frac{3}{5}$

(D) $\frac{3}{4}$

(E) 1

474. The figure shows a portion of the graph of $y = (1.5)^x$ and a circle with center (3, 1). The two meet at the point indicated on the figure. Which is nearest to the area of the circle in square units?

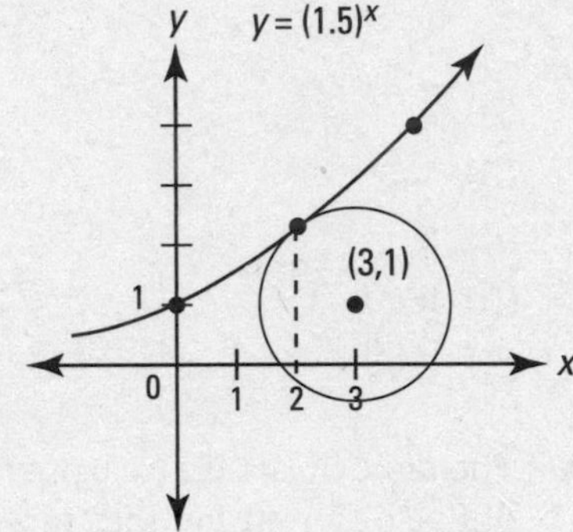

© John Wiley & Sons, Inc.

(A) 2.56π

(B) 3.20π

(C) 4.50π

(D) 10.24π

(E) 15

475. The figure shows the graph of $y = |f(x)|$. Which of the following could be graph of $y = f(x)$?

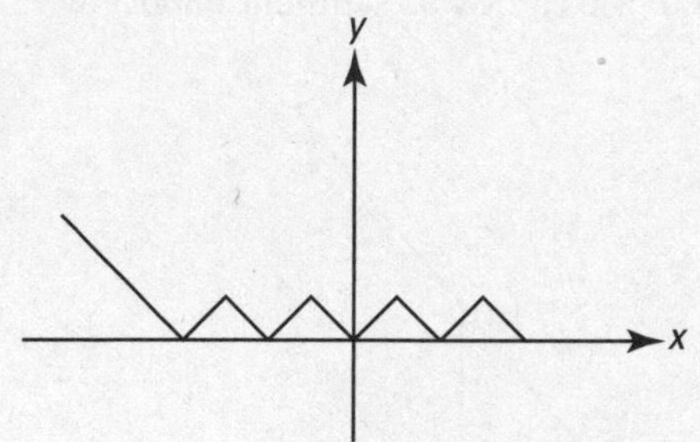

© John Wiley & Sons, Inc.

(A)

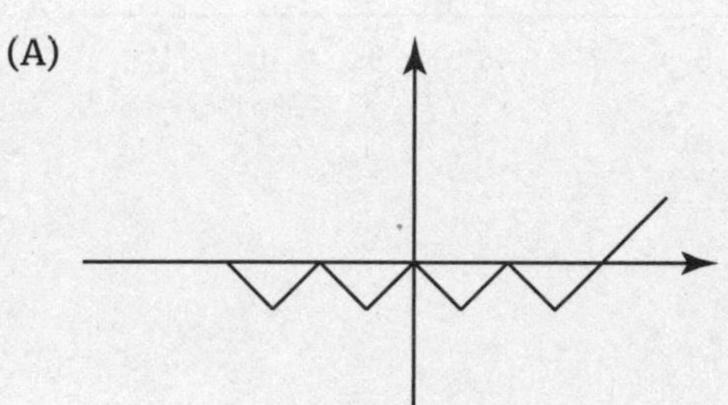

© John Wiley & Sons, Inc.

(B)

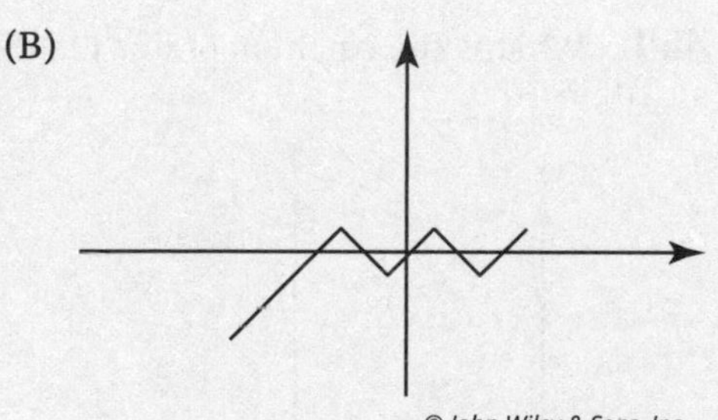

© John Wiley & Sons, Inc.

(C)

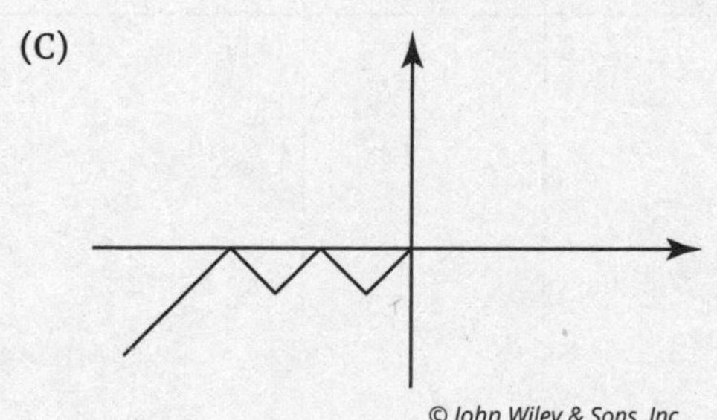

© John Wiley & Sons, Inc.

(D)

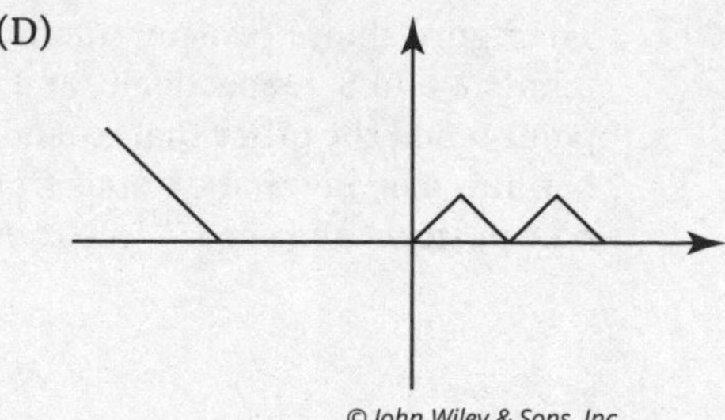

© John Wiley & Sons, Inc.

(E)

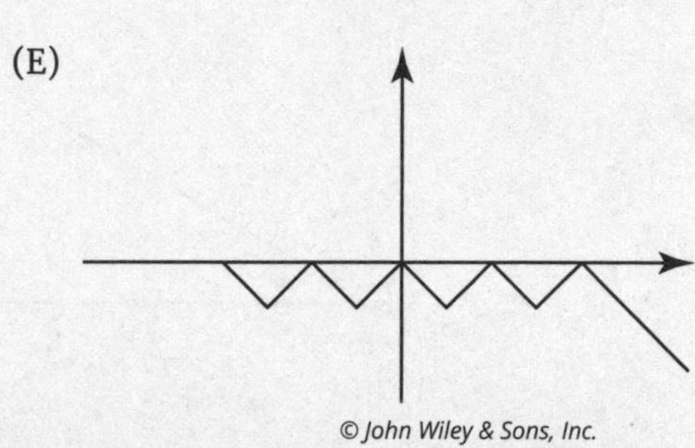

© John Wiley & Sons, Inc.

476. Each face of the pictured cube consists of 16 small squares. Three of the faces are shaded as shown. The shading on the other three faces is such that on opposite faces the reverse squares are shaded. For example, if one face has only the upper left corner shaded, its opposite face will have the other 15 squares shaded (every square but the one in the upper left corner). What is the total number of shaded squares on all 6 faces of the cube?

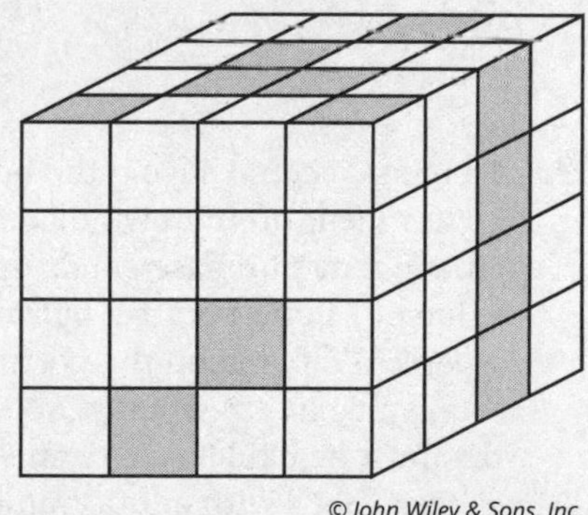

© John Wiley & Sons, Inc.

(A) 32

(B) 48

(C) 64

(D) 80

(E) 96

477. The figure shows two congruent segments (a and b) that are perpendicular to the number line at points 4 and 8, respectively, and that end when they intersect two rays, one that extends from point 0 and the other that extends from point 6. Segment b is moved to the right along the number line. The ray that extends from point 6 is rotated until it intersects the top of segment b at its new position and $\cos x° = \cos y°$. How many units to the right was segment b moved?

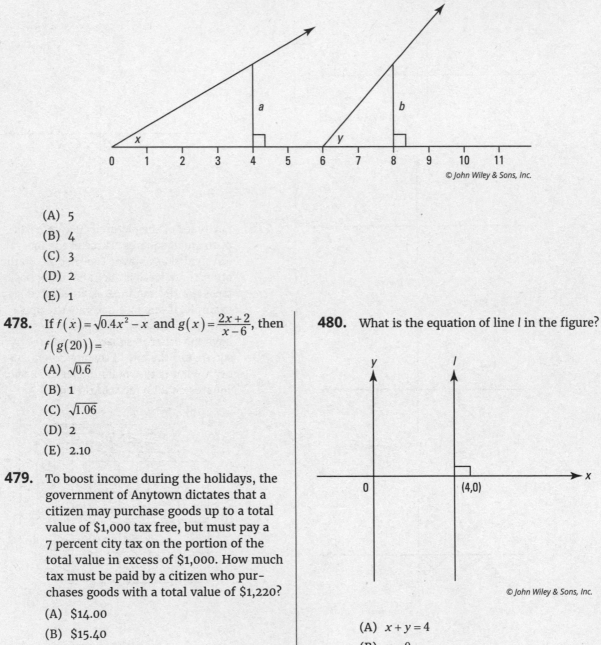

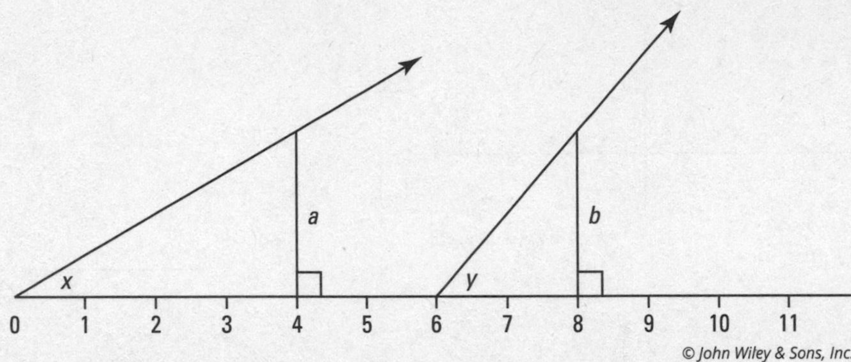

(A) 5
(B) 4
(C) 3
(D) 2
(E) 1

478. If $f(x) = \sqrt{0.4x^2 - x}$ and $g(x) = \dfrac{2x+2}{x-6}$, then $f(g(20)) =$

(A) $\sqrt{0.6}$
(B) 1
(C) $\sqrt{1.06}$
(D) 2
(E) 2.10

479. To boost income during the holidays, the government of Anytown dictates that a citizen may purchase goods up to a total value of $1,000 tax free, but must pay a 7 percent city tax on the portion of the total value in excess of $1,000. How much tax must be paid by a citizen who purchases goods with a total value of $1,220?

(A) $14.00
(B) $15.40
(C) $54.60
(D) $70.00
(E) $87.40

480. What is the equation of line l in the figure?

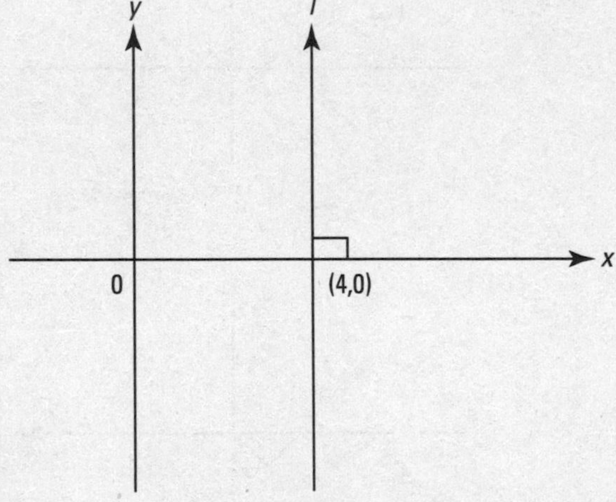

(A) $x + y = 4$
(B) $x = 0$
(C) $y = x + 4$
(D) $y = 4$
(E) $x = 4$

481. Jasmine sets up a monthly budget of her expenses. She uses a circle graph to give her a visual picture of her budget. The size of each sector on her circle graph is proportional to the amount of the budget it represents. What portion of the graph represents the sector Jasmine's monthly rent payment, which is 35% of her budget?

(A) $252°$

(B) $189°$

(C) $130°$

(D) $126°$

(E) $63°$

482. If $100 - x > x - 70$, what must be true about the value of x?

I. It is closer to 75 than it is to 100

II. $x > 85$

III. $x < 87.5$

(A) I only

(B) II only

(C) II and III only

(D) I and III only

(E) I, II, and III

483. In the figure, $\overline{OA} = \overline{AB} = \overline{BO}$, what is the slope of segment OA?

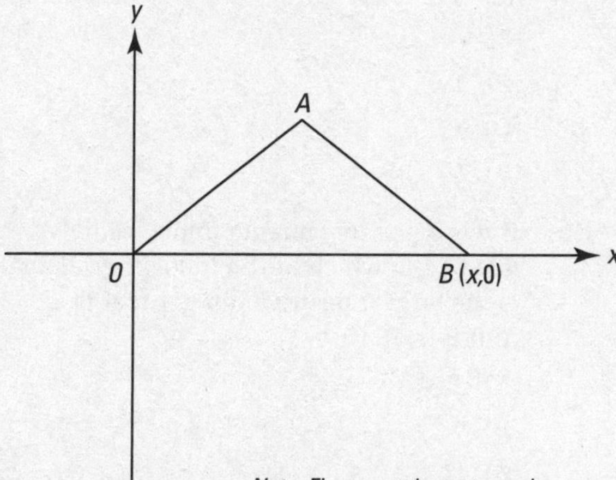

(A) $\sqrt{3}$

(B) $\frac{\sqrt{3}}{2}$

(C) $-\sqrt{3}$

(D) $-\frac{\sqrt{3}}{2}$

(E) Cannot be determined

484. Sofa King is having is annual clearance sale. The price of a certain style of couch was discounted by 20 percent and then further reduced by an additional 20 percent. By what percent did the final price decrease from the original price?

(A) 40%

(B) 38%

(C) 36%

(D) 30%

(E) 20%

485. If $f(x) = ax^2 + bx + c$ for all real numbers x and if $f(0) = 2$ and $f(1) = 5$, then $a + b =$

(A) 0

(B) 1

(C) 2

(D) 3

(E) 4

486. If n is a positive integer and n^2 is divisible by 98, which of the following values is the largest positive integer that is a multiple of n?

(A) 2

(B) 7

(C) 14

(D) 28

(E) 56

487. Angelo and Isabella are both salespersons. In any given week, Angelo earns $550 in base salary plus 8 percent of the portion of his sales above $1,000 for that week. Isabella earns 10 percent of her total sales for any given week. For what amount of weekly earnings would Angelo and Isabella earn the same amount?

(A) $23,500

(B) $24,500

(C) $25,500

(D) $26,500

(E) $27,500

488. The figure shows a portion of the graph of $y = 2^x$. What is the sum in units squared of the areas of the three inscribed triangles?

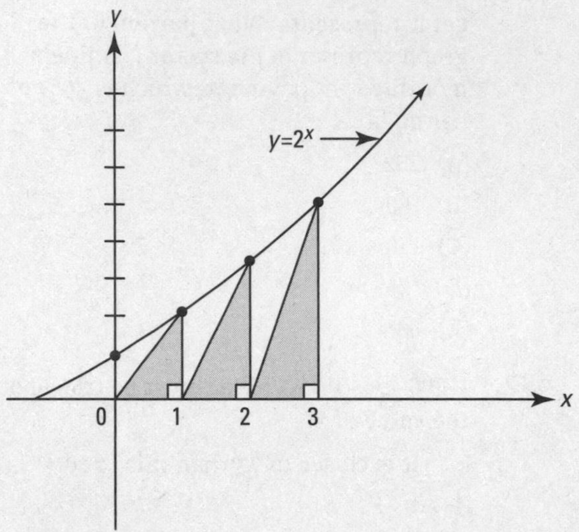

© John Wiley & Sons, Inc.

(A) 3.5

(B) 4

(C) 6

(D) 7

(E) 14

489. In the figure, $z \tan\Theta =$

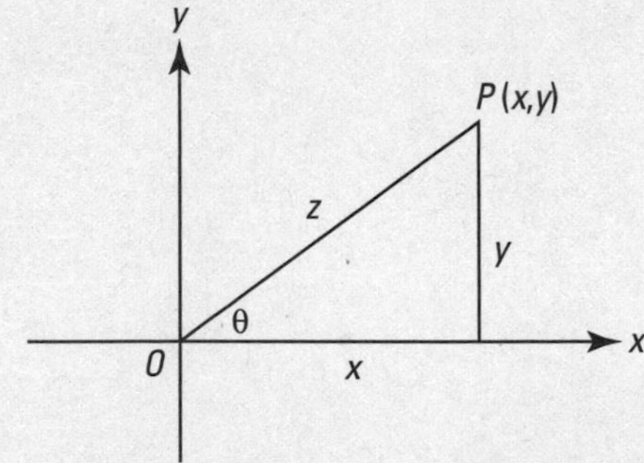

© John Wiley & Sons, Inc.

(A) z^2

(B) $z(x + y)$

(C) zxy

(D) $\frac{zx}{y}$

(E) $\frac{zy}{x}$

490. In the figure, $\frac{a+b}{b}=\frac{5}{2}$. What does b equal?

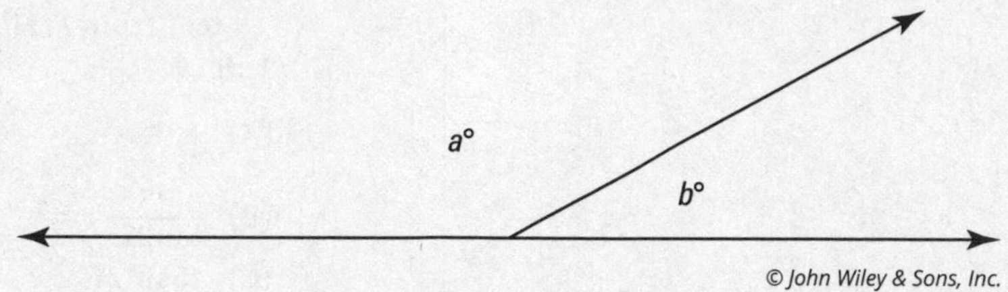

(A) 63
(B) 72
(C) 81
(D) 99
(E) 108

491. If $\sqrt{7x+1}=5.3$, then $x=$

(A) 4.36
(B) 3.87
(C) 3.13
(D) 2.53
(E) 1.26

492. $\overline{BX}$ bisects $\angle ABY$ and $\overline{BZ}$ bisects $\angle YBC$. The measure of $\angle YBZ$ is 60°. What is the measure in degrees of $\angle ABX$ in the figure?

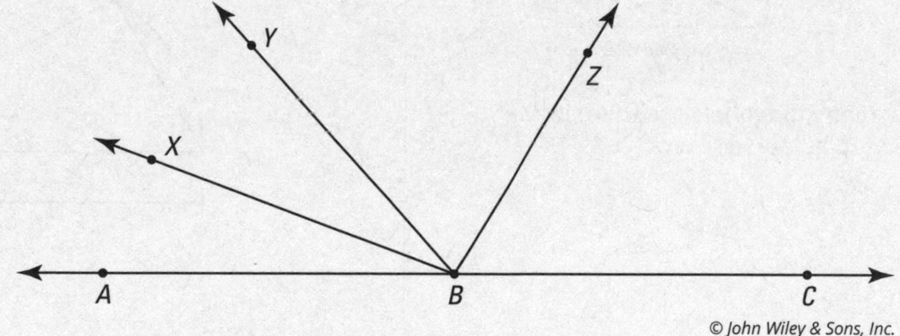

(A) 15
(B) 20
(C) 25
(D) 30
(E) 60

493. If $2x - 6y = 3z$ and $x + z = -2y$, what is the value of y in terms of z?

(A) $y = -2z$

(B) $y = -\frac{1}{2}z$

(C) $y = 2z$

(D) $y = 1$

(E) $y = -\frac{5}{7}x$

494. Which of the following could be the coordinates of the center of a circle tangent to the negative y-axis and the positive x-axis?

(A) (−3, 3)

(B) (0, −3)

(C) (3, −2)

(D) (3, 0)

(E) (3, −3)

495. As shown in the figure, a hexagon has 9 diagonals.

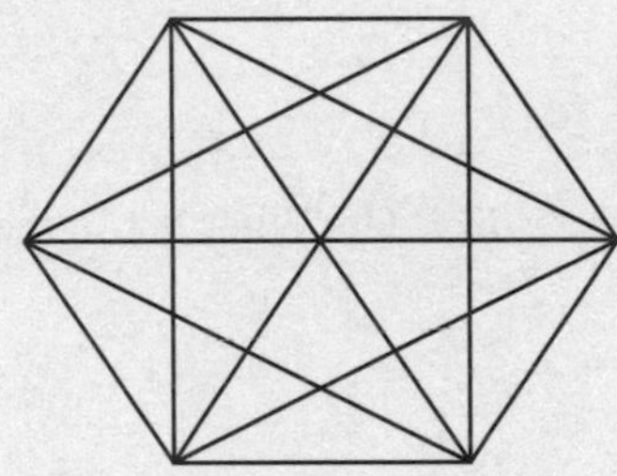

© John Wiley & Sons, Inc.

How many diagonals are there in the nonagon below?

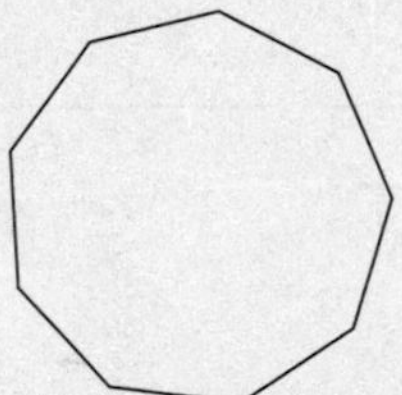

© John Wiley & Sons, Inc.

(A) 9

(B) 12

(C) 27

(D) 36

(E) 81

496. From a point P on the ground, the angle of elevation to a ledge on a building is 27°. The distance to the base of the building is 45 feet from P. How many feet high is the ledge?

(A) $\dfrac{45}{\sin 27°}$

(B) $\dfrac{45}{\tan 27°}$

(C) $45 \sin 27°$

(D) $45 \cos 27°$

(E) $45 \tan 27°$

497. Under which of the following conditions is $\dfrac{yx}{y-x}$ negative?

(A) $0 < y < x$

(B) $0 < x < y$

(C) $x < y < 0$

(D) $y < 0 < x$

(E) Under none of the conditions listed above

498. The figure shows a triangle inscribed in a semicircle. What is the perimeter of the triangle in terms of Θ?

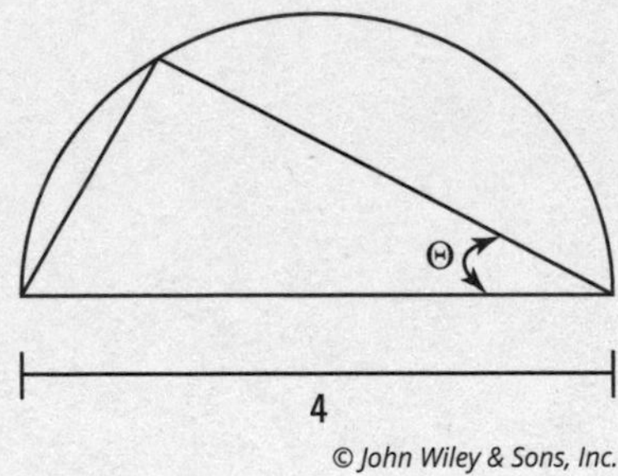

© John Wiley & Sons, Inc.

(A) 8

(B) $8 \sin\Theta \cos\Theta$

(C) $4(\sin\Theta + \cos\Theta + 1)$

(D) $4 \tan\Theta + 4$

(E) 16

499. A large square lies in a single plane. P and Q are two different points in that square. Which of the following represents the set of all points inside this square that are closer to P than to Q?

(A) the interior of a smaller square inside the square

(B) the interior of a small circle inside the square

(C) the region of the plane on one side of a line

(D) a pie slice region of the plane

(E) the region of the plane bound by a parabola

500. Which of the following is the slope of the equation of this line $3x+4=2y$ on the xy-coordinate plane?

(A) -3

(B) $-\frac{3}{2}$

(C) $-\frac{2}{3}$

(D) $\frac{3}{2}$

(E) 2

501. In the figure, sector AOB has an area of 60π square units and $\angle ACB=36°$. What is the circumference of the circle with center O?

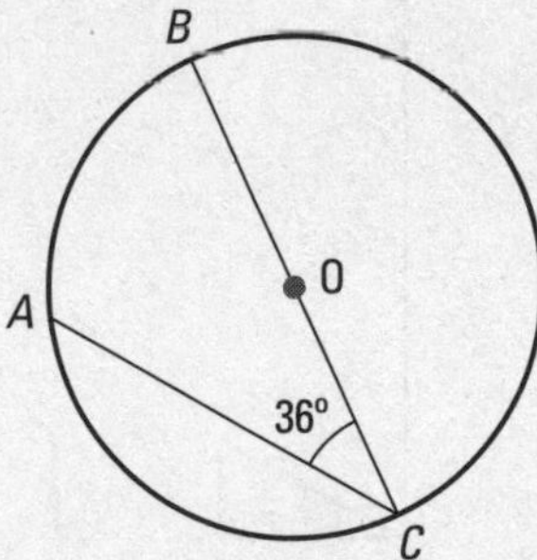

© John Wiley & Sons, Inc.

(A) $\sqrt{\frac{60}{\pi}}$

(B) $10\sqrt{3}\pi$

(C) $20\sqrt{3}\pi$

(D) $\frac{60}{\pi}$

(E) 300π

502. $|5(-3)+4|=?$

(A) -14

(B) -11

(C) 5

(D) 11

(E) 14

503. Given that $p=-64$ and $x=15$, $\sqrt{\frac{p}{-x-1}}=?$.

(A) -4

(B) -2

(C) $\sqrt{2}$

(D) 2

(E) 4

504. What is the value of a in the (a, b) solution to the following system of equations?

$$b=2a-7$$
$$b=5-a$$

(A) -4

(B) -1

(C) $\frac{5}{7}$

(D) 2

(E) 4

505. What vector is the result of adding the vectors $(-1, 2)$, $(3, -2)$, and $(4, 1)$?

(A) $(6, 1)$

(B) $(5, 5)$

(C) $(5, -5)$

(D) $(2, 1)$

(E) $(-6, -12)$

506. What is the y-intercept of the line given by the equation $-2y+5x=8$?

(A) -8

(B) -4

(C) 4

(D) $\frac{5}{2}$

(E) 8

507. A 30:60:90-degree triangle has a hypotenuse that measures 24 units. What is the measure in units of the leg opposite the angle that measures 60°?

(A) 6

(B) 12

(C) $12\sqrt{2}$

(D) $12\sqrt{3}$

(E) 48

508. A store sells colored markers individually or in packs of 3. The price of one marker is 10% more than the price of each marker when sold in the 3-pack. Jodie purchases two 3-packs of colored markers and one individual marker and pays a total of $1.42. How much does one marker cost when sold individually?

(A) $0.20

(B) $0.22

(C) $0.23

(D) $6.00

(E) $7.10

509. In the standard *xy*-coordinate plane, the *x*-coordinate of the midpoint of a line segment with endpoints (−7, 4) and (−1, 4) is:

(A) −8

(B) −4

(C) 0

(D) 4

(E) 8

510. A copy machine makes hundreds of copies of a corporation's annual report. It copies 600 pages in the first hour, after which it breaks. One hour later, the mechanic fixes the copy machine, and it resumes making copies at the rate of 600 pages per hour. To make up for lost time, the company employs the services of another copy machine that works at the same rate. The second machine begins making copies at the same time that the first machine resumes copying. The two copy machines working together finish copying two hours later. The graphs of the number of pages copied (c) as a function of time (t) would most resemble which of the following?

(A)

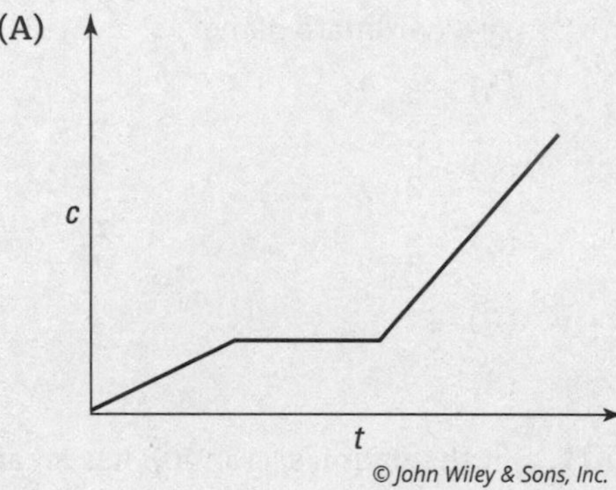

(B)

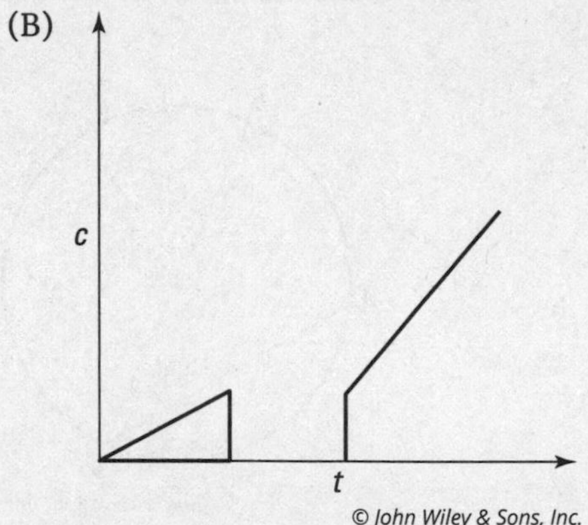

(C)

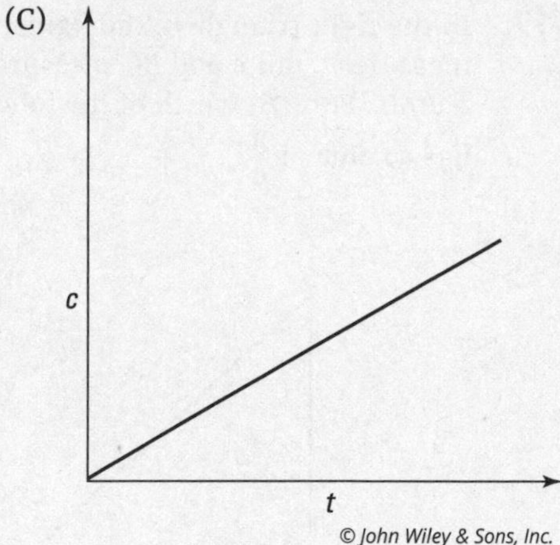

(D)

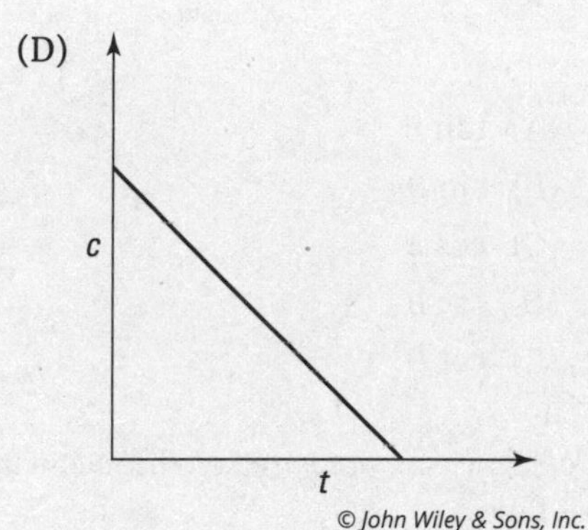

(E)

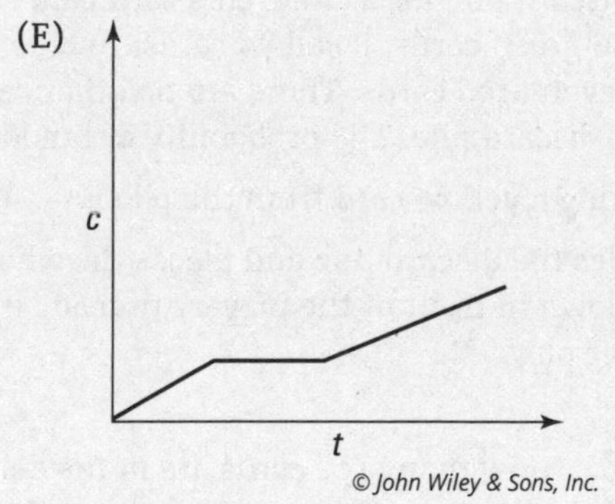

511. Whenever $5(6n-m)-l=0$, m is equal to this expression:

(A) $\frac{30n-l}{5}$

(B) $-\frac{30n+l}{5}$

(C) $l-6n$

(D) $6n+5l$

(E) $\frac{l}{5}+30n$

512. What is the least common multiple of 70, 90, and 110?

(A) 70

(B) 270

(C) 6,930

(D) 69,300

(E) 693,000

513. In $\triangle ABC$ below, D and E are endpoints of a line that is parallel to $\overline{BC}$. If it can be determined, what is the ratio of the area of $\triangle ADE$ to the area of $\triangle ABC$?

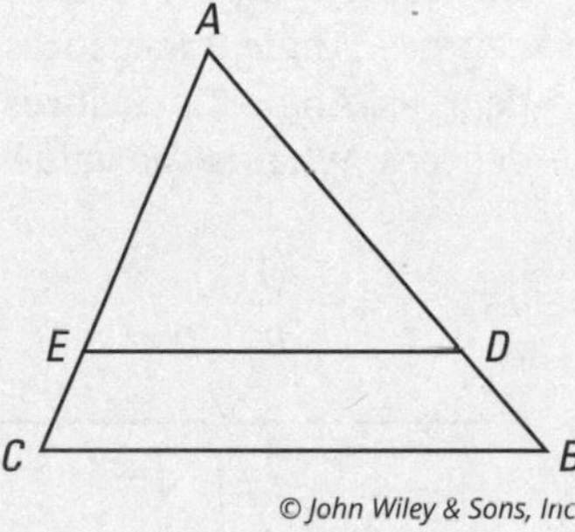

(A) 1:2

(B) 1:3

(C) 2:3

(D) 1:4

(E) Cannot be determined from the information

514. If $t+7=p$ and $t+9=q$, what is the value of $q-p$?

(A) 16

(B) $2t+16$

(C) $2t-2$

(D) $2t-16$

(E) 2

515. The perimeter of a parallelogram is 92 inches. The length of one side is 12 inches. What are the lengths in inches of the other 3 sides?

(A) 12, 12, 68

(B) 12, 12, 34

(C) 12, 28, 28

(D) 12, 34, 34

(E) 12, 44, 44

516. Lines l and m are parallel, and lines p, o, and l intersect at the same point. Angles A, B, and C are designated as shown on the figure. Angle A measures $(4x+19)$ degrees. Angle B measures $(2x-16)$ degrees. Angle C measures $(x+16)$ degrees. What is the value of x?

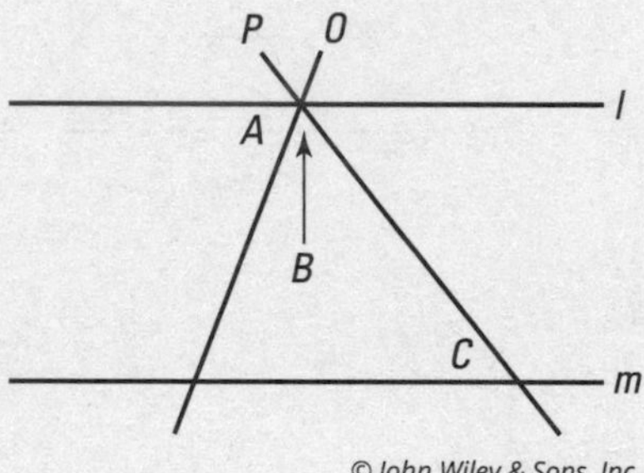

© John Wiley & Sons, Inc.

(A) 7

(B) 23

(C) 45

(D) 90

(E) 151

517. In the right triangle in the figure, $\overline{AB}$ measures 5 units and $\overline{BC}$ measures 4 units. For $\angle B$, which of the following has a value of $\frac{3}{4}$?

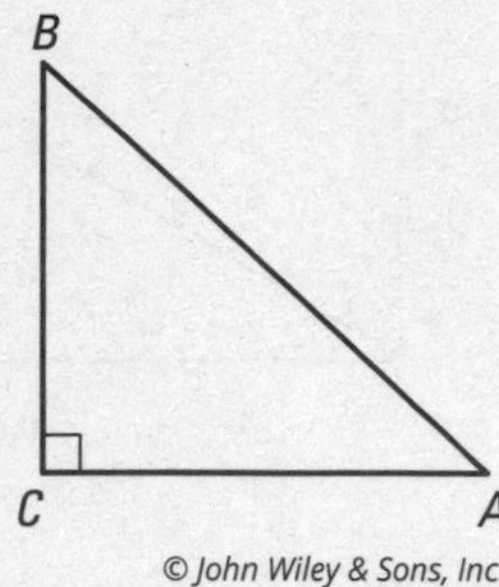

© John Wiley & Sons, Inc.

(A) tan B

(B) sin B

(C) cos B

(D) csc B

(E) cot B

Questions 518–520 are based on the following information.

The discard pile for a children's card game contains 6 green cards, 8 yellow cards, 10 blue cards, and several red cards. There are no other cards in the discard pile. The probability of randomly choosing a yellow card from the pile is $\frac{1}{4}$. Armando shuffles the discard pile and places the whole pile face down in front of the players to ready it for further play.

518. How many red cards are in the discard pile when Armando places it in front of the players?

(A) 6

(B) 10

(C) 14

(D) 24

(E) 32

519. To put a card into play, the players flip over the top card of the newly shuffled discard pile. What is the probability that the first player will flip over a green card?

(A) $\frac{3}{16}$

(B) $\frac{1}{4}$

(C) $\frac{5}{16}$

(D) $\frac{5}{12}$

(E) $\frac{17}{32}$

520. If Armando creates a pie chart to show the accurate percentages of each of the four colors in the discard pile, what would be the degree measure of the pie chart sector that shows the percentage of yellow cards?

(A) 8°

(B) 25°

(C) 45°

(D) 90°

(E) 270°

521. Which of the following would express the 21st term of the geometric sequence represented by 3, $9b$, $27b^2$. . .?

(A) $(3b)^{21}$

(B) $3^{21}b^{20}$

(C) $3^{20}b^{21}$

(D) $3b^{20}$

(E) $9b^{21}$

522. A class of 30 biology students completed a final exam with a possible score range of 1 to 100 points. The teacher recorded each student's exam score as a whole number. The median score for the class was an 83. No student received a score of 83, and 20% of the class received a score equal to or higher than 88. How many students received scores of 84, 85, 86, or 87?

(A) 4

(B) 6

(C) 8

(D) 10

(E) 15

523. Which of the following could be the equation of a line graphed in the standard *xy*-coordinate plane that includes points (0, 4) and (−3, 0)?

(A) $3x-4y=12$

(B) $4x-3y=12$

(C) $4y-3x=12$

(D) $3y-4x=12$

(E) $3y+4x=12$

524. Which of the following is equivalent to $\frac{7}{\frac{3}{5}}$?

(A) 3

(B) $4\frac{1}{5}$

(C) 5

(D) 7

(E) $11\frac{2}{3}$

525. If $f(x)=x-4$, what is $f(x+2)$?

(A) $x-2$

(B) $x-1$

(C) $2x-1$

(D) $2x-4$

(E) $2x+4$

526. Polygon ABCD below is a trapezoid. What is the measure in degrees of $\angle DBC$?

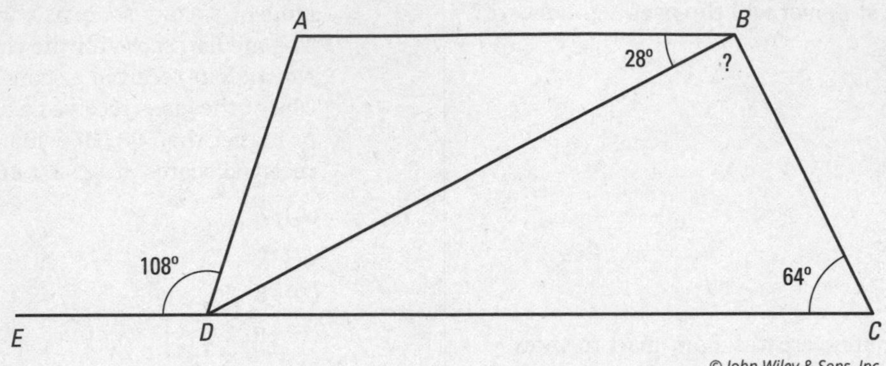

(A) 28
(B) 45
(C) 62
(D) 88
(E) 108

527. If $0° \leq x \leq 90°$ and $\tan x = \frac{24}{7}$, what is the value of $\cos x$?

(A) $\frac{7}{24}$
(B) $\frac{24}{25}$
(C) $\frac{7}{25}$
(D) $\frac{15}{7}$
(E) $\frac{25}{7}$

528. What is the value of $y \times 3^x$ when $x = 2$ and $y = 5$?

(A) 3
(B) 10
(C) 12
(D) 45
(E) 225

529. $\frac{1}{5}$ of a number is equal to $\frac{3}{4}$ of 11 more than that number. What is the number?

(A) −15
(B) −11
(C) $\frac{33}{9}$
(D) 11
(E) 165

530. In the figure below, *A*, *B*, and *C* are collinear. The measure of $\angle ABD$ is 4 times that of $\angle DBC$. What is the measure of $\angle ABD$?

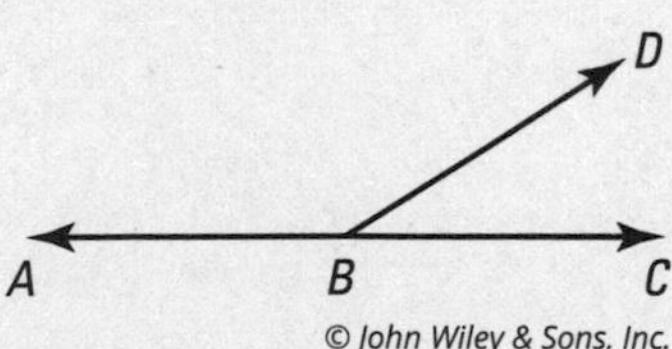

(A) 36°
(B) 45°
(C) 72°
(D) 108°
(E) 144°

531. For which of following values for x is $\log_6 4 + \log_6 x = 2$?

(A) $\frac{1}{2}$

(B) $\frac{4}{3}$

(C) 2

(D) 9

(E) 32

532. A circle with a radius of 6 centimeters is circumscribed inside a square. What is the area in square centimeters of the portion that is outside of the circle but inside the square?

(A) $36-36\pi$

(B) 36π

(C) $36-12\pi$

(D) $144-12\pi$

(E) $144-36\pi$

533. What is the solution to $\frac{5}{6}+\frac{1}{12}+\frac{2}{3}$?

(A) 12

(B) $\frac{19}{12}$

(C) 1

(D) $\frac{9}{12}$

(E) $\frac{8}{21}$

534. The Marquez family is adding a rectangular pool to the backyard. When filled completely to the top with water, the pool will have a volume of 4,032 cubic feet and a consistent depth of 6 feet. If the pool has a perimeter of 124 feet, which of the following could be the dimensions of its length and width?

(A) 6×112

(B) 14×48

(C) 12×50

(D) 24×28

(E) 31×31

535. On the number line below, the distance between A and D is 42 units. The distance between A and C is 25 units. The distance between B and D is 23 units. What is the distance in units between B and C?

(A) 5

(B) 6

(C) 8

(D) 10

(E) 13

536. What is the volume in cm^3 of a circular cylindrical canister with a diameter of 2 centimeters and height of 8 centimeters?

(A) 8π

(B) 16π

(C) 32π

(D) 64π

(E) 128π

537. Which of the following is equal to 2.43×10^{-5}?

(A) 2,430

(B) 243

(C) 0.0243

(D) 0.000243

(E) 0.0000243

538. If a 12-gallon tank of gas costs $36 to fill up, how much does it cost to fill up a 16-gallon tank of gas?

(A) $40

(B) $42

(C) $46

(D) $48

(E) $50

539. Simplify $\left(\frac{2x}{y^3}\right)\left(\frac{x^3y^2}{8}\right)$.

(A) $\frac{x^4}{4y}$

(B) $\frac{x^4}{y}$

(C) $\frac{xy^2}{4}$

(D) $4x^4y$

(E) $\frac{2x^3y^2}{8y^3}$

540. What would the slope be of any line in the standard *xy*-coordinate plane that is perpendicular to the line *l* below?

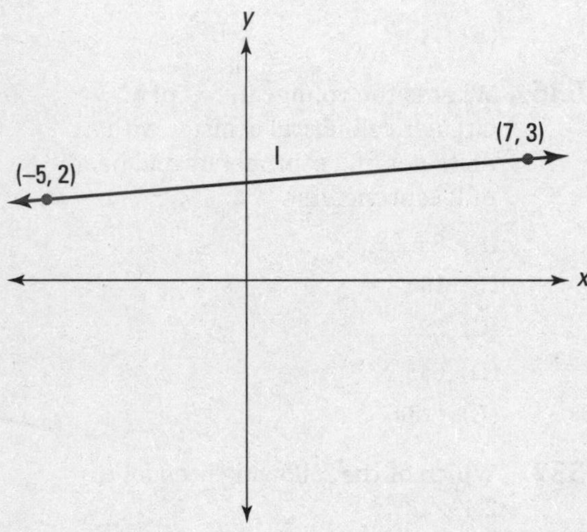

© John Wiley & Sons, Inc.

(A) −12

(B) −2

(C) $-\frac{1}{12}$

(D) $\frac{1}{12}$

(E) 2

541. What is the distance in the standard *xy*-coordinate plane between the points (−2, 1) and (3, −2)?

(A) $\sqrt{15}$

(B) $\sqrt{10}$

(C) $\sqrt{34}$

(D) 3

(E) 2

542. If $y = 4x - h$ and $x = h + 4$, then what is the value of *y* expressed in terms of *x*?

(A) $y = 3x$

(B) $y = 3x - 4$

(C) $y = 3x + 4$

(D) $y = -4$

(E) $y = \frac{3}{4}x$

543. A secret code is created by combining any 2 letters from the English alphabet and any 2 one-digit numbers between and including 0 and 9. How many different code combinations are possible if numeric digits can be repeated but letters cannot?

(A) 71

(B) 72

(C) 60,840

(D) 65,000

(E) 67,600

544. The area of a circle is 144π. What is the circumference?

(A) 6π

(B) 12π

(C) 24π

(D) 72

(E) 72π

545. For what values of x does $x^4 - 20x^2 - 64 = 0$?

(A) 16 and −4 only

(B) −16 and 4 only

(C) 1, 4, −1, and −4 only

(D) 4 only

(E) 4, 2, −4, and −2 only

546. The first five terms of an arithmetic series are 1, .75, 0.5, 0.25, and 0. What is the sixth term?

(A) −0.25

(B) −0.05

(C) 0.25

(D) 1

(E) 1.25

547. What is the measure of angle b in the following figure where lines C and D are parallel?

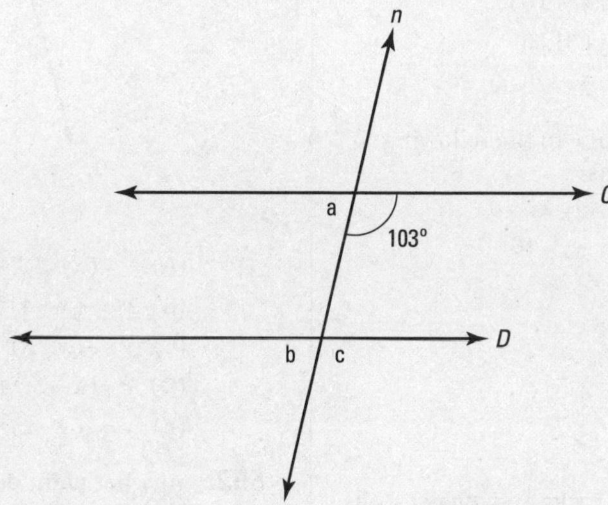

(A) 37°

(B) 43°

(C) 63°

(D) 77°

(E) 103°

548. Corrina is making birdhouses to sell for a wildlife charity. To complete her creations, she visits the hardware store to purchase only these items: *m* feet of bamboo dowel rods at \$0.50 per foot, *n* boxes of nails at \$4.50 per box, and 10 precut wooden platform boards at \$1 per board. Which of the following expresses Corrina's total expenditure in dollars at the hardware store?

(A) $(m + \$0.50)(n + \$4.50) + \$10.00$

(B) $m + \$0.50 + n + \$4.50 + \$10.00$

(C) $\$0.50m + \$4.50n + \$10.00$

(D) $\$0.50m + \$4.50n + \$1.00$

(E) $(\$0.50m)(\$4.50n) + \$10.00$

549. What is the value of *y* in the following system of equations?

$$4x + 2y = 4$$
$$x - y = 16$$

(A) 10

(B) 6

(C) 0

(D) −6

(E) −10

550. Sheila has 4 black socks and 2 navy socks in her laundry pile. If she randomly selects one sock from the pile, sets it aside, and then picks another sock from the pile, what is the chance that she will select the navy pair?

(A) $\frac{1}{15}$

(B) $\frac{2}{15}$

(C) $\frac{1}{5}$

(D) $\frac{1}{3}$

(E) $\frac{4}{5}$

551. Which of the following functions is represented on the standard *xy*-coordinate plane below?

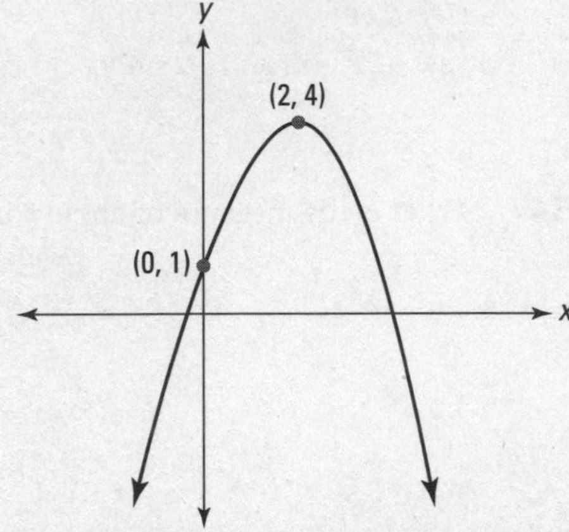

(A) $y = (x + 4)^2 - 2$

(B) $y = -(x + 4)^2 + 2$

(C) $y = -(x + 2)^2 + 4$

(D) $y = (x - 2)^2 + 4$

(E) $y = -(x - 2)^2 + 4$

552. At what point does $5x + 2y = 10$ intersect the *y*-axis in the standard *xy*-coordinate plane?

(A) $(-\frac{5}{2}, 0)$

(B) (5, 0)

(C) $(0, -\frac{5}{2})$

(D) (0, 5)

(E) (0, 10)

553. To accommodate a wheelchair, a couple places a triangular ramp from the ground to the base of a doorway as shown below. Given that the base of the doorway is 15 inches directly above the ground and the base of the ramp is 36 inches, what is the length in inches of the ramp?

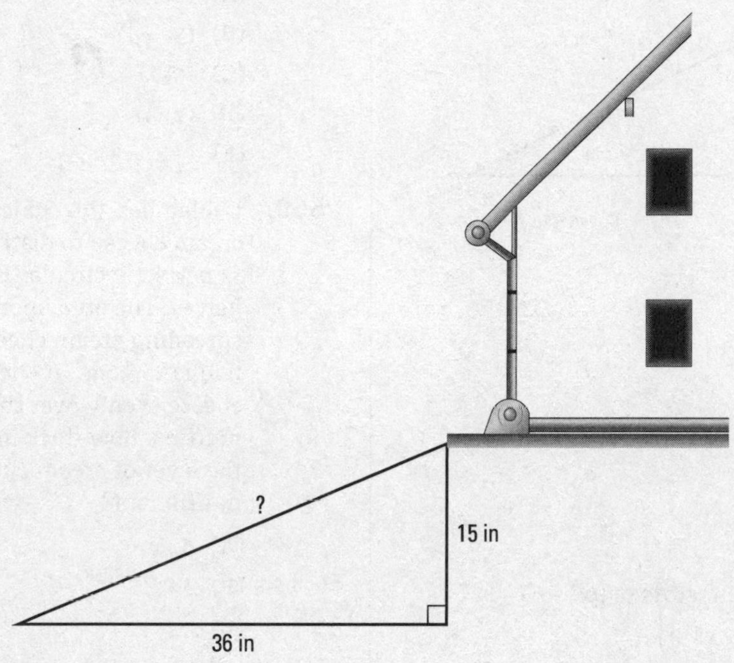

(A) $\sqrt{51}$

(B) 15

(C) 36

(D) 39

(E) 51

554. All-day amusement park passes are sold for $24 for adults and $13 for children. The amusement park sells 105 passes in one hour and collects a total of $2,201. How many adult passes were sold in that hour?

(A) 29

(B) 65

(C) 76

(D) 87

(E) 89

555. Which of the following represents all possible solutions for x the inequality $-2x-7<3x+5$?

(A) $x<-\frac{12}{5}$

(B) $x>-\frac{12}{5}$

(C) $x>\frac{12}{5}$

(D) $x>\frac{5}{12}$

(E) $x>-\frac{5}{12}$

556. In the right triangle below, what is $\sin A$?

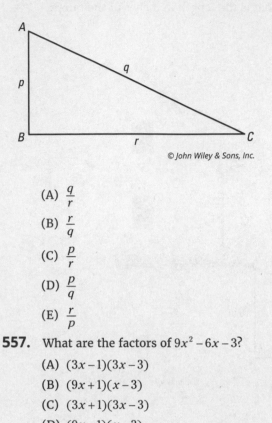

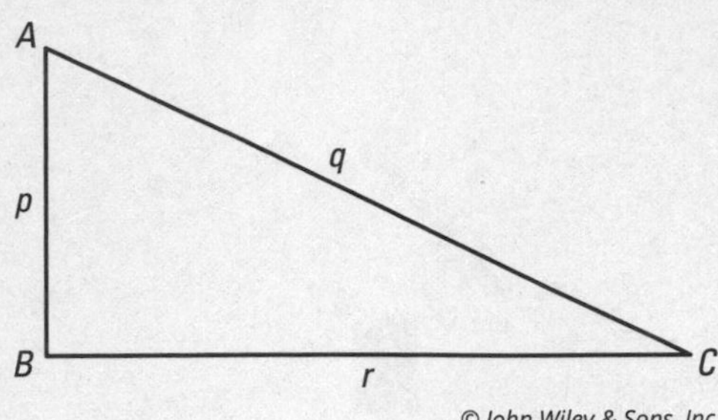

(A) $\frac{q}{r}$

(B) $\frac{r}{q}$

(C) $\frac{p}{r}$

(D) $\frac{p}{q}$

(E) $\frac{r}{p}$

557. What are the factors of $9x^2 - 6x - 3$?

(A) $(3x-1)(3x-3)$

(B) $(9x+1)(x-3)$

(C) $(3x+1)(3x-3)$

(D) $(9x-1)(x-3)$

(E) $(3x+2)(x-3)$

558. When Mr. Albright looks at his grade book after he has returned graded quizzes to his class of 20 students, he realizes he forgot to record a quiz score for one of the students. He sees that he previously recorded an average of 89 for the 20 quiz scores. When he totals the 19 scores in his grade book, he gets a sum of 1,680. What quiz score should Mr. Albright record for the missing entry?

(A) 88

(B) 89

(C) 92

(D) 94

(E) 100

559. What coordinate point in the standard *xy*-coordinate plane is the endpoint of a line segment whose other endpoint is (−1, 3) and whose midpoint is (2, −1)?

(A) (0.5, 1)

(B) (5, −5)

(C) (5, 1)

(D) (2, 3)

(E) (−2, −5)

560. Delilah has 300 cubic centimeters of cream cheese to distribute evenly on 12 perfectly circular English muffin halves. The area upon which she will be spreading cream cheese on each muffin half is 25π cm^2. If she spreads the cream cheese evenly over the area of the muffins, how thick in centimeters will the layer of cream cheese be atop each muffin half?

(A) 5

(B) 5π

(C) π

(D) 12

(E) 12π

561. In the standard xy-coordinate plane, the quadrilateral $ABCD$ is reflected over the y-axis to form quadrilateral $A_1B_1C_1D_1$. At what set of coordinates would point C_1 lie?

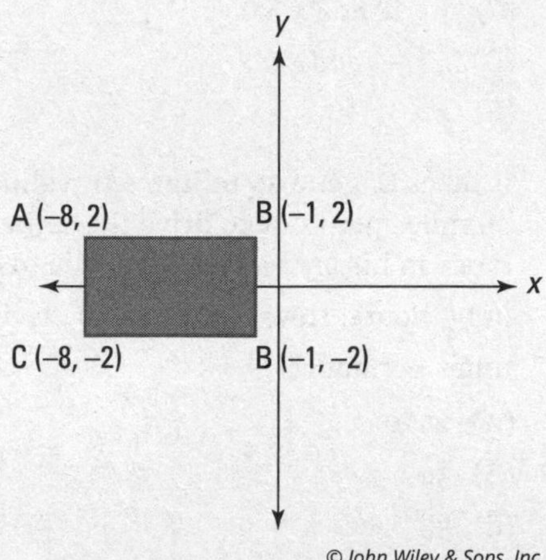

© John Wiley & Sons, Inc.

(A) (8, −2)

(B) (1, −2)

(C) (2, −4)

(D) (8, 2)

(E) (−8, −2)

562. William decided to give 15% of the money he won in a local lottery to his favorite charity and put the rest in his savings account. If he put $2,575.50 in savings, how much money did he win in the lottery?

(A) $5,655.50

(B) $3,030.00

(C) $3,000.50

(D) $1,000.00

(E) $756.56

563. For all pairs of real numbers x and y where $2x = 5y + 8$, what does y equal?

(A) $\frac{x-4}{5}$

(B) $\frac{2x}{5} - 8$

(C) $\frac{2x+8}{5}$

(D) $\frac{2x-8}{5}$

(E) $2x - 8$

564. The polygon below has interior 90° angles. The sides of the polygon have measures as marked. What is the value of $x - y$?

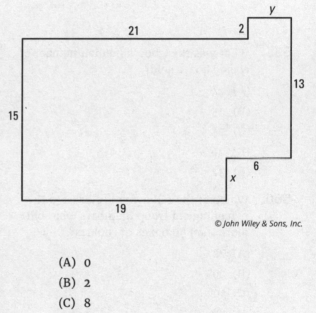

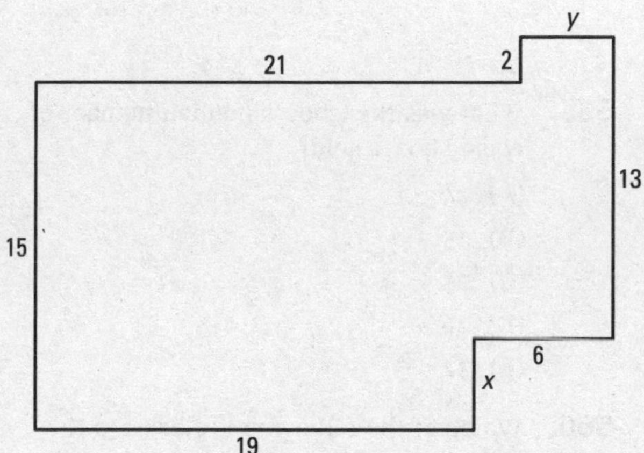

© John Wiley & Sons, Inc.

(A) 0

(B) 2

(C) 8

(D) 21

(E) 25

Questions 565–567 are based on the following information.

The following stem and leaf plot shows the number of boxes of cookies sold by 22 members of a Tiger Scout troop.

Number of Boxes of Cookies Sold per Scout	
1	2 5 7 8 8
2	2 3 3 4 5 5 5
3	2 4 4 4 8 9 9
5	0 2
6	1

565. What was the troop's median number of cookie boxes sold?

(A) 24

(B) 25

(C) 25.5

(D) 26

(E) 32

566. Which of the following is closest to the percentage of troop members who sold more than 50 boxes of cookies?

(A) 22%

(B) 20%

(C) 10%

(D) 9%

(E) 2%

567. Next year, the troop wants to increase its average number of boxes sold per member to 35. If the number of troop members remains at 22, how many additional boxes will each trooper need to sell on average next year for the troop to reach this goal?

(A) 3

(B) 5

(C) 32

(D) 35

(E) 110

568. Which of the following expresses all values of x that make the solution of $x^2 + x - 12$ positive and nonzero?

(A) $x > 12$

(B) $-4 < x < 3$

(C) $x > 12$ and $x < 0$

(D) $x < -4$ and $x > 3$

(E) $x > 3$

569. It takes Eugene 55 minutes traveling at 45 miles per hour to drive the same distance in his car as it takes Nadia to drive in $1\frac{1}{4}$ hours. How fast is Nadia driving in miles per hour?

(A) 25

(B) 30

(C) 33

(D) 60

(E) 75

570. A car's starting velocity is 20 meters per second as it pulls away from a stop sign. The physics equation for velocity is $v = at + v_0$ where t stands for time and v_0 is the initial velocity. What is the car's acceleration (a) in meters per square second if it takes it 5 seconds to reach 30 meters per second and it accelerates uniformly?

(A) 130

(B) 30

(C) 5

(D) 2

(E) 1

571. For all $a \neq 0$ and $b \neq 0$, $\frac{(4a^4b^3)^2}{2a^2b^{-2}} = ?$

(A) $8a^6b^8$

(B) $8a^6b^4$

(C) $8a^4b^7$

(D) $2a^6b^8$

(E) $2a^4b^7$

572. Of the 315 gems for sale at jewelry wholesaler, $\frac{2}{5}$ are emeralds, $\frac{1}{7}$ are rubies, and $\frac{3}{7}$ are sapphires. The remaining gems are of a type other than emeralds, rubies, and sapphires. How many of the wholesaler's gems are NOT emeralds, rubies, or sapphires?

(A) 5

(B) 7

(C) 9

(D) 35

(E) 306

573. What is the *maximum* possible sum of two integers that have a product that ranges between −5 and 0 exclusive?

(A) −5

(B) 3

(C) 5

(D) 7

(E) There is no limit to the value of the sum of the two integers.

574. Which of the following represents the equation of a circle in the standard *xy*-coordinate plane that is tangent to the *x*-axis at 3 units and to the *y*-axis at 3 units?

(A) $x^2 + y^2 = 9$

(B) $(x+3)^2 + (y-3)^2 = 9$

(C) $(x-3)^2 + (y-3)^2 = 9$

(D) $(x-3)^2 + (y-3)^2 = 6$

(E) $(x+3)^2 - (y+3)^2 = 6$

575. What is the distance of a line in the standard *xy*-coordinate plane with endpoints of (−3, −1) and (4, −2)?

(A) 5

(B) $\sqrt{47}$

(C) $5\sqrt{2}$

(D) $\sqrt{58}$

(E) 50

576. What is the length to the nearest tenth of side *a* on the triangle below?

Note: The law of cosines for non-right triangles states that $a^2 = b^2 + c^2 - 2bc\cos A$ when *A* is the angle opposite side *a*.

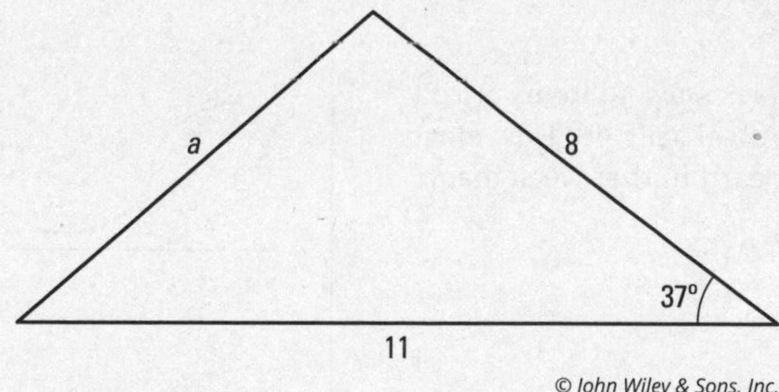

(A) $a = \sqrt{185 - (176\cos 37°)}$

(B) $a = 185 - (176\cos 37°)$

(C) $a = \sqrt{1{,}304\cos 37°}$

(D) $a = \sqrt{185 - (176\cos 73°)}$

(E) $a = 185 - (176\cos 73°)$

Questions 577–579 are based on the following information.

Aspen runs a consignment shop in which she sells used items for other people, whom she refers to as consignees. Her consignment agreement stipulates that Aspen will sell the consignees' items and split the gross sales with them so that Aspen retains 60% of gross sales after taxes and provides 40% to the corresponding consignee.

She has found a store space to rent for $350 per month, including all utilities. She pays 2 sales clerks, Jack and Angel, to help her run her store. Jack earns $15/hour and works 40 hours/week. Angel works 30 hours/week and makes $12/hour but receives an additional $1 for every item she sells over the price of $10. Aspen figures her advertising costs to be $1 per customer visit; she has furnished the store with items she already owns and has no other expenses.

577. If Aspen sells an antique table for $227, which includes a sales tax of 6%, how much did she give to the consignee who provided the table?

(A) $85.35

(B) $90.80

(C) $128.03

(D) $136.20

(E) $227.00

578. In one week, Jack sells 50 items priced over $10 and Angel sells 60. How much more did Jack earn in that week than Angel?

(A) $90.00

(B) $150.00

(C) $180.00

(D) $230.00

(E) $600.00

579. In January, Aspen has expenses of rent, 4 weeks of regular payroll and payroll taxes for Jack and Aspen, and advertising. One hundred customers visit the store, and 500 items are sold at an average price after taxes of $100 per item. Jack sells 300 items that cost more than $10, Angel sells 30 that cost more than $10 and 50 that cost less than $10, and Aspen sells 100. Payroll taxes for Jack and Aspen total $100. Considering total gross sales after taxes and total expenses, does Aspen's store make a profit in January?

(A) No, her expenses exceeded gross sales after taxes by $320 in January.

(B) No, her expenses exceeded gross sales after taxes by $20 in January.

(C) Yes, her gross sales after taxes exceeded expenses by $20 in January.

(D) Yes, her gross sales after taxes exceeded expenses by $120 in January.

(E) Yes, her gross sales after taxes exceeded expenses by $220 in January.

580. Which one of the following equations is represented by the graph below?

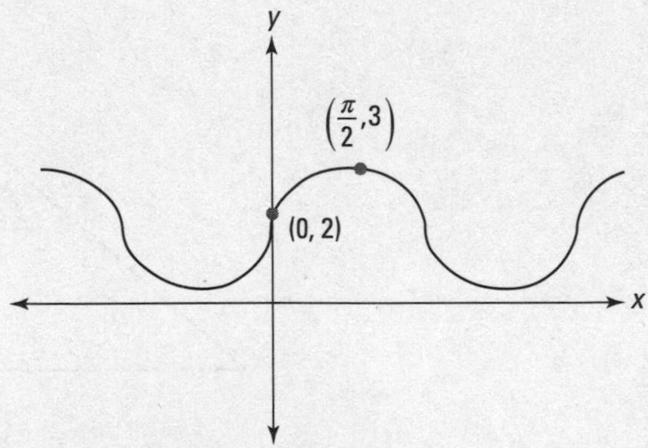

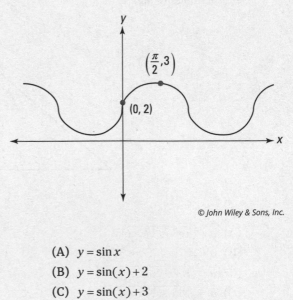

(A) $y = \sin x$

(B) $y = \sin(x) + 2$

(C) $y = \sin(x) + 3$

(D) $y = \tan x$

(E) $y = \tan x + 2$

581. Geoff invests \$1,200 in a certificate of deposit (CD) that earns 1.05% in interest compounded biannually, which means that he earns 1.05% of his existing money twice per year. The money he makes in interest is added to his account balance and rounded to the nearest cent. After 2 years, the CD matures. Geoff decides to use \$400 of the funds to purchase a tablet and invest the remaining balance in another CD. How much money did Geoff invest in this second CD?

(A) \$800.00

(B) \$850.40

(C) \$851.20

(D) \$1,250.40

(E) \$1,251.20

582. Harry conducts a poll to determine his classmates' favorite musical instruments. On the day Harry conducted the poll, 20% of the class was away on a field trip. Of the students who were present, 37.5% chose the guitar, 25% chose the drums, 18.75% chose the piano, 12.5% chose the saxophone, and 6.75% chose the flute. No other instruments were chosen and all present students including Harry participated in the poll. If 6 students choose the piano, how many students are in Harry's class?

(A) 32

(B) 40

(C) 48

(D) 50

(E) 52

583. What is the slope of a line on the *xy*-coordinate plane with endpoints of (2, 5) and (10, 4)?

(A) −8

(B) $-\frac{1}{8}$

(C) $\frac{1}{8}$

(D) $\frac{4}{3}$

(E) 8

584. Which is closest to the distance, to the nearest mile, represented by a line with endpoints of (7, 6) and (−1, −2) if each unit in the *xy*-coordinate plane is equivalent to 2 miles?

(A) 5

(B) 11

(C) 14

(D) 17

(E) 18

585. The regular polygon below has 6 congruent sides and 6 congruent interior angles. Two of the sides are extended until they meet at point *A*. What is the measure of $\angle A$?

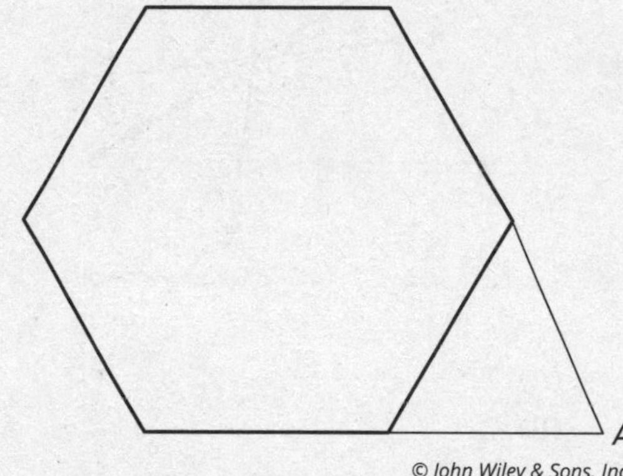

© John Wiley & Sons, Inc.

(A) 160°

(B) 120°

(C) 72°

(D) 60°

(E) 35°

586. What is the set of all real solutions to the equation $|x|^2 + 3|x| - 4 = 0$?

(A) {1, −1}

(B) {3, −3}

(C) {1, 3}

(D) {1, −1, 0}

(E) {1, −1, 3, −3, 0}

587. The edges of a cube are each 4 inches long. What is the cube's surface area in square inches?

(A) 8

(B) 16

(C) 36

(D) 64

(E) 96

588. The figure below shows three straight lines that intersect at point M. If $\angle EMF$ measures 47° and $\angle AMB$ measures 29°, what is the degree measure of $\angle CME$?

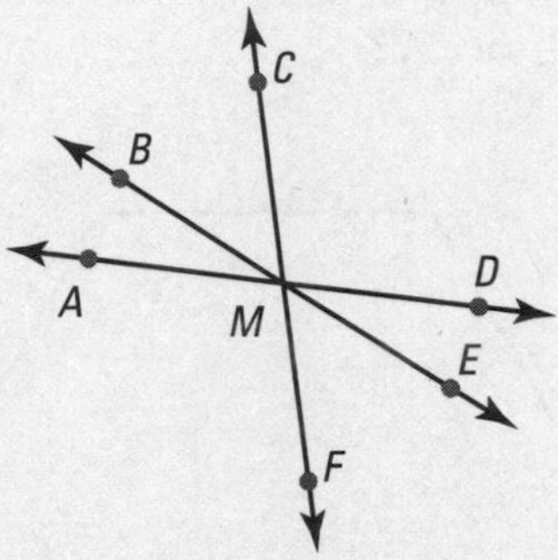

© John Wiley & Sons, Inc.

(A) 72°

(B) 76°

(C) 104°

(D) 133°

(E) 151°

589. Circle C below has a center point C, and the line that contains points M and Q is tangent to Circle C at point M. If $\overline{MC}$ and $\overline{PQ}$ are parallel, all of the following must be true EXCEPT:

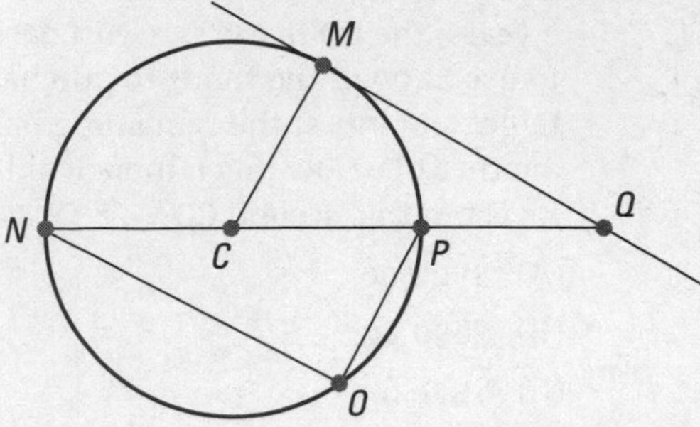

© John Wiley & Sons, Inc.

(A) $\angle CQM = \angle ONP$.

(B) $\triangle NOP$ is similar to $\triangle CMQ$.

(C) $\angle N$ measures $\frac{1}{2}$ minor arc PQ.

(D) Arc PN measures 180°.

(E) The measure of $\angle CQM = \frac{1}{2}$ the measure of minor arc MN.

590. For $i^2 = -1$, $(3+i)^2 = ?$

(A) 10

(B) $8 + 6i$

(C) 8

(D) $10 + 6i$

(E) $6 + 2i$

591. Which of the following could be the equation of the ellipse centered on the origin of the xy-coordinate plane shown below.

Note: The coordinate unit on the x-axis is the same length as the coordinate unit on the y-axis.

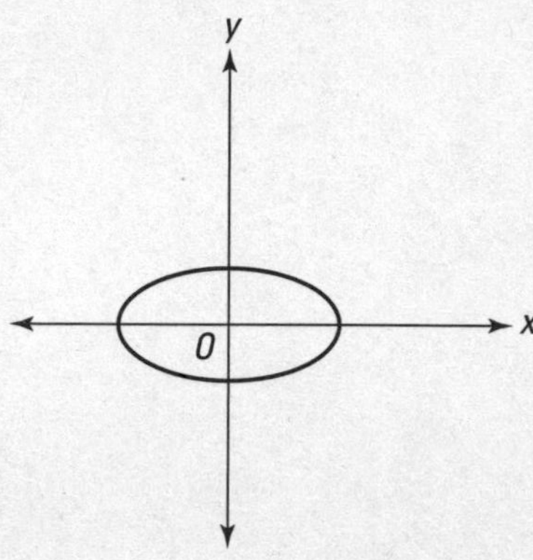

© John Wiley & Sons, Inc.

(A) $x^2 + y^2 = 25$

(B) $(x-5)^2 + (y-4)^2 = 16$

(C) $\frac{x^2}{25} + \frac{y^2}{16} = 1$

(D) $\frac{(x-5)^2}{25} + \frac{(y-4)^2}{16} = 1$

(E) $\frac{(x+5)^2}{25} + \frac{(y+4)^2}{16} = 1$

592. There is a straight, 36-mile road between Sacramento and Lodi. If Julian leaves Sacramento at 4:00 p.m. traveling 55 miles per hour and Emmett leaves Lodi at the same time traveling 65 miles per hour, at how many miles from Sacramento will the two pass each other?

(A) 10

(B) 16

(C) 19.5

(D) 22.5

(E) 39

593. In the right triangle shown below, the lengths in units are marked for two sides. What is tan A?

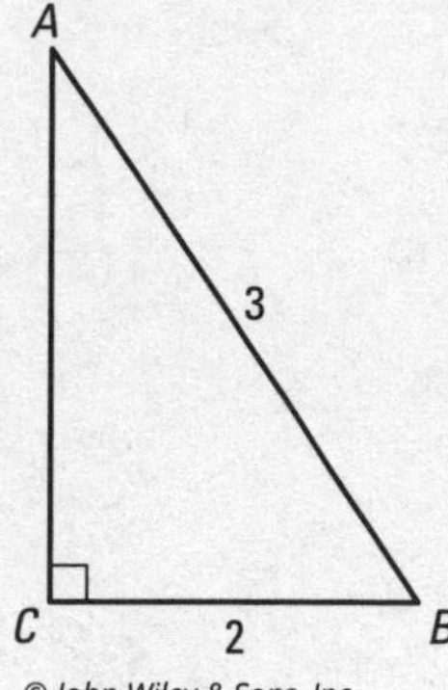

© John Wiley & Sons, Inc.

(A) $\frac{2}{\sqrt{5}}$

(B) $\frac{2}{\sqrt{13}}$

(C) $\frac{\sqrt{13}}{3}$

(D) $\frac{3}{2}$

(E) $\frac{\sqrt{5}}{2}$

594. Which of the following properly orders the four fractions from least to greatest?

(A) $\frac{5}{6} < \frac{4}{5} < \frac{9}{7} < \frac{7}{3}$

(B) $\frac{4}{5} < \frac{5}{6} < \frac{9}{7} < \frac{7}{3}$

(C) $\frac{7}{3} < \frac{9}{7} < \frac{5}{6} < \frac{4}{5}$

(D) $\frac{5}{6} < \frac{7}{3} < \frac{9}{7} < \frac{4}{5}$

(E) $\frac{4}{5} < \frac{5}{6} < \frac{7}{3} < \frac{9}{7}$

595. What is true about the solution set for this equation: $3^{(b^2-4)} = 1$?

(A) It contains 1 positive value, 1 negative value, and 0.

(B) It contains 2 positive numbers and 2 negative numbers.

(C) It contains 1 positive value and 1 negative value.

(D) It contains a value of 0 only.

(E) It contains 1 imaginary number.

Chapter 3

The Reading Test

The ACT Reading Test is pleasingly predictable. You always encounter 40 questions in four passages categorized as fiction, social science, humanities, and natural science — and always in that order. Each passage contains 10 questions, and most ask you to regurgitate details directly from the passage. Others require you to summarize main points or draw logical inference about the passage contents.

Keep your eye on the ticker because timing is crucial. You have a scant 35 minutes to answer all 40 questions, which boils down to a little under 9 minutes per passage. Keep alert and focused on your answer possibilities to maximize your efforts.

The Problems You'll Work On

When working through the questions in this chapter, be prepared to do the following:

- Choose the most easily justified answer from four possibilities.
- Scan the passages to locate key words from the questions and answers.
- Discover that often two of the four answers are clearly incorrect.
- Interpret vocabulary in the context of a passage.
- Compare the ideas in two similar passages.

What to Watch Out For

Trap answers include the following:

- Enticements to rely on your own knowledge or opinion
- Ideas that aren't directly supported by the passage
- Facts that are true but don't answer the question
- Words and phrases that suggest value judgments, such as *too much* or *not enough*
- Terms that leave no room for exception, such as *first*, *never*, or *all*

Prose Fiction

Questions 596–605 are based on the following information.

This passage is adapted from the novella "Notes from the Underground" by Fyodor Dostoyevsky, translated by Constance Garnett.

I am a sick man. . . . I am a spiteful man. I am an unattractive man. I believe my liver is diseased. However, I know nothing at all about my disease, and do not know for certain what ails me. I don't consult a doctor for it, and never have, though I have a respect for medicine and doctors. Besides, I am extremely superstitious, sufficiently so to respect medicine, anyway (I am well-educated enough not to be superstitious, but I am superstitious). No, I refuse to consult a doctor from spite. That you probably will not understand. Well, I understand it, though. Of course, I can't explain who it is precisely that I am mortifying in this case by my spite: I am perfectly well aware that I cannot "pay out" the doctors by not consulting them; I know better than anyone that by all this I am only injuring myself and no one else. But still, if I don't consult a doctor it is from spite. My liver is bad, well — let it get worse!

I have been going on like that for a long time — twenty years. Now I am forty. I used to be in the government service, but am no longer. I was a spiteful official. I was rude and took pleasure in being so. I did not take bribes, you see, so I was bound to find a recompense in that, at least. (A poor jest, but I will not scratch it out. I wrote it thinking it would sound very witty; but now that I have seen myself that I only wanted to show off in a despicable way, I will not scratch it out on purpose!)

When petitioners used to come for information to the table at which I sat, I used to grind my teeth at them, and felt intense enjoyment when I succeeded in making anybody unhappy. I almost did succeed. For the most part they were all timid people — of course, they were petitioners. But of the uppish ones there was one officer in particular I could not endure. He simply would not be humble, and clanked his sword in a disgusting way. I carried on a feud with him for eighteen months over that sword. At last I got the better of him. He left off clanking it. That happened in my youth, though. But do you know, gentlemen, what was the chief point about my spite? Why, the whole point, the real sting of it lay in the fact that continually, even in the moment of the acutest spleen, I was inwardly conscious with shame that I was not only not a spiteful but not even an embittered man, that I was simply scaring sparrows at random and amusing myself by it. I might foam at the mouth, but bring me a doll to play with, give me a cup of tea with sugar in it, and maybe I should be appeased. I might even be genuinely touched, though probably I should grind my teeth at myself afterwards and lie awake at night with shame for months after. That was my way.

I was lying when I said just now that I was a spiteful official. I was lying from spite. I was simply amusing myself with the petitioners and with the officer, and in reality I never could become spiteful. I was conscious every moment in myself of many, very many elements absolutely opposite to that. I felt them positively swarming in me, these opposite elements. I knew that they had been swarming in me all my life and craving some outlet from me, but I would not let them, would not let them, purposely would not let them come out. They tormented me till I was ashamed: they drove me to convulsions and — sickened me, at last, how they sickened me! Now, are not you fancying, gentlemen, that I am expressing remorse for something now, that I am asking your forgiveness for something? I am sure you are fancying that . . . However, I assure you I do not care if you are. . . .

It was not only that I could not become spiteful, I did not know how to become anything; neither spiteful nor kind, neither a rascal nor an honest man, neither a hero nor an insect. Now, I am living out my life in my corner, taunting myself with the spiteful and useless consolation that an intelligent man cannot become anything seriously, and it is only the fool who becomes anything. Yes, a man in the nineteenth century must and morally ought to be preeminently a characterless creature; a man of character, an active man is preeminently a limited creature. That is my conviction of forty years. I am forty years old now, and you know forty years is a whole lifetime; you know it is extreme old age.

596. Information in the passage suggests that the narrator grinds his teeth when he is:

(A) struggling at work.

(B) avoiding contact with others.

(C) feeling anxious or worried.

(D) spreading animosity.

597. Throughout the passage, the narrator can best be described as expressing:

(A) eager expectation.

(B) profound pessimism.

(C) amused melancholy.

(D) angry conviviality.

598. The narrator makes all of the following assertions about himself EXCEPT that he:

(A) acts out of spite.

(B) could never become spiteful.

(C) has a bad liver.

(D) may have an unhealthy heart.

599. When the narrator states "I am well-educated enough not to be superstitious, but I am superstitious" in lines 7–10, he most nearly means that:

(A) he is superstitious because he does not trust doctors.

(B) information he has gained through a university education should cause him to be more logical than he really is.

(C) he is superstitious despite rational evidence to the contrary.

(D) if he were better educated, he would seek medical attention.

600. When the narrator states in lines 50–51 that he "might foam at the mouth," he most nearly means that:

(A) he hungers for something sweet, such as a doll or sugared tea.

(B) he may display signs of aggression.

(C) his illness may be rabies.

(D) he is easily amused despite his seemingly angry demeanor.

601. The primary function of the fourth paragraph within the context of the passage as a whole is to:

(A) cast doubt on previous statements about the narrator's character to lead to an ultimate conclusion about his inability to control his character.

(B) provide the first indications that the narrator considers himself to be a shameful liar.

(C) identify the opposite elements that swarm inside the narrator.

(D) portray the narrator as a generally kind and moral individual, worthy of forgiveness, despite prior isolated incidents of cruelty.

602. The narrator's desire to "find a recompense," as it is described in line 25, most nearly means that he wishes to:

(A) issue a punishment.

(B) seek monetary gain at others' expense.

(C) compensate for other transgressions.

(D) enjoy a much-needed source of amusement.

603. The narrator indicates that he does not see a doctor for which of the following reasons?

(A) Failing to visit a doctor will hurt himself and others.

(B) He has misgivings about the medical profession.

(C) A visit to a doctor is not necessary because the narrator is acutely aware of the nature of his condition.

(D) He does not consult a doctor because he wants his liver condition to worsen.

604. Information in the passage suggests that this narrative takes place during which period?

(A) Between 1700 and 1800

(B) Between 1800 and 1900

(C) Between 1900 and 1950

(D) Between 1950 and present day

605. The narrator makes which of the following generalizations about petitioners from his experiences working for the government?

(A) The petitioners were primarily frightened and weak, which made the narrator look on them with contempt.

(B) Most petitioners, especially the officers, were unbearably arrogant.

(C) The narrator's behavior caused unhappiness for most of the petitioners.

(D) Most petitioners tried to bribe the narrator with offers of money.

Social Science

Questions 606–615 are based on the following information.

This passage is adapted from "Personality, Personality Disorder, and Violence: An Introduction" by Mary McMurran from *Personality, Personality Disorder and Violence: An Evidence-Based Approach* edited by Mary McMurran and Richard Howard (Wiley 2009).

In mitigating antisocial behavior and violence, a psychological explanation or psychiatric diagnosis needs to identify specific deficiencies that impair the agency of the person diagnosed. The deficiency may affect the capacity of a person to make rational decisions, impair the control a person has over his or her behavior, and/or impair the degree of awareness of the harm caused by the act. People with personality problems or personality disorders are usually viewed as being responsible for their behavior and not warranting excuse or mitigation in the same way as those with mental illness or learning disabilities. The basis of this view lies in the perceived normality of people with personality disorders. They face the same challenges in the same way as the rest of us in relation to controlling their emotions and impulses. We all, at times, have to control anger and aggression under provocation and express our anger appropriately. We all have to practice negotiation, compromise, and fair play to achieve what we want without bullying, intimidating, or abusing others. The truth is, we all come to these challenges with different personal resources, and some are better equipped than others to control their emotions, relate well to other people, and act in nonviolent ways. Indeed, a dimensional approach to personality disorders would likely place people with personality problems and personality disorders at the far end of a continuum that includes the normal range of experiences and behaviors.

A disorder may excuse or mitigate antisocial and violent behavior because the individual is not fully aware of the legal or moral imperative to refrain from this behavior or because that person does not fully understand the harmful consequences of that act. Intellectual disability and dementia are examples of such disorders. In any caring society, people who are seriously mentally impaired are unlikely to be punished for violent acts. In relation to people with antisocial personality disorder, there is an assumption of knowing the consequences but nonetheless being unable to exercise control over behavior. In relation to psychopathy, the case has been made that psychopathic individuals' lack of emotional capacities reduces their responsibility for their actions in that they do not really understand the implications of their antisocial and aggressive acts, either for others or for themselves. This has far-reaching implications for the administration of criminal justice.

If we hold people responsible for their actions, then a proportionate punishment is a reasonable option; yet, a final consideration to be taken into account is the effect of punishment on the individual. Punishment can lead to behavior change when it is immediate and inevitable (note that neither of these is typical of punishments in relation to crime). If the individual can understand the punishment in relation to the deed, and if punishment is likely to lead to a change in attitude or behavior, then perhaps punishment proportionate to the deed is warranted. An analogy is reprimanding a child for a misdeed. The child may not fully understand why the misdeed transgresses social or moral rules, but through the reprimand he or she begins to learn appropriate behavior. Concerning people with antisocial personality disorder, violent behavior may be explicable in terms of biopsychosocial disadvantage; hence there is mitigation of culpability, yet that individual may nevertheless be able to learn from punishment.

Concerning people with psychopathy, biopsychosocial disadvantage may again mitigate culpability, but the nature of the disorder may mean that the individual will not learn from punishment. Hence, to punish is purely for society to signal its disapproval. Some philosophers believe that punishment should be only a just desert and should not be administered to effect behavior change. Indeed, punishment is not the most effective way to reduce recidivism overall; hence, while punishment may be a necessary signal of society's disapproval and a means of exacting retribution for a crime, it is through treatment that behavior change is most likely to occur. For offenders with personality problems or personality disorders, treatment takes place within either a criminal justice context or a forensic mental health setting or, most probably, a combination of both of these over time. Thus, there is usually a combination of punishment and treatment. However, not all offenders with personality problems or personality disorders are considered treatable. Issues that need to be considered in making the decision to offer treatment or not are: Can appropriate treatment targets be identified? If they can, do treatments that have a positive effect on these treatment targets exist? An understanding of personality problems, personality disorder, and violence is required to identify and address the treatment needs of these offenders.

606. The overall tone of the passage can best be described as:

(A) informational.

(B) argumentative.

(C) negative.

(D) instructional.

607. The author of the passage makes all of the following assertions about punishment EXCEPT:

(A) when immediate, punishment can encourage behavioral change.

(B) when inevitable, punishment can encourage behavioral change.

(C) adults are more likely to respond to punishment and modify their behavior than are children.

(D) punishment is not the most effective way to prevent or minimize recidivism.

608. Which of the following does the author NOT consider an effective method of achieving what one wants?

(A) Fair play

(B) Intimidation

(C) Negotiation

(D) Compromise

609. The author would most likely disagree with which of the following statements?

(A) Comprehensive treatment is more likely to encourage behavioral change than punishment alone.

(B) Children will learn to modify their behavior from punishment even if they do not understand the social or moral rules they have broken.

(C) People with personality disorders and those without face the same challenges in controlling anger.

(D) A combination of treatment and punishment stimulates behavioral change in all offenders.

610. When the author says a dimensional approach to personality disorders would likely place people with personality problems and personality disorders at the far end of a continuum in lines 27–30, she most likely means that:

(A) those with personality problems and disorders should not be held to the same standard of behavior as the rest of the population.

(B) those with personality problems and disorders exhibit behavior that is considered normal, but just barely.

(C) those with personality problems and behaviors behave no differently than those who do not have these issues.

(D) those with personality problems and behaviors may actually be better equipped to deal with emotions than others.

611. The author attributes the fact that people who have severe mental handicaps tend to be punished less for their actions to:

(A) prison overcrowding.

(B) their propensity to be more adversely affected by punishment.

(C) a caring society.

(D) their inability to learn from punishment.

612. The author notes that disorders may help excuse antisocial or violent behavior for all of the following reasons EXCEPT that those with disorders:

(A) do not always understand why laws exist to limit certain types of behavior.

(B) do not always understand that their actions may be considered morally reprehensible.

(C) cannot always comprehend that consequences exist for their actions.

(D) are better helped by treatment in a forensic mental health setting.

613. Which of the following is a good synonym for the word *mitigate*, as it appears in line 74?

(A) Mask the symptoms of

(B) Diminish the consequences of

(C) Encourage

(D) Control

614. The author states which of the following as a condition for justifying a punishment proportionate to an action?

(A) The offender recognizes that punishment for the action is inevitable.

(B) The punishment issued will likely encourage a change in behavior.

(C) The perpetrator fully realizes the moral and societal implications of the action and resolves to never commit a crime in the future.

(D) The person is unaware of how the action negatively affects the lives of others.

615. Which of the following does the author consider a condition that inhibits an individual's capability to fully comprehend the consequences of an action?

(A) Physical impairment

(B) Antisocial behavior

(C) Dementia

(D) Narcissism

Humanities

Questions 616–625 are based on the following information.

Passage A is adapted from *Such Stuff as Dreams: The Psychology of Fiction* by Keith Oatley (Wiley 2011). Passage B is adapted from *Who Was William Shakespeare?: An Introduction to the Life and Works* by Dympna Callahan (Wiley-Blackwell 2013)

Passage A is by Keith Oatley

Dream was an important word for William Shakespeare. In his earliest plays he used it with its most common meaning, of a sequence of actions, visual scenes, and emotions that we imagine during sleep and that we sometimes remember when we awake, as well as with its second most common meaning of a waking fantasy (day-dream) of a wishful kind. Two or three years into his playwriting career, he started to use it in a subtly new way, to mean an alternative view of the world, with some aspects like those of the ordinary world, but with others unlike. In the dream view, things look different from usual.

In or about December 1594, something changed for Shakespeare. What changed was his conception of fiction. He started to believe, I think, that fiction should contain both visible human action and a view of what goes on beneath the surface. His plays moved beyond dramatizations of history as in the three *Henry VI* plays, beyond entertainments such as *The Taming of the Shrew*. They came to include aspects of dreams. Just as two eyes, one beside the other, help us to see in three dimensions so, with our ordinary view of the world and an extra view (a dream view), Shakespeare allows us to see our world with another dimension. The plays that he first wrote when he had achieved his idea were *A Midsummer Night's Dream* and *Romeo and Juliet.*

In *A Midsummer Night's Dream* it is as if Shakespeare says: Imagine a world a bit different from our own, a model world, in which, while we are asleep, some mischievous being might drip into our eyes the juice of "a little western flower" so that, when we awake, we fall in love with the person we first see. This is what happens to Titania, Queen of the Fairies. Puck drips the juice into her eyes. When she wakes, she sees Bottom the weaver, who — in the dream world — has been turned into an ass, and has been singing.

Passage B is by Dympna Callahan

Shakespeare's comedies, some of which press the genre to the very edges of its boundaries, address a great range of experience. What all the plays have in common is that they demonstrate the way that comedy is an intrinsically social genre about how men and women go about the business of interacting with one another so as to achieve a certain connectedness, either as conjugal pairs or as a cohesive community. Using information about Shakespeare's day-to-day life in Stratford and London, one can examine the extraordinary power and complexity of the comic perspective. A discussion of *The Comedy of Errors,* for example, may revolve around the fact that Shakespeare had two sisters who were named Joan. Extensive archival evidence has shown how the early modern practice of duplicate naming operated and how it illuminates the treatment of social identity in the play. *The Taming of the Shrew* pays homage to Shakespeare's rural Warwickshire roots. Indeed, the play proves insistently domestic in being a comedy of marriage rather than a comedy of courtship. An analysis of *Love's Labour's Lost* should take into consideration Shakespeare's connections with the translator John Florio, who lived for a time at the French Embassy in London, as a way of beginning to understand what the representation of brilliant and glittering French court culture might mean in England. An analysis of *A Midsummer Night's Dream* may take into consideration Shakespeare's creative and conceptual engagement both with his female sovereign and with the sovereignty of art that he sets so skillfully against the flora and fauna of his native place. In contrast, an examination of *The Merchant of Venice* considers all that Shakespeare encountered that was not marked by familiarity and domesticity, particularly those Jews and Italians who were, like himself, entertainers for the court.

Questions 616–619 are about Passage A.

616. Oatley lists all of the following as interpretations of the word *dream* EXCEPT:

(A) a waking fantasy.

(B) an alternate view of the world.

(C) imagined scenes and emotions that are typically forgotten upon awaking.

(D) the scenes, actions and emotions experienced during sleep.

617. The primary purpose of the second paragraph (lines 14–29) is to:

(A) list the various names of Shakespeare's works that demonstrate his new interest in dreams.

(B) describe the primary interpretations of what constitutes a dream.

(C) demonstrate that Shakespeare changed the focus of his plays in a way that incorporated elements of dreams.

(D) confirm Shakespeare's reliance on historical fact in his later works.

618. Oatley suggests that which of the following Shakespearian works is a dramatization of history?

(A) *Romeo and Juliet*

(B) *Henry VI, Part I*

(C) *A Midsummer Night's Dream*

(D) *The Taming of the Shrew*

619. According to Oatley, Shakespeare's later works often included a "dream view" in an effort to:

(A) make them more entertaining.

(B) add a more comedic element.

(C) give the reader a look at the world through another dimension.

(D) allow himself more creative freedom.

Questions 620–623 are about Passage B.

620. As it is used in line 45, *intrinsically* most nearly means:

(A) oddly.

(B) radically.

(C) humorously.

(D) fundamentally.

621. Callahan states that *The Taming of the Shrew* contains elements of Shakespeare's early life in:

(A) Warwickshire

(B) Stratford

(C) Venice

(D) London

622. Callahan mentions all of the following as influences for elements in Shakespeare's comedies EXCEPT:

(A) Shakespeare's sisters and daily life in Stratford.

(B) Jews and Italians who were entertainers for the court.

(C) Shakespeare's connections with John Florio and the Queen of England.

(D) aspects of ordinary life mixed with an alternative dream view, unlike anything from day-to-day life in Stratford.

623. According to Callahan, which of the following is common to all Shakespearian comedies?

(A) References to the way both men and women conduct business

(B) Characters who are based on Shakespeare's family members

(C) Human connections between couples or within communities

(D) Themes of familiarity and domesticity

Questions 624–625 are about both passages.

624. The two passages have which of the following in common?

(A) Both discuss Shakespeare's reliance on the concept of dreams.

(B) Both describe the inspirations behind some of Shakespeare's most notable works.

(C) Both offer an overview of Shakespeare's early life.

(D) Both reference how Shakespeare's geographic upbringing played a role in his most notable works.

625. Which of the following images from Oakley's passage would Callahan likely cite as a specific example of one of Shakespeare's influences?

(A) Two eyes, one beside the other, in *A Midsummer Night's Dream*

(B) The "little western flower" in *A Midsummer Night's Dream*

(C) Titania in *A Midsummer Night's Dream*

(D) Historical events in *The Taming of the Shrew*

Natural Science

Questions 626–635 are based on the following information.

This passage is adapted from *Anatomy & Physiology of Farm Animals*, 7th Edition, by Rowan D. Frandson, W. Lee Wilke, and Anna Dee Fails (Wiley 2009).

All living things, both plants and animals, are constructed of small units called cells. The simplest animals, such as the ameba, consist of a single cell that is capable of performing all functions commonly associated with life. These functions include growth (increase in size), metabolism (use of food), response to stimuli (such as moving toward light), contraction (shortening in one direction), and reproduction (development of new individuals of the same species).

A typical cell consists of three main parts, the cytoplasm, the nucleus, and the cell membrane. In complex animals, certain cells specialize in one or more the functions of the animal body. A group of specialized cells is a tissue. For example, cells that specialize in conducting impulses make up nerve tissue. Cells that specialize in holding structures together make up connective tissue. Various tissues are associated in functional groups called organs. The stomach is an organ that functions in digestion of food. A group of organs that participate in a common enterprise make up a system. The stomach, liver, pancreas, and intestines are all part of the digestive system.

The primary types of tissues include (1) epithelial tissues, which cover the surface of the body, line body cavities, and form glands; (2) connective tissues, which support and bind other tissues together and from which, in the case of bone marrow, the formed elements of the blood are derived; (3) muscle tissues, which specialize in contracting; and (4) nervous tissues, which conduct impulses from one part of the body to another.

In general, the epithelial tissues are classified as simple (composed of a single layer) or stratified (many-layered). Each of these types is further subdivided according to the shape of the individual cells within it. Simple epithelium includes squamous (platelike) cells, cuboidal (cubic) cells, columnar (cylindrical) cells, and pseudostratified columnar cells.

Simple squamous epithelium consists of thin, platelike cells. They are much expanded in two directions but have little thickness. The edges are joined somewhat like mosaic tile covering a floor. A layer of simple squamous epithelium has little tensile strength and is found only as a covering layer for stronger tissues. Simple squamous epithelium is found where a smooth surface is required to reduce friction. The coverings of viscera and the linings of body cavities and blood vessels are all composed of simple squamous epithelium.

Cuboidal epithelial cells are approximately equal in all dimensions. They are found in some ducts and in passageways in the kidneys. The active tissue of many glands is composed of cuboidal cells. *Columnar epithelial cells* are cylindrical. They are arranged somewhat like the cells in a honeycomb. Some columnar cells have whip-like projections called cilia extending from the free extremity. Pseudostratified columnar epitheliumis composed of columnar cells. However, they vary in length, giving the appearance of more than one layer or stratum. This type of epithelium is found in the upper respiratory tract, where the lining cells are ciliated.

Stratified epithelium consists of more than one layer of epithelial cells and includes stratified squamous, stratified columnar, and transitional epithelia. *Stratified squamous epithelium* forms the outer layer of the skin and the lining of the first part of the digestive tract as far as the stomach. In ruminants, stratified squamous epithelium also lines the forestomach (rumen, reticulum, and omasum). Stratified squamous epithelium is the thickest and toughest of the epithelia, consisting of many layers of cells. From deep to superficial, these layers include the basal layer (stratum basale), the parabasal layer (stratum spinosum), intermediate layer (stratum granulosum), and superficial layer (stratum corneum). The deepest layer, the stratum basale, contains the actively growing and multiplying cells. These cells are somewhat cuboidal, but as they are pushed toward the surface, away from the blood supply of the underlying tissues, they become flattened, tough, and lifeless and are constantly in the process of peeling off. This layer of cornified (keratinized) dead cells becomes very thick in areas subjected to friction. Calluses are formed in this manner.

Stratified columnar epithelium is composed of more than one layer of columnar cells and is found lining part of the pharynx and salivary ducts. *Transitional epithelium* lines the portions of the urinary system that are subjected to stretching. These areas include the urinary bladder and ureters. Transitional epithelium can pile up many cells thick when the bladder is small and empty and stretch out to a single layer when completely filled. Glandular epithelial cells are specialized for secretion or excretion. Secretion is the release from the gland cell of a substance that has been synthesized by the cell and that usually affects other cells in other parts of the body. Excretion is the expulsion of waste products.

626. Which of the following best outlines the format of the passage?

(A) The passage begins with general statements about the makeup of living things, provides more specific details, and ends with a general conclusion about biological components.

(B) The passage opens with a general theory about all living things and follows with a series of support evidence for that theory.

(C) The passage lays a foundation of general facts that leads to more specific information about one element of that foundation and then more specific detail about one type of that element.

(D) The passage draws a general conclusion and then supports it by discussing a variety of opinions on the validity of that statement.

627. According to the passage, if epithelial tissue is simple, then it is composed of:

(A) a single cell.

(B) a single layer.

(C) multiple layers.

(D) multiple cells.

628. According to the passage, all of the following are considered functions commonly associated with life EXCEPT:

(A) reproduction.

(B) food breakdown.

(C) impulse control.

(D) contraction.

629. According to the passage, which of the following functioning together is an example of a system?

(A) Liver, intestines, and pancreas

(B) Cytoplasm, nucleus, and membranes

(C) Tissues, cells, and organs

(D) Bones, muscles, and nerves

630. Which of the following is likely true of the types of epithelial cells in the upper respiratory tract?

(A) They are organized a bit like the cells of a honeycomb.

(B) They contain more than one layer or stratum.

(C) They are similar to epithelial cells found in lining of the digestive tract.

(D) They are somewhat cuboidal.

631. The type of tissue that conducts impulses is known as:

(A) epithelial.

(B) connective.

(C) muscle.

(D) nervous.

632. All of the following are primary components of a cell EXCEPT:

(A) cytoplasm.

(B) membrane.

(C) tissue.

(D) nucleus.

633. According to the passage, which of the following is true about glandular epithelial cells?

(A) They are the sole components of the pituitary and adrenal glands.

(B) They line the pharynx.

(C) They line the stretchable parts of the urinary system.

(D) They specialize in secreting or excreting.

634. Where would one most likely find simple squamous epithelium?

(A) Within the inner layers of a large muscle, such as the quadricep

(B) Along the surface of the muscles that pump the blood into the heart

(C) In the lining of the first part of the digestive tract

(D) As the lining of the pharynx and salivary ducts

635. Which of the following do the authors say form when keratinized dead cells thicken in places where they are subject to friction?

(A) Flattened cuboidal cells

(B) Stratified squamous epithelium

(C) Calluses

(D) Warts

Prose Fiction

Questions 636–645 are based on the following information.

This passage is adapted from the short story "Brown Wolf" by Jack London.

From the thicket-covered hillside came a crashing of underbrush, and then, forty feet above them, on the edge of the sheer wall of rock, appeared a wolf's head and shoulders. His braced forepaws dislodged a pebble, and with sharp-pricked ears and peering eyes he watched the fall of the pebble till it struck at their feet. Then he transferred his gaze and with open mouth laughed down at them.

"You Wolf, you!" and "You blessed Wolf!" the man and woman called out to him. The ears flattened back and down at the sound, and the head seemed to snuggle under the caress of an invisible hand.

They watched him scramble backward into the thicket, then proceeded on their way. Several minutes later, rounding a turn in the trail where the descent was less precipitous, he joined them in the midst of a miniature avalanche of pebbles and loose soil. He was not demonstrative. A pat and a rub around the ears from the man, and a more prolonged caressing from the woman, and he was away down the trail in front of them, gliding effortlessly over the ground in true wolf fashion.

In build and coat and brush he was a huge timber-wolf; but the lie was given to his wolf-hood by his color and marking. There the dog unmistakably advertised itself. No wolf was ever colored like him. He was brown, deep brown, red-brown, an orgy of browns. Back and shoulders were a warm brown that paled on the sides and underneath to a yellow that was dingy because of the brown that lingered in it. The white of the throat and paws and the spots over the eyes was dirty because of the persistent and ineradicable brown, while the eyes themselves were twin topazes, golden and brown.

The man and woman loved the dog very much; perhaps this was because it had been such a task to win his love. It had been no easy matter when he first drifted in mysteriously out of nowhere to their little mountain cottage. Footsore and famished, he had killed a rabbit under their very noses and under their very windows, and then crawled away and slept by the spring at the foot of the blackberry bushes. When Walt Irvine went down to inspect the intruder, he was snarled at for his pains, and Madge likewise was snarled at when she went down to present, as a peace-offering, a large pan of bread and milk.

A most unsociable dog he proved to be, resenting all their advances, refusing to let them lay hands on him, menacing them with bared fangs and bristling hair. Nevertheless he remained, sleeping and resting by the spring, and eating the food they gave him after they set it down at a safe distance and retreated. His wretched physical condition explained why he lingered; and when he had recuperated, after several days' sojourn, he disappeared.

And this would have been the end of him, so far as Irvine and his wife were concerned, had not Irvine at that particular time been called away into the northern part of the state. Biding along on the train, near to the line between California and Oregon, he chanced to look out of the window and saw his unsociable guest sliding along the wagon road, brown and wolfish, tired yet tireless, dust-covered and soiled with two hundred miles of travel.

Now Irvine was a man of impulse, a poet. He got off the train at the next station, bought a piece of meat at a butcher shop, and captured the vagrant on the outskirts of the town. The return trip was made in the baggage car, and so Wolf came a second time to the mountain cottage. Here he was tied up for a week and made love to by the man and woman. But it was very circumspect love-making. Remote and alien as a traveller from another planet, he snarled down their soft-spoken love-words. He never barked. In all the time they had him he was never known to bark.

To win him became a problem. Irvine liked problems. He had a metal plate made, on which was stamped: "Return to Walt Irvine, Glen Ellen, Sonoma County, California." This was riveted to a collar and strapped about the dog's neck. Then he was turned loose, and promptly he disappeared. A day later came a telegram from Mendocino County. In twenty hours he had made over a hundred miles to the north, and was still going when captured.

636. Which of the following is the most accurate chronological listing of events in the story from earliest to most recent?

(A) Walt and Madge meet the wolf while hiking; they try to win his affection by feeding him at their home; Walt takes a train trip; Wolf follows him home, and Walt makes him a collar.

(B) Wolf meets Walt and Madge on a hiking trail; they realize the dog doesn't have the coloring of a wolf; the dog follows them to their mountain cottage; the dog is captured in Mendocino County.

(C) The brown dog drifts to Walt and Madge's mountain cottage seeking food and affection; the dog disappears but then reappears when Walt takes a train trip; the dog joins them on a trail; Walt gives the dog a collar.

(D) Wolf stays at the mountain cottage for a few days then leaves; Walt sees Wolf outside a train window; Wolf stays with Walt and Madge for at least a week; they meet Wolf on a hiking trail.

637. The point of view from which the passage is told can best be described as that of:

(A) Walt Irvine.

(B) the man who called to the wolf.

(C) a first-person omniscient narrator.

(D) an unidentified commentator.

638. The passage suggests that the section of the story during which Walt rides the train takes place:

(A) in southern Oregon near its border with California.

(B) north of the mountain cottage.

(C) near Sonoma County.

(D) in Mendocino County.

639. When the author says the wolf ". . .with open mouth laughed down at them," (line 8) he most likely means to indicate that the wolf:

(A) was amused by Walt and Madge's appearance.

(B) was happy to see Walt and Madge.

(C) intended to harm Walt and Madge.

(D) felt superior to Walt and Madge.

640. The word *precipitous*, as it is used in line 16, most nearly means:

(A) hasty.

(B) wet.

(C) rocky.

(D) steep.

641. When the author notes in lines 24–25, that ". . .the lie was given to his wolfhood by his color and marking," he is likely trying to say that:

(A) wolves' colors are usually gray or black and never brown.

(B) the wolf's colors and markings made him appear as though he was wearing a hood.

(C) the animal's colors revealed that he was not a timber-wolf.

(D) the creature was a wolf with doglike features.

642. The passage indicates all of the following about the animal EXCEPT:

(A) he continued to reject the couple's demonstrations of affection.

(B) he never barked.

(C) he was capable of traveling long distances.

(D) he had the physique of a wolf.

643. The main point of the last paragraph is to demonstrate to the reader:

(A) the extent of the animal's stubborn determination to get away from Walt and Madge.

(B) the efforts couple made to keep the dog from running away.

(C) Walt's resolve to provide care for the dog.

(D) Walt's desire to deal with complex situations.

644. Which of the following best summarizes the author's sentiments when he says, "The man and woman loved the dog very much; perhaps this was because it had been such a task to win his love" (lines 36–38)?

(A) The man and the woman could not help but love the dog that showed them deep affection.

(B) The effort it took to love the dog made the dog's presence that much more valuable.

(C) From the moment they found him, Walt and Madge felt the same abundant love for the dog that he felt for him.

(D) The man and woman strove in vain to win the dog's affection.

645. As it is used in line 75, the word *circumspect* most nearly means:

(A) guarded.

(B) speculative.

(C) short-lived.

(D) tender.

Social Science

Questions 646–655 are based on the following information.

This passage is adapted from *Women, Wealth, and Giving: The Virtuous Legacy of the Boom Generation*, by Margaret May Damen and Niki Nicastro McCuistion (Wiley 2009).

In 2030, of the 57.8 million American boomers, 54 percent will be women. And it is women worldwide who make the largest slice of the pie when it comes to making consumer purchasing decisions, estimated at $20 trillion annually, including 91 percent of homes, 60 percent of automobiles, and 51 percent of consumer electronics.

Today, women control almost 60 percent of the nation's wealth, and evidence indicates they will inherit and manage even more wealth in the future. And since women outlive men by an average of five years, in the next twenty years, it is predicted that 80 percent to 90 percent of women will be in charge of their families' financial affairs sometime in their life. With the majority of the estimated $41 trillion that is expected to be transferred through estate settlements and trusts passing through their hands, women will have a defining role in the reshaping of the American Dream for future generations. There is no question; women are indeed where the money is.

Even better, they are using the "power of the purse" to profoundly influence our economy and our society. The Center for Women's Business Research states that 54 percent of businesswomen make all of their philanthropic decisions independent of advice or counsel from anyone. And since women are the key decision makers in the managing and disposing of wealth, they will be, as management guru Tom Peters affirms, "the largest 'national' economy on earth."

While men may still earn more money, women give as much to charity, yet they do so differently. In today's challenging economic, political, and sociological times, women have the power to accelerate their ability to do good and change the face of society. A case in point is the 2008 national elections. Women made contributions to candidates in unprecedented numbers. Women increasingly realize their own tremendous potential to apply their charitable dollars to shaping the future of society and the world. Women are where the money is; they matter. "If you don't get more women in politics," says Marie C. Wilson, founder and president of the White House Project, "you won't get more women on boards that have the possibility for change. If you don't fund political work and power, you don't get the change you need."

More and more women are becoming aware of the power of money to truly make a difference in their local and global community. One of our interviewees, Dallas boomer Brenda Pejovich, an entrepreneur who devotes significant time to serving on state agency and nonprofit boards and supporting political causes, says that one of the reasons she gives to political organizations is to be heard and to raise awareness for women's issues, She emphasizes, "We [women] need to understand that while volunteering time is important, we need to support the causes we believe in with our checks so that we have a seat at the table. Women have a major impact on policy and the more involved we are, the more effectively we can influence decisions that are important to us and our families. By increasing our participation in the competition for ideas, women will continue to contribute to a better society. It's our checks that influence, and it's never been more important to open our wallets and give."

For women born between 1943 and 1964, the first decade of the twenty-first century is a defining time. Women of this generation are entering the next phase of their biological life. This fresh vigor — as anthropologist Margaret Mead calls it, the "post menopausal zest" — brings with it new assets, freedom, networks, and knowledge that allow boomer women to take on unique challenges, give more creatively, become even more authentic, and engage in pursuits that can bring a greater sense of meaning, joy, and balance. For boomer women, the rite of passage to "post menopausal zest" is a signal to reconnect with the voice of their soul, to find original songs from the heart, to dance to an unfamiliar beat, and to create authentic ways of making those challenging situations better.

"Our time on this earth is so short," says Vi Nichols Chason, co-president of the Martin County Women Supporting the Arts. "I think often of how important taking action is every time I hear the lyrics of the Beatles' song 'Hey Jude.'" She runs through a few lines of that familiar boomer-generation song that urges us to give sad songs happy endings.

646. According to the passage, women make about 90 percent of the decisions concerning the purchase of:

(A) cars.

(B) homes.

(C) electronics.

(D) furniture.

647. The authors attribute the fact that between 80 and 90 percent of women will one day be in charge of family finances to the fact that:

(A) women will one day make more than men.

(B) men are not always responsible when it comes to consumer decisions.

(C) a woman's worth will, at some point, be recognized.

(D) most women outlive men.

648. The authors use the example of women's donations to political candidates in record numbers to demonstrate all of the following EXCEPT:

(A) women are willing to give to charity despite their lower earning power.

(B) the power women have when they get behind important causes.

(C) men and women differ in terms of how they give to charitable causes.

(D) in terms of total dollars, men donate less to political causes than women do.

649. The authors link all of the following to what anthropologist Margaret Mead refers to as "post-menopausal zest" EXCEPT:

(A) new assets.

(B) freedom.

(C) more time to relax.

(D) a chance to reconnect with one's soul.

650. According to the passage, Marie C. Wilson would most likely agree with which of the following statements?

(A) Women should find ways to immerse themselves in politics.

(B) "Hey Jude" is a sad song with a happy ending

(C) Financial contributions are just as important as, if not more important than, volunteering one's time.

(D) Women should not be afraid to dance to an unfamiliar beat.

651. The authors suggest that the era when women boomers in America outnumber men boomers is during:

(A) the first decade of the twenty-first century.

(B) the 1960s.

(C) the third decade of the twenty-first century.

(D) the early 1940s.

652. The primary purpose of the passage's final paragraph is to:

(A) demonstrate the need for women to achieve their goals.

(B) demonstrate the differences between the goals of boomers and those of younger generations.

(C) urge women to write songs with happy endings.

(D) reconnect with the voice of their soul.

653. Which of the following individuals urged boomer women to engage in pursuits that bring them a greater sense of meaning, joy and balance?

(A) Brenda Pejovich

(B) Margaret Mead

(C) Vi Nichols Chason

(D) Marie C. Wilson

654. The passage makes all of the following assertions about women EXCEPT that:

(A) women are the key decision makers when it comes to managing and disposing of wealth.

(B) the first 10 years of the 20th century is defining time for women of a certain age.

(C) women make about 60 percent of automobile purchasing decisions.

(D) women make nearly half of all consumer electronics purchasing decisions.

655. All of the following could serve as synonyms for *unprecedented*, as it is used in line 39, EXCEPT:

(A) customary

(B) never before seen

(C) record

(D) unparalleled

Humanities

Questions 656–665 are based on the following information.

This passage is adapted from *Italian Renaissance Art: Understanding Its Meaning*, by Christiane L Joost-Gaugier (Wiley 2013).

There is no such thing as "progress" in art. Unlike modern concepts of science, art cannot be "dated" or outmoded. One work of art is not more important because it was made after another. Nor does it make its predecessor obsolete. In fact, some of the most valuable works of art are some of the oldest known to us — a Sumerian statue, an Egyptian crown, a Greek tombstone, for example. So, we may ask, why does time matter: Why do we study the history of art and not just "art"?

Time is not an enemy invented by the gods to confuse us. On the contrary, in the history of art it is our friend. By paying attention to it we can understand many things that might otherwise elude us. A work of art can, for example, be remarkable in the year that its features were invented, whereas the very same work of art copied a generation later may have less or little value. Even so, in the big picture of the history of art, one hundred years is not much. An ancient Egyptian temple, for example, might be dated within several hundred years, or even a thousand, because styles and materials did not change much in ancient Egypt. But in the Italian Renaissance, a hundred years is a stellar leap in the chronological ordering of artistic events. This is even more true when we take into account that time is colored by geographic locality, for in different places developments occur at different paces. When we think about such things we can more easily extract the significance of a work of art.

Both Masaccio's Trinity and Pontormo's Deposition were important commissions, about a hundred years apart, and both were painted for churches in Florence. Both represent the same subject, the dead Christ. Yet they are completely different.

The painting by Masaccio depicts the wounded and lifeless body of Christ hanging from a cross which is grasped from behind by the hands of God the Father. Christ is being mourned by two figures who stand below in the space of the picture and worshipped by two figures who kneel in front praying in what seems to be our space. One of the mourners looks out at us and gestures to us, inviting us to enter the picture and participate in the sorrow they feel. The other figures pray: They are us. The object of their attention is the mortal figure of Christ, who has expired after a long agony and tragic death. Though dead, Christ is victorious: for, standing behind him, God the Father enlarges the image of Christ so as to allow it to dominate the picture space. Christ is the center and the focal point. By dropping the floor out of our sight and articulating the receding coffers of the ceiling to assure that we are seeing it from below, the artist suggests to us that we are looking up with reverence and respect. Thus the eye ascends slowly to its ultimate destination in the center, the figure of Christ being displayed to us by God himself.

Above the center, a huge barrel vault is represented in perspective, ingeniously imagined for the first time in the history of painting. Its compartments diminish so that the fresco appears to be hollowed out of the actual wall it was painted on. It creates a chamber that defines and measures a space that is clearly structured and related to the space of the viewer. Inside the cube of space, the mourners stand on a platform; the worshippers kneel on the ground in a space of their own — their space is our space. A rational light enters the scene from our world, illuminating the fresco from the front and casting shadows behind the forms it defines. The colors illuminated by this light are earthy and naturalistic. Their chromatic accents convince us that the forms they describe really do exist and really do project. All the figures, including the divine ones of Christ and God the Father, are naturalistically formed. They behave in rational ways. Their actions, thoughts, and struggles are clear. They are ennobled figures participating in an ennobled drama.

656. The author notes all of the following similarities between Pontormo's Deposition and Masaccio's Trinity EXCEPT:

(A) both were significant commissions.

(B) both were painted within the same century.

(C) neither can become outdated.

(D) both were owned by Florentine churches.

657. According to the passage, the effect of the way Masaccio's Trinity manipulates architectural elements to position its viewers serves to:

(A) invite them to share in the sorrow of the mourners and pray.

(B) convince them that the scene is real and the figures are rational.

(C) encourage them to look upon the central figure with awe and reverence.

(D) allow them to determine the actual time period in which the scene takes place.

658. According to the passage, how many figures are depicted in Massacio's Trinity?

(A) 4

(B) 5

(C) 6

(D) A number greater than 6

659. When the author notes in line 2 that art cannot be "dated," she most nearly means that:

(A) knowing the creation dates of some pieces of art is nearly impossible.

(B) works of art do not become obsolete as new works are created.

(C) the study of art history is necessary to appreciate older works of art.

(D) that much like modern science, art becomes progressively more relevant over time.

660. Which of the following original techniques does Massacio use to incorporate the viewer into the painting's setting?

(A) The representation of a barrel vault

(B) Earthy and naturalistic colors

(C) Gesturing figures

(D) The placement of smaller figures around a larger central figures

661. Which of the following does the author offer as evidence to back up her claim in line 49 that "Christ is victorious"?

(A) Christ is still a popular subject in art despite his death.

(B) Christ is the focal point of the painting.

(C) God supports Christ's lifeless body from behind.

(D) A rational light illuminates Christ's head.

662. When the author states that the figures in Masaccio's Trinity are naturalistically formed, she is most likely saying:

(A) the figures were drawn by hand.

(B) the figures are representative of real people with real emotions.

(C) the paints used to create the figures were made from natural resources.

(D) painting the figures came naturally to the seasoned artist.

663. *Ennobled* as it is used in line 81 most closely means:

(A) dignified.

(B) insignificant.

(C) royal.

(D) infallible.

664. Which of the following does the author consider an insignificant amount of time when it comes to "the big picture of the history of art?"

(A) 50 years

(B) 100 years

(C) 500 years

(D) 1,000 years

665. In relation to the rest of the passage, the fourth paragraph serves to:

(A) discuss artistic techniques used to create the painting.

(B) show how Masaccio's Trinity differs from Pontormo's Deposition.

(C) emphasize the importance of the figures surrounding Christ.

(D) explain how the artist distinguishes the key figure in the painting.

Natural Science

Questions 666–675 are based on the following information.

This passage is adapted from *Natural Disasters in a Global Environment*, by Anthony N. Penna and Jennifer S. Rivers (Wiley 2013).

Supervolcanoes, those rare geological events, pose the most catastrophic threat to life on this planet. No super-eruption of Mt. Toba's magnitude has occurred during the Common Era (CE). It is the most studied of all known supervolcanoes in geological time, even though no precise measurements exist of its ejected material in either solid or gaseous states. Only cylinders of ice from the Greenland Sheet Project 2 (GISP2), measured for trapped gases, provide information about the magnitude of the Toba eruption.

The eruption was identified as the Younger Toba Tuff (YTT), to distinguish it from previous supervolcanoes at the same site. The Middle Toba Tuff (500,000 years Before Present; BP), the Oldest Toba Tuff (840,000 years BP), and the Haranggoal Dacite (1.2 million years BP) preceded it. The magma reservoirs from these older eruptions remained thermally stagnant for thousands of years, while the magma from the YTT began to accumulate and become more active for at least 100,000 years before its eruption.

Its eruption expelled 6.7 mi (2,800 km) of dense lava. The largest recorded eruption of Mt. Tambora in Indonesia in 1815 (whose effects historians have identified as "the year without a summer") was minimal when compared to the Younger Toba Tuff. Scientists estimated its explosive capacity at 3,500 times greater than the 1815 explosion. As fractures opened in the roof of YTT's magma chamber, massive outflows of dense magma covered 7,700 mi (19,930 km) of Sumatra during a 9-to-14-day period.

Combining the magnitude of the eruption with its intensity of around 7.8 million tons per second (7.1 billion kg/s), scientists estimated that the plume height was 20 ± 3 mi (32 ± 5 km).

Once the plume became airborne, its gas content of H_2S (hydrogen sulfide) oxidized rapidly into H_2SO_4 (sulfuric acid). Approximately 3.8 million tons (3.5 billion kg) of H_2S would oxidize into 11 million tons (10 billion kg) of H_2SO_4. However, since these estimates are subject to re-evaluation with further research, they should be accepted cautiously. Confirmation of such high readings in the atmosphere is recorded in the Greenland Ice Sheet. With an error margin of five years, these high readings about 70,000 years ago are greater than at any time in the 110,000-year record of the GISP2.

Additional evidence of the magnitude of this monumental event is found in the deposits of Toba tephra ejected during the volcanic explosion and spread across a wide expanse of the Indian Ocean and the South China Sea and beyond, including the surrounding areas of Borneo, Sumatra, Sri Lanka, Malaysia, Vietnam, and the Arabian Sea. Mt. Toba deposited at least 1,000 yd^3 (765 m^3) of ash and several gigatons of volcanic gases across this vast expanse. Additional discoveries of YTT tephra appear as deep-sea drilling continues to date ash deposits of 4 in (10 cm) or more. These covered at least 1% of Earth's surface with 3,700 yd^3 (2,829 m^3) of dense rock equivalent (DRE). Researchers have uncovered as much as 35 in (90 cm) of ash in Malaysia. With each new discovery, the magnitude of this supervolcano grows and its estimated impact on the global climate system becomes clearer.

Scientists Michael R. Rampino and Stephen Self argued that the possible effects of the Toba eruption was the onset of a "volcanic winter" creating conditions suggested by the exchange of nuclear weapons that would create a cloud of ash caused by fireballs blocking out the energy from the sun. In the latitudes from 30° to 70°N, drops in temperatures ranging from 9 to 27°F (5 to 15°C) would have been possible, with deep freezes in the midlatitudes. Temperatures below normal in the range of 5.4 to 9°F (3 to 5°C) may have continued for several years. More snow and sea ice would have accumulated, thereby accelerating cool conditions and leading to decades of long winters and shorter summers.

Evidence from the Vostok ice core from Antarctica indicates that the global drop in temperatures of 7.2°F (4°C) occurred between 80,000 and 75,000 years ago. Although Rampino and Self acknowledged that global cooling had begun before the Toba super-eruption, they believed that the aerosol cloud accelerated the push toward full glacial conditions. Although the cloud cover would disperse in the short term, elevated levels of sulfuric acid (H_2SO_4) and the clouds that it created would remain in the atmosphere for at least five years after the eruption. The estimated amounts of stratospheric H_2SO_4 from the supervolcano range from 100 megatons (Mt) to 10 gigatons (Gt), with 6 Gt of sulfuric acid remaining in the stratosphere for five years, a figure that coincides with the amounts found in the ice cores.

666. The primary purpose of the passage is to:

(A) show that supervolcanoes, though rare, are the most dangerous threat to Earth's existence.

(B) explain how supervolcanoes may cause catastrophic changes to Earth and its atmosphere.

(C) compare the eruption of Mt. Toba to other volcanic eruptions.

(D) describe in detail the eruption of Mt. Toba and its effects.

667. Given that the authors of the passage refer to Mt. Toba as "the most studied of all known supervolcanos in geological time," one may find it surprising that:

(A) the supervolcano is considered a catastrophic threat to human life.

(B) ice cylinders are used to garner information about the supervolcano's eruption.

(C) no precise measurements exist of its projected material.

(D) Mt. Toba could potentially create a volcanic winter.

668. According to the passage, scientists Stephen Self and Michael R. Rampino feared that the effects of a Mt. Toba eruption could potentially lead to:

(A) the end of human and animal life.

(B) a volcanic winter.

(C) the end of several continents.

(D) global warming.

669. In comparison to the Younger Toba Turf eruption, the most considerable recorded eruption of Mt. Toba was:

(A) relatively insignificant.

(B) equal in terms of ejected material.

(C) far more significant.

(D) equal in terms of deadliness.

670. The authors reference all the following as evidence of the magnitude of the YTT eruption EXCEPT:

(A) deposits of Toba tephra spread across the Indian Ocean.

(B) deposits of Toba tephra in the South China Sea.

(C) evidence of Toba tephra in the earth's surface across the entire planet.

(D) YTT tephra uncovered by deep-sea drilling.

671. According to the passage, the high readings in the atmosphere recorded in the Greenland Ice Sheet are subject to an error margin of about:

(A) 1 year
(B) 5 years
(C) 10 years
(D) 100 years

672. As it is used in line 19, *stagnant* most closely means:

(A) flowing.
(B) cool.
(C) unchanging.
(D) temperate.

673. According to the passage, during which of the following periods did the earth experience no super-eruptions that rivaled the size of Mt. Toba's?

(A) BP period
(B) Volcanic winter
(C) The year without summer
(D) Common Era

674. The primary purpose of the seventh paragraph (lines 69-83) is to:

(A) point out the magnitude of a Toba eruption.
(B) demonstrate how Toba's eruption could lead to long summers and short winters.
(C) pinpoint where Toba's deposits were found after they were ejected from the supervolcano.
(D) demonstrate the differing opinions of scientists.

675. According to the passage, evidence uncovered in Antarctica's Vostok ice core suggests that the worldwide drop in temperatures of about 7 degrees likely occurred between:

(A) 300,000 and 200,000 years ago
(B) 200,000 and 100,000 years ago
(C) 80,000 and 75,000 years ago
(D) 50,000 and 25,000 years ago

Prose Fiction

Questions 676–685 are based on the following information.

This passage is adapted from the short story "The Grass is Greener" by Julia Diament.

She gave one last glance in the rearview mirror as the car rolled down the driveway. Seeing her mother blink back tears, she quickly looked away. It was hard enough leaving the small town that had served as her home, comfort zone, and safety net for the last 22 years — seeing her mother feign strength as the last of her little ones flew the coop only made the whole process that much harder.

Just like that, there she was, alone in the car with nothing but the open road in front of her. Only 2,500 miles to go until she reached her destination, a small, desert town in central Arizona she'd never seen before.

When she'd told her family, friends, and employer of her plans to venture into unchartered territory, she was met with mixed reactions. Particularly disappointing was the response of the manager of the restaurant where she worked.

"The grass is always greener," he said in response to her plan to start life anew in a drastically different environment.

Always a pessimist, she thought, and while she didn't exactly expect him to swing from the chandeliers upon hearing her news, a simple "good luck" would have sufficed.

"I give you two years," he snorted instead.

But she brushed off his comments, filled with excitement, anticipation, and determination to one day have the last laugh. She'd lived in the same small Northeastern town since she was born, and the time had finally come to spread her wings and explore potentially greener pastures, regardless of the careless comments made by those who had yet to venture more than 50 miles from everything they'd ever known.

The trip itself was eye opening. She'd never driven more than two hours at a time on her own, and here she was, embarking on a whole bunch of firsts: Her first solo cross-country drive, her first night alone in a hotel room, her first time putting down roots without the rest of her family, and the first time committing to a new home having not seen it first.

The journey was not without its share of speed bumps, either. There was the exorbitant speeding ticket in rural Texas, not to mention the empty gas tank that coincided with sighting of the "Prison area — Do not stop for hitchhikers" sign. Then there was the anxiety attack that occurred somewhere across the New Mexican desert as the realization sunk in that she had better find a job immediately upon arrival if she ever wanted to eat again.

The moments of panic did not stop when she arrived at her final destination either. She spent many nights on a deflated air mattress, endured the trials of living with a stranger with odd culinary and housekeeping habits, and made it through the general hiccups involved with any move: undelivered mail, poor cell phone reception, and the inability to find items she was *certain* she had packed. In time, these matters had a way of working themselves out, and before long, she was feeling genuinely happy, and, dare she say, at home in her new environment.

Years later, while visiting home one December on a holiday break, she stopped into the restaurant where she used to wait tables, hoping to show the manager who'd made the "grass is always greener" comment just how successful her big move had been, despite the negativity of so many naysayers. To her dismay, he had since been fired, and, last anyone had heard, was now mowing lawns and working odd jobs to make ends meet.

I guess the grass is *always greener,* she thought to herself, feeling just a small amount of satisfaction at the misfortune of the man who had been so quick to rain on her parade several years back. As she returned to what had fast become her home away from home in the desert, and her lucrative job, growing group of friends, and satisfying romantic relationship, she couldn't help but remember her vow to have the last laugh. While she didn't take too kindly to the "grass is always greener" metaphor, she thought if the day ever came when she ran into her old manager, she knew exactly what to say: She who laughs last, laughs best.

676. The use of the word *exorbitant* in line 45 most likely indicates that the traveler:

(A) was traveling far above the posted speed limit.

(B) considered the amount of the ticket unreasonable.

(C) considered the ticket to be an unanticipated expense.

(D) believed she was unfairly given the ticket.

677. When the narrator says the traveler didn't expect her manager to "swing from the chandeliers" (lines 23–24), she most likely means:

(A) she did not expect him to become overwhelmed by excitement.

(B) she did not expect him to offer her a raise to stay at the job.

(C) she did not expect him to give her a going away party at a fancy restaurant.

(D) she did not want him to have a breakdown upon hearing the news of her impending departure.

678. The traveler's attitude as conveyed in the last paragraph can best be described as:

(A) frustrated.

(B) thoughtful.

(C) bitter.

(D) sarcastic.

679. Overall, the traveler is most likely to say that her move across the country was:

(A) a complete failure because she experienced anxiety and loneliness.

(B) a valuable learning experience that had both negative and positive aspects.

(C) a primarily hazardous journey that made her wish she were back with her family and former employer.

(D) completed solely because of boredom with her life in a small town in the Northeast.

680. That the restaurant manager who once made the "grass is always greener" comment eventually found himself mowing lawns is an example of:

(A) resentment.

(B) redundancy.

(C) irony.

(D) predestination.

681. All of the following were matters of concern for the traveler during her road trip EXCEPT:

(A) hitchhiking prisoners.

(B) staying alone in a hotel.

(C) driving a manual transmission.

(D) living apart from her family.

682. When the manager utters his "grass is always greener" comment, he is most likely implying that:

(A) the traveler is likely to be pleased with the aesthetics of her new home.

(B) his own life is superior to the traveler's.

(C) the traveler's new life in a new area of the country will not be as great as she thinks it will.

(D) the traveler will never find a job like the one she is leaving.

683. Which of the following was true for the traveler once she moved into her new home?

(A) She bought a new, more comfortable bed.

(B) She misplaced and was unable to locate many items that she had brought with her from home.

(C) She was afflicted by a particularly lengthy bout of hiccups.

(D) She had a roommate who prepared different foods from the ones she was used to.

684. Which of the following statements best describes the function of the tenth paragraph (lines 54–65) in the passage as a whole?

(A) It indicates that, although the journey and transitional period were not without hardship, the traveler was able to overcome the obstacles that stood in her way and eventually feel comfortable with her move.

(B) It outlines many of the arguments that can be made against moving across the country.

(C) It provides insight into the neurotic and worrisome nature of the traveler.

(D) It provides evidence to support the passage's main theme that although travels are educational, in the end there's no place like home.

685. If the traveler was to describe her manager in one word, that word would most likely be:

(A) insecure.

(B) passive.

(C) optimistic.

(D) negative.

Social Science

Questions 686–695 are based on the following information.

Passage A is adapted from *Plato within Your Grasp*, by Brian Proffitt (Wiley 2004). Passage B is adapted from *Why Plato Wrote* by Danielle S. Allen (Wiley 2010).

Passage A is by Brian Proffitt

Even though Plato was raised in an antidemocratic family and he himself tended to lean away from democracy, he resisted joining his family in ruling Athens. This was a surprising decision because his great mentor, Socrates, was also a critic of the old Athenian government, believing that nobility could not be found in leadership by the masses.

In fact, Socrates's teachings would be forever linked to the Thirty Tyrants because they parroted his works in order to justify their actions. Perhaps it was the Tyrants' actions that repelled Plato, for the Thirty certainly shaped the modern definition of the word *tyrant* with their violence and cruelty toward the conquered citizens of Athens.

Even though Socrates had many negative beliefs about democratic government, he refused to actively involve himself in politics, preferring to stay out of such worldly affairs. Such neutrality may have influenced Plato to stay out as well. After a mere eight months, the Thirty Tyrants were violently overthrown and replaced by a new democracy in 403 BCE. This new democracy, a far cry from the old government, was a far more conservative and religious group of men — and it was also a group that never forgot a grudge. After regaining power from the Thirty Tyrants, the new democracy craftily began to take their revenge on the members of that short-lived oligarchy and anyone who helped support the Tyrants.

They found the perfect target in Socrates. Although Socrates had maintained all along that he didn't want to actively participate in political affairs (and indeed, he never did), the new government of Athens nonetheless saw him as the embodiment of all that was wrong with the Tyrants' rule. What gave the ruling power the excuse to finish Socrates once and for all was Socrates's continued insistence that his search for truth and virtue was motivated by a divine dream. This dream was a sign to him that he should continue to teach the young men of Athens a noble and virtuous lifestyle — a lifestyle that the Athenian government perceived as decidedly antidemocratic.

In 399 BCE, Socrates was arrested and charged with corruption of youth, participating in odd religious practices, introducing new gods, and atheism (though how one could believe in new gods and still be an atheist is a point that seems to have been lost on the Athenian government).

Passage B is by Danielle S. Allen

When Plato, son of Ariston and Perictione, was born to an aristocratic family in Athens in 424/3 BCE, he had two elder brothers, Adeimantus and Glaucon, roughly eight and five years older. Glaucon, at least, would soon be an aspiring politician. Plato also had two uncles, Critias and Charmides, who were intensely involved in Athenian politics and who, in 404/3 BCE, joined a group of aristocrats in an oligarchic take-over of the democratic city. It seems they invited young Plato to join them. He was then just twenty, the age at which young Athenian men usually got involved in politics, but he declined the invitation. Some years earlier his life had already taken an interesting turn; he had met the famous wise man Socrates, who lived from 469 to 399 BCE. Now, at age twenty, he began to follow Socrates formally.

The word *philosopher* wasn't yet much in use during the years that Socrates frequented the Athenian city center and market-place or agora; Socrates would generally have been called a Sophists. This word literally means "wise man" but came to have the negative connotation of "sophist," a person who fast-talks his way out of moral, intellectual, and practical quandaries or trickily leads others into them. Plato probably met Socrates in his early or mid-teens, and even then earned the older man's admiration; he would have been sixteen in 408 to 407 BCE, which appears to have been the year that Socrates undertook to educate Plato's older brother Glaucon in wise political leadership, a conversation that both Xenophon and Plato record. Xenophon represents Socrates as having struck up the conversation with Glaucon as a favor to Plato, so the latter must by then already have been a regular associate of Socrates.

Plato's record of such a conversation occurs, of course, in the very famous dialogue, The Republic, in which Socrates leads Glaucon (and Adeimantus too) through an answer to the question, "What is justice?" Over the course of the conversation, Socrates builds an argument for a utopia led by philosopher-kings and queens and protected by a class of guardian-soldiers, including both men and women, who hold their property in common, have egalitarian gender relations, and enjoy open marriages.

Questions 686–689 are about Passage A.

686. Proffitt suggests that Plato likely avoided getting involved in politics because:

(A) his mentor, Socrates, also avoided politics.

(B) his mentor, Socrates, requested that he stay out of the political landscape.

(C) he preferred to devote his time to religion.

(D) his family was antidemocratic.

687. Given the context of the passage, the term *oligarchy*, as it is used in line 28, most likely means:

(A) a ruling family has all the control.

(B) a single individual has all the control.

(C) a small group of people have all the control.

(D) an entire society has all the control.

688. Proffitt lists all of the following as reasons the new Athenian government sought to silence Socrates EXCEPT:

(A) he ultimately did pursue a political role after the fall of the Thirty Tyrants.

(B) they believed he was corrupting the youth of Athens.

(C) they didn't believe his claims that a divine dream motivated his desire to spread the word about living a noble and virtuous lifestyle.

(D) they viewed him in the same manner in which they viewed the Thirty Tyrants.

689. According to Proffitt, the Athenian government considered which of the following characteristics as antidemocratic?

(A) conservativism

(B) virtue

(C) religiousness

(D) devotion

Questions 690–692 are about Passage B.

690. Which of the following words would perhaps be the best equivalent of the term *sophist*, as defined by Allen?

(A) politician

(B) wise person

(C) intellectual

(D) smooth talker

691. According to Allen, Socrates considered all of the following criteria necessary for creating a utopia EXCEPT:

(A) open marriages.

(B) egalitarian gender relations.

(C) monogamy.

(D) leadership by philosopher-kings and queens.

692. According to Allen, Plato and Socrates most likely met before Plato reached the age of:

(A) 10.

(B) 16.

(C) 25.

(D) 40.

Questions 693–695 are about both passages.

693. Which of the following statements would both Proffitt and Allen likely consider to be true?

(A) Socrates' beliefs will forever be linked to those of the Thirty Tyrants.

(B) Socrates also taught Plato's brother, Glaucon.

(C) Plato's family members took part in an oligarchic takeover of Athens.

(D) Socrates and Plato likely had a mentor/mentee relationship.

694. Which of the following statements most accurately summarizes the content of each passage?

(A) The first passage concentrates on Socrates and Plato's political involvement, or lack thereof, and the second focuses more on the relationship between the two men.

(B) The first passage focuses more on the life of Plato, while the second passage focuses more on Socrates.

(C) The first passage discusses why Socrates was ostracized, while the second focuses on why he was beloved.

(D) The first passage discusses Socrates' earliest years, while the second passage focuses more closely on his later life.

695. Proffitt and Allen present passages that are generally:

(A) similar in that both authors treat their subject with nostalgia.

(B) similar in that both authors present their subjects in a way that is primarily informative and scholarly.

(C) dissimilar in that while Proffitt's passage is primarily informative, Allen's passage presents ideas by using a literary narrative.

(D) dissimilar in that Proffitt is largely critical of Socrates and Allen sings his praises.

Humanities

Questions 696–705 are based on the following information.

This passage is adapted from the book *A History of Ancient Egypt* by Marc Van De Mieroop (Wiley 2010).

When we think about peoples of the past, we intuitively try to imagine what they would have looked like in real life and to visualize their physical features, dress, and general appearance. Popular culture regularly portrays ancient Egyptians, and the various ways in which this has happened shows how impressions change over time. Take Queen Cleopatra, for example, the last ruler of the country at least partly of Egyptian descent. The repeated filming of the story of Shakespeare's *Antony and Cleopatra* shows how the image of this woman has changed. The 1963 Hollywood blockbuster featured the British-born Caucasian Elizabeth Taylor as the queen; in a 1999 movie made for TV a Latin-American actress of mixed Chilean-French parentage, Leonor Varela, played the part. A calendar issued somewhat earlier by an American beverage company entitled "Great Kings and Queens of Africa" included a depiction of Cleopatra as a black African woman. These changes in the queen's representation did not result from scholarly reconsiderations of ancient data, but from changing perceptions in the popular mind about the context of ancient Egypt.

It was only recently that scholars started to acknowledge the African background of Egyptian culture as a consequence of contemporary cultural identity politics that tried to replace the dominant western-centered views on world history with a greater focus on Africa's contributions. One manifestation of these ideas, Afrocentricity, highlights the ancient Egyptians as black Africans who brought about many of the cultural innovations credited to the ancient Greeks. Initially Egyptologists bluntly dismissed these proposals, but in recent years a greater willingness to engage with them has developed. This new attitude has not made it easier to visualize the ancient Egyptians, however, as their relationship with other African peoples is not obvious, as is true for Egypt's overall contacts with the rest of Africa. While ancient Egypt was clearly "in Africa," it was not so clearly "of Africa." Archaeological and textual evidence for Egyptian contacts in the continent beyond its immediate neighbors is so far minimal and limited to the import of luxury items. The contributions of Egypt to other African cultures were at best ambiguous, and in general Egypt's interactions with Asiatic regions were closer and more evident. Was the same true for the population of the country and did the ancient Egyptians leave any reliable data that could guide our imagination?

There exist countless pictures of humans from ancient Egypt, but it is clear that these were not intended as accurate portraits, except for some late examples from Ptolemaic and Roman times. Men and women appear in standardized depictions where physical features, hairdos, clothing, and even posture characterize them as Egyptians. The representations of foreigners are equally uniform: Nubians have dark skin and braided hair while Syrians have lighter skin and pointed beards. Clothing often also sets apart various peoples. The artists were intent upon showing the opposition between Egyptians and foreigners, not to make clear their individual appearances. The perception of who was Egyptian could change according to the intended audience. For example, a prince from Upper Nubia in the 14th century, Hekanefer, appears in two different guises. In the tomb of the Egyptian viceroy at Thebes Hekanefer has typical Nubian features and dress, while in his own burial in Nubia he looks fully Egyptian. He wanted his own people to see him as a member of the Egyptian ruling class, whereas to the Egyptian viceroy of his country he was a Nubian subject, clearly distinct from Egyptians.

The homogeneity of Egyptians in ancient depictions is deceptive. Over the millennia Egyptian society constantly integrated newcomers with various origins, physical features, and customs. But unless there was a reason to make the difference explicit, they all appeared alike in stereotypical depictions. They were all Egyptians, not people with Nubian, Syrian, Greek, or other backgrounds. Some scholars have tried to determine what Egyptians could have looked like by comparing their skeletal remains with those of recent populations, but the samples are so limited and the interpretations so fraught with uncertainties that this is an unreliable approach.

696. One of the main arguments the author is trying to make in this passage is:

(A) popular culture often plays a greater role than historical fact in shaping our impressions of the appearances of ancient Egyptians.

(B) the majority of the images that exist of ancient Egyptians differ greatly and therefore it is nearly impossible for scholars to get an accurate idea of their true appearance.

(C) common artistic portrayals of Egyptians suggest that they share both African and Greek roots.

(D) the best way to determine the appearance of ancient peoples is by comparing their skeletal remains with those of recent populations.

697. The author mentions the various versions of *Antony and Cleopatra* in order to:

(A) demonstrate to the reader, through the various portrayals of Cleopatra, the uncertainties that exist regarding the appearances of ancient Egyptians.

(B) show the various ways in which historical data may be interpreted.

(C) give the reader an example of how popular culture often dictates the common perception of ancient Egypt more than scholarly reconsiderations of ancient data.

(D) call attention to the fact that the common perception of the appearance of ancient Egyptians is likely to continue to evolve over time.

698. As it is used in line 78, *homogeneity* most nearly means:

(A) small, tight-knit community.

(B) uniform appearance.

(C) diversity.

(D) elements that are not of the same kind or nature.

699. According to the passage, the results of scholarly comparisons of the skeletal remains of ancient Egyptians to recent populations:

(A) were inadequate and inconclusive.

(B) helped shape the common portrayal of Egyptians in Hollywood and popular culture.

(C) provided better descriptions of traits of ancient Egyptians than historical data.

(D) gave the first solid proof of the skeletal similarities between ancient Egyptians and black Africans.

700. The author describes the two different guises of Prince Hekanefer in order to demonstrate:

(A) the difference in appearance of Nubians and Syrians.

(B) how the questions that arose in terms of how Hollywood should portray Cleopatra were also of concern to ancient Egyptian artists.

(C) the changing perception of the appearance of the ancient Egyptian due to scholarly comparisons of skeletal remains.

(D) that the perception of who was considered Egyptian was subject to change based upon the intended audience.

701. All of the following are synonyms for the word *fraught* as it is used in line 90, EXCEPT:

(A) laden.

(B) loaded.

(C) lacking.

(D) burdened.

702. Which of the following statements best describes the function of paragraph three (lines 53–77) as it relates to the rest of the passage?

(A) It explains how ancient Egyptian art shaped ideas regarding the common physical traits of foreigners, regardless of historical accuracy.

(B) It links the ideas that were expressed through ancient art concerning the appearance of Egyptians to those expressed in modern day popular culture and Hollywood glamorization.

(C) It highlights the similarities between ancient images of Egyptians and ancient images of black Africans.

(D) It provides an explanation of how the appearances of royals and those in the ruling class are depicted differently in ancient art than those of the common citizen.

703. The author is most likely to agree with which of these statements regarding the portrayal of the ancient Egyptian in common forms of art?

(A) The creators of ancient Egyptian portraits were less concerned with portraying physical accuracy than modern popular culture has been.

(B) The uniform appearance of Egyptians in ancient depictions is generally accurate.

(C) Syrians are typically portrayed more accurately in ancient portraiture than Nubians are.

(D) Members of ancient Egyptian society, regardless of their origins, have typically been portrayed stereotypically.

704. When the author states that "Nubians have dark skin and braided hair while Syrians have lighter skin and pointed beards," he is intending to show:

(A) that the common perception of the way ancient Egyptians look is based more on cultural interpretations than historical accuracy.

(B) that the common portrayal of the ancient Egyptian stems from a variety of origins.

(C) how to determine who was Nubian and who was Syrian from interpreting ancient art.

(D) that those depicted with braided hair in ancient art were likely members of the ruling class.

705. According to the final paragraph, as newcomers integrated into Egyptian society over the millennia:

(A) the depiction of Egyptians remained generally the same regardless of the varying cultural differences of the newcomers.

(B) they were depicted differently depending on whether they came from Nubia or Syria.

(C) the physical characteristics of Egyptians changed to more closely match the depictions of ancient Egyptians in Hollywood.

(D) the way ancient Egyptians were depicted in portraits became more historically accurate.

Natural Science

Questions 706–715 are based on the following information.

This passage is adapted from *Geology of the Alps* by O. Adrian Pfiffner (Wiley 2014).

From a geological perspective, the European continent has a highly checkered history. Although the Alps are an integral component of this continent and are, essentially, a spectacular mountain chain, their origin lies in the recent geological history of the continent. In order to understand the geological structure of Europe, the individual regions need to be classified according to the age of their consolidation. In this case, the term consolidation is taken to mean the welding of continents, following on from the motion of plates. Almost all of the mountain chains in Europe originated as a result of plate movements, where an ancient ocean was swallowed up in a subduction zone and the continental blocks subsequently collided with each other. The density of continental crust is relatively low and, therefore, buoyancy acts against it sinking to greater depths once it has entered a subduction zone. As a result, continental crust remains close to the surface and is compressed. During this process, the uppermost portions of the crust are pushed upwards and gradually build a mountain chain. This process is called *orogenesis*, or mountain-building.

A number of such collisions between continents, or *orogenies*, have occurred during the geological evolution of Europe. Accordingly, we distinguish between Caledonian, Variscan, and Alpine orogens. The continental plates involved in these collisions were North America, Siberia, Baltica/Europe, and Africa and are also called *terranes*. Europe has also been subdivided into Eo-, Palaeo, Meso- and Neo-Europe, based on the relative ages of these orogenies. It must be noted that the terranes mentioned above contain rock units that are relics of even older, fully eroded mountain chains.

Eo-Europe is a large geological structure, a welded block that experienced no further orogenies after the Precambrian. Two geological provinces are distinguished within Eo-Europe: the Baltic Shield and the Russian Platform.

The Baltic (or Fennoscandian) Shield is a convex bulge or shield covering a large area, which is composed of a highly metamorphic crystalline basement. Multiple, very ancient and fully eroded mountain chains can be distinguished within these series of rock formations. The oldest rocks in the Baltic Shield are 3 to 3.5 billion years old and were encountered in a deep drill core obtained in the region of Kola, to the south of the White Sea, as well as in Lapland.

The Russian Platform is the sedimentary cover over the Baltic Shield and is composed of Neoproterozoic non-metamorphosed sediments, overlain by Cambrian rocks as well as a series of rock formations that extend into the Cenozoic. In the southeast, the platform plunges beneath the foreland of the Caucasus, to the north of the Caspian Sea, and in the east and west, beneath the forelands of the Ural and Carpathian Mountains. The internal structure of the plate contains local depressions or basins with thick sedimentary successions as well as zones with a thin sedimentary cover. The sediments of the Russian Platform reflect the later phases of mountain-building that took place at its margins. Examples are the famous Old Red Sandstone, continental fluviatile sediments of the Middle to Late Devonian that are the erosional product from the (Caledonian) mountains in Norway and Scotland, the Permo-Triassic continental lagoon sediments in the foreland of the Urals and the Cenozoic continental formations in the foreland of the Caucasus and Carpathians. Sediments of the Russian Platform are usually marine deposits in the center (with the exception of the Early Carboniferous coal swamps in the area of Moscow), but the sea retreated towards the south after the Early Cretaceous and the Russian Platform became subaerial.

Palaeo-Europe refers to the Caledonian orogen that extends across Scandinavia to Ireland. Other parts are found in Greenland and the Appalachians. This broad geographical distribution is sufficient to indicate that later plate movements fragmented this Early Palaeozoic mountain chain. Plate movements responsible for this were, for example, the opening up of the North Sea from the Permian onwards and the opening up of the North Atlantic starting in the Jurassic.

Meso-Europe includes the Variscan orogen that originated in the Late Palaeozoic. With the exception of the Urals, the Variscan mountain chain can be followed as a continuous range, which in Germany and France is generally completely eroded and covered with younger sediments.

Finally, Neo-Europe comprises a series of mountain chains that originated in the Jurassic (Turkey), in the Cretaceous (parts of the Alps and Pyrenees), but mainly in the Cenozoic. These mountain chains are often winding and arc-shaped. In addition to the Alps, good examples are the Carpathians and the Betic Cordillera–Rif–Tell–Atlas system.

706. According to the author, which of the following provides the best description of terranes?

(A) The oldest rocks in the Baltic Shield
(B) Continental plates
(C) Sediments of the Russian Platform
(D) Mountain chains

707. The author's tone in the passage can best be described as:

(A) cynical.
(B) enthusiastic.
(C) persuasive.
(D) scholarly.

708. The author uses the terms "arc-shaped" and "winding" to describe:

(A) mountain chains in Neo-Europe.
(B) the Variscan mountain chain.
(C) early Palaeozic mountains.
(D) the Baltic Shield.

709. The author attributes the formation of nearly all of Europe's mountain chains to:

(A) shifting icebergs.
(B) volcanic activity.
(C) collisions between continental blocks.
(D) accumulation of a sedimentary cover.

710. According to the passage, the Baltic Shield's oldest rocks are approximately how many years old?

(A) 3.5 million
(B) 100 million
(C) 1 billion
(D) 3 billion

711. The passage establishes all of the following EXCEPT:

(A) the number of continental collisions that occurred during the geological evolution of Europe.
(B) the plate movements responsible for the fragmenting of an Early Palaeozoic mountain chain.
(C) the location of the White Sea relative to the region of Kola.
(D) the shape of a Eo-European geological structure.

712. The passage suggests that Eo-European geological structure:

(A) is the largest in the European region.
(B) contains no evidence of eroded mountain chains.
(C) can be found in Greenland and the Appalachians
(D) did not experience further major plate movements.

713. According to the passage, the designations of Eo-, Palaeo, Meso-, and Neo-relate to which of the following?

(A) Regions in Europe that contain examples of mountains chains created by orogenesis
(B) The eras when the continents that formed these subdivisions' geological structures came together
(C) The mineral content of particular subdivisions of European geological structures
(D) Shapes of mountain chains in various regions of Europe

714. As it is used in line 79, *subaerial* most likely means:

(A) in the atmosphere.
(B) below the ocean.
(C) on the earth's surface.
(D) underground.

715. The author makes all of the following assertions about the Russian Platform EXCEPT that:

(A) it covers the Baltic Shield.

(B) its sediments are marine deposits.

(C) its sediments reflect a phase of mountain formation.

(D) it is part of Neo-Europe.

Prose Fiction

Questions 716–725 are based on the following information.

This passage is adapted from *Middlemarch*, by George Eliot (1874).

The human soul moves in many channels, and Mr. Casaubon, we know, had a sense of rectitude and honorable pride in satisfying the requirements of honor, which compelled him to find other reasons for his conduct than those of jealousy and vindictiveness. The way in which Mr. Casaubon put the case was this:

"In marrying Dorothea Brooke I had to care for her well-being in case of my death. But well-being is not to be secured by ample, independent possession of property; on the contrary, occasions might arise in which such possession might expose her to the more danger. She is ready prey to any man who knows how to play adroitly either on her affectionate ardor or her quixotic enthusiasm; and a man is standing by with that very intention in his mind — a man with no other principle than transient caprice, and who has a personal animosity towards me — I am sure of it — an animosity which he has constantly vented in ridicule, of which I am as well assured as if I had heard it. Even if I live I shall not be without uneasiness as to what he may attempt through indirect influence. This man has gained Dorothea's ear; he has fascinated her attention; he has evidently tried to impress her mind with the notion that he has claims beyond anything I have done for him. If I die — and he is waiting here on the watch for that — he will persuade her to marry him. That would be calamity for her and success for him. She would not think it calamity; he would make her believe anything; she has a tendency to immoderate attachment which she inwardly reproaches me for not responding to, and already her mind is occupied with his fortunes. He thinks of an easy conquest and of entering into my nest. That I will hinder! Such a marriage would be fatal to Dorothea. Has he ever persisted in anything except from contradiction? In knowledge he has always tried to be showy at small cost. In religion he could be, as long as it suited him, the facile echo of Dorothea's vagaries. When was sciolism ever disassociated from laxity? I utterly distrust his morals, and it is my duty to hinder to the utmost the fulfillment of his designs."

The arrangements made by Mr. Casaubon on his marriage left strong measures open to him, but in ruminating on them his mind inevitably dwelt so much on the probabilities of his own life that the longing to get the nearest possible calculation had at last overcome his proud reticence and had determined him to ask Lydgate's opinion as to the nature of his illness.

He had mentioned to Dorothea that Lydgate was coming by appointment at half past three, and in answer to her anxious question, whether he had felt ill, replied, "No, I merely wish to have his opinion concerning some habitual symptoms. You need not see him, my dear. I shall give orders that he may be sent to me in the yew-tree walk, where I shall be taking my usual exercise."

When Lydgate entered the yew-tree walk he saw Mr. Casaubon slowly receding with his hands behind him according to his habit, and his head bent forward. It was a lovely afternoon; the leaves from the lofty limes were falling silently across the somber evergreens, while the lights and shadows slept side by side; there was no sound but the cawing of the rooks, which to the accustomed ear is a lullaby, or that last solemn lullaby, a dirge. Lydgate, conscious of an energetic frame in its prime, felt some compassion when the figure which he was likely soon to overtake turned around and in advancing towards him showed more markedly than ever the signs of premature age — the student's bent shoulders, the emaciated limbs, and the melancholy lines of the mouth.

"Poor fellow," he thought, "some men with his years are like lions; one can tell nothing of their age except that they are full grown."

"Mr. Lydgate," said Mr. Casaubon with his invariably polite air, "I am exceedingly obliged to you for your punctuality. We will, if you please, carry on our conversation in walking to and fro."

"I hope your wish to see me is not due to the return of unpleasant symptoms," said Lydgate, filling up a pause.

716. Which of the following best expresses the same idea as that given in the first sentence of the passage?

(A) Mr. Casaubon is justifiably proud of not being jealous or vindictive.

(B) Mr. Casaubon justified his actions to himself in a way that didn't make him seem jealous or vindictive.

(C) Mr. Casaubon was ashamed of his jealousy and vindictive toward those who pointed it out to him.

(D) Mr. Casaubon is afraid of his wife's jealousy and vindictiveness.

717. Mr. Casaubon feels that leaving his money to Dorothea in case of his death would:

(A) be unfair to his children from a previous marriage.

(B) leave her vulnerable to fortune-hunters.

(C) be the right and proper thing to do.

(D) be fair because getting his money was the only reason that Dorothea married him in the first place.

718. Which of the following may be inferred about the animosity of the man who Mr. Casaubon fears is "standing by" to take Dorothea after Mr. Casaubon's death (line 16)?

(A) He has never directly expressed any animosity toward Mr. Casaubon.

(B) He has valid reasons for his animosity, which Mr. Casaubon is uneasily aware of.

(C) His intentions toward Dorothea are not honorable.

(D) He was a rival of Mr. Casaubon's for Dorothea long ago.

719. According to the second and third paragraphs, Mr. Casaubon:

(A) is afraid that the other man has been corrupting Dorothea.

(B) has convinced himself that frustrating the other man is his responsibility.

(C) hopes to avoid a confrontation with the other man.

(D) is uneasily aware that Dorothea prefers the other man to him.

720. By stating "his mind inevitably dwelt so much on the probabilities of his own life," the author suggests in lines 47–48 that:

(A) Mr. Casaubon believes that Lydgate is the man he describes in the second paragraph of the passage.

(B) thinking about the arrangements he made on his marriage has caused Mr. Casaubon so much anguish that he is feeling ill.

(C) Mr. Casaubon is under the impression that he may die soon.

(D) Mr. Casaubon is afraid that Dorothea will find out about the arrangements he made on their marriage and desires Lydgate's opinion on how to conceal them from her.

721. When Lydgate says "some men with his years are like lions" (lines 77–78), he most likely means that Mr. Casaubon:

(A) was less mature than other men his age.

(B) was not as aggressive as other men his age.

(C) appeared older than other men his age.

(D) worried more about growing old than other men his age did.

722. Which of the following attitudes best describes Lydgate's feelings upon seeing Mr. Casaubon?

(A) confusion

(B) discomfort

(C) self-pity

(D) ebullience

723. It is reasonable to conclude that the author's reason for describing the loveliness of the day (lines 64–70) is most likely to:

(A) show Lydgate's tranquil frame of mind.

(B) contrast the beauty of the surroundings with the unattractiveness and frailty of Mr. Casaubon.

(C) foreshadow impending doom to Mr. Casaubon and his wife.

(D) emphasize Mr. Casaubon's wealth in comparison to his physical well-being.

724. The author indicates that Lydgate's comment in lines 84–85 was:

(A) a professional pleasantry with which he always began a visit.

(B) intended to encourage Mr. Casaubon to discuss his illness.

(C) designed to make Mr. Casaubon conscious of his infirmity.

(D) offered to end an awkward silence.

725. The author most likely intends for the reader's attitude toward Mr. Casaubon to:

(A) change from contempt toward the man at the beginning of the passage to pity for him at the end.

(B) become progressively less tolerant of the man and more disgusted with his behavior as the reader moves through the passage.

(C) become indifferent because, by the end of the passage, the reader no longer cares what happens to Mr. Casaubon but instead focuses on Lydgate.

(D) become gradually more understanding because, toward the end of the passage, the reader finally comprehends the reasons Dorothea married her husband.

Social Science

Questions 726–735 are based on the following information.

This passage has been adapted from *Surveying Cultures: Discovering Shared Conceptions and Sentiments*, by David R. Heise (Wiley 2010).

In traditional sample surveys, one person's measurements are presumed unpredictable from measurements on another person. For example, one person's age offers no clues about another person's age. Consequently, knowledge about variations and central tendencies in a population has to be built up piecemeal from many individual measurements. A statistical methodology has developed to guide the process of making inferences about a population from a sample of people, and this methodology is so fundamental in social science that it frequently is treated as the only viable framework for acquiring and interpreting survey data.

However, work in psychological anthropology and in sociology has clarified that some surveys are conducted in order to ascertain normative features shared by everyone, such as beliefs and sentiments deriving from culture. In this case, information from one person does predict information from others: For example, one person in a traditional society reporting that fathers usually are husbands foreshadows others saying the same thing. When people all provide the same information, it is redundant to ask a question over and over. Only enough people need be surveyed to eliminate the possibility of errors and to allow for those who might diverge from the norm. Romney, Weller, and Batchelder's mathematical-statistical analysis of ethnographic data gathering demonstrated that as few as a half-dozen expert respondents can provide a very clear picture of some types of shared norms.

In population surveys, large variances in variables are sought to register the extent and shape of social controversies and to enable causal inferences. However, a survey of culture is intended to build a descriptive database regarding norms, and therefore lack of variability on every item is the ideal, since response variation confounds the delineation of norms. Surveys of cultures do seek variations, but across items rather than across respondents. For example, when describing a culture, the difference in the average evaluation of doctor versus the average evaluation of robber is the interesting variation, rather than differences in evaluations of doctor or robber by respondent A versus respondent B. Stable individual differences actually count as errors when surveying cultural norms because individual deviance obscures underlying uniformity. Consequently, usual notions of reliability no longer hold in culture surveys.

An occasional complaint about surveys of culture is that the respondents providing the data are too few and are not selected randomly from general populations. However, this criticism — posed from the perspective of traditional survey methods — is tangential for ethnographic data gathering. The aim in ethnography is not to describe a population of individuals but, instead, to describe a culture that is being reproduced within some group. Properly chosen respondents are those whose responses are quintessential for their culture, and the more normative the respondents' beliefs and sentiments, the fewer of them are needed to obtain an accurate view of the culture. Whereas there is no notion of respondent goodness in surveying a population, other than representativeness of the sample as a whole, proficiency in the target culture is a key desideratum in choosing respondents for a survey of culture. Indeed, lack of cultural expertise is a legitimate basis for culling respondents or for assigning less weight to a respondent's answers.

The usual procedure in a survey of a population, of sampling individuals in a political unit, is inefficient in surveys of culture because desirable respondents for a survey of culture typically are not evenly distributed throughout a politically defined population. Rather, the best respondents for a culture survey are persons who reproduce the culture — the denizens of settings where the culture is being regenerated. For example, if interested in the middle-class culture that sustains the basic social institutions of American society (e.g., commerce, education, medicine, politics), a researcher would seek representative settings in which the activities of those institutions occur and question individuals at those sites about cultural matters. If interested in the culture that sustains black community life, the researcher would go to the homes, churches, and leisure venues where black culture is reproduced and question people at those sites. This emphasis on behavior settings in which culture is reproduced contrasts with the sampling frame in traditional survey research, where individuals themselves are the sampling units, even when geography is a practical consideration in sampling schemes for acquiring respondents.

So surveys of culture differ fundamentally from surveys of populations in at least three respects: (1) questions are asked about matters of agreement rather than about issues that generate diversity of response; (2) respondents are graded on the basis of their expertise; and (3) respondents are acquired by visiting settings where cultural reproduction takes place rather than by random sampling of people in a large geographic area delineated by political boundaries.

726. The main purpose of the passage can best be described as an effort to:

(A) describe how surveys of culture differ from another fundamental type of sociological methodology.

(B) define which respondent groups are most likely to yield accurate results for both population and cultural surveys.

(C) examine the fundamental differences between population and cultural surveys to prove that surveys of culture provide superior results.

(D) explain why surveys of culture are reliable even though they may be based on the responses of a few individuals.

727. What was a key finding of Romney, Weller, and Batchelder in regards to obtaining an accurate sampling of normative features shared by a given society?

(A) At least a dozen respondents are required to paint an accurate picture of a society's normative features.

(B) As few as six individuals can provide enough information to indicate shared norms within a given society.

(C) The most effective respondents are those who reproduce within the same culture.

(D) Significant variances in variables are desired in order to enable causal inferences and chronicle the extent and shape of social controversies.

728. It can be reasonably inferred that *tangential*, as it is used in line 59, most likely means:

(A) crucial.

(B) outdated.

(C) inconclusive.

(D) not particularly relevant.

729. Which of the following does the author state is a fundamental difference between surveys of culture and surveys of populations?

(A) Respondents to surveys of populations are graded based on expertise.

(B) Surveys of culture can provide accurate information with only five respondents, whereas surveys of population require a larger field of respondents.

(C) Cultural survey respondents are selected from areas where the culture is being regenerated, whereas population survey respondents are chosen from within a political unit.

(D) Questions in surveys of culture seek to find diversity among responses, whereas those in surveys of population typically encourage similarity among responses.

730. According to the passage, which of the following does the author mention as the goal of ethnography?

(A) To define the quintessential elements of a particular culture

(B) To describe a population of individuals

(C) To uncover information about a given population using as few respondents as possible

(D) To determine normative features shared by everyone within a geographical boundary

731. Which of the following does the author cite as occasional criticism of surveys of culture in lines 54–57?

(A) There is no notion of respondent goodness in surveying a population.

(B) Cultural respondents are chosen from within settings where cultural reproduction takes place as opposed to large geographic areas.

(C) Surveys of culture sometimes rely on information from too small of a respondent group, and respondents are always selected randomly from general populations.

(D) Surveys of culture sometimes rely on information gathered from too small of a respondent group, and respondents are not always selected randomly from general populations.

732. What connection does the author make between the beliefs of survey respondents and the quantity of respondents in gathering accurate information?

(A) The greater the dissension among survey respondents, the smaller the number of respondents necessary to obtain an accurate view of the culture.

(B) The greater the dissension among survey respondents, the greater the number of respondents necessary to obtain an accurate view of the culture.

(C) The more homogenous the beliefs of the respondents, the smaller the number of respondents necessary to obtain an accurate view of the culture.

(D) The more homogenous the beliefs of the respondents, the higher the number of respondents necessary to obtain an accurate view of the culture.

733. According to the information in lines 75–80, what does the author consider inefficient in relation to surveys of culture?

(A) Surveying those who reproduce the culture — that is, the denizens of settings where the culture is being regenerated

(B) Analyzing behavior settings in which culture is reproduced

(C) Sampling a population within political boundaries

(D) Selecting a respondent group based on cultural expertise

734. The author uses the example of black community life in the fifth paragraph (lines 90–94) primarily to:

(A) show an instance of middle-class culture.

(B) demonstrate how a lack of cultural expertise can be grounds for removing someone from a survey group.

(C) indicate the types of questions commonly found on a cultural survey.

(D) provide support for the theory that the best respondents for cultural surveys are those from the behavior settings that reproduce the culture.

735. Which of the following is the best synonym for *desideratum* as it is used in line 71?

(A) deciding factor

(B) detraction

(C) reason

(D) stumbling block

Humanities

Questions 736–745 are based on the following information.

Passage A is adapted from *A Companion to Greek Mythology* by Ken Dowden and Niall Livingston (Wiley 2011). Passage B is adapted from *Ancient Greeks from Homer to Alexander - The Evidence*, by Joseph Roisman (Wiley 2011).

Passage A is by Ken Dowden and Niall Livingston

Everyone knows the Greeks had myths. But the use of the word *myth* in modern times only goes back to its use in 1783 by arguably the first modern theorist of mythology, Christian Gottlob Heyne.

Myth is therefore as much a product of the modern history of ideas from the end of the Enlightenment onwards as it is an objective product of ancient Greece. It is more than mere stories, but in describing that 'more' and conducting the interpretation of myth we play out the intellectual history of our own times — the romantic and anthropological revolutions of the 19th century, and the crises, grand theories, interdisciplinary certainties, and doubt triumphant of the 20th century. And on top of all this there lurks behind mythology its failure to be scripture, to provide the holy books the Greeks surely ought to have had in order to be an intelligible nation to us and to our 19th-century forebears.

It is vital to realize that there is no one thing called "myth," and for that reason there is no definition that will satisfy all significant uses of the word. *Myth* (which derives from the Greek word *mythos,* not always "myth" in our sense) refers to a network of Greek stories to which it is conventional to apply the term *myth.* This is a matter of empirical fact, not philosophy or circular definition. We know a Greek myth when we see one and have need of no definitions, guidance, or codes of practice to identify it as such. It is, however, not a random network but has a strong core of a system that was on occasion told as a system. Thus, Apollodoros' Library (first century AD) may serve to define that system for us, as his lost predecessor, "Hesiod," had in the Catalogue of Women. Anything that forms part of this is myth.

Anything that looks like this is myth. Homer, himself, knew an astonishing repertoire of myths and then, like a tragedian, but one much more wayward and self-confident, bent the mythology he had inherited to develop his own economical but panoramic epics.

Passage B is by Joseph Roisman

Scholarly interest in the Homeric epics goes back to ancient times. It has often focused on the so-called Homeric Question, which may be more aptly termed the Homeric Controversy. Readers have failed to agree on the identity of Homer; the time and the manner by which the *Iliad* and the *Odyssey* were composed or edited; the origins of the epics and their unique language; and the historicity of the poems.

Briefly, already in ancient times readers doubted whether Homer was a historical figure or if he wrote both the *Iliad* and the *Odyssey*. Many modern scholars would answer both questions in the positive. They assume that he wrote, or orally composed, first the *Iliad* and then the *Odyssey,* based on oral traditions. Indeed, the epics reveal their oral origins in their language, which used a special rhythmic form, the hexameter, and many repetitive descriptive words or phrases (epithets) that were well suited to recitations.

Students of history are particularly interested in how historical the events and the society described in the epics are and to what period they should be dated. The *Iliad* in particular describes a long war between a large Greek expedition and a well-fortified Troy. The nineteenth-century excavator Heinrich Schliemann identified the site of Troy in the mound of Hissarlik in Asia Minor near the Dardanelles. Yet the site has revealed the existence of nine cities as well as sub-settlements dating from the Bronze Age to Roman times. Identifying which of these is the Troy of the Trojan War has been a bone of scholarly contention since Schliemann. The Greeks could not have mounted a large expedition following the destructions and consequent decline of many Bronze Age sites around 1200. This means that only Troy VIh, ca. 1300, or Troy VIi (formerly known as VIIa), ca. 1210–1180, would be good candidates. Yet both were relatively small settlements that appear to have suffered no human destruction, although recent excavators of the site interpret some findings as signs of a much larger site and even of human destruction for Troy VIi.

Many scholars agree that the Homeric epics may retain ancient memories, but that they also project on mythical times realities that better fit the poet's own era, perhaps between the second half of the eighth century and the first half of the seventh.

Questions 736–738 ask about Passage A.

736. Dowden and Livingston make all of the following assertions about myths EXCEPT that:

(A) the word *myth* is attributed to Christian Gottlob Heyne.

(B) they were more than mere stories.

(C) they all have bases in truth.

(D) the term was coined in 1783.

737. When Dowden and Livingston state, "We know a Greek myth when we see one" (line 28), they most likely mean:

(A) Greek myths are so entrenched in global history and culture that they are easily recognizable.

(B) facets of Greek myths are easily distinguishable from other types of myths, such as Roman myths.

(C) Greek myths are easily recognizable because of the prevalence of references to their characters in modern literature.

(D) Greek myths are defined by clear codes of practice that provide easily recognizable guidance regarding their components.

738. As it is used in line 39, *tragedian* most likely means:

(A) an individual with a tragic past.

(B) a writer of tragedies.

(C) an expert in tragedies.

(D) an actor who plays tragic roles.

Questions 739–742 ask about Passage B.

739. According to Roisman, which of the following does "a descriptive word or phrase" best define?

(A) An epic

(B) An epithet

(C) A poem

(D) A myth

740. Roisman states that the excavation of the mound of Hissarlik in Asia Minor exposed all of the following EXCEPT:

(A) nine cities.

(B) sub-settlements from the Bronze Age and Roman times.

(C) possible evidence of larger sites and war-related destruction.

(D) the definitive site of the Troy of the Trojan War.

741. When Roisman notes that the Homeric Question may ". . .be more aptly termed the Homeric Controversy," he is most likely referring to all of the following EXCEPT that:

(A) doubts remain regarding whether Homer was an actual historical figure.

(B) opinions differ regarding when Homer's works were authored.

(C) questions exist about the true identity of Homer.

(D) disagreement exists on whether the *Illiad* and the *Odyssey* originated in oral traditions.

742. According to Roisman, modern scholars who believe Homer either wrote or orally composed the *Iliad* and the *Odyssey* cite which of the following as evidence to back their claims?

(A) The Homeric Question

(B) Apollodoro's Library

(C) The use of hexameter

(D) Homer's reliance on myths

Questions 743–745 ask about both passages.

743. Which of the following may be derived only by combining information contained in both passages?

(A) The *Iliad* and the *Odyssey* are the result of a recalcitrant manipulation of traditional Greek myths.

(B) Traditional oral storytelling incorporated descriptive words and phrases and repetition to help storytellers remember their tales.

(C) The concept of myth is at once a product of modern times and ancient Greece.

(D) Greek epic myths, such as the *Iliad* and the *Odyssey*, are better understood as records of ancient events than they are as interpretations of the mores of their times.

744. The authors of both passages discussed each of the following EXCEPT:

(A) Homer

(B) the ancient Greeks

(C) Troy

(D) mythical times

745. From information gained from reading both passages, one could make all of the following assertions about Homer EXCEPT that:

(A) he was intensely knowledgeable about mythology.

(B) he likely lived near the mound of Hissarlik in Asia Minor around 1200.

(C) there is disagreement over his true identity.

(D) there has been interest in his works since ancient times.

Natural Science

Questions 746–755 are based on the following information.

This passage is adapted from *The Case for Pluto: How a Little Planet Made a Big Difference* by Alan Boyle (Wiley 2009).

Out amid the cornfields of Iowa, my friend Chief built a monument to Pluto, the picked-on planet.

The red, oval-shaped plaque was smaller than a stop sign, with a pimple of polished steel sticking up from the surface to represent Pluto's size. It was mounted on a metal pole by the side of a blacktop road, four miles west of the town of Mount Vernon, population 3,628.

Chief, who got his nickname during childhood because he was part Native American, was one of my best friends in high school. Now he's a professor at the University of Iowa and has become an amateur astronomer of some repute. A few years ago, he and other volunteers started up a group called the Mount Vernon Solar Tourist Society and erected the plaques just for fun, to show how big and empty our solar system is.

You can't understand the distances that separate the planets just by looking at a schoolroom poster. They're usually displayed right next to each other like some kind of celestial police lineup, with pea-sized Pluto pictured right alongside his big brothers Uranus and Neptune.

To provide a better sense of scale, folks like Chief have laid out scores of mini–solar systems around the world. It's the best way to relate the size of the planets to the immense distances involved. For example, the scale model in Washington, D.C., has a five-inch-wide sun, and plaques depicting the planets are lined up along the National Mall for a third of a mile. Boston's planetary parade extends more than 9 miles, leading out from an 11-foot-wide sun. And you'd have to drive more than 180 miles to get from Stockholm's solar stand-in (actually the round-domed Stockholm Globe Arena) to a 5-inch-wide Pluto perched on a monument in Sweden's Dellen Lake district.

The Mount Vernon Solar Tourist Society set up a five-foot-wide sun at the city park and planted plaques leading west along First Avenue, plus an "Asteroid Crossing" road sign next to Cornell College's campus to mark an imaginary asteroid belt. That sign shows up in a fair number of pictures on the Internet, but few if any of the photographers have figured out that it's actually part of a set.

Each of the nine planetary plaques displays a list of facts about the world in question and includes a scaled-down circle of bright steel to represent the planet's relative size. Pluto's circle was about as small as the artist could make it, as big around as a pebble that gets caught between your tires on a gravel road.

Even when the plaques were being put up, the society was having second thoughts about Pluto. One of the inscriptions on its plaque read, "If Pluto was discovered today, it would not be called a planet, but a minor planet."

Since then, Pluto has suffered putdowns galore. It was left out when New York's American Museum of Natural History remodeled its planetary exhibits. More and more worlds like Pluto were found on the solar system's rim, and in 2005 astronomers determined that one of them was actually bigger than Pluto.

If that newfound world — known at first as Xena (the Warrior Princess) and later named Eris (the Goddess of Discord) — had been accepted into the planetary clan, Chief might have had to add one more monument to the set. It would have been about seven miles out of town, by my calculation. And for a while, it looked as if things were heading in that direction.

A committee charged with settling the question drew up a proposal that would have boosted the solar system's official planet count to twelve, including Eris, as well as Pluto's largest moon, Charon, and the asteroid Ceres. But in 2006 when the proposal came up for a vote by the International Astronomical Union (IAU), the world body that deals with astronomical names and definitions, it was hooted down. Instead, a few hundred astronomers voted to throw Pluto and the other lesser worlds into a different class of celestial objects, known as "dwarf planets."

That might not sound so bad. After all, a dwarf planet is still a planet, just as a dwarf galaxy is still a galaxy, and just as a dwarf star (like our sun) is still a star. Right?

Wrong.

746. The author's primary purpose in writing this passage is to:

(A) explain why he considers Pluto to be the "picked-on planet" and how its relative size and distance to other planets in the solar system has been misrepresented.

(B) argue that Pluto should be categorized as a planet rather than dwarf planet.

(C) argue that Pluto should remain under the categorization of dwarf planet.

(D) highlight that classrooms and scale models in various U.S. and worldwide cities misrepresent Pluto's size and distance in relation to other planets in the solar system.

747. Which of the following is NOT a reason that the author gave for considering Pluto to be "the picked-on planet"?

(A) The Mount Vernon Solar Tourist Society's put up a plaque that read, "If Pluto was discovered today, it would not be called a planet, but a minor planet."

(B) Several hundred astronomers voted to throw Pluto into a new class of celestial objects called "dwarf planets."

(C) Various scale models throughout the nation failed to include Pluto in their models of the solar system.

(D) New York's American Museum of Natural History failed to include Pluto in its remodel of planetary exhibits.

748. The author describes in detail the solar system models in Washington, D.C.; Boston; and Stockholm in order to:

(A) offer a clearer sense of scale than the standard schoolroom poster depiction does.

(B) show that different cities have different ideas regarding Pluto's size and distance from other planets in the solar system.

(C) provide background information as to why the International Astronomical Union voted down the proposal to boost the solar system's official planet count to 12.

(D) demonstrate how Pluto is a "picked-on planet" all over the world.

749. *Repute*, as it is used in line 13, most likely means:

(A) degree.

(B) ignominy.

(C) opinion.

(D) standing.

750. When the author mentions the Greek mythological characters of Xena and Eris, he refers to:

(A) names that were used to identify a Pluto-like world that has been discovered in recent years along the solar system's rim.

(B) two of Pluto's biggest moons.

(C) new planets that the International Astronomical Union voted not to include in the solar system's official planet count.

(D) proposed new names for Pluto by astronomers who voted to change its distinction from "planet" to "dwarf planet."

751. According to the passage, which of the following is true about Mount Vernon Tourist Society's model of the solar system?

(A) It is larger than the model in Boston.

(B) Its asteroid belt is likely more famous than its sun.

(C) It is smaller than the model that is set up along the National Mall.

(D) Its model of Pluto is actually a piece of gravel from a road near Cornell College.

752. Chief and his colleagues most likely erected the plaques displayed throughout Mount Vernon in order to:

(A) compete with similar scale-models on display in Boston; Washington, D.C.; and Stockholm.

(B) demonstrate why Pluto and the other planets in the solar system are often displayed side-by-side like some sort of celestial police line-up.

(C) garner more attention for the Mount Vernon Solar Tourist Society to help promote their celestial theories.

(D) demonstrate the massive nature of the solar system.

753. According to the passage, which of the following were considered for inclusion into the solar system's official planet count?

(A) the dwarf planets

(B) Ceres and Xena

(C) the worlds on the rim of the solar system that were like Pluto

(D) the asteroids in the asteroid belt

754. The primary purpose of the fourth paragraph (lines 18–23) is to:

(A) provide interesting but irrelevant information.

(B) give an explanation as to why Chief felt Pluto suffered "putdowns galore."

(C) offer a visual representation of how small Pluto is in relation to the rest of the planets in the solar system.

(D) present a necessary transition to the subsequent paragraph by showing how the locations of the planets are normally represented.

755. It is reasonable to infer from the passage that:

(A) as scientific study of the solar system continues, the official planet count is subject to change.

(B) Pluto is smaller than its largest moon.

(C) Pluto's largest moon, Charon, will likely replace Pluto as one of the nine planets in the solar system.

(D) Pluto will likely be officially reclassified as a planet before the year 2020.

Prose Fiction

Questions 756–765 are based on the following information.

This passage is adapted from the story "The Jewel of Seven Stars" by Bram Stoker (1903).

It all seemed so real that I could hardly imagine that it had ever occurred before; and yet each episode came, not as a fresh step in the logic of things, but as something expected. It is in such a wise that memory plays its pranks for good or ill; for pleasure or pain; for weal or woe. It is thus that life is bittersweet, and that which has been done becomes eternal.

Again, the light skiff, ceasing to shoot through the lazy water as when the oars flashed and dripped, glided out of the fierce July sunlight into the cool shade of the great drooping willow branches — I standing up in the swaying boat, she sitting still and with deft fingers guarding herself from stray twigs or the freedom of the resilience of moving boughs. Again, the water looked golden-brown under the canopy of translucent green; and the grassy bank was of emerald hue. Again, we sat in the cool shade, with the myriad noises of nature both without and within our bower merging into that drowsy hum in whose sufficing environment the great world with its disturbing trouble, and its more disturbing joys, can be effectually forgotten. Again, in that blissful solitude the young girl lost the convention of her prim, narrow upbringing, and told me in a natural, dreamy way of the loneliness of her new life. With an undertone of sadness she made me feel how in that spacious home each one of the household was isolated by the personal magnificence of her father and herself; that their confidence had no altar, and sympathy no shrine; and that there even her father's face was as distant as the old country life seemed now. Once more, the wisdom of my manhood and the experience of my years laid themselves at the girl's feet. It was seemingly their own doing; for the individual "I" had no say in the matter, but only just obeyed imperative orders. And once again the flying seconds multiplied themselves endlessly. For it is in the arcana of dreams that existences merge and renew themselves, change and yet keep the same — like the soul of a musician in a fugue. And so memory swooned, again and again, in sleep.

It seems that there is never to be any perfect rest. Even in Eden the snake rears its head among the laden boughs of the Tree of Knowledge. The silence of the dreamless night is broken by the roar of the avalanche; the hissing of sudden floods; the clanging of the engine bell marking its sweep through a sleeping American town; the clanking of distant paddles over the sea. . . . Whatever it is, it is breaking the charm of my Eden. The canopy of greenery above us, starred with diamond-points of light, seems to quiver in the ceaseless beat of paddles; and the restless bell seems as though it would never cease. . . .

All at once the gates of Sleep were thrown wide open, and my waking ears took in the cause of the disturbing sounds. Waking existence is prosaic enough — there was somebody knocking and ringing at someone's street door.

I was pretty well accustomed in my Jermyn Street chambers to passing sounds; usually I did not concern myself, sleeping or waking, with the doings, however noisy, of my neighbours. But this noise was too continuous, too insistent, too imperative to be ignored. There was some active intelligence behind that ceaseless sound; and some stress or need behind the intelligence. I was not altogether selfish, and at the thought of someone's need I was, without premeditation, out of bed. Instinctively I looked at my watch. It was just three o'clock; there was a faint edging of grey round the green blind which darkened my room. It was evident that the knocking and ringing were at the door of our own house; and it was evident, too, that there was no one awake to answer the call. I slipped on my dressing-gown and slippers, and went down to the hall door.

When I opened it there stood a dapper groom, with one hand pressed unflinchingly on the electric bell whilst with the other he raised a ceaseless clangour with the knocker. The instant he saw me the noise ceased; one hand went up instinctively to the brim of his hat, and the other produced a letter from his pocket. A neat brougham was opposite the door, the horses were breathing heavily as though they had come fast. A policeman, with his night lantern still alight at his belt, stood by, attracted to the spot by the noise.

756. It can be reasonably inferred from the passage that the narrator's visitor:

(A) came bearing a letter from the young girl mentioned in the second paragraph.

(B) came bearing news of the young girl mentioned in the second paragraph.

(C) came bearing urgent news that couldn't wait until dawn.

(D) came to the wrong house.

757. What do the details in the passage suggest the narrator is referring to when he says "Whatever it is, it is breaking the charm of my Eden" (lines 51-52)?

(A) Thoughts of the young girl mentioned in the second paragraph

(B) Loud knocks at his door

(C) The contents of the letter the narrator receives when he opens the door

(D) The noise made by boats in the waterways near the author's home.

758. All the following statements can be reasonably inferred given the content of the passage EXCEPT:

(A) the gentlemen who arrived at the home of the narrator came bearing news of an urgent nature.

(B) the description in the second paragraph of the young girl was not the first time the narrator had thought about her.

(C) the narrator was well known to the policeman who stood outside his door.

(D) the narrator had resided in his Jermyn Street quarters for some time before the evening the late night visitors arrived.

759. Which of the following statements best describes the way the third paragraph functions in the passage as a whole?

(A) It offers a glimpse into the mind of the narrator and his idea of paradise.

(B) It gives the reader a glimpse into the pessimistic nature of the narrator.

(C) It offers a glimpse into the semi-conscious mind of the narrator as he wavers somewhere between the dream described in the beginning of the passage and the real life occurrence toward the end.

(D) It clarifies for the reader the exact moment the narrator snaps back into reality from his dream.

760. The statement "There was some active intelligence behind that ceaseless sound; and some stress or need behind the intelligence" (lines 67–69) functions in the passage to indicate the narrator:

(A) should not ignore the late-night knocking in the same manner as he usually ignored noises at night in the neighborhood.

(B) thought whoever was at the door had come bearing ominous news.

(C) thought whoever was knocking was very wise.

(D) knew who was standing on the other side of the door before he opened it.

761. Which of the following statements is true regarding the narrator's dream as it is described in lines 9–23?

(A) It took place in the spring.

(B) The narrator allowed the young girl to guide the boat as he took in the beauty of the natural scene surrounding them.

(C) It describes the day that the narrator first met the young girl.

(D) The boat ride provided the narrator and the young girl with a temporary escape from their problems.

762. The narrator is likely to agree with which of the following statements regarding Eden?

(A) Dangers exist even in Eden.

(B) Only in Eden does perfect, uninterrupted silence exists.

(C) Only in Eden can one truly rest peacefully.

(D) It is the place the narrator expects to see the young girl discussed in paragraph two.

763. It is reasonable to infer from the context of the passage that the "brougham" at the narrator's door (line 86):

(A) was an individual who accompanied the groom and the policeman as a safety precaution given the nature of the late-night visit.

(B) was a method of transportation.

(C) was the author of the letter the groom carried.

(D) was of a dangerous nature.

764. As it is used in line 19, *myriad* most likely means:

(A) loud.

(B) artificial.

(C) unpleasant.

(D) numerous.

765. It can be reasonably inferred that the young girl mentioned in the second paragraph:

(A) was a romantic interest of the narrator.

(B) was discontented with her home life.

(C) was a figment of the narrator's imagination and didn't exist outside of his dream.

(D) was the narrator's idea of feminine perfection.

Social Science

Questions 766–775 are based on the following information.

This passage is adapted from the book *Your Creative Brain* by Shelley Carson (Wiley 2010).

You are in possession of one of the world's most powerful supercomputers, one that has virtually unlimited potential not only to change your life, but also to change your world.

This supercomputer has the ability to adapt to ever-changing environments, understand subtle patterns, and make connections between seemingly unrelated things. It can design skyscrapers, cure life-threatening illnesses, and send humans into space.

It can make you successful, rich, happy, and fulfilled . . . and it's located right inside your skull. The supercomputer I am talking about is your brain, that miracle machine that allows you to do everything from brushing your teeth in the morning to presenting complex facts and figures to your boss in the afternoon.

Think about it: Our brains have shepherded us through some pretty amazing evolutionary developments in record time. In the past 10,000 years, we've invented the wheel, built the pyramids in Egypt, discovered penicillin, developed the Internet, and sent devices of our own making beyond the outer regions of our solar system.

To put it into perspective, consider the fact that the turtle has been around for roughly 220 million years and has yet to make an innovative lifestyle improvement.

So what separates us from the turtle? The answer is: our creative brain. Our brain allows us to feel, love, think, be, and, most important, create.

You may think that creativity is a gift only certain types of people possess, like the Einsteins, Mozarts, or Shakespeares of the world. However, the latest neuroscience research suggests that creative mental functioning involves a set of specific brain activation patterns that can be amplified through conscious effort and a little practice. These are skills that anyone can master. By learning how and when to turn the volume up or down in certain parts of the brain, you can develop your creative potential to achieve greater success and life fulfillment.

But the purpose of enhancing creativity is not only for enrichment; it's a vital resource for meeting the challenges and dangers, as well as the opportunities, of the accelerated-change climate of the twenty-first century.

The information and technology explosion, along with cyber-communication and globalization, is transforming the way we learn, the way we do business, and the way we form relationships with each other. The rule books for virtually *every* aspect of human endeavor and interaction — from corporate life to personal life to dating and even parenting — are being rewritten right in the middle of the game. So if all the old bets are off, how do you survive and thrive? The most important asset you have for negotiating this rapidly changing world is *your creative brain.*

Your creative brain can lead you to discover a new and better way to manage some aspect of your business. It can help you to express your unique life experience in a way that inspires or educates others. You can use it to ensure that the best traditions of the past get incorporated into the future or to add beauty to your environment. Your creative brain can even reshape your vision of retirement so that you continue to grow and prosper throughout the decades ahead. There is truly no limit to the potential of your creative brain.

Regardless of your mission for the future, it is crucial that you develop your creative capacities. By developing your creative brain, you can not only adapt to the changing world, but you can make a contribution to that change. By developing your creative brain, you will also prime your brain to discover, innovate, and produce your original contribution to what is shaping up to be a twenty-first-century Golden Age.

Before we go further, let's define exactly what we mean by that nebulous term *creativity*. Though philosophers and writers have come up with a number of definitions for *creative*, there are two elements to the definition that virtually all of us who study creativity agree need to be present in the creative idea or product. First, the creative idea or product needs to be *novel* or *original*, and second, it has to be *useful* or *adaptive* to at least a segment of the population. Note, for example, that the scribblings of a toddler who has just learned to hold a crayon are *novel* . . . but, as a product, they are not considered *useful* or *adaptive*.

You can take these elements of novel/original and useful/adaptive and apply them to virtually any aspect of your life to increase your productivity and happiness. You can also apply them to the betterment of your community and to the enrichment of society. When you learn to use your creative brain more efficiently, there is no limit to the innovative ideas, products, and new ways of doing things that you can explore.

766. If the author were to summarize the message of the entire passage in one statement, which of the following statements would best accomplish this task?

(A) There is no other species, past or present, with the same potential as the human being to continue to make innovative lifestyle improvements.

(B) When the creative potential of the human brain is maximized, there is essentially no limit to the types of innovative and evolutionary developments we can expect to see as time progresses.

(C) The information and technology explosion has forced human beings to maximize the potential of their creative brains in order to stay afloat in an increasingly tech-heavy society.

(D) Human beings are subject to fall into the same trap as the turtle and eventually cease evolutionary advancements unless they learn to maximize the full potential of the creative brain.

767. The author uses the example of a turtle to:

(A) highlight the advancements the human brain has been able to make in just a small fraction of time.

(B) point out what sets the human being and the turtle apart from other species.

(C) prove that humans are the only creatures on earth that have the ability to create.

(D) compare the lifestyle improvements of the turtle and the human being over the course of millions of years of evolution.

768. Which of the following does the author mention as a discovery that came as a result of the latest neuroscience research?

(A) Human beings' ability to send devices of their own making into the farthest regions of the solar system

(B) The invention of the Internet

(C) The fact that creativity is a gift that only certain types of people possess

(D) That human beings can learn to activate different parts of the brain through conscious effort and practice

769. The author uses *nebulous* to define creativity in line 82 likely because:

(A) creativity has many definitions.

(B) trying to define creativity is impossible.

(C) attempts by philosophers and writers to define creativity have resulted in cloudy explanations at best.

(D) there is one clear definition for creativity.

770. Which of the following changes is NOT included in the author's description of the results of the information and technology explosion?

(A) Changes in human interaction and relationships

(B) Changes in the way people raise their children

(C) Changes in the corporate world

(D) Changes in the way people travel

771. Which of the following would most likely fall under the author's definition of *creative?*

(A) The scribbling of a toddler because it is original and useful

(B) The invention of a new way to preserve foods that does not require refrigeration

(C) A new way to toast bread that requires more time to prepare than a toaster does

(D) An exact rendering of an artistic masterpiece by a new artist

772. What are some of the benefits of creativity as specifically stated in the passage?

(A) A person can assimilate old customs in a way that functions in future environments.

(B) One is able to resign oneself to living in the same way as one has for decades.

(C) People can live exactly the way they did during the Golden Age of England.

(D) It makes it easier to avoid new technology, cyber-communication, and globalization because they may be dangerous.

773. The main function of the second, third, and fourth paragraphs in relation to the rest of the passage is to:

(A) define the term *supercomputer* as the author uses it in paragraph one.

(B) provide real-life examples of just how limitless the capabilities of the creative brain are.

(C) summarize 10,000 years of human advancement.

(D) make the reader aware of the fact that, without learning to maximize their creative brains, humans would still be living like cavemen.

774. As it is used in line 18, *shepherded* most nearly means:

(A) shielded.

(B) guided.

(C) fielded.

(D) limited.

775. The author would likely disagree with which of the following statements about the human creative brain?

(A) When human beings learn to use their creative brains more efficiently, it leads to more enriched, successful and fulfilling lives.

(B) Our best shot at adapting to an ever-changing informational and technological society is to hone our creative thinking skills.

(C) Essentially every aspect of human life, from familial relationships to corporate success, can experience improvements as we continue to explore our creative brains.

(D) The Einsteins and Mozarts of the world were able to maximize their intellectual potential because they were born with an inherent sense of creativity uncommon in the human race.

Humanities

Questions 776–785 are based on the following information.

Passage A is adapted from *Reading Romantic Poetry* by Fiona Stafford (Wiley 2012). Passage B is adapted from *Reading Modernist Poetry* by Michael H. Whitworth (Wiley 2010).

Passage A is by Fiona Stafford

Byron knew that pleasurable poetry was not dependent on cheerful subjects, and his work, like that of many other fine poets in the Romantic period, also dealt with memories of loss, sadness, despair, or disappointment. Indeed, "the joy of grief" became a critical touchstone in the later eighteenth century, following the extraordinary, international success of James Macpherson's ancient, isolated, and deeply despondent bard, Ossian. According to some Enlightenment thinkers, including David Hume, sad recollections were generally more pleasurable than happy ones because of the mind's natural tendency to compare the past with the present. While a bad memory might prompt gratitude for current well-being, thoughts of happier times now gone were likely to produce more melancholy reflections. To gaze back obsessively on "the times of old" was to emphasize the uncongenial nature of the present, or to deny any hope for a better future. The enormous international popularity of Ossian, however, suggests that many late eighteenth-century readers were deriving deep pleasure from the poems of an old man, left with nothing but memories of a better world now gone. Ossianic gloom appealed partly because it was seen to affect those overflowing with sensibility — the widely admired capacity for fine feeling. Readers moved to tears by an affecting lament were readers possessed of a soul. With the mid-eighteenth-century cult of feeling, poems that dwelled on graveyards, darkness, and ruin became very popular, and so the pleasures of memory seemed closely allied to the pleasures of melancholy.

During the Romantic period, however, many of the prevailing cultural trends were questioned, complicated, or even rejected, and although the taste for ruins and melancholy was by no means forgotten, the forms it assumed were rather different. Ruined castles and abbeys, no longer necessarily sites for meditations on the transience of human life or vanished societies, were now seized as settings for exciting Gothic narratives, with room for supernatural elements difficult to accommodate in more realistic, modern situations. Poems such as Coleridge's "Christabel," Scott's "The Lay of the Last Minstrelor," and Keats's "The Eve of St. Agnes" all included medieval architecture to create an otherworldly atmosphere in which anything seemed possible. Darkness and gloom often seemed the most congenial conditions for imaginative freedom, so even a tale filled with terrors offered pleasurable reading, if well told.

From a radical perspective, too, the ruins of monumental buildings might be a cause for celebration as much as sorrow. The great castle of the Bastille in Paris roused passionate feelings across the Channel, long before the start of the French Revolution.

Passage B is by Michael H. Whitworth

Why might the hand, channel for the writer's expression, have become so detached from the mind and the body? Of course the profusion of autonomous hands in Eliot's poetry is partly a consequence of his employing techniques of metonymy, of substituting a part for the whole; but as the hand is the writer's instrument, I would like to suggest that these hands emblematize two important aspects of modern poetry. One is the impersonality of modernist writing: The writer remains detached from his or her creation. As James Joyce's Stephen Dedalus puts it, using another memorable image of hands, "The artist, like the God of the creation, remains within or behind or beyond or above his handiwork, invisible, refined out of existence, indifferent, paring his fingernails." Joyce's artist keeps control of his hands, but we might take Eliot's independent hands as signs of a creative faculty that is detached from the rest of the human subject.

The other aspect is to do with agency: While in some cases the subject appears to have delegated its work to disembodied hands, in others the hands have escaped altogether. The "automatic" and the weak hands are particularly interesting in this regard, and emblematize the idea that the writer, in common with all individuals in the twentieth century, has suffered a loss of agency. Individuals either fail to achieve anything at all, because they are too weak, or they achieve something unintended, because something comes between the mind and the hand. Eliot's lines in "The Hollow Men" put it more abstractly and more starkly: "Between the conception / And the creation / Between the emotion / And the response / Falls the Shadow." It is curious to note Eliot's initial experience of writing book reviews using a typewriter: "I find that I am sloughing off all my long sentences which I used to dote upon. Short, staccato, like modern French prose. The typewriter makes for lucidity, but I am not sure that it encourages subtlety." Eliot's hands not only have a mind of their own, but in conjunction with the typewriter they have evolved a prose style of their own.

Questions 776–779 ask about Passage A.

776. Which of the following best summarizes the main idea of passage A?

(A) Poems are most enjoyable when their themes are cheerful.

(B) Poetic subject matter does not have to be joyful for a poem to be enjoyable.

(C) Reading material that is somber will likely make the reader somber; likewise, cheerful images most often produce joyful feelings.

(D) Images of ancient building in poetry can be invoke pleasurable memories or sorrowful ones, depending on the perspective of the reader.

777. Stafford notes that all of the following works relied on medieval architecture to set the atmosphere EXCEPT:

(A) Coleridge's "Christabel"

(B) A cycle of extremely popular poems by the bard Ossian

(C) Scott's "The Lay of the Last Minstrelor"

(D) Gothic narratives

778. According to Stafford, a poem's ability to provoke readers to reflect on bad memories has a tendency to make those readers:

(A) feel particularly melancholy.

(B) question their satisfaction with their current situations and surroundings.

(C) accept more gratefully their current circumstances.

(D) reflect on their current surroundings and vow to avoid repeating prior mistakes.

779. Stafford attributes the sentiment that people have a natural tendency to compare the past with the present to:

(A) Macpherson

(B) all Enlightenment thinkers

(C) Byron

(D) Hume

Questions 780–783 ask about Passage B.

780. *Emblematize*, as it is used in line 85, most closely means to:

(A) publicize

(B) delegate

(C) exacerbate

(D) epitomize

781. According to Whitworth, Eliot makes all of the following assertions about the typewriter EXCEPT that it:

(A) makes for lucidity.

(B) produces a new prose style that he dotes upon.

(C) lacks subtlety.

(D) encourages brevity.

782. When Whitworth mentions the concept of "agency" in line 87, he most likely refers to:

(A) an entity's ability to act and exist in a given environment.

(B) an organization dedicated to offering a particular service.

(C) a government office or entity.

(D) one's ability to write clear prose.

783. As they are described by Whitworth, the writer's hands symbolize two important aspects of modernist poetry. These separate but complementary aspects are:

(A) detachment from the handiwork and lack of creative ability.

(B) joy and grief.

(C) impersonality and loss of control over creativity.

(D) handwriting sentences and typing them.

Questions 784–785 ask about both passages.

784. Statements from Stafford and Whitworth suggest that the works of Joyce and Eliot were written:

(A) after the works of romantic poets.

(B) with medieval architectural imagery.

(C) during the romantic period.

(D) after the romantic period but before the modernist period.

785. Which of the following is common to the discussions of both Stafford and Whitworth?

(A) Both use direct statements from the poets themselves to support their points.

(B) Both describe some of the ways a certain classifications of writers executed their craft and suggest reasons for these manners of writing.

(C) Both refer to the role of the writer's hand to support their points regarding the engagement of the poet.

(D) Both provide a general critique of the poetic style of the period they discuss and suggest ways that the style could be improved.

Natural Science

Questions 786–795 are based on the following information.

This passage is adapted from the book *Applied Turf Grass Science and Physiology* by Jack Fry and Bingru Huang (Wiley 2004).

Photosynthesis takes place mostly in leaf mesophyll cells, which contain chloroplasts. Chloroplasts are cellular organelles that contain green chlorophyll molecules capable of absorbing the light needed for photosynthesis. Photosynthesis is basically a two-step process whereby green leaves convert solar energy to chemical energy (light reaction) that is used to produce energy-rich carbohydrates (food) using carbon dioxide (CO_2) and water (H_2O) (dark reaction). The first step requires light, and thus is referred to as the light reaction. The fixation of CO_2 into carbohydrates is light independent, and thus is called the dark reaction (even though the process occurs during the daytime).

Photosynthesis occurs only when sufficient light is available. Except for turf grasses growing in shade, light intensity does not normally limit turf photosynthesis. Very high light intensities may bleach chlorophyll and retard photosynthesis, but plants that typically grow under such conditions have evolved mechanisms for protection, such as thick leaf cuticles or hairy leaves to reflect light.

Plant injury resulting from high light intensity is due not to the light per se but to an excess of light energy over that utilized by photosynthesis. When light reaching the leaves is not used for photosynthesis, the excess energy triggers production of free radicals that can damage cells (oxidative damage). This often occurs when light intensity is high but photosynthesis is inhibited due to stress from temperature extremes, drought, or excessive soil water. When light intensity is at a low level where photosynthesis and respiration reach equilibrium and the net carbon gain is zero, no plant growth will occur. This light level is the light compensation point (LCP). Leaves exposed to light levels below the LCP for an extended period of time will eventually senesce. Both LSP and LCP vary among turf grass species and with temperature and CO_2 concentration.

Under high irradiance, warm-season grasses maintain a higher rate of photosynthesis than cool-season grasses. However, cool-season grasses have a lower LCP and exhibit higher photosynthetic rates under low light levels compared to warm-season grasses. Photosynthetic rates of both warm-season and cool-season grasses exhibit a diurnal pattern on clear, sunny days, increasing from sunrise, reaching a maximum around noon, and then decreasing to the lowest levels by sunset.

Photosynthesis is affected by light duration because it occurs only during daylight. Increasing light duration may not increase the rate of carbon fixation, but the total amount of carbon fixed by photosynthesis will increase due to increased light exposure. Sunlight has all the colors of visible light and is composed of different wavelengths. Not all wavelengths are equally effective in driving photosynthesis, however. Most photosynthetic activity is stimulated by blue and red wavelengths — chlorophylls absorb blue and red light and carotenoids absorb blue light. Green light is reflected, thus giving plants their green color. Green-yellow and far red are transmitted through the leaf.

Light quality is important under artificial light (some turf managers have resorted to using supplemental artificial light) and shade. Turf in the shade of a tree receives primarily green-yellow and far-red wavelengths. Artificial lights emit a different pattern of wavelengths: Fluorescent lights are highest in the blue and yellow-orange region of the spectrum but low in the red, and incandescent (tungsten) lights are poor in the blue region, moderate in the green region, and high in the red and far red region of the spectrum, with up to 50 percent of their output in the infrared region.

Nutrient availability is equally important for photosynthesis in both warm- and cool-season grasses. Nitrogen and magnesium are essential constituents of the chlorophyll molecule, and iron serves as an activator for enzymes involved in chlorophyll synthesis. Sulfur is involved in photosynthetic electron transport and is a constituent of several iron-sulfur proteins that are intermediates in the process, as are manganese and copper. Chlorine is required for photosynthetic oxygen evolution. Lack of nutrients also induces stomatal closure, leading to reduced photosynthesis. Potassium acts as an osmoregulator, and its accumulation promotes the maintenance of cell turgor and stomatal opening, thus affecting photosynthesis.

Leaves contain chlorophyll, which traps the sun's energy, and the photosynthetic rate typically increases with increasing chlorophyll content. Plants with greater leaf area also have higher rates of canopy photosynthesis. Damaged, senescent, or diseased leaves have lower photosynthetic rates than healthy leaves. As leaf angle increases, lower leaves become shaded and total light absorption decreases, resulting in lower photosynthetic rates. Pubescent leaves reflect more light and are less photosynthetically efficient.

786. The authors of the passage are primarily concerned with:

(A) discussing the impacts of light energy and photosynthesis on warm-season and cool-season grasses.

(B) arguing in favor of warm-season grasses, which are less prone to oxidative damage than cool-season grasses.

(C) exploring the important role of photosynthesis in sustaining turf grass production.

(D) comparing different kinds of turf grasses according to their responses to various levels of light energy.

787. It can be reasonably inferred from the passage that a plant with very large green leaves:

(A) contains less chlorophyll.

(B) has a high rate of canopy photosynthesis.

(C) has a low rate of canopy photosynthesis.

(D) may experience a slower rate of photosynthesis.

788. Which of the following would the authors likely agree is true of incandescent lights?

(A) They are highest in the blue and yellow-orange region.

(B) They exhibit a diurnal pattern.

(C) They are lower in the green and blue regions than the red.

(D) Up to 75 percent of their output is in the infrared region.

789. In the context of the passage, which of the following is the best definition for the word *senesce* (line 38)?

(A) Grow faster

(B) Grow slower

(C) Turn darker green

(D) Die back

790. According to the passage, which of the following is an important difference between warm-season and cool-season grasses?

(A) Cool-season grasses can better withstand higher light intensities such as those found nearer the equator, while warm-season grasses are better suited to northern climates.

(B) Warm-season grasses can handle the higher light levels of summer, while cool-season grasses can grow during under the lower light conditions of winter.

(C) Most of the photosynthesis in warm-season grasses takes place during the day, while cool-season grasses usually photosynthesize at night.

(D) Warm season grasses use only the blue and red spectrums of light for photosynthesis, while reflecting harmful green light.

791. Which of the following can be inferred from the discussion on oxidative damage in lines 27–29?

(A) Oxidative damage most frequently occurs about one hour after sunrise and one hour before sunset.

(B) Homeowners should water their lawns as often as possible because damage to grass is caused by drought and not simply by light intensity.

(C) Damage to grass occurs because of the high intensity of light and homeowners can do nothing to preserve their lawns.

(D) Both overwatering and underwatering a lawn can inhibit photosynthesis and damage grass.

792. According to the passage, each of the following is true of turf grass photosynthesis EXCEPT that:

(A) its rate depends only on the amount of light energy.

(B) it occurs only during daylight.

(C) it is stimulated by blue and red wavelengths of light.

(D) it is inhibited by temperature extremes.

793. As it is used in line 48, which of the following is the best definition for the word *diurnal*?

(A) Active only during the daytime

(B) Occurring twice a day

(C) Occurring every other day

(D) Back and forth

794. When the authors speak of plants with "evolved mechanisms for protection" (line 21), these mechanisms are used to protect against:

(A) free radicals that can damage cells.

(B) chemical energy.

(C) very high light intensities.

(D) chlorophyll.

795. According to the authors, one of the ways that nutrient availability is critical for photosynthesis is that:

(A) nitrogen and sulfur make up the essential components of chlorophyll.

(B) sulfur is a constituent of proteins that help along the process.

(C) chlorine reduces photosynthetic oxygen evolution.

(D) potassium helps promote the maintenance of stomatal closure.

Chapter 4

The Science Test

This section of the ACT tests your ability to work with science information — and your endurance under time pressure. In just 35 minutes, you face 40 questions distributed over six passages with six or seven questions each, which gives you a little less than six minutes to spend on each passage.

Although some questions expect you to know some foundational science terms and concepts, the majority of the science test answers are right there in the passage in front of you. No calculators are allowed, so all math calculations require only simple calculations or easy estimations.

The Problems You'll Work On

When working through the questions in this chapter, be prepared to do the following:

- Analyze data represented on tables and graphs.
- Sift through text for information on experiment procedure and set up.
- Consider science topics from all areas of biology, chemistry, and physics.
- Read your answer options carefully and use them to help you focus.
- Discover that often two of the four answers are clearly incorrect.
- Compare the opinions of two or more scientist or students.

What to Watch Out For

To maximize your score, avoid these counterproductive and time-sucking activities:

- Reading the passage before you examine the questions
- Neglecting to identify the column headings on tables and the axis designations on graphs
- Believing you need to know a bunch of science concepts to answer the questions
- Spending more than a minute on any one question instead of marking it for later and moving on
- Failing to quickly eliminate answers that contain irrelevant data or blatantly contradict information in the passage

Questions 796–802 are based on the following information.

Circadian rhythms drive human and animal behaviors, such as activity, sleep, metabolism, and mating. A scientist hypothesizes that exposure to light and dark regulate these rhythms by altering the production of a hormone called melatonin. To evaluate the importance of light and dark in regulating circadian rhythms, the scientist conducts a set of experiments.

Experiment 1

Over the course of one week, the scientist encloses three mice and exposes them to 24-hour periods of varying exposure to light and dark. During each 24-hour period, the mice receive 12 consecutive hours of artificial light and 12 consecutive hours of complete darkness. At 15-minute intervals, the scientist notes the activity levels of the mice and records his findings. Furthermore, every 15 minutes during Day 7, the scientist collects a small blood sample from the mice to measure their level of melatonin.

At the end of one week, the scientist graphs the mice's activity levels in Figure 1, with black bars indicating the periods of continuous activity. The scientist then graphs the mice's levels of melatonin as shown in Figure 2.

Figure 1

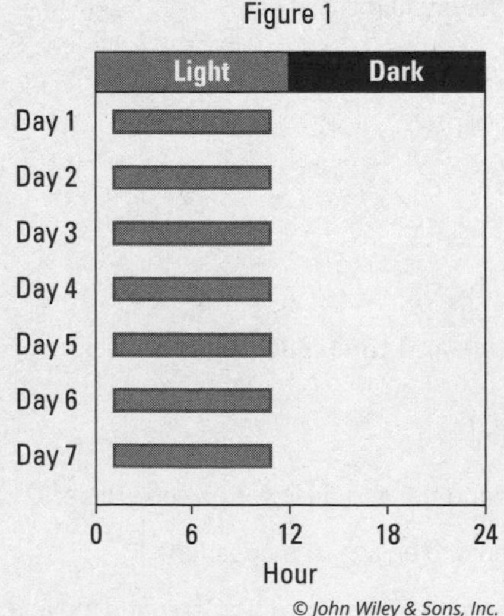

Experiment 2

The scientist then conducts a similar experiment in which he studies the activity levels of mice exposed only to darkness over the course of one week. Figure 3 graphs the mice's resulting activity levels, and Figure 2 records their melatonin levels on Day 7.

Figure 2

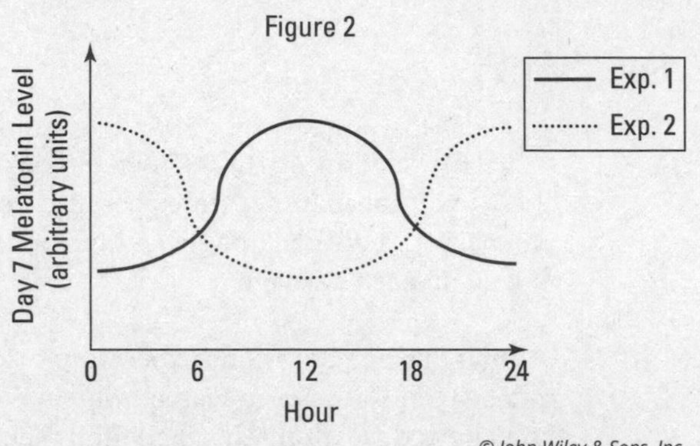

Figure 3

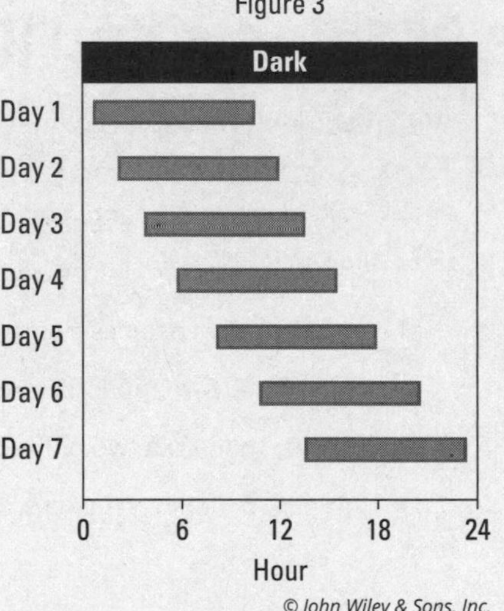

796. Approximately how long were the mice active each day during Experiment 1?

(A) 10 hours

(B) 6 hours

(C) 18 hours

(D) 24 hours

797. What aspect of the study was varied between Experiments 1 and 2? Compared to Experiment 1, in Experiment 2

(A) the number of mice used was greater

(B) the amount of daily mouse activity decreased

(C) the mice experienced only darkness

(D) the mice experienced equal daily exposure to light and darkness

798. Based on the results of both experiments, which of these statements is a valid conclusion the scientist could reach?

(A) Mice are more active during the day than during the night.

(B) Peak melatonin levels in mice closely coincide with the onset of periods of inactivity.

(C) Mice produce more melatonin during the day than during the night.

(D) There is no clear relationship between melatonin production and activity levels in mice.

799. The scientist conducts a third experiment during which the mice experience darkness from hours 0 to 12 and light from hours 13 to 23. Based on the results of Experiments 1 and 2, when would peak melatonin production most likely occur on Day 7?

(A) Hour 18

(B) Hour 5

(C) Hour 1

(D) Hour 0

800. The scientist wants to conduct another experiment to support to his hypothesis. Which of the following experiments would best provide that additional support?

(A) Repeat the two experiments with two mice.

(B) Repeat Experiment 2 but with 24 hours of daily light exposure.

(C) Repeat Experiment 1 and measure oxygen levels in the blood instead of melatonin.

(D) Repeat Experiment 2 with 12 hours of daily light exposure and 12 hours of daily darkness.

801. Melatonin pills have been approved for use in humans. Based on information in the passage, when should a physician advise his patients to take melatonin pills if they wanted to get a better night's sleep?

(A) Before bedtime

(B) In the morning

(C) With meals

(D) Every 4 hours

802. If the scientist had collected melatonin levels over the course of Day 4 during Experiment 2, what would most likely represent the graph for melatonin level?

(A)

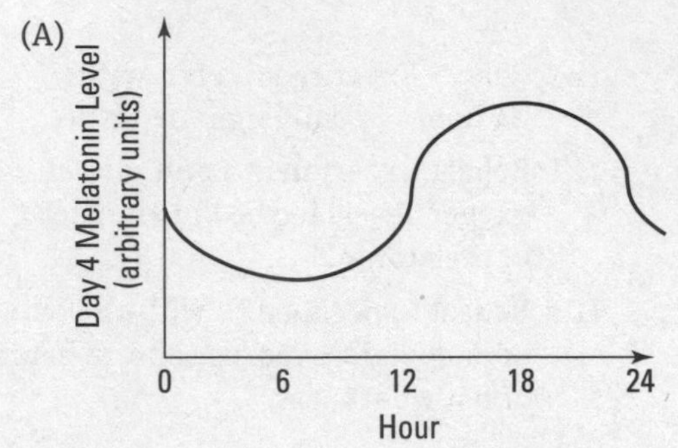

© John Wiley & Sons, Inc.

(B)

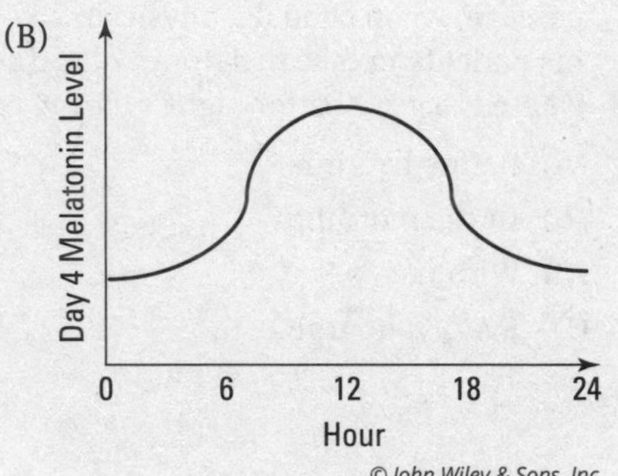

© John Wiley & Sons, Inc.

(C)

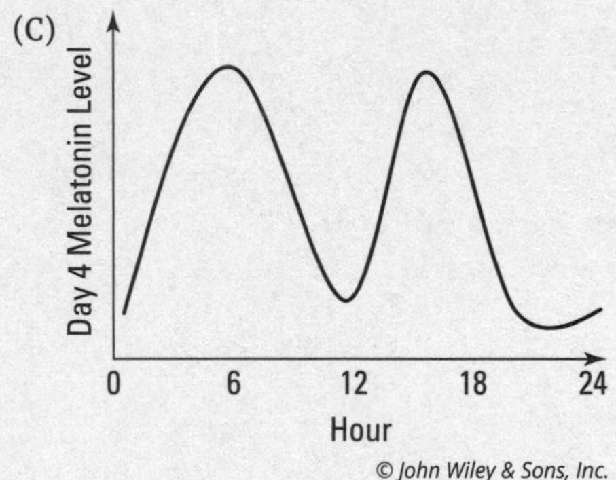

© John Wiley & Sons, Inc.

(D)

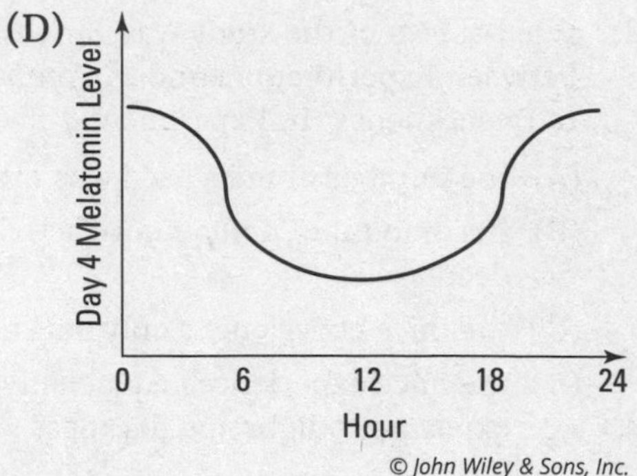

© John Wiley & Sons, Inc.

Questions 803–809 are based on the following information.

The Krebs Cycle is a key part of metabolism that helps create energy for cells. To start the cycle (shown in Figure 1), a 2-carbon molecule called Acetyl-CoA (created from Glucose) is combined with a 4-carbon molecule (Oxaloacetate) to create a 6-carbon molecule (Citrate). Over the course of the rest of the cycle, the energy stored in Citrate is used to create other molecules (NADH, $FADH_2$ and GTP), all of which go on to produce ATP, the primary energy source of the cell, as documented in Table 1.

Figure 1

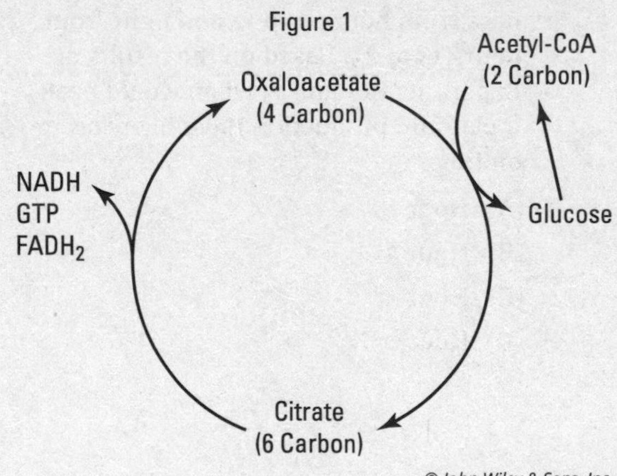

© John Wiley & Sons, Inc.

TABLE 1

Molecule	ATP created per 1/molecule
NADH	2.5
$FADH_2$	1.5
GTP	1

A scientist, using an exact measuring system, applied different amounts of glucose to a cell and measured the resulting outputs from the Krebs Cycle. The results are recorded in Table 2.

TABLE 2

Number of Glucose Molecules Applied	Number of Acetyl CoA Created	Number of NADH Created	Number of GTP Created	Number of $FADH_2$ Created
1	2	6	2	2
10	20	60	20	20
20	40	120	40	40
30	60	180	60	60

803. Based on the results of the experiment and information in the passage, how many NADH are produced per one turn of the Krebs Cycle?

(A) 1

(B) 2

(C) 3

(D) 6

804. In the experiment described in the passage, what is the independent variable?

(A) Number of Glucose molecules applied

(B) Number of Oxaloacetate molecules created

(C) Number of Acetyl-CoA created

(D) Number of turns of Krebs Cycle

805. A certain cell needs 600 ATP to survive for a day. Based on information in the passage, how many Glucose molecules will the cell need for the day?

(A) 1

(B) 10

(C) 20

(D) 30

806. The scientist has isolated the step in the Krebs Cycle that occurs between Citrate and Oxaloacetate. She notes that in addition to NADH, $FADH_2$, and GTP, the 1-carbon gas CO_2 is also created. How many molecules of this gas are likely created in this step?

(A) 1

(B) 2

(C) 3

(D) 4

807. The scientist finds that ATP inhibits the reaction between Oxaloacetate and Acetyl-CoA. What effect does this reaction have on NADH production?

(A) It increases because more Citrate is produced.

(B) It decreases because more Acetyl-CoA is produced.

(C) It decreases because less Citrate is produced.

(D) It increases because more Glucose is used.

808. Removal of which molecule would have the most significant effect on cellular ATP production?

(A) GTP

(B) NADH

(C) $FADH_2$

(D) Acetyl-CoA

809. Which is the most appropriate graph of the relationship between number of glucose molecules applied and number of $FADH_2$ created during the experiment?

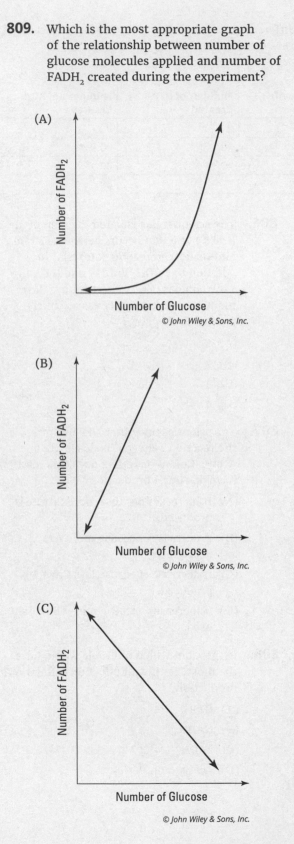

(A)

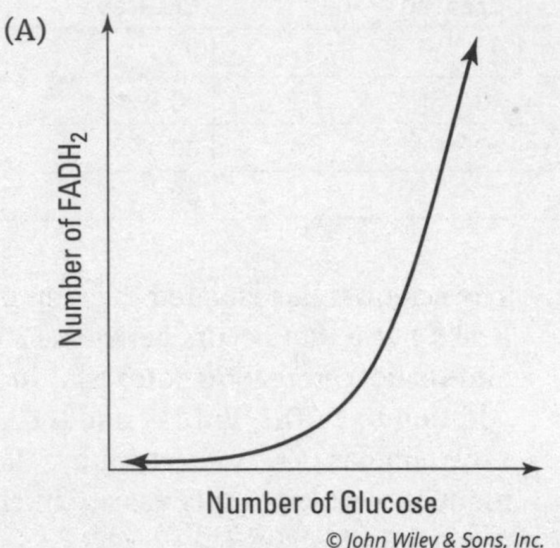

(B)

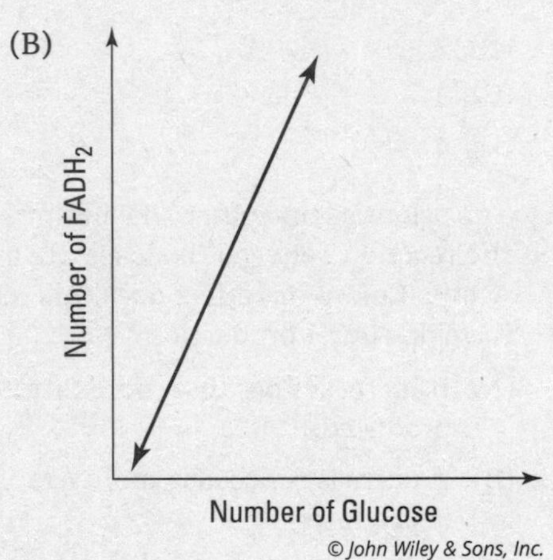

(C)

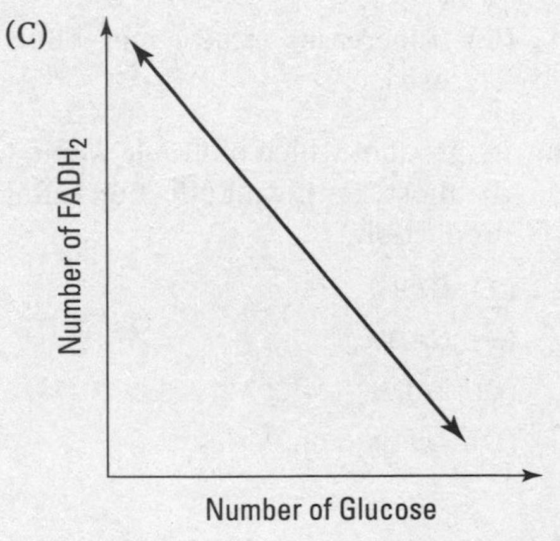

(D)

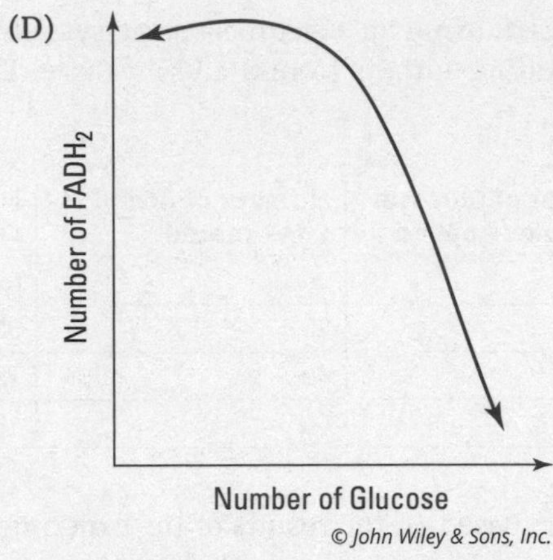

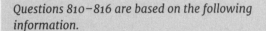

Questions 810–816 are based on the following information.

A tire company is testing a variety of new materials (A, B, C, and D) for its new line of tires. It subjected each new material to testing by creating prototype tires and calculating the stopping distance (the length the car travels from the time brakes are applied to the moment the car come to a complete stop) needed for each tire type when installed on a test car. Table 1 displays data on each material's performance on a variety of surface types.

TABLE 1

Material	Stopping Distance Dry Concrete	Stopping Distance Wet Concrete	Stopping Distance Ice	Stopping Distance Dirt
A	51ft	66ft	80ft	66ft
B	44ft	69ft	74ft	69ft
C	56ft	61ft	85ft	61ft
D	62ft	77ft	90ft	77ft

During the test, as the tires on the car are sliding across each material, they experience kinetic friction. Kinetic friction and the force acting to slow the car are related by the following equation:

$$F_{stop} = \mu_{kinetic} \times W$$

Where F_{stop} is the stopping force, $\mu_{kinetic}$ is the coefficient of kinetic friction, and W is the weight of the vehicle. $\mu_{kinetic}$ values are only dependent on the types of surface materials sliding against one another. Table 2 displays $\mu_{kinetic}$ values for the tires on each surface type.

TABLE 2

Material	$\mu_{kinetic}$ Dry Concrete	$\mu_{kinetic}$ Wet Concrete	$\mu_{kinetic}$ Ice	$\mu_{kinetic}$ Dirt
A	0.79	0.65	0.55	0.65
B	0.90	0.61	0.59	0.61
C	0.75	0.69	0.50	0.69
D	0.69	0.56	0.49	0.56

810. What are the independent variables for the stopping distance study?

(A) Material and stopping distance

(B) Vehicle weight and material

(C) Material and surface type

(D) F_{stop} and stopping distance

811. Which material had the shortest stopping distance on dry concrete?

(A) Material A

(B) Material B

(C) Material C

(D) Material D

812. Which combination of vehicle weight and tire material would generate the greatest stopping force (F_{stop})?

(A) 2,000-pound vehicle using material A on dry concrete

(B) 2,000-pound vehicle using material D on dirt

(C) 1,000-pound vehicle using material A on dry concrete

(D) 1,000-pound vehicle using material D on ice

813. Across all tire materials and surfaces, what is the relationship between $\mu_{kinetic}$ and stopping distance?

(A) As $\mu_{kinetic}$ increases, stopping distance increases.

(B) As $\mu_{kinetic}$ decreases, stopping distance decreases.

(C) As $\mu_{kinetic}$ increases, stopping distance does not change.

(D) As $\mu_{kinetic}$ decreases, stopping distance increases.

814. The tire company develops a new material that when tested on dirt has a stopping distance of 76 feet. What is the nearest estimate for its $\mu_{kinetic}$?

(A) 0.90

(B) 0.45

(C) 0.55

(D) 0.20

815. The tire company desires to produce the safest tires on the market. It increases the width of its tires and keeps the weight the same. Based on the information given, using these tires will

(A) increase the stopping force because $\mu_{kinetic}$ is dependent on tire width

(B) decrease the stopping force because $\mu_{kinetic}$ is dependent on tire width

(C) not change the stopping force because $\mu_{kinetic}$ is not dependent on tire width

(D) will not change the stopping force because $\mu_{kinetic}$ is not dependent on vehicle weight

816. When two objects have contact with each other without motion (such as a book on a table), the force (F_{static}) is the product of the coefficient of static friction (μ_{static}) and the object's weight. Anti-lock brake systems (ABS) were designed to keep tires from sliding during rapid braking. Given the information in the passage, what is a possible explanation for the reason a car with an ABS will stop faster than one without an ABS?

(A) μ_{static} is greater than $\mu_{kinetic}$.

(B) μ_{static} is less than $\mu_{kinetic}$.

(C) An ABS increases μ_{static}.

(D) An ABS increases $\mu_{kinetic}$.

Questions 817–823 are based on the following information.

Hydrodynamics is the science that describes how fluids behave in motion. For example, as water flows through a pipe, its velocity and pressure are subject to change depending on the shape and size of the pipe. Figure 1 shows water being pumped through a pipe that increases in diameter. Water exits the pipe at the end. The pump has two settings. On low, it pumps water at $10m^3$ / sec. On high, it pumps water at $20m^3$/ sec.

Figure 1

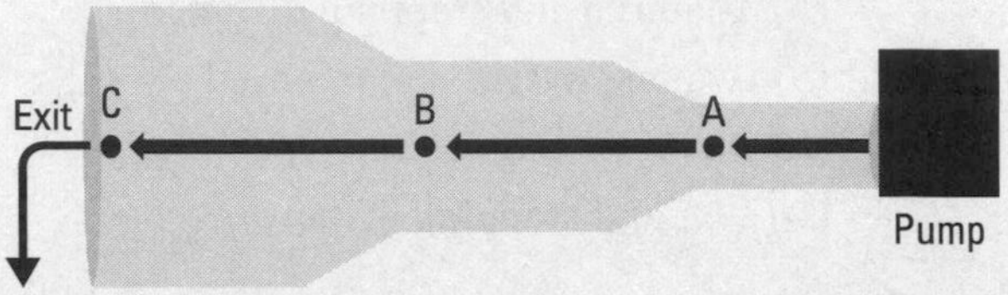

© John Wiley & Sons, Inc.

Data are collected about characteristics of the water flowing through the pipe at the three different points (A, B, and C) for both settings. Table 1 displays the data results.

TABLE 1

	Pipe Diameter (m)	Pressure (kPa)		Density (kg / m³)		Velocity (m/s)	
Point	high and low	low	high	low	high	low	high
A	1.0	193.6	470.5	1,000	1,000	12.7	25.5
B	2.0	107.4	125.6	1,000	1,000	3.2	6.4
C	3.0	101.3	101.3	1,000	1,000	1.4	2.8

817. What is the velocity of the water at point A when the pump is set to low?

(A) 1.0 m/s

(B) 12.7 m/s

(C) 12.7 kPa

(D) 3.2 m/s

818. According to the data, what effect does changing the setting of the pump from high to low have on the density of the water flowing through the pipe?

(A) The water's density increases.

(B) The water's density decreases.

(C) The water's density remains the same.

(D) The water's density changes depending on the point in the pipe.

819. Suppose a fourth section of pipe with a diameter of 4.0 meters was attached to the exit end of the current pipe. The velocity of water flowing through this pipe with the pump set to low would be

(A) greater than 12.7 m/s

(B) between 3.2 m/s and 12.7 m/s

(C) between 1.4 m/s and 3.2 m/s

(D) less than 1.4 m/s

820. Based on Table 1, which action would lead to the greatest decrease in water pressure at point A when the pump is on the high setting?

(A) Increase pipe length.

(B) Increase water temperature.

(C) Double pipe diameter.

(D) Change pump setting from high to low.

821. When the pump setting is changed from low to high, the velocity of the water

(A) does not change

(B) approximately doubles

(C) approximately triples

(D) approximately quadruples

822. Which of the following combinations would result in the highest water velocity?

(A) Pump setting: low; pipe diameter: small

(B) Pump setting: low; pipe diameter: large

(C) Pump setting: high; pipe diameter: small

(D) Pump setting: high; pipe diameter: large

823. When selecting a pipe material for water systems, engineers have a variety of options. Certain materials begin to crack under pressures greater than those supported by the system. Using information about different pipe materials provided by the table below, which material from this table would be the best option for this pipe system?

Material	Maximum Pressure Rating (kPA)
Clay	310.7
Lead	355.2
Copper	406.9
Polyvinyl chloride	488.5

(A) Clay

(B) Lead

(C) Copper

(D) Polyvinyl chloride

Questions 824–830 are based on the following information.

Matter can exist in three different phases: solid, liquid, or gas. A matter's state is determined by its temperature and the pressure of its physical surroundings. With a change in temperature or pressure, matter can undergo a phase change from one state to another. Table 1 provides several phase changes.

TABLE 1

Phase change with increasing energy	Phase change with decreasing energy
Melting: solid to liquid	Freezing: liquid to solid
Vaporization: liquid to gas	Condensation: gas to liquid
Sublimation: solid to gas	Deposition: gas to solid

A triple-point diagram is a chart used to describe what state a certain compound will take given a certain temperature and pressure. Figure 1 shows the triple-point diagrams for water (*a*) and carbon dioxide CO_2 (*b*).

Figure 1

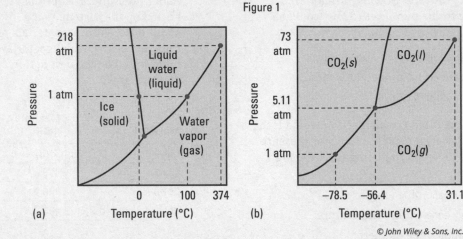

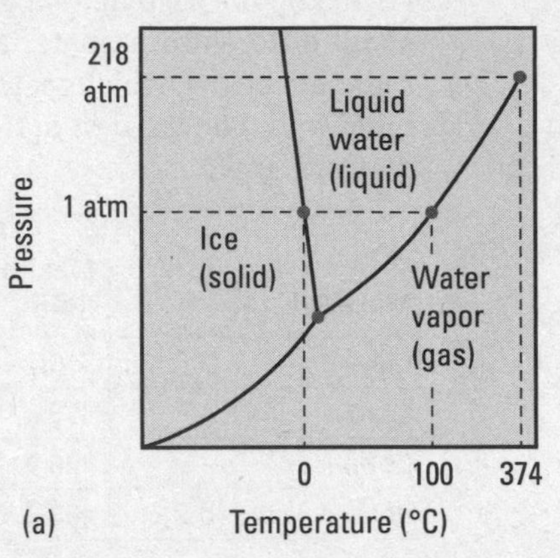

824. At low pressures, when water vapor is cooled, it becomes ice. What is this transition called?

(A) Deposition

(B) Condensation

(C) Sublimation

(D) Freezing

825. According to Figure 1, in what state or states can water exist at 100°C?

(A) Solid only

(B) Liquid only

(C) Gas or liquid

(D) Gas or solid

826. At 1 atm pressure and −10°C, which of the following describes the states of water and CO_2?

(A) Water: liquid; CO_2: liquid

(B) Water: solid; CO_2: gas

(C) Water: gas; CO_2: solid

(D) Water: solid; CO_2: solid

827. Dry ice is the solid form of CO_2. Manufacturers use liquid CO_2 to produce dry ice. What must the manufacturers do to liquid CO_2 to create dry ice?

(A) Slowly increase the temperature at low pressures

(B) Slowly increase the temperature at high pressures

(C) Slowly decrease the temperature at low pressures

(D) Slowly decrease the temperature at high pressures

828. The pressure at sea level is 1 atm. What is the maximum temperature of liquid water at sea level?

(A) 31.1°C

(B) 0°C

(C) 100°C

(D) 374°C

829. A pressure cooker is a culinary device used to cook foods at pressures higher than 1 atm (the atmospheric pressure at sea level). It accomplishes this task by sealing in the steam created from boiling liquid water, which increases the internal pressure of the device. Pressure cookers generally operate at about 2 atm. What is the likely advantage of cooking with a pressure cooker?

(A) Cooking at higher pressures (2 atm) increases the maximum temperature of liquid water, which reduces cooking time.

(B) Cooking at higher pressures (2 atm) decreases the maximum temperature of liquid water, which reduces cooking time.

(C) Cooking at higher pressure (2 atm) forces liquid water to undergo sublimation, which reduces cooking time.

(D) Cooking at higher pressure (2 atm) has no advantages over cooking at 1 atm.

830. What is the temperature of solid CO_2 that undergoes sublimation at 1 atm?

(A) 100°C

(B) 31.1°C

(C) –56.4°C

(D) –78.5°C

Questions 831–837 are based on the following information.

The monarch butterfly (*Danaus plexippus*) migrates south for the winter. In the early fall, the butterflies leave their habitats in United States and Canada and make their journey to sites in central Mexico. In early spring, the butterflies make a return trip to their original habitats across the United States and Canada. This feat, covering up to 4,500 miles, is one of the longest insect migrations in the world. Because of the length of the trip, no single butterfly makes the entire journey. It can take up to five generations of butterfly to travel to and from the wintering sites. Entomologists have proposed three main theories for how the butterflies manage to migrate with such exceptional precision on an annual basis.

Geographical Features Theory:

Monarch butterflies use large geographic landmarks to navigate to central Mexico. These features include large mountain ranges, rivers, lakes, and oceans. Butterflies often roost transiently at these large landmarks during their trip.

Sun Compass Theory:

Monarch butterflies use the location of the sun to orient themselves along the north/south axis. The location of the sun in the sky varies with the time of day and season. Using an internal circadian clock, the butterflies "know" how to orient themselves based on the sun's location at a given time and season.

Magnetic Compass Theory:

Monarch butterflies have magnetic-sensitive cells in their antennae that orient them along the magnetic north/south axis. During the fall, these cells point them south, and during the spring, they point north. In this manner, the butterflies always have a reliable way to navigate.

831. For which of the three theories are butterflies most dependent on the position of the sun?

(A) Geographic features theory

(B) Sun compass theory

(C) Magnetic compass theory

(D) None of the theories

832. Based on information in the passage, in the early fall, monarch butterflies migrate from

(A) east to west

(B) west to east

(C) south to north

(D) north to south

833. Which of the following responses provides accurate summarizes of the theories?

(A) **Sun compass:** The butterflies always fly toward the sun. **Magnetic compass:** The butterflies use magnets to orient themselves.

(B) **Geographic features:** The butterflies use mountains to navigate. **Sun compass:** The butterflies use the sun to orient themselves.

(C) **Sun compass:** The butterflies use the sun to orient themselves. **Magnetic compass:** The butterflies use magnets to orient themselves.

(D) **Geographic features:** Butterflies use landmarks to navigate. **Magnetic compass:** The butterflies use the sun to orient themselves.

834. A scientist puts a group of *Danaus plexippus* in a large cylindrical tank that is shielded from the Earth's magnetic field. In the tank, he creates his own magnetic field that can be rotated. He orients his artificial magnetic field so that its magnetic North Pole is located in a position that is actually west. If the season is currently early spring and the magnetic compass theory is correct, in which *actual* direction will the butterflies fly?

(A) North

(B) South

(C) East

(D) West

835. Entomologists find that butterflies have trouble navigating on cloudy days. If true, this finding provides evidence that calls into question which theory or theories?

(A) Magnetic compass theory and geographic features theory

(B) Sun compass theory and magnetic compass theory

(C) Sun compass theory only

(D) Magnetic compass theory only

836. Which of the following pieces of evidence, if true, would provide the most support for the geographic features theory?

(A) Removing a gene responsible for butterfly coloration patterns interferes with their navigation ability.

(B) Butterflies consistently change direction when encountering a large river.

(C) Construction of a large dam along a major river does not affect butterfly migration.

(D) Global warming has forced butterflies to migrate earlier in the season.

837. Global warming may force butterflies to migrate earlier in each season. Which migration mechanism or mechanisms would be most affected by global warming?

(A) Magnetic compass theory only

(B) Sun compass theory only

(C) Geographical features theory only

(D) Geographical features theory and magnetic compass theory

Questions 838–844 are based on the following passage:

The Cretaceous-Tertiary extinction (K-T) happened between 65 and 66 million years ago and is commonly known for the extinction event that killed the dinosaurs. Around 75% of life on Earth, including dinosaurs, many plants, fish, and some mammals, ceased to exist after the K-T event. Two scientists present theories to explain the K-T extinction event:

Scientist 1

The K-T extinction was precipitated by the collision of a large asteroid with the earth. The initial impact of this asteroid caused large tsunamis and earthquakes, immediately killing anything within thousands of miles. It also led to rapid changes to

Earth's climate. The massive dust cloud created by the impact blocked the sun, causing global temperatures to plummet. Fiery chunks of rock, exploding from the impact site, ignited huge fires across the planet. These fires decreased oxygen levels and increased CO_2 levels in the atmosphere, leading to a greenhouse effect and climate change. All of these combined factors led to the massive K-T extinction. The main evidence for this impact theory is the 110-mile wide Chicxulub crater near the eastern coast of Mexico.

Scientist 2

The massive K-T extinction was caused by huge volcanic activity on the Earth. These volcanos, especially those that formed the Deccan Plateau in western India, became active during the same time as the K-T extinction. The volcanos spewed around 1.5 million square kilometers (580,000 square miles) of lava over the period of thousands of years. At the same time, these volcanos pumped CO_2, ash, and poisonous chemicals into the atmosphere. Eventually, this process would lead to ocean acidification, killing plankton and small marine life essential for food chain stability. Reduced solar intensity from the greenhouse gases, coupled with loss of food killed off much of the plant and animal life over the period of thousands of years, causing the K-T extinction.

838. Which of these concepts is consistent with only Scientist 1?

(A) Rapid destruction

(B) Increased CO_2

(C) Climate change

(D) Food chain instability

839. Fossils from the K-T extinction are hard to find around the Chicxulub crater. How would Scientist 1 best account for this phenomenon?

(A) There was nothing living in that area at the time.

(B) The volcanos responsible for the extinction burned away all evidence of life.

(C) The impact of the asteroid and the resulting explosion burned or buried most evidence of life.

(D) No fossils formed because of the slow die-off caused by climate change.

840. Rocks dated to the time of the K-T extinction contain abnormally high levels of iridium. This finding would best support Scientist 1 if which of the following statements is true?

(A) Iridium is a common element in Earth's crust.

(B) Iridium is stored in magma.

(C) Iridium is found in high concentrations around the Deccan Plateau.

(D) Iridium is only common in meteors.

841. Which of these factors is common to the theories of both scientists?

(A) Climate change

(B) Asteroid impact

(C) Volcanic activity

(D) Chicxulub

842. Many scientists believe that a combination of the theories presented by both Scientist 1 and Scientist 2 played a role in the K-T extinction. What evidence would best support this conclusion?

(A) The Chicxulub crater is larger than originally thought.

(B) Food chain instability was present before the Chicxulub crater appeared.

(C) Large lava flows have been found to release more CO_2 than fires of similar size.

(D) Climate change was widespread during the K-T extinction.

843. What must be true about fossils from the K-T extinction for the Scientist 2's theory to be true?

(A) The fossils show evidence of rapid death.

(B) Only fossils of plankton and marine life are present.

(C) Many fossils show evidence of starvation.

(D) All fossils are buried in old lava flows.

844. According to both theories, plants and animals that thrived after the K-T extinction would have to adapt to

(A) lower sea levels

(B) increased access to food

(C) widespread lava

(D) increased atmospheric CO_2

Questions 845–850 are based on the following passage:

A circuit is built with a battery, three switches and resistors, and an electric motor. As shown in Figure 1, current flows from the battery (+), through one of the switches (S) as long as the switch is closed, through a resistor (R), and then to the motor (M) to cause the motor to turn.

Figure 1

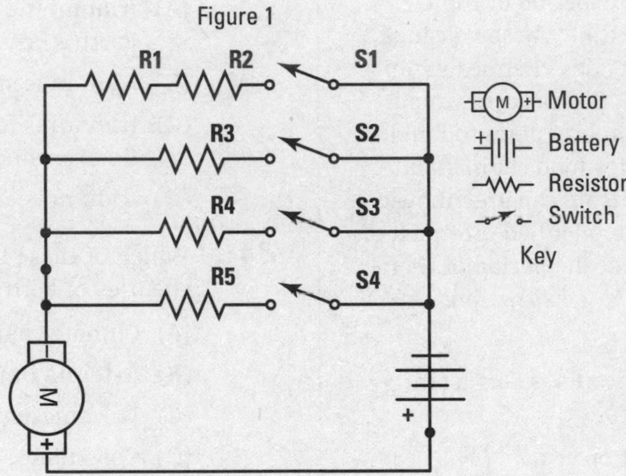

© John Wiley & Sons, Inc.

The corresponding resistance in ohms for each resistor is listed in Table 1. The battery produces a steady 12 volts of energy.

TABLE 1

Resistor	Resistance (ohms)
R1, R2, R5	1
R3	2
R4	4

Each switch is closed one at a time. The experimenter observed the resulting power output (J/s) and recorded the data along with the current measured in amps. Table 2 displays the record.

TABLE 2

Closed Switch	Power Output (J/s)	Current (Amps)
1	72.0	6.0
2	72.0	6.0
3	36.0	3.0
4	144.0	12.0

845. Closing which switch causes the motor to generate the most power?

(A) 1

(B) 2

(C) 3

(D) 4

846. What best describes the relationship in Table 8 between current and power?

(A) As current increases, power decreases.

(B) As current increases, power increases.

(C) As current decreases, power does not change.

(D) As current decreases, power increases.

847. Which of the following does not vary based on which particular switch is closed?

(A) Current through the motor

(B) Resistance

(C) Power output

(D) Voltage produced by the battery

848. What is most likely the total resistance in the circuit when Switch 1 is closed?

(A) 1 ohms

(B) 2 ohms

(C) 3 ohms

(D) 4 ohms

849. A student wants to create the circuit below. Which two resistors should he use to minimize the power output from the motor?

(A) R1 and R2

(B) R3 and R2

(C) R3 and R4

(D) R2 and R5

850. What are the dependent variables measured when the experimenter closes each switch?

(A) Voltage and power

(B) Power and resistance

(C) Resistance and current

(D) Current and power

851. What is the relationship between total resistance and current? As resistance:

(A) increases, current increases.

(B) increases, current does not change.

(C) decreases, current decreases.

(D) decreases, current increases.

Questions 852–857 are based on the following passage:

Biochemical enzymes are small proteins that help regulate the rate of chemical reactions in the body. They usually function by reducing the amount of energy needed to transition from reactant to product during a reaction. Enzyme kinetics investigates how quickly products are created from reactants in the presence of an enzyme. A typical enzyme kinetics graph, as shown in Figure 1, displays how reaction rate (V, in mol/s) changes with substrate (the molecule to which the enzyme binds) concentration, [S].

Figure 1

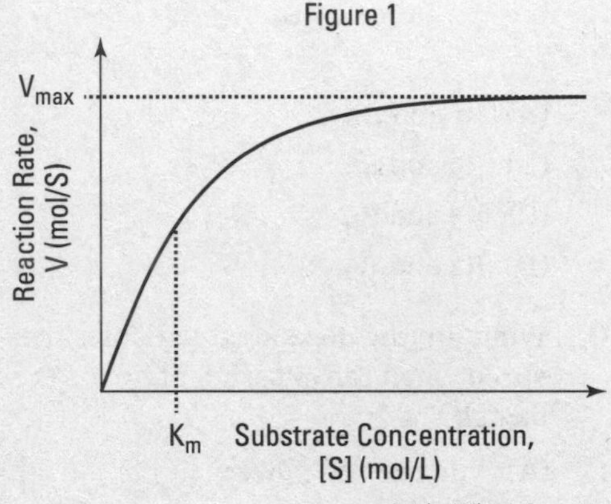

Other salient points on an enzyme kinetics graph include V_{max} and K_m,V_{max} is simply the point at which adding more substrate will not change the reaction rate. K_m is the point at which the reaction rate reaches $\frac{V_{max}}{2}$. A lower K_m corresponds to an enzyme that has more affinity for its substrate. A pharmaceutical company is testing a new medication to help replace the almylase enzyme, which binds to and breaks down carbohydrates in the digestive tract. The company tests four new versions of the drug in the lab and records the data in Table 1.

TABLE 1

Drug Version	K_m (mol/L)	V_{max} (mol/s)
A	10	6
B	35	12
C	20	15
D	8	21

852. Which drug version results in the highest possible reaction rate?

(A) A

(B) B

(C) C

(D) D

853. Which amylase has the lowest affinity for carbohydrates?

(A) A

(B) B

(C) C

(D) D

854. Most of the time, the concentration of unprocessed carbohydrates in the digestive tract is low. Of the available drugs, which one will function best at lowest concentrations of carbohydrates?

(A) A

(B) B

(C) C

(D) D

855. During competitive inhibition, chemicals that are not involved with the reaction interfere with the binding of true substrate to the enzyme. Drug A is tested with and without a competitive inhibitor and the following kinetic graph is generated. Based on the graph, what is the effect of competitive inhibitors if a solid line indicates Drug A tested with a competitive inhibitor and the dashed line indicates Drug A tested without? The presence of a competitive inhibitor

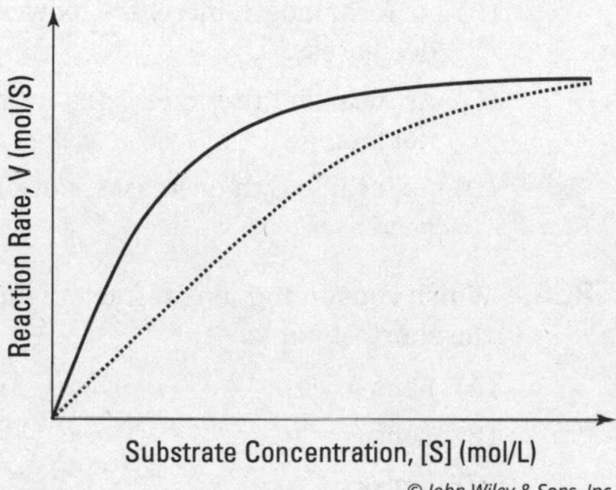

© John Wiley & Sons, Inc.

(A) decreases maximum reaction rate

(B) increases maximum reaction rate

(C) increases K_m

(D) decreases K_m

856. Based on Figure 1, what is the effect of adding more substrate to a reaction? Adding more substrate causes

(A) an increase in reaction rate

(B) increase V_{max}

(C) increase K_m

(D) change in reaction energy

857. Patients with Phenylketonuria (PKU) have a mutated form of the enzyme phenylalanine hydroxylase, which breaks down the protein phenylalanine (Phe). The mutated enzyme cannot break down Phe, and it builds up in organs such as the brain, where it can cause intellectual disability. The mutated form of phenylalanine hydroxylase likely has

(A) increased K_m, and increased V_{max}

(B) decreased K_m and decreased V_{max}

(C) increased K_m and decreased V_{max}

(D) decreased K_m and increased V_{max}

Questions 858–863 are based on the following passage:

Lenses are used every day for items such as glasses, telescopes, and lasers. Lenses work by refracting light in a controlled manner to create an image. There are two basic types of lenses, converging and diverging. Diverging (convex) lenses are thicker in the middle and bend light inward (toward their center) as shown in Figure 1.

Figure 1

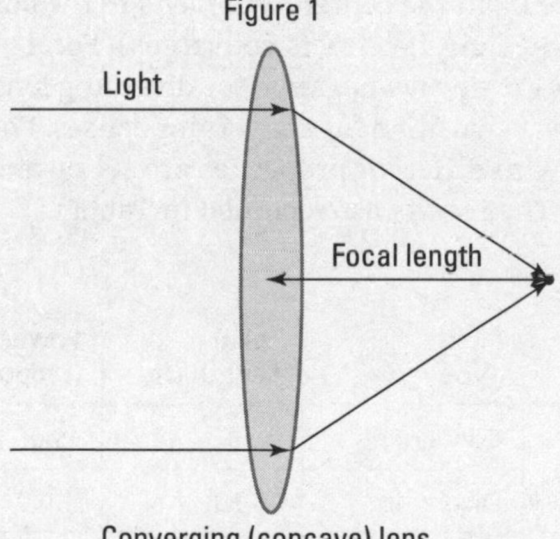

Converging (concave) lens

© John Wiley & Sons, Inc.

Diverging (concave) lenses are thinner in the middle and bend light outward (away from the center) as shown in Figure 2.

Figure 2

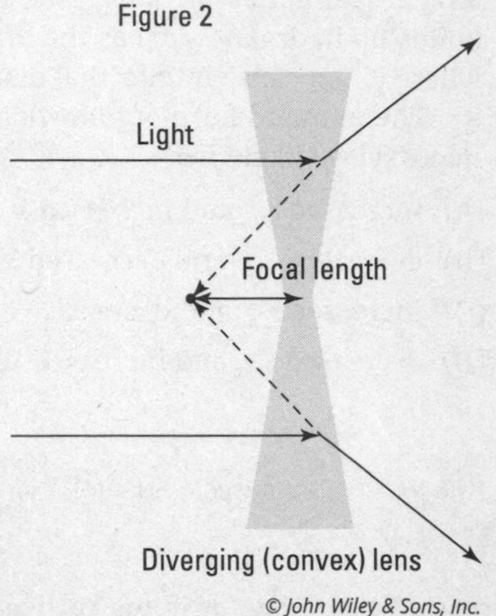

Diverging (convex) lens

© John Wiley & Sons, Inc.

The strength of a lens is measured by its power. Power is calculated by the following equation:

$$P = \frac{1}{f}$$

In the equation, *f* is the lens's focal length (the distance from the center of the lens to the point where the light it refracts converges). Focal lengths are always negative for diverging lenses and always positive for converging lenses. Four lenses with different properties are set up and tested. The results are recorded in Table 1.

TABLE 1

Lens	Type	Focal Length (f)	Power (Diopter)
A	Converging	0.10	10.0
B	Diverging	–0.10	–10.0
C	Converging	0.30	3.33
D	Diverging	–0.40	–2.50

858. Which of the four lens types is/are concave?

(A) Lens A only

(B) Lens B only

(C) Lenses A and C

(D) Lenses B and D

859. What is the relationship between the absolute value of power and the absolute value of focal length?

(A) As focal length increases, power increases.

(B) As focal length increases, power decreases.

(C) As focal length increases, power does not change.

(D) As focal length decreases, power decreases.

860. Which converging lens refracts light at the shortest angle?

(A) Lens A

(B) Lens B

(C) Lens C

(D) Lens D

861. When two lenses are placed right next to each other, their power increases. Which combination of lenses would result in the shortest overall focal length?

(A) Lenses A and B

(B) Lenses A and D

(C) Lenses C and D

(D) Lenses C and A

862. The human eye uses a lens to focus incoming light directly onto the retina. When the focal length of the lens is too short, the resulting condition is called myopia. Which of the following is true about the myopic human eye?

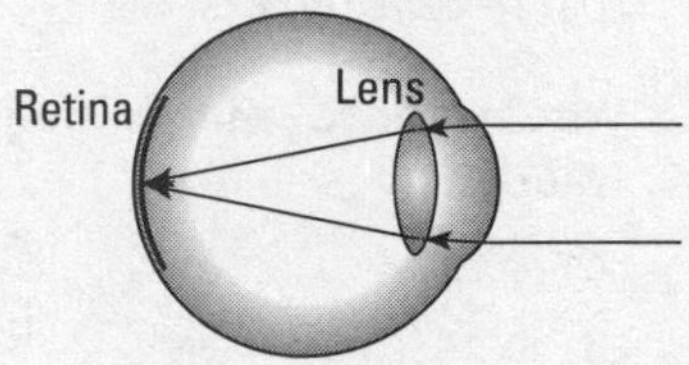

© John Wiley & Sons, Inc.

(A) The lens is too strong, and the focal point is in front of the retina.

(B) The lens is too weak, and the focal point is in front of the retina.

(C) The lens is too strong, and the focal point is behind the retina.

(D) The lens is too weak, and the focal point is behind the retina.

863. When the focal length of the human eye lens is too long, the resulting condition is called hyperopia. What type of lens should be used to correct a hyperopic eye?

(A) Diverging

(B) Concave

(C) Convex

(D) Either concave or convex

Questions 864–869 are based on the following passage:

Thin layer chromatography (TLC) is a popular laboratory technique in organic chemistry for separating chemicals of different polarities. In TLC, a strip of glass coated in a polar substrate is placed vertically into a liquid solvent. As shown in Figure 1, a small amount of the chemical solution is dabbed near the bottom of the strip, where it meets the solvent. As the solvent is drawn up the strip, it pulls the test solution along with it.

Figure 1

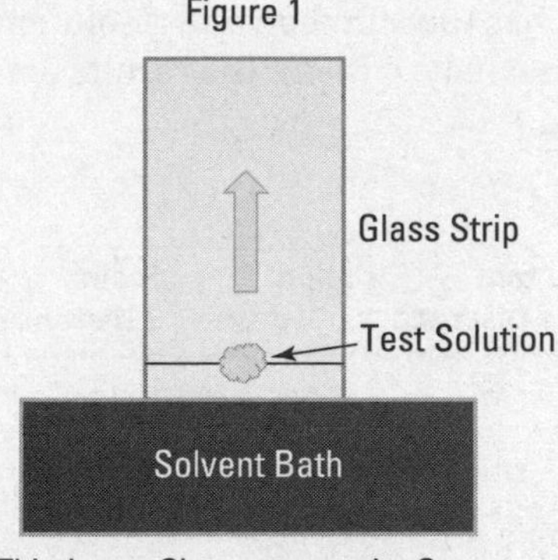

Thin Layer Chromatography Setup

© John Wiley & Sons, Inc.

Polar molecules in the test solution interact more strongly with the polar substrate on the glass than nonpolar molecules. Therefore, polar molecules move more slowly than nonpolar ones. In this way, the chemical constituents of a test solution of many components can be separated.

After the strip runs for a set amount of time, it is removed and the components of the test solution can be visualized as different stains along the strip as demonstrated in Figure 2.

Figure 2

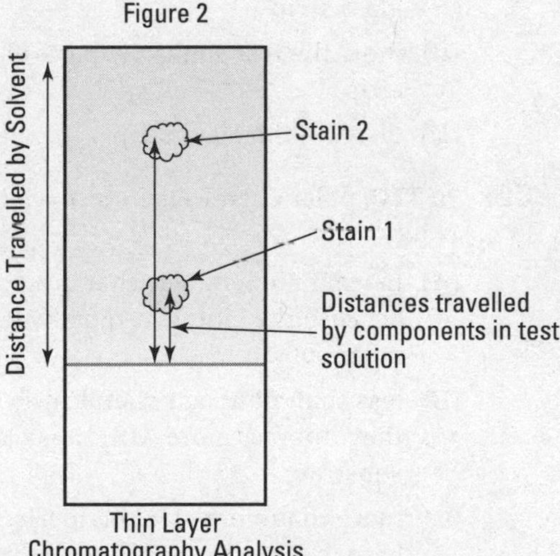

Thin Layer Chromatography Analysis

© John Wiley & Sons, Inc.

To calculate the retention factor (R_f), the distance of each stain from the bottom is compared to how far the solvent travelled. The equation for R_f value is

$$R_f = \frac{\text{distance of stain}}{\text{distance of solvent}}$$

A chemist has four unknown test solutions and uses TLC to analyze them. His results are provided in Table 1.

TABLE 1

Test Solution	Stain 1 Distance	Stain 2 Distance	Stain 3 Distance	Solvent Distance
1	3 cm	8 cm	0 cm	20 cm
2	5 cm	7 cm	0 cm	20 cm
3	5 cm	10 cm	12 cm	20 cm
4	10 cm	15 cm	18 cm	20 cm

864. How many different chemicals of different polarities were present in test solution 1?

(A) 1

(B) 2

(C) 3

(D) 4

865. The purpose of the solvent bath in TLC is to

(A) keep the test solution cold

(B) interact with the polar coating of the glass strip

(C) draw the test solution up the glass strip

(D) dissolve the glass strip

866. In TLC, polar chemicals in test solutions travel

(A) more than nonpolar chemicals because they interact more with the polar substrate

(B) less than nonpolar chemicals because they interact more with the polar substrate

(C) more than nonpolar chemicals because they interact less with the polar substrate.

(D) the same distance as nonpolar chemicals because they interact less with the polar substrate

867. How far did the most nonpolar chemical in test solution 4 travel in the experiment?

(A) 8 centimeters

(B) 10 centimeters

(C) 15 centimeters

(D) 18 centimeters

868. What is the R_f value of stain 1 in test solution 2?

(A) 0.10

(B) 0.25

(C) 0.50

(D) 0.75

869. Which test solution contained the most polar chemical?

(A) 1

(B) 2

(C) 3

(D) 4

870. Which of these combinations of polarity and solvents would lead to the highest R_f value?

(A) very polar test solution; fast moving solvent

(B) somewhat polar test solution; fast moving solvent

(C) nonpolar test solution; slow moving solvent

(D) nonpolar test solution; fast moving solvent

Questions 871–876 are based on the following passage

Schizophrenia is a mental disorder that affects 24 million people across the world. It is characterized by symptoms such as confused thinking, hallucinations, cognitive decline, abnormal perception of reality, and reduced social activity. These symptoms are managed with anti-psychotic medications, but few that suffer from schizophrenia fully recover. The neurological underpinnings of schizophrenia are not well understood. There are a variety of anatomical and functional changes that have been observed in patients, including reduced frontal lobe volume, overactive D_2 dopamine receptors, and enlarged lateral ventricles. However, there is significant debate as to what causes these changes.

Environmental Hypothesis

One theory about schizophrenia is that environmental factors influence its development. For example, it has been found that people that grow up in with abusive parents or experience a childhood trauma have a significantly elevated risk for developing schizophrenia. Cannabis use has also been linked to the disease in those who are already at risk. Lastly, the environment that a developing fetus is exposed to in utero has been found to correlate to the disease. Fetuses that experienced periods of infection, hypoxia (low oxygen), or malnutrition are more likely to become schizophrenic later in life.

Genetic Hypothesis

It is also theorized that genetics plays a large role in the development of schizophrenia. Its heritability (how much of an influence genetics has in the development of a particular trait) has been estimated to be as high as 80%. Furthermore, having a first-degree relative affected by schizophrenia increases risk significantly. Studies have revealed that mutations in dysbindin and neuregulin genes may be important in these inheritance patterns.

871. According to the environmental hypothesis, the most likely person to develop schizophrenia is someone who

(A) has a biological parent with schizophrenia

(B) has a brother with schizophrenia

(C) was born to a mother who was infected with *C. trachomatis* during pregnancy

(D) was born to a mother who smoked cigarettes during pregnancy.

872. Schizophrenia is more likely to occur in children who have parents with the disease. Which of the following, if true, would provide a justification for this occurrence for a scientist who holds to the environmental hypothesis?

(A) Genetic material that contains a propensity toward schizophrenia is passed down from the parents to the children.

(B) Schizophrenic parents have a higher incidence of abusive parenting methods than do parents who do not have the disease.

(C) Children born in the 21st century are more likely to use cannabis products.

(D) Once they are born, children of schizophrenics are exposed to many infections.

873. There is likely a consensus between the environmental and genetic hypotheses about

(A) how the disease is transmitted

(B) whether cannabis increases the risk for contracting the disease

(C) the role of the dysbindin gene in contracting the disease

(D) the types of anatomical changes in the brain that cause the disease

874. The mutated dysbindin phenotype is inherited in an autosomal recessive fashion. If a man displaying the phenotype has children with a woman carrying (but not displaying) the mutation allele, what proportion of their children would display the mutated phenotype?

(A) 0

(B) $\frac{1}{4}$

(C) $\frac{1}{2}$

(D) $\frac{3}{4}$

875. Recently, scientists have thought that schizophrenia is most likely caused by a combination of environmental and genetic factors. Which of the following statements, if true, would provide the best evidence for this combined theory?

(A) Schizophrenia is found to occur most often in those older than 15.

(B) Schizophrenia occurs most often in those who experienced a childhood trauma and have mutations in the neuregulin gene.

(C) Not all those who use cannabis develop schizophrenia.

(D) D_2 dopamine receptors are found to be more overactive in those who have mutations in dysbindin.

876. Which combination of statements best characterizes a component of each hypothesis?

(A) Environmental: Malnutrition *in utero* is linked to schizophrenia.
Genetic: Enlarged lateral ventricles cause schizophrenia.

(B) Environmental: Enlarged lateral ventricles cause schizophrenia.
Genetic: Dysregulin mutations are heritable factors in schizophrenia.

(C) Environmental: Increased cannabis use causes overactive D_2 receptors.
Genetic: Parents with schizophrenia are more likely to have children with the disease.

(D) Environmental: Malnutrition *in utero* is linked to schizophrenia.
Genetic: Dysbindin mutations are heritable factors in schizophrenia.

Questions 877–882 are based on the following passage:

Diabetes is a disease that affects a person's ability to regulate the concentration of blood glucose. Chronic hyperglycemia (too much blood glucose) or hypoglycemia (too little blood glucose) can result in serious medical complications. Therefore, those with diabetes must keep track of their blood glucose. Many use a glucometer, a device that measures the amount of glucose in the blood. A small amount of blood (usually from the fingertip) is applied to a test strip, and after a few seconds, the concentration of glucose is displayed on the screen. The test strip contains two essential chemicals that react with the blood glucose, glucose oxidase and ferricyanide. The reaction follows these steps:

- Step 1: Glucose oxidase removes electrons from blood glucose.
- Step 2: The glucose oxidase donates the electrons it gained from the blood glucose to the ferricyanide.
- Step 3: The ferricyanide with its electrons (now known as ferrocyanide), donates its electrons to an electrode in the test strip.

- Step 4: The constant stream of electrons across the electrode creates an electric current.
- Step 5: The glucose meter senses the current.
- Step 6: Based on the amount of current, the glucose meter displays a corresponding concentration of glucose.

A scientist uses a similar procedure, taking blood with known levels of glucose and directly measuring the current across the electrode. The results are displayed in Figure 1.

Figure 1

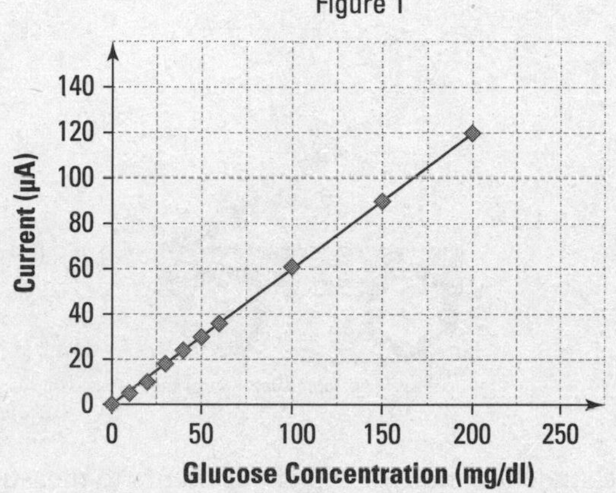

© John Wiley & Sons, Inc.

877. What is the variable directly measured by the test strip?

(A) current
(B) glucose concentration
(C) glucose oxidase concentration
(D) ferricyanide concentration

878. What is the relationship between glucose concentration and current? As glucose concentration:

(A) increases, current decreases.
(B) increases, current remains unchanged.
(C) increases, current increases.
(D) decreases, current increases.

879. Contamination by other molecules can affect the result of a glucose test. Based on this chart, which of the following molecules would most likely distort the test results?

Molecule	Electrons Donated to Glucose Oxidase
Glucose	2
Mannose	3
Fructose	1
Dextrose	4
Lactose	6

(A) mannose
(B) fructose
(C) dextrose
(D) lactose

880. Healthy blood glucose levels range from 80 to 100 mg/dl. What is the corresponding current range for healthy blood glucose levels?

(A) 10–100 μA
(B) 45–60 μA
(C) 80–100 μA
(D) 135–170 μA

881. When the pH of the blood decreases, the resultant blood glucose reading may be increased. Which of the following statements provides an explanation for this event?

(A) Decreased pH causes glucose to donate fewer electrons to glucose oxidase, resulting in a higher current and a higher glucose reading.

(B) Decreased pH causes glucose to donate more electrons to glucose oxidase, resulting in a higher current and a higher glucose reading.

(C) Decreased pH causes glucose to donate more electrons to glucose oxidase, resulting in a lower current and a higher glucose reading.

(D) Decreased pH causes glucose to donate more electrons to the electrode, resulting in a lower current and a higher glucose reading.

882. The chemical term for gaining electrons is *reduction*, while the chemical term for losing electrons is *oxidation*. Given the information provided by the passage, which of the following set of statements is true?

(A) Glucose is oxidized; glucose oxidase is reduced and oxidized.

(B) Glucose is reduced; glucose oxidase is only reduced.

(C) Glucose is oxidized; glucose oxidase is only oxidized.

(D) Glucose is reduced; glucose oxidase is reduced and oxidized.

Questions 883–889 are based on the following passage:

To launch tennis balls from varying angles and at different speeds, a student builds the catapult shown in Figure 1. The tennis ball is propelled out of the catapult with velocity V and angle θ.

Figure 1

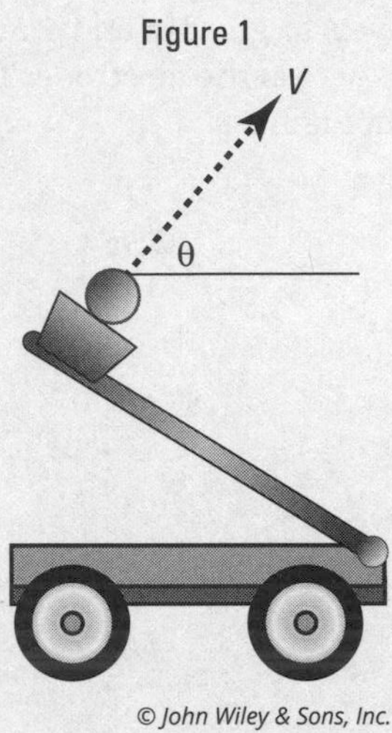

The student conducts two experiments to measure the distance between the launch site and where the ball lands.

Experiment 1

The student varies θ, launches the ball at a constant 15 m/s, and measures the distance travelled. The results are provided in Figure 2.

Figure 2

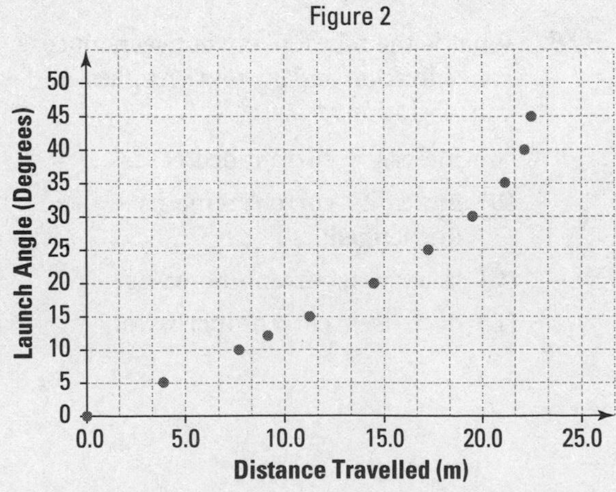

Experiment 2

In the second experiment, the student varies the launch velocity of the ball, launches it at a constant 45° angle, and measures the distance travelled. The measurements are recorded in Figure 3.

Figure 1

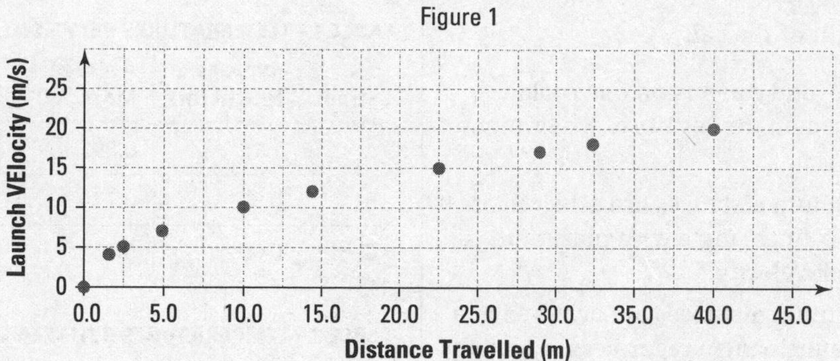

883. What is the dependent variable common to both experiments?

(A) Launch velocity

(B) Launch angle

(C) Distance travelled

(D) Height of tennis ball

884. Which launch angle achieved the maximum distance travelled?

(A) 10°

(B) 20°

(C) 35°

(D) 45°

885. Which combination of launch angle and launch velocity results in the greatest increase in distance travelled?

(A) 45° launch angle and increasing launch velocity from 5 m/s to 10 m/s

(B) 45° launch angle and increasing launch velocity from 10 m/s to 15 m/s

(C) 15 m/s launch velocity and increasing launch angle from 20° to 30°

(D) 15 m/s launch velocity and increasing launch angle from 10 degrees to 15 degrees

886. The student conducts a third experiment by repeating Experiment 2 but using a 30° launch angle. What would be the most likely result of this third experiment when compared to Experiment 2? The third experiment would result in

(A) greater distance travelled at each velocity tested

(B) less distance travelled for each velocity tested

(C) the same distance travelled for each velocity tested

(D) variable distances travelled depending on the velocity tested

887. Gravity acts equally on objects regardless of mass. The student launches a tennis ball of the same size but with twice the mass of the first ball tested. He uses a launch angle of 45° and a launch velocity of 15 m/s. What is the best estimate of the distance the ball will travel?

(A) Between 8 and 10 meters

(B) About 11 meters

(C) Between 12 and 18 meters

(D) About 22 meters

888. What is the independent variable in Experiment 1?

(A) Distance travelled

(B) Launch velocity

(C) Launch angle

(D) Weight of the ball

889. What is a valid conclusion one could reach based on the results of Experiments 1 and 2?

(A) Maximum distances are achieved at a 45° launch angle with maximum launch velocity.

(B) Maximum distances are achieved at a 45° launch angle regardless of launch velocity.

(C) Maximum distances are achieved at a 35° launch angle with maximum launch velocity.

(D) Maximum distances are achieved at a 35° launch angle regardless of launch velocity.

Questions 890–895 are based on the following passage.

Climate change poses risks for the future of agriculture. Increases in global temperatures, atmospheric CO_2 and acidic rain will affect crop health and output. To test the hardiness of plants against these changes, an agricultural scientist conducts a series of experiments in carefully controlled greenhouses.

Experiment 1

A team of scientists planted three strains of wheat in the first greenhouse. They set the temperature to fluctuate between 65° and 80° Fahrenheit, which are the average night and day ground temperatures in many wheat-producing areas. In the second greenhouse, they planted the same three strains of wheat in the same soil with the same nutrients but increased the temperature fluctuation to between 75° and 90° Fahrenheit. Over the same five-month growing season, each greenhouse received the same amount of water daily. Throughout the season, the scientists observed plant height, mass, and survival rate for each greenhouse. At the end of the season, they reported the final data in Tables 1 and 2.

TABLE 1 – TEMPERATURES BETWEEN 65° AND 80°F

Strain	Average Height (m)	Average Mass (kg)	% plant survival throughout season
A	1.10	0.89	95%
B	0.90	0.77	92%
C	0.90	0.75	90%

TABLE 2 – TEMPERATURES BETWEEN 75° AND 90°F

Strain	Average Height (m)	Average Mass (kg)	% plant survival throughout season
A	0.90	0.69	75%
B	0.70	0.57	70%
C	0.80	0.65	80%

Experiment 2

The scientists repeated Experiment 1, but instead of varying temperature, they varied the pH of the water used to irrigate the wheat. With ground temperatures ranging between 65° and 80° Fahrenheit, the first greenhouse received water with a normal pH (pH = 5.6). The second greenhouse received the same temperature settings, but the water used to hydrate the plants had a lower pH (pH = 4.2). Throughout the growing season, the scientists observed plant height, mass, and survival rate for each greenhouse. At the end of the season, they reported the final data in Tables 3 and 4.

TABLE 3 – WATER WITH PH = 5.6

Strain	Average Height (m)	Average Mass (kg)	% plant survival throughout season
A	1.10	0.89	95%
B	0.90	0.77	92%
C	0.90	0.75	90%

TABLE 4 – WATER WITH PH = 4.2

Strain	Average Height (m)	Average Mass (kg)	% plant survival throughout season
A	0.71	0.59	65%
B	0.69	0.47	50%
C	0.80	0.65	80%

890. What was the independent variable in Experiment 1?

(A) Average height

(B) Average mass

(C) Percent survival through season

(D) Temperature

891. What was the effect of increasing temperature in Experiment 1? When temperature was increased

(A) plant height decreased and plant survival increased

(B) plant height increased and plant mass decreased

(C) plant height decreased and plant mass increased

(D) plant height decreased and plant survival decreased

892. Which plant strain or strains were least affected by changes in water pH?

(A) strain A

(B) strain B

(C) strain C

(D) Both strains A and B

893. Which chart best summarizes the results for the second greenhouse in Experiment 1?

(A)

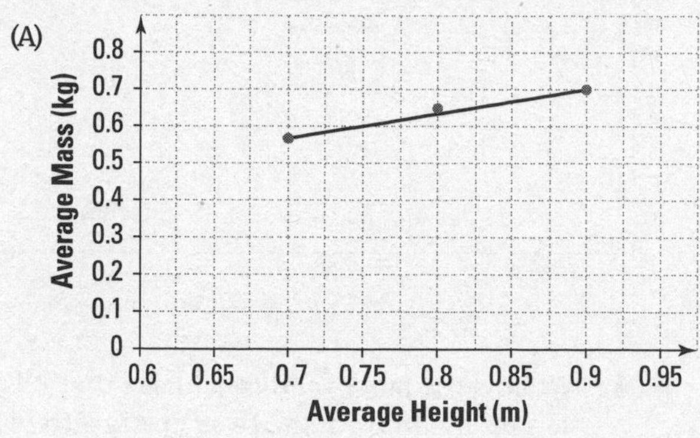

© John Wiley & Sons, Inc.

(B)

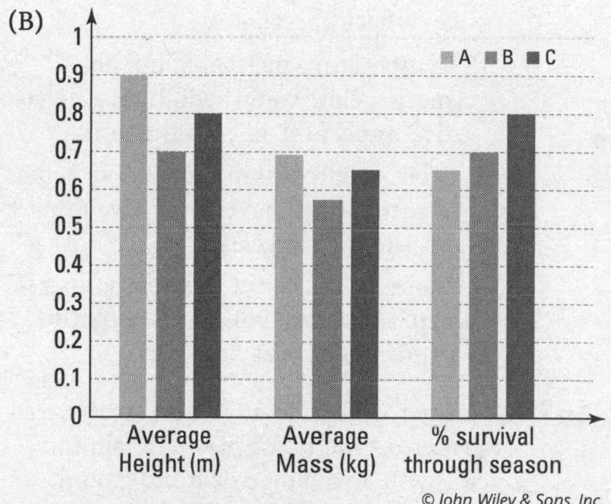

© John Wiley & Sons, Inc.

(C)

Average Height (m)

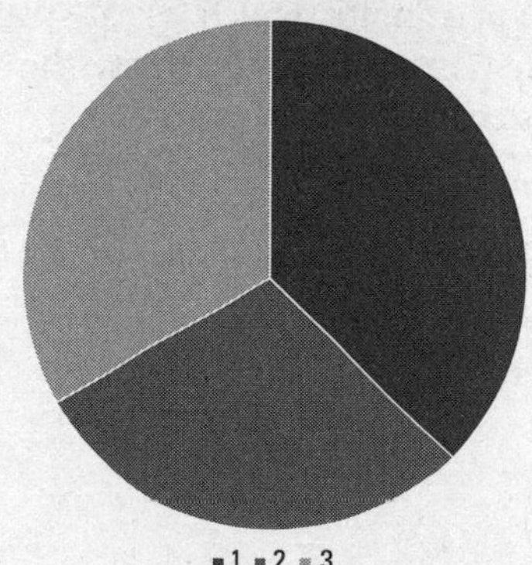

© John Wiley & Sons, Inc.

(D)

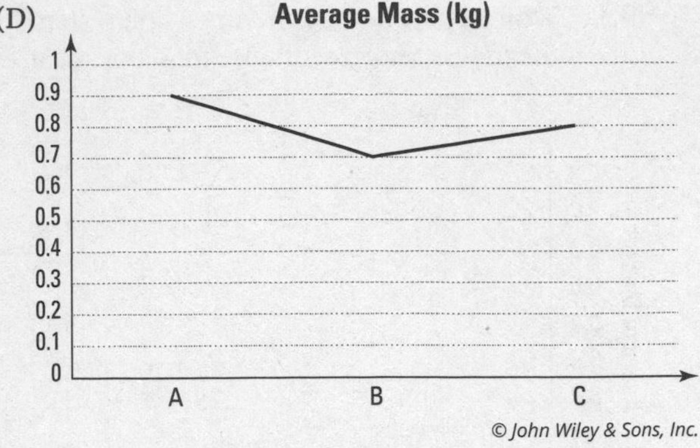

894. What is the most valid conclusion that can be drawn from the two experiments?

(A) More-acidic water and warmer temperatures will have a negative impact on wheat harvests.

(B) Temperature increases, but not more-acidic water, will have a negative impact on all crop harvests.

(C) More-acidic water and warmer temperatures will have a negative impact on all crop harvests.

(D) More-acidic water, but not temperature increases, will have a negative impact on wheat harvests.

895. A farmer lives in an area that is predicted to receive 3 inches of pH = 4.2 rain this year, with an average daytime ground temperature of 80° degrees. The farmer does not anticipate any issues with insects or pests. Based on the results of the two experiments, which wheat strain should the farmer plant to achieve the highest survival rate?

(A) Strain A

(B) Strain B

(C) Strain C

(D) Either Strain A or B

Questions 896–900 are based on the following passage:

Transformation is an important technique in molecular biology through which a short piece of circular bacterial DNA (called a plasmid) is incorporated into a bacterial strain. The bacteria of interest is treated with high concentrations of calcium ions to open small pores in the bacterial membrane. Then, the plasmid containing the gene of interest is applied to the bacteria. This plasmid, in addition to the gene of interest, may also contain a "reporter gene." This gene usually codes for a fluorescent or colorful protein that indicates that the plasmid has been successfully incorporated into the bacteria's genome.

A scientist is hoping to study the effect of a plasmid that has been thought to confer resistance to the antibiotic *ampicillin*. The scientist conducts the following experiments.

Experiment 1

The scientist used the standard transformation procedure to apply a plasmid to a stain of the *e. coli* bacteria. This plasmid contained a gene thought to confer resistance to the antibiotic *ampicillin*, as well as a reporter gene, known as GFP, that glows green under UV light. The scientist applied this strain of *e. coli* to a petri dish (dish 1) containing growth medium. In a separate dish (dish 2) containing only growth medium, the scientist applied normal *e. coli* that has not been transformed. The scientist allowed the bacteria to grow over a period of two days and recorded the results in Table 1.

TABLE 1

Dish	Contains	Total Area of Growth
1	Plasmid + growth medium	35.0 cm^2
2	No plasmid + growth medium	35.1 cm^2

Experiment 2

The scientist used the standard transformation procedure to apply a plasmid to a stain of the *e. coli* bacteria. This plasmid contained the antibiotic resistance gene and the GFP gene. The scientist applied this strain of *e. coli* to a petri dish (dish 3) containing growth medium and the antibiotic, *ampicillin.* In a separate dish (dish 4) containing *ampicillin* and growth medium, the scientist applied normal *e. coli* that has not been transformed. The scientist allowed the bacteria to grow over a period of two days and recorded the results in Table 2.

TABLE 2

Dish	Contains	Total Area of Growth	Glow under UV?
3	Plasmid + growth medium + ampicillin	17.5 cm^2	Yes
4	No plasmid + growth medium + ampicillin	0.0 cm^2	No

896. What is the main difference between the two experiments?

(A) Only Experiment 2 *e. coli* were transformed with the antibiotic resistance plasmid.

(B) Experiment 1 *e. coli* grew for a longer period of time than *e. coli* in Experiment 2.

(C) Experiment 2 *e. coli* plates contained an antibiotic; in Experiment 1 the plates did not.

(D) Only Experiment 1 *e. coli* had plasmids containing GFP.

897. What was the independent variable in Experiment 1?

(A) Total area of growth

(B) Glow under UV light

(C) Length of growth period

(D) Presence of plasmid in bacteria

898. What was the purpose of the GFP protein in the experiment? The GFP protein was included to

(A) confer antibiotic resistance

(B) signal successful transformation of the bacteria

(C) increase growth potential of *e. coli*

(D) help incorporate the plasmid into the bacterial genome

899. Comparison of which two dishes shows that the plasmid makes *e. coli* resistant to ampicillin?

(A) 1 and 3

(B) 2 and 4

(C) 1 and 2

(D) 3 and 4

900. Assuming the bacteria on dishes 1 and 2 grew to their full potential, and the same total number of bacteria were placed on each dish initially, approximately what percent of bacteria placed in dish 3 successfully incorporated the plasmid into their genome?

(A) 25%

(B) 50%

(C) 75%

(D) 100%

Questions 901–907 are based on the following information.

Low- or no-carbohydrate diets have risen and fallen in popularity in recent years. Low-carbohydrate diets are based on the belief that the main cause of obesity is eating refined carbohydrates, most notably sugar, flour, and high-fructose corn syrup. Followers of low-carbohydrate diets restrict their carbohydrate intake in order to help switch the body's metabolism from burning glucose as fuel to burning stored body fat. This process starts when insulin levels are low, typically before eating. Conversely, high-calorie carbohydrates impact the body by increasing the amount of sugar in the blood following a meal. Two scientists discuss the safety and effectiveness of a low-carbohydrate diet.

Scientist 1

Any diet that condones unlimited consumption of bacon, eggs, and butter cannot be considered healthy for the human body. Not one major governmental or science-based organization in the world argues in support of the low-carbohydrate diet and its encouragement of unrestricted amounts of meat. The theories behind low-carbohydrate dieting are based upon poorly controlled and administered studies and unsubstantiated rhetoric. The risks inherent with a high-protein, low-carbohydrate diet, such as heart disease and additional concerns for individuals suffering from gout or kidney disorder, are not worth the short-term weight loss that may occur.

Scientist 2

Simply put, a low-carbohydrate intake leads to increased fat burning. Lowering carbohydrate consumption and increasing protein intake forces the body to utilize existing stored fat as fuel for the body because one is not getting fuel through the consumption of food. Most low-carbohydrate diets are designed not only for short-term use and effectiveness but also to coincide with nutritional supplementation to ensure that the body remains in a healthy balance.

901. Both Scientist 1 and Scientist 2 would consider a primary component of low-carbohydrate dieting to be:

(A) lowering the body's metabolism.

(B) increasing fat burning.

(C) raising one's intake of protein.

(D) placing oneself at risk for heart disease.

902. With which of the following statements about low-carbohydrate diets would both Scientist 1 and Scientist 2 most likely agree?

(A) Low-carbohydrate dieting poses serious health risks.

(B) Whether nutritional supplementation is necessary should be determined on a case-by-case basis.

(C) It is a bad idea to consume large amounts of bacon, eggs, and butter.

(D) Short-term weight loss is a likely result.

903. Scientist 1's argument presupposes which of the following?

(A) The health benefits of weight loss are not sufficient to overcome the risks associated with a low-carbohydrate diet.

(B) Most of the people who begin a low-carbohydrate diet suffer from gout or kidney disease.

(C) The risks of a low-carbohydrate diet can be minimized by the use of nutritional supplements.

(D) Obesity is caused by eating unlimited amounts of meat.

904. Scientist 2 claims that with a low-carbohydrate diet, the body does not get fuel from consuming food. If this statement is true, which of these statements must also be true?

(A) Scientist 2 does not consider glucose to be food.

(B) Protein consumption does not fuel the body.

(C) Scientist 2 believes that heart disease is caused by the body's not getting enough food.

(D) A person on a low-carbohydrate diet experiences profound starvation.

905. Given that all the following statements are true, which would provide the most effective argument against the assertion of Scientist 1?

(A) There is a positive correlation between consuming large amounts of meat and developing certain kinds of cancer.

(B) The consumption of high-fiber carbohydrates has been found to promote good digestive health.

(C) A healthy diet relies on broad consumption of varying types of food, including both carbohydrates and proteins.

(D) A recent study has shown that eating protein makes a person feel fuller faster than eating carbohydrates, which means that people who consume primarily protein tend to eat significantly less than those who eat less protein.

906. Which of the following statements about low-carbohydrate diets is most consistent with the view of Scientist 2?

(A) People who eat a low-carbohydrate diet without taking nutritional supplements are putting themselves at risk for kidney disease.

(B) There are some studies that show that eating unrestricted amounts of meat for a short period of time does not cause adverse health issues.

(C) By observing proper precautions, most people can receive health benefits from eating a low-carbohydrate diet.

(D) More heart disease is caused by obesity than by eating unlimited amounts of meat.

907. Based on the information in the passage, eating which of the following would most likely prevent the body from burning fat as fuel?

(A) Sugar cookie

(B) Slice of Canadian bacon

(C) Pat of butter

(D) Cheese omelet

Questions 908–913 are based on the following information.

Body Mass Index, or BMI, is a tool used to determine whether an individual is at a healthy weight relative to height, assuming that the individual has an average body type and is more than 20 years of age. Calculating BMI has grown in popularity as an effective factor in determining whether one is over or underweight or obese. Professionals calculate Body Mass Index using this formula:

$$BMI = \frac{weight(kg)}{height^2(m^2)}$$

Individuals may be categorized depending on their BMI figures. BMI figures and their corresponding categories are represented in Table 1. To determine the BMI of its patients, a clinic took the measurements of four adult patients and recorded the information in Table 2.

TABLE 1

BMI Range	Category
< 18.5	Underweight
18.5 - 24.9	Healthy
25 - 29.9	Overweight
> 30	Obese

TABLE 2

	Height in Meters	Weight in Kg	BMI
Julia	1.73	77.30	25.83
Brian	1.78	77.30	24.4
Corbin	1.42	32.70	16.1
Tawny	1.68	85.50	30.3

908. According to standard BMI measurements, which of the patients listed in Table 2 maintains the healthiest weight?

(A) Julia

(B) Brian

(C) Corbin

(D) Tawny

909. An individual with a height of 1.70 meters who weighs 85.7 kilograms would fall into which of these categories?

(A) Underweight

(B) Healthy weight

(C) Overweight

(D) Obese

910. Which of the following sets of measurements is most likely from an individual who falls into the underweight category?

(A) 17.3 m; 77.3 kg

(B) 1.85 m; 90.9 kg

(C) 1.45 m; 38.6 kg

(D) 1.42 m; 55 kg

911. If Julia were to lose 10 percent of her body weight, her new BMI would place her in the category of:

(A) underweight.

(B) healthy.

(C) overweight.

(D) obese.

912. Which of the following relationships is correct? BMI increases as:

(A) height decreases.

(B) weight decreases.

(C) height only increases.

(D) both height and weight increase.

913. A factor that could hinder deriving an accurate BMI result from the table is:

(A) waist circumference.

(B) overall health.

(C) nationality.

(D) age.

Questions 914–920 are based on the following information.

While most organisms perform aerobic cellular respiration (ACR), only plants (known as primary producers) engage in photosynthesis. The process of photosynthesis uses light energy to take in carbon dioxide (CO^2) and give out oxygen (O^2). In very simple terms, the process of ACR takes in O^2 and gives out CO^2 and energy. No animals (also known as consumers) or protists (some of which can be decomposers) engage in photosynthesis. Table 1 classifies a few organisms by type.

TABLE 1

Organism	Type
Moss	Nonvascular plant
Slime molds	Protist
Sponge	Animal
Fish	Animal
Rose	Vascular plant
Mushroom	Protist
Spider	Animal

One of the organisms listed in Table 1 was isolated and sealed in a large container in a laboratory with windows open to the outside. The organism was given the basic nutrients it needed to survive. Researchers monitored the concentrations of CO^2 and O^2 in the container over the course of 24 hours. The graph in Figure 1 shows the results of the measurements.

Figure 1

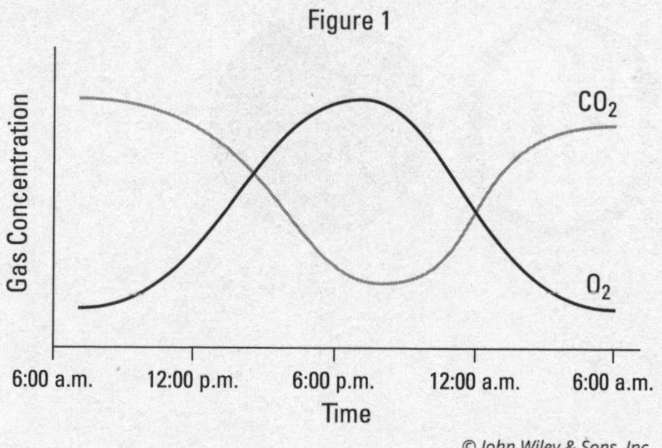

© John Wiley & Sons, Inc.

914. The most likely explanation for the event that occurred at 6:00 p.m. is that the:

(A) organism in the container fell asleep.

(B) organism in the container died.

(C) lights in the laboratory were turned off and the sun set.

(D) container started to leak.

915. Which of the following is a complete list of organisms from Table 1 that do NOT perform photosynthesis?

(A) Sponge, fish, spider

(B) Moss, slime molds, rose, mushroom

(C) Slime molds, sponge, fish, mushroom, spider

(D) Moss, rose

916. According to the passage, which of the organisms listed in the table do NOT require O^2 to produce energy?

(A) Moss

(B) Mushroom

(C) Fish

(D) All listed organisms likely require O^2.

917. What is most likely true about the organism in the container?

(A) It can perform only photosynthesis.

(B) It can perform photosynthesis and ACR.

(C) It can perform only ACR.

(D) It can perform neither photosynthesis nor ACR.

918. The organism in the container most likely functions as:

(A) a primary producer.

(B) a consumer.

(C) a decomposer.

(D) something other than a primary producer, consumer, or decomposer.

919. The organism in the container is most likely:

(A) moss.

(B) a mushroom.

(C) a sponge.

(D) slime mold.

920. If the researchers kept the organism in the container with the basic nutrients necessary for the organism's survival and moved the container to a room with no windows or doors open to the outside and no source of electricity, the likely result would be that:

(A) The CO^2 and O^2 levels would remain stable for the full 24-hour period.

(B) The CO^2 levels would increase a little and the O^2 levels would decrease a little.

(C) The O^2 levels would increase significantly and the CO^2 levels would decrease significantly.

(D) The results of the experiments would be the same as those of the original experiment.

Questions 920–927 are based on the following information.

A student studied the effectiveness of certain antibiotics in killing bacteria.

Experiment 1

The student placed a culture of unknown bacteria on four different Petri dishes, each of which contained a high-nutrient medium. Small paper circles were soaked with two different antibiotics. Paper circles marked with an "A" were soaked in penicillin. Paper disks marked with a "B" were soaked in erythromycin. A single "A" disk was placed in Petri Dish 1, a single "B" disk was placed in Petri Dish 2, and Petri Dish 3 received one "A" and one "B" disk. Petri Dish 4 did not contain a paper disk. The bacteria were then allowed to grow for 24 hours. Figure 1 shows the patterns of bacterial growth (indicated by the dark shaded areas) on each of the Petri dishes. The lightly shaded circles in the figure represent the antibiotic-soaked disks

Figure 1

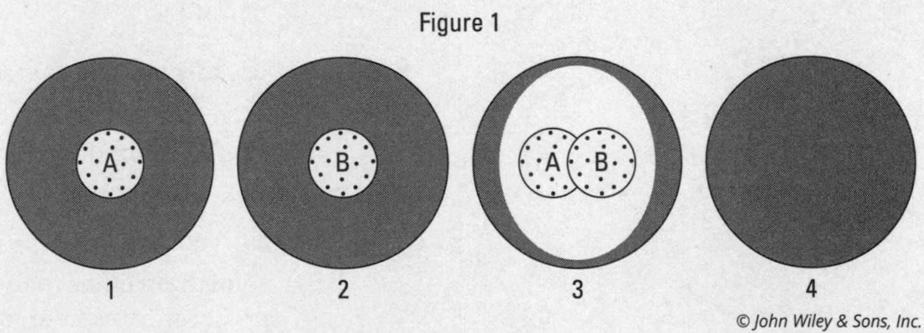

Experiment 2

The student then took some of the bacteria from Petri Dish 1 and placed it in new Petri Dish 5 with a "B" disk and took some of the bacteria from Petri Dish 2 and placed it in a new Petri Dish 6 with an "A" disk. The results of the bacteria growth in these dishes after 24 hours are represented in Figure 2.

Figure 2

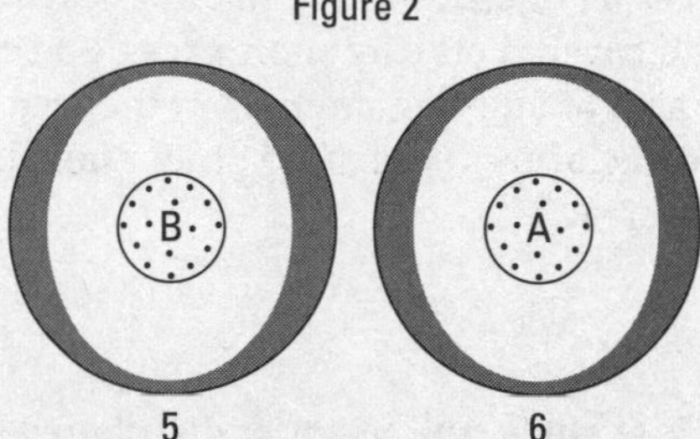

© John Wiley & Sons, Inc.

921. Which of the dishes in Experiment 1 represented the control?

(A) Dish 1

(B) Dish 2

(C) Dish 3

(D) Dish 4

922. Which of the following provides the best explanation for the inclusion of the high-nutrient medium in the four dishes?

(A) The medium is necessary to encourage bacteria growth.

(B) The medium is necessary to inhibit bacteria growth.

(C) The medium is necessary to encourage an increase in the amount of the antibiotic.

(D) The medium is necessary to encourage a decrease in the amount of the antibiotic.

923. Another effective control for Experiment 1 would be:

(A) a dish with bacteria and a paper disk that has been soaked in a third antibiotic such as streptomycin.

(B) a dish with bacteria and a paper disk that has not been soaked in any substance.

(C) a dish with bacteria and a paper disk that has been soaked in bleach.

(D) a dish with no bacteria.

924. Which of the following is the best explanation for the results of the two experiments?

(A) Erythromycin and penicillin have the same effect on the bacteria in the petri dishes.

(B) The bacteria are immune to both penicillin and erythromycin.

(C) Specific bacteria in the culture are immune to either penicillin or erythromycin but not both simultaneously.

(D) Dishes 1 and 2 must be contaminated with a substance that promotes bacteria growth.

925. Which of the following best describes the relationship between Experiment 1 and Experiment 2?

(A) Experiment 2 provides results that contradict the results of Experiment 1.

(B) The results of Experiment 2 provide further proof for a conclusion reached by Experiment 1.

(C) Experiment 2 results in information that is unrelated to the results of Experiment 1.

(D) Experiments 1 and 2 use completely different methods to reach the same conclusion.

926. Studies show that erythromycin is one of the only antibiotics effective in the treatment of infections of the prostate gland, penicillin is effective against most forms of meningitis, erythromycin is not effective against meningitis, and both antibiotics are effectively used to kill *Staphylococcus*. Based on the results of Experiment 2, it is reasonable to conclude that:

(A) the bacteria in Dish 1 at the end of Experiment 1 are of the type that causes prostate gland infections.

(B) the bacteria in Dish 2 at the end of Experiment 1 are of the type that causes meningitis.

(C) neither the bacteria in Dish 1 nor the bacteria in Dish 2 at the end of Experiment 1 are *Staphylococci*.

(D) the bacteria in Dish 3 at the end of Experiment 2 are *Staphylococci*.

927. Based on the student's experiments, what is reasonable to conclude about the two antibiotics?

(A) The level of effectiveness of either antibiotic depends on the particular type of bacteria to be controlled.

(B) Generally, antibiotic A is more effective at killing bacteria than is antibiotic B.

(C) Using the two antibiotics together will always be more effective in killing bacteria than using one of them alone.

(D) Neither of the two antibiotics is particularly effective for fighting bacteria.

Questions 928–934 are based on the following information.

A behavioral scientist was studying the behavior of a certain species of rodents that normally lives in habitats with both open grassy areas and areas with fairly dense bushes. Most of the known predators of these rodents are nocturnal. The scientist prepared a large, controlled living area for the rodents by placing lots of bushes and small trees on one side of the habitat, leaving the other half covered only by short grass. She cleared the test area of all other animals in the area and provided enclosures so that no other animals could enter the area.

Study 1

For her first study, the scientist distributed seeds and other foods common to the rodents equally over the entire habitat and released the rodents into the area. The scientist tracked the rodents' movements within the area during the daylight hours of one day and recorded her data in Figure 1.

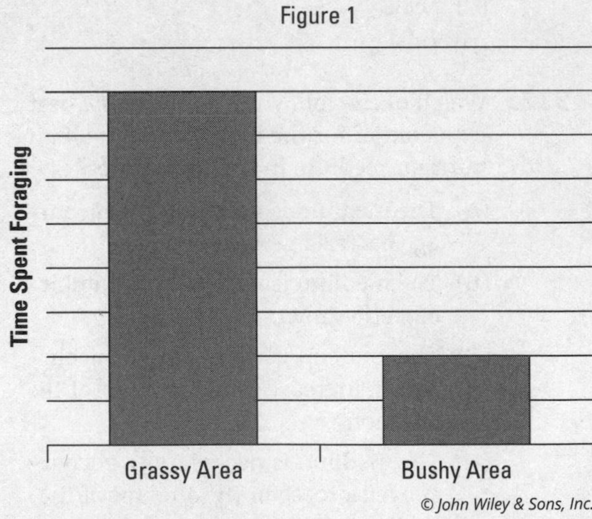

Study 2

The scientist then distributed the food in the controlled area in the same manner as she did for Study 1. She placed a model of a hawk, which is a predator of the rodents, above the controlled habitat and observed the rodents' movements during the daylight hours of another day. She recorded the results of her observations in Figure 2.

Figure 2

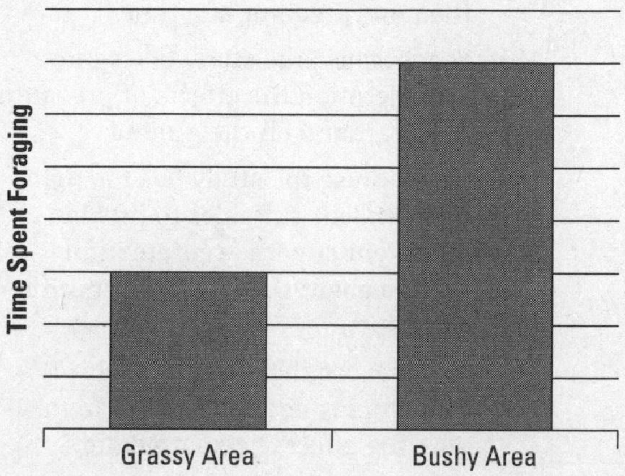

Time Spent Foraging

Grassy Area

Bushy Area

© John Wiley & Sons, Inc.

Study 3

For her last study, the scientist removed the hawk model from the area and distributed food. She placed twice as much food in the area with the bushes and trees as she did in the grassy area. Her observations of the rodents' movements over the next day-long hours of daylight are recorded in Figure 3.

Figure 3

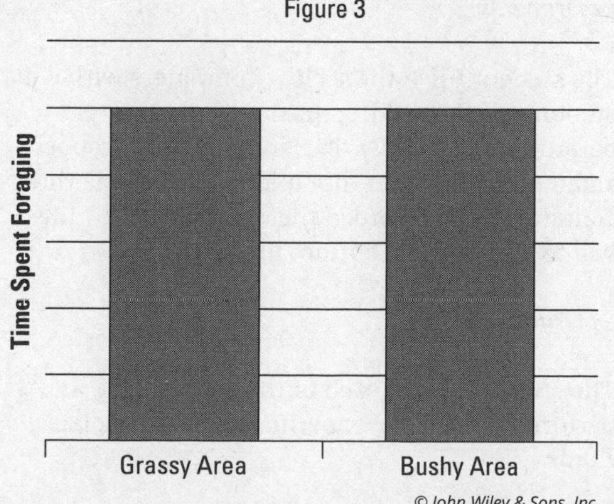

© John Wiley & Sons, Inc.

928. Which of the following provides the best explanation for why the scientist observed the rodents' behavior during daylight hours?

(A) The scientist wanted to observe the rodents' behavior during the hours when their predators were less present.

(B) The scientist wanted to observe the rodents' behavior during the hours when their predators were more present.

(C) The scientist wanted to observe the predators' behavior during the hours when the rodents were most active.

(D) The scientist wanted to observe the predators' behavior during the hours when the rodents were least active.

929. Given the information recorded by the scientist in all three studies, which of the following hypotheses is best supported by the results of Study 1?

(A) Some rodents established territories in the bushy area and forced all others into the grassy area.

(B) The rodents had no preference for either area.

(C) The rodents were less likely to face competition in the grassy area.

(D) It was easier for the rodents to find the food in the grassy area.

930. Which of the following is the best explanation for the results of Study 2?

(A) More rodents foraged in the bushy area because they were not as hungry as they were the day before.

(B) More rodents foraged in the bushy area because they were seeking shelter from the sun.

(C) Fewer rodents foraged in the grassy area because they felt safe there.

(D) Fewer rodents foraged in the grassy area because they were leaving food for the hawk.

931. What is the most reasonable conclusion to draw from the results of Study 3?

(A) The rodents ate more food when they foraged in the bushy area than they did when they foraged in the grassy area.

(B) Rodents can find food more easily if there is more of it available.

(C) Rodents prefer to forage in the grassy area and will forage in the bushy area only if they run out of food in the grassy area.

(D) When they foraged in the grassy area, the rodents were less efficient food seekers than when they foraged in the bushy area.

932. The scientist decides to conduct a fourth study in the same controlled area under the same conditions as Study 1. The only variation she makes to Study 4 is that she records data only during the hours when there is no daylight. Given what is known about the rodents, a reasonable hypothesis for the results of this study would be:

(A) the rodents will spend three times as much time foraging in the bushy area as in the grassy area.

(B) no rodents will forage in the bushy area.

(C) no rodents will forage in the grassy area.

(D) the rodents will spend more time foraging in the bushy area than they spent in the bushy area in Study 1.

933. What is an independent variable in all three studies?

(A) Rodent movement while foraging for food

(B) Food placement

(C) Presence of a predator

(D) Air temperature

934. The scientist would like to further explore the effect of the presence of specific predators on the rodents' behavior. She is contemplating setting up another study in the same controlled environment in which she places a model of a hawk overhead and a model of another known predator, the bobcat, in the bushes. Will this study be adequate to meet her goal?

(A) Yes, because the study allows the scientist to study the effects of more than one predator at a time.

(B) Yes, because the study takes into consideration the effects of predators in the air and on the ground.

(C) No, because the study has too many independent variables to provide the scientist with accurate information about the effects of specific predators.

(D) No, because the use of models of predators is not appropriate to measure the effect of real predators.

Questions 935–941 are based on the following information.

A student conducted several experiments to test the relative viscosity of three kinds of fluids other than water at different temperatures. Viscosity refers to the ability of a fluid to resist flow. The results of the student's experiments are recorded in Figure 1.

Experiment 1

The student filled three clear containers with equal amounts of three different fluids at room temperature (about 25°C). The student then dropped a small metal ball into the fluid in each of the three containers and recorded the time it took for the ball to travel to the bottom in each case.

Experiment 2

The student cooled each of the fluids to 0°C and performed the same experiment on the cooled fluids.

Experiment 3

For the final experiment, the student heated the fluids to 100°C and performed the same task on the heated fluids.

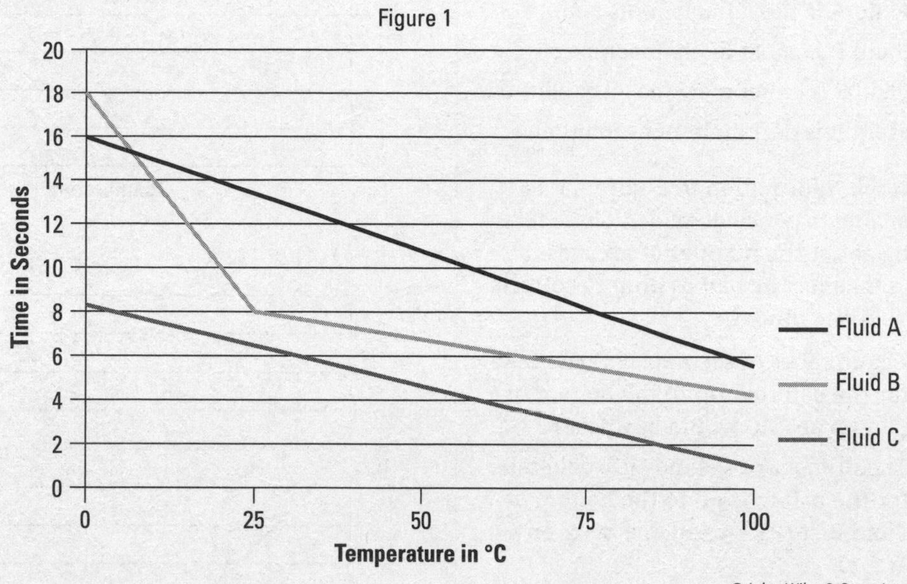

935. At a temperature of 75°C, the time it took Fluid A to reach the bottom of container is closest to which of the following:

(A) 2 seconds.

(B) 6 seconds.

(C) 8 seconds.

(D) 10 seconds.

936. Based on the results of the experiments, it is reasonable to conclude about the relative viscosities of the fluids that:

(A) Fluid A is less viscous than Fluid B.

(B) at increased temperatures Fluid A and Fluid B have the same viscosity.

(C) all three fluids have virtually the same viscosity at every temperature.

(D) at some temperatures some fluids have the same viscosity, and at other temperatures they do not.

937. Which of the following is true about the relationship between temperature and viscosity for the three fluids?

(A) For all fluids, there is an inverse relationship between temperature and viscosity.

(B) For all fluids, there is a positive correlation between temperature and viscosity.

(C) The relationship between temperature and viscosity is negative for Fluid C and positive for Fluid B.

(D) The relationship between temperature and viscosity is static for all three fluids.

938. The student is told that the three fluids are motor oil, machine oil, and olive oil and that motor oil has a higher viscosity than olive oil. From this information, the student can draw the conclusion that:

(A) Fluid A is most likely motor oil.

(B) Fluid B is most likely machine oil.

(C) Fluid C is either machine oil or olive oil.

(D) Fluid B is definitely not motor oil.

939. Given the information in Figure 1, it is reasonable to conclude which of the following about the number of seconds it would take for the ball to drop to bottom of one of the fluids?

(A) The number of seconds it would take for the ball to drop to the bottom of Fluid A at 75°C would be about 6.

(B) The number of seconds it would take for the ball to drop to the bottom of Fluid B at 125°C would be between 6 and 4.

(C) The number of seconds it would take for the ball to drop to the bottom of Fluid B at 80°C would be just about 1.

(D) The number of seconds it would take for the ball to drop to the bottom of Fluid C at 25°C would be about 4.

940. If the student were to conduct further experiments on Fluid C at progressively increasing temperatures up to over 225°C, which of these graphs would depict the most accurate representation of the likely results?

(A)

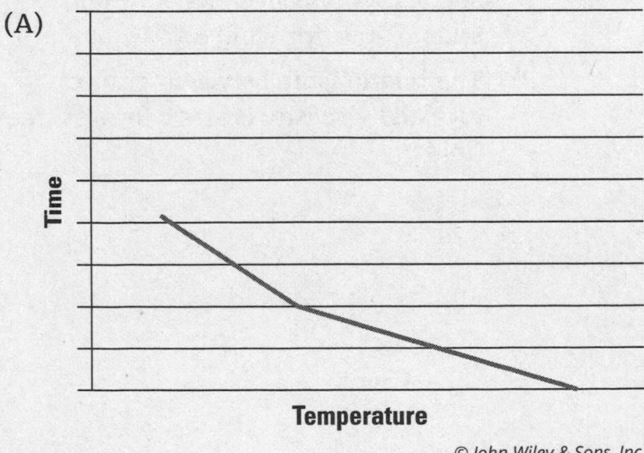

© John Wiley & Sons, Inc.

(B)

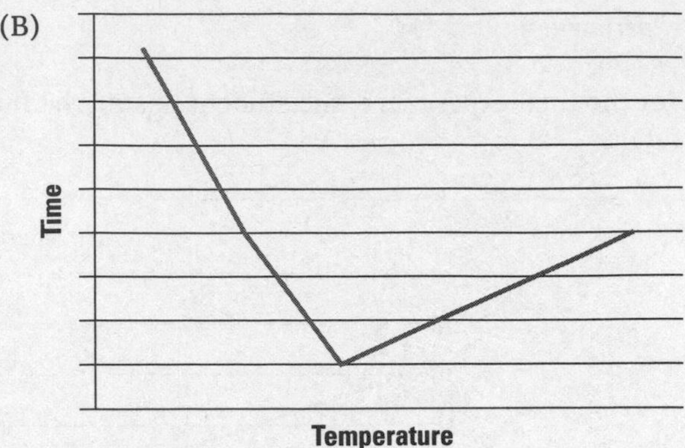

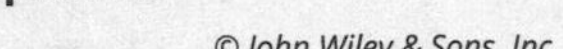

© John Wiley & Sons, Inc.

(C)

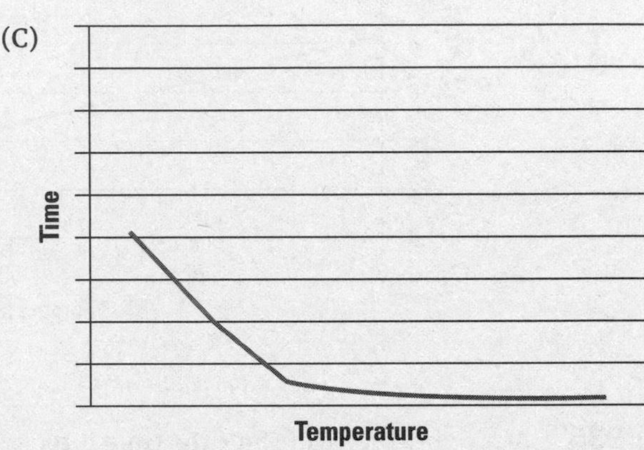

© John Wiley & Sons, Inc.

(D)

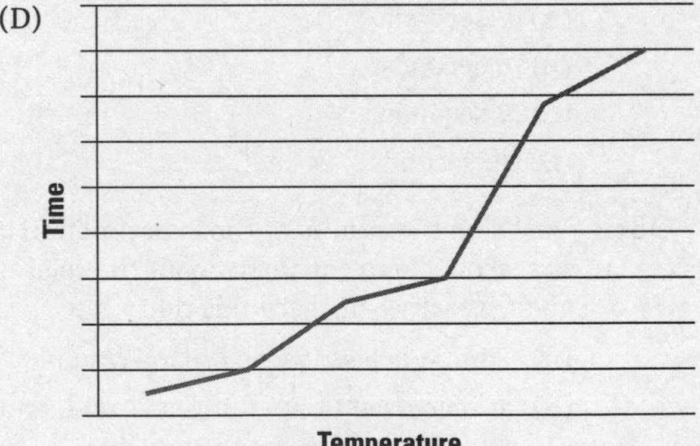

© John Wiley & Sons, Inc.

941. The student conducted the exact same group of experiments using H_2O and recorded the results in Table 1. Which of the following is a reasonable explanation for the data?

TABLE 1

Temperature in °C	Time in seconds
25°C	1
0°C	---
100°C	0.6

(A) H_2O is more viscous at 0°C than the other three tested fluids are.

(B) In the second experiment the student conducted, the H_2O was a solid.

(C) If the student were to record the results for H_2O on the graph in Figure 1, the line for H_2O would have a greater slope than Fluid A's line.

(D) It is impossible to find the relative viscosity of H_2O using the student's experiments.

Questions 942–948 are based on the following information.

In the study of physics, energy is a property that measures the ability of an object to perform work on another object. An object that contains higher energy levels is therefore able to perform more work. There are two common types of energy that many objects can possess: kinetic energy and potential energy.

Kinetic energy relates to the speed at which an object is moving and the momentum that object has because of its mass and speed. An object moving at a fast speed has more kinetic energy than a slow-moving object of the same mass. Also, an object with a large mass moving at a specific speed has more kinetic energy than another object with lower mass moving at the same speed. The kinetic energy of a moving object can be written as $E_k = 0.5mv^2$, with E_k being kinetic energy, m as mass, and v as velocity, or speed.

Potential energy can be present in both stationary and moving objects, and has to do with the gravitational potential energy stored within an object because of its relation to the Earth's gravitational field. An object further from the Earth's surface has more potential energy because it has the potential to fall toward the Earth. The farther away from the earth, or higher, an object is, the farther down it can fall, slide, or roll and the higher its potential energy.

For example, consider a skier skiing on a snowy slope as shown in Figure 1 below. The skier starts at the left side of the figure and skis from left to right. The skier's speed varies as she goes up and down the hills, and after she reaches the right side of the figure, she stops moving.

Figure 1

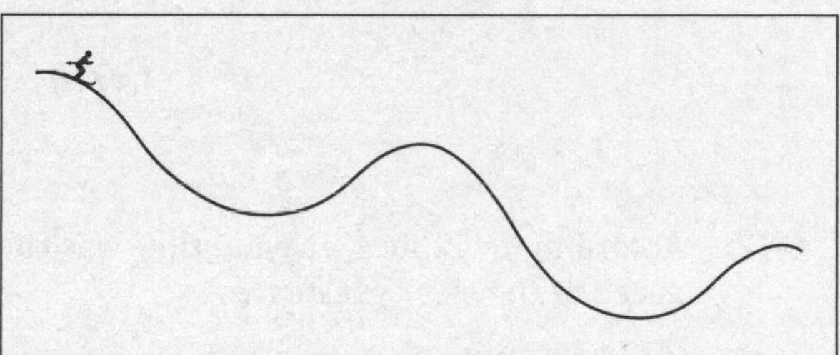

The speed of the skier in Figure 1 is shown below in Table 1. A time of 0 seconds represents the time at leftmost side of Figure 1, and a time of 5 seconds occurs at the rightmost side of Figure 1. Time is measured in seconds (s) and speed is measured in meters per second (m/s).

TABLE 1

Time (s)	Speed (m/s)
0	2
1	4
2	7
3	3
4	10
5	0

The skier's kinetic energy and potential energy vary as she travels across the slope, as shown in the graph in Figure 2. The skier's total energy level decreases as she skis because of losses to friction against the snow beneath the skis as well as air drag. Energy is measured in joules (J).

Figure 2

Kinetic and Potential Energy of a Skier

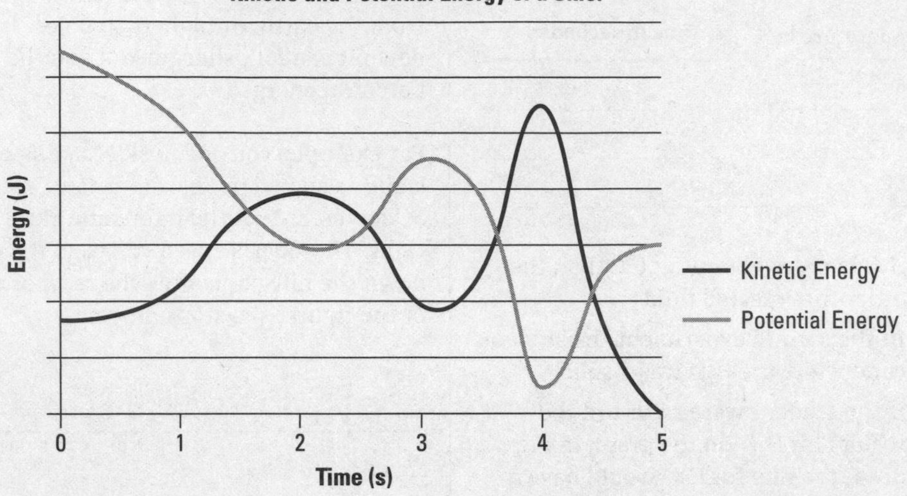

© John Wiley & Sons, Inc.

942. According to Table 1, at what time was the speed of the skier greatest?

(A) 2 seconds

(B) 3 seconds

(C) 4 seconds

(D) 5 seconds

943. The graph shows that the greatest increase in the skier's kinetic energy occurred between:

(A) 1 and 2 seconds.

(B) 2 and 3 seconds.

(C) 3 and 4 seconds.

(D) 4 and 5 seconds.

944. Given the information in the passage, which of the following best describes the general relationship between the skier's energy and speed?

(A) The skier experiences greater potential energy at greater speeds.

(B) The skier experiences greater kinetic energy at lower speeds.

(C) There is no apparent relationship between the skier's speed and kinetic energy.

(D) The skier experiences greater kinetic energy at greater speeds and less kinetic energy at lower speeds.

945. Based on Figure 2, as potential energy decreases, kinetic energy:

(A) increases only.

(B) decreases only.

(C) remains constant.

(D) increases then decreases.

946. Which of the following best describes the skier's motion between 2 and 3 seconds?

(A) The skier is traveling downhill.

(B) The skier is traveling uphill.

(C) The skier is traveling on a flat surface.

(D) The skier is motionless.

947. Kinetic energy is most directly related to:

(A) height.

(B) speed.

(C) time.

(D) distance.

948. To best increase potential energy, the skier should engage in which of the following activities?

(A) Adopt a compressed body position to reduce air drag

(B) Push on ski poles to increase speed

(C) Wax the skis to reduce friction

(D) Ride a chair lift back to the top of the mountain

Questions 949–955 are based on the following information.

When the human body is exposed to doses of ionizing radiation, tissue damage can occur and cause adverse health effects. Typical sources of radiation include radioactive decay of elements, and cosmic rays from outer space. Health effects vary widely, ranging from a mild headache to severe nausea and fever. The effects also depend greatly upon the quantity of radiation exposure and the amount of time over which the exposure occurred. The unit of measurement for absorbed radiation is called the Gray (Gy) and is equal to one joule of energy absorbed by one kilogram of matter.

Precise data for the health effects of exact doses of ionizing radiation on humans is not available because that would require a very controlled scientific environment, and it would be unethical to purposefully injure test subjects for data. However, there have been less-controlled cases where humans have been exposed to varying doses of ionizing radiation. Following these cases, studies were performed to estimate the amount of radiation exposure received and to correlate this with the severity of adverse health effects. Table 1 shows data on the health effects of various levels of ionizing radiation doses. For each dosage range, 100 humans who were estimated to have that level of dosage were studied. For each symptom, the number of humans who experienced it in the group of 100 is shown.

TABLE 1

Estimated Dosage (Gy)	Number of humans who experienced symptom		
	Nausea	Headache	Fever
1–2	23	14	0
2–6	74	52	64
6–8	85	77	100
8–30	94	86	100
> 30	100	100	100

In addition to the total number of incidents of each symptom, the number of headaches over time was also studied. Figure 1 shows how many cases of headache there were for each dosage level over time.

Figure 1

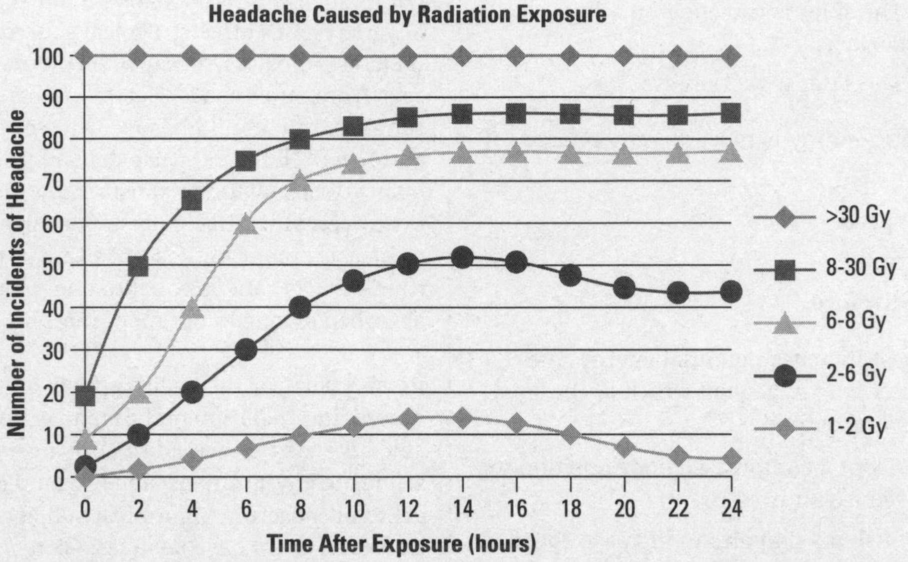

Headache Caused by Radiation Exposure

949. Based on Table 1, those people who were exposed to a radiation dose of greater than 30 Gy experienced:

(A) the most symptoms.

(B) the fewest symptoms.

(C) no symptoms.

(D) varying numbers of symptoms.

950. Based on Figure 1, over time to the number of incidents of headaches in those exposed to 1 to 2 Gy:

(A) increased only.

(B) decreased only.

(C) increased then decreased.

(D) decreased then increased.

951. Suppose a person has been exposed to radiation and is experiencing a headache but not a fever. Based on Table 1, that person most likely received what amount of radiation?

(A) 1 to 2 Gy

(B) 2 to 6 Gy

(C) 6 to 8 Gy

(D) 8 to 30 Gy

952. Based on Table 1, a person that receives a radiation dose of 2 to 6 Gy is most likely to experience which of the following?

(A) No symptoms

(B) Fever

(C) Headache

(D) Nausea

953. Table 1 and Figure 1 best support which of the following conclusions about radiation exposure? Increased radiation results in:

(A) fewer symptoms because higher doses of radiation result in fewer cases of headaches, nausea, and fever.

(B) more symptoms because higher doses of radiation exposure result in more cases of headaches, nausea, and fever.

(C) more fevers than headaches because the humans experienced more fevers than headaches at higher dosages of radiation.

(D) more headaches than fevers because the humans experienced more headaches than fevers at higher dosages of radiation.

954. For those who received 6 to 8 Gy of radiation, the number of headaches increased the most during how many hours after exposure?

(A) Between 0 and 2

(B) Between 4 and 6

(C) Between 8 and 10

(D) Between 12 and 14

955. For which levels of radiation exposure did the number of headache incidents decrease after several hours after exposure?

(A) > 30 Gy

(B) 8 to 30 Gy and 6 to 8 Gy

(C) 2 to 6 Gy and 1 to 2 Gy

(D) 1 to 2 Gy only

Questions 956–962 are based on the following information.

The Moon has many influences on humankind, including physical effects on the Earth itself and societal effects on humans. The Moon is responsible for the changing tides of the ocean and has been studied for thousands of years by astronomers. Lunar cycles have a significant impact on human society, serving as the origin of the current month system. Two scientists speculate about the formation of the Moon as discussed below.

Scientist 1

The Moon formed as a result of a giant body impacting the Earth. This collision occurred after the Earth was formed, meaning that the Moon is younger than the Earth. The body that impacted the Earth was roughly the size of Mars, which is slightly more than half the size of the Earth. The impact resulted in a great deal of matter being ejected from the Earth and forming a large cloud of debris near the Earth. Gravitational forces caused this cloud to slowly solidify into a spherical shape, creating the Moon.

The Moon's angular momentum and orbit around the Earth are a result of the swirling of the debris originally caused by the giant impact. The composition of the Moon is very similar to that of the Earth's crust and mantle, or outer layer. The Moon has much less iron than the Earth, suggesting that most of the core of the Earth was not ejected, and the majority of the material which makes up the Moon comes from the outer portions of the Earth, as well as the outer portions of the giant impacting body.

Scientist 2

The Moon and the Earth formed at roughly the same time, both originating from the same cloud of gas and dust. The two bodies drew material to themselves as a result of gravitational forces. During the beginning stages of their formation, the Earth and Moon were flat discs orbiting around each other, but as time progressed, they slowly coalesced into their present spherical shapes. The large craters present on the Moon's surface demonstrate that it is very old and was formed around the same time as the Earth. Though the Earth's thick atmosphere protects it from small impacts, the Moon's atmosphere is thin and provides little shielding from asteroids.

The Moon's current orbit around the Earth is a result of the swirling dust and gases that were the basis for both bodies. The Moon and Earth have been locked into their existing orbital patterns since their formation, explaining the regularity of lunar cycles seen today. Many of the elements found on the Earth are found also on the Moon, suggesting that they formed from some of the same matter. The differences in composition are explained by the fact that the swirling cloud of gas and dust from which the Moon and Earth were formed was not entirely homogeneous.

956. According to Scientist 1, which of the following is true about the age of the Moon?

(A) The Moon is the same age as the Earth.

(B) The Moon is younger than the Earth.

(C) The Moon is older than the Earth.

(D) The age of the Moon is not known.

957. Which of the following statements is NOT consistent with Scientist 2's theory?

(A) A large collision caused the Moon to form.

(B) The Moon orbits the Earth.

(C) At one point in its formation, the Earth was shaped like a flat disc.

(D) The Moon and Earth formed from similar matter.

958. Which of the following discoveries would cause the most doubt about the validity of Scientist 2's theory?

(A) Evidence of large impacts on the Earth's surface early in its history

(B) Samples from the Moon showing that it is composed of material similar to the Earth's

(C) Evidence that the oldest craters on the Moon are much younger than the geologic age of the Earth

(D) Samples from the Moon showing less iron is present on the Moon than on the Earth

959. Which of the following best describes how each of the two scientists explains the formation of the Moon?

(A) Scientist 1: Cloud of gas and dust. Scientist 2: Impact of a large body

(B) Scientist 1: Earth spun too fast and split. Scientist 2: Cloud of gas and dust.

(C) Scientist 1: Impact of a large body. Scientist 2: Earth spun too fast and split.

(D) Scientist 1: Impact of a large body. Scientist 2: Cloud of gas and dust.

960. Which of the following must be true about the Moon for Scientist 1 to be correct?

(A) The Moon is composed of material similar to the Earth's crust and mantle.

(B) The Moon is covered in craters and other geologic features.

(C) The Moon's orbit is perfectly circular.

(D) The Moon's atmosphere is much thinner than that of the Earth.

961. Which of the following statements is supported by both theories?

(A) The Moon is younger than the Earth.

(B) The Moon and the Earth are composed of some common matter.

(C) The Moon has no atmosphere.

(D) The Earth's core is less dense than that of the Moon.

962. Which of the following statements is consistent with Scientist 1 but not with Scientist 2?

(A) Gravitational forces played a role in the formation of the Moon.

(B) The Earth's diameter is roughly four times larger than that of the Moon.

(C) The Earth's atmosphere protects it from small impacts.

(D) Some of the matter that makes up the Moon was once part of the Earth.

Questions 963–969 are based on the following information.

An engineer is designing a piping system to supply water to a home. Two studies are conducted to determine the effects on volumetric flow rate of the water when the pipe diameter and water velocity are varied. Volumetric flow rate is measured in gallons per minute (GPM), and represents how much water can be supplied to a home in a given amount of time. Figure 1 shows a pipe of diameter D with water flowing through it at a velocity V.

Figure 1

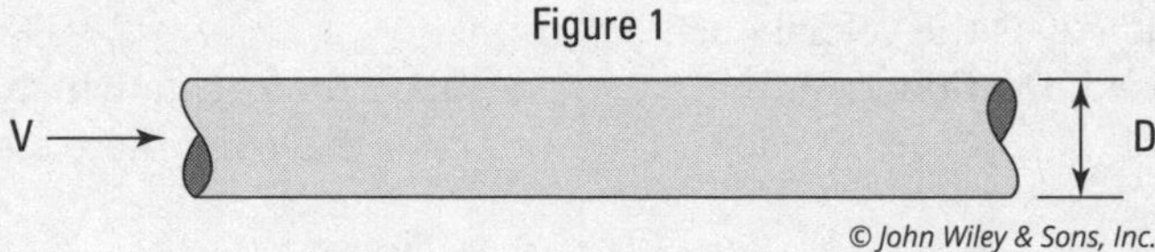

Study 1

The diameter, D, of the pipe was varied while the velocity of the water, V, was held constant at 5 feet per second (ft/s). Figure 2 shows how varying the diameter, which was measured in inches, changed the flow rate.

Figure 2

Effect of Diameter on Flow Rate

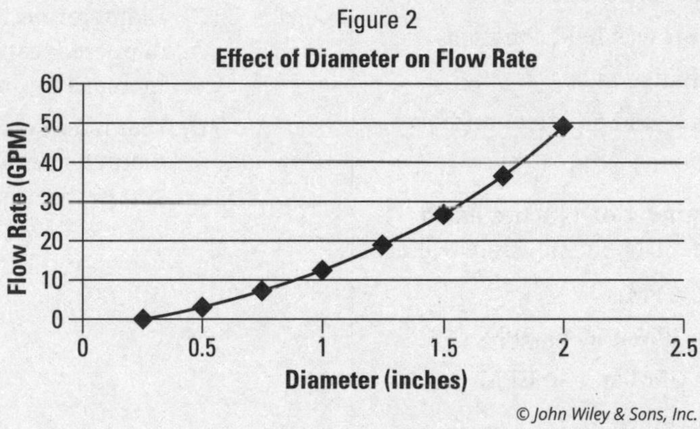

Study 2

The velocity, V, of the water flowing in the pipe was varied while the diameter of the pipe, D, was held constant at 1 inch. Figure 3 shows how varying the velocity changed the flow rate.

Figure 3

Effect of Velocity on Flow Rate

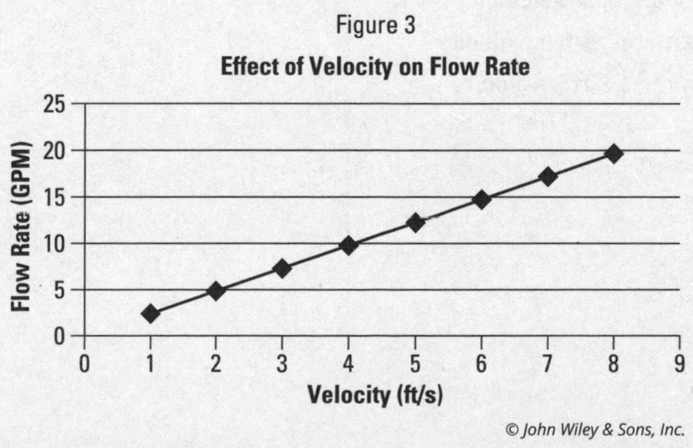

963. According to Study 1, the flow rate with a pipe diameter of 1.5 inches was closest to which of the following values?

(A) 5 GPM

(B) 12 GPM

(C) 28 GPM

(D) 36 GPM

964. According to Study 2, as the velocity of the water increased, the flow rate:

(A) increased.

(B) decreased.

(C) stayed the same.

(D) was not measured.

965. Which of the following is NOT true about Study 1?

(A) Velocity was held constant.

(B) Pipe diameter was held constant.

(C) Flow rate changed.

(D) Pipe diameter had an effect on flow rate.

966. Given a pipe diameter of 3 inches and a water velocity of 5 ft/s, the flow rate will be:

(A) less than 10 GPM.

(B) between 10 GPM and 30 GPM.

(C) between 30 GPM and 50 GPM.

(D) greater than 50 GPM.

967. Which of the following combinations of diameter and velocity would produce a flow rate of 10 GPM?

(A) 0.5-inch diameter, 5 ft/s velocity

(B) 1-inch diameter, 4 ft/s velocity

(C) 1.5-inch diameter, 5 ft/s velocity

(D) 2-inch diameter, 8 ft/s velocity

968. When a 1-inch diameter pipe is used and the water velocity is increased from 2 ft/s to 4 ft/s, according to Study 2, by about how much will the flow rate increase?

(A) 5 GPM

(B) 10 GPM

(C) 15 GPM

(D) 20 GPM

969. Increasing which of the following would have the more significant affect on flow rate?

(A) Velocity because doubling velocity results in a 100 percent increase in flow rate.

(B) Velocity because a 100 percent in velocity results in an approximate 300 percent increase in flow rate.

(C) Diameter because a 50 percent in diameter results in a 50 percent increase in flow rate.

(D) Diameter because a 100 percent in diameter results in an approximate 300 percent increase in flow rate.

Questions 970–976 are based on the following information.

Certain genes produce certain traits in an organism. The offspring of complex organisms result from a combination of genes from two different parents. Every individual has two genes for every trait, and each parent passes on only one of its two genes for each trait (this gene is also called an allele) so that the offspring ends up with two alleles for every trait, one from the mother and one from the father as shown in Figure 1.

Figure 1

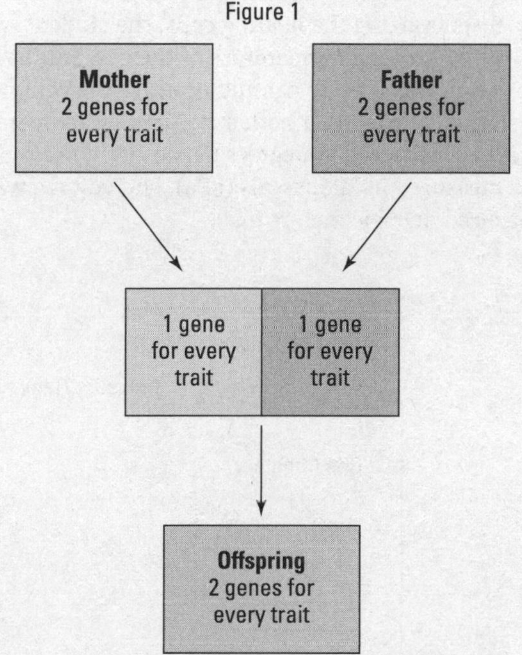

© John Wiley & Sons, Inc.

The combination of the two alleles that individuals possess for a certain trait is called their genotype. How that combination of traits is expressed physically is called the phenotype. Often one allele is dominant over another, recessive, allele. This means that the trait of the dominant allele is the only one that is expressed even though the individual also possesses the allele for the other trait. In cases of incomplete dominance, the combination of the dominant and recessive alleles produces a phenotype that is different from either of the traits held by the separate alleles.

A certain species of animal has two alleles for height. The *H* allele holds the trait for the tall phenotype, while the *h* allele codes for the short phenotype. The trait for height for this animal is incompletely dominant. Figure 2 displays a family tree showing some of the genotypes and phenotypes where the lines indicate the relationship between parents and offspring.

Figure 2

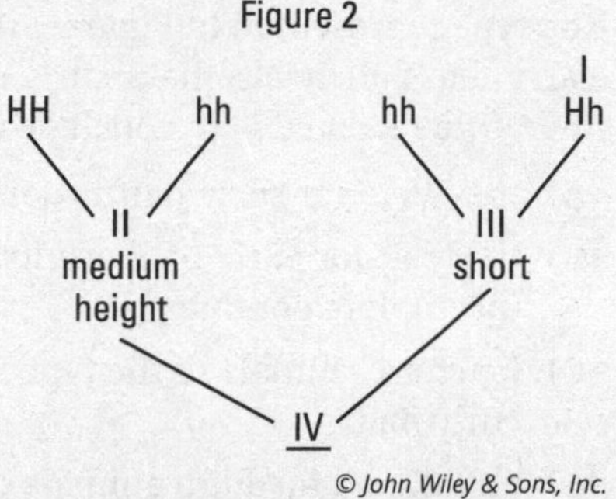

© John Wiley & Sons, Inc.

970. The relationship between the two alleles in the family tree in Figure 2 is best described as:

(A) the *H* is dominant and the *h* is recessive.

(B) the *H* is recessive and the *h* is dominant.

(C) incomplete dominance.

(D) indeterminable from the information.

971. The phenotype of animal I must be:

(A) tall.

(B) short like animal III.

(C) the same as the phenotype for animal IV.

(D) medium.

972. What are the chances that animal IV will have the same phenotype as animal II?

(A) 0 percent

(B) 25 percent

(C) 50 percent

(D) 100 percent

973. If animal III were to mate with a tall animal, the genotype of their offspring would be:

(A) *Hh* only.

(B) either *HH*, *Hh*, or *hh*.

(C) medium only.

(D) tall, medium, or short.

974. Geneticists have found that animals of the type represented in Figure 2 that carry the *H* allele also have curly hair. It is therefore reasonable to conclude that:

(A) the allele for curly hair is dominant.

(B) the trait for curly hair results from incomplete dominance.

(C) no short animals of the type have curly hair.

(D) all tall and medium animals of the type have curly hair.

975. If animal III mates with another animal with the same genotype, what is the percent chance that their offspring will be tall?

(A) 0 percent

(B) 25 percent

(C) 50 percent

(D) 100 percent

976. Animal III mates with an animal who has a tall genotype, and they produce six offspring. How many of their offspring will possess a genotype different from the parents'?

(A) 0

(B) 2

(C) 3

(D) 6

Questions 977–983 are based on the following information.

A student conducted an experiment to examine the effects of temperature and volume on the pressure of a gas. The student used a gas chamber to perform the experiments, carefully controlling the temperature, pressure, and volume of the gas within the chamber. The mass of the gas used remained constant throughout both experiments.

The gas chamber was set up as shown in Figure 1, with heating coils outside the chamber walls, and a piston that served as the bottom wall of the chamber. By energizing the heating coils, the student was able to control the temperature of the gas. Similarly, the piston was used to carefully control the volume of the gas. Throughout both experiments, temperature was measured in degrees Celsius (°C), pressure was measured in kilopascals (kPa), and volume was measured in cubic meters (m^3).

Figure 1

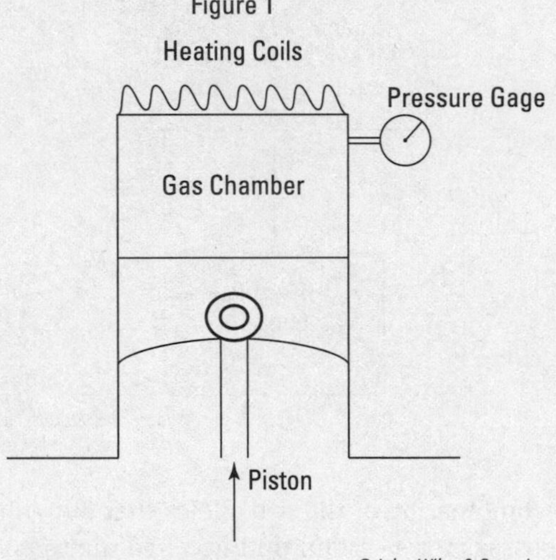

Experiment 1

In the first experiment, the student kept the volume of the chamber constant and increased the temperature using an outside heat source. At each 5°C temperature increment, the student recorded the pressure of the gas within the chamber. Table 1 shows the temperatures used and the corresponding pressure data.

TABLE 1

Temperature (°C)	Pressure (kPa)	Volume (m^3)
25	24.8	0.50
30	25.2	0.50
35	25.6	0.50
40	26.0	0.50
45	26.5	0.50
50	26.9	0.50

Experiment 2

In the second experiment, the student kept the temperature of the chamber constant but changed the volume by moving a piston in the chamber, as shown in Figure 1. By moving the piston further into the chamber, the volume of the gas was decreased because there was less space for the gas to occupy. The piston was moved slowly to ensure that the temperature of the chamber remained at 25°C. Table 2 shows the volumes used and the corresponding pressure data.

TABLE 2

Temperature (°C)	Pressure (kPa)	Volume (m^3)
25	12.4	1.00
25	16.5	0.75
25	24.8	0.50
25	49.6	0.25

977. In Experiment 1, which of the following properties of the gas was held constant?

(A) Temperature

(B) Pressure

(C) Volume

(D) None of the above

978. Suppose the student performs the experiment again under the same conditions at a temperature of 25°C. When the pressure measures 14.4 kPa, the volume of the gas in m^3 would be closest to:

(A) 1.25.

(B) 0.88.

(C) 0.62.

(D) 0.33.

979. Which of the following temperature and volume combinations was used in both experiments?

(A) Temperature of 25°C Volume of 0.50 m^3

(B) Temperature of 25°C Volume of 1.00 m^3

(C) Temperature of 40°C Volume of 0.50 m^3

(D) Temperature of 40°C Volume of 1.00 m^3

980. Which of the following best describes the procedure used in Experiment 2?

(A) Volume was held constant and temperature was varied.

(B) Pressure was held constant and temperature was varied.

(C) Volume was varied and temperature was varied.

(D) Temperature was held constant and volume was varied.

981. If the student wanted to conduct the same experiment with a variable that he had not already examined, he should vary the gas:

(A) temperature.

(B) volume.

(C) type.

(D) pressure.

982. Which of the following conclusions is best supported by Experiments 1 and 2?

(A) As the volume of the gas was increased, the pressure increased.

(B) As the volume of the gas was decreased, the pressure increased.

(C) As the temperature of the gas was increased, the pressure decreased.

(D) As the temperature of the gas was decreased, the pressure increased.

983. Which of the following is difference between the two experiments? In the second experiment:

(A) temperature varied.

(B) volume remained constant.

(C) temperature remained constant.

(D) pressure varied.

Questions 984–990 are based on the following information.

When solid materials are subjected to an outside force, they become compressed and temporarily change in length until the force is removed. Deformation is a measurement of this change in length. A student conducted a series of studies to determine what factors affect the deformation that an object experiences. The student conducted the studies using blocks of material and placed weights on top to provide the compressing force. The student used a precision laser device to measure the deformations and recorded them micrometers μm, which are one-millionth of a meter. Figure 1 shows the configuration the student used to conduct the studies. The original length of the block is labeled as L1, while the compressed length of the block is labeled as L2. The difference in original and compressed lengths is the deformation, *d*.

Figure 1

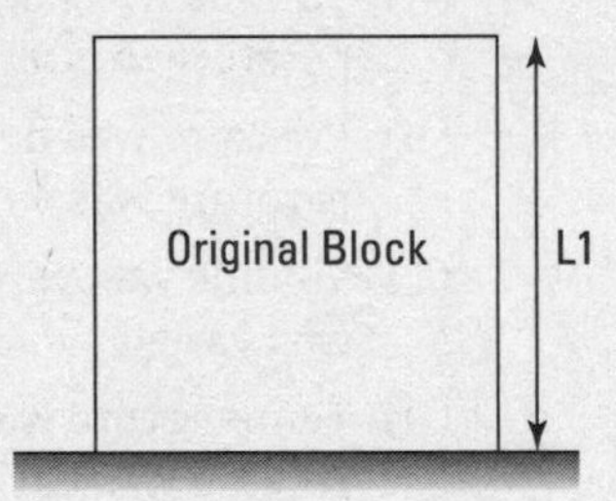

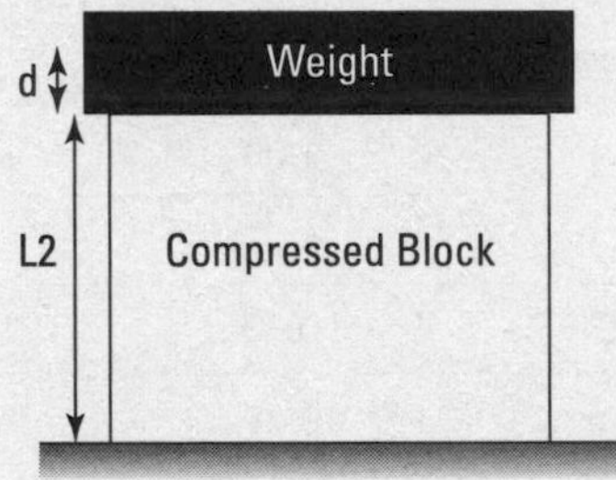

Study 1

In Study 1, the material that the block was made from was varied to examine the how deformation changes with material type. The original size of each block was a 20-centimeter (cm) cube. The weight used to compress the block had a mass of 50 kilograms (kg). Table 1 shows the results of Study 1.

TABLE 1

Block Material	Deformation (μm)
Rubber	24.525
Steel	0.012
Aluminum	0.081
Concrete	0.036
Plastic	1.066

Study 2

For Study 2, the student used one of the blocks from Study 1 and varied the mass of the weight placed on top of the block. For each different mass, the deformation was recorded. Table 2 shows the results of Study 2.

TABLE 2

Mass of Weight (kg)	Deformation (μm)
10	4.905
20	9.810
30	14.715
40	19.620
50	24.525

Study 3

For Study 3, the student varied the dimensions of the block, using plastic to create five blocks of varying lengths. Each block was a cube, with all sides being of the same length. Table 3 shows the results of Study 3.

TABLE 3

L1 (cm)	Deformation (μm)
10	2.133
20	1.066
30	0.711
40	0.533
50	0.427

984. Which of the following best represents what was varied in each study?

(A) Study 1, Block Material; Study 2, Block Length; Study 3, Weight Mass

(B) Study 1, Weight Mass; Study 2, Block Material; Study 3, Block Length

(C) Study 1, Block Length; Study 2, Weight Mass; Study 3, Block Material

(D) Study 1, Block Material; Study 2, Weight Mass; Study 3, Block Length

985. In Study 1, which material experienced the least deformation?

(A) Steel

(B) Aluminum

(C) Concrete

(D) Plastic

986. According to Study 3, what length of plastic block would most likely experience a deformation of 0.474 μm when loaded with a mass of 50 kg?

(A) 12 centimeters

(B) 27 centimeters

(C) 36 centimeters

(D) 45 centimeters

987. According to Tables 1 and 2, which material was most likely used in Study 2?

(A) Steel

(B) Rubber

(C) Concrete

(D) Plastic

988. Which conclusion is best supported by the data from the studies?

(A) A lighter weight causes more deformation in the block.

(B) A heavier weight causes less deformation in the block.

(C) A larger block experiences less deformation.

(D) A smaller block experiences less deformation.

989. Based on Study 1 and Study 3, which of the following would most likely experience the most deformation?

(A) A 20-centimeter rubber block

(B) A 30-centimeter rubber block

(C) A 40-centimeter steel block

(D) A 20-centimeter steel block

990. Which of the following expresses the equation for finding *d*?

(A) L2 – L1

(B) L1 – L2

(C) L1 + L2

(D) $\frac{L1}{L2}$

Questions 991–996 are based on the following information.

When light travels through a material, such as air, water, or glass, it travels at a specific speed. When a light wave approaches a boundary between two different materials at an angle, the speed of the wave changes and the light is refracted, causing a change in the direction of the light wave. This refraction can be illustrated with a laser beam shined at an angle across a material boundary.

Figure 1 shows how the angle of the laser beam changes when it enters a different material.

Figure 1

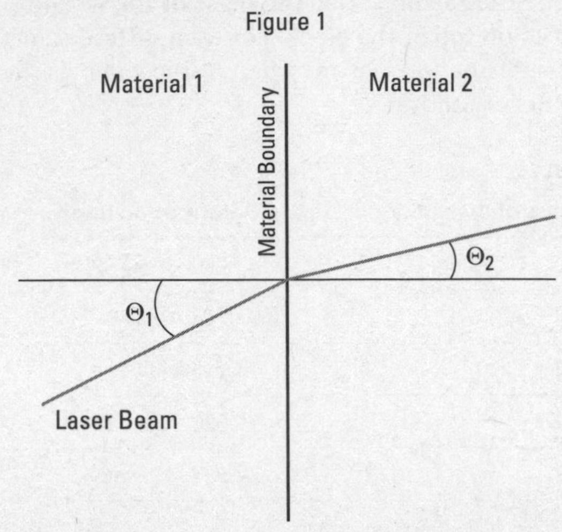

© John Wiley & Sons, Inc.

Each material has a specific refractive index, n, which describes how light is refracted within that material. The angle of refraction is unitless. The relationship between the angle of incidence, θ_1, and the angle of refraction, θ_2, is described by Snell's law:

$$n_1 \sin(\theta_1) = n_2 \sin(\theta_2)$$

Table 1 shows the angle of refraction, θ_1, for various angles of incidence, θ_2, across different material boundaries.

TABLE 1

Material 1	Material 2	θ_1 (degrees)	θ_2 (degrees)
Air (n_1=1.0)	Water (n_2=1.3)	10	8
		20	15
		30	23
Air (n_1=1.0)	Diamond (n_2=2.4)	10	4
		20	8
		30	12
Glass (n_1=1.6)	Water (n_2=1.3)	10	12
		20	25
		30	38

991. According to Table 1, when a laser beam travels from air into diamond with an angle of incidence (θ_1) of 20 degrees, what will be the angle of refraction (θ_2)?

(A) 4°

(B) 8°

(C) 12°

(D) 25°

992. When a laser beam travels from air into water, as the angle of incidence (θ_1) increases, the angle of refraction (θ_2):

(A) increases.

(B) decreases.

(C) is unchanged.

(D) is the same as that from glass into water.

993. Suppose a laser beam is traveling across a boundary from glass ($n_1 = 1.6$) to water ($n_2 = 1.3$) and the angle of refraction (θ_2) is 30 degrees. What is closest to the angle of incidence?

(A) 4°

(B) 10°

(C) 24°

(D) 38°

994. When a laser beam travels from a material with a higher index of refraction (higher n_1) into a material with a lower index of refraction (lower n_2), the angle of refraction (θ_2):

(A) is smaller than the angle of incidence (θ_1).

(B) is larger than the angle of incidence (θ_1).

(C) is the same as the angle of incidence (θ_1).

(D) is unknown.

995. Which of the following conclusions about refraction of a laser beam is supported by the data?

(A) A smaller difference between n_1 and n_2 results in a greater difference between θ_1 and θ_2.

(B) A greater difference between n_1 and n_2 results in a smaller difference between θ_1 and θ_2.

(C) A difference between n_1 and n_2 results in no difference between θ_1 and θ_2.

(D) A greater difference between n_1 and n_2 results in a greater difference between θ_1 and θ_2.

996. According to information in the passage, which of the following expresses a relationship between θ_1 and θ_2 for glass and water?

(A) $(1.6)\sin 30° = (1.3)\sin 38°$

(B) $(1.0)\sin 30° = (1.3)\sin 15°$

(C) $(1.6)\sin 30° = (1.3)\sin 25°$

(D) $(1.0)\sin 30° = (1.3)\sin 23°$

Chapter 5

Writing Test Questions

If you choose to complete the ACT Writing Test, you have 40 minutes to examine an issue and three possible perspectives and write one essay. Be sure to present a clear and logical analysis with specific supporting detail and use language precisely. Write your essay by hand and be sure it's legible.

REMEMBER

Your essay is *not* an analysis of the validity of each of the three provided perspectives. Rather, create and support a thoughtful, persuasive argument that advances your opinion on the issue.

The Problems You'll Work On

When working through the practice essays based on the sample topics in this chapter, be prepared to do the following:

- Declare your position and support it with sound reasoning and examples.
- Communicate clearly so your point can be understood by someone who doesn't know the topic.
- Critically think about how a topic fits in the big picture.
- Support your thesis and topic sentences with specific examples from your own personal experience.
- Consider the complexity of the argument by acknowledging and addressing counterarguments to your position.

What to Watch Out For

Your challenge is to complete a quality essay in 40 minutes. Avoid these common pitfalls:

- Stating a wishy-washy thesis rather than a clear opinion
- Focusing on an analysis of the three perspectives instead of your own opinion
- Rushing into the essay without spending about 10 minutes to organize your thoughts and create a rough outline
- Making general statements without the support of specific examples or precise vocabulary

Follow these instructions for Questions 997–1001:

Write a unified, coherent essay in which you evaluate multiple perspectives on the given issue. Your essay should do the following:

- Examine and assess the given perspectives
- Present and support your own perspective on the issue
- Clarify the relationship between your view and those provided in the perspectives

Your perspective may agree completely with one or more of the perspectives, or it may be completely different. Make sure you support your thesis with clear, logical reasoning and specific, relevant examples.

Make sure your essay contains these necessary features:

- **A clear position:** Did you take a stand and stick to it? Remember that which side you take isn't a big deal. How well you support your position makes or breaks your essay. You should take only a few seconds to choose which side to argue before you start writing.
- **A clear understanding of the complexity of the issue:** Top essays include a careful analysis of possible positions to weigh the pros and cons of all to arrive at the best possible solution.
- **Consideration of the three perspectives:** You don't need to thoroughly examine all three perspectives, but make sure you address each one somewhere in the support for your own opinion.
- **A strong thesis:** Did you create a thesis that answers the question posed by the prompt and sets up your essay? Try to slip in some of the wording from the prompt. Make sure your thesis introduces the two or three main points you use to back up your stand on the issue.
- **A steady focus:** Every element of your essay should be about your thesis. Make sure you didn't stray off topic.
- **Good organization:** We know it sounds boring, but your essay must have an introduction, body, and conclusion. Make sure you devote each paragraph in the body to a discussion of one of your two or three main supporting points. Check out the hamburger organization plan that we outline in Chapter 18 to help you evaluate the organization of your essay.
- **Excellent examples:** Professional essay readers really love to see creative, descriptive examples that strengthen your points. Vivid details draw readers in and endear them to your writing prowess.
- **Clear and interesting writing:** Check your essay for sentence structure variety, precise word choice, and impeccable spelling, grammar, and punctuation.

997. Educators and school administrators have proposed implementing a ban on possessing cellphones on school grounds for all area high school students. A recent survey reveals that more than one third of high school students have used their cellphones to cheat on high school exams. Administrators argue that, because cellphones are small and easy to conceal during an exam, the only way to ensure that students do not cheat with their cellphones is by banning cellphones altogether. Students and many parents oppose the ban, stating that banning cellphones from school would deprive students of a means of communicating with parents and would decrease student safety. They cite recent instances of school violence that were reported to the outside through students' cellphones.

Read and carefully consider these perspectives. Each suggests a particular way of thinking about the proposed ban on student cellphone possession on school grounds.

Perspective 1: Just as most haven't for hundreds of years, today's students do not need cellphone access while at school. It is an unnecessary distraction, and there are other phones available for use in an emergency.

Perspective 2: Cellphones are part of the modern way of life, and they are necessary for safety as well as convenience. Students should have access to their cellphones throughout the day because they aren't going to have time to travel to the office or another landline location if an emergency occurs.

Perspective 3: Students should not be refused the right to possess their cellphones on school grounds. However, teachers should have the right to collect cellphones at the start of class and then return them afterward, after the day's work is performed.

998. In response to recent incidences of school violence, a high school has encouraged teachers to listen in to students' conversation during periods of downtime in the classroom. School administrators believe that students do not have and should not expect to have a right to privacy in the classroom and that increased teacher attention and awareness can help increase the safety of all students. The theory is that, when teachers are more in tune with what's being said in their classrooms, tragedies such as the one that took place at Columbine High School may be avoided.

Read and carefully consider these perspectives. Each suggests a particular way of thinking about the proposed listening-in policy discussed in the prompt.

Perspective 1: Asking teachers to listen in on high school students, some of whom are legal adults, is an egregious invasion of privacy that can be likened to installing video cameras in bathroom stalls.

Perspective 2: In this day and age, you simply cannot be too careful, and evidence has shown that many instances of school violence have been foiled by people listening in and speaking up. The listening in policy may also help reduce instances of bullying on high school campuses.

Perspective 3: Whether teachers should listen in on student conversations is really a nonissue. If students are speaking loudly enough to be overheard, then no invasion of privacy is taking place. If they want matters to stay private, they can speak in hushed tones or save the conversation for later.

999. Physicians have been prescribing pregnant women with extreme morning sickness certain anti-nausea medications for years, and while these drugs are approved by the U.S. Food and Drug Administration for use among cancer patients, they have not been specifically tested for side effects on pregnant populations due to the ethical considerations involved in doing so. Thus, doctors are prescribing the drug for what are considered "off-label" purposes. Many women who took these medications are now giving birth to babies with severe birth defects, and many attribute these defects to their use of the medications.

Consider the following perspectives regarding a pregnant woman's use of prescription-label drugs for off-label purposes.

Perspective 1: Any doctor who prescribes a prescription drug for any use other than its intended one should be prosecuted under federal law. Without prior testing to determine whether a drug is safe for use by pregnant women, the risk is simply too great, and it is a physician's job to keep the mother and baby safe to the fullest extent possible.

Perspective 2: Though it is risky to give a pregnant woman an anti-nausea medication that has not been tested on pregnant populations, going through pregnancy with severe morning sickness and the nutritional deficiencies it can cause is no safer. Most pregnant women who take these drugs during pregnancy give birth to healthy babies without birth defects.

Perspective 3: By prescribing pregnant women anti-nausea medications that haven't been specifically tested on this population, these women are essentially becoming the very human guinea pigs it's considered "unethical" to formally test. At least a formal clinical trial would likely furnish critical information about the safety and effectiveness of these drugs when used by pregnant women.

1000. What bathroom individuals who identify as transgendered should legally use has become an increasingly hot-button issue in recent years, with several major nationwide retailers taking their own stances and enacting their own guidelines. The results thus far have been mixed, with some shoppers supporting the decisions of these retailers and others decrying it.

Consider the following perspectives regarding public bathroom use by transgendered individuals.

Perspective 1: Transgendered individuals should simply use whichever bathroom corresponds with their anatomy. If they have male anatomy, they should use the men's room, and vice versa.

Perspective 2: Transgendered individuals should have the right to use the bathroom intended for use by whichever sex they identify with. If they were born female and have not undergone gender reassignment surgery but still choose to live life as a man, they should be able to use the men's bathroom.

Perspective 3: Business and public places should have to have unisex bathrooms available after they reach a certain size to avoid issues with discrimination. Businesses that are too small to offer unisex bathrooms should simply have several single bathrooms that are intended for use by either sex.

1001. In recent years, many fast food industry workers have gone on strike and engaged in other efforts to try to boost their hourly wages to about $15. They argue that anything less will likely keep them below the poverty line, even if they work full-time, and that the current federal minimum wage is simply not sufficient enough to cover the typical cost of living. Others argue against a $15-per-hour rate for workers within the fast food industry, arguing that most of these jobs don't require much of an educational background and therefore shouldn't reward workers with a salary more than twice the federal minimum wage.

Consider the following perspectives regarding whether fast food workers should receive at least $15 an hour.

Perspective 1: Not all fast food workers are there because they are uneducated. On the contrary, tough economic times have landed people from all walks of life in these positions, and people who work full-time to support themselves and their families should be compensated appropriately for doing so.

Perspective 2: A raise for fast food workers is not an outlandish request, but a raise to $15 an hour is above and beyond a reasonable hike. This amount is more than some workers with degrees make, such as many who work in the nonprofit industry, and salary should be commensurate with one's skill set and level of education.

Perspective 3: Most positions in the fast food industry require minimal skills and education, and therefore, those who hold these positions should not expect to receive more than the federal minimum wage. The minimum wage is set after the nationwide cost of living is taken into account, so the government will raise it when it deems appropriate, and fast food industry workers should wait until this occurs.

2 The Answers

IN THIS PART . . .

Review the answers to all 1,001 questions.

Study the answer explanations to better understand the concepts being covered.

Chapter 6

The Answers

Chapter 1

1. B. One obvious

That comma at after *obvious* is wrong. You never put a comma between a preceding adjective and the noun it describes. Choice (B) corrects the problem by eliminating the comma. Choice (C) doesn't work because *obvious* starts with a vowel sound, and the article you use before a word that starts with a vowel sound is *a*, not *an*.

Choice (D) incorrectly moves the comma between *one* and *obvious*. The only time you use a comma to separate two adjectives that come before a noun is when the adjectives are coordinate adjectives.

You can tell whether you should put a comma between adjectives that describe the same noun if you can answer yes to these two questions about them. Could you replace the comma with *and*? If you reversed the order of the adjectives would the meaning stay the same? In this case, *and* between *one* and *obvious* doesn't make sense and you can't logically reverse their order. Therefore, Choice (D) is wrong.

2. C. campaigns is

When you see a verb in the underlined part, check to see that it agrees with the subject. The subject of the sentence is *goal*, and *goal* is singular. The verb *are* is plural. To make sure the verb and subject get along, you have to make the verb singular. Choices (C) and (D) correctly change *are* to *is*, but Choice (D) improperly switches *campaigns* to *campaign*. The correct answer is Choice (C).

3. A. NO CHANGE

The underlined portion is fine as it is. The addition of *those* in Choice (B) adds *those*, which adds an unclear reference to people who haven't yet been mentioned. Choice (C) makes the subject singular so that it no longer agrees with the plural verb *don't*. If you read Choice (D) in place of the underlined words, you see that it's not only wordy and weak but also improper. You'd need to put *who* after *people* for the construction to make sense.

4. B. themselves

Theirselves isn't a word. Neither is *themself*. Cross out Choices (A) and (D). Because the pronoun refers to the plural noun *people*, it can't be singular. That means that Choice (C) can't be right. The proper form of the reflexive pronoun is *themselves*, which makes Choice (B) the right answer.

5. C. and it can be ferocious

This sentence sounds weird because it's not quite clear what noun *ferocious* describes. Choice (D) clarifies that it's the competition that's ferocious, but its construction creates a comma splice. You can't join two independent clauses with just a comma and no conjunction. Eliminate Choice (B) because it improperly uses the possessive form of it to mean it's. The answer that solves the modifier problem without creating a new error is Choice (C).

6. A. NO CHANGE

Both *organization* and *field* are nouns. Whenever you have two nouns right next to each other, the first noun "possesses" the other. The way the original sentence presents the possessive form of *organization* is just fine. The best answer is Choice (A).

Choice (B) isn't possessive, and Choice (C) pluralizes the noun. Choice (D) is way off. There's nothing in the rest of the sentence that would indicate that the organization is a field.

7. A. where it is now

Place descriptive information as close to the word or word it describes as possible. The underlined portion provides examples of the types of fields of activity an organization may have. Therefore, it's best right where it is.

The underlined portion would fit after *field*, but Choice (B) would leave "of activity" hanging all by itself after the list with a dash after it. Putting the list after the first three words of the sentence makes no sense at all. Cross out Choice (C). Choice (D) makes the underlined portion improperly describe types of organizations rather than types of activities.

8. **B. are, in effect, in competition**

Almost always *affect* is used as a verb and *effect* is a noun. "In effect" means "to have the effect of." "In affect" is never a proper construction. Eliminate Choices (A) and (C). Choice (D) is missing the comma before "in effect" that shows that the phrase is an aside. Because there's a comma after the phrase, there also needs to be one before it. The answer that uses the proper phrase and doesn't make a new mistake is Choice (B).

9. **D. sister organizations,**

The underlined portion uses the possessive form of *sister*. Even though *sister* is usually a noun, in this sentence it's used as an adjective to describe the type of organization. The intended meaning of *sister* in this context is to indicate an organization that's similar and connected to yours in some way, like a sister city. Adjectives can't take possessive form. The only answer that eliminates the possessive form is Choice (D).

10. **C. a necessary transition between the third and fourth paragraphs**

First analyze the purpose of the sentence in question. The first sentence of the fourth paragraph serves as a necessary transition to the subsequent sentence. Without it, "more typically" in the next sentence makes no sense, and you don't who *they* refers to. The sentence is definitely significant, which means Choice (A) is wrong. You know Choice (B) isn't right because the author doesn't suggest that people support only one organization earlier in the passage. Nor does the sentence summarize what the author knows about nonprofits as suggested by Choice (D). The best answer is Choice (C).

11. **B. library, homeless shelter, and symphony orchestra**

The underlined portion contains a list of more than two elements. You punctuate lists by placing commas after each element and putting *and* before the last element. Choice (A) contains no commas. Choice (C) puts a comma after *and*, which is never proper. Choice (D) gets it all messed up by putting the *and* after the first element. The answer the gets it right is Choice (B).

12. **D. organizations that protect whales in the Pacific, support medical research in the Amazon, or care for orphans in Africa.**

When you see a list in an underlined part, check it for parallel construction. All of the elements in the list should begin with the same grammatical form. This list describes organizations that *protect*, *support*, or *providing*. Two present tense verbs and one that in –*ing* form isn't parallel construction. Choose Choice (D) to fix the problem. It describes organizations that *protect*, *support*, or *care*. All elements are present tense verbs. Problem solved.

13. B. organization, trying

The pronoun *who* refers only to people. An organization is a thing, not a person. Cross out Choices (A) and (C). Choice (D) gets rid of *who* but creates an awkward and wordy construction. The best answer is Choice (B). It gets rid of *who* and keeps the construction clearer and more concise than the other option.

On the ACT you're always looking for the best answer of the four possible choices. Sometimes the right answer doesn't seem like the words you'd use if you were writing the sentence. As long as an answer presents a better way to form the words than the other choices do, it's the one to pick.

14. B. support

Support and *backing* mean the same thing, so you don't need both of them. The only answer than rids the sentence of its redundancy problem is Choice (B).

15. D. hard-nosed terms, public relations

The underlined part uses a semicolon after an introductory phrase (you know it's a phrase because it begins with a preposition). The proper punctuation mark after a beginning phrase is a comma. Choice (C) is out because it places the comma after the subject of the sentence rather than after the phrase. The colon is only proper after an independent clause (never a phrase), Choice (B) is wrong. The correct answer is Choice (D).

16. B. 2, 3, 4, 1

Hmmm. . .the sentence doesn't sound right the way it is. You can confidently cross out Choice (A). The other options give you the choice of beginning the sentence with "in West Africa" or sticking with the existing beginning. "In West Africa" would make a handy beginning phrase, and you already know that the sentence is awkward the way it is. Besides, Choice (D) constructs a sentence without a subject: "Rather than through the media and peers, are taught through dance. . . ." Try the configurations in Choices (B) and (C).

Choice (C) creates the same problem as Choice (D): "In West Africa, are taught through dances. . . ." The answer has to be Choice (B). It's the only one that takes care of the awkward construction of the original sentence without depriving the sentence of a subject.

17. C. provides a sense

The power of dance doesn't provide *for* the sense of belonging; it provides *a* sense of belonging. Choice (C) corrects the problem.

Choice (D) creates a subject/verb agreement problem. The verb should be singular to go with the singular subject *power*. If you read the complete sentence with Choice (B) included, you see that that option introduces a *that* and creates an incomplete thought, "power provides that the sense of belonging".

Always reread your answer choice in the context of the sentence to make sure it fits. This step often alerts you to a new error an answer choice creates that you may miss otherwise.

18. D. their

A pronoun immediately before a noun (such as *age*) has to be in possessive form. The proper possessive form they is their. Pick Choice (D). Choice (A) is an adverb, and Choices (B) and (C) introduce another subject and verb into the sentence.

19. B. rhythms. Each

This sentence is a fused sentence: It contains two complete thoughts, but no punctuation separates them. You can correct the problem by separating it into two different sentences, putting a comma and *and* between *rhythms* and *each*, or by inserting a semicolon after *rhythm*. The only answer that gives you one of these fixes is Choice (B).

Choice (C) makes the sentence a comma splice, and Choice (D) creates a run-on sentence.

20. B. its

The underlined portion uses the contraction of *it is* when it needs the possessive form of *it*, which is *its*, Choice (B). If you read the other choices in the sentence, you can immediately exclude them.

21. C. Kuku, Yole, Sonsorne, and Sinte.

The underlined portion punctuates the series incorrectly. A list of single words needs just commas and a final *and* to separate the items. Choice (C) provides the fix.

22. A. Sinte, and each one has a distinctive beat.

Find the answer that relates best to the information in the passage. The passage is about dances rather than the way words sound, so you can cross out Choice (B). Choice (C) repeats information from the sentence before this one, so it's not relevant. Choice (D) is obviously wrong. The passage is informational rather than experiential, which means the author's rhythm preferences don't belong in this particular essay. The best answer is Choice (A). It provides new information (the beats are different) about the topic discussed in the paragraph.

23. **B. Beyla, located**

The sentence that begins with *locate* is a fragment. To make the sentence complete, use a comma to join it to the sentence before it. Choice (B) fixes the problem. A comma is proper because the second part of the new sentence provides descriptive (but not absolutely necessary) detail about Beyla's location.

For the semicolon in Choice (C) and the comma and conjunction in Choice (D) to work, the rest of the sentence would have to express a complete thought. It doesn't, so they're both wrong.

24. **D. most commonly**

The parts of speech are all messed up in the underlined part. *Common* is an adjective, but it is supposed to tell how often Kuku is played. Words that tell how are adverbs. Choice (C) also contains *common*. Cross it out along with Choice (A). Choice (B) contains the adverb form *commonly*, but it has the adverb *mostly* to define *commonly*. You use adjectives to modify adverbs. Choice (D) gets it right.

25. **C. women's**

Cross out Choices (A) and (D). The plural of woman is women, so there's never a right time to use *womens* or *womans'*. The nouns *women* and *dance* are right next to each other, so you need to put *women* in possessive form. Choice (C) does the trick.

26. **D. hollowed logs called Krins,**

The pronoun *which* introduces nonessential dependent clauses and always needs a comma to separate the words that come after it from the words that come before it, so eliminate Choice (A). Conversely, the pronoun *that* introduces essential dependent clauses and shouldn't have a comma before it. Choice (B) is out.

Between Choices (C) and (D), Choice (D) states the explanation of the logs' construction much more succinctly. The ACT credits answers that convey ideas clearly and concisely.

27. **C. Yes, because the sentence does not provide information that is relevant to understanding how Kuku is performed.**

First, concentrate on the proposed deletion to determine its purpose in the paragraph. The sentence is about fishing tools, which is unrelated to the paragraph's topic about the performance of Kuku. Check the answers to see which matches this observation.

Choice (A) contradicts the observation. Knowing that the women used fishing tools isn't essential to understanding how the Kuku is currently performed. Though it's true that the sentence provides the reader with information about the use of fishing tools, this truth isn't a reason to keep the sentence. Cross out Choice (B). The underlined sentence doesn't contradict anything the author has said so far, so Choice (D) can't be right. The answer that best states the earlier observation about the sentence's lack of relevance is Choice (C).

28. **D. The rhythm of Yole comes from the Temne people, who live in Sierra Leone near the Guinean border.**

When you see a lengthy underlined part, you're usually dealing with the proper positioning of descriptive elements. The construction of the original sentence indicates that the Guinean border comes from the Temne people, which doesn't make sense. Choices (B) and (C) correct that problem, but Choice (B) make the border rather than the rhythm the main idea of the sentence, and both answers include awkward arrangements of prepositional phrases in the descriptions.

The answer that properly positions the descriptive elements and most clearly presents the main idea that the rhythm of Yole comes from the Temne people is Choice (D).

29. **A. NO CHANGE**

The underlined portion is best as is. The addition of *most* in Choice (B) is unnecessary. Choice (C) incorrectly uses *most* to mean *almost*. Choice (D) is redundant and changes the meaning of the sentence.

30. **C. Yes, because the essay presents the benefits of the dances and gives some details about the way some of them are performed.**

For questions that ask about the passage as a whole, first check the passage title. The title indicates that the passage is about West African dances, so it's likely that the essay describes West African dances, so concentrate on Choices (C) and (D). The writer summarizes the benefits of dance to the West African culture in the first sentences of the essay. The rest of the essay provides a few details about some of the dances, including where they come from and how and where they're performed. That seems to meet the intended goal for the reason expressed Choice (C). He doesn't focus on a comparison of earlier dances to modern dances, and this comparison wouldn't fulfill the intention stated in the question, so Choice (D) is wrong. A quick skim of Choices (A) and (B) reveals that they are untrue. The best answer is Choice (C).

31. B. When I grocery shop, the one area

The original sentence contains a dangling participle because the beginning phrase doesn't describe the subject. The way the sentence is constructed, the area is doing the grocery shopping. Choice (A) has to be wrong.

The only choice that corrects the problem is Choice (B); it changes the beginning phrase to a clause.

32. D. irrationally

The underlined phrase is an adverb phrase that describes how the area overwhelms. Adverbs correctly describe verbs, but the one-word adverb in Choice (D) accomplishes the task more concisely. The other two choices propose a noun or an adjective to describe how the author is overwhelmed, and nouns and adjectives don't describe verbs.

33. A. NO CHANGE

The underlined portion is fine the way it is. You may not like the quotation marks, but the only choice that doesn't have them is Choice (B), and that option puts a question mark at the end of a declaratory statement. Choice (C) places a comma between *fresh* and *breath*, but that would be proper only if fresh and breath were coordinating (or related) adjectives. *Breath* is a noun, so Choice (C) is wrong. *Inside* isn't nonessential, so no reason exists for the comma before it in Choice (D).

34. D. I've

Underlined verbs usually indicate either a tense or subject/verb agreement problem. In this case, the issue is the verb tense. The author uses present tense throughout the essay, but the underlined verb is future tense. Choice (A) is wrong. Choice (B) is past tense, so it's not right. There's nothing in the sentence to indicate that the author ought to have done something she shouldn't, so Choice (C) doesn't make sense. Choice (D) is the best answer. It's puts the verb in present tense, and the contraction's proper because it fits with the casual tone of the passage.

35. B. whitening effect

As they're tested on the ACT, *effect* is used as a noun and *affect* is a verb. Choice (A) uses affect as a noun, so it's wrong. Putting *whitening* in the possessive form doesn't solve the problem. Cross out Choice (C). You may think that Choice (D) works because it seems like *affects* is now correctly a verb showing what whitening does. But that change doesn't work with the rest of the sentence. Choice (B) correctly changes the noun to effect.

36. **C. there**

Their is the possessive form of *they*, and no noun follows their in this sentence to justify the possessive form. Cross out Choice (A), and look for the adverb that shows location, which is *there*. The answer is Choice (C). The other choices introduce a verb that doesn't work in the sentence.

37. **A. NO CHANGE**

The paragraph seems fine the way it is, but read the other options just to make sure you haven't missed something. The *however* in sentence 2 indicates that there should be an idea before it that the sentence contradicts, and *it* needs something to refer to. Sentence 2 wouldn't make a good first sentence for this paragraph. Cross out Choice (B). In fact, because *it* in sentence 2 refers to the tube of toothpaste in sentence 1, sentence 1 has to come before sentence 2. None of the other choices put sentence 1 before sentence 2, so you know that Choice (A) is the right answer.

38. **C. past, but**

Passed is the past tense of the verb *pass*. The proper word for the underlined part is the noun *past*. Cross out Choices (A) and (B). The difference between the remaining two choices is the comma before *but*. You need the comma because but is a conjunction that separates two independent clauses, and you put a comma before conjunctions that join two complete thoughts. Choice (C) is correct.

39. **B. one**

This question should be a "gimme." *Won* is a verb, the past tense of win. It sounds like the correct word *one* but has a completely different meaning. Eliminate Choices (A) and (C). There's no need to separate *one* from the rest of the sentence. Pick Choice (B).

40. **A. NO CHANGE**

Even if you're fuzzy on when to use who and whom, you can eliminate Choices (B) and (C). The *a* before *woman* tells you that the noun isn't plural.

Who is the subject form of the pronoun, and whom is the object form. If the pronoun is the subject of a clause, use who.

In this case, the pronoun is the subject of a clause ("who needed her teeth to be whiter"), so you need the subject form.

If you have trouble figuring out whether the relative pronoun should be a subject or an object, substitute both forms of a personal pronoun for who or whom. If you put the objective form *her* in the clause, you'd get "her needed her teeth to be whiter." That means the objective form doesn't work in this sentence, and *whom* has to be wrong.

41. A. NO CHANGE

This question tests your knowledge of when to use commas. *But* is a conjunction, and the rule regarding conjunctions and commas is that you need a comma before the conjunction when the conjunction joins two independent clauses. There are a lot of words on the other side of *but*. Those words don't form a complete thought, however, which means you don't need a comma before *but*. Cross out Choice (B). The other two choices put a comma before or after "at the same time." If "at the same time" is an aside, it has to have commas on either side of it. Neither of the options fulfills this rule. Therefore, the author must not intend the phrase to be an aside, and the underlined portion is correct the way it is, Choice (A).

42. B. teeth yellow, such as coffee and blueberries,

Eliminate Choices (A) and (C) because you don't use *as* by itself to compare one noun to another. You can use *as* to compare an action to another action, which means *as* would be okay in this sentence if you added *do* after blueberries: "things. . .that make teeth yellow as coffee and blueberries do." But the choices don't give you that option. Cross out Choice (D). The semicolon would work only if the rest of the sentence were an independent clause, and it's not. The right answer is Choice (B).

43. C. No, because the list would interrupt the flow of the author's story.

You probably figured out right away that the list wasn't a good idea. Jump to the no options to see which is best. The problem with the list isn't its placement. Choice (D) is out. The list doesn't belong anywhere in the essay. Pick Choice (C).

Just to be sure you have somehow missed the relevance of proposed list, check out the yes choices. The essay isn't an informative piece on how to whiten teeth. It's a personal account of why the author decided to switch toothpastes. Cross out Choice (A). A list of consumables would shed no light on the author's personality (other than that she can't tell the difference between relevant detail and mindless minutiae that would put even a barista to sleep!). Eliminate Choice (B).

44. A. NO CHANGE

The point of the last paragraph is that the author has decided to switch from her old toothpaste to a new brand because the new brand promises to provide her with whiter teeth. The answer that best maintains that idea is Choice (A). If the old toothpaste hasn't been whitening her teeth and her goal is whiter teeth, the switch to a new brand makes sense.

Choice (B) is illogical. If the writer's toothpaste works just fine, why should she switch? The paragraph is about toothpaste's whitening effect, not the way it tastes. There's no justification for Choice (C). Choice (D) is redundant. If something's a standby, it's something you've used for a long time.

45. **D. No, because the essay is a personal account rather than an analysis.**

Reading the title may not give you an immediate knowledge of whether the answer is yes or no, so do a bit more digging. The essay is a casual, first-person account of the author's personal experience with switching to another toothpaste. An analysis would include statistical data and reasoned reporting based on the experiences of many consumers. Neither Choice (A) nor Choice (B) recognize that the essay is based on just one experience and therefore fails to analyze the conditions that influence a wide group of consumers. The best answer is Choice (D).

If you picked Choice (C), you realized that the essay didn't fulfill the assignment, but you neglected to focus on the main requirement of the assignment. The assignment asked for the conditions that cause consumers to change brands rather than information about the actual brands they switch to. The lack of brand name in the essay isn't as much a problem as the fact that it doesn't present an analysis.

46. **C. the modern-day melodrama**

The underlined portion puts a comma between *modern* and *day*, which means that modern and day would have to be coordinating (or related) adjectives. Day is a noun, so Choice (A) can't be right. Day isn't an aside, so there's no reason to surround it with commas. Cross out Choice (D). For Choice (B) to work, *todays* would have to be possessive (today's) rather than plural. The best answer is Choice (C). It's proper to hyphenate an adjective and noun combination when they function together to describe a noun that follows them.

47. **D. good guys or bad guys,**

The *and* that comes after the underlined portion is a conjunction that separates two independent clauses (each expresses a complete thought). Therefore, the underlined portion has to end with a comma; otherwise, the sentence is a run on. Choice (C) doesn't end with a comma, so it's wrong. Choice (B) creates a sentence fragment. Cross it out. Putting a comma before *or* the way Choice (A) does suggests that "or bad guys" is nonessential, which isn't true. The correct answer is Choice (D). It eliminates the comma after the first *guys* and maintains the comma after the second.

48. **B. bland,**

Boring and *bland* mean the same thing, and the sentence doesn't need both of them. Choice (C) exchanges one repetitive word for another, so it doesn't solve the problem. Choice (D) eliminates one of the redundant adjectives, but it omits the necessary comma before the conjunction that follows it to separates two independent clauses. The best answer is Choice (B).

49. A. NO CHANGE

You can leave the underlined part the way it is. There's no reason to place commas anywhere. Mark Choice (A).

If you picked Choice (C), you probably thought there was a redundancy problem, but *worried* and *helpless* don't mean the same thing. Plus, both Choice (C) and Choice (B) incorrectly places a comma between the adjective and the noun it describes.

50. C. good;

The two ideas in the sentence are similar, but the transition word *but* in the original sentence implies that they're contrasting. Cross out Choice (A) and consider the others. Choice (D) also shows contrast; cross it out. There isn't a cause and effect relationship between wanting to play bad characters and the fact that evil expressions are more fun, so Choice (B) isn't logical. The best answer is Choice (C). Two complete ideas joined by a semicolon in one sentence conveys similarity between the ideas.

51. D. than helpless ones.

The underlined part uses the adverb *then* to make a comparison instead of the correct word *than*. Cross out Choice (A), and, while you're at it, mark through Choice (B), too. It has the same problem and is unnecessarily wordy. Choices (C) and (D) correct the error, but Choice (C) uses unnecessary words to say the same thing. Choice (D) is correct.

The more direct construction is almost always best.

52. A. Where it is now

If you put the sentence after sentence 1, the paragraph talks about how actors like to play bad characters more than good ones before you discuss the differences between playing bad and good characters. Putting the sentence after sentence 3 or sentence 4 separates the introduction of the close up from descriptive detail about it.

Although the sentence seems a little out of place where it is now, the placements suggested by other options are worse. Choice (A) is the best answer.

53. C. stock expressions

It's unclear what the pronoun *those* refers to. The only answer that clearly defines *those* is Choice (C), which replaces the pronoun with a specific noun.

54. **B. every scene; for instance,**

The sentence is a comma splice because it uses a comma to join two independent clauses. Cross out Choices (A) and (D), which make the same error. One proper way to punctuate two independent clauses in the same sentence is with a semicolon. Pick Choice (B).

You may be able to get by with using a colon in this circumstance, but Choice (C) incorrectly omits the essential comma necessary after *for instance*.

55. **C. When the camera pulls away,**

"The camera pulling away" is a beginning phrase, and beginning phrases describe the subject of the sentence. In this sentence, the subject is *audience*. The audience doesn't pull the camera away. Choice (A) can't be right. Choice (B) has the camera doing the pulling away, but the rest of the answer doesn't flow with the remainder of the sentence. Choices (C) and (D) correct the modifier error by changing the beginning phrase to a clause, but Choice (C) makes more sense. The audience doesn't see the results *because* the camera pulls away. The results are revealed *when* the camera pulls back.

56. **A. Whereas**

Choices (B), (C), and (D) have similar meanings. They and the underlined word convey the same idea: that of "in the same way." The answer choice that doesn't belong with the others and is therefore an inappropriate alternative is Choice (A). *Whereas* shows contrast instead of similarity.

57. **B. characters breathe deeply and heave their shoulders**

The sentence is a fragment. Breathing and heaving look like verbs, but they don't function as verbs. The answer choice that changes them so that they function as verbs is Choice (B). Choice (C) changes the words to their verb forms, but *that* is the subject that goes with them, so there's still no verb that goes with *characters*. Choice (D) has the same problem as Choice (C), and it incorrectly puts a comma after *shoulders*.

58. **C. hold**

This question tests your ability to choose the word that has the most precise meaning. The verb that goes best with "their ground" in the context of this sentence is Choice (C). The author intends to say that the characters remain in the same place. You know this because the next sentence implies that they don't engage in overt physical demonstrations. Choice (B) implies a territorial challenge that isn't supported by the passage. Choices (A) and (D) conjure up images of the characters hugging or grabbing the ground, which doesn't make sense if they're also lifting their hands.

59. **B. examples of the common types of poses soap opera characters strike to portray emotions**

The sentences come after the sentence that state there are stock (or common) physical poses. They provide specific examples of common poses. Choice (B) is the best answer.

You can eliminate Choice (A) because the sentences describe physical actions rather than facial expressions. Examples of overt physical demonstrations appear in the last sentence, so Choice (C) is wrong. The author talks about close ups of facial expressions earlier in the passage, so there's nothing that links the two sentences to what the audience may see in close ups.

60. **B. emotion are**

The underlined portion has a subject/verb agreement problem. The verb *is* is singular. That doesn't agree with the plural subject *demonstrations*. Choice (C) also has a singular verb that doesn't agree with the plural noun. Choice (B) correctly changes the verb to *are*. Choice (D) changes the verb to past tense, which isn't appropriate for an essay that's written in the present tense.

A noun that's the object of a preposition in a prepositional phrase (like *emotion* in "of emotion") can't be the subject of a sentence or clause because a noun can't be an object and a subject at the same time.

61. **B. "Philosophy: Who Needs It?"**

Titles of essays aren't italicized (italics are reserved for longer works). You designate titles of essays with quotation marks. The answer has to be either Choice (B) or Choice (C). The question mark is part of the title, so it needs to go inside the ending quotation mark. The correct answer is Choice (B).

62. **D. questions:**

A semicolon separates independent clauses. The list following the semicolon isn't a complete thought, so Choice (A) is wrong. The proper punctuation mark for introducing a series of examples is the colon as long as the colon is preceded by a complete thought. The clause before the colon is an independent clause, so Choice (D) works. The comma after "such as" in Choice (C) and the lack of punctuation in Choice (A) are both improper constructions.

63. C. also correspond to

The questions aren't literally the branches of philosophy. They relate or fall in line with the branches. Cross out Choices (A) and (B). It's more precise to say that the questions correspond to the branches of philosophy than to say they represent the branches. Choice (D) makes it sound like the question may be doing legal work for the branches! Choice (C) is the best way to phrase the underlined portion.

64. D. philosophy, which are metaphysics, epistemology, and ethics.

The way the underlined portion is punctuated is confusing. It looks like philosophy is included in the list of branches of philosophy. Distinguish the list from *philosophy* by adding "which are." Choice (D) takes care of the problem. Choice (C) improperly punctuates the simple list with semicolons, and Choice (B) neglects to place a comma before the awkward use of *being*.

65. A. NO CHANGE

There's nothing wrong with the underlined portion as it is. Choices (B) and (D) have unjustified commas. If you wish to make *arguably* an aside, you have to put commas on both sides. Choice (C) provides the proper punctuation for an aside but incorrectly changes *most* to *more*. You use more to compare two elements, and there are more than two elements of human survival. Stick with Choice (A).

66. B. concur

The underlined words are a casual way of saying that other philosophers agree with the preceding statement. Eliminate Choice (C) because it has an opposite meaning. The meaning of Choice (A) implies that philosophers are friendly with each other rather than that they agree with the previous statement. Choice (D) means agree, but it suggests that agreement has resulted after giving into to an opposing opinion. The answer that most nearly conveys the meaning of the underlined words is Choice (B).

67. D. cave dwellers

The word that follows *dwellers* is a preposition rather than another noun, so there's no need for the possessive form in the underlined words. Pick Choice (D), which contains the proper plural construction.

ANSWERS 1–100

68. C. people have avoided the study of philosophy

The sentence with the underlined portion is a fragment with no verb. Choice (B) introduces a verb *are*, but it's part of a relative clause and not the main verb of the sentence. Choice (D) includes a word that looks like a verb (avoiding), but it can't be a main verb without another helper verb. The only choice that makes the sentence complete is Choice (C).

69. D. reason

"Reason why. . . is because" is redundant. *The reason, the why,* and *because* have the same meaning. Choice (B) includes the unnecessary preposition *for*. Choice (C) is wrong because you use *which* to introduce nonessential clauses, so *which* should be preceded by a comma. Choice (D) is all you need to get the meaning across.

70. B. their

The pronoun is followed by a noun. The comfort zones belong to them, so you need the possessive form of *they* instead of the adverb *there*. Choice (B) fixes the problem.

71. C. Philosophy requires a deep thought process,

Choice (B) gets the point across in the most descriptive and succinct fashion. Philosophy deals with the way one thinks about things, but it's not exactly a process of thought. Choices (A) and (B) are imprecise. And Choice (B) introduces a verb tense that suggests that philosophy won't be a deep thought process in the future. Choice (D) introduces the second person (you), but the rest of the passage employs third person.

72. D. make them leave a level of discomfort for which they are unprepared.

The choice that doesn't convey the same meaning as the original is Choice (D). The others say that new ideas will push people out of their comfort zone. Choice (D) states the opposite, that new ideas will push people out of their discomfort.

73. B. the feeling of insignificance they experience

"A feeling. . .they can feel" is redundant and a poor use of descriptive language. Eliminate Choices (A) and (C). Choice (D) uses passive instead of active voice, which makes Choice (B) the better answer of the two.

74. C. this breadth

There's no clear reference for the pronoun *this*. It could refer to philosophy, human life, human mindset, or perhaps everything. The only answer that clarifies the reference is the one that eliminates the pronoun completely. Choice (C) accomplishes this task by introducing a noun that defines what creates the sense of insignificance.

75. D. Some philosophical theories

The beginning phrase describes the subject of the sentence, but it makes no sense that theories study philosophy, so you have to change the construction of the original sentence. Cross out Choice (A). Choice (B) sounds okay until you read it in the context of the sentence. Then you find out that it doesn't make sense. That leaves you with Choices (C) and (D). Examine Choice (C). The construction corrects the problem with the theories studying philosophy. In Choice (C), *some* study philosophy. But it's the *theories*, not *some*, that suggest that human perception may be wrong. The description isn't clear in Choice (C). The best answer is Choice (D), which eliminates the problem beginning phrase and clearly states that the theories provide the suggestion that human perception may be wrong.

76. B. human error is, by far,

The trouble with the underlined portion is the comma after *far*. There's no reason to put a comma there unless "by far" is an aside, but "by far" as an aside isn't punctuated properly unless it has commas before and after. Choice (C) takes away the problem comma, but it adds a new error by eliminating the verb. You must have a verb, so Choice (C) can't be right. Choice (D) punctuates "human error" as the nonessential phrase, but if you take those words out of the sentence, you have no subject. Choice (B) properly places commas on either side of the nonessential phrase.

77. B. most frequent

The underlined portion has a redundancy issue. *Common* and *frequent* mean the same thing, so you don't need both. The only answer that eliminates one of the words and corrects the repetitiveness is Choice (B).

78. A. NO CHANGE

The punctuation is proper in the underlined part. The words before the comma make up a complete sentence, and the words after it are a complete sentence.

When you join two independent clauses with a conjunction such as *and*, you need to put a comma before the conjunction.

Choice (B) puts the comma in the wrong place; an answer with a comma after a coordinating conjunction is almost always incorrect. Choice (C) incorrectly omits the comma. Choice (D) is punctuated correctly, but it changes the meaning of the sentence by replacing *and* with *but*.

79. C. Each of us has had

The subject and verb don't agree. It's not that they're arguing. It's that the subject *each* is singular, and the verb *have* is plural. A singular subject has to have a singular verb. The singular form of *have* is *has*, Choice (C). Choice (D) changes *have* to *had*, but it also mistakenly changes the verb tense from present to past.

80. D. after sentence 5

The underlined sentence begins with "the same is true." So the sentence has to follow a sentence with the same idea as the one in the underlined sentence. Deleting a whole folder of important documents isn't the same as developing a new document. The sentence doesn't fit where it is. Cross out Choice (A).

If you put the sentence after sentence 1, deleting a whole folder of documents would be the same as human error's being a cause of business disasters. That's not a great comparison, so Choice (B) isn't right.

Putting the sentence after sentence 2 would make deleting documents the same as the negligible impact on your business operations. Nothing fits so far. Eliminate Choice (C) and hope that putting the sentence after sentence 5 makes more sense. Writing over new text in an old document that you'll need again is similar to deleting a folder of documents. Choice (D) is the best answer.

81. C. our work, we hit

Most of sentence 5 uses the first person plural *we*, but *hit* without a subject implies the command form that means *(you) hit*. To keep person the same throughout the sentence add *we* before *hit* just like it's done in Choice (C).

82. D. single simple solution

The comma after *single* is no good. There's no reason to separate the adjective from the noun it describes. Eliminate Choice (A), and while you're at it, Choice (C), because that option also separates the adjective from the noun that follows it. Choice (B) doesn't help. Adding a comma before single makes it an aside, but single is an essential part of the idea that there isn't just one solution that's simple.

Choice (D) corrects the punctuation problem and correctly switches the order of the adjectives. *Simple* describes the kind of solution, so it goes next to the noun. Single describes the kind of simple solution, so it comes before both words.

83. **C. ourselves**

The underlined word isn't followed by a noun, so the possessive form can't be right. Eliminate Choice (A). The proper form of the reflexive pronoun is *ourselves*. Choice (D) improperly suggests that the businesses make the errors. You can't blame them, so you have to choose Choice (C).

84. **B. their**

They're is the contraction of *they are*. It doesn't make sense to say that "managers hope that they are employees will be careful." The answer isn't Choice (A) or Choice (D). Because the pronoun *they* is followed by the noun *employees*, you need to put the pronoun in possessive form. The possessive form of *they* is *their*, Choice (B).

85. **D. when employees inadvertently delete a file, managers**

The pronouns in the underlined portion don't have clear references. You can guess, but you don't know for sure whether *they* refers to employees or managers. The choice that clears up the references is Choice (D). Choice (C) also incorrectly omits the necessary comma after *file*.

86. **A. NO CHANGE**

The sentence is okay the way it is. The comma after *so* is necessary to separate the beginning dependent clause from the rest of the sentence. Choices (C) and (D) change the meaning of the sentence.

87. **B. a few weeks have passed**

The underlined verb has a tense problem. It switches from the present tense used in the rest of the paragraph to the simple past tense. Choice (B) changes the verb to the proper present tense form "have passed." Choice (C) mistakenly changes the verb *passed* to the noun *past*. Choice (D) omits the *a* and changes the meaning of the sentence.

88. **D. Omit the underlined portion and capitalize *The*.**

Choices (B) and (C) change the original transition to show contrast and cause and effect, respectively. *While* means "at the same time" The corrective action isn't taken at the same time as the backup drive is forgotten. The *and* merely extends the thought and isn't necessary. The option that best keeps the original meaning intact is Choice (D), just taking the *and* out of the sentence

89. D. runs nervously through

Nervous describes how *someone* was running, and words that tell how something is done are adverbs. The adverb form of nervous is *nervously*. Choice (D) makes the change without eliminating the verb from the sentence the way Choice (C) does.

90. D. No, because although it describes the types of human errors that occur in the office environment, the passage does not provide an explanation of how to avoid them.

This passage doesn't describe how to avoid employee error, so it wouldn't meet the needs of the business owner. The best answer is Choice (D). The passage gives examples of employee errors, so Choice (C) is wrong. But the business owner isn't seeking examples of errors, which means that Choice (A) isn't right. The passage specifically states that there's not a simple solution to making human errors, so Choice (B) is wrong.

91. B. October 12, 1875,

The right way to punctuate a date is to put commas on both sides of the year. So Choice (B) is the correct answer.

92. D. he was already marked for deviance

The next sentence says that Crowley was born with a birthmark. You can't give yourself a birthmark, so it doesn't make sense to say he marked himself. Eliminate Choice (A) and check your other options. Choice (C) doesn't work. The comma after *he* replaces the verb with a nonessential phrase, which creates an incomplete thought.

You may be a little confused, because the remaining choices are in passive voice. This sentence is one of those instances where passive voice is appropriate. It's not important who gave Crowley the mark. The point is that he was marked at birth. Choice (B) is wordy and confusing. It uses the phrase "behavior that is deviant" to express something that can be stated as a simple adjective and noun "deviant behavior" or a simple noun, *deviance*. Plus, the placement of *already* makes it sound like the behavior, rather than Crowley, was already deviant. The best answer is Choice (D). It omits *himself* without creating sentence structure problems.

93. A. NO CHANGE

The sentence is punctuated properly. The words before the comma create a complete thought, and the words after the comma are a complete thought. A conjunction *and* joins the independent clauses, so the comma before the conjunction is proper. Stick with Choice (A).

The presences of *and* after the punctuation makes the semicolon, colon, and dash in the other choices improper for this sentence.

94. B. Crowley was born into a Protestant family; his father was an influential preacher.

A beginning phrase always describes the subject of the sentence. The way this sentence is written, it sounds like Crowley's father was born into a Protestant family. The paragraph is about Crowley, not his father, so the sentence should be revised to reflect that it's Crowley who was born into a Protestant family rather than his father.

Choice (C) doesn't change the subject of the sentence. It just changes *his* to *Crowley*. You already know that the dad the sentence refers to belongs to Crowley. Choice (D) makes *preacher* the subject. The sentence doesn't intend to tell you that the preacher was born into Protestant family. The best answer is Choice (B). It corrects the problem by changing the beginning phrase to an independent clause. That correction clarifies that Crowley is the one who was born into a Protestant family. It also changes *dad* to *father* to maintain the more formal style of the rest of the passage.

95. C. an additional detail that supports the author's point that Crowley engaged in deviant behavior from an early age

Examine the underlined words. They provide additional information about Crowley through a statement about his mother's negative name for him. Check the answers to find the one that most closely states this purpose.

The author doesn't suggest that there's a cause and effect relationship between Crowley's mother's name for him and his rejection of Christianity. If anything, the construction of the sentence suggests the opposite, that his mother called him "The Beast" because he rejected Christianity. Cross out Choice (B). The clause doesn't provide transition, and the last sentences don't present a point that contrasts with the rest of the paragraph. Choice (D) isn't right.

The clause is either a minor detail about Crowley's family life or an additional supporting example. Although the clause mention's Crowley's mother, it doesn't provide much insight into what family life was like for him. The clause presents another example that supports the author's point that Crowley's deviant behavior began at birth and continued throughout his life. The best answer is Choice (C).

96. B. he turned

The sentence doesn't have a subject, so it's a fragment. Choices (B) and (D) introduce a subject, but the verb tense in Choice (D) indicates that he was continually turning. Choice (B)'s simple past tense shows that the turning point happened just once in the past. Choice (B) is best.

97. D. the supernatural

The pronoun *it* doesn't have a clear reference. It's singular, so it could rename *occult* or *magic*. Replacing *it* with *them* would be better because *them* could refer to both the *occult* and *magic*. The answers don't give you the option of choosing *them*, however. "Them all" suggests more than two things, so it's not ideal. The best answer is Choice (D). This answer replaces *it* with a specific noun.

98. C. a life of deviant behavior, violent actions, and devotion to the powers of darkness

The original sentence has a problem with parallel construction. All of the elements of the series should have the same grammatical form, but the first (deviant behavior) is a noun and adjective combination, the second (acting) is a gerund, and the third (was devoted to the powers of darkness) is a verb and object. Pick Choice (C) because it changes all three elements to nouns: behavior, actions, and devotion.

If you picked Choice (B) or Choice (D) you can pat yourself on the back for at least noticing that *violent* should be changed to an adverb. Choice (D) also eliminates the redundancy "throughout his life." But Choice (D) still has a parallelism issue; *acting* and *devoted* have different grammatical forms.

99. A. NO CHANGE

The sentence is best the way it is. The possessive form is correct because *one* and *bent* are two adjacent nouns. When you see a noun directly followed by another noun, the first noun should be in the possessive form.

Choice (B) incorrectly changes *one's* to the plural form of *one*. Choice (C) creates an unclear pronoun reference. Choice (D) uses additional unnecessary words to say essentially the same thing as the original.

100. C. after sentence 3

The underlined sentence, sentence 1, mentions Crowley's followers. The only other sentence in the paragraph that mentions Crowley is sentence 3, so it's likely that sentence 1 should come either before or after sentence 3. Focus on Choices (B) and (C). Sentence 3 logically follows sentence 2. Sentence 2 introduces the concept of nurture, and sentence 3 relates the nurture theory to Crowley. You wouldn't want to separate these two thoughts with another sentence. Sentence 1 goes best after sentence 3. It continues the idea that Crowley's personality isn't a product of the way he was raised. Choice (C) is the most logical placement for the sentence.

101. **B. it is**

Choice (A) is wrong because *its* is the possessive form of *it*. There's no noun after *its* for it to possess. Choice (C) doesn't make sense, so the answer has to be Choice (B) or Choice (D). They mean the same thing, but Choice (D) is less formal. The author doesn't use contractions anywhere else in the passage. Choose the more formal Choice (B).

102. **D. whether a person is evil**

You use *if* to introduce a condition that has to be met before another thing happens. Use *whether* to present two alternatives. In this case, you're determining between the two alternatives of whether a person is evil and whether a person is not evil. Therefore, it's better to use *whether* than *if*. Cross out Choices (A) and (B). The *or not* isn't wrong, but it's unnecessary. Additionally, Choice (C) contains a contraction that doesn't jive with the style of the rest of the passage. Choice (D) is the best answer.

103. **A. but**

Like *however* in the passage, all of the answer choices convey contrast, but when you plug each of the choices into the sentence, you see that *but* doesn't fit. That's because *however* is used as an adverb in this sentence, and *but* functions as only a conjunction or a preposition.

104. **D. A better explanation for Crowley's personality would be the nature theory.**

The best transition will join the Crowley example to the overall idea of whether nature or nurture determines personality. Choice (B) doesn't mention Crowley and is too general. Choice (C) doesn't link the two sentences, and its example is contrary to the nature theory. Under the nature theory, Crowley's twin would be like him. What Crowley's followers think about either theory is irrelevant, so Choice (A) is out. The best answer is Choice (D). It links Crowley's personality to the nature theory. The next sentence goes to give a little explanation of what the nature theory is about.

105. **B. twins who are raised under different conditions**

The comma in the original sentence has no purpose, so cross out Choice (A). Adding a comma to the other end of the underlined portion makes the concept of "raised under different conditions" a nonessential element. However, that thought is necessary to the meaning of the sentence. It's not identical twins who support the nature theory; it's specifically identical twins who are raised in different environments. So any answer choice that sets that thought off with commas has to be wrong. Additionally, Choice (D) creates an incomplete thought. The only answer that gets it right is Choice (B).

106. C. is communicated

There's a problem with the underlined portion, but it's not that *communicated* is used inappropriately. The subject of the sentence is *history*, which is singular. Therefore, the verb also needs to be singular. The only choice that changes the plural verb *are* to the singular form is Choice (C).

If you had trouble finding the subject, remember that "migration and destruction" aren't the subjects of the sentence because they're part of the prepositional phrase "of constant migration and destruction of community." Nouns can't be objects of prepositions and subjects at the same time.

107. A. specific documentation of the source of the author's materials

The underlined portion tells you who translated the Codex into the version the author used to write the essay. It provides no information about the legend, its origins, or the reason for its being recorded in the Codex. The best answer has to be Choice (A).

108. D. humans, yet it ended with

There's a problem with the last two words of the underlined portion. They don't make sense with the rest of the sentence. The legend didn't end the flood; it ended *with* a flood. The rest of the choices include *with*, but Choices (B) and (C) create an incomplete thought in the second part of the sentence. Choice (B) has a subject, *ending*, but no verb. Choice (C) doesn't have a subject or a verb. The proper construction is Choice (D). It includes the subject *it*, which clearly refers to the noun *legend*, and it includes the verb *ended*.

109. A. NO CHANGE

The underlined part is fine the way it is. "Four Jaguars" renames the second sun, which means it's an *appositive*, so it's proper to set the title off with commas on either side. None of the other choices punctuates the title properly. For Choices (C) and (D) to work, they'd have to have commas on both sides of the nonessential information.

110. A. NO CHANGE

You use *like* to compare one thing to another. Generally, you use *as* to compare the way one thing is done to the way another thing is done. The underlined portion correctly uses like to compare one sun to another.

Choice (B) mistakenly uses *as* to compare one thing, the second sun, to another thing, the third sun. Choice (D) wrongly uses *like* instead of *as* to compare actions. Choice (C) introduces a prepositional phrase that makes no sense in the context of the sentence.

111. **D. fire and gravel**

You have no idea what *it* refers to. It could be the third sun, or perhaps the blaze, or maybe something else. Making the pronoun plural in Choice (B) does nothing to solve the problem. The only answer that clarifies what rained down with the gravel is Choice (D).

112. **C. existed**

The way that the underlined portion is constructed indicates that "existing as it did under the rule of Quetzalcoatl" is an aside that provides a little more information about Four Winds. However, there's no comma after Quetzacoatl, so the aside is punctuated improperly. Choices (B) and (D) propose different ways of making the same error. The best answer is Choice (C). It changes *existing* to a verb so that the sentence has a compound verb.

113. **A. NO CHANGE**

The preposition that goes best with *scattered* is *throughout*. To scatter is to distribute randomly over a wide area. Choices (C) and (D) suggest that the monkeys landed either next to the forests and mountains or in some place in between them. Neither of those ideas indicates a wide area. Choice (B) conveys that the monkeys landed in the forests and mountain, but it doesn't suggest that they were spread out over a wide area the way that throughout does. Choice (A) is the best preposition for the phrase.

114. **C. No, because it conveys a negative tone that is not consistent with the rest of the paragraph.**

Without the addition, the paragraph is just a series of descriptions of how each of the five suns ends. The sentence ties the five descriptions together by showing that all of them end in human destruction. This information also relates to the previous paragraph that says that the legend communicates the disruption and destruction of the Mexica people. The answer that best summarizes the value of the addition is Choice (B).

Choice (C) is wrong because the rest of the paragraph is full of negative ideas. The sentence provides transition from the first paragraph to the second, so Choice (D) doesn't cut it. Choice (A) is true. The sentence definitely tells the reader that people lived by the legend, but that fact isn't relevant to the rest of the paragraph that is all about the details of the legend and not who lived by them.

ANSWERS
101–200

115. D. suns is just

The underlined part contains the possessive form of *suns*. There's no noun after *suns'*, so there's nothing for suns to possess. You need the plural form *suns*. Choice (B) corrects the possessive problem, but it mistakenly changes *is* to the plural form *are*. The subject of the sentence is story, so the verb needs to be singular.

You may have been enticed by Choice (C) because it changes *just* to *only*, but it creates an awkward contraction of *sun is*. This contraction is a problem for three reasons: it makes *sun* singular; it links sun with *is*, but sun isn't the subject that goes with the verb *is*; and a contraction doesn't fit in with the more formal style of the rest of the passage.

116. D. legend, it helps

The words that come before the semicolon make up a beginning dependent clause. You know that because they don't express a complete thought without the help of the rest of the sentence. You separate a beginning dependent clause from the rest of the sentence with a comma instead of a semicolon, a period, or no punctuation at all. Choice (D) punctuates the sentence properly and changes the verb from the inappropriate present perfect to the more appropriate simple present.

117. B. information that clarifies the difference between myth and what really happened to the Mexica people

You can work this question out by the process of elimination. Cross out Choice (D) immediately. The passage doesn't mention anything having to do with Armageddon. Choice (A) can't be right. Without the underlined part, the passage would mistakenly suggest that the native people experienced actual disasters that were very similar to those described in the legend. Your clue that Choice (C) is wrong is the word *extensive*. It would be hard to provide evidence of anything extensive in as few words as are included in the underlined part.

The best answer has to be Choice (B). The underlined words tell you that the real disaster weren't exactly like the one in the legend.

118. A. NO CHANGE

The clause is best the way it is. The other choices change from active to passive voice and exhibit a lack of parallel structure.

119. B. because

"Due to the fact that" is wordy. "Due to" is better. In this case, however, "due to" doesn't work with the rest of the sentence. That the "Tolltecs disbanded due to the city of Tollan fell" doesn't make sense. The only logical substitute is Choice (B): The Tolltecs disbanded *because* the city of Tollan fell.

Don't move on to the next question until you read the answer you've chosen in the context of the sentence. If you picked Choice (D) without substituting it into the sentence, you would have gotten this fairly easy question wrong.

120. **C. which**

The city has already fallen in the previous sentence, so the people's wandering for seven years didn't cause the city to fall. Choices (A) and (B) don't make sense in the context of the paragraph. If you omit the underline part altogether with Choice (D), however, you lose the subject of the final clause and the sentence becomes "The people wandered for seven years, resulted in the dispersal. . . ." You need to include *which* to give the clause a subject. Choice (C) is the correct answer.

121. **B. However, although**

The sentence makes some sense the way it is, but Choice (B) is better because it provides a greater contrast between the thought in the first sentence and the thought in this sentence. The previous sentence tells you that acting *seems* to be similar to big screen acting. The next sentence tells you that even though there are similarities, television acting is different. The *although* shows the contrast between the ideas in the sentence itself. You need to add the *however* in Choice (B) to show the contrast between the two ideas in the first and second sentence. Choice (C) creates a comma splice. Choice (D) includes a word that incorrectly shows similarity rather than contrast.

122. **A. NO CHANGE**

The sentence is best as is. The phrase after *two* in the underlined portion provides a nonessential example of one of the ways that television and big screen acting are similar. Therefore, it should be set aside from the rest of the sentence with commas on both sides. You can easily eliminate Choice (D). The semicolon separates two independent clauses, and the words that come after the semicolon in this sentence don't create a complete thought.

123. **D. has a tendency toward**

Choice (D) doesn't fit in the context of the sentence even though "tend to be" and "have a tendency toward" have almost the same meaning. With Choice (D) inserted, the first part of the sentence reads "acting for television has a tendency toward more superficial." All of the other choices make sense in the sentence, so you can eliminate them as being *not* acceptable.

ANSWERS 101–200

124. **C. than**

The proper comparison construction is "more. . .than." Choice (C) is the best answer.

125. **A. a beginning phrase that introduces the sentence but does not add vital information**

Eliminate wrong answers. The three-word phrase introduces an example of one of the differences between television and movie acting, but it isn't an example itself. Choice (D) is out. The examples that follow the first sentence aren't numbered, so Choice (C) is wrong. The phrase isn't necessary to link the first and second paragraphs. Cross out Choice (B). The best answer is Choice (A). The phrase provides a little introduction, but it isn't necessary and the sentence would lose little without it.

126. **C. significantly less**

You use *fewer* with plural nouns and *less* with singular nouns. *Time* is singular, so television requires *less* time, Choice (C). Choice (D) uses *less*, but it presents an awkward construction.

127. **C. for each episode, less taped footage to draw from, and less time to edit the final product.**

The original sentence incorrectly uses semicolons to punctuate a simple series. Choice (D) doesn't solve the problem by introducing a colon. Choice (B) is punctuated correctly, but it changes the construction and the meaning of the sentence. It makes it sound as though less preparation time results in less taped footage and less time to edit. This cause and effect relationship doesn't make sense in the context of the sentence. The best answer is Choice (C). It corrects the punctuation problem without changing the meaning of the sentence.

128. **D. lack depth**

One-dimensional and *lacking depth* mean the same thing, so you don't need both of them to describe the characters. Choice (D) corrects the redundancy in the clearest way.

129. **D. No, because the sentence contains comparison language but doesn't provide a specific comparison.**

The sentence doesn't provide transition to the next paragraph, so you can eliminate Choice (B). The passage is about the difference between television and movie actors, not about the negative aspects of television acting, so Choice (C) isn't best. The goal of writing isn't to include as many examples as possible. You can eliminate Choice (A). The best answer is Choice (D). The sentence says that actors are much more spontaneous, but it doesn't tell you exactly what they are much more spontaneous than.

130. **B. in other words**

The phrase "on the other hand" shows contrast. Choices (A), (C), and (D) also show contrast. "In other words" shows similarity. So Choice (B) is the least acceptable alternative because it changes the meaning of the sentence.

131. **D. This gives them**

The underlined portion creates a sentence fragment. *Giving* looks like a verb, but it's really just a part of a verb trying to do the job of a verb. You need to pick the choice that adds a subject and verb to the sentence. Choices (B) and (C) maintain the same *ing* form, so they don't solve the problem. The answer that gives the sentence a subject and verb is Choice (D).

132. **C. also affect**

Effect is almost always a noun, but this sentence incorrectly uses it as a verb. The proper verb is *affect.* Choice (D) uses *affecting*, but it changes the verb tenses so that it's inconsistent with the rest of the passage. The answer that corrects the word confusion and maintains the proper verb tense is Choice (C).

133. **A. NO CHANGE**

By definition, a variety is diverse, so Choices (B) and (D) are redundant. The underlined portion is fine the way it is. Choice (C) isn't redundant, but it changes the meaning of the sentence.

134. **D. their last**

The underlined portion calls for the possessive form of *they*, which is *their.* So the best answer is Choice (D). Choice (C) employs the possessive form, but it uses a singular pronoun to refer to the plural noun *actors.*

135. **A. Yes, because the passage states that television acting is different from movie acting and then provides specific ways that the two types of acting differ.**

The question asks you to determine whether the author has written an essay that *contrasts* the two types of acting. To contrast means to expose the differences. Because the essay focuses on the differences between television and movie acting, it fulfills the goal of the assignment. Choice (A) is the best answer.

Choice (B) is untrue; pointing out similarities would be comparing rather than contrasting the two types of acting. Contrasting doesn't require specific acting examples, so Choice (D) isn't the best answer.

136. A. NO CHANGE

The underlined portion is right. As a general rule, numbers under 10 and any number that begins a sentence should be written out in words, so eliminate Choices (B) and (D). A noun doesn't follow *dramatists*, so the possessive form in Choice (C) is wrong.

137. C. stage:

The punctuation in the underlined portion creates a comma splice. The words to the left of the comma form a complete thought, and the words to the right of the comma form a complete thought. When you use a comma to separate two independent clauses, you need to include a conjunction. None of the answer choices contains a conjunction, so you have to come up with another way to fix the problem.

You may have jumped on Choice (D) immediately. It appears to solve the comma splice issue by splitting the clauses into two separate sentences. If you look at Choice (D) carefully, though, you see that it omits the verb *were*, which makes the second sentence a fragment.

Choice (B) changes the second clause to a phrase. That solves the comma splice, but it creates an unclear descriptive phrase that sounds like the playwrights are *being* the stage. Check Choice (C) to see if it offers a better solution.

Choice (C) ends the first clause with a colon. You can do that because the first clause is an independent clause, and one of the most important rules for using colons is that they follow a complete thought. The colon introduces a specific description of the topic in the initial independent clause. Choice (C) provides a proper punctuation of the sentence and is the best answer.

138. D. No, because the paragraph is specifically about fifth-century Greek drama.

Check for relevance. The paragraph is primarily about fifth-century Greek drama. It gives a little of its history, specifies three of its major dramatists, describes the way that the actors dressed, and mentions the chorus. The dramatists of the time make up just one element of the paragraph. Therefore, it is inappropriate to insert a sentence that's about Greek dramatists from other times. Choice (D) is the best answer.

The paragraph isn't primarily about Greek dramatists, the influence of Greek drama, or dramatists in general, so Choices (A), (B), and (C) have to be wrong.

139. D. Actors, accompanied by a chorus and dressed in masks and platform shoes,

This question has a reference problem. The underlined portion makes it sound as though the platform shoes were accompanied by a chorus. Choose the answer that moves things around so that it's clear that it's the actors who are accompanied by a chorus.

Choices (B) and (C) clarify that it's the actors, not the shoes, who are accompanied by a chorus, but they create problems with parallel structure. Choice (B) provides three descriptions of the actors: they are dressed in platform shoes, accompanied by a chorus, and they have masks on. The first two descriptions have the same construction, participle phrases ("dressed in platform shoes" and "accompanied by a chorus"). The last description is an independent clause ("they have masks on"). Choice (C) omits the awkward clause, but it still contains a lack of parallelism that you may not have noticed. The first and last descriptions in the list ("dressed in platform shoes" and "accompanied by a chorus") are participle phrases, but the middle description is a simple noun and adjective (platform shoes).

Choice (D) reduces the three descriptions to two participle phrases. The actors are "accompanied by a chorus" and "dressed in masks and platform shoes." Problem solved!

140. B. 1, 3, 2

Approach this question methodically. The answers give you the option of beginning with any of the three sentences and ending with either sentence 2 or sentence 3. Because you have fewer ending sentence options, consider the best ending sentence first.

The last sentence of the paragraph should lead into the first sentence of the next. The next paragraph begins "Their tragedies." *Their* must refer to a group. The subject of sentence 3 is *actors*, and the subject of sentence 2 is *dramatists*. The tragedies more logically belong to the dramatists who wrote them than the actors who play in them. Therefore, sentence 2 should end the first paragraph. Eliminate Choices (A) and (C).

The remaining task is for you to decide whether sentence 1 or sentence 3 provides a better introduction. Sentence 1 presents the primary topic of the paragraph and the entire passage, fifth-century Greek drama. Sentence 3 is merely a subtopic about Greek drama at that time. The best order for the sentences is the one in Choice (B).

141. B. usual

All options are meanings of *inevitable*. Three of them duplicate the particular meaning of *inevitable* in the context of this sentence. The other, the one that's meaning is slightly different, is the correct answer.

You can approach this question by eliminating the three answer choices that have similar meanings to each other. Then check to make sure that the one left over doesn't fit as well in the sentence.

Unavoidable and *inescapable* are obvious synonyms. If you can't avoid something, you can't escape it. Cross out Choices (A) and (C). Eliminating the next answer may be a little more difficult. When you think carefully, though, you see that if something's unavoidable or inescapable, it's certain to happen. Eliminate Choice (D) because it fits better with the other two answer choices than Choice (B) does.

Inevitable can mean *usual*, but the point of the sentence and the rest of the paragraph is that the tragic hero has a flaw that prevents him from controlling what happens to him. The tragic hero's movement from good fortune to destruction isn't *usual*, it's *certain*.

142. **A. NO CHANGE**

The original construction conveys the cause and effect relationship in the most succinct way. Choice (A) is the best answer.

Choice (B) uses an unnecessary phrase and superfluous clause to say the same thing, and *since* isn't a good substitute for *because*. Choice (C) is shorter than the original, but that's because it omits a necessary preposition.

143. **B. humans'**

You know there's more than one human because the pronoun that refers to *humans* later in the sentence (their) is plural. So eliminate Choices (A), (C), and (D) because they're singular. The only plural answer is Choice (B). It properly shows that the inability to control their fates belonged to humans.

144. **C. resulted**

The verbs in the rest of the passage are in past tense. The verbs in Choices (A) and (B) are present tense, so they don't fit. Choice (D) is past tense, but its past perfect construction indicates that a continual action in the past without a definite end. The hero's attempts resulted in increased suffering. Period. The simple past in Choice (C) is the most appropriate tense.

145. **A. NO CHANGE**

The best transition sentence is the one that's already in the passage. Eliminate Choice (C) because it illogically compares *those* (referring to tragedies) to Sophocles. Sophocles wrote tragedies, but he wasn't himself a tragedy. Choice (D) also has sentence structure problems. Sophocles's tragedy was titled *Oedipus Tyrannus*, so the phrase that tells you that fact should come directly after *tragedy* in the sentence. The way that Choice (D) is constructed, the hero is called *Oedipus Tyrannus*, which could be true if the name wasn't in the italicized title form. Choice (B) can't be best. The third paragraph is specifically about Sophocle's *Oedipus Tyrannus*, and Choice (B) provides no introduction to the play or indication of who Oedipus is. Choice (A) provides the best transition.

146. **B. ascertains**

The sentence has no verb. *Learning* may look like a verb, but it's only part of a verb and it's incapable of functioning as a verb on its own. We might say it's codependent, but for now we'll leave that diagnosis to the poor verb's psychologist.

Choice (C) changes the terminology, but it doesn't correct the sentence fragment. Choice (D) provides a verb, but the construction doesn't flow well with the rest of the sentence. It's awkward to say that Oedipus stumbles upon "that he cannot escape," because there's no clear object for the preposition *upon*.

The best answer is Choice (B). It provides a verb that fits into the sentence.

Don't get hung up on whether *ascertain* is a better verb for the sentence than *learn*. There's nothing inherently wrong with learn in the sentence. The answers just don't give you that option. Take what you're given and move on.

147. **B. He learns that his attempts to escape his fate serve to worsen his destruction**

The action in the next clause is the lamentation of the chorus over the cruelty and inevitability of fate. The correct answer must indicate that Oedipus is a victim of cruel and inevitable fate. Any option that suggests he had control over his situation has to be wrong. So eliminate Choices (A), (C), and (D). That leaves you with just one choice. The best answer has to be Choice (B) because it shows that Oedipus had no control over his fate.

148. **A. NO CHANGE**

The sentence tells you that Euripides' plays are different. The word that indicates this contrast is *however*, Choice (A). Choice (B) shows cause and effect, but the sentence doesn't give a reason for the difference between the dramatists' plays. For *mostly* to work, the sentence would have to suggest a small way that the two plays were the same. Cross out Choice (C). *Supposedly* suggests that the rest of the paragraph's going to show you how the plays really aren't all that different, but that's not what happens. The paragraph tells you that Euripides' plays are indeed different. The best answer is Choice (A).

149. D. passage would avoid stating an unnecessary redundancy

The fact that Euripides is one of the three great dramatists of the fifth century is already mentioned in the first paragraph of the passage. The underlined portion is redundant and unnecessary. The best answer is Choice (D).

150. A. as it is now.

Don't give up on this one too quickly. It's really fairly easy. You know that paragraph 4 comes after paragraph 3 because paragraph 4 compares Euripides to what's already been said about Sophocles. Cross out Choices (B) and (D) because they put paragraph 4 before paragraph 3.

It should be obvious to you that paragraph 1 is the introductory paragraph. It's more general than paragraph 2. So paragraph 1 must come before paragraph 2. Eliminate Choice (C). The passage is already arranged correctly, so Choice (A) is correct.

151. D. OMIT the underlined portion.

An answer option to omit the underlined part is a signal to check for irrelevance or redundancy. In this case, the underlined words add no relevant information, and Choices (B) and (C) are irrelevant and wordy. The best choice is to omit "and on."

152. B. amazing and unique

Eliminate Choices (A) and (D) because the only time a comma before a coordinating conjunction, such as *and*, is proper is when the *and* joins two independent clauses or when it comes at the end of a series of three or more elements. Choice (C) is also wrong. It's almost never proper to put a comma after a conjunction. Choice (B) correctly eliminates the comma.

153. A. NO CHANGE

The punctuation is proper in the underlined part. The words before the semicolon make up a complete sentence, and the words after it are a complete sentence.

Choice (B) creates a comma splice, and Choice (C) is a fused sentence.

If you pick Choice (D), you've failed to read the whole sentence. Beginning the second clause with *which* doesn't make sense.

154. **A. more specific details about the restaurant's offerings.**

Focus on the information provided in the sentence. The writer provides a list of three specific dishes she enjoyed at Wokamama. The information doesn't tell you how many times she visited the restaurant or about foods available in other restaurants, so Choices (C) and (D) must be wrong.

The sentence tells you what kinds of foods the writer ate and liked at the restaurant but doesn't explain why. That explanation comes two sentences before. The primary purpose of the sentence in question is to provide examples of the kinds of dishes the writer liked best, which is expressed by Choice (A).

155. **D. My travels provided other encounters with Asian fusion.**

Read the second paragraph to determine its primary topic. It seems to discuss a restaurant in Amsterdam that offered a menu similar to Wokamama's. The writer doesn't say that Wok the Walk is less satisfying, so Choice (B) is out. The paragraph doesn't mention other London restaurants, so Choice (A) isn't a good option. You have to eliminate Choice (C) because it repeats information offered later in the essay. The best answer is Choice (D). It links the information in the second paragraph about the writer's discovery in Amsterdam to the type of cuisine described in the first paragraph.

156. **D. In Amsterdam, I found a place that**

The arrangement of Choices (A), (B), and (C) indicate that *it* or *they* were in Amsterdam. Neither of these pronouns appropriately refers to the person who was "in Amsterdam." Choice (D)'s introduction of *I* as the subject of the sentence clearly identifies that the writer is the one who is in Amsterdam.

157. **B. Wokamama, which offered a**

Eliminate Choice (A) because the semicolon doesn't connect two independent clauses. Choice (B) is out for a similar reason: The comma before *but* is proper only to connect two complete thoughts. Choice (D)'s addition of *was* contains an unnecessary second verb. The properly punctuated and more clearly constructed version is Choice (B).

158. **B. after *place*.**

Place the underlined part as close as possible to the noun that is called Wok the Walk. The rest of the paragraph makes clear that the Amsterdam restaurant is called Wok the Walk. The best reference for that restaurant is *place*. So Choice (B) is best.

159. **C. meals**

Choices (A) and (D) contain an unclear pronoun. You can't circle a prior noun that *it* refers to. Choice (B) changes the pronoun to plural form, which does nothing to clarify the situation. The best answer is Choice (C) because it clarifies that *meals* can be eaten in or at home.

160. **D. tasty**

Because tasty, delicious, and delectable all have pretty much the same meaning, the only answer that isn't redundant is Choice (D).

161. **B. when I discovered after I arrived back in the States that one had been pretty close to me in**

Find the answer that orders the words most clearly and logically. The writer gets bummed when she finds out that a Wok the Walk had been near her back in London. She wasn't bummed that she arrived back in the States, so Choice (A) is out. She didn't arrive back to the States in London, so Choice (C) is wrong. Choice (D) contains passive voice ("one was discovered"), so Choice (B) expresses the thought best.

162. **A. NO CHANGE**

Check the answers for comma errors. Choice (B) omits the comma after town that separates the beginning phrase from the main clause. The missing comma before *due* also suggests that the writer is back in the States *because* of the lack of good Asian restaurants. Choice (C) contains a comma pair that incorrectly indicates that "of good Asian restaurants" is a nonessential phrase. Choice (D) improperly places a comma between *restaurants* and the preceding adjective *Asian* that describes them. The best punctuation is in Choice (A). It properly uses commas to designate that "due to the lack of good Asian restaurants" does not describe why the writer is back in the States.

163. **A. NO CHANGE**

The rest of the paragraph is primarily in present tense, so stick with the present tense form of the verb as presented in Choice (A). All other answers are in past tenses.

164. **D. Happily,**

To select the best transition word, check the preceding sentence and the sentence that contains the underlined word to determine how they're related. The prior sentence says that Panda Panda doesn't taste right. It's followed by the discovery that the writer's preferred restaurants may come to her town. Therefore, *happily* makes the most sense. That Panda Panda's food doesn't taste right doesn't cause the other restaurants to expand, so Choice (B) is out. Both Choices (A) and (C) provide contrasting transitions. The two sentences don't convey opposing ideas, and the two answers can't both be right, so eliminate Choices (A) and (C). The most logical transition is Choice (D).

165. **D. No, because the essay doesn't directly relate appreciation of foreign food to appreciation of foreign cultures.**

You can eliminate Choices (B) and (C) because they aren't true. The essay doesn't discuss the writer's appreciation for London culture so much as it describes her appreciation for a particular Asian restaurant in London. Choice (A) is true, but providing examples of foods the writer likes better than American options doesn't necessarily show her general appreciation for London culture. The best answer is Choice (D). Check the title. The essay doesn't talk about the writer's appreciation for any element of London other than its Wokamama restaurant.

166. **A. NO CHANGE**

Stick with Choice (A). The proper punctuation mark is the comma. The words before the punctuation don't express a complete thought. Therefore, the semicolon and comma paired with *and* can't be right because their job is to join two independent clauses. Eliminate Choices (B) and (D), which are wrong. The colon must be preceded by a complete thought, so Choice (C) is also incorrect.

167. **B. today's rapid-paced**

Even though two adjectives come between *today* and *landscape*, you still need possessive form. Whenever you see a noun followed directly by another noun (including the adjectives that describe the second noun), you need to put the first noun in possessive form. Eliminate Choices (A). There is only one today, so eliminate the plural form in Choice (D).

The comma after *rapid-paced* is improper; it fails the *and* test because you can't replace the comma with *and.* Pass on Choice (C) and select Choice (B).

168. **C. quickly and effectively**

The underlined words describe the way the verb *work* is performed, so they need to be adverbs. The only choice contains two adverbs is Choice (C).

169. C. No, because it interrupts the transition between this paragraph and the one that follows.

The question asks you to determine whether adding the proposed statement to the end of the first paragraph is appropriate. This paragraph introduces the importance of developing business partnerships. Although the statement regards business, it doesn't directly pertain to building partnerships. The answer is likely *no*.

You can eliminate Choice (D) because it isn't true. The entire essay is about making businesses more successful. Choice (C) provides the better rationale for not adding the statement. The last sentence of the first paragraph sets up the beginning of the second paragraph by introducing the idea of partnerships. A statement about research and development disturbs this flow.

You can check the *yes* answers to be sure you haven't missed something. Choice (B) is true but doesn't relate to the topic of the first paragraph. Choice (A) is false. The proposed statement doesn't summarize the paragraph's main point about the necessity of partnerships.

170. D. achieve

To maintain the parallel structure of the series in the sentence, you need the infinitive form of achieve: the opportunity to gain, develop, and *achieve*.

Choices (A), (B), and (C) provide verb forms that aren't consistent with the rest of the elements of the series.

171. A. NO CHANGE

The question directs you to the requirement in the rest of the sentence, which is to adapt to quickly changing markets. The state that relates most direct to adapting quickly is nimbleness, or agility. Pick Choice (A).

Nothing in the sentence suggests that businesses should be cautious, so Choice (B) is clearly wrong. *Evolvement* implies slow change rather that quick adaptation, so Choice (C) isn't best. Choice (D) is weak. To achieve an accomplishment is redundant.

172. A. NO CHANGE

Believe it or not, the dash is the best way to punctuate this sentence. It's preceded by an independent clause, so the dash acts as a colon to set up clarifying information. In other words, "they're not just marginalized (that is to say) they're eliminated.

If you aren't sure, check the other options. Choice (C) incorrectly replaces the contraction of "they are" with the possessive form of they. Choice (B) creates a comma splice. The clauses on either side of the comma are both independent. Putting no punctuation between the two complete thought creates a fused sentence in Choice (D).

173. C. company's

Because the noun *company* is followed by another noun competitiveness, you need to put company in possessive form. Eliminate Choice (B). The article *a* in front of company indicates that the noun is singular. The singular possessive is Choice (C) rather than Choice (D). Choice (A) is completely wrong because it creates a plural possessive with the singular spelling of company.

174. A. NO CHANGE

The sentence is best the way it is. The following two paragraphs explain first the reasons why businesses resist partnerships all together and then the reasons that past partnerships have been limited in scope. Choice (A) sets up both of these topics.

The rest of the essay doesn't provide solutions to the resistance toward partnerships, nor does it indicate that businesses should approach partnerships with caution. Eliminate Choices (B) and (D). Choice (C) references only the next paragraph and not the rest of the essay.

175. C. Just like a corporation that lacks communication between its divisions,

Choices (A) and (B) contain a faulty comparison. They say that a company is like two divisions. The answer that creates the most accurate comparison is Choice (C). It compares a company that fails to integrate and share information to a corporation that lacks communication. Choice (D) improperly uses *as* instead of *like* to compare nouns.

176. B. its

The construction *it's* is the contraction of *it is.* You wouldn't say "fails to integrate it is business processes," so Choice (A) is wrong.

Quickly eliminate Choice (D) because *its'* doesn't exist in the English language. The underlined pronoun renames the singular noun *company*, so the singular pronoun *its* (not the plural pronoun *their*) is correct.

177. B. Consequently,

Note the capitalized LEAST in the question. You're seeking the answer that doesn't fit with the meaning conveyed by the underlined portion. *Similarly* indicates that the idea in the preceding sentence and the idea in the sentence with the underlined portion are alike. Choices (A), (C), and (D) also show a similarity between the two ideas. Choice (B) is wrong because *consequently* indicates a cause and effect relationship between the ideas rather than strict similarity.

178. D. more closely

You need an adverb to describe the way the companies work. Choices (A) and (C) are adjectives (and "more close" should be *closer*), so they're incorrect. Choice (B) is an adverb phrase, but Choice (D) states the same idea in much more precisely.

179. D. Have begun

The participle form of *begin* (the one you use with the helping verb *to have*) is *begun*, not *began*. *Began* is the past tense form. So the proper verb form is provided in Choice (D): companies *have begun* communicating.

Choice (C) incorrectly switches the tense from present to past. Choice (B) uses the participle form without the necessary helping verb.

180. A. point A in paragraph 1.

The potential addition begins with *but*, so it needs to follow an idea that it contrasts with. The ideas presented before point A states that a company always has customers and suppliers. It would logically follow to say that, in contrast, not every company has partners, especially because the following sentence talks about the value of having partners.

Placing the sentence at point B isn't logical. The sentence repeats rather than opposes the idea presented before point B. Putting it before point C doesn't work because the fact that not every company has partners isn't a logical reference for the pronoun *these* in the sentence that follows point C. Point D in the last paragraph is too late in the essay for the writer to introduce the idea the not every company has partners.

181. D. pillaged

Pillage means "loot, raid, and steal," so any answer other than Choice (D) is redundant.

182. B. lost

The subject, *army*, is singular, so eliminate the plural verbs in Choices (A) and (C). Choice (D) isn't conjugated, which leaves Choice (B) — the only conjugated singular verb.

183. A. NO CHANGE

The comma paired with the conjunction in the original is the best way to join the two independent clauses in the sentence. Choice (B) incorrectly omits the comma before the conjunction, and inappropriately joins the two thoughts with *and* instead of *but*. Choice (C) requires a semicolon before the subjunctive adverb *however.* And even though an independent clause precedes the comma in Choice (D), what follows isn't a more specific way of saying it took time. The proper punctuation is in Choice (A).

184. **D. Alaric, marched**

In Choice (A), the sentence is incomplete; *marching* isn't conjugated, so the sentence has no main verb. Choice (B) provides a verb, but it's in present instead of past tense. Choice (C) is incorrect because the first clause is dependent and therefore not a complete thought capable of ending with a period. The answer that creates a complete sentence in past tense is Choice (D).

185. **C. However,**

The sentence before the transition word states that the Romans tried to pay off the raiders. The following sentence indicates that the Visigoths attacked. So *even though* the Senate tried to pay them off, the Visigoths defeated Rome. The proper transition should show contrast, which is provided with *however* in Choice (C).

Notice you can easily eliminate Choices (A) and (B) because they provide the same cause and effect transition. They can't both be right, so they must both be wrong.

186. **D. rebuffed**

Find the answer that is most unlike *defeated.* Though the rest of the choices mean that Rome was overthrown, Choice (D) indicates that it was ignored. Romans likely wished the Visigoths had ignored them!

187. **B. existed**

The clause after *stability* is an essential description of who had supplied the authority and stability. Therefore, you need to eliminate that the comma after stability in Choices (A) and (C). You do need the comma before *confusion* to separate the beginning phrase from the main clause. The properly punctuated answer is Choice (B).

188. **D. OMIT the underlined portion.**

Whenever you see the option to omit the underlined part, check it for irrelevance or redundancy. You already know from the first part of the sentence that the Romans were without stability, so eliminate Choices (A) and (B); *unstableness* is just another way of saying "instability." *Disarray* is another way of saying "confusion," so Choice (C) is wrong. The best option is to get rid of the underlined part altogether.

189. A. NO CHANGE

The best use of prepositions in in Choice (A). The estate owners trade farmers *for* (not *from* or *with*) their land and labor.

190. B. No, because the addition provides details that are already stated elsewhere in the essay.

From the preceding sentence, you know that the feudal structure is a pyramid. The next paragraph begins with information that states the kind is on top, so the proposed addition is redundant and shouldn't be added. Choice (B) is best.

191. C. keeps and thick, strong, siege-proof curtain walls

Eliminate Choices (B) and (D) because the, *and* construction is only proper when you're ending a series of three of more items or joining together two independent clauses. Neither is happening here.

The difference between Choices (A) and (C) is the comma before curtain. The noun that thick, strong, and siege-proof are describing is "curtain walls." You know that because it sounds wrong to insert *and* between siege-proof and curtain. For a series of adjectives before a noun, place commas between them only when you could also insert an *and.* Therefore, Choice (C) is proper.

192. C. These bastions

When you look for the noun that the pronoun *these* renames, you see several possibilities. It could mean walls, keeps, or castles. Because the reference is unclear, Choice (A) is incorrect. The same is true for Choice (B) and (D). The only answer that provides clarity is Choice (C), which replaces the pronoun with the actual noun that had the latest luxuries.

193. D. NO CHANGE

Eliminate Choice (A) because it uses the plural verb *were* to go with a singular subject, *cathedral.* Choice (B) is wrong because it lacks the necessary comma before *which.* The pronoun which introduces nonessential clauses and therefore must be set apart from the rest of the sentence with commas. Choice (C) makes the nonessential part of the clause just "which was led," but the entire clause is nonessential, so the comma after *led* is wrong. Notice that the best answer, Choice (D), not only corrects the punctuation but also simplifies the sentence.

194. **A. Though he fortified his kingdom against attackers,**

Keeping peace with the nobles is an additional king's duty. Choices (B), (C), and (D) convey this idea. Choice (A) improperly indicates that fortifying the kingdom and making peace with the nobles are opposite goals.

195. **B. The successful accomplishment of these goals resulted in a feudalistic system that lasted for centuries.**

Choice (B) summarizes the paragraph by referencing its discussion of the duties of a feudal king; it also references the main topic of the essay, which was to describe the rise feudalism

Choice (A) summarizes the paragraph but not the passage as a whole (and it includes the nondescript noun *things*), so it's not your best bet. Choice (D) contradicts information in the beginning of the essay that claims the Roman government was overthrown. Choice (C) introduces a new topic about the role of other society members and fails to summarize the paragraph and the essay.

196. **D. many students choose to earn an associate degree.**

The lengthy group of underlined words follows a beginning participle phrase. Whenever a sentence begins with a phrase containing an -ing word or other verb participle, the subject needs to be the entity that performs the action. The action in the phrase is *securing*. Those doing the securing of a diploma are the students. The only answer that makes students the subject of the sentence is Choice (C).

197. **B. industry, has become**

Choice (A) is wrong. You need the comma after industry to close the descriptive clause that begins earlier with *which*. When Choice (C) changes *has become* to *becoming*, the sentence loses its verb. Adding *and* in Choice (D) is also a problem because the only time a comma before a coordinating conjunction such as *and* is proper is when the *and* joins two independent clauses or when it comes at the end of a series of three or more elements. Choice (D) changes the sentence's main clause to "this degree and has become."

Choice (B) correctly places the comma after industry to close the clause without messing with the main verb.

198. **A. NO CHANGE**

A reflexive pronoun such as *itself* isn't a nonessential element and therefore shouldn't be surrounded by commas. Eliminate Choice (C). Placing a single comma anywhere between a subject and verb is never correct. Choices (B) and (D) both violate this rule. So the correct answer is Choice (A).

199. C. administrative

The question tells you to clarify the last part of the sentence, so focus your attention there. The two factors concern program location and length, which are administrative concerns. Location and length are certainly tangible, so Choice (A) is wrong. Nothing in the last part of the sentence justifies that the considerations are crucial, so Choice (B) is out. You know Choice (D) is wrong because the following sentence says that program content is similar. The most justifiable answer is Choice (B).

200. A. Yes, because the statement provides more detailed information to support the sentence that precedes it.

The information in the sentence that precedes the proposed addition states that different programs have similar curricula. The addition relates to that statement and provides more detailed insight into the content of the similar courses. So Choice (A) is best.

Choice (B) isn't true. The preceding statement informs the reader about the similarities in curricula. Because the details relate to the preceding sentence, Choice (C) also untrue. Although the sentence begins with ways programs may differ, it also provides information about how they are the same, so Choice (D) is out.

201. C. comprehensive

Broad and *comprehensive* have essentially the same meaning, so including both adjectives is redundant. Choice (B) doesn't correct the redundancy, and Choice (D) introduces a new synonym for comprehensive. The best answer is Choice (C) because comprehensive by itself is sufficient to convey the general nature of the discussion.

202. A. NO CHANGE

The underlined pronouns stand in for *a graduate*, which is a singular noun. Eliminate Choice (B) because it's a plural pronoun. Choice (C) is out because you don't use *it* to refer to people. Choice (D) sounds as though the associate degree is prepared to enter the nursing profession. Choice (A) provides the set of singular pronouns that correctly refer to the singular noun.

203. B. more specific information about the types of possible working environments for nurses.

The underlined part contains specific examples of the locations where nurses may find work. Choice (B) is the closest representation of this function. The list of work environment isn't detailed enough to justify Choice (A). The paragraph doesn't compare the opportunities available to associate degree earners versus advanced program participants, so Choice (C) is wrong. The underlined list contains no explanations, so Choice (D) isn't right.

204. **D. OMIT the underlined portion and capitalize *some*.**

When you add a subordinating conjunction like *while* to the beginning of an independent clause, you create a dependent clause. Dependent clauses can't stand alone as sentences. Choice (A) is wrong, and so are Choices (B) and (C) because they, too, begin the clause with subordinating conjunctions. The only way to create a complete sentence is to delete the subordinating conjunction as provided by Choice (D).

205. **B. side.**

The best answer is Choice (B). The other choices contain information that is either redundant (option) or vague (things).

206. **A. NO CHANGE**

The possessive form of *they* is *their*, so Choice (A) is correct. Choice (B) defines a location, and Choice (C) is the contraction of *they are*. Choice (D) doesn't work because *an* must apply to all three elements of the subsequent series, and you can't refer to "an career opportunities."

207. **B. people; part**

First, check the semicolon in Choice (B). Semicolons are easy to evaluate. If you see an independent clause before the semicolon and after it (which is the case in Choice (B)), you've likely found the correct answer. Choice (A) is a comma splice, Choice (C) is a fused sentence, and Choice (D) makes no sense.

208. **C. continue**

The subject that pairs with the underlined verb is the singular noun *need*. Therefore, the verb needs the singular form *continues* provided by Choice (C). All other options are plural.

209. **A. NO CHANGE**

The most succinct and clear way to express the thought is Choice (A). Choices (B) and (C) are redundant: Global and world-wide have the same meaning. Choice (D) uses relative clauses ("that has opportunities" and "that span the globe") to provide the same details as the adjective (global) and adjective phrase (with global opportunities) in Choice (A).

ANSWERS 201–300

210. A. where it is now.

The best location for the second paragraph is where it is now. It offers more specific information about the degree program introduced in the first paragraph, so it shouldn't precede paragraph 1. Paragraph 3 provides information regarding what happens after completion of the program discussed in paragraph 2, so it should follow paragraph 2. Paragraph 4 summarizes the essay; adding specific detail after the summary creates disorganization.

211. D. No, because although the essay mentions that nurses may pursue advanced degrees, it does not state how the resulting opportunities differ from those available to holders of an associate degree.

The explanations for Choices (A) and (B) are true for the essay, but they don't support the specific goal provided in the question. Just because the essay discussed a career available through an associate or a more advanced degree doesn't mean it actually compared the opportunities offered by each degree. Choice (C) is wrong because its explanation is untrue. The essay doesn't compare opportunities of an associate degree with those offered by more advanced degrees. The best answer is Choice (D).

212. A. NO CHANGE

Because the sentence references *your* instinct, *you* in Choice (A) is proper. Your instinct would talk only to you, not to one, them, or people.

213. B. specific types of natural disturbances.

The underlined portion is a more detailed list of the unexpected changes plant communities have to deal with. Choice (B) is right.

The phrase doesn't provide explanations or means of protection, so Choices (A) and (D) are wrong. Choice (C) is untrue because the underlined list items are changes that aren't human or animal generated.

214. A. NO CHANGE

The verbs in the rest of the paragraph are in present tense, so eliminate the past tense form in Choice (D). The subject is the plural *events*, so the verb form also must be plural. The only plural option is Choice (A).

215. C. quinquennial,

The best answer is Choice (C). *Quinquennial* means every five years, so Choice (C) gives you a clear idea of the number of years between fires. The other answers tell you the fires are frequent, but they don't tell you how frequent.

216. **B. grasses but only**

The comma and conjunction combination is incorrect. The only time a comma before *but* is proper is when it joins together two independent clauses. The group of words that follow *but* isn't an independent clause, so Choice (A) is wrong. Choice (D) is wrong because it adds *they*, which forms an independent clause and therefore requires a comma before *but*. Choice (C) doesn't make sense. The properly punctuated answer is Choice (B).

217. **B. reduce**

Reduce and *diminish* have the same meaning, so you don't need them both. Eliminate Choice (A) and pick Choice (B).

The other answers use more words to convey the same meaning as Choice (B), so they're out. The ACT rewards the most precise answers.

218. **A. NO CHANGE**

You know Choice (C) is wrong. The words after the semicolon don't express a complete thought. Choice (D) makes no sense. Between Choice (A) and (B), you've got to go with the dash to set off the nonessential descriptive information that follows the main clause.

219. **D. after *fires*.**

The underlined phrase answers the question "for how long," so it's an adverb phrase. It should be placed as close to the verb it describes as possible. The fires weren't strong enough for more than 200 years, so Choice (A) is wrong. The fires didn't destroy for more than 200 years, so Choices (B) and (C) are out. The best option is Choice (D); the pine trees weathered the fires for more than 200 years.

220. **C. have evolved**

The sentence tells you the species adapted when it classifies it as "disturbance-adapted"; the answer that clears the redundancy is Choice (C).

221. **D. for example,**

Be sure to read the preceding sentence to uncover its main idea: Some species have evolved to depend on disturbances. The sentence with the underlined transition tells you that the lodgepole pine needs fire. So the second sentence provides an example of the fact provided in the first. The best transition between the ideas is Choice (D).

222. **B. their**

The underlined pronoun refers to the plural noun *trees*, so the proper answer is the plural possessive pronoun *their*. Choice (C) is the contraction of *they are*.

223. **B. a community with a high degree of diversity**

A single comma that falls anywhere between the subject and verb of a sentence is always incorrect, which means Choices (A) and (D) must be wrong. Both place a single comma between *community* and *has*. Choice (C) places commas around the prepositional phrase "of diversity," but the phrase defines *degree* and therefore is essential. Prepositional phrases are rarely nonessential. The answer with no punctuation errors is Choice (B).

224. **A. where it is now.**

The sentence is best right where it is. The paragraph defines resilience in sentence 2, and sentence 3 refers to resilience. Therefore, sentence 3 should follow sentence 3. You know Choice (C) is wrong because sentence 5 provides an example of sentence 4 rather than sentence 3.

225. **B. before paragraph 1.**

Paragraph introduces disturbances, and paragraph 1 discusses them in more detail. Therefore, paragraph 2 logically belongs before paragraph 1. Pick Choice (B).

226. **D. Stress**

The sentence contains a comma paired with *and*; this combination joins two independent clauses. The only answer that creates a beginning independent clause is Choice (D). The others begin with subordinating conjunctions, which create dependent clauses.

227. **B. NO CHANGE**

The subject, army, is singular, so eliminate the plural verbs in Choices (A) and (C). Choice (D) isn't conjugated, which leaves Choice (B) — the only conjugated singular verb.

228. **A. Kept, because it provides a helpful transition to an idea in the following sentence.**

Easily eliminate Choices (B) and (D). The passage clearly indicates elsewhere that many people get the flu, but it doesn't specifically state that those people could be the reader's loved ones. Choice (D) is incorrect because second person is used throughout the passage. The best answer is Choice (A). The underlined part sets up the rest of the passage by reminding readers that their family members may suffer from the flu and therefore require pampering.

229. D. raunchy

The first three answers are other ways to define the flu virus as nasty. Choice (D) has a sleazy connotation that isn't appropriate for describing a virus.

230. A. NO CHANGE

The sentence before the transition word states that eating oats helps fight the flu. The next sentence says that those with the flu have a hard time getting oats into their systems. The ideas are contrasting, so *however* is the best transition and Choice (A) is correct.

Notice you can easily eliminate Choices (B) and (C) because they provide the same transition. You can't choose both, so you must choose neither. Choice (D) is clearly improper; that eating oats is a flu remedy doesn't cause people with the flu to be unable to make oatmeal.

231. B. know,

The word *know* ends the dependent clause that begins with *as*. Use a comma to separate a dependent clause that comes before the main clause. Choice (B) is correct. Choices (C) and (D) have to be wrong because the semicolon and colon aren't preceded by an independent clause.

232. D. one is

The pronoun in the underlined part has an unclear reference. You don't know who *they* refers to. Choice (B) doesn't correct the issue and creates a new error by substituting the possessive form of *they*. Choice (C) also contains an unclear pronoun. The best answer is Choice (D), which eliminates the pronoun altogether.

233. D. OMIT the underlined portion and capitalize *many*.

Whenever you see the option to omit the underlined part, check it for irrelevance or redundancy. You already know from the rest of the sentence that the Madison businesses have the information, so you don't need the underlined part in any form. The best option is to get rid of the underlined part altogether.

ANSWERS 201–300

234. **B. include and compose a specialized note to your sick loved one, and they**

Choice (A) isn't logical. It states that businesses allow you to design, compose, and provide delivery. You aren't providing delivery; the companies are. Choice (C) lacks parallel structure. The series is two verbs (design, compose) and a clause (they provide delivery), and it contains the same wordy construction as Choice (A). Choice (D) incorrectly sounds as though your sick loved one is providing delivery. The best answer is Choice (B). It eliminates the unnecessary words and corrects the lack of parallel structure.

235. **C. businesses offer numerous items with oats to further promote a speedy recovery**

A comma before an infinitive verb such as "to further promote" is almost never proper, so Choices (A) and (B) are wrong. Using a single comma to separate a verb, such as promote, from its object (a speedy recovery) is also incorrect. So Choice (D) is out. The correctly punctuated answer is Choice (B).

236. **C. Many college students have shared**

The answer that expresses the thought in the most precise way is Choice (C). The others contain unnecessary relative clauses ("that have shared" and "who have shared").

237. **A. NO CHANGE**

The words that follow *and* don't create an independent clause, so the comma and conjunction in Choice (B) and the semicolon in Choice (C) can't be right. Choices (A) and (D) are properly punctuated, but *but* doesn't logically join the two ideas in the sentence. Choice (A) is best.

238. **A. NO CHANGE**

The bakeries have already come up with the idea, so present tense isn't proper. Eliminate Choice (B). Choice (C) uses the wrong participle form with *had*; the proper construction is had come. Choice (D) incorrectly pairs a singular verb with a plural subject.

239. **A. Point A in paragraph 1**

The first paragraph introduces the flu, so this sentence that provides general information about the flu is best placed in the first paragraph.

240. B. Yes, because the essay directs information about care packages toward blog writers.

Eliminate Choice (C) because the primary audience is people who have readers. People who have readers are generally writers. Choice (D) isn't correct. The title indicates that the essay is about the flu care packages, which are a service rather than a lifestyle.

Choice (A) is true; the passage does discuss the benefits of eating oats when one has the flu, but that fact doesn't relate to the goal of persuading others to promote a service. The best answer is Choice (B). The essay promotes the care package to blog writers so they'll tell their readers about it.

ANSWERS 201–300

241. A. NO CHANGE

Apply the he/him test. Substitute the underlined *whom* with *he* and *him* to see which you like better. If it's *he,* the correct answer is *who;* if it's *him,* the correct answer is *whom.* It's better to say you want to spend the rest of your life with *him* than it is to say you want to spend the rest of your life with *he*. So Choice (A) is correct. The other clue that *whom* is correct is the preceding preposition; you need the objective form *whom* because it's the object of the preposition *with.*

Choice (C) is wrong because *which* doesn't refer to people. Choice (D) is out because the sentence doesn't make sense if you omit *whom.*

242. B. it's

Try *it is* instead of *its* to determine which is best. "It is time to start thinking" sounds good, so the correct answer is the contraction of it is, or it's. Select Choice (B). Choice (D) must be wrong; *its'* doesn't exist in the English language.

243. A. NO CHANGE

The underlined punctuation separates two independent clauses, so Choices (B) and (C) have to be wrong. Choice (B) creates a fused sentence; Choice (C) is a comma splice. Choice (D) is punctuated correctly, but the cause and effect relationship indicated by *so* isn't an appropriate transition between the two clauses.

244. C. minimal anxiety.

Stress and *anxiety* have similar meanings, so it's redundant to include both. Eliminate Choices (A) and (B). Because the sentence refers to stress in the first independent clause, Choice (C) is a more precise option than Choice (D).

245. D. a shortened timeline

The underlined pronoun has no clear reference, so you must replace it with the actual noun that forces you to be more flexible. Choice (D) is best.

246. C. schedule and stick

The *and* doesn't join two independent clauses, so the comma in Choice (A) is incorrect. A comma after *and* is rarely correct, so eliminate Choice (B). Choice (D) creates a comma splice elsewhere in the sentence. Removing the *and* creates an independent clause after *forever*, which makes the comma after *forever* improperly join two independent clauses.

247. A. NO CHANGE

You can easily eliminate Choices (B) and (D); "one of the most biggest" incorrectly contains two qualifiers and "most big" is improper. Choice (C) expresses the underlined idea with fewer words, but it also creates a problem with subject/verb agreement. The subject of Choice (A) is the singular *one*, which properly pairs with the singular verb *involves*. Choice (C) changes the subject to the plural *decisions*, which doesn't fit with the singular *involves*. Choice (A) is best.

248. B. this maxim applies to

Eliminate Choice (C) phrase isn't a proverb. It isn't a cliché, and even if you aren't sure about that, you know Choice (D) isn't correct because the following sentence doesn't justify that the phrase ruins wedding planning. Choice (A) contains a mixed metaphor. Rules don't ring. The best answer is Choice (B). The phrase can be classified as a maxim that applies to wedding planning.

249. B. bridesmaids' dresses

The dresses belong to the bridesmaids, so you need the possessive form. Eliminate Choice (C). There is more than one bridesmaid; otherwise, *bridesmaid's* would have been preceded by an article such as *a* or *the*. The proper plural possessive form is Choice (B).

250. B. alterations

The underlined pronoun has no clear reference, so you must replace it with the actual noun that should be placed at the top of the to-do list. Choice (B) is best.

251. A. NO CHANGE

Sentence 4 refers to the wedding budget discussed in the first sentences and sets up the new topic of wedding details in the next paragraph. Therefore, it is a good first sentence of the second paragraph, and the break should come before it and after sentence 3. Choice (B) correctly places the paragraph break, but it incorrectly states that sentence 3 is the last to mention the budget topic. Choice (A) is best.

252. C. tasks

Choices (A) and (D) are out because they are vague. Choice (B) is redundant. The most precise answer is Choice (C).

253. D. send save-the-dates, or at least invitations,

The answer that properly designates the nonessential elements with a set of commas is Choice (D). You can remove "at least" from the sentence and the main clause still makes sense. The single comma before the preposition in Choice (B) has no purpose. Choices (A) and (C) improperly include *or* in the nonessential element.

254. B. carefully — twice — because

This sentence uses a dash to set apart nonessential information, which is fine as long as you use a set of dashes instead of a dash and a comma. Eliminate Choices (A) and (C). The comma after because in Choice (D) has no purpose. The properly punctuated option is Choice (B).

255. C. point C.

The addition references a dream destination. Therefore, the best location is point C, right after the sentence about booking a honeymoon.

256. B. The economic model in the industrial nations for new infrastructure development such as railways and canals was a mixture of private and municipal development in the 19th century, a time in which electricity supply could be said to have become an industry.

The key to answering this question correctly is to focus on the nonessential description. Determine exactly what is "a time in which electricity supply could be said. . . ." The element of the sentence that defines a time is "the late 19th century." So the answer that places the description immediately after the late 19th century, Choice (B), is correct. The other options improperly describe *development* or *canals* as "a time."

257. **D. then expanded**

The underlined part is the second of a compound verb: "rulings that first increased. . .and then expanded." So the past tense form in Choice (D) properly completes the combination.

258. **A. NO CHANGE**

Eliminate Choices (B), (C), and (D) because they have commas between nouns and the descriptive prepositional phrases that follow them. The only answer that doesn't commit this error is Choice (A).

259. **B. For example,**

The idea following the underlined word presents a specific example of the general regulation attempts mentioned in the preceding sentence. The best transition is Choice (B).

260. **C. initiated**

The sentence in Choice (A) is incomplete; it has no main verb. The subject is Samuel Insull and New York and Wisconsin. The action this compound subject took is to initiate. Therefore, you need the conjugated form of the verb in Choice (C). The other options fail to create a complete sentence.

261. **B. examples of the types of entities that required electricity.**

Lighthouses and street lighting aren't types of electricity, so Choice (A) is out. The words contain no explanation, so eliminate Choice (C). Lighthouses and street lights are sources of light, but the information is relevant to the paragraph on electricity products, Choice (D) is out.

The underlined part begins with "such as," which indicates that what follows are examples. The sentence is about early installations that used electricity. Choice (B) is best.

262. **D. the municipality contracted directly with utilities with names such as Illinois Power and Light that raised debt and equity from private investors.**

Analyze the sentence carefully. The information set apart by commas in Choice (A) isn't nonessential. The municipality didn't contract directly with utilities with names; it contracted with utilities with names such as Illinois Power and Light. Similarly, Choice (C) improperly sets apart essential information. Therefore, the commas in Choices (A) and (C) are improper. Choice (B) is wrong because clauses beginning with which are nonessential; therefore, there should be a comma before *which*. But the last clause of the sentence is essential: the municipality contracted specifically with utilities that raised debt and equity from private investors. Choice (D) corrects the problem by changing *which* to *that* and removing the commas.

263. **D. point D.**

The sentence has to come somewhere after the first sentence, which introduces and defines the installations. Eliminate Choice (A). The sentence seems like it could go at point B, but placing it there breaks the flow between the mention of electricity in the first sentence and the statement that the product was light not electricity in the second sentence. The third sentence provides additional clarification about the light product mentioned in the second sentence, and placing the sentence in the question at point C would interrupt the flow of those ideas. By process of elimination, the most logical placement is at point D, where the sentence sets up the discussion of the development of additional civic buildings in the last paragraph.

264. **A. NO CHANGE**

You use number to refer to plural nouns such as buildings, so Choices (B) and (C) are wrong. Choice (D) incorrectly uses the adverb *increasingly* to describe the noun *number.* The correct answer is Choice (A).

265. **B. were**

Choice (A) creates a sentence fragment; *being* isn't a conjugated verb. The passage is in the past tense, so the proper conjugated verb tense is Choice (B).

266. **B. under the 1926 Electricity Supply Act, the UK created the General Electricity Board,**

The *and* that follows the underlined part joins two independent clauses, so the underlined words must end with a comma to accompany the conjunction. Eliminate Choices (A) and (D).

The better answer between Choices (B) and (C) is the active voice option in Choice (B). Given the choice between active (the U.K. created the board) and passive voice (the board was created by the U.K.), choose active.

267. **D. began**

The paragraph is in the past tense, and the past tense of *to begin* is *began,* Choice (D).

268. **C. Europe and**

The underlined *and* doesn't join together two independent clauses, so the comma preceding it is improper. Eliminate Choices (A) and (D). A comma after *and* is almost always incorrect. Choice (C) correctly removes all commas.

269. **A. NO CHANGE**

The third paragraph references years in the 20th century, so the events in the last paragraph happened after those in the 19th century mentioned in the first paragraph. Eliminate Choice (D). Because the third paragraph talks about new utilities, it must immediately follow the original utilities discussed in paragraph 2. The best ordering is no change.

270. **B. No, because the essay covers the rise of electricity markets in earlier centuries but not in current markets.**

Choice (D) is out because it isn't true. The essay does mention U.S. markets throughout the essay. Choices (A) and (B) are true, but they don't directly support the goal of providing a *complete* history. The essay's title reveals that the passage is about just the rise of the markets. The best answer is Choice (C).

271. **C. "snowbird" or**

The comma before the conjunction *or* doesn't join two independent clauses, so it needs to go. Eliminate Choices (A) and (D). A comma after a coordinating conjunction such as *or* is almost always wrong, so Choice (B) is out. The correctly punctuated answer is Choice (C).

272. **A. NO CHANGE**

The underlined pronoun renames someone, a singular indefinite pronoun. Someone is a person, so you wouldn't refer to the pronoun as *its*. Indefinite pronouns aren't second person, so *your* isn't appropriate, even though most of the essay uses second person. Eliminate Choices (C) and (D). Choice (B) is a contraction rather than a possessive pronoun — you wouldn't say "they are time" — so it's out. The remaining answer must be correct. In standard written English, referring to singular indefinite pronouns as "his or her" is the best option. Choice (A) is best.

273. **A. NO CHANGE**

In this sentence, *however* is an aside rather than a conjunctive adverb, which means it's part of the first independent clause that precedes the coordinating conjunction *so*. The words following *so* also form an independent clause, which means you need a comma before *so* to properly join them to the first independent clause. Therefore, Choice (A) is correct; it properly sets *however* apart with a pair of commas, the second of which properly pairs with *so* to join the independent clauses.

Because the first independent clause ends with *however*, the semicolon and colon in Choices (B) and (C) can't be right. Commas after coordinating conjunctions are rarely correct, so Choice (D) is out.

274. B. yours

The underlined singular pronoun *it* has no clear reference. It appears to refer to *cars*, but *cars* is plural, so Choices (A), (C), and (D) are wrong. The best answer is Choice (B), which may refer to cars and specifically those that are yours.

275. D. wasteful

There is no reason to add a bunch of meaningless words and clauses when the single word *wasteful* conveys the intended meaning. The most precise answer is Choice (D).

276. A. NO CHANGE

Choice (A) provides the reader with the most specific images of the kinds of grime that ruin paint. You have no idea what *it* refers to. Merely stating that a variety of substances exists doesn't provide the reader with concrete images, so Choices (C) and (D) are out. Choice (B) indicates where the grime comes from, but it doesn't provide the specific substances that Choice (A) does.

277. D. period, for

The question asks for the least desirable alternative, so eliminate answers that convey a similar meaning to the underlined part. *But* means *in contrast*, which means that the answers that also convey contrast, such as *however*, *though*, and *nonetheless*, are incorrect. The answer that's different is Choice (D); *for* as a conjunction means *because*.

278. C. No, because the sentence introduces a new dilemma that is unrelated to the essay's main idea.

The essay in general is about protecting cars, so a sentence about potential damage to houses is irrelevant. The answer that conveys this reasoning best is Choice (C). Although Choices (B) and (D) are true about the essay, they don't provide clear reasons for adding or omitting the sentence. Choice (A) is untrue; the essay is primarily about protecting cars and not about dirt damage.

ANSWERS 201–300

279. **D. OMIT the underlined part.**

You can easily eliminate Choices (B) and (C) because they have exactly the same meaning. They can't both be right, so they must both be wrong. Choice (A) isn't much different. Consider Choice (D). What if you omitted the underlined word? Do you really need to know that a vehicle parked on the street is outside? It's hard to imagine a car on the street that would be *inside*! The underlined part is redundant, and Choice (D) is best.

280. **C. are**

Being and *creating* are participles (verb parts) that can't be main verbs without a helper. So Choices (A) and (B) are sentence fragments. The sentence needs a conjugated verb. Both Choices (C) and (D) deliver, but Choice (D) introduces a past tense verb into a present tense essay. Choice (C) is best.

281. **A. NO CHANGE**

The preposition that best connects "worry" and "criminals and critters" is *about*: you with worry *about* criminals and critters, not *from*, *on*, or *by* them. Choice (A) is best.

282. **D. Furthermore,**

Rain and snow aren't examples of criminals and critters, so Choice (A) is out. Criminals and critters don't cause rain and snow, so the cause and effect relationship suggested by Choice (B) is wrong. Rain and snow aren't opposite to criminal and critters, though; they're all car damage causers. So Choice (C) isn't the proper transition. The best answer is Choice (D). Rain and snow are additional, or further, elements to worry about.

283. **D. you're**

When you apply the "it is" test, you see that Choice (B) works better than Choice (A): It is smart to fill the car with oil. Be sure to check all answers, though, before you select Choice (B) and move on. Consider Choice (D). Notice that the sentence contains a beginning phrase with an action word (washing), which is a participle. A beginning participle phrase describes the subject of the sentence. But *it* isn't washing the car, *you* are. The better answer between Choices (B) and (D) is Choice (D).

Choice (C) doesn't exist, so always eliminate it when you see it as an answer option.

284. **A. NO CHANGE**

Eliminate Choices (B), (C), and (D) because they're in the past tense. The rest of the paragraph is present tense.

285. **B. dangerous**

The way this sentence uses *prove* suggests that it's a linking verb rather than an action verb. Therefore, it should be followed by the adjective form *dangerous* rather than the adverb form *dangerously* or the noun *danger*. Choice (B) is best.

286. **D. are**

The subject of the clause is "alcohol and drug use and abuse," which is plural. Therefore, you need a plural verb. Eliminate Choices (A) and (C). The rest of the verbs in the paragraph are in the present tense, so Choice (D) is best.

287. **B. exist regarding**

The sentence in Choice (A) is incomplete. *Regarding* isn't a conjugated verb. The remaining choices contain conjugated verbs, but only Choice (B) presents the correct plural form and present tense.

288. **A. NO CHANGE**

The punctuation is correct in Choice (A). You need the comma after *drinking* to provide the partner to the comma pair that sets apart "or needing to drink to fit in" as a nonessential phrase.

289. **B. effect**

As a general rule, the verb is *affect*, and the noun is *effect*. You need the noun form here, so Choice (B) is correct. Choices (C) and (D) have alternative meanings that aren't appropriate for the sentence.

290. **A. NO CHANGE**

The best preposition for the job is Choice (A). The use has a negative effect *by* impairing one's judgment — not *as*, *on*, or *for* impairing.

291. **D. judgment, becoming a coping device,**

The sentence in Choice (A) has a problem with parallelism. The negative effects are by impairing, becoming, or promoting. All elements of the series are noun participles. *Coping* in Choice (B) is used as an adjective to describe *device* rather than as a noun like the other members of the series. The answer that maintains parallel structure is Choice (D).

ANSWERS 201–300

292. C. engage in risky behaviors

The only choice that suggests danger is Choice (C). Risky behaviors are more specifically dangerous than things, acts, or activities.

293. B. surrounds

Choice (A) isn't a complete sentence because surrounding isn't a conjugated verb. The rest of the paragraph is in present tense, so the best answer is the present tense option in Choice (B).

294. B. familiar

Choice (A) is redundant. The sentence describes the exposure as common at the beginning. Choices (C) and (D) don't convey the intended meaning, so Choice (B) is best.

295. C. Deleted, because the statistics presented are not directly relevant to the statements made in the first sentences of the paragraph.

The statistics presented in the sentence support the premise that alcohol is abused by more people than other drugs, but the main purpose of the paragraph is to show that drug and alcohol use are more prevalent because of media exposure. Therefore, the statement should be deleted for the reason stated in Choice (C).

296. C. colleagues'

Because *colleague* and *research* are both nouns, you need to put *colleague* in possessive form. Eliminate Choices (B) and (D). Elsewhere, the passage clarifies that Bedard-Gilligan has several colleagues, so the plural version in Choice (C) is correct.

297. D. research shows that assaults are more violent when alcohol is involved

The sentence is about a current fact, so all verbs should be in present tense. The only answer that maintains present tense is Choice (D).

298. D. others

Choice (D) uses one word to convey the same meaning as the other answers. It's the most precise, concise construction.

299. A. NO CHANGE

The punctuation in Choice (A) is proper. The nonessential descriptive clause consists of all words after the comma. The underlined part has no other nonessential elements, so the comma placement in Choices (B), (C), and (D) is incorrect.

300. D. before paragraph 3

The information in paragraph 4 sets up the more specific, related information in paragraph 3. Paragraph 4 links the societal influences mentioned in the first two paragraph with the tendency to diminish sexual assault in situations where those involved are under the influence of drugs and alcohol as described in paragraph 3.

Another big clue is that the fourth paragraph refers to Michele Bedard-Gilligan by her first and last name in the paragraph 4 but by her last name in paragraph 3. Therefore, the best placement for paragraph 4 is before paragraph 3.

Chapter 2

301. E. 210

Eliminate Choices (B) and (C) right away because neither is divisible by 2. Choice (A) is less than 15, so you know it can't be right. 60 is divisible by 15 and 2 but not 7, so Choice (D) can't be correct. The answer must be 210. When you divide 210 by 2, 7, and 15, you get a nice whole number each time.

302. C. 496

Substitute values for the variables in the formula and solve:

$$\begin{aligned} 0.80(120)+100(4) &= \text{Cost} \\ 96+400 &= \text{Cost} \\ 496 &= \text{Cost} \end{aligned}$$

Jenny would pay the contractor $496 to paper her room.

ANSWERS 301–400

303. **B. −5 and 1**

You can solve for the values of x by setting both expressions equal to 0 and solving for x for both. You can eliminate Choices (C), (D), and (E) because you have two different answers.

$$(x+5)=0$$
$$x=-5$$

$$(x-1)=0$$
$$x=1$$

The answer is Choice (B).

304. **D.** $\frac{1}{2}$

Put the numbers in order: −4, −3, $\frac{1}{2}$, 11, 18. The one in the middle, $\frac{1}{2}$, is the median. It's as simple as that. If you picked Choice (C), you forgot to list the numbers in numerical order first.

305. **B. $21.60**

Multiply $16 by 0.35 (which is the same as 35 percent) to get $5.60. Add that to the original $16, for a total of $21.60.

You can take a small shortcut for problems like this one. Multiply 16 by 1.35, because that's the same as 135 percent, to get $21.60 without the additional step.

306. **A. 15 inches**

This problem requires just simple subtraction and knowledge that there are 3 feet in a yard. That means that $1\frac{2}{3}$ yards is 3 feet + 2 feet, or 5 feet, for a total of 60 inches. Subtract: 60 − 30 = 30; 30 − 15 = 15.

You can eliminate Choices (C) and (E) immediately because you're cutting off whole inches, not fractions.

307. **C. $200,000**

The three friends averaged $40,000 each, which means their total earnings were $120,000 ($3\times 40{,}000=120{,}000$). Create the equation where T stands for Total: 120,000 = 60 percent T or $120{,}000=0.6T$. Divide both sides by 0.6:

$$T=\frac{120{,}000}{0.6}$$
$$T=200{,}000$$

308. D. *a* could be −7 or +4

One of the two parenthetical expressions must equal zero, because the product of zero and anything else is zero. That means that either $a=-7$ (because $-7+7=0$) or $a=4$ (because $4-4=0$). So the correct answer is Choice (D).

If you answered Choice (E), you likely worked this problem too quickly. Adding a number to or subtracting a number from 0 doesn't necessarily result in 0.

309. D. 625

Whenever you see "average" in an ACT math question, quickly jot down a version of the average formula so you can get a better visual of what variable you're solving for and what you need to find it:

$$A=\frac{\text{sum}}{\#}$$

If the telemarketer wants to average 100 calls a day for 10 days, he needs to make 1,000 total calls in those 10 days:

$$100=\frac{\text{sum}}{10}$$
$$1{,}000=\text{sum}$$

He currently makes 375 calls ($75\times5=375$). Subtract: $1{,}000-375=625$.

310. E. The angle may be acute, obtuse, or right.

Knowing geometry vocabulary helps with this question. A right angle measures 90 degrees, an *obtuse angle* is more than 90 degrees, and an *acute angle* is greater than 0 but less than 90 degrees. The interior angles of a triangle total 180 degrees. If two angles measure less than 90 degrees, the third angle could measure 90 degrees, as in the case of a 45:45:90-degree triangle. It could be obtuse, as in the case of a 30:30:120-degree triangle. It could also be acute, as in the case of 60:60:60-degree triangle.

311. E. $a-15$

The easiest way to approach this problem is to first consider the last term in the expression, the −15. What are the factors of −15 that sum to −14? They could only be $(a-15)$ and $(a+1)$. When you multiply $(a-15)(a+1)$, you get the desired quadratic, $a^2-14a-15$. Because $a+1$ isn't an option, the answer has to be Choice (E).

ANSWERS 301–400

312. D. $2\frac{2}{5}$ mph

A couple of ACT math questions simply give you a formula and ask you to solve for one of the variables. You just have to plug in the values for the other variables and solve the equation.

The answers reveal that you're searching for mph, which the problem tells you corresponds with *r*. So you know you're solving the equation for *r*. All you need are values for *d* and *t*. The biker's time (*t*) is 3 hours and 20 minutes, which is $3\frac{1}{3}$, or $\frac{10}{3}$, hours, so substitute $\frac{10}{3}$ for *t* in the equation. The distance (*d*) is 8 miles. Plug 8 in for *d* and solve the equation for *r*:

$$\begin{aligned} d &= rt \\ 8 &= r\frac{10}{3} \\ 24 &= r10 \\ 2.4 &= r \end{aligned}$$

2.4 isn't in the answer choices, so you need to convert it to a fraction. 0.4 is $\frac{4}{10}$ or $\frac{2}{5}$, so the correct answer is $2\frac{2}{5}$.

313. C. 24

Find the percentage of green-eyed and brown-eyed children in the class by adding the probabilities of choosing either one: $\frac{1}{8}+\frac{1}{4}=\frac{1}{8}+\frac{2}{8}=\frac{3}{8}$. If $\frac{3}{8}$ the children don't have blue eyes, the other $\frac{5}{8}$ of the children do have blue eyes. That means the number of children with blue eyes, 15, is $\frac{5}{8}$ the

$$15 = \frac{5}{8}x$$

number of total children: $120 = 5x$

$$24 = x$$

So the total number of children in the class is 24.

314. A. 144

Set up equations from the wording of the question: $a = 5 + b$ and $a = b = -15$. Substitute the value of *a* in the first equation for *a* in the second equation and solve for *b*:

$$\begin{aligned} (5+b)+b &= -15 \\ 5+2b &= -15 \\ 2b &= -20 \\ b &= -10 \end{aligned}$$

So $b^2 = 100$.

315. **B. 19**

Perimeter is the sum of the four sides. To find this sum, multiply double the sum of the length and width.

$$\begin{aligned} 2(4.5+5) &= P \\ 2(9.5) &= P \\ 19 &= P \end{aligned}$$

316. **D. 4**

First, combine like terms: $3p = 9p - 24$. Next, to get all of your p's on one side of the equation and your numbers on the other, subtract $3p$ from both sides of the equation and add 24 to both sides of the equation: $-6p = -24$. Finally, to get the variable by itself, divide both sides of the equation by -6: $p = 4$.

If you picked Choice (A), you incorrectly combined like terms by multiplying the coefficients together instead of adding or subtracting them. Choice (B) is the result of thinking that you could cancel out each $2p$ on both sides of the equation. However, each $2p$ has a different sign, so they can't cancel each other out.

ANSWERS 301–400

317. **C. 180**

When two parallel lines are cut by a line that goes through both of them, the angles across from each other are equal. Additionally, supplementary angles add to 180 degrees. The little square in the angle across from angle x tells you that it's a right angle. Right angles equal 90 degrees. Because angle x is across from the right angle, it also measures 90 degrees.

Angles x and y are corresponding angles. They're in the same spot along the intersections of parallel lines l and m and the line that crosses those lines. Corresponding angles are equal. That means that angle y also measures 90 degrees. When you add the two angles together, you get 180 degrees because $90 + 90 = 180$.

318. **B. $54.16**

To find 4% of $1,354, multiply the amount by 0.04. The result is $54.16. You know the answer can't be Choice (E). Jordy wouldn't earn more than he sold!

319. **A. $\frac{2}{7} > \frac{1}{8} > 0.02$**

Convert the fractions to decimals to compare the three values. $\frac{1}{8} = 0.125$, which is greater than 0.02. So eliminate answers that show $\frac{1}{8}$ to be less than 0.02. $\frac{3}{7} \approx 0.429$, so it's greater than $\frac{1}{8}$. The proper order is Choice (A).

Choices (D) and (E) present values in a way that suggests order from least to greatest, so they must be wrong.

320. B. 12

First, solve the equation for x:

$$\begin{aligned} 7x+10&=31 \\ 7x&=21 \\ x&=3 \end{aligned}$$

Then multiply 3 by 4 to get 12.

321. E. 4

Substitute the values for variables in the expression and solve, making sure you properly follow the rules for adding and subtracting:

$$\begin{aligned} x-y+z&=? \\ 3-(-2)+(-1)&=? \\ 3+2-1&=4 \end{aligned}$$

322. B. −8

Simply substitute 2 for y and follow the order of operations:

$$\begin{aligned} (y-4)(y+2)&=? \\ (2-4)(2+2)&=? \\ (-2)(4)&=? \\ -8&=? \end{aligned}$$

323. C. 84

Eliminate Choices (D) and (E) right away because there's no way that Justin's average increases when he divides by 8 instead of 7. Any answer greater than 96 has to be wrong.

You know Justin's average score when the sum is divided by 7. You can put that information into the average formula to figure out the sum of Justin's scores:

$$\begin{aligned} 96&=\frac{\text{sum}}{7} \\ 96\times 7&=\text{sum} \\ 672&=\text{sum} \end{aligned}$$

Substitute the sum into the average formula to determine Justin's average over 8 tests:

$$\begin{aligned} A&=\frac{672}{8} \\ A&=84 \end{aligned}$$

ANSWERS 301–400

324. C. 5

To solve this relatively easy basics operation problem, first find the two values you need to compare:

$$3-0.5=2.5$$

$$1-0.5=0.5$$

To find out how many times 0.5 goes into 2.5, just divide:

You know that 25 divided by 5 is 5, so 0.5 goes into 2.5 five times, which means that 2.5 is 5 times greater than 0.5, and $3-0.5$ is 5 times greater than $1-0.5$.

If you picked Choice (A), you found the difference between to the two values instead of the quotient.

325. A. $-\frac{3}{2}$

If the product of two factors equals 0, then at least one of the factors must be 0 (because anything times 0 equals 0). So, one of the factors in this equation must equal 0. You know it's not the second one, because y doesn't equal 5, and y would have to equal 5 for the second term to result in 0.

So you need to create an equation that makes the first factor equal 0 and solve for y:

$$\left(\frac{3}{y}+2\right)=0$$

$$\frac{3}{y}=-2$$

$$3=-2y$$

$$-\frac{3}{2}=y$$

326. A. $800

The formula for area of the carpet is $l\times w$, which is 10×16, or 160 square feet. The total price is 160×5, which is $800.

327. E. $29-x$

If Emilio will be 35 years old in 6 years, he is 29 right now $(35-6=29)$. Therefore, to determine how old he was x years ago, simply subtract x from his current age of 29: $29-x$.

ANSWERS 301–400

328. E. greater than 16

Find the value of a:

$$\begin{aligned} 3a+2 &> 14 \\ 3a &> 12 \\ a &> 4 \end{aligned}$$

When you square both sides of the inequality, you find $a^2 > 16$.

329. E. 32

Add the numbers in the ratio: $3+5=8$. The total must be a multiple of 8 (or, looking at it another way, the total must be evenly divisible by 8). Only Choice (E) is a multiple of 8.

330. D. II and III

For Roman numeral questions like this one, consider statements I, II, and III individually and eliminate answers based on your findings.

When you multiply a fraction by its reciprocal, you always get 1. You know the values in statement I aren't reciprocals of each other because they don't have a product of 1: $\frac{1}{15} \times -\frac{1}{15} = -\frac{1}{225}$. Eliminate answers that include statement I, which means Choices (A), (C), and (E). You're left with Choices (B) and (D), which both contain statement III, so you just need to consider statement II.

Evaluating statement II may be a little tricky. The two values don't look like reciprocals at first glance. And you may be tempted to pick Choice (B) without working out statement II.

When you multiply $\frac{\sqrt{2}}{1}$ and $\frac{\sqrt{2}}{2}$, you get 1:

$$\frac{\sqrt{2}}{1} \times \frac{\sqrt{2}}{2} = \frac{2}{2}$$

331. D. 256

Don't let all those 3s and 4s and cubes intimidate you. As long as you notice that the first part of the question says that $3x^3 = 4$, you can work this problem out very quickly. All you have to do is substitute the $3x^3$ for 4 in the second equation. That gives you $4(4)^3$. $4^3 = 64$ and $4 \times 64 = 256$.

332. C. 27

Solve for x in the first equation:

$$\begin{aligned} 3x+2 &= 14 \\ 3x &= 12 \\ x &= 4 \end{aligned}$$

Then plug that value into the second: $(4-1)^3 = 3^3 = 27$.

If you picked Choice (D), you incorrectly applied the exponent to each term in the second expression $4^3 - 1^3 = 63$.

333. C. 28

The hypotenuse is the longest side of a right triangle, so Choices (D) and (E) are wrong.

You could apply the Pythagorean theorem to find the measure of the other leg, but it's quicker to notice that the given hypotenuse and leg lengths are multiples by 7 of a 3:4:5 right triangle, where 3, 4, and 5 are the ratio of the short leg, long leg, and hypotenuse. The leg that measures 21 centimeters must be the short leg, so the longer leg is $4 \times 7 = 28$.

334. D. $-\frac{3}{5}$

Order the equation in slope-intercept form: $y = mx + b$. The m value will be the slope.

$$3x = 30 - 5y$$
$$5y + 3x = 30$$
$$5y = -3x + 30$$
$$y = -\frac{3}{5}x + 6$$

335. A. $\frac{12}{49}$

Because Julian has extracted and retained 3 cards from the box, the total number of remaining cards when he reaches in his hand for the fourth time is 49 ($52 - 3 = 49$). He has pulled 1 green card, so the number of remaining green cards is 12 ($13 - 1 = 12$). He has a 12 in 49 chance of randomly choosing a green card on his fourth try.

If you picked Choice (D), you didn't take into consideration the 3 cards Julian had already pulled from the box.

336. C. 218

To find the average, divide the total number of miles the bus traveled all week by the number of days in a week, 7.

$1{,}525 \div 7 = 217.857$, which is approximately 218 miles.

ANSWERS 301–400

ANSWERS 301–400

337. C. $a=b$

An easy way to deal with percentages is to use the number 100. In this case, say that $(a+b)=100$. Then 6 percent of 100 = 6. That means that 12 percent of b is 6. Solve for b:

$$\begin{aligned}0.12b&=6\\b&=50\end{aligned}$$

If $a+b=100$, then a = 50 and a = b.

338. E. $4x=36$

The key to this question is knowing that an integer is a whole number (for example, 1.5 is not an integer). For Choice (A) to be true, x would have to be 5, which is not *between* 5 and 12. For Choice (B) to be true, x would have to be 16, which is too large. For Choice (C) to be true, x would have to be 5.25, which is not an integer. For Choice (D) to be true, x would have to be 74.5, which is both too large and not an integer. Only Choice (E) works because if $4x=36$, $x=9$.

339. B. $8\sqrt{2}$

The area of a square is s^2. In this case, that's 8^2, or 64 units. That means the area of the triangle is also 64. The area of a triangle is $\frac{1}{2}b\times h$. For an isosceles right triangle, the base and height are the same length, so the area is $\frac{1}{2}x\times x$, or $\frac{1}{2}x^2$.

Apply this equation to the triangle in the question:

$$\begin{aligned}A&=\frac{1}{2}x^2\\64&=\frac{1}{2}x^2\\128&=x^2\\\sqrt{128}&=x\\\sqrt{64}\times\sqrt{2}&=x\\8\sqrt{2}&=x\end{aligned}$$

The two legs of the triangle each measure $8\sqrt{2}$.

340. E. 90

At first, you may think you need to apply trigonometry to find the angle. But look for the easier way. You can solve this problem very quickly if you recognize that the triangle's ratio of 10:24:26 is double the ratio of 5:12:13, which is common ratio for the sides of right triangles. The angle formed by the two shorter sides of a right triangle is the 90 degree angle.

341. **E. \$21.00**

This problem is easier than it looks. If the jackets cost \$3,336 for 12, each jacket when purchased by the dozen costs \$278 because \$3,336 divided by 12 is \$278. The price per jacket drops from \$299 to \$278, a difference of \$21.

342. **A.** $y+n+15$

A simple way to approach this problem is to plug in numbers. Say that Claude is 100 years old now. Let $n=10$. That means that 10 years ago, Claude was 90, which makes $y=90$. In 15 years, he will be 100 (his current age) + 15, which is 115. Look for an answer that works out to 115 when you plug in your values for y and n. The answer is Choice (A) because $y(90)+n(10)+15=115$.

343. **A.** $36x^8y^{12}$

Follow the order of operations: PMDAS. First, square the first expression: $\left(2x^3y^4\right)\left(2x^3y^4\right)=4x^6y^8$. Then square the second: $\left(3xy^2\right)\left(3xy^2\right)=9x^2y^4$. Multiply these products: $(4x^6y^8)(9x^2y^4)$.

The product of 4 and 9 is 36, so cross out Choices (C), (D), and (E).

When you multiply like coefficients, you add their exponents. Because $(x^6)(x^2)=x^8$, the answer has to be Choice (A). It's the only answer with the proper x value.

344. **C. 20**

You can eliminate Choices (D) and (E) because the width of the room on the plan is greater than its length and therefore the length of the actual room must be greater than its width of 15 feet.

To find the ratio of the plan to the actual bedroom, set up a proportion. The ratio of the plan's bedroom length to the actual bedroom length is 18 inches to 15 feet. The answer has to be in feet, so change inches to feet. The 18 inches is the same as 1.5 feet and the 24 inches is the same as 2 feet, so the ratio of the plan's width to the room's width in feet is $\frac{1.5}{15}$ and the proportion to find the width is $\frac{1.5}{15}=\frac{2}{x}$.

Cross-multiply and solve for x:

$$1.5x=(2)(15)$$
$$1.5x=30$$
$$x=20$$

The homeowner's bedroom measures 20 feet wide.

ANSWERS 301–400

345. C. 540

You can find the interior angles of any polygon by using this formula: $(n-2)\times 180°$, where n stands for the number of sides. So $n=5$ and $(5-2)180=3(180)=540$.

346. D. $8\sqrt{3}$

If the given circle has an area $\frac{3}{4}$ the other circle, the other circle is larger and must have a greater radius, so eliminate Choices (A) and (B).

The area of a circle is πr^2, where r is the radius. So the area of the first circle with a radius of 12 is 144π. Because the area of the given circle is $\frac{3}{4}$ the area of the first, the larger circle (L) must have an area of 192π:

$$144\pi = \frac{3}{4}L$$
$$576\pi = 3L$$
$$192\pi = L$$

To find the radius of a circle whose area is 192π, apply the area formula again:

$$A = \pi r^2$$
$$192\pi = \pi r^2$$
$$192 = r^2$$
$$\sqrt{192} = r$$
$$\left(\sqrt{64}\right)\left(\sqrt{3}\right) = r$$
$$8\sqrt{3} = r$$

The larger circle has a radius of $8\sqrt{3}$ inches.

347. B. 3

In this arrangement with repetition problem, you have 2 choices for the first station (flour or corn tortillas), 4 choices for the second station (steak, chicken, pork, or guacamole), 2 choices for the third station (black or pinto beans), and s number of choices for the last station (s number of salsas). The problem states that there are 48 different burrito possibilities, so you can set up an equation to solve for s.

Use the multiplication principle and solve:

$$2\times 4\times 2\times s = 48$$
$$16s = 48$$
$$s = 3$$

ANSWERS 301–400

348. **A.** $> 132°$

Clearly the other angle measure has something to do with 132° because $180 - 48 = 132$. But because angles *A* and *B* measure $< 48°$, they have to sum to 47° or less. So the other angle has to measure at least 133°. Therefore, the answer can't be 132° or any answer that indicates less than 132°. The only possibility is Choice (A).

349. **D. 7.5**

A quarter inch on the graph paper represents a foot in the office. You can set up a proportion to find the number of inches on the paper that indicate a 30-foot long wall:

$$\frac{\frac{1}{4}}{1} = \frac{x}{30}$$
$$x = 30\left(\frac{1}{4}\right)$$
$$x = 7.5$$

350. **E. $640.50**

To find Denny's gross earnings, you must add the amount he earned for working 40 hours to the amount he earned for working the additional 14 hours. His regular earnings are $420.00 ($40 \times 10.50 = 420$). Determine his additional earnings by multiplying the number of hours over 40 (14) by the proper hourly wage: $1.5 \times 10.50 = 15.75$. His additional earnings, therefore, are $15.75 \times 14 = 220.50$. Add 420 to 220.50 to get total gross earnings of $640.50 for the week.

351. **C. 40%**

Give this problem a real value to work with. Say the 2014 price of the tablet is $100. If the price increased 25% between 2014 and 2015, its 2015 price is $125. The next year the price was $\frac{1}{4}$ less its 2014 price of $100, which means it cost $75 in 2016. To find the percent decrease between 2015 and 2016, subtract the two prices and divide the difference by the 2015 price:

$$125 - 75 = 50$$
$$\frac{50}{125} = 0.4$$

The percent decrease from 2015 to 2016 is 40%.

ANSWERS 301–400

352. C. 54°

The total number of tourists is the sum of 2,000 + 3,200 + 1,400 + 1,770 + 2,400 + 1,030 is 11,800. The French make up $\frac{1,770}{11,800}$, or 15 percent of the total. A circle has 360 degrees, and 15 percent of 360 is 54. The arc on the circumference created by the section representing the French measures 54 degrees, and the central angle measures the same number of degrees as the arc its endpoints create.

353. E. $L = 0.25\left(\sqrt{625} + 25\right)$

Glance at the answers to make sure you know what this word problem is asking for before you start doing any math. It doesn't want the solution to the equation but rather the equation itself. For these types of questions, working backward is often easier. "25 percent of the resulting sum" means 0.25 times the total of all else, so you can eliminate Choices (A) and (D). Neither multiplies by 0.25. Adding the square of 5 is simply + 25. Choice (C) is wrong because it multiplies rather than adds 25. And + 25 doesn't belong under the square root sign, which means you can cross out Choice (B). Only Choice (E) remains.

354. E. $(x+y)^2 - 16$

When you multiply two trinomials (which is a fancy way of saying a number with three terms), just distribute one term at a time from the first set of parenthesis to the other three terms in the other set of parenthesis.

So, in this problem, you multiply the first term of the first set (x) by the first term of the second set (x) and get x^2. Then you multiply the first term of the first set by the second term of the second set and get xy. Then you multiply the first term of the first set by the third term of the second set and get $-4x$.

Multiply the second term of the first expression by each of the terms in the second expression to get yx, y^2, and $-4y$. Complete the process with the third term of the first expression to get $4x$, $4y$ and -16. Combine the nine terms to get this expression:

$$x^2 + xy - 4x + yz + y^2 - 4y + 4x + 4y - 16.$$

Then, combine like terms. Remember that xy and yx are the same term, and recognize that the $4x$ and $-4x$ and the $4y$ and $-4y$ cancel each other out. So, after combining, you get $x^2 + 2xy + y^2 - 16$. This isn't an answer option, so there must be something more you can do.

Simplify $x^2 + 2xy + y^2$ to $(x+y)^2$. The answer is $(x+y)^2 - 16$.

355. B. 0.237

Write out the average formula: $A=\frac{\text{sum}}{\#}$ and fill in what you know. You can find the sum of the starters' averages by completing the formula:

$$0.252=\frac{\text{sum}}{9}$$
$$2.268=\text{sum}$$

You can find the sum of the reserves in the same way:

$$0.225=\frac{\text{sum}}{11}$$
$$2.475=\text{sum}$$

Use the average formula once more to find the batting average for all 20 team members:

$$A=\frac{2.268+2.475}{20}$$
$$A=\frac{4.743}{20}$$
$$A=0.23715$$

ANSWERS 301–400

356. B. $-1<z<9$

The absolute value bars make the expression $z-4$ positive in all cases. Consider the values that make $|z-4|=5$. They're both 9 and –1. Those two numbers become your limits. 9 and higher or –1 and lower makes the absolute value equal to or greater than 5. The problem asks for the values that make it less than 5. Any value that is less than 9 but greater than –1 will work. The answer that represents this set of values is $-1<z<9$.

357. C. 151

When $\overline{OA}$ and $\overline{OB}$ form a straight line, they will from a straight angle and measure 180 degrees.

A straight angle measures 180 degrees.

The diagram indicates that the original angle is less than the straight angle. So all you have to do is subtract the degree of rotation from 180 degrees. 180 – 29 = 151. $\angle AOB$ measured 151 degrees before $\overline{OA}$ was rotated.

Choice (E) is incorrect because it adds 29 degrees to 180 degrees instead of subtracting it.

358. C. 125

This is really just a substitution problem. The first equation tells you what to put into the parentheses of the second equation.

Because $10x^4 = 5$, you can substitute 5 for $10x^4$ in the second equation: $5(5)^2 = ?$

Then follow the order of operations to solve the problem. The expression simplifies to 5(25), which equals 125.

Another way to solve the problem is to recognize that $5(5)^2$ is the same as $5^1 \times 5^2$, which is 5^3 and equals 125.

359. C. negative and less than the *x*-intercept of *l*

Drawing a diagram may be your best strategy for this problem.

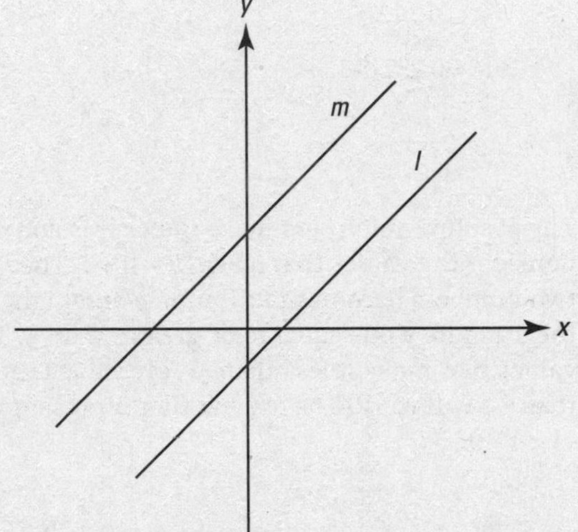

© John Wiley & Sons, Inc.

The figure shows a possible placement for line *l*. It slopes from left to right and the point where it crosses the *x*-axis (the *x*-intercept) is positive (to the right of the *y*-axis). Its *y*-intercept has to be negative (below the *x*-axis). If line *m* is parallel to line *l* and has a positive *y*-intercept (above the *x*-axis), then its *x*-intercept must be negative (left of the *y*-axis) and is clearly less than that of line *l*.

360. D. 204

You can solve this problem by setting up an equation.

The product of the three numbers in the horizontal row is 6 times 12 times 3, which is 216. So, the sum of the three numbers in the vertical column is 216.

$$x + 12 + y = 216$$
$$x + y = 204$$

361. D. 400

You can solve this problem by setting up an equation that represents the sum of the three separate trip portions. Let x = the total distance in miles. Traci stopped to rest after she traveled $\frac{1}{3}$ of the total distance, so the first part of the trip is $\frac{1}{3}x$. She stopped again after she traveled $\frac{1}{4}$ of the distance remaining between her first stop and her destination, which is the total distance she traveled minus the first part of her trip. You can represent the second part of the trip mathematically like this: $\frac{1}{4}\left(x - \frac{1}{3}x\right)$. The third part of the trip is the remaining 200 miles.

Add up the three parts of the trip to get the total distance.

$$\frac{1}{3}x + \frac{1}{4}\left(x - \frac{1}{3}x\right) + 200 = x$$
$$\frac{1}{3}x + \frac{1}{4}\left(\frac{2}{3}x\right) + 200 = x$$
$$\frac{1}{3}x + \frac{1}{6}x + 200 = x$$
$$2x + x + 1200 = 6x$$
$$3x + 1200 = 6x$$
$$1200 = 3x$$
$$400 = x$$

362. B. $94 - b$

Knowing that the two unlabeled angles in each triangle are supplementary and therefore add to 180 degrees helps you solve for "a in terms of b." So does knowing that the three angles of a triangle always add up to 180 degrees.

Solving for "a in terms of b" means that you find out what a equals without finding a number value for b. That means that your answer will have the b variable in it.

The value of the unlabeled angle in the left triangle is equal to $180 - 60 - a$, or $120 - a$. The value of the unlabeled angle in the right triangle is

ANSWERS 301–400

$180-26-b$, or $154-b$. Set up an equation that adds the two values to equal 180 and solve for "a in terms of b:"

$$\begin{aligned}(120-a)+(154-b)&=180\\274-a-b&=180\\94-a-b&=0\\94-b&=a\end{aligned}$$

363. E. $\frac{15\sqrt{2}}{2}$

Draw a line from point E to point F. The question gives you the length of this line and indicates that $\angle ECF$ is a right angle. Therefore, the triangle formed by drawing chord EF is a right triangle.

Segments CE and CF are radii of the circle just like r and therefore have the same length as r. This tells you that ΔECF is an isosceles right triangle.

The ratio of the sides of a 45:45:90 triangle is $s:s:s\sqrt{2}$, where s is the measure of the legs of the triangle and $s\sqrt{2}$ is the measure of the hypotenuse.

Chord EF, with a length of 15 units, is the hypotenuse of the right triangle. To find the length of its legs, divide 15 by $\sqrt{2}$. The length of r is $\frac{15}{\sqrt{2}}$. Then eliminate the radical from the denominator: $\frac{15}{\sqrt{2}}\times\frac{\sqrt{2}}{\sqrt{2}}=\frac{15\sqrt{2}}{2}$.

364. E. $\frac{8}{3}$

Treat function problems like substitutions. The value of the function is $\frac{1}{1.5x}$ for any value of x you plug in that is greater than 0. Because 0.25 is greater than 0, you just substitute 0.25 for x in the equation and solve:

$$\frac{1}{1.5(0.25)}=\frac{1}{0.375}$$

This fraction contains a decimal in the fraction and doesn't appear in the answers, so convert the denominator to a fraction to come up with the ultimate solution.

$$\frac{1}{0.375}=\frac{1}{\frac{375}{1000}}=\frac{1}{\frac{3}{8}}$$

When you divide 1 by a fraction, the answer is the reciprocal of the fraction in the denominator:

$$\frac{1}{\frac{3}{8}}=\frac{8}{3}$$

It may be easier and quicker to solve this problem by converting the decimals to fractions before you tackle it.

$$\frac{1}{1.5(0.25)}=\frac{1}{\frac{3}{2}\times\frac{1}{4}}=\frac{1}{\frac{3}{8}}=\frac{8}{3}$$

365. C. 45

The information tells you that line *l* bisects the angle formed by the *x* and *y*-axes. The *x* and *y*-axes are perpendicular to each other and therefore form a 90 degree angle. To bisect means to cut in half. So the angle formed by line *l* and the *y*-axis is half of 90 degrees, or 45 degrees.

366. B. $6\sqrt{2}$

Because line *m* is perpendicular to the *x*-axis, the triangle in the figure is an isosceles right triangle. Line *l* bisects the right angle at point *O*, so it cuts the 90-degree angle into two 45 degree angles. If the angle formed by segment *OB* and the *x*-axis measures 45 degrees, the other angle of the triangle must also measure 45 degrees.

When you know that the triangle is an isosceles right triangle, you can apply the ratio of its sides to find the side lengths of the triangle.

The base of the triangle is one of the legs, and the end of the leg has the same *x*–coordinate as point *A*. You know that because the end of the base of the triangle is the same distance from the *y*-axis as point *A*. To figure out the *x*-coordinate of point *A*. you just add 2 to the *x*-coordinate of point *C*. Why 2? The problem tells you that segment *CA* measure 2 units. The *x*-coordinate of point *C* is 4. $4 + 2 = 6$, so point *A* is 6 units from the *y*-axis and the measure of each of the legs of the right triangle is 6 units.

Don't stop there and pick Choice (C). The question asks for the length of the hypotenuse, not the leg length.

Because the hypotenuse of an isosceles right triangle is $s\sqrt{2}$, the length of segment *OB* measures $6\sqrt{2}$ units.

367. C. (–6, 3)

When you reflect a shape across a line the near points stay near, the far points stay far, and the distances from the reflection line remain the same. It's like you lift the circle from the right side of line *l* and flip it like a blanket over to the left side of line *l*.

Because line *l* runs on a 45-degree angle through the origin, the *x* and *y* coordinates will be reflected in the quadrant on the other side of the reflection line, which is Quadrant II in the upper left.

The *x*-coordinate of point *A* is 6. Point *A*'s *y*-coordinate is –3, the same as point *C*'s. So the original coordinates of point *A* are (6, –3).

The points in the upper left quadrant of the coordinate plane have negative *x*-coordinates and positive *y*-coordinates, which is the opposite of the lower right quadrant where circle originally resided. So the coordinates of point *A* on the reflected circle become the opposite of what they were: (–6, 3).

368. D. 15

To determine in what percent of the trials a 3 came up more than 2 times, you have to divide the number of trials with more than two rolls of 3 by the total number of trials, which is 100.

The first two bars on the left of the graph show the number of trials with two or fewer rolls of 3. The first bar shows 35 rolls and the second shows 50. 50 + 35 = 80, which means that 85 of the trials resulted in one or two rolls of 3. But the question doesn't ask for the number of trials with two or fewer rolls of 3, so don't pick Choice (E).

Because there were 85 trials of two or fewer rolls of 3, there must have been 15 trials where a 3 was rolled more than 2 times: 100 − 85 = 15. And 15 is 15% of 100.

369. A. Sum: −2 Product: −15

When you see a quadratic equation, you likely need to find its factors. Then you can find its solutions.

Focus on the last term of the equation and ask yourself which two values equal −15 when they're multiplied together. The possible combinations are 3 and −5, −3 and 5, 1 and −15, and −1 and 15.

To narrow down the options, notice that the coefficient of the second term in the original equation is 2. Figure out which of the number combinations results in a value of 2 when they're added together. Only −3 and 5 add up to 2.

So the factors of the quadratic equation are $(x - 3)(x + 5)$. You know that's true because if you multiply these two expressions using the FOIL method, you end up with the original quadratic equation. When you set the two expressions equal to zero and solve for x, you find out that the two roots of the quadratic equation are −5 and 3. The product of −5 and 3 is −15, and their sum is −2. The correct answer is Choice (A).

370. B. $\frac{9}{20}$

To solve for the lowest portion of the job that can be done by two people in an hour, choose the two slowest people, Steve and Jack.

Jack completes $\frac{1}{5}$ of the job in 1 hour (it takes him 5 hours total, so in 1 hour he completes 1 out of 5 hours, or $\frac{1}{5}$ of the job). Similarly, Steve finishes $\frac{1}{4}$ of the job in 1 hour. Add $\frac{1}{5}$ and $\frac{1}{4}$:

$$\frac{1}{4}+\frac{1}{5}=\frac{4}{20}+\frac{5}{20}=\frac{9}{20}$$

371. **A. 5**

Perhaps the fastest and easiest way to solve this problem is to consider the possibility of the answer choices. Start with Choice (A) because it's the shortest answer.

If one side is 5 and the area is 75, the other side would have to be 15:

$$\begin{aligned} lw &= 75 \\ 5l &= 75 \\ l &= 15 \end{aligned}$$

Try 15 and 5 to see whether they produce a perimeter of 40:

$$\begin{aligned} 2(15)+2(5) &= 40 \\ 30+10 &= 40 \end{aligned}$$

That works! The shortest side is 5.

You could also solve this problem by setting up two equations with two unknowns, one for perimeter and one for area, but it may take you longer:

$$2l+2w=40$$

$$lw=75$$

First, divide each term in the perimeter equation by 2 and solve for l:

$$\begin{aligned} 2l+2w &= 40 \\ l+w &= 20 \\ l &= 20-w \end{aligned}$$

Substitute 20 − w for l in the area equation and solve for w:

$$\begin{aligned} lw &= 75 \\ (20-w)w &= 75 \\ 20w-w^2 &= 75 \\ 0 &= w^2-20w+75 \\ 0 &= (w-15)(w-5) \\ w &= 15 \text{ and } w=5 \end{aligned}$$

Because the problem asks you for the length of the *shorter* side, you know the answer is 5 feet.

372. **B. 40**

Don't spend a bunch of time worrying about what basis points are in this question. They're just units of measurement.

ANSWERS 301–400

This question really wants to see what you know about proportions. You know that 5 percent equals 100 basis points. You can use a proportion to find out how many basis points 7.5 percent equals.

$$\frac{5\%}{100} = \frac{7.5\%}{x}$$
$$\frac{0.05}{100} = \frac{.075}{x}$$

Cross-multiply:

$$0.05x = 7.5$$
$$x = 150$$

You could figure out the basis points for 5.5 percent in the same way, but you don't have to take the time to do the calculations. All of the answer choices begin with 4, so you know that the basis points for 5.5 percent begins with the value that results in a number that begins with 4 when it's subtracted from 150. The value also has the same decimal placement as 150 because 7.5 and 5.5 have the same decimal placements. So you know that the number of basis points for 5.5 percent is 110, and the difference between the two basis points values of 150 and 110 is 40.

373. B. –8

Simply substitute and then follow the order of operations. When you substitute 2 for y in the second equation, you get $(2-4)(2+2)$. Solve inside the parenthesis first, and you get $(-2)(4) = -8$.

374. D. 18

To determine the perimeter of triangle *ADG*, you need to add up segments *AD*, *DG*, and *AG*. You can find the lengths of these segments by adding up the lengths of their sub segments.

Because triangle *CDE* is equilateral and *AD* and *DG* are straight lines, triangles *DCE*, *BDF*, and *ADG* are similar and equilateral.

Therefore, segments *BD* and *DF* both equal 4 because $\overline{BF} = 4$. That means segments *AD* and DG both equal 6 because $\overline{BD} = 4$ and $\overline{AB} = 2$ and $4 + 2 = 6$. The same calculations apply to *DG* (*FG* also equals 2). Because triangle *ADG* is equilateral, *AG* also must equal 6. So the perimeter is $6 + 2 + 6 = 18$.

375. C. (7, 5)

When you know either the diameter of the circle, you can find the coordinates of *C*. That's because *C*'s x-coordinate is the value of *A*'s x-coordinate plus the diameter of the circle.

The diameter is twice the radius, and you can find the radius of the circle by checking the coordinates of points *A* and *B*. Both *A* and *B* use the variable m in the values for their y coordinates. The radius that starts at center O and ends at point B is parallel to the y-axis. So, if you can figure out the difference between the y coordinates of O and B, you know the value of the radius of the circle. Because O is on the same horizontal line as A, O, like A, also has a y-coordinate of $m+3$. B has a y-coordinate m. The difference between O and B is $m+3-m$, which is 3. So the radius of the circle is 3 and its diameter is 6.

To determine C's x-coordinate, just add the length of the diameter (6) to the value of A's x-coordinate (1) to get 7. C's x-coordinate is 7, so the answer can't be Choice (B), (D), or (E).

C's y-coordinate is the same as the y-coordinate of O. Because O is one radius length below D, you can find O's y-coordinate by subtracting the value of the radius (3) from the y-coordinate of D (8) to get 5. The answer is (7, 5).

376. **A. Chris leaves one of his clients, drives to another client, stays there a few days, and then returns home**

The graph shows that at the beginning of the week Chris is 200 miles from home. Sunday, he travels farther away, presumably to another client, with whom he spends Monday and Tuesday. Wednesday he travels back to the point that is 0 miles from his home. In other words, he drives home. The answer that describes this schedule is Choice (A).

For Choice (D) or (E) to be right, the graph would have to start at 0. The graph for Choice (C) would have to camp out at 0 for a couple of days in the middle of data.

Choice (B) is meant to trap those who didn't include the days that Chris stayed over at the location of the second client.

377. **D.** $x+2y=6$

The question asks for the answer that's *not* an equation of one of the lines. That means that you eliminate answers that *are* equations of one of the boundary lines.

The left and right boundary lines of the shaded shape are the vertical lines $x=2$ and $x=4$, so eliminate Choices (A) and (C). Horizontally, the shape is bound on the bottom by the x axis, which has an equation of $y=0$. So eliminate Choice (B). You know that the equation of the topmost horizontal line has to be either $x+2y=6$ or $x+3y=6$ because those are the two remaining choices.

An easy way to determine which one is right is by using the slope intercept formula and plugging in what you know. The slope intercept formula is $y=mx+b$, where m is the slope of the line and b is the y-intercept.

From the graph, you can see that the y-intercept (the point where the line intercepts the y-axis) is 2 and that the slope (the rise over run) is equal to $-\frac{2}{6}$, which is $-\frac{1}{3}$. Plug these values into the appropriate places in the equation:

$$y = -\frac{1}{3}x + 2$$

Then manipulate the equation into the format in the answer choices by multiplying all expressions by 3 and then adding x to both sides:

$$\begin{aligned} y &= -\frac{1}{3}x + 2 \\ 3y &= -x + 6 \\ x + 3y &= 6 \end{aligned}$$

The equation of the top line is $x + 3y = 6$, so eliminate Choice (E). The equation that doesn't represent one of the lines is Choice (D).

378. D. $120,000

Use the equation the question gives you to solve this problem. First, substitute 200 for p to see how many airlines tickets were sold:

$$\begin{aligned} t &= 1{,}000 - 2p \\ t &= 1{,}000 - 2(200) \\ t &= 1{,}000 - 400 \\ t &= 600 \end{aligned}$$

Then multiply the 600 tickets by $200 per ticket to get $120,000.

379. E. $x = \frac{15}{\sin 35°}$

The triangle in the figure is a right triangle, which means you can use SOHCAHTOA to find the length of one of its sides. The figure gives you the value of the angle's opposite side and you're trying to figure out the value of the hypotenuse. Sine deals with the opposite side and the hypotenuse, so you can eliminate any answers that apply cosine or tangent. That leaves you with either Choice (A) or (E).

Use the formula for sine to determine which is correct:

$$\begin{aligned} \sin\Theta &= \frac{\text{opposite}}{\text{hypotenuse}} \\ \sin 35° &= \frac{15}{x} \\ \sin 35° x &= 15 \\ x &= \frac{15}{\sin 35°} \end{aligned}$$

380. D. $\frac{3}{2}$

These similar triangles are mirror images of each other. Therefore, you have to keep careful track of which sides correspond to which.

It's pretty obvious that *W* corresponds to 4, but *Y* corresponds to *X* not 7. This is actually quite helpful because the problem asks you to figure out the value of $\frac{Y}{X}$.

All you have to do is set up a proportion:

$$\frac{Y}{X} = \frac{W}{4}$$

Substitute 6 for *W*, $\frac{Y}{X} = \frac{6}{4} = \frac{3}{2}$.

381. C. $\frac{1}{5}$

The pie chart displays Welch's rent expense as 20 percent of total expenses, but all the answer choices are fractions. To convert 20 percent to a fraction, put 20 over 100 and simplify. When you divide both the numerator and denominator by 20, you get $\frac{1}{5}$. If you picked Choice (E), you forgot that percent means per one hundred.

382. D. $27,450

You can use the percentages on the chart to determine the amount the company spends on salaries and rent each month. Salaries make up 41% of expenses, and 41% of $45,000 is $18,450 $0.41 \times \$45,000 = \$18,450$. Don't pick Choice (C), though. You're not through. You have to add rent costs to the total salaries. Eliminate Choices (A) and (B) along with Choice (C) because you know that the total the company spends on salaries plus rent is more than they spend on salaries alone. The rent expense is 20% of $45,000, or $9,000, $0.20 \times \$45,000 = \$9,000$. Add $9,000 to $18,450 to get $27,450. You don't actually have to add the numbers together to know the right answer. The right answer has to end in 450. Eliminate Choice (E).

383. B. 6%

Under the reduced spending policy, total expenses equal $40,000. The question asks you to find what percentage of $40,000 makes up travel expenses. To do that, you have to know how much the company now spends on travel. Rent and salaries aren't touched, so the company still spends $27,450 on those two categories. The question tells you that the company spends $10,125 on supplies and miscellaneous goods. If you add that figure to the rent and salaries figure and subtract the total from $40,000, you end up with the travel total:

$$\begin{aligned} \$27,450 + x + \$10,125 &= \$40,000 \\ x + \$37,575 &= \$40,000 \\ x &= \$2,425 \end{aligned}$$

You know you can calculate the answer, so eliminate Choice (E). Just figure out what percent $2,425 is of $40,000:

$$\$2,425 = \frac{x}{100} \times \$40,000$$
$$0.060635 = \frac{x}{100}$$
$$6.0635 = x$$

Travel expenses make up just a little over 6% of Welch Inc.'s total monthly expenses. If you picked Choice (A), you figured your percentage using the old monthly total of $45,000.

384. **A. (6, 3)**

Because coordinates *B* and *C* have the same *y*-coordinate of 5, you know that the sides of the rectangle are parallel to the axes. That means that vertex *B* and vertex *A* must have the same *x*-coordinate. The *x*-coordinate of *A* is 2, so *g* must equal 2. Vertex *C* must have the coordinates (6, 5) because $g+4=2+4=6$. Finally, *D* must have the same *x*-coordinate as *C* and the same *y*-coordinate as *A*, which means that *D*'s coordinates are (6, 3).

385. **C. 520**

There are 2 choices for the first character (M or F), 10 choices for the second character (0, 1, 2, 3, 4, 5, 6, 7, 8, and 9), and the 26 letters of the alphabet for the third character. All you do is multiply the possibilities: $2 \times 10 \times 26 = 520$.

If you picked Choice (B), you thought there were 9 numbers from 0 to 9 instead of 10. Choice (A) results from incorrectly adding the numbers instead of multiplying them.

386. **B. $5\sqrt{2}$**

The figure indicates that the triangle formed by *E*, *F*, and *C* is a right triangle. Segments *CE* and *CF* link the center of the circle to a point on the circle. Therefore, they are radii of the circle and have the same length of 5. That means that triangle *ECF* is a 45:45:90 triangle with sides in this ratio: $s:s:s\sqrt{2}$.

Chord *EF* is the hypotenuse of the right triangle. The length of one of the equal sides is 5. Therefore, the measure of chord *EF* is $5\sqrt{2}$.

387. E. 4

The function tells you that its value is $\frac{1}{x^2}$ for any value of x you plug in that's greater than zero. 0.5 is greater than zero, so you can just substitute 0.5 for x in the fraction and solve:

$$f(0.5) = \frac{1}{(0.5)^2}$$
$$f(0.5) = \frac{1}{0.25}$$
$$f(0.5) = 4$$

388. C. 100

Word problems usually require you to translate English into math language. Let L = Larry and G = Greg. "As many as" means multiply. The equation for the first part of the first sentence is $L = \frac{2}{3}G$.

Plug in numbers you know. The question tells you that Larry has 50 dogs. Substitute 50 for L and solve for G:

$$50 = \frac{2}{3}G$$
$$150 = 2G$$
$$75 = G$$

Greg has 75 dogs.

Now you can set up an equation that allows you to solve for the number of dogs Ralph has:

$$G = \frac{3}{4}R$$
$$75 = \frac{3}{4}R$$
$$300 = 3R$$
$$100 = R$$

Ralph has 100 dogs to take care of.

You can also work this problem backwards from the answers. Try the middle value of 100. If Ralph has 100 dogs, Greg has 75, and therefore Larry has 50. Choice (C) works! If it didn't, you'd just try another.

389. B. 23

You can answer this question the long way by simply listing and counting the multiples: 15, 18, 21, 24, 27, 30, 33, 36, 39, 42, 45, 48, 51, 54, 57, 60, 63, 66, 69, 72, 75, 78, and 81. (The *inclusive* means you include 15 and 81 in your total.) There are 23 multiples.

You can save time by subtracting 15 from 81, which results in 66. Then, you divide by 3 because you're counting by threes, which gives you 22. You're not finished, though. Add 1 because the set includes 15 and 81. The answer is 23.

390. D. 7,500

Set up an equation from this word problem. Make x equal to the measurement you're supposed to figure out, the area of the park in square yards. 80 percent of the park is a field that has a length of 120 yards and width of 50 yards. That means the area of the football field is 6,000 square yards:

$$A = lw$$
$$A = (120)(50)$$
$$A = 6{,}000$$

Now, you just need to find the area of the total park. Remember that "of" means multiply, so 80 percent of the total is expressed as 0.80 times x:

$$0.80x = 6{,}000$$
$$x = 7{,}500$$

391. E. 42

The distance formula is rate multiplied by time = distance, so time = distance divided by rate. Substitute the known values into the equation and solve for time:

$$t = \frac{d}{r}$$
$$t = \frac{140}{200}$$
$$t = \frac{7}{10}$$

But you're not done yet. The key to this problem is noticing that it asks for how many *minutes* the travel takes, not hours.

Multiply $\frac{7}{10}$ hours times 60 minutes per 1 hour: $\frac{7}{10} \times \frac{60}{1} = \frac{420}{10} = 42$ minutes.

392. A. 2

You can answer this question super quickly when you recognize that when you multiply numbers with the same exponents, the exponents stays the same. That means in this multiplication problem all of the exponents on either side of the equation must have the same value:

$$35^c = (5 \times 7)^c = 5^c \times 7^c$$

ANSWERS 301–400

Because the value of the exponents on the right side of the equation is 2, c must be 2.

You can also figure the answer by simplifying the right side of the equation and then play with your calculator to find out what power of 35 that is. The right side of the equation simplifies as follows: $5^2 \times 7^2 = 25 \times 49 = 1{,}225$.

So $35^c = 1{,}225$. Turns out 1225 is 35 times 35 or 352. c still equals 2.

393. B. 9

You can set up an equation to figure out Dora's age, which means you can eliminate Choice (E). Let D stand for Dora's age now. "As old as" means times or multiply. It's pretty clear that you should multiply Dora's age 6 years ago by 3 to get Dora's age now: D is 3 times Dora's age 6 years ago.

The last part of the equation is to translate Dora's age 6 years ago into math language. Dora's age 6 years ago is Dora's age now less 6 years: $D-6$. You've got your complete equation:

$$D = 3(D-6)$$

Solve for D and you're done:

$$\begin{aligned} D &= 3D-18 \\ D+18 &= 3D \\ 18 &= 2D \\ 9 &= D \end{aligned}$$

Dora's 9 years old.

394. B. 49

The right side of the equation equals 0, so the left side of the equation must also equal 0. Find a value for x that makes the left side of the equation equal 0. If x equaled 0, the equation would work out, but 0 isn't an answer choice. You'll have to work harder. You can factor out the x on the left side, which gives you $x(x-49)$. Now it's easy to see that $x = 49$. That's the only number that produces a sum of 0 in the parentheses and makes the equation right.

If you picked either Choice (D) or Choice (E), you were thinking about the solution set to $x^2 - 49 = 0$. However, the solution set to that equation would be 7 and −7, and there can't be two right answers to a question.

395. D. $\frac{3}{r}$

This question merely requires that you know how to divide by a fraction.

When you divide by a fraction, you multiply by the reciprocal. In this case, change the first division bar to a multiplication symbol and then flip the fraction underneath to $\frac{6}{4r}$. Then, multiply to get $\frac{2}{1}\times\frac{6}{4r}=\frac{12}{4r}=\frac{3}{r}$.

396. C. (0, –3)

The equation $3x-5y=15$ intersects the y-axis at the point that has a x-coordinate of 0, or in other words, where $x=0$. Eliminate Choices (A) and (D) because they don't contain an x-coordinate of 0. To find the y-coordinate, all you have to do is substitute 0 for x in the given equation:

$$\begin{aligned}3(0)-5y&=15\\-5y&=15\\y&=-3\end{aligned}$$

The point's coordinates are (0, –3).

397. D. 56%

To determine in what percent of the trials there were 7 or more made baskets, you have to divide the number of trials with 7 or more made baskets by 50, which is the total number of trials.

Starting with the 5th bar from the left, the number of trials where the players made 7 or more baskets is $18+5+3+2=28$ trials, and 28 divided by 50 is 0.56 or 56%.

To convert from a decimal to a percentage, move the decimal two digits to the right and add a percentage sign. Reverse these directions to go from a percentage to a decimal.

Choice (A) isn't the correct answer because it's the percentage of trials where more than 7 made baskets occurred (instead of 7 or more). If you picked Choice (B), you divided the 28 trials by 100 total trials instead of 50.

398. A. $210<c+d<290$

To find the sum of the interior angles of a polygon, you use this formula: $180°\times(n-2)$, where n is the number of sides in the polygon.

If you can't remember that formula, simply divide the shape into triangles. The sum of the interior angles in each triangle measures 180 degrees, so for each triangle add 180 degrees and you get the sum of all the angles in the polygon.

The polygon in this problem has 4 sides, so you know its interior angles add up to 360 degrees. The problem tells you that the sum of angles *a* and *b* is more than 70 degrees. The lowest possible value for $a + b$ is 71 degrees. If $a+b=71°$ at its lowest, then $c+d=360°-71°$, or $289°$, at its highest. That means that $c+d<290°$. The answer that states $c+d<290$ is Choice (A).

Double-check the rest of the information to make sure Choice (A) is the right answer. The problem says that $a+b<150$. If $a+b<150$, then its highest value is 149 degrees the lowest the sum of *c* and *d* can be is $360-149=211$. Choice (A) works.

399. **D.** $\cos 36° \times 20$

The figure gives you values for the hypotenuse of the triangle and the side that's adjacent to the appropriate angle. Those values call for cosine because CAH in SOHCAHTOA translates to cosine = $\frac{\text{adjacent}}{\text{hypotenuse}}$. Plug the known values in the equation and solve for *x*:

$$\cos 36° = \frac{x}{20}$$
$$\cos 36° \times 20 = x$$

400. **C. –4**

It may be faster to solve this problem by considering each of the answer choices instead of working in out. Substituting Choice (A), –16, for *x* would make $x^2=256$. Choice (B), –5, would make $x^2=25$. Neither of these answers makes $x^2-1\leq 15$. Cross them out. If you substitute –4 for *x*, x^2 would be 16 and $16-1=15$. Because 15 is equal to 15. Choice (C) works, and it's a smaller number than Choice (D) or Choice (E). You don't have to work any harder to know that the correct answer is Choice (C).

If you choose to solve for *x* to solve the problem, you get this:

$$x^2-1\leq 15$$
$$x^2\leq 16$$
$$x\leq 4 \text{ or } -4$$

That means the set of numbers that could be *x* is $\{-4, -3, -2, -1, 0, 1, 2, 3, 4\}$ and of those –4 is the smallest value.

401. **A.** $\frac{1}{3}\pi$

First, find the circumference of the entire circle by plugging the values you know into the circumference formula:

$$C = 2\pi 5$$
$$C = 10\pi$$

Then find what portion of the circle the arc comprises by putting its degree measurement over 360 degrees. You can find the degree measurement of the arc by knowing that angle *ROS* is an inscribed angle and an inscribed angle measures half of the central angle and half of its intercepted arc. In other words, the measurement of angle *ROS* is half the degree measurement of the arc. Multiply 6 and 2 and you know that the arc measures 12 degrees and that the arc is $\frac{12}{360}$ or $\frac{1}{30}$ of the circle.

Finally, to find the length of the arc, multiply the circumference of the circle by the portion of the circle the arc makes up:

$$10\pi \times \frac{1}{30} = \frac{10}{30}\pi = \frac{1}{3}\pi$$

402. E. $\sqrt{5}$

This one's easy when you know the distance formula: $\sqrt{(x_2 - x_1)^2 + (y_2 - y_1)^2}$.

Make sure you keep your point designations straight. $x_1 = 9$, $x_2 = 8$, $y_1 = 4$, and $y_2 = 6$. Plug the values into the equation and solve:

$$\begin{aligned}\sqrt{(8-9)^2 + (6-4)^2} &= D\\ \sqrt{(-1)^2 + (2)^2} &= D\\ \sqrt{1+4} &= D\\ \sqrt{5} &= D\end{aligned}$$

ANSWERS 401–500

403. C. 8.75

The union of two sets consists of one of all of the numbers that appear in set A and set B. So, set C consists of 2, 4, 5, 6, 8, 10, 15, and 20. Notice that you only include one 10 in set C.

The average of a set of numbers is their sum divided by the number of members in the set. Add up the numbers in set C, and you get a grand total of 70. Now divide by the number of elements in the union of the two sets: 70 divided by 8 is 8.75.

404. E. $\frac{3x+4y}{7}$

Read the question carefully. It asks you to figure the cost *per pound* of the mixture. *Per* means divide. You'll eventually divide the cost by the number of pounds.

Set up an equation to determine the cost of the total mixture. The cost of the mixture is $3x$ (total cost of dried cherries) + $4y$ (total cost of dried apples).

The total number of pounds is 7 (3 + 4). So the final equation is the cost divided by number of pounds: $\frac{3x+4y}{7}$, which is the answer in Choice (E).

405. B. $\frac{1}{20}$

The small ticks are placed at $\frac{1}{5}, \frac{2}{5}, \frac{3}{5}$, and $\frac{4}{5}$. The large ticks are placed at $\frac{1}{4}$, $\frac{2}{4}$, and $\frac{3}{4}$. The least common denominator for all ticks is 20, so the tick marks in ascending order are placed at $\frac{4}{20}, \frac{5}{20}, \frac{8}{20}, \frac{10}{20}, \frac{12}{20}, \frac{15}{20}$, and $\frac{16}{20}$. The least distance between tick marks on this number line is $\frac{1}{10}$.

406. C. 1,410

Consider this to be a function problem with $h(t)$ as $f(x)$. Functions are really just fancy substitution problems. To solve this function, simply substitute 2 for t on the right side of the equation, and then solve for $h(t)$:

$$h(2) = 1{,}454 - 16(2)^2 + 8(2) + 4$$
$$h(2) = 1{,}454 - 16(4) + 16 + 4$$
$$h(2) = 1{,}410$$

407. D. 1

Cosecant (csc), secant (sec), and cotangent (cot) are essentially defined as the reciprocals of sine, cosine, and tangent, respectively, you know and love. Here are their formulas:

$$\csc\Theta = \frac{1}{\sin\Theta} = \frac{\text{hypotenuse}}{\text{opposite}}$$
$$\sec\Theta = \frac{1}{\cos\Theta} = \frac{\text{hypotenuse}}{\text{adjacent}}$$
$$\cot\Theta = \frac{1}{\tan\Theta} = \frac{\text{adjacent}}{\text{opposite}}$$

When you know these equations, a problem like this one becomes a piece of cake. You can substitute $\frac{1}{\cos 3\Theta}$ for $\sec^2(3\Theta)$. That changes the question to $\frac{1}{\cos 3\Theta} \times \cos 3\Theta$. The two $\cos 3\Theta$ cancel each other out to give you 1.

408. C. 45

The easiest way to solve this problem is to plug each of the answer choices into the given equation and pick the one that doesn't make the expression true.

Choice (A) gives you 1. Plug 1 into the equation:

$$1 + 3 = 4^n$$
$$4 = 4^1$$

This would make n = 1, which is positive. Because Choice (A) works, it isn't right.

If you substitute the 13 in Choice (B), you get this:

$$13 + 3 = 4^n$$
$$16 = 4^2$$

2 is a positive value for *n*, so eliminate Choice (B).

Choice (C) asks you to substitute 45 into the equation:

$$45 + 3 = 4^n$$
$$48 = 4^?$$

While it may seem like 4 could be a root of 48, it's not. 45 doesn't work in the equation, so Choice (C) is the correct answer. You can mark Choice (C) and go on, or you can check the last two answers just to be sure.

If you plug 61, Choice (D), into the equation, you get this:

$$61 + 3 = 4^n$$
$$64 = 4^3$$

3 is a positive integer, so Choice (D) can't be right.

Choice (E) is 253:

$$253 + 3 = 256$$
$$256 = 4^4$$

This makes $n = 4$, a positive integer. Choice (E) makes the equation true, so it's a wrong answer.

As you move through the answer choices, notice a trend? Answers that made the equation work created values that could have a root of 4 when you add 3.

409. D. $\sqrt{19}$

To help you solve this problem, draw a picture.

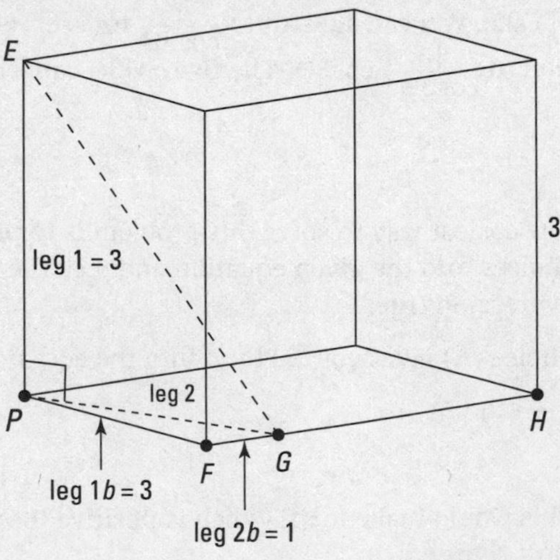

Create a right triangle with segment *EG* as the hypotenuse. Leg 1 is the segment created by point *E* and the unnamed point directly below it (we've named it *P* for clarity). Leg 2 is the segment created by *P* and *G*. Mark the two legs in with dashes so you can see them.

Because it's an edge of the cube, the distance of leg 1 of the right triangle is 3 units. The distance of leg 2 is trickier to determine. You actually need to set up second right triangle to solve for that. Leg 1*b* of this second right triangle is the segment created by *P* and point *F*, and leg 2*b* will be segment *FG*.

You know these two values: leg 1*b* is an edge of the cube and measures 3 units; leg 2*b* is segment *FG*, which measures 1 unit because *G* is one-third of the distance from *F* to *G* and $\frac{1}{3} \times 3 = 1$.

Use the Pythagorean theorem to solve for the length of leg 2 using what you know about the lengths of leg 1*b* and leg 2*b*.

$$\begin{aligned} 3^2 + 1^2 &= c^2 \\ 9 + 1 &= c^2 \\ 10 &= c^2 \\ \sqrt{10} &= c \end{aligned}$$

Segment *EG* is the hypotenuse of a right triangle with legs measuring 2 and $\sqrt{10}$. Again, apply the work of your buddy Pythagoras.

$$\begin{aligned} 3^2 + \sqrt{10}^2 &= c^2 \\ 9 + 10 &= c^2 \\ 19 &= c^2 \\ \sqrt{19} &= c \end{aligned}$$

410. **D.** $45 + 15\sqrt{3}$

If a right triangles has angles in the ratio 1:2:3, it must be 30:60:90 triangle. The largest angle is the one that measures 90 degrees. The sum of the other two angles is also 90 degrees, so the smallest angle must measure 30 degrees:

$$\begin{aligned} x + 2x &= 90 \\ 3x &= 90 \\ x &= 30 \end{aligned}$$

The ratio of sides in a 30:60:90 triangle is $s : s\sqrt{3} : 2s$, where *s* stands for the shortest side. So, if the shortest side of the triangle is 15, the other two sides measure $15\sqrt{3}$ and 30. Add the three sides together to get a perimeter of $45 + 15\sqrt{3}$.

411. **B. Increase its length by 2 units**

Use what you know about trigonometry to answer this question. SOHCAHTOA tells you that $\sin = \frac{\text{opposite}}{\text{hypotenuse}}$. So, for the sines of *x* and *y* to be equal, the ratios of the opposite sides and hypotenuses of the two triangles need to be equal. When you examine the two triangles, you see that the ratio of the opposite sides of each triangle, segment *CB* to segment *FE*, is 8:16, which simplifies to 1:2. The same proportion is true for the two bases of the triangles. The ratio of segment *AB* to segment *DE* 6:12, or 1:2. For the angle measurements to be equal, the hypotenuses of the two triangles must also have a 1:2 ratio. The current ratio of segment *AC* to segment *DF* is 10:18, or 5:6. To change segment *DF* to make the ratio 1:2, you have to add length to segment *DF* so that the length of segment *DF* is twice the measurement of *AC*. Cross out Choices (D) and (E) because they decrease length from segment *DF*.

Segment *DF* measures 10 units. When you multiply 10 by 2, you get 20. To make segment *DF* measure 20 units, you have to add 2 units to 18. In other words, you have to increase its length by 2. The answer is Choice (B).

412. **C. $x^2y + 3xy^2 - 7$**

Remove the parentheses and distribute the minus sign:

$$3x^2y + xy^2 - 4 - 2x^2y + 2xy^2 - 3$$

Then combine like terms:

$$3x^2y - 2x^2y + xy^2 + 2xy^2 - 3 - 4 = x^2y + 3xy^2 - 7$$

When you distribute the minus sign, it changes the sign of every element in the parentheses. Knowing to distribute negative 1 to all terms in the second set of parentheses is a commonly tested concept on the ACT.

413. **A. (–1, 6)**

To find the midpoint, determine the average of the *x*-coordinates and *y*-coordinates of the endpoints. The *y*-coordinates are the same, so the midpoint's *y*-coordinate is also 6. Eliminate Choices (B) and (D).

To find the average of –4 and 2, add the coordinates and divide by 2:

$$\frac{-4+2}{2} = -1$$

414. **B. 72**

Add the numbers in the ratio: 3 + 5 = 8. The total must be a multiple of 8, eliminating Choices (A) and (D). Try the remaining answers.

If the total is 72, there are 9 groups of 8 because $8 \times 9 = 72$. Multiply each element of the ratio by 9:

$$3 \times 9 = 27$$

So there are 27 lollypops.

$$5 \times 9 = 45$$

There are 45 chocolate bars.

When you subtract 27 from 45, you get 18. Choice (B) must be correct, and you don't need to check the other options.

415. **C. 10**

Instead of working out complex calculation, first examine the answer choices. Based on the second equation, you can eliminate Choices (D) and (E). Neither 13 + 4 nor 12 + 4 is less than 16.

Then plug the remaining options into the first equation. Because you're determining which answer results in a value greater than 16, start with the greatest value, 10.

If x is 10 in the first expression, then $10 + \frac{4}{5}(10) = 10 + 8 = 18$, which is certainly more than 16. The first equation is valid.

Try the second: $10 + 4 > 16$. This inequality is also true, so the answer must be Choice (C).

You can try the other options, but neither $x = 7$ nor $x = 8$ results in a value greater than 16.

416. **B. 7**

This question tests your ability to translate English into algebra. "A third" means $\frac{1}{4}$ and "of" means multiply. The product of 8 and 3 translates to 8×3. So far you've got $\frac{1}{4} \times (8 \times 3)$. "Is" means = and "four less than $2x$" means $2x - 4$. The final translated equation is $\frac{1}{4} \times (8 \times 3) = 2x - 4$. Now just solve for x:

$$\begin{aligned} \frac{1}{4} \times (8 \times 3) &= 2x - 4 \\ \frac{1}{4} \times 24 &= 2x - 4 \\ 6 &= 2x - 4 \\ 10 &= 2x \\ 5 &= x \end{aligned}$$

ANSWERS 401–500

417. **E.** $\frac{1}{36}$

The only way to roll a 12 with two dice is to roll double sixes. The probability of rolling any number on a six-sided die (one of a pair of dice) is 1 out of 6, or $\frac{1}{6}$. Multiply consecutive probabilities: $\frac{1}{6}$ for the first die times $\frac{1}{6}$ for the second die is $\frac{1}{36}$.

418. **E. 32**

The sides of an isosceles right triangle are in the ratio $s:s:s\sqrt{2}$, where s is one of the equal sides. The equation for the perimeter (p) of an isosceles right triangle, then, is $2s+s\sqrt{2}=p$ You know the perimeter of the triangle is $16+8\sqrt{2}$, which means that s must be 8. The two legs of the triangle represent its base and height.

Use that information to find the area:

$$\frac{1}{2}bh=A$$
$$\frac{1}{2}(8)(8)=A$$
$$32=A$$

419. **A. 4.4**

The formula for the volume of a rectangular solid (a litter box or a fish tank, for instance) is $l\times w\times h$. So the volume of the former box is $12\times 24\times 4=1{,}152$. The new box will have the same volume of 1,152 cubic inches. The sides of its base are 50 percent longer than those of the former box. If one side of the former box is 12 inches, the new box has a side of $12+0.5(12)$, which is 18. If the other side of the former box is 24, the second tank has a side of length $24+0.5(24)$, which is 36. Apply what you know to the volume formula and solve for h to find how many inches tall the new box measures:

$$18\times 36\times h=1{,}152$$
$$648h=1{,}152$$
$$h=1.\overline{77}$$

The new box is approximately 1.7 units tall.

420. **A.** $9+3\sqrt{3}$

You can find the base of triangle ABC by applying the formula for the area of a triangle. The area is $50\sqrt{3}$ square units and the height is $10\sqrt{3}$ units:

$$\frac{1}{2}10\sqrt{3}b=50\sqrt{3}$$
$$5\sqrt{3}b=50\sqrt{3}$$
$$5b=50$$
$$b=10$$

The base is 10, which means the triangle must be a 30:60:90-degree triangle. A right triangle with a long leg length that is $\sqrt{3}$ times its short leg length has angle measures of 30:60:90 degrees. Because similar figures have the same angle measures, triangle *DEF* is also a 30:60:90-degree triangle, which means its base is $\sqrt{3}$ times its height and its hypotenuse is double its short side. Therefore, the sides of triangle *DEF* are 3, $3\sqrt{3}$, and 6.

Add the three sides to find the perimeter: $3+6+3\sqrt{3}=9+3\sqrt{3}$.

---

421. **E.** $\frac{\sqrt{256}}{\sqrt{4}}$

An irrational number is a decimal that never ends or repeats. All of the choices are irrational except Choice (E). The square root of a number that is not a perfect square is irrational. The values under the square root signs of the fraction in Choice (E) are perfect squares, so its value is $\sqrt{256}$, which is 16, divided by $\sqrt{4}$, which is 2. Choice (E) equals 8, which is a rational number.

---

422. **A. 5**

The straight lines indicate absolute value, which is always positive. Therefore, $3-3a$ must equal 12 or −12. For $3-3a=12$, $a=-3$, which is not one of the answer choices. For $3-3a=-12$, and $a=5$, which is Choice (A). If you chose Choice (C), you forgot to change the sign when you moved the 3 to the other side of the equal sign.

You can also take a simple shortcut by plugging in the answer choices. The ACT is nice enough to give you the answer for each problem; all you have to do is substitute each answer choice to see which one could be a value for *a*.

---

423. **D. 1:1**

Don't let the information about the triangles' areas distract you. This problem is much easier than it looks. The sum of the interior angles of any triangle is 180° no matter what the size of the triangle is. Because the interior angles of both triangles total 180°, the ratio is 180:180, or 1:1.

---

424. **C.** $25y-6x$

To give the question context, plug in easy values for the variables. Say the cars cost 10 cents (x) each for a total cost of 60 cents. Matt forked over 3 quarters(y), for a total of 75 cents. His change is the difference: $75-60=15$. Go through each answer choices, plugging in 10 for x and 3 for y. The answer that comes out to be 15 is the winner. When you try Choice (A), you get $3-60=-57$. Nope. Choice (B) gives you $25(3)+6(10)=135$, which isn't right. Choice (C) is $25(3)-6(10)=15$. You have your answer.

425. D. 85

Arc *AB* has the same degree measure as the central angle. Because the central angle measures 72 degrees, minor arc *AB* also measures 72 degrees. The ratio of the arc length to the circumference is equal to the ratio of the arc degree measurement to 360°. $\widehat{AB} = \frac{72}{360}$ or $\frac{1}{5}$ of the circumference. Set up the proportion and cross-multiply to find the circumference:

$$\frac{17}{C} = \frac{1}{5}$$
$$1C = (5)(17)$$
$$C = 85$$

426. A. 52

To visualize the scene, record the paths of Debbie and Jaspar. Mark point *A* on your booklet. Draw a straight line vertically (north) from *A* to mark Debbie's travels. From the same point, draw a straight horizontal line to the right (east) for Jaspar's walk. Connect the end points of Debbie and Jaspar's lines and mark the distance as 65 yards. You get a right triangle:

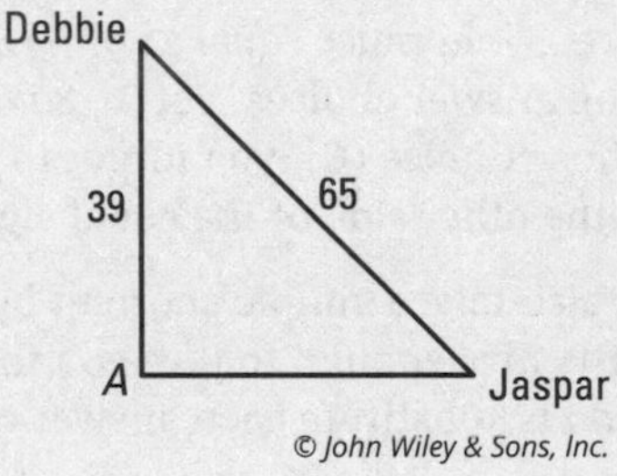

© John Wiley & Sons, Inc.

You could apply the Pythagorean theorem to find the long leg of the triangle, but note that both 39 and 65 are divisible by 13 to get a ratio of 3:5 of short leg:hypotenuse. This must be a 3:4:5 right triangle. Simply multiply 4 by 13 to get the measure of the long leg, 52 yards, which is the distance Jaspar walks.

427. D. (2, −2)

Choice (A) doesn't have an *x*-coordinate of 2, so it's wrong.

Plug 2 in for *x* in the equation and solve for *y* to get the *y*-coordinate:

$$x^2 - y = 6$$
$$(2)^2 - y = 6$$
$$4 - y = 6$$
$$-y = 2$$
$$y = -2$$

The coordinates are (2, −2).

ANSWERS 401–500

428. **A.** $-\frac{5}{12}$

To find the slope of the given line, put it in the slope-intercept form:

$$5y-12x=35$$
$$5y=12x+35$$
$$y=\frac{12}{5}x+7$$

So the slope of the given line is $\frac{12}{5}$.

To determine the slope of a perpendicular line, flip the fraction and change the sign. The slope has to be negative, so eliminate Choices (C), (D), and (E). Flip the numerator and denominator to get $-\frac{5}{12}$.

429. **B. −1.5**

Create the number sequence with the information you're given:

1	2	3	4	5
?	-6	?	?	0.75

Because the sequence is geometric, you multiply by the same value to find each term. The second term is negative and the fifth is positive, so you must be multiplying by a negative value. Therefore, the fourth term must be negative and you can eliminate Choices (D) and (E).

You could spend time determining the common ratio between each term, but it's likely faster to try out the remaining answer choices. If the fourth term is Choice (C), −0.5, the common ratio would be −15 because 0.75 divided by −0.5 is −15. When you multiply −6 by −15, you get 90 for the third term and −1,350 for the fourth term, so Choice (C) doesn't work.

When you apply Choice (B), you have a fourth term of −1.5. Divide 0.75 by −1.5 to find the common ratio: $\frac{0.75}{-1.5}=-0.5$.

If −0.5 is the common multiplier, the third term would be 3: $-6\times-0.5=3$. The fourth term would be −1.5: $3\times-0.5=-1.5$. That works, so the fourth term must be −1.5, Choice (B).

430. **C. 300°**

The merry-go-round rotates 5 times in a minute (or 60 seconds), it rotates 1 time in 12 seconds: $\frac{60}{5}=12$. So the ride moves 360° in 12 seconds. You know the number of degrees it rotates in 10 seconds has to be less than 360° but not much less. The answer can't be Choice (E), (A), or (B).

If the ride moves 360° in 12 seconds, it rotates 30° per second. In 10 seconds, it rotates 10 times that or 300°.

You could also solve this problem by setting up a proportion using the total number of degrees the ride travels in 5 rotations:

$$\frac{5(360)}{60} = \frac{x}{10}$$
$$\frac{1,800}{60} = \frac{x}{10}$$
$$60x = 18,000$$
$$x = 300$$

431. **C. 12**

To create an infinite number of solutions, the two equations must be equal. Each of the terms in the second equation must be exactly 4 times the terms in the first equation. To make the final term in the second equation equal to 4 times the final term in the first, the value must be 48: $12 \times 4 = 48$. Therefore, a must be 12 because that's the value for a that makes the two equations equal.

432. **E. 9**

Note that k is a constant. To figure out its value, plug the initial values for x and y into the proportion and solve for k:

$$\frac{3}{27} = \frac{k}{18}$$
$$27k = 54$$
$$k = 2$$

When you know k is 2, you can plug in 6 for y in the proportion and solve for x:

$$\frac{x}{27} = \frac{2}{6}$$
$$6x = 54$$
$$x = 9$$

When $y = 6$, $x = 9$.

433. **B. $10\sqrt{3}$**

The altitude (or height) divides the equilateral triangle into two 30:60:90 triangles, as shown here:

ANSWERS 401–500

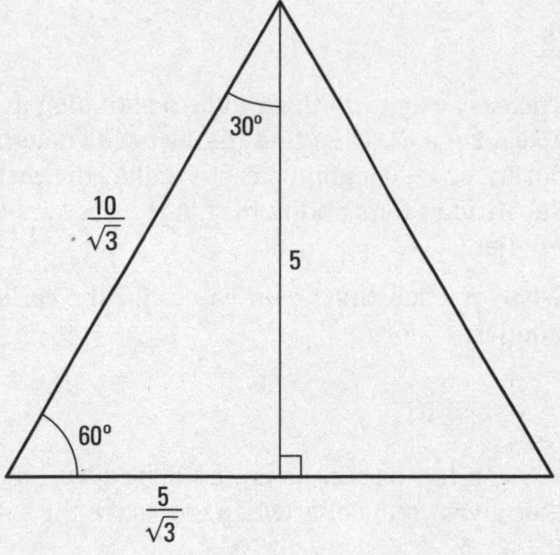

You know this because an altitude creates a right angle with the base and an equilateral triangle has three 60-degree angles. So the bottom-left angle of the triangle is 60 degrees and the angle at the top measures 30 degrees, half of the 60-degree angle.

The ratio of the sides of a 30:60:90 triangle is $s : s\sqrt{3} : 2s$, where s is the measure of the short leg and the long leg measures $s\sqrt{3}$, Use this information to find the length of the short side of one of the 30:60:90 triangles:

$$s\sqrt{3} = 5$$
$$s = \frac{5}{\sqrt{3}}$$

Therefore, each side of the original triangle is $2\frac{5}{\sqrt{3}}$ or $\frac{10}{\sqrt{3}}$, and the perimeter is $3\frac{10}{\sqrt{3}}$. Rationalize the denominator:

$$3\frac{10}{\sqrt{3}} \times \frac{\sqrt{3}}{\sqrt{3}} = \frac{30\sqrt{3}}{3} = 10\sqrt{3}$$

434. **E. 3**

Try substituting values to help you solve this problem. Use a number like 12 that is divisible by 4 to represent the total capacity of the water tank. If the tank holds 12 gallons of water, it holds 9 gallons when it is $\frac{3}{4}$ full. In one hour, the tanks fills one quarter of 12 gallons, or 3 gallons. If it continues to fill at the same rate, it will reach 9 gallons in 3 hours:

$$\frac{1}{3} = \frac{x}{9}$$
$$3x = 9$$
$$x = 3$$

In 3 hours the tank will be $\frac{3}{4}$ full.

ANSWERS 401–500

435. E. $\frac{t}{12n}$ dollars

The easy way to do this problem is to plug in easy values for the variables. Let $n=1$. Then find the cost of 12 doughnuts (so $t=12$). If one dozen, or 12, doughnuts cost 1 dollar, the cost of t doughnuts is 1 dollar. Substitute 1 for n and 12 for t in the answers to see which one equals 1 dollar.

When you substitute your values for the variables in Choice (A), you get 1 dollar:

$$\frac{12}{(12)(1)}=1$$

You can try the other answers to be sure, but Choice (A) is the only one that gives you 1 dollar when you make the substitutions.

436. A. 5

First, find out how many 45-minute increments are in 4.5 hours, or 270 minutes: $\frac{270}{45}=6$. Ferah, therefore, processes 6 batches of 200 mailings, or 1,200 mailings. Mickey assembles 600 in 2.5 hours, or 1,200 in 5 hours.

Don't bother figuring out how many mailings Mickey produces in 1 minute, in 45 minutes, or in any other increment. That's way too much work. Because 1,200 is 2 times 600, Mickey works for 2 times 2.5 hours, or 5 hours.

437. D. 84%

To make this problem easier, give this problem real numbers. For percentage problems, 100 is a good choice. Say that a lawnmower was originally \$100. A 50 percent increase raises the price to \$150: $100+(100\times 0.50)=150$. A 20 percent drop in that price puts the cost at \$120: $150-(150\times 0.2)=120$. Decreasing that price another 30 percent drops the price to \$84: $120-(120\times 0.3)=84$. Now you can easily see that the August price of 84 dollars is 84 percent of the May price of \$100.

438. B. 10

To create an infinite number of solutions, the two equations must be equal. Before you start your analysis, order the two equations similarly:

$$x+2y=15$$
$$2x+4y=3a$$

The reordering reveals that each of the terms in the second equation must be exactly 2 times the terms in the first equation. So the last term in the second equation has to be 30 ($15 \times 2 = 30$).

Therefore, a must be 10 because that's the value for a that makes the last term 30 and the two equations equal.

439. **E. 10**

The distance the tire travels in one revolution is its circumference. If the tire revolves 15 times in 300π yards, each revolution has a circumference of 20π: $\frac{300\pi}{15} = 20\pi$. When you know the circumference, you can apply the formula to find the radius:

$$C = 2r\pi$$
$$20\pi = 2r\pi$$
$$20 = 2r$$
$$10 = r$$

440. **A. prime**

Prime numbers have no positive integer factors other than 1 and themselves, so the product of any two prime numbers cannot be prime. That value would have at least four factors: 1, itself, and the two prime numbers that multiplied together produced its value.

441. **C. $256 - 64\pi$**

To find shade area, subtract the area of the unshaded figure from the total area. The total area in the figure is the area of the square. The side of the square measures 16 units, so the area of the square is 16^2, or 256 square units.

The unshaded figure is a circle. To find the area of a circle, you need to know its radius. Notice that the diameter of the circle measures the same as the side of the square. So the diameter of the circle is 16 units and its radius is half that — 8 units. Apply that value to the area formula:

$$A = \pi r^2$$
$$A = \pi 8^2$$
$$A = 64\pi$$

Subtract 64π from 256 to get an area of $256 - 64\pi$ for the unshaded portion of the figure.

ANSWERS 401–500

442. C. $\sqrt{45}$

Simply plug in −2 for *x* the equation and solve for *y*:

$$-2^2+y^2=49$$
$$4+y^2=49$$
$$y^2=45$$
$$y=\pm\sqrt{45}$$

443. B. $2a^2+2a+13$

You can, of course, apply FOIL to multiply each expression and then add the products. But it's more efficient to remember that $(a+b)^2=(a^2+2ab+b^2)$. Substitute 3 for *b*: a^2+6a+9. Next recall that $(a-b)^2=(a^2-2ab+b^2)$. Substitute 2 for *b*: a^2-4a+4. Stack and add the two equations:

$$\begin{array}{r} a^2+6a+9 \\ \underline{a^2-4a+4} \\ 2a^2+2a+13 \end{array}$$

You can eliminate Choices (D) and (E) immediately because you know that $a^2+a^2\neq a^2$. Narrow down the answers as you go to avoid making a careless mistake.

444. E. $\frac{23}{50}$

The jar originally holds a total of 105 marbles. After the shopper selects the marbles and places them in a bag, 100 marbles remain (105 − 5 = 100). Of those 100 marbles, 48 are green because the shopper has taken 2 of the original 50 green marbles from the jar. So the probability of the shopper selecting a green marble next is $\frac{48}{100}$, or $\frac{23}{50}$.

445. B. $\frac{r}{t}$

For this problem, you need to know that tan = opposite/adjacent. The length of the side opposite the 30-degree angle *is* r, and the length of the side adjacent to the angle is *t*. Therefore, $\tan 30°=\frac{r}{t}$

446. D. $-2<x\leq 3$

The unshaded point means that point is not included on the graph. Therefore, −2 is not part of the graph and you can eliminate Choices (C) and (E). The shaded circle means that point is included on the graph. Look for an answer that says the graph can be equal to 3. Choices (D) works.

Choices (A) and (B) are far too broad. Numbers greater or less than −2 travel infinitely in one direction.

447. **D.** $\frac{5b}{2ac}$

Get the terms that have y and x in them on one side and all the terms that have nothing to do with y and x on the other side:

$$2ay - \frac{5b}{c} = 2ax$$
$$2ay - 2ax - \frac{5b}{c} = 0$$
$$2ay - 2ax = \frac{5b}{c}$$
$$2a(y - x) = \frac{5b}{c}$$
$$y - x = \frac{5b}{2ac}$$

448. **E.** $-\frac{b}{a}$

Apply the slope equation to solve this type of problem:

$$slope = \frac{y_2 - y_1}{x_2 - x_1}$$

Substitute the appropriate x- and y-coordinates into the equation:

$$slope = \frac{b-(-b)}{-a-a}$$
$$slope = \frac{2b}{-2a}$$
$$slope = -\frac{b}{a}$$

449. **A.** $\frac{72}{\cos 22°}$

The length of Beam B is the hypotenuse of the right triangle. Tangent doesn't include the hypotenuse, so you can eliminate Choices (B) and (D).

The other answers contain the cosine and sine of either a 68° angle or a 22° angle. The figure shows a 68°. You know that the angle formed by Beam B and the concrete slab is also 68° because it and the 68° angle are alternate interior angles.

Apply the sine ratio because you know the side opposite the 68° angle and you're trying to find the hypotenuse:

$$\sin 68° = \frac{72}{x}$$
$$\sin 68° x = 72$$
$$x = \frac{72}{\sin 68°}$$

ANSWERS 401–500

But this answer isn't available. Consider the other angle in the triangle. It must measure 22°. Apply cosine to this angle because you know its adjacent side and you're solving for the hypotenuse:

$$\cos 22° = \frac{72}{x}$$
$$\cos 22° x = 72$$
$$x = \frac{72}{\cos 22°}$$

This answer is there!

450. **B.** $\sqrt{142}$

Finding distance on the coordinate plane means apply the distance formula: $d = \sqrt{(x_1 - x_2)^2 + (y_1 - y_2)^2}$

Plug the values for x and y into the formula and solve:

$$d = \sqrt{(3-(-8))^2 + (4-(-7))^2}$$
$$d = \sqrt{(11)^2 + (11)^2}$$
$$d = \sqrt{121+121}$$
$$d = \sqrt{142}$$

451. **D.** $\frac{1}{\sec^2 \theta}$

The key to answering this question is to remember the equation $\cos^2 \theta + \sin^2 \theta = 1$. So the numerator in the fraction is equal to 1.

$$\frac{\sin^2 \theta + \cos^2 \theta}{\sec^2 \theta} = \frac{1}{\sec^2 \theta}$$

452. **D. 6**

Get rid of the machine and a half by doubling to get three machines. Twice as many machines produce twice as many widgets, three, in the same number of hours.

Don't stop there and choose Choice (A). The machines produce 3 widgets in 36 hours, but the question asks you for the number of widgets they produce in 72 hours. Because 72 hours is double the time, you just have to double the widgets: $3 \times 2 = 6$

453. **C.** $16 \sin 56°$

The unknown height is opposite the 56° angle. Because 16 is the hypotenuse, you can use the sine formula: $\frac{\textit{opposite}}{\textit{hypotenuse}}$. So $\sin 56° = \frac{x}{16}$.

Solve for x:

$$16\sin 56° = x.$$

454. **E. $\frac{4}{5}$ only**

Tangent values refer to the legs of a right triangle. If one leg is 3 and the other is 4, the triangle in question is a 3:4:5 right triangle, and the hypotenuse must be 5. Because cosine includes the hypotenuse at the bottom, eliminate answer that don't contain 5 or place it in the numerator: Choices (C) and (D).

In tangent ratios, the adjacent side is in the denominator, so the side adjacent the angle is 4. Cosine ratios place the adjacent side in the numerator, so eliminate Choice (B) because it doesn't have 4 in the numerator. You have Choices (A) and (E) remaining.

Because $\tan\theta$ is positive, $\sin\theta$ and $\cos\theta$ must both be positive or both be negative. On the unit circle, between 0 and $\frac{\pi}{2}$ in radians, $\sin\theta$ and $\cos\theta$ are both positive. But between $\frac{\pi}{2}$ and π, $\sin\theta$ is positive and $\cos\theta$ is negative, ruling out any possibility that θ is between $\frac{\pi}{2}$ and π and establishing that $\cos\theta$ cannot be negative.

455. **B. 4**

Figure out how many wolves existed in the refuge in 2014, subtract the number of wolves introduced in 2010, and you've got your answer.

You could figure out the number of wolves by multiplying the population each year by 12 percent and adding the yearly totals. From 2010 to 2011, the number of wolves grew to 8.96 ($0.12\times 8 = 0.96$ and $8 + 0.96 = 8.96$). From 2011 to 2012, those 8.96 wolves grew to 10.04 wolves ($0.12\times 8 = 8.96$; $8.96 + 8.96 = 10.04$). Likewise, the 10.04 wolves became 11.25 wolves from 2002 to 2003. And from 2013 to 2014 the wolf population grew from 11.25 wolves to 12.60 wolves.

Subtract the initial 8 wolves from those around in 2014 and you get 4.60 wolves: $12.6 - 8 = 4.6$.

Don't think the answer should be 5. 0.6 of a wolf is not a whole wolf, so the answer is 4 rather than 5.

You can solve this problem more quickly if you remember the formula for exponential growth, $NV = IV \times (1+P)^{Y}$, where NV is the new value, IV is the initial value, P is the percent increase, and Y is the number of years.

The initial value of the wolves when they were introduced into the wild was four pairs, which is 8 total wolves. The rate of increase was 12 percent, or 0.12, per year. The number of years was 2014 – 2010, or 4.

ANSWERS 401–500

Plug the numbers into the formula to find the new number of wolves in 2014.

$$NV = 8 \times (1 + 0.12)^4$$
$$NV = 8 \times (1.12)^4$$
$$NV = 8 \times 1.57351936$$
$$NV = 12.59$$

Subtract 8 and you come up with a 4-wolf difference.

If you picked Choice (A), you may have missed that the number of wolves introduced in 2010 was 4 *pairs* and figured the growth based on an initial number of 4 wolves rather than 8. Be sure to read the questions carefully to avoid these kinds of costly mistakes.

456. **D.** $\frac{abc}{b-c}$

To figure out the answer, first find the lowest common denominator (LCD) for the fractions in the denominator. The LCD of two variables is the product of the two variables, so the LCD of $\frac{1}{b} - \frac{1}{c}$ is *bc*. Multiply each numerator by the variable you multiplied by in the denominator.

$$\frac{1}{b} \times \frac{c}{c} = \frac{c}{bc}$$
$$\frac{1}{c} \times \frac{b}{b} = \frac{b}{bc}$$

The expression now looks like this: $\frac{a}{\left(\frac{b-c}{bc}\right)}$

To divide the fraction, multiply by the reciprocal:

$$\frac{a}{\left(\frac{b-c}{bc}\right)} = \frac{a}{1} \times \frac{bc}{b-c} = \frac{abc}{b-c}$$

457. **B.** $300 < t + u + v < 380$

The sum of the interior angles of a pentagon is 540 degrees.

The problem tells you that the degree measurement of $r + s$ is more than 160. So, the lowest $r + s$ can be is 161 and the highest the degree measurement of $t + u + v$ can be is 379, because $540 - 161 = 379$. In math terms, $t + u + v < 380$.

The second half of the equation says that the degree measurement of $r + s$ has to be less than 240. If the degree measurement of $r + s$ is less than 240, then the highest it can measure is 239 degrees and the lowest $t + u + v$ can measure is $540 - 161 = 301$. In math language, the second half of the answer is that the degree measurement of $t + u + v < 300$, which is the same thing as saying $300 > t + u + v$.

Combine these two pieces of information in one happy math expression: $300 > t + u + v < 380$.

ANSWERS 401–500

458. **C.** $n(n-1)$

Avoid the debilitating effects of brain damage trying to figure out the answer to this problem by simply examining each answer choice to see if it fits the pattern. The one that fits is the right answer.

You know from the figure that the 2nd arrangement has 2 squares, the 3rd arrangement has 6 squares, and the 4th arrangement has 12 squares. Substitute 2, 3, and 4 for *n* in each answer choice. The one that results in answers of 2, 6, and 12 is correct. Start with the answer choices that are easiest to plug in.

Choice (A)'s pretty simple to evaluate. Substitute 2, 3, and 4 for *n* in 2*n*. When you plug in 2, you get 4: 2(2) = 4. The answer should be 2, so Choice (A) doesn't work. When you substitute 2 for *n* in Choice (B), you get 8: $2(2)^2 = 2 \times 4 = 8$. Choice (B) is wrong.

Try Choice (C). Plug 2 into the expression: $2(2-1) = 2(1) = 2$. That works. Substitute 3 for *n*: $3(3-1) = 3(2) = 6$. 4 works, too, so Choice (C) has the right formula.

459. **D.** $\overline{CA}, \overline{AB}, \overline{CB}$

Find the distance between each of the points. Then line them up from shortest to longest.

You can solve this problem using the distance formula. Apply the formula to find the distance between each of the three points. The distance formula is $d = \sqrt{(y_2 - y_1)^2 + (x_2 - x_1)^2}$.

You don't need to work out the formula to find the distance between Point *C* and Point *A*. They have the same *y*-coordinate, and there's a 1-unit distance between their *x*-coordinates, so the length between them is 1.

To find the length of segment *AB*, substitute the coordinates of each end point into the distance formula and solve for *d*.

$$d(\overline{AB}) = \sqrt{(y_2 - y_1)^2 + (x_2 - x_1)^2}$$
$$d(\overline{AB}) = \sqrt{[0-(-1)]^2 + [(-1)-1]^2}$$
$$d(\overline{AB}) = \sqrt{1^2 + (-2)^2}$$
$$d(\overline{AB}) = \sqrt{1+4}$$
$$d(\overline{AB}) = \sqrt{5}$$

You know that segment *AB* is longer than segment *CA*. $\sqrt{5}$ has to be greater than 2 because $\sqrt{4}$ is 2 and $\sqrt{5}$ is greater than $\sqrt{4}$. Cross out Choices (A) and (B) because they place segment *AB* before segment *CA*.

To pick the right answer from the remaining choices, you have to know the length of segment *CB*. Apply the distance formula again:

$$d\left(\overline{CB}\right)=\sqrt{\left[0-(-1)\right]^2+\left[(-1)-2\right]^2}$$
$$d\left(\overline{CB}\right)=\sqrt{1^2+(-3)^2}$$
$$d\left(\overline{CB}\right)=\sqrt{1+9}$$
$$d\left(\overline{CB}\right)=\sqrt{10}$$

Segment *CB* is greatest.

460. A. $2\frac{1}{2}$

To get a handle on this problem, you may want to draw yourself a quick picture of the information in the question. When you see what you're dealing with, the question is easy to answer.

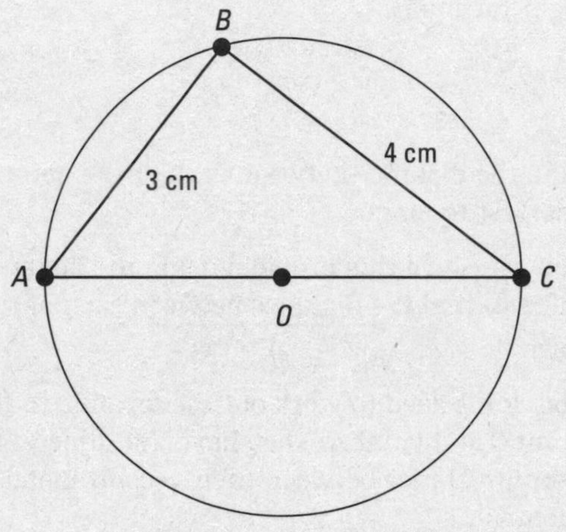

The picture shows an inscribed angle in a semicircle. An inscribed angle in a semicircle is a right angle. So, triangle *ABC* is a right triangle. Not only that, the triangle is a special right triangle, a 3:4:5 right triangle. If the two legs measure 3 and 4, the hypotenuse must measure 5.

The hypotenuse of the triangle is the diameter of the circle. And the radius is half the diameter. So the radius is half of 5 or $2\frac{1}{2}$.

461. E. 45 tan 50°

To find the area of a parallelogram, you multiply the lengths of its base and height. Finding the base of *EFGH* is easy. Just add the lengths of the two segments that make up the top of the parallelogram. Because $4+5=9$, the base of the parallelogram measures 9 units.

The height is of the parallelogram is the length of the dashed line (a) in the figure. That line is one of the legs in a right triangle. Use what you know about the angle measurements of the parallelogram to find the length of that side.

Start with angle *HEF*. The figure tells you it measures 130 degrees.

The opposite angles in a parallelogram are equal and the sum of the four angles is 360 degrees. So, angle *HGF* also measures 130 degrees because it's opposite angle *HEF*. The sum of angles *HGF* and *HEF* is 260 degrees, which leaves 100 degrees to split equally between the measurements of the other two angles. Angles *EFG* and *EHG* each measure 50 degrees.

Take a moment to consider what you know about the right triangle. One of its angles measures 50 degrees. The side adjacent to that angle measures 5 units. And you need to know the length of the side that's opposite the 50-degree angle, side a. Sounds like this is a job for tangent!

Plug the numbers in to the tangent formula and solve for a.

$$\tan 50° = \frac{a}{5}$$
$$5 \tan 50° = a$$

That gives you the height of the parallelogram. Just multiply the height by the base and you get the area:

$$9 \times 5 \tan 50° = 45 \tan 50°$$

462. **D. 24**

This question gives you a little break from geometry and trigonometry. To calculate how many $1\frac{3}{4}$ pieces can be cut from four 12-foot long wood pieces, divide 12 by $1\frac{3}{4}$, ignoring the remainder (scrap wood), and then multiply by 4. Start by converting $1\frac{3}{4}$ to a mixed fraction: $1\frac{3}{4} = \frac{7}{4}$. Set up an equation and solve for x:

$$x = \left[\frac{12}{\left(\frac{7}{4}\right)}\right]$$
$$x = \left(\frac{12}{1} \times \frac{4}{7}\right)$$
$$x = \frac{48}{7}$$

48 divided by 7 is 6 with a remainder of 6. You have to throw away the remainder because that's scrap wood. So you can get 6 pieces that measure $1\frac{3}{4}$ feet from each 12-foot length. The answer isn't 6, though. You still have three additional 12-foot pieces of wood. Each of those pieces can also be cut into 6 lengths. The maximum number of $1\frac{3}{4}$ lengths you can get from the 4 larger pieces of wood is 24. The correct answer is Choice (D).

ANSWERS 401–500

463. D. $s = u^9$

The language in the first part of the question just tells you that whenever you see two positive integers on either side of that goofy little diamond symbol, the first integer is equal to the cube of the second. The second part of the questions tells you that you're solving for *s* and your answer has the *u* variable in it.

To solve *s* for *u*, identify the two simultaneous equations: $s \Diamond t$ means $s = t^3$ and $t \Diamond u$ means $t = u^3$. Because you're solving for *s* in terms of *u*, you have to make the *t*s disappear.

The second equation has solved for *t* in terms of *u*, so you know you can substitute u^3 for *t* in the first equation. Solve for *s* and you're done!

$$s = t^3$$
$$s = \left(u^3\right)^3$$
$$s = u^9$$

464. B. $\sqrt{10}$

This problem involves two equations and substitution. The question gives you the equation of the line, $y = 4$.

The second equation you need to know is the one for the circle.

The general equation for a circle is $(x-h)^2 + (y-k)^2 = r^2$, where (*h*, *k*) are the (*x*, *y*) coordinates of the center of the circle and *r* is the radius. So here's the equation for this circle:

$$(x-2)^2 + (y-3)^2 = r^2$$

Start with the equation for the circle, and then plug in the *x*- and *y*-coordinates of the intersection point. You know that $y = 4$. The problem tells you that the *x*-coordinate is 5 at the intersection point. Just substitute and solve for *r*.

$$(5-2)^2 + (4-3)^2 = r^2$$
$$3^2 + 1^2 = r^2$$
$$10 = r^2$$
$$\sqrt{10} = r$$

465. A. 8

The ultimate mix with 3 liters of concentrate should result in a beverage that's 27 percent orange juice concentrate and the rest water.

Percentages can be expressed as ratios. The best way to solve the problem is to set up a proportion with amount of concentrate on top and the total liquid in the beverage on the bottom on both sides of the equal sign.

The left side of the equation shows the portion orange juice concentrate makes of the final beverage: $\frac{27}{100}$. You put 27 over 100 because percent means "per hundred."

On the right side of the proportion, you put the amount of concentrate over the total amount of the beverage mixture. The question tells you that the amount of concentrate is 3 liters. The total amount is of beverage is concentrate plus water, or $3+x$. Set up the proportion and solve for *x*:

$$\frac{27}{100}=\frac{3}{3+x}$$
$$3(100)=27(3+x)$$
$$300=81+27x$$
$$219=27x$$
$$8.11=x$$

Round to the nearest whole liter to find that the diner should mix 8 liters of water with the 3 liters of concentrate.

466. **E.** $16\sqrt{3}$

The formula for the area of a triangle is $A=\frac{1}{2}bh$. The question tells you that the length of the base (diameter *XY*) is 8 units. The height of the triangle is the measure of segment *CO*, as shown in the figure.

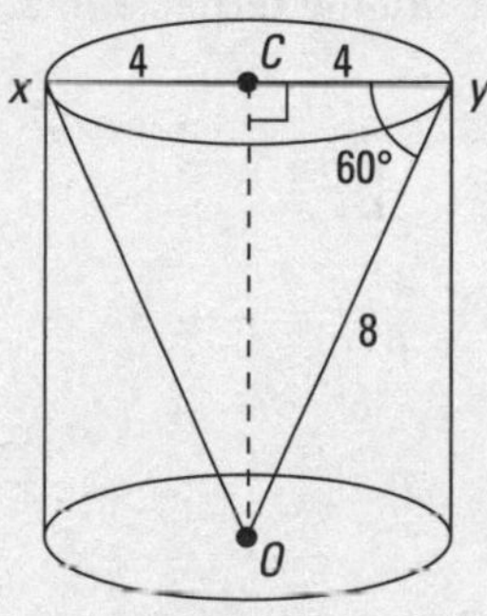

© John Wiley & Sons, Inc.

Because the *XYO* is equilateral, you know that segment *OY* measures 8 units and that angle *XYO* measures 60 degrees. To find the measure of *CO*, use the ratio for 30:60:90-degree triangles, which is $s:s\sqrt{3}:2s$ where *s* is the measure of the smallest side and 2*s* is the hypotenuse. Because $s=4$ in this triangle, the measure of *CO* is $4\sqrt{3}$.

But the answer isn't Choice (B). You still have to find the area. Multiply the height by 8 and divide by 2:

$$A=\frac{1}{2}\times 8\times 4\sqrt{3}$$
$$A=16\sqrt{3}$$

ANSWERS 401–500

467. A. b^4c^8

To get the expression in its simplest form, solve for one of the variables in terms of the other two. When you examine the answers, you see that the ACT gurus want the answers in terms of *b* and *c*, which means you have to solve for *a*.

When you're not sure what variable to solve for when you simplify an expression, check out the possible answers for clues.

One way to get *a* by itself on one side of the equation is to divide a^5 by *a* on the right side of the equation. That eliminates the *a* in the denominator: $a^5b^4c^3 = \frac{a^4b^2}{b^{-2}c^{-4}}$.

Then you can divide both sides of the equation by a^4, which leaves just one *a* on the left side: $ab^4c^3 = \frac{b^2}{b^{-2}c^{-4}}$.

The b^{-2} in the denominator is the same as b^2 in the numerator. Likewise, the c^{-4} in the denominator is the same as c^4 in the numerator. Solve for *a*:

$$ab^4c^3 = b^2b^2c^4$$
$$ab^4c^3 = b^4c^4$$
$$ac^3 = c^4$$
$$a = c$$

When you know that $a = c$, you can substitute *c* for *a* in the original expression, combine terms, and eliminate the variable *a* from the expression:

$$a^5b^4c^3 = \frac{c^5b^2}{cb^{-2}c^{-4}}$$
$$a^5b^4c^3 = \frac{c^5b^2}{b^{-2}c^{-3}}$$
$$a^5b^4c^3 = c^8b^4$$

468. D. 25

To help you through this problem, look for something familiar. The presence of the equation $\sin^2\Theta + \cos^2\Theta = 1$ may not be immediately obvious, but you can find it with a little problem solving.

Simplify the expression, making sure that you distribute the negative sign through the terms in the second set of parentheses.

$$\left[\cos^2\Theta + 6 - \left(-\sin^2\Theta + 2\right)\right]^2 = ?$$
$$\left(\cos^2\Theta + 6 + \sin^2\Theta - 2\right)^2 = ?$$
$$\left(\cos^2\Theta + \sin^2\Theta + 4\right)^2 = ?$$
$$\left(1 + 4\right)^2 = ?$$
$$5^2 = 25$$

469. E. Family E

You don't need to calculate each family's ratio to answer this question. Glance through the figures for recycled waste and eliminate any families that recycle less than 50 percent of what they throw away.

The only family with a value for recycled material that is more than half of its value for tossed material is Family D (30 is more than half of 55).

470. A. $-\frac{2}{3}$

When you first looked at this problem, you may have panicked. How do two equations give you information about one straight line? The answer is simple: simultaneous equations.

To get rid of that meddlesome r, you could solve one equation for r and substitute what you get into the other equation.

A quicker option may be to solve both equations for r and set the results equal to each other. When you solve the first equation for r, you get $r = \frac{x+2}{4}$.

When you solve the second equation for r, you get $r = \frac{y-1}{-3}$.

Set the expressions equal to each other: $\frac{x+2}{4} = \frac{y-1}{-3}$.

Cross multiply and distribute:

$$\begin{aligned} -3(x+2) &= 4(y-1) \\ -3x-6 &= 4y-4 \\ -3x &= 4y+2 \end{aligned}$$

To solve for the x-intercept, just substitute 0 for y in the equation.

$$\begin{aligned} -3x &= 4(0)+2 \\ -3x &= 2 \\ x &= -\frac{2}{3} \end{aligned}$$

471. D. $9\sqrt{2}$

To find the area of triangle *ABC*, you have to determine the length of both its base and height. The height is *AB*, which is an edge of the cube and therefore measures 6 cm. To figure out base *BC*, draw a right triangle as shown.

ANSWERS 401–500

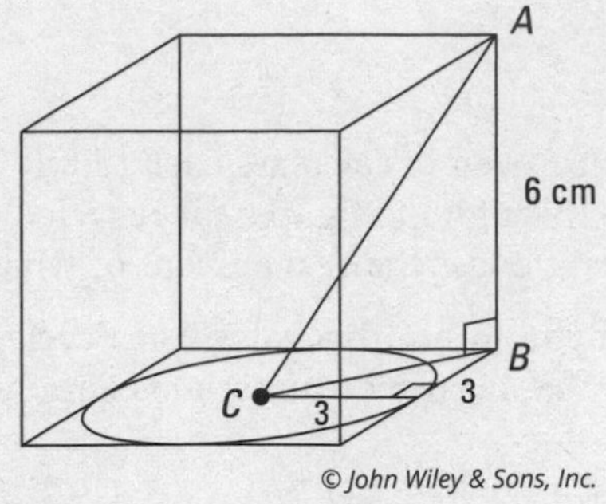

© John Wiley & Sons, Inc.

Both legs of this little triangle measure 3 because one is half of the edge length and the other is the radius of the circle (which also has to be 3 because the circle is inscribed). Now you're on a roll. If the legs are equal lengths, the triangle is a 45:45:90 triangle with a side ratio of $s:s:s\sqrt{2}$. So the measure of *CB* is $3\sqrt{2}$.

But that's just the measure of *BC*, and the question asks for the area of *ABC*. The height of *ABC* is 6 centimeters. The base is $3\sqrt{2}$. Plug these values into the formula for area:

$$A = \frac{1}{2}6 \times 3\sqrt{2}$$
$$A = 9\sqrt{2}$$

ANSWERS 401–500

472. B. $\frac{\log 4 \log 6}{\log 3 \log 5}$

Looking at the answer choices tells you you're dealing with a logarithm problem. Because you're solving for $\frac{x}{z}$ and none of the answers has a *y* variable, you need to get rid of the *y* variables in the original equations. You can do this by solving both equations for *y* and them setting them equal to each other. Then, you can manipulate the equation to solve for $\frac{x}{z}$. First, take the log of both sides of the first equation and solve for *y*:

$$3^x = 4^y$$
$$x\log 3 = y\log 4$$
$$\frac{x\log 3}{\log 4} = y$$

Then, take the log of both sides of the other equation and solve for *y*:

$$5^y = 6^z$$
$$y\log 5 = z\log 6$$
$$y = \frac{z\log 6}{\log 5}$$

Set the equations equal to each other and move terms around until you've solved for $\frac{x}{z}$:

$$\frac{x\log 3}{\log 4} = \frac{z\log 6}{\log 5}$$
$$\frac{x\log 3}{z\log 4} = \frac{\log 6}{\log 5}$$
$$\frac{x}{z\log 4} = \frac{\log 6}{\log 3\log 5}$$
$$\frac{x}{z} = \frac{\log 4\log 6}{\log 3\log 5}$$

473. C. $\frac{3}{5}$

Applying what you know about algebra operations, solve the equation for a:

$$2 + \frac{3}{a} = 4 + 5a$$
$$\frac{3}{a} = 2 + 5a$$
$$3 = a(2 + 5a)$$
$$3 = 2a + 5a^2$$
$$0 = 5a^2 + 2a - 3$$

Factor the quadratic equation:

$$5a^2 + 2a - 3 = 0$$
$$(5a - 3)(a + 1) = 0$$

Set both factors equal to 0 and solve for a:

$$a = \frac{3}{5}, a = -1$$

Because $-1 < 0$ and isn't an answer option, the correct choice is $\frac{3}{5}$.

474. A. 2.56π

Don't let the equation with the x exponent throw you. Just use a couple of familiar formulas.

The formula for the area of a circle is $A = \pi r^2$. So find the radius of the circle, apply it to the formula, and you're done.

The radius is the distance from (3, 1) to the point on the circle that intersects with the graph. Find the coordinates of that point, and you can use the handy dandy distance formula to discover the length of the radius.

ANSWERS 401–500

The point's x-coordinate is obvious. The dotted line on the figure indicates that it's 2. The y-coordinate, then, is what you get when you plug 2 in for x in the equation of the curve:

$$y=(1.5)^2$$
$$y=2.25$$

The y-coordinate is 2.25. So the coordinates of the second point are (2, 2.25).

With the coordinates of the two points, you can use the distance formula to find the radius.

$$d=\sqrt{(1-2.25)^2+(3-2)^2}$$
$$d=\sqrt{(-1.25)^2+(1)^2}$$
$$d=\sqrt{1.5625+1}$$
$$d=\sqrt{2.5625}$$

The radius of the circle is $\sqrt{2.5625}$. Plug that value into the area formula (Don't bother to find the square root of 2.5625 because you just square it again in the area formula):

$$A=\sqrt{2.5625}^2\pi$$
$$A=2.5625\pi$$

ANSWERS
401–500

475. E.

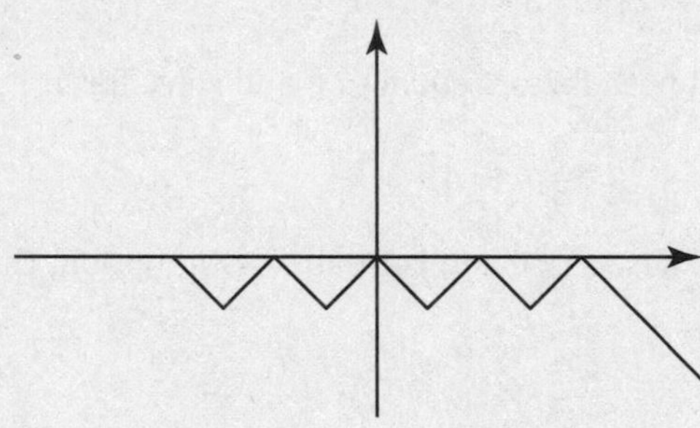

© John Wiley & Sons, Inc.

The key to solving this problem is knowing the definition of absolute value. The *absolute value* of a number is simply its absolute distance from zero (like on a number line) and will always be positive.

This figure, then, is the positive version of whatever makes up $f(x)$. You have to figure out just exactly what that *whatever* is. There are several possibilities, but a correct answer will have the same basic pattern as the original. It will just be reflected below the x-axis.

Eliminate answers that can't be right. Choice (D) disconnects the straight line from the rest of the graph. It doesn't maintain the same general pattern as the original, so it's wrong. Choices (B) and (C) eliminate two of the four original zigzags, so they can't be right. Choice (A) has the proper number of zigzags, but the straight line goes off in the wrong direction, across the x-axis. The only answer that shows a representation of the pattern of the original figure reflected below the x-axis is Choice (E). It provides the mirror image of original pattern below the x-axis, and the original could be the absolute value (positive version) of this pattern.

476. **B. 48**

At first this question may have overwhelmed you, but if you think about it logically, it's really downright simple. If each side and its opposite have the reverse squares shaded, then for every two sides of the cube, the equivalent to one side of the cube is completely shaded. With three sets of opposite sides, the area is the equivalent of three completely shaded sides. Multiply 16 squares by 3 sides, and you get 48 shaded cubes.

477. **D. 2**

For the cosines of x and y to be equal, the angles have to be equal. The angles will be equal when the vertical and horizontal legs of the two right triangles formed by the number line, rays, and segments are equal. The problem tells you that the segments are congruent, which means the vertical legs are already equal.

The horizontal leg of the left right triangle measures 4 units. To make the horizontal legs equal, horizontal leg of the right triangle on the right must also measure 4 units. Don't pick Choice (B), though. The question doesn't ask for the total length of the horizontal leg. It asks for the number of units segment b had to move to create a leg that's 4 units long. Segment b needs to move two units to the right — from 8 to 10 — so that the horizontal leg of the right triangle on the right also measures 4 units.

478. **A. $\sqrt{0.6}$**

Functions are really just fancy substitution problems. This one combines two functions, which means you have to perform two substitutions. Work from inside the parentheses out (that's easy because you're used to working this way under the standard order of operations).

The problem asks you to find $f\left(g(20)\right)$. In other words, solve $g(x)$ for $g(20)$ in the second equation, and then plug what you get in for x in the other equation.

Substitute 20 for x in $g(x)$:

$$g(x)=\frac{2(20)+2}{20-6}$$
$$g(x)=\frac{42}{14}$$
$$g(x)=3$$

Now substitute 3 for x in the equation for $f(x)$:

$$f(x)=\sqrt{0.4(3)^2-3}$$
$$f(x)=\sqrt{3.6-3}$$
$$f(x)=\sqrt{0.6}$$

479. **B. $15.40**

The first $1,000 of purchases is tax-free, so you don't need to consider the first $1,000. Subtract $1,000 from $1,220 to find the amount of purchases that will actually be taxed:

$$1{,}220-1{,}000=220$$

To find the amount of tax due, you multiply 220 by 7 percent (or 0.07).

You don't have to take the time to fully work out the calculation. Estimate to save time. 200 is close to 220 and 200 times 0.07 is 14.00, so the amount has to be a little more than $14.

480. **E. $x=4$**

Line l is vertical line. For a vertical line, the x-coordinate always stays the same. Only the y-coordinate changes. Therefore, line l always has an x-coordinate of 4, which makes the equation of the line $x=4$.

481. **D. 126°**

There are 360 degrees in a circle. Jasmine's monthly rent payment represents 35% of the circle. To determine the number of degrees that make up Jasmine's rent payment on the graph, just multiply 360° by 0.35 to get 126°.

ANSWERS 401–500

482. D. I and III only

As you evaluate the statements, eliminate answer choices along the way. Solve the inequality for x:

$$\begin{aligned} 100 - x &> x - 70 \\ 170 - x &> x \\ 170 &> 2x \\ 87.5 &> x \end{aligned}$$

That means that statement III must be true. You can eliminate Choices (A) and (B) because they don't contain statement III. It's probably easier to evaluate statement II than statement I. The solution tells you that $x < 87.5$, so x could be greater than 85, equal to 85, or less than 85. It could be true that $x > 85$, but it doesn't have to true. Cross out Choices (C) and (E) because they contain statement II. The answer is Choice (D).

You didn't even have to evaluate statement I to answer this question correctly. Using process of elimination, you know that statement I must be true. You can check it if you want. 87.5 is equal distance between 100 and 75. If x must be less than 87.5, x has to be closer to 75 than 100.

483. A. $\sqrt{3}$

To find slope, you apply the slope formula, which is the change in the y-coordinates divided by the change in x-coordinates, or $\text{slope}(m) = \frac{y_2 - y_1}{x_2 - x_1}$. To do that you need to know the coordinates for two points on the line segment. You know that point A has coordinates of $(x, 0)$, and you don't know the coordinates of Point O. You may be tempted to pick Choice (E) and move on. But just because you don't know all of the coordinates of the points doesn't mean that you can't figure out the slope of the segment. Your biggest clue that you can solve this one is that all the segments of the triangle are equal, meaning that the triangle in the figure is equilateral. That means you can determine the lengths of the sides in terms of x. Then when you calculate the slope of the segment, the x terms will cancel each other out and you'll have your value.

Eliminate Choice (E). You can also eliminate Choices (C) and (D) because you can tell by looking at segment OA that its slope is positive.

Here's what you do to choose between the remaining answers:

Draw an altitude from A to the midpoint (M) of segment OB. Label segment OA as measuring x units. Segment OB also measures x units, and each half of OB (OM and MB) measures $\frac{1}{2}x$ units, like this:

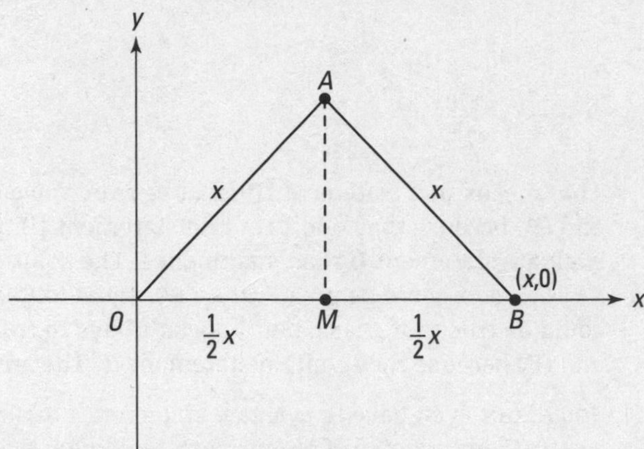

At this point, you may recognize that the slope of OA equals AM divided by OM because the length of AM is the change in the y-coordinates and the length of OM is the change in the x-coordinates. You know that $OM = \frac{1}{2}x$. All that remains is to find the length of AM.

Because triangle AOM is half of an equilateral triangle, it must be a 30:60:90-degree triangle. You know this because each of the angles in an equilateral triangle measures 60 degrees, and angle AOM is one of those angles. Angle AMO measures 90 degrees, which means that angle OAM has to measure 30 degrees. In 30:60:90 triangles, the longer leg is equal to the measure of the shorter leg multiplied by $\sqrt{3}$. Segment AM is the longer leg of the triangle, so it measures $\frac{1}{2}x \times \sqrt{3}$ or $\frac{\sqrt{3}}{2}x$.

When you know the length of segment OM and segment AM, you can plug them into the slope formula and solve:

$$\text{slope}(m) = \frac{AM}{OM}$$

$$\text{slope}(m) = \frac{\frac{\sqrt{3}}{2}x}{\frac{1}{2}x}$$

$$\text{slope}(m) = \frac{\sqrt{3}}{2} \times \frac{2}{1}$$

$$\text{slope}(m) = \frac{2\sqrt{3}}{2}$$

$$\text{slope}(m) = \sqrt{3}$$

484. C. 36%

The easiest way to solve this problem is to apply actual numbers to the circumstances. To simplify your life, use a nice round percentage-friendly figure like $100.

If the couch originally cost $100, a 20 percent discount would result in a new price of $80:

$$100 \times 0.20 = 20$$
$$100 - 20 = 80$$

When you discount the price of the couch another 20 percent, you get a new price of $64:

$$80 \times 0.20 = 16$$
$$80 - 16 = 64$$

But you're not finished yet. You need to calculate the total percent decrease, which is just the difference between the original and final prices divided by the original price:

$$100 - 64 = 36$$
$$\frac{36}{100} = 36\%$$

485. D. 3

The problem gives you two values for *x* and the equation for *f*(*x*) and wants to know the sum of *a* and *b*. If you figure out the value of *c*, you're in business. To accomplish this, perform two separate substitutions.

First, plug in 0 and 2 for *x* and *f*(*x*) respectively and solve for *c*:

$$2 = a(0)^2 + b0 + c$$
$$2 = 0 + 0 + c$$
$$2 = c$$

Do the same thing using 1 and 5 for *x* and *f*(*x*) respectively. This time you can substitute 2 for *c*:

$$5 = a(1)^2 + b(1) + 2$$
$$3 = a + b$$

486. C. 14

Consider what the question tells you. You know that 98 goes into n^2. So, think of a multiple of 98 that's a perfect square. $98 \times 2 = 196$ and 196 is a perfect square. If 196 is n^2, then *n* is 14 because $\sqrt{196} = 14$. The largest integer in the answer choices that is a multiple of 14 is 14. 7 and 2 go into 14, too, but they're smaller values than 14.

487. A. \$23,500

To figure out the amount of weekly earnings it takes for Angelo and Isabella to earn the same amount of money, create an equation that sets Angelo's and Isabella's weekly earnings equal to each other with *x* representing the unknown of weekly sales.

Weekly earnings for each salesperson are equal to base salary plus commission. So Angelo's earnings are $550+0.08(x-1{,}000)$ and Isabella's are 0.10*x*. Set up the equation and solve:

$$\begin{aligned}550+0.08(x-1{,}000)&=0.10x\\550+0.08x-80&=0.10x\\470&=0.02x\\23{,}500&=x\end{aligned}$$

488. D. 7

This problem may look scary, but don't give up too quickly. Figure out the area of each triangle using the formula $A=\frac{1}{2}h$ and add them together.

Each of the bases of the three triangles measures 1 unit (0 to 1, 1 to 2, and 2 to 3 on the graph). The height of each triangles is the *y*-coordinate of the graph of $y=2^x$. To determine the *y*-coordinate at each point, plug the appropriate *x*-coordinate into the function. The height of the first triangle is 2 ($y=2^1=2$); the height of the second triangle is 4 ($y=2^2=4$); and the height of the third triangle is 8 ($y=2^3=8$). All that's left is to figure out the areas of the triangles and add them up:

$$\begin{aligned}A&=\tfrac{1}{2}b_1h_1+\tfrac{1}{2}b_2h_2+\tfrac{1}{2}b_3h_3\\A&=\tfrac{1}{2}(1)(2)+\tfrac{1}{2}(1)(4)+\tfrac{1}{2}(1)(8)\\A&=1+2+4\\A&=7\end{aligned}$$

489. E. $\frac{zy}{x}$

Apply your trusty tool SOHCAHTOA, which reminds you that $\tan\Theta=\frac{\text{opposite}}{\text{hypotenuse}}=\frac{y}{x}$. Therefore, $z\tan\Theta=z\times\frac{y}{x}=\frac{zy}{x}$.

490. B. 72

The key to this problem is to recognize that *a* and *b* are supplementary angles, which means they add up to 180 degrees:

$$a+b=180$$

ANSWERS 401–500

Now all you have to do is substitute 180 for $a+b$ in the original equation and solve:

$$\frac{180}{b}=\frac{5}{2}$$
$$5b=360$$
$$b=72$$

491. **B. 3.87**

To solve for *x*, break out the variable from the radical cage in that it's trapped in. To organize its escape, square both sides of the equation and simplify:

$$\sqrt{7x+1}\times\sqrt{7x+1}=5.3\times5.3$$
$$7x+1=28.09$$
$$7x=27.09$$
$$x=3.87$$

492. **D. 30**

It's important to recognize that the measures of the four angles in the figure add up to 180 because they lie along a straight line.

Knowing that line *BZ* bisects (cuts exactly in half) angle *YBC* tells you that angle *YBZ* and angle *ZBC* are equal. Angle *YBZ* measures 60 degrees, which means that angle *ZBC* also measures 60 degrees. The measures of angle *YBZ* and *ZBC* account for 120 of the total 180 degrees allotted for the four angles, which leaves you with 60 degrees to allocate to the remaining two angles. Because line *BX* bisects angle *ABY*, those two remaining angles are equal. The two angles together measure 60 degrees, so each individual angle must measure 30 degrees ($30+30=60$). Angle *ABX* measures 30 degrees.

493. **B.** $y=-\frac{1}{2}z$

The problem gives you two simultaneous equations. Often the easiest way to solve for one of the variables is to stack the equations. Because you're solving for *y* in terms of *z*, you need to eliminate the *x* variable. First, arrange the equations in a similar order:

$$2x-6y=3z$$
$$x+2y=-z$$

Find the term you can multiple the terms in the second equation by that will allow you to get rid of the *x* variable. Notice that multiplying the equation by –2 will do the trick:

$$2x-6y=3z$$
$$-2(x+2y=-z)$$

ANSWERS 401–500

Then distribute the value and add the expressions:

$$\begin{aligned}
2x - 6y &= 3z \\
\underline{-2x - 4y} &\underline{= 2z} \\
-10y &= 5z \\
y &= -\frac{5}{10}z \\
y &= -\frac{1}{2}z
\end{aligned}$$

494. E. (3, −3)

To help you visualize the problem, draw a picture like the one in this figure.

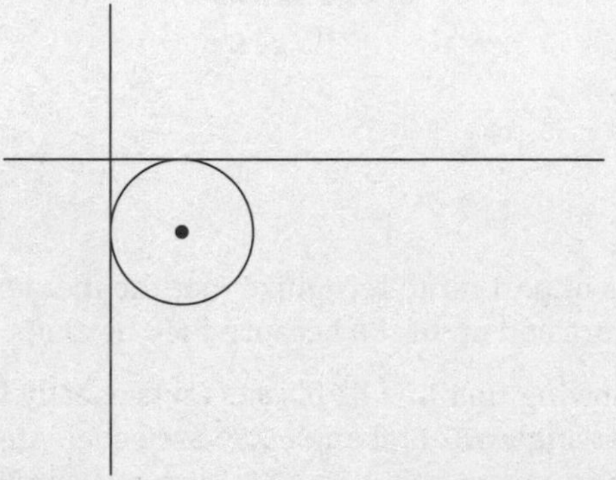

© John Wiley & Sons, Inc.

The circle in the question is tangent to the negative y-axis and the positive x-axis. That means it sits in the lower right quadrant of the coordinate plane, and two of its points (its uppermost and leftmost points) are touching the axes. Because the center is of a circle is the same distance from all points on the circle, the center of your circle must be the same distance from each of the axes. You can eliminate any answers that don't have the same absolute value for each of the coordinates, which means you should cross out Choices (B), (C), and (D). That leaves you with Choices (A) and (E), but Choice (A), with a negative x-coordinate and a positive y-coordinate, would incorrectly place the circle in the upper left quadrant of the plane. The only answer that satisfies the requirements is Choice (E).

495. C. 27

This one's quick and easy if you know the formula for finding the number of diagonals in a regular polygon: $D = \frac{n}{2}(n-3)$, where D stands for the number of diagonals and n stands for the number of sides the polygon has. The nonagon has 9 sides. Apply the formula and you've got your answer:

$$D = \frac{9}{2}(9-3)$$
$$D = 4.5(6)$$
$$D = 27$$

496. E. $45\tan 27°$

Do yourself a favor and draw a picture like the one in the figure. The distance to the base of the building, the height of the ledge, and the line that connects Point P to the ledge form a right triangle.

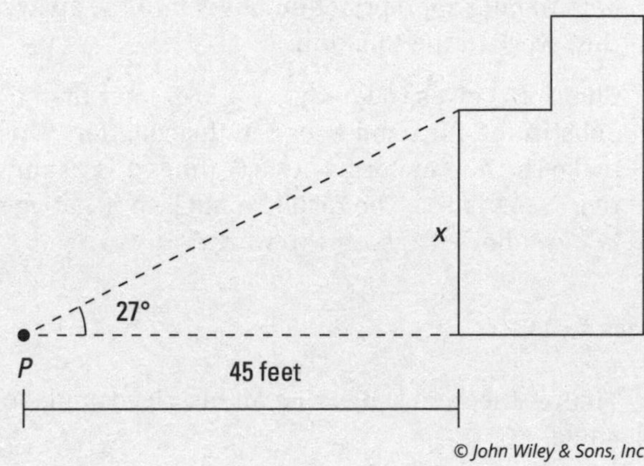

© John Wiley & Sons, Inc.

The height of the ledge (x) is the side opposite the angle measuring 27 degrees. The 45-foot line is the side adjacent to the 27-degree angle. Use what you know, the measurement of the angle and the length of the adjacent angle, to find the length of the opposite side, x.

SOHCAHTOA tells you that tangent is the division of the opposite side by the adjacent side. Because you know you're dealing with tangent, you can cross out Choices (A), (C), and (D) that contain sine and cosine. Create the formula and solve for x:

$$\tan 27° = \frac{x}{45}$$
$$x = 45\tan 27°$$

497. A. $0 < y < x$

To solve this problem, you apply the rules for combining signs for mathematical operations. The bottom line is that for $\frac{yx}{y-x}$ to be negative, either the numerator has to be positive and the denominator negative or the numerator has to be negative and the denominator positive.

That's valuable information for sure, but you have to consider the situation more deeply:

For the numerator (the product yx) to be positive, both y and x have to be positive or both have to be negative.

For the numerator to be negative, either y or x has to be negative.

For the denominator (the difference of $y-x$) to be positive, x has to be less than y if x and y are both positive or both negative, and y cannot be negative if x is positive.

For $y-x$ to be negative, y has to be less than x if they are both positive or both negative, and y cannot be positive if x is negative.

If it makes your brain ache to hang on to all of that information, it may help to plug appropriate numbers into the answer choices to see how they work in the equation.

Choice (A) gives you $0 < y < x$. 1 is greater than 0 and 2 is greater than 1. Substitute 1 for y and 2 for x in the equation. This substitution would make the numerator positive (1 times 2 is 2) and the denominator negative (1 − 2 is −1). The result would be a negative number (2 divided by −1 is −2). Choice (A) seems to work.

498. C. $4(\sin\Theta+\cos\Theta+1)$

Thales' theorem states that an inscribed angle in a semicircle is a right angle.

If you were unaware of this theorem, you might have guessed that one of the angles of the given triangle was a right angle because some of the possible answers involve sine and cosine. The hypotenuse of the right triangle is the diameter of the circle and equal to 4. You know that 4 is one of the side measurements that you'll be adding to the lengths of the other two sides to find the perimeter of the triangle.

Use SOHCAHTOA to help you figure out the lengths of the other two sides. Both sine and cosine involve the hypotenuse. Use cosine to find the adjacent side length:

$$\cos\Theta=\frac{\text{adjacent}}{4}$$
$$\text{adjacent}=4\cos\Theta$$

Use sine to figure out the opposite side:

$$\sin\Theta=\frac{\text{opposite}}{4}$$
$$\text{opposite}=4\sin\Theta$$

Add the three sides to find perimeter: $4\sin\Theta+4\cos\Theta+4$. When you extract the common factor of 4, you come up with the correct answer: $4(\sin\Theta+\cos\Theta+1)$.

499. C. the region of the plane on one side of a line

This question requires you to consider the worth of each of the answer choices. It's probably easier to answer this question if you draw a picture. Create a big square on your test booklet and put Points P and Q inside the square as shown in the figure. We've put P on the left and Q on the right, but it doesn't really matter where you put them. To enhance the visual, you can draw in the line segment that connects the two points, like this:

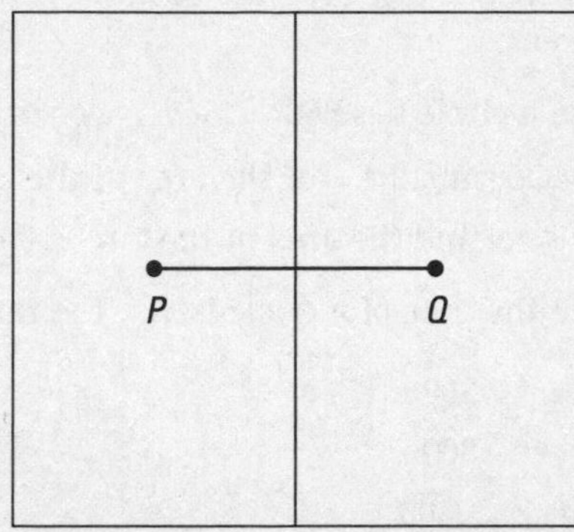

When you look at what you've drawn, it's clear that a smaller square or small circle wouldn't take in all of the points that are closer to P. They'd just include a portion of them. Cross out Choices (A) and (B).

Read Choice (C) and draw a long line perpendicular to this connecting segment and have it intersect the segment halfway between the two points. Examine what you have drawn; everything on the long perpendicular line is the same distance from P and Q. Everything to the left of the line — the half plane that contains P — is closer to P. Choice (C) works.

If you have time, you can consider that last two answers, but neither Choice (D) nor (E) makes sense. There's nothing about the shape of a parabola or a pie slice that would take into account all of the points in a square that are closer to P.

500. D. $\frac{3}{2}$

Rearrange the formula in the slope-intercept form:

$$3x + 4 = 2y$$
$$-2y = -3x - 4$$
$$y = \frac{3}{2}x + 2$$

The value in front of the x is the slope.

501. **C.** $20\sqrt{3}\pi$

To find the circumference of the circle, you need to know its radius. Examine the figure to determine what you know. Because the angle measure of *ACB* is 36 degrees, the measure of minor arc *AB* is twice that, or 72 degrees. The problem also gives you the area of the sector. Use these facts to find the circle's radius.

To visualize sector *AOB*, draw a straight line from point *A* to point *O* on the figure. Because arc *AB* measures 72 degrees, angle *AOB* also measures 72 degrees.

Because a circle has 360°, $\angle AOB = \frac{72}{360}$ or $\frac{1}{5}$ of the circle, so the area of sector *AOC* must be $\frac{1}{5}$ of the area of the circle. Multiply the area of sector *AOB* by 5 to find the area of the circle: $60\pi \times 5 = 300\pi$.

Because the area of a circle is πr^2, the radius of this circle must be $10\sqrt{3}$:

$$\pi r^2 = 300\pi$$
$$r^2 = 300$$
$$r = \sqrt{300}$$
$$r = \sqrt{100 \times 3}$$
$$r = 10\sqrt{3}$$

When you know the circle's radius, you can apply the formula for circumference:

$$C = 2(10\sqrt{3})\pi$$
$$C = 20\sqrt{3}\pi$$

ANSWERS 501–600

502. **D.** 11

This question tests absolute value and order of operations. Because absolute value is always positive, eliminate Choices (A) and (B). Order of operations dictates that you first multiply 5 and –3 to get –15. Then add 4 to get –11. Absolute value is the number of spaces a number is from 0 on the number line. Because –11 is 11 spaces from 0, the answer must be Choice (D).

503. **D.** 2

Substitute the given values for the variables and solve:

$$\sqrt{\frac{-64}{-15-1}} = ?$$
$$\sqrt{\frac{-64}{-16}} = ?$$
$$\sqrt{4} = ?$$
$$2 = ?$$

504. E. 4

The question asks you to solve for a, so you need to eliminate the b values from the system. Because both equations are equal to b, you can set the expressions on the right sides of both equations equal to each other and solve for a:

$$\begin{aligned} 2a-7&=5-a \\ 3a&=12 \\ a&=4 \end{aligned}$$

505. A. (6, 1)

To add the vectors, you simply add the three x values (the first values in each of the parentheses) to get the x value of the new vector and the three y values (the second values in each of the parentheses) to get the y value of the new vector:

$$\begin{aligned} -1+3+4&=6 \\ 2+(-2)+1&=1 \end{aligned}$$

The vector is (6, 1).

506. B. −4

Put the equation in the slope-intercept form, $y=mx+b$, where b is the y-intercept:

$$\begin{aligned} -2y+5x&=8 \\ -2y&=-5x+8 \\ y&=\frac{-5}{-2}x+\frac{8}{-2} \\ y&=\frac{5}{2}x-4 \end{aligned}$$

The b value in the equation is −4.

507. D. $12\sqrt{3}$

Eliminate Choice (E). The hypotenuse is the largest side of a right triangle, so the long leg can't be greater than the hypotenuse.

Apply the side ratio for a 30:60:90-degree triangle, which is $s:s\sqrt{3}:2s$, where s is the measure of the short leg, $s\sqrt{3}$ is the measure of the long leg, and $2s$ is the measure of the hypotenuse. If the hypotenuse in this

ANSWERS 501–600

right triangle measures 24 units, the short side (the side opposite the smallest angle) is 12:

$$2s = 24$$
$$s = 12$$

Therefore, the measure of the long leg (the leg opposite the 60° angle) is $12\sqrt{3}$.

508. B. $0.22

You can set up an equation to solve this problem. Let x equal the price of a single marker in the 3-pack. So the cost of a 3-pack is $3x$. Jodie bought 2 of them, so multiply $3x$ by 2. Then add in another $x + 10\%x$ for the individual marker. The sum totals $1.42:

$$\begin{aligned} 2(3x) + 1.10x &= 1.42 \\ 6x + 1.10x &= 1.42 \\ 7.10x &= 1.42 \\ x &= 0.2 \end{aligned}$$

Remember that x is the price of each marker in the 3-pack, so don't pick Choice (A). You have to multiply x by 1.10 to get the price of a marker sold individually. The price is 0.20 + 0.02, or $0.22.

Questions that require you to create an equation may be more quickly solved using backsolving. First, you'd eliminate Choices (D) and (E) because they're way too expensive to be the price of a single marker. Then try Choice (C). If a single marker sold individually costs $0.23, a 3-pack would cost 3 times 10% less than 0.23 (which is 0.207), or $0.621. It's unlikely that a pack of markers would carry such an odd price, so Choice (C) is likely incorrect. If you want to take it further to be sure, multiply 0.621 times 2 and add 0.23. You get $1.472, which isn't what Jodie paid. Try 0.22. If a single marker is 0.22, a 3-pack would cost 0.20×3 or $0.60. Jodie's purchase would be $2(0.6) + 0.22$, which sums to the $1.42 she spent. Choice (B) is correct.

509. B. −4

To find the x-coordinate of the midpoint of a line segment, you simply find the average of the x-coordinates of the two endpoints. This line segment has endpoint x-coordinates of −7 and −1. Find their average:

$$\begin{aligned} \frac{-7 + -1}{2} &= x \\ \frac{-8}{2} &= x \\ -4 &= x \end{aligned}$$

510. **E.**

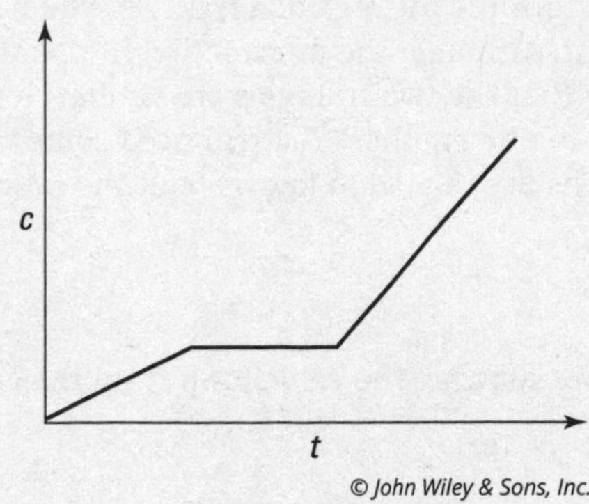

Approach the problem systematically. First, look for a graph that shows that after one hour of copying, the number of copies remains the same for one hour. This narrows the field quickly to Choices (A) and (E), which look almost exactly alike. The difference, however, is that the line that represents the number of copies created in the last two hours has a greater slope in Choice (A). Because two machines work together during the last two hours, the number of copies will increase at twice the rate of the first hour. Therefore, Choice (A) is more representative of the event than is Choice (E).

511. **A.** $\frac{30n+1}{5}$

To answer this question, solve the expression for m:

$$\begin{aligned} 5(6n-m)-l&=0\\ 30n-5m-l&=0\\ -5m&=-30n+l\\ m&=\frac{-30n+l}{-5}\\ m&=\frac{(30n+l)}{5} \end{aligned}$$

512. **C. 6,930**

The answer must be divisible by 70, 90, and 110, so Choices (A) and (B) must be wrong. Choices (C), (D), and (E) are divisible be the three values, but Choice (C) is the lesser value.

513. E. Cannot be determined from the information

To determine the area of a triangle, you need to know its base and height. Although the information in the question is sufficient to determine that the two triangles are similar, it isn't enough to figure out their ratio to one another. You still need some indication of how their side lengths are related to know about the ratio of their areas.

514. E. 2

Simply subtract the value for p from the value for *q*:

$$(t+9)-(t+7)$$

Distribute the negative through the second term:

$$t+9-t-7$$

And solve:

$$t+9-t-7=2$$

The *t*s cancel out, so Choices (B), (C), and (D) have to be wrong. If you forgot to distribute the negative, you mistakenly ended up with Choice (A).

515. D. 12, 34, 34

A parallelogram has two sets of equal sides. One side of this parallelogram is 12 inches, so there has to be one other 12-inch side. All choices provide another 12-inch side, so keep on. The other two sides have to be the same length, so Choices (A) and (B) must be wrong.

Eliminate answers with side lengths that don't sum to 92 when you add their sum to the fourth 12-inch side. Choices (C) and (E) don't result in a perimeter of 92 inches, so Choice (D) has to be the answer.

You could also solve this question by setting up an equation to solve for the length of one of the other two sides:

$$\begin{aligned}12+12+x+x&=92\\24+2x&=92\\2x&=68\\x&=34\end{aligned}$$

516. B. 23

Use what you know about angles to help you answer this question. Notice that lines *p* and *o* form a triangle with line *m*. Its interior angles sum to 180 degrees. You know the measures of angles *B* and *C*. When you know the measure of the third interior angle, you can create an equation to solve for *x*. The other angle measure you're given is angle *A*. Could angle *A* be the value of the third interior angle? You bet! Notice that angle *A* corresponds with (is equal to) the third interior angle on the opposite side of the transversal *o*. Set up the equation and solve for *x*:

$$\begin{aligned}(4x+19)+(2x-16)+(x+16)&=180\\7x+19&=180\\7x&=161\\x&=23\end{aligned}$$

517. **A. tan B**

The side that measures 3 units is opposite angle *B*. The side adjacent to angle *B* measures 4 units. The trig ratio of opposite over adjacent is tan (remember TOA). So the answer has to be Choice (A).

518. **C. 14**

If the discard pile contains 8 yellow cards and the probability of choosing a yellow card is 1 out of 4, there must be a total of 32 cards in the discard pile because $\frac{1}{4}$ is the same as $\frac{8}{32}$. Now subtract the number of blue and yellow cards from that total to determine the number of red cards: 32 – 10 – 8 = 14 red cards.

519. **A.** $\frac{3}{16}$

First, you need to know the number of cards in the shuffled discard pile. If the discard pile contains 8 yellow cards and the probability of choosing a yellow card is 1 out of 4, there must be a total of 32 cards in the discard pile because $\frac{1}{4}$ is the same as $\frac{8}{32}$.

The pile has a total of 6 green cards, so the probability that a green card is the top card is $\frac{6}{32}$, or $\frac{3}{16}$ after you simplify the fraction.

520. **D. 90°**

Whenever the ACT gives you a question involving a portion of a circle and you see the answers are presented in terms of degrees, you know you're determining a portion of circle's total of 360 degrees.

If the probability of choosing a yellow card from the pile is $\frac{1}{4}$, then the number of yellow cards must make up 25% of the total number of cards in the discard pile.

Be careful. The answer isn't Choice (B). The question asks for the number of degrees represented in the yellow card sector of the pie chart, so you need to change the percentage to degrees. You can create a proportion:

$$\frac{1}{4} = \frac{x}{360}$$
$$4x = 360$$
$$x = 90$$

Out of a total of 360 degrees on the pie chart the number of degrees in the yellow card sector is 90.

521. **B. $3^{21}b^{20}$**

Because the first number in this series is 3 and the next values are $9b$ and $27b^2$, the common multiplier in the geometric series is $3b$. The first term in the series is 3. To reach the 21st term, you need to find 20 additional terms multiplied by $3b$: $3(3b)^{20}$. Expand $(3b)^{20}$ to $3 \times 3^{20} \times b^{20}$, and combine terms by adding the exponents:

$$3^1 \times 3^{20} \times b^{20} = x$$
$$3^{21} \times b^{20} = x$$

The correct answer is Choice (B).

Choice (A) would make sense if the first term were $3b$ instead of 3.

522. **C. 8**

Analyze the information provided. The class has an even number of students, so the median is determined by finding the average of the two middle values. If the median score is 83, but no one received an 83, the two middle values must be 82 and 84 because the average of 82 and 84 is 83. So you know that the 16th value when you list the scores from least to greatest has to be 84. You also know the class has a total of 14 scores equal to or above 84.

The question indicates that 6 ($20\% \times 30 = 6$) of those 14 scores are 88 or greater. Therefore, the remaining 8 spots must be scores of 84, 85, 86, or 87.

523. **D. $3y - 4x = 12$**

The standard form of the equation of a line is $y = mx + b$, where m is the slope and b is the y-intercept. Knowing that the line contains point (0, 4) tells you that the y-intercept for this line is 4 because where $x = 0$, $y = 4$. So the correct answer will be an equation where $b = 4$.

Next, determine the slope of the line using the formula for rise over run: $m = \frac{y_2 - y_1}{x_2 - x_1}$.

Plug the coordinates into the equation:

$$m = \frac{0-4}{-3-0}$$
$$m = \frac{4}{3}$$

The value for m in the equation is $\frac{4}{3}$.

The answer that gives you an equation where $b = 4$ and $m = \frac{4}{3}$ when you solve for y is Choice (D):

$$3y - 4x = 12$$
$$3y = 4x + 12$$
$$y = \frac{4}{3}x + 4$$

524. E. $11\frac{2}{3}$

Divide the fraction by multiplying its reciprocal:

$$\frac{7}{1} \times \frac{5}{3} = \frac{35}{3}$$

$\frac{35}{3}$ isn't an answer choice, so you need to convert to a mixed fraction. Choices (A), (C), and (D) aren't mixed fractions, so eliminate them all.

When you consider the remaining two answers, you know Choice (E) must be correct even without completing the conversion. When you divide 35 by 3, you get a whole number of 11 instead of 4.

525. A. $x - 2$

The first expression in this function problem gives you the equation for the output. The second tells you what value to input for x in the first. To find $f(x+2)$, you plug in $(x+2)$ for x in the first expression:

$$f(x+2) = (x+2) - 4$$
$$f(x+2) = x + 2 - 4$$
$$f(x+2) = x - 2$$

526. D. 88

A trapezoid has parallel bases, so $\overline{BD}$ is a transversal that crosses parallel lines. Therefore, $\angle BDC$ and $\angle DBA$ are corresponding, or equal, and both measure 28 degrees. Because $\angle BDC$ and $\angle BCD$ are two of the interior angles of a triangle and $\angle DBC$ is the third, all you have to do to find $\angle DBC$ is to add 28 and 64 and subtract the sum from 180:

$$180 - (28 + 64) = \angle DBC$$
$$180 - 92 = \angle DBC$$
$$88 = \angle DBC.$$

$\angle DBC$ measures 88 degrees and the answer is Choice (D).

527. C. $\frac{7}{25}$

Apply SOHCAHTOA. Knowing that $\tan x = \frac{24}{7}$ tells you that the opposite side is 24 and the adjacent side is 7 because tangent is TOA, or opposite over adjacent. Cosine is CAH, so the correct answer will have the adjacent side, 7, in the numerator and the hypotenuse in the denominator. Eliminate Choices (B), (D), and (E) because they don't have 7 in the numerator.

You know two sides of the triangle, so you could apply the Pythagorean theorem to find the hypotenuse, but don't bother. The answer choices tell you the only other side length possibility is 25, and one of the Pythagorean triples is 7-24-25, so save some time and pick the only answer that puts the hypotenuse of 25 in the denominator, Choice (C).

528. D. 45

Follow the order of operations by first solving the exponent. Because $x = 2$, and $3^2 = 9$ the value of the second term is 9. When you multiply value of y, which is 5, by 9, you get 45, which is Choice (D).

Choice (E) is the result when you mistakenly multiply the two values before you solve the exponent.

529. A. −15

ANSWERS 501–600

Conduct an English/math translation: x represents the number you're trying to find, *of* means multiply, *is* means equals, and "more than" means add. So the equation is $\frac{1}{5}x = \frac{3}{4}(x+11)$. Be careful to multiply the second fraction by the sum of x and 17; otherwise, you may incorrectly pick Choice (E).

Solve the equation for x:

$$\begin{aligned}\frac{1}{5}x &= \frac{3}{4}(x+11)\\ \frac{1x}{5} &= \frac{3(x+11)}{4}\\ 4x &= 15(x+11)\\ 4x &= 15x+165\\ -11x &= 165\\ x &= -15\end{aligned}$$

Notice that you can cross-multiply to save time.

You can also find the answer by backsolving. Plug the answers into your equation until you find the one that fits. $\frac{1}{5}$ of −15 is −3 and $\frac{3}{4}$ of −4 is also −3, so Choice (A) works.

530. E. 144°

Because the value of $\angle ABD$ measures 4 times that of $\angle DBC$, $\angle ABD = 4x$ and $\angle DBC = x$. Because *A*, *B*, and *C* are collinear, the sum of $\angle DBC$ and $\angle ABD$ is 180°. To find the measure of $\angle ABD$, set up an equation and solve for *x*:

$$4x + x = 180$$
$$5x = 180$$
$$x = 36$$

Don't stop there and pick Choice (A), though. The value of *x* is the measure of $\angle DBC$. Multiply 36 by 4 to get 144°, which is 4*x* and the measure of $\angle ABD$.

531. D. 9

When you add logs with the same base, you solve by multiplying: $\log_6(4x) = 2$.

Then you can plug in the options for *x*. Choice (D) is correct. The product of 4 and 9 is 36, which is the value you get when you multiply 6 by itself two times.

Choice (E) incorrectly adds 4 and *x*.

532. E. $144 - 36\pi$

This question is actually a shaded area question. To find the area in question, you must find the area of the square and subtract the area of the circle. It may help to draw a picture like the one below.

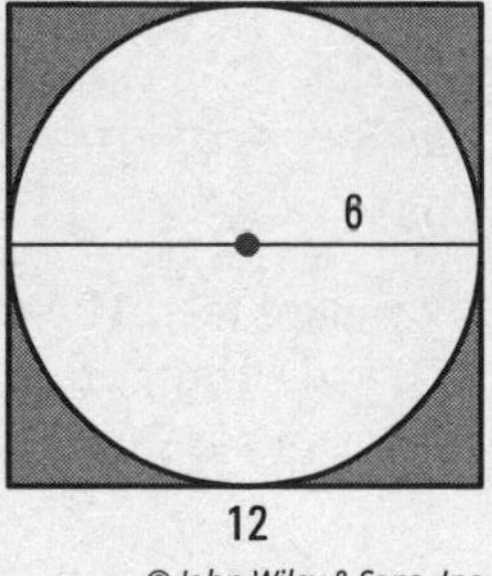

© John Wiley & Sons, Inc.

It's easy to see that because the radius of the circle is 6 centimeters, the diameter of the circle and the sides of the square are 12 centimeters.

Eliminate Choice (A) because its value is negative, and the area can't be negative. Find the area of the square by squaring the side length: $12^2 = 144$, so you can automatically narrow your options to Choice (D) or (E).

ANSWERS 501–600

Apply the area formula for a circle ($A = \pi r^2$) by replacing r with 6. The circle's area is 36π. The answer that presents the difference between the two areas is Choice (E).

If you picked Choice (D), you used the circumference formula rather than the area formula.

533. B. $\frac{19}{12}$

To solve this expression, change the fractions so they have the same denominator. The least common denominator of this set of fractions is 12. The second fraction doesn't change because its denominator is already 12. Convert $\frac{5}{6}$ to $\frac{10}{12}$ and $\frac{2}{3}$ to $\frac{8}{12}$.

Add the numerators and place the sum over the common denominator of 12:

$$\frac{10}{12} + \frac{1}{12} + \frac{8}{12} = \frac{19}{12}$$

534. B. 14×48

When you know the area and perimeter of the rectangular pool, you can determine which answer provides its correct width and length. The question gives you the perimeter — 124 feet. The perimeter is the sum of the pool's sides. So first get rid of any answer choice that doesn't add up to 124 when you add up the sides that would make up the given dimensions. The only answers that result in a sum of 124 are Choices (B), (C), and (E).

The question doesn't give you the pool's area, but it does give you its volume. The formula for volume is the product of the length, width, and height. You know the pool's height (depth) is 6 feet. So the area will be the pool's volume divided by 6:

$$\begin{aligned} V &= lwh \\ 4{,}032 &= lw(6) \\ 672 &= lw \end{aligned}$$

The area is 672 square feet. The only one of the remaining answers of Choices (B), (C), and (E) that results in a product of 672 when you multiply the two dimensions is Choice (B), $14 \times 48 = 672$.

535. B. 6

Label the whole line from A to D with a distance of 42, from A to C with 25, and from B to D with 23. The distance between B and C is the overlapping portion of the three distances. Add the distance from A to C and the distance from B to D to get 48. Subtract 42 from 48 to get the distance of the overlap; the length between B and C is 6. Choice (B) is the answer.

536. A. 8π

The volume of any regular solid is the product of its height and the area of its base. The base of this solid is a circle, so the formula for the volume of this cylinder is $V_c = \pi r^2 h$. To solve for V, you need the radius of the base and the height of the cylinder. The diameter is 2 centimeters. The radius is half that, or 1 centimeter. Apply the formula:

$$V_c = (1)^2(8)\pi$$
$$V_c = (1)(8)\pi$$
$$V_c = 8\pi$$

537. E. 0.0000243

When converting a number in scientific notation, the easiest trick to just move the decimal to the right the same number of places as the power of the 10. In this case, moving the decimal to the right −5 positions is the same as moving it to the left 5 positions. Write the number with extra zeros on each end and no decimal point in your test booklet. The number looks something like this:

000002430000

Place the decimal in its original position between the 2 and the 4 and move it to the left 5 places to come up with the answer 0.0000243.

538. D. $48

To solve this problem, set up a proportion and solve. Keep the dollars and gallons in the same respective positions:

$$\frac{36}{12} = \frac{x}{16}$$
$$12x = 576$$
$$x = 48$$

539. A. $\frac{x^4}{4y}$

To simplify the expressions, combine like variables. First, multiply the numerators: $(2x)(x^3y^2) = 2x^4y^2$.

Then multiply the denominators: $(y^3)(8) = 8y^3$.

The result is $\frac{2x^4y^2}{8y^3}$.

Divide the y terms: $\frac{y^2}{y^3} = \frac{1}{y}$.

The coefficients reduce to $\frac{1}{4}$. The result is $\frac{x^4}{4y}$.

ANSWERS 501–600

540. A. −12

The slope of a perpendicular line is the opposite reciprocal of the slope of the line it intersects. The figure shows line *l* with a positive slope, so the slope of a perpendicular line has to be negative. Eliminate Choices (D) and (E).

To choose among the remaining answers, find the slope of the given line. The graph shows that the given line travels through the points (−5, 2) and (7, 3). Plug values into the slope equation to solve:

$$m = \frac{y_2 - y_1}{x_2 - x_1}$$

$$m = \frac{3-2}{7-(-5)}$$

$$m = \frac{1}{12}$$

Switch the sign to negative and flip the numerator and denominator. The slope is −12.

541. C. $\sqrt{34}$

You can solve this question is by plugging the given values into the distance formula and solving:

$$d = \sqrt{(y_2 - y_1)^2 + (x_2 - x_1)^2}$$

$$d = \sqrt{(-2-1)^2 + (3-(-2))^2}$$

$$d = \sqrt{3^2 + 5^2}$$

$$d = \sqrt{9+25}$$

$$d = \sqrt{34}$$

542. C. $y = 3x + 4$

To eliminate *h*, rearrange and stack the equations and add:

$$\begin{aligned} y &= 4x - h \\ \underline{-4} &\underline{= -x + h} \\ y - 4 &= 3x \end{aligned}$$

Solve the equation for *y*:

$$\begin{aligned} y - 4 &= 3x \\ y &= 3x + 4 \end{aligned}$$

ANSWERS 501–600

543. D. 65,000

Determine the total pool of elements you have to create code combinations. You can repeat numbers, and there are 10 separate digits from 0 to 9. Letters cannot be repeated, and there are 26 possibilities in the English alphabet. Apply the multiplication principle by multiplying the total possibilities for each element of the code. There are 10 for the first position, 10 for the second, 26 for the third, and 25 for the fourth (because you can't repeat the letter in the third position). The product of 10, 10, 26, and 25 is 65,000.

544. C. 24π

To find the circumference of a circle, you need to know its radius. The question doesn't give you the radius of the circle, but you find the radius from the area.

Apply the area formula and solve for *r*:

$$144\pi = \pi r^2$$
$$144 = r^2$$
$$12 = r$$

Then you plug the value of the radius in the formula for circumference:

$$C = 2\pi 12$$
$$C = 24\pi$$

545. E. 4, 2, −4, and −2 only

When you see a quadratic equation, your first thought should be to find its binomial factors. When you factor, you'll likely discover the next step.

Find the square root of the first term: x^2. Then consider the last term of −64 and ask yourself what factors of −64 have a sum of −20. Those two factors are −16 and −4, so the binomial factors of the quadratic are $(x^2 - 16)(x^2 - 4)$.

At this point, you may be tempted to pick Choice (A), but you aren't through; you can factor the terms further. Notice that the binomial factors are the difference of perfect squares. Finding their factors is easy. The two factors are the sum and difference of the square roots of each perfect square in the expression. So when you factor $(x^2 - 16)$, you get $(x+4)(x-4)$. When you factor $(x^2 - 4)$, you get $(x+2)(x-2)$. The fully factored quadratic is $(x+4)(x-4)(x+2)(x-2) = 0$. The expression in its entirety equals 0 when any one of these factors equals 0. Set each equal to 0, and you see that the full set of values for *x* that solve the equation are 4, 2, −4, and −2, which is Choice (E).

546. A. −0.25

An *arithmetic series* is a series of values between which is added a common value. Because each value decreases by 0.25, the common value in this series is −0.25 The next term after 0 is $0 + (-0.25)$, or −0.25

547. D. 77°

Angle *a* and the 103° are supplementary, which means their sum measures 180°. So the measure of angle *a* is $180 - 103$ or 77°. Because lines *C* and *D* are parallel and crossed by a transversal, angle *a* corresponds with angle *b*, which means they have the same degree measure. So angle *b* also measures 77°.

548. C. $\$0.50m + \$4.50n + \$10.00$

When you see *total* in the last sentence, you know that the formula involves addition. You just have to find the answer that correctly adds the totals of each of the three types of items Corrina has to buy. Choices (A) and (E) multiply the cost of the bamboo and nails, so eliminate them right away.

The total cost for the bamboo is 0.50 times the number of feet Corrina needs: 0.50*m*. Eliminate Choice (B) because it doesn't contain 0.50*m*. Similarly, the total cost for the nails is 4.50 times the number of boxes she needs: 4.50*n*. The cost of the boards is $1 times 10 or $10. Eliminate Choice (D) because it doesn't include $10. The answer must be Choice (C).

If the proper formula isn't immediately obvious to you, substitute numbers for the variables in the problem to see which answer works out.

Pick easy numbers to work with. Say that Corrina bought 10 feet of bamboo for $0.50 a foot and 10 boxes of nails for $4.50 a foot. That means that $m = 10$ and $n = 10$. Because 10 times $0.50 is $5 and 10 times $4.50 is $45, Corrina spent $50 on bamboo and nails. She also spent $10 for platforms (1 times $10). The total cost is $60. Plug your made-up numbers into the answer choices to see which one equals 60.

Choice (C) is the only answer that equals $60 because $\$0.50(10) + \$4.50(10) + \$10.00 = \$60.00$.

549. E. −10

To solve a series of equations, you must cancel out one of the variables. Because the question asks that you find *y*, it makes sense to cancel out *x* in order to isolate *y*. To do this, multiply the bottom equation by −4 and stack the two equations like this:

$$4x + 2y = 4$$
$$-4x + 4y = -64$$

ANSWERS 501–600

When you add the equations, the x terms cancel, the y terms add to $6y$, and the sum of the right side of the equation is −60: $6y = -60$. When you solve for y, you get −10.

550. A. $\frac{1}{15}$

Before you find the chance Sheila will pick two navy socks, you first have to find the chance that the first sock she picks will be navy. That chance is $\frac{2}{6}$ or $\frac{1}{3}$ because 2 out of 6 socks are navy. Multiply that fraction by the probability that the second sock she chooses will also be navy. The second probability isn't also $\frac{1}{3}$ because Sheila has already picked a navy sock from the pile and set it aside. After she chooses the first navy sock, 5 socks remain in the pile and only 1 is navy. So the chance that the second sock she picks will be navy is actually $\frac{1}{5}$. The chance that both socks Sheila picks will be a navy pair results from multiplying $\frac{1}{3}$ by $\frac{1}{5}$, which is $\frac{1}{15}$. Pick Choice (A).

551. E. $y = -(x-2)^2 + 4$

You can tell from the graph that the parabola faces downward, so the x^2 term in the vertex form of the parabola equation has to be negative. Right away, you can eliminate Choices (A) and (D). You can also tell that the graph has a vertical displacement of 4 (the y-coordinate of the vertex). Vertical displacement is indicated by the term that is added to or subtracted from the x^2 term. This means that you can get rid of Choice (B).

The difference between Choices (C) and (E) is that Choice (C) adds the 2 in parenthesis and Choice (E) subtracts the 2. When the parabola moves in a positive direction horizontally, the number is subtracted from, not added to, x inside the parenthesis. This means that the correct answer is Choice (E).

552. D. (0, 5)

The point on the x-axis that also lies on the y-axis has an x-coordinate of 0, and the x-coordinate is the first number in the ordered pair. So eliminate Choices (A) and (B) because they don't have x-coordinates of 0. You know the answer is Choice (C), (D), or (E).

Substitute 0 for x in the equation and solve for y:

$$\begin{aligned} 5(0) + 2y &= 10 \\ 2y &= 10 \\ y &= 5 \end{aligned}$$

The point that $5x + 2y = 10$ intersects the y-axis is (0, 5), Choice (D).

You can also approach this problem by applying slope intercept form of the equation of a line: $y = mx + b$, where b is the y-intercept. When you solve for y, you get

$$5x + 2y = 10$$
$$2y = -5x + 10$$
$$y = -\frac{5}{2}x + 5$$

So you know the y-intercept is 5. The only answer with a y-coordinate of 7 is Choice (D).

553. D. 39

This question concerns a simple right triangle. The ramp length is the hypotenuse. The lengths of the sides of this triangle are those of the Pythagorean triple 5-12-13 times 3, so the ramp length is 3×13, or 39 inches.

You can also solve for c in the Pythagorean theorem ($a^2 + b^2 = c^2$), but it's much faster to rely on common side ratios of right triangles.

554. C. 76

To find the number of adult passes sold, create a system of equations. The equation for the total number of adult and child passes sold in the hour is represented by the expression $a + c = 105$, where a is the number of adult passes sold and c is the number of children's passes sold.

Create another equation to represent the amount collected: $\$24a + \$13c = \$2,201$.

Now you can backsolve from the answers to determine which works. Start with the middle value in Choice (C). If the number of adult passes was 76, the number of child passes would be 29:

$$76 + c = 105$$
$$c = 29$$

When you substitute 76 for a and 29 for c in the second expression, you get \$2,201: $\$24(76) + \$13(29) = \$2,201$. Choice (C) must be the answer. If Choice (C) hadn't worked, you'd just try another answer.

You could also solve this problem by solving the system of equations for a. Multiply the first equation by -13 to get $-13a - 13c = -1,365$ and add that equation to $24a + 13c = \$2,201$:

$$24a + 13c = \$2,201$$
$$-13a - 13c = -1,365$$

The result is $11a = 836$. Solve for a:

$$11a = 836$$
$$a = 76$$

The number of adult passes is 76.

ANSWERS 501-600

555. **B.** $x > -\frac{12}{5}$

Solve the inequality just as you would an ordinary equation. Move all the constants to the right and all the x terms to the left:

$$\begin{aligned} -2x - 7 &< 3x + 5 \\ -2x &< 3x + 12 \\ -5x &< 12 \\ x &> -\frac{12}{5} \end{aligned}$$

Choice (B) is the answer.

Choice (A) is wrong because you must change the direction of the sign when you divide both sides of an inequality by a negative value.

556. **B.** $\frac{r}{q}$

The equation you use to find sine is SOH, $\sin = \frac{\text{opposite}}{\text{hypotenuse}}$. The hypotenuse is side q, so eliminate answers that don't have q in the denominator. That leaves you with Choices (B) and (D).

The side opposite to angle A is r, so the numerator is r, and $\sin A = \frac{r}{q}$.

557. **C.** $(3x+1)(3x-3)$

Rather than attempt to factor this complex quadratic, make your job easier by multiplying the answer possibilities. Eliminate Choice (E) because its first terms don't multiply to $9x^2$.

For the rest, you just need to figure out the middle term because the first and last terms of each answer choice are the same.

Start with Choice (C). The product of the outer terms is $-9x$; the inner terms multiply to $3x$. The sum of the outer and inner terms is $-6x$, so Choice (C) is correct.

If you find the middle term of the other answers, you see that none comes out to be $-6x$.

558. **E.** 100

Set up the average equation and plug in what Mr. Albright knows. The average of the 20 scores was 89. The sum of 19 of those scores is 1,680, and x represents the missing score:

$$\begin{aligned} A &= \frac{\text{sum of scores}}{\text{\# of scores}} \\ 89 &= \frac{1{,}680 + x}{20} \\ 1{,}780 &= 1{,}680 + x \\ 100 &= x \end{aligned}$$

Mr. Albright should enter 100 in place of the missing score.

559. B. (5, −5)

The midpoint of a line segment is just the average of both the *x*- and *y*-coordinates of the endpoints. Use this information to find the *x*-coordinate of the other endpoint:

$$2 = \frac{-1+x}{2}$$
$$4 = -1 + x$$
$$5 = x$$

Eliminate any answers that don't have an *x*-coordinate of 5. You're down to Choices (B) and (C).

Find the *y*-coordinate:

$$-1 = \frac{3+y}{2}$$
$$-2 = 3 + y$$
$$-5 = y$$

The answer is Choice (B).

560. C. π

The question asks for thickness, which suggests a third dimension, so you'll likely need to apply the volume formula. For a circular cylinder, that formula is the area of the circular base times the height: $V = \pi r^2 h$.

The area of each muffin half is 25π cm^2. Plug this value and the volume measurement into the volume formula to find the height, or thickness, of the cream-cheese layer. Be careful, though. The volume provided is for the whole amount of cream cheese, but the area is for just one muffin half. You need to divide the volume by 12 first to determine the volume measure for one muffin half:

$$\frac{300}{12} = 25$$

Apply the formula for volume:

$$25 = 25\pi h$$
$$\pi = h$$

The correct answer is Choice (C).

561. A. (8, −2)

The original point *C* lies at (−8, −2). The whole quadrilateral is reflected over the vertical *y*-axis, but you just need to focus on the reflected point *C*. The point will land in Quadrant IV, so the *x*-coordinate is positive and the *y*-coordinate is negative. Eliminate Choices (D) and (E).

ANSWERS 501–600

The y-coordinate of the point doesn't change because the y-axis is a vertical line. You can eliminate Choice (C) because it doesn't contain a y-coordinate of −2.

The original x value of point C is −8, which is 8 units to the left of the y-axis, so reflected point C is 8 units to the right of the y-axis. This makes the y value of reflected point C equal to 8 and the point (8, −2), which is Choice (A).

562. **B. $3,030.00**

First, eliminate Choices (D) and (E). If William gave some money away, he started out with more than $2,575.50.

Set up an equation. If William gave 15% of his winnings and ended up with $2,575.50 in savings, the $2,575.50 is 85% of what he originally received. You can write 85% as 0.85, and *of* means multiply, so the equation is $0.85x = \$2{,}575.50$. Solve for x.

$$\begin{aligned} 0.85x &= 2{,}575.50 \\ x &= 3{,}030 \end{aligned}$$

Choice (B) is correct.

563. **D.** $\frac{2x-8}{5}$

Solve the equation for y:

$$\begin{aligned} 2x &= 5y+8 \\ 2x-8 &= 5y \\ \frac{2x-8}{5} &= y \end{aligned}$$

564. **A. 0**

Use the provided measures to determine the value of x and y. Add the two vertical left side lengths: $15+2=17$. The sum of the vertical side lengths on the right side is therefore 17. Use that information to solve for x:

$$\begin{aligned} 13+x &= 17 \\ x &= 4 \end{aligned}$$

Solve for y in the same way. The sum of the bottom horizontal side lengths is 25 $(19+6)$. So $y+21=25$ and $y=4$.

Therefore, $x-y=4-4=0$

565. **B. 25**

This stem and leaf plot presents a set of values in terms of their tens and ones digits. The left column is the tens digit, and the right column is the ones digit for each of the numbers of cookie boxes sold. The median of a

ANSWERS 501–600

set of even numbers is the average of the two middle values. In this set of 22 values, the middle values are the 11th and 12th values. Count the first 10 leaves in the stem and leaf plot. The next two values are both 25, so the median value is 25.

566. **D. 9%**

To find the number of members who sold more than 50 boxes, focus on the last two rows in the plot. The values represented by those two rows are 50, 52, and 61. Only two are greater than 50. So 2 out of 22 members sold more than 50 boxes:

$$\frac{2}{22} = 0.\overline{09}$$

This is closest to 9%.

567. **B. 5**

Apply the average formula to find the current year's average number of boxes sold. To find the sum, you need to add all the values represented on the plot: $\begin{matrix} 12+15+17+(2\times18)+22+(2\times23)+24+(3\times25)+32+(3\times34) \\ +38+(2\times39)+50+52+61=660 \end{matrix}$

$$A = \frac{\text{sum of boxes}}{\text{\# of boxes}}$$
$$A = \frac{660}{22}$$
$$A = 30$$

Apply the formula again to determine the total number of additional boxes the troop needs to sell next year to achieve an average of 35 boxes sold per member:

$$35 = \frac{660 + x}{22}$$
$$770 = 660 + x$$
$$110 = x$$

This number is total number of additional boxes the troop needs to sell next to reach its goal, but the question asks for the average number each member needs to sell to achieve an average of 35 boxes per member. So divide 110 by 22: $\frac{110}{22} = 5$.

On average, each troop member needs to sell 5 additional boxes to reach an average of 35 boxes per troop member.

568. **D. $x < -4$ and $x > 3$**

This question is asking for all values of x that would make the quadratic equal to a number greater than 0. To solve it, factor the polynomial to give you $(x+4)(x-3)$. So the values for x that would make the expression equal to 0 are $x = -4$ and $x = 3$.

ANSWERS 501–600

To find the values for x that make the expression greater than 0, consider that the expression is positive when both factors equal positive values or when both factors have negative values. The first factor is positive when $x > -4$ and the second factor is positive when $x > 3$, so both factors are positive when $x > 3$. At this point, you know the answer is Choice (D) because it's the only option that includes $x > 3$ and one other set of values for when the factors are both negative. Choice (E) doesn't take into consideration that the expression will be positive when both of its factors are negative.

Another way to approach this question is by substituting answer choices into the expression. Eliminate Choices (A) and (C) because although it's true that values over 12 make the solution greater than 0, so do some values that are less than or equal to 12. Choice (D) is wrong because values greater than 5 make the expression positive and some values less than 3 (say 2) make the expression negative. To evaluate Choice (D), try 4 and −5 for x in the expression. Both make its solution greater than 0, so Choice (D) is right and Choice (E) is wrong.

---

569. **C. 33**

Set up a simple equation. Because Eugene and Nadia both travel the same distance, you can set up an equation where Eugene's miles = Nadia's miles. Remember to convert minutes to hours because the unit is miles per hour rather than miles per minute. In hours, 55 minutes is $\frac{55}{60}$ or $\frac{11}{12}$ of an hour. Multiply Eugene's speed times the number of hours he spent in the car and set it equal to the amount of hours Nadia spent in the car times Nadia's speed:

$$(45)\left(\frac{11}{12}\right) = (x)\left(1\frac{1}{4}\right)$$

$$\frac{495}{12} = x\frac{5}{4}$$

$$\frac{495}{12} \div \frac{5}{4} = x$$

$$\frac{495}{12} \times \frac{4}{5} = x$$

$$\frac{1{,}980}{60} = x$$

$$33 = x$$

Nadia's speed is 33 miles per hour, which is Choice (C).

---

570. **D. 2**

This word problem gives you a formula and asks you to solve for one of the variables. All you have to do is plug in the proper values for the other variables and solve.

You're asked to find the acceleration (a). Reformat the equation so you're solving for a. Subtract v_0 from both sides and then divide both sides by t.

ANSWERS 501–600

The equation to solve for acceleration is $a = \frac{v - v_0}{t}$. Now find the values for the other variables. You know that initially the car travels 20 meters per second, so plug in 20 for v_0 to get $a = \frac{v-20}{t}$. Next, note that the time that the car accelerates is 5 seconds, so plug in 5 for t: $a = \frac{v-20}{5}$. You're told that the final velocity is 30 meters per second, so substitute 30 for v and solve:

$$a = \frac{30-20}{5}$$

$$a = \frac{10}{5}$$

$$a = 2$$

571. A. $8a^6b^8$

This question requires basic simplification. Begin by canceling terms. Because the whole numerator is squared, you first need to square every term in the parentheses.

$$4^2 = 16$$

Divide the coefficients of 16 and 2 to get 8; eliminate Choices (D) and (E) because they don't have a coefficient of 8. Continue by squaring the variables in the numerator. When you take an exponent to another power, you multiply the exponents:

$$(a^4)^2 = a^8$$

$$(b^3)^2 = b^6$$

The new expression is $8\left(\frac{a^8b^6}{a^2b^{-2}}\right)$.

Divide the variables by subtracting the exponents:

$$\frac{a^8}{a^2} = a^6$$

$$\frac{b^6}{b^{-2}} = a^8$$

Combine the components to get a final answer of $8a^6b^8$.

If you picked Choice (B), you subtracted the 2 from 6 when you worked with the b exponents. When you subtract a negative value, you actually add the value. If you picked Choice (C), you added the exponents when you squared them instead of multiplying them.

572. C. 9

The problem doesn't give you the fraction that represents the other gems, so you need to make that determination. Add the fractions for emeralds, rubies, and sapphires by first finding the common denominator (35) and then adding the numerators and placing the sum over the common denominator:

$$\frac{2}{5}+\frac{1}{7}+\frac{3}{7}=\frac{14}{35}+\frac{5}{35}+\frac{15}{35}=\frac{34}{35}$$

Then subtract the result from the whole to find the fraction of gems that aren't emeralds, rubies, and sapphires:

$$\frac{35}{35}-\frac{34}{35}=\frac{1}{35}$$

So $\frac{1}{35}$ of the 315 gems aren't emeralds, rubies, and sapphires. *Of* means multiply: $\frac{1}{35}\times 315=9$.

The number of gems that aren't emeralds, rubies, and sapphires is 9.

573. B. 3

The most efficient way to approach this problem is likely by trying each of the answer choices. The question asks for the *maximum* sum, so start with the greatest answer. Consider Choice (D). Possible integers that add up to 7 are 8 and −1, but their product is −8, which doesn't fit within the given range. Choice (D) is wrong, and therefore Choice (E) is also. You may have thought 7 could work because $7+0=7$ and $7\times 0=0$, but *exclusive* in the question means that −5 and 0 aren't included in the possible range of values.

Try 5. The integers 6 and −1 have a sum of 5, but their product, −6, doesn't fit within the range. Consider 3, Choice (B): 4 and −1 have a sum of 3 and their product is −4, which fits in the range of values. When you know 3 works, pick Choice (B) and move on. You don't have to check Choice (A) because it wouldn't be the *maximum* value even if it worked.

574. C. $(x-3)^2+(y-3)^2=9$

For this problem, you need to know the general equation for a circle: $(x-h)^2+(y-k)^2-r^2$, where h and k are the x- and y-coordinates of the center of the circle and r is its radius.

Because the circle is tangent to the x and y at 3 units, the radius of the circle is 3. Eliminate Choices (D) and (E) because they don't have 3^2 on the right side of the equation.

Choice (A) is wrong because it's the equation for a circle with a center on the origin (0, 0). There's no way this circle's center is on the origin if it's touching both axes.

Choice (B) adds rather than subtracts within the first parentheses, which would be true only if the center were (−3, 3).

Choice (C) is the only equation in proper format for a circle with a center point of (3, 3)

575. C. $5\sqrt{2}$

Apply the distance formula:

$$d=\sqrt{(y_2-y_1)^2+(x_2-x_1)^2}$$
$$d=\sqrt{(-2-(-1))^2+(4-(-3))^2}$$
$$d=\sqrt{(-1)^2+7^2}$$
$$d=\sqrt{50}$$
$$d=5\sqrt{2}$$

576. A. $a=\sqrt{185-(176\cos 37°)}$

The question gives you the equation you need: $a^2=b^2+c^2-2bc\cos A$. Plug values from the figure into this equation. The only angle measure provided is the 37° angle, which is angle *A* because it is opposite side *a*. Substitute 37° for *A* in the equation. Eliminate Choices (D) and (E) because they don't have the correct angle measure. It doesn't matter which side is *b* or *c*; just plug in 8 and 11 for the two side lengths. You get this solution:

$$a^2=11^2+8^2-2(11)(8)\cos 37°$$
$$a^2=121+64-(22)(8)\cos 37°$$
$$a^2=185-(176\cos 37°)$$
$$a=\sqrt{185-(176\cos 37°)}$$

The correct answer is Choice (A). Choice (B) is wrong because it neglects to take the square root of the right side. If you picked Choice (C), you didn't follow the proper order of operations.

577. A. $85.35

The passage tells you that Aspen gives 40% of gross sales after taxes to the consignee. Eliminate Choice (E) because Aspen wouldn't give the whole amount to the consignee. Because Aspen doesn't include taxes in the amount she provides the consignee, you have to subtract 6% of $227 before you calculate the 40%: $227-227(0.06)=213.38$.

40% of $213.38 is $85.35.

578. C. $180.00

During the week in the question, Jack earned $15/hour for 40 hours, or $600. Angel earned $12/hour for 30 hours, which is $360. She also earned $60 for the 60 items she sold for a total of $420 for the week. $\$600-\$420=\$180$.

If you picked Choice (D), you mistakenly calculated a commission for Jack. Only Angel receives the commission.

ANSWERS 501–600

579. **B. No, her expenses exceeded gross sales after taxes by $20 in January.**

The question tells you to consider total gross sales after taxes and total expenses. To figure out gross sales after taxes, multiply the number of items sold (500) by the average sale after taxes ($100): $500 \times \$100 + \$5{,}000$.

Aspen's expenses are rent, payroll, and advertising. Monthly rent is always $350. Four weeks of payroll for Jack is always $15/hour for 160 hours, or $2,400. Aspen makes $12/hour for 120 hours, or $1,440, *plus* $1 for the 30 items she sold for over $10. Her total January payroll, therefore, is $3,870. Add payroll taxes of $100 for a total payroll cost of $\$600 + \$3{,}870 + \$100 = \$4{,}570$.

Aspen has one additional expense, advertising. She had 100 customer visits at $1 per visit for a total of $100.

Add total January rent, payroll, and advertising: $\$350 + \$4{,}570 + \$100 = \$5{,}020$.

When you subtract expenses from gross sales after taxes, Aspen has a negative balance of $40: $5{,}000 - 5{,}020 = -20$.

The answer is Choice (B). If you picked Choice (D) or (E), you likely forgot to add the advertising and/or payroll taxes into expenses. If you picked Choice (A), you likely mistakenly gave Jack a $1 per item commission.

580. **B. $y = \sin(x) + 2$**

Consider the graph in the question. You can eliminate Choices (D) and (E) because the graph of tangent functions would be vertical rather than horizontal.

The graph intersects the *y*-axis at (0, 2), so when $x = 0$, $y = 2$. You can eliminate Choice (A). The equation for sin *x* would intersect the *y* axis at (0, 0). This graph is the regular sin *x* graph moved up by 2, which is the equation in Choice (B). When you substitute 0 for *x* in $y = \sin(x) + 2$, you get a *y* value of 2.

581. **C. $851.20**

Geoff begins with an initial CD investment of $1,200. Every 6 months he makes 1.05% on his existing money. So after the first 6 months, Geoff has 1.0105 times the $1,200 initial investment, or $1,212.60. But the balance doesn't increase by $12.60 every 6 months because Geoff makes 1.05% on the new existing balance. So after one year, he has 1.0105 times $1,212.60 instead of $1,200, which is a balance of $1,225.33. At a year and a half, Geoff has 1.0105 times $1,225.33, or $1,238.20. Six months later the CD matures after another 1.05% is added to Geoff's balance. $\$1{,}238.20 \times 1.0105 = \$1{,}251.20$.

The amount Geoff invests into a second CD is $1,251.20 less the $400 he uses to purchase the tablet: $\$1{,}251.20 - \$400 = \$851.20$

ANSWERS 501–600

582. B. 40

The question states that 18.75% of students who responded to the poll is equal to 6 students. You can set up a simple proportion where x is the number of students who responded to the poll and 18.75% is represented in fraction form: $\frac{18.75}{100} = \frac{6}{x}$. When you cross multiply, you get $18.75x = 600$. Divide both sides by 18.75 to discover that $x = 32$. But don't stop there and pick Choice (A). 32 is the number of students in Harry's class who responded in the poll rather than the total number of students in the class. You know that 20%, or $\frac{1}{5}$, didn't participate in the poll. That means that 80%, or $\frac{4}{5}$, did participate. Set up another proportion where $\frac{4}{5} = \frac{32}{x}$ and x is the total number of students in Harry's class. When you cross multiply, you get $4x = 160$. Divide both sides by 4 to find that $x = 40$. So Harry's class has 40 students. The answer is Choice (B).

583. B. $-\frac{1}{8}$

The equation to find slope is $m = \frac{y_1 - y_2}{x_1 - x_2}$. Simply plug in values in this question. When you plug the values into the slope equation and solve, you get this:

$$m = \frac{5-4}{2-10}$$

$$m = -\frac{1}{8}$$

ANSWERS 501–600

584. C. 14

Apply the distance formula:

$$d = \sqrt{(y_2 - y_1)^2 + (x_2 - x_1)^2}$$

$$d = \sqrt{(6-2)^2 + (7-1)^2}$$

$$d = \sqrt{(4)^2 + (6)^2}$$

$$d = \sqrt{16 + 36}$$

$$d = \sqrt{52}$$

Multiply the distance by 2 to get the approximate number of miles:

$$2\sqrt{52} = \text{miles}$$

$$2\sqrt{4 \times 13} = \text{miles}$$

$$4\sqrt{13} = \text{miles}$$

The square root of 13 is between the square root of 9 and the square root of 16, or somewhere between 3 and 4. The product of 4 and 3 is 12; the product of 4 and 4 is 16. The only answer that falls between 12 and 16 is Choice (C). If you use the square root key on your calculator, you find that the distance is approximately 14.42 miles.

585. D. 60°

The formula for finding the interior angle measures of a regular polygon is as follows, where *n* represents the number of sides in the polygon:

$$\frac{180(n-2)}{n}$$

Apply the formula to the figure in the question to find the measure of each interior angle in the polygon:

$$\frac{180(6-2)}{6}=\frac{180(4)}{6}=\frac{720}{6}=120$$

So each angle in the hexagon measures $120°$. The angles in the triangle that's formed by the two extended sides must each be $60°$ because two of those angles form a straight line with the two $120°$ angles in the hexagon and $180-120=60$. If two angles in a triangle each measure $60°$, the third angle, $\angle A$, must also measure $60°$.

586. A. {1, –1}

Try backsolving to solve this problem. Choice (A) provides two solutions for *x*. When you put 1 in place for *x* in the equation you get this:

$$\begin{aligned}|1|^2+3|1|-4=0\\1+3-4=0\end{aligned}$$

It's true that $4-4=0$, so 1 works. You know that –1 works, too, because the 1 and –1 have the same absolute value. You can eliminate Choices (B) and (C) because they don't contain both 1 and –1. Choice (D) offers up 1 and –1 along with 0. If you move too quickly, you may think that 0 works too, but when you substitute 0 for *x* in the equation, you get this:

$$\begin{aligned}|0|^2+3|0|-4=0\\0-4\neq0\end{aligned}$$

Choices (D) and (E) are wrong, and Choice (A) is correct.

587. E. 96

The formula for the surface area of a cube is $6s^2$, which makes sense because the cube has 6 sides and each has an area of s^2. The question tells you that the edges of the cube each measure 4 inches. The edges of the cube are the sides of the squares that make up the cube's sides. Plug in 4 for *s* in the formula and solve:

$$\begin{aligned}SA&=6(4)^2\\SA&=6(16)\\SA&=96\end{aligned}$$

588. **D. 133°**

Scan the figure to determine which angles are equal. $\angle AMB$ and $\angle DME$ are vertical angles, so they're equal. $\angle DME$ also measures 29°. The same goes for $\angle EMF$ and $\angle BMC$. They're equal, so $\angle BMC$ also measures 47°. The remaining two angles, $\angle CMD$ and $\angle AMF$, are also vertical angles and equal. The degree measures of the 6 angles in the figure total to 360° because they circle around the center point *M*. Create an equation to solve for the degree measure of the remaining two angles:

$$\begin{aligned} 2(47)+2(29)+x+x &= 360 \\ 94+58+2x &= 360 \\ 2x &= 208 \\ x &= 104 \end{aligned}$$

Hang on, though. This is the degree measure of $\angle CMD$, but the question asks for the measure of $\angle CME$. You need to add 29° to 104° for a degree measure of $\angle CME = 133°$.

589. **E. The measure of $\angle CQM = \frac{1}{2}$ the measure of minor arc *MN*.**

Eliminate answers that have to be true. Choice (A) is true. The two angles are corresponding angles along the transversal *QN* that crosses the parallel lines $\overline{MC}$ and $\overline{PQ}$.

Choice (B) is true. Similar triangles have the same angle measures. $\angle CQM = \angle ONP$, and $\angle MCP = \angle OPN$ because they, too, are corresponding angles along the transversal *QN*. $\angle CMQ = \angle NOP$ because both are right angles. The line tangent to the circle is perpendicular to the radius where they intersect. And the triangle formed by the diameter of the circle and angle that emanates from a point on the circle is a right triangle

Choice (C) is true. The endpoints of $\angle N$ form minor arc *PQ*, and the angle formed at the point on a circle has half the degree measure of the arc formed by its endpoints on the circumference of the circle.

Choice (D) is true; arc *PN* has to be half the circle because it's formed by a diameter of the circle.

Choice (E) has to be the false and therefore correct answer. $\angle CQM$ doesn't have its point on the circumference of the circle, so it doesn't measure $\frac{1}{2}$ of arc *MN*.

590. B. $8+6i$

To square the expression, multiply $(3+i)$ by $(3+i)$ and substitute –1 for i^2:

$$(3+i)(3+i)=?$$
$$9+3i+3i+i^2=?$$
$$9+6i+i^2=?$$
$$9+6i+(-1)=?$$
$$8+6i=?$$

591. C. $\frac{x^2}{25}+\frac{y^2}{16}=1$

The equation of an ellipse that is centered on the origin of the *xy*-coordinate plane looks like this, where *a* is the radius along the *x*-axis, *b* is the radius along the *y*-axis, and *x* and *y* are coordinates of any point on the ellipse:

$$\frac{x^2}{a^2}+\frac{y^2}{b^2}=1$$

The equation of an ellipse is always equal to 1, so eliminate Choices (A) and (B). Choices (D) and (E) are equations for ellipses that aren't centered on the origin, so they're also wrong. The answer must be Choice (C).

592. C. 19.5

To solve this question, set up proportion. Divide Julian's distance traveled by his speed and Emmett's distance traveled by his speed so that hours = hours. Assign the distance Emmett travels to be *x* because that signifies the distance from Sacramento. Because the total distance between Sacramento and Lodi is 36 miles, the distance Julian traveled can be represented as $36-x$. The proportion looks like this: $\frac{x}{65}=\frac{36-x}{55}$.

Cross multiply and solve:

$$55x=65(36-x)$$
$$55x=2{,}340-65x$$
$$120x=2{,}340$$
$$x=19.5$$

593. A. $\frac{2}{\sqrt{5}}$

The trig ratio for tan is TOA. To find tan *A*, put the side opposite angle *A* over the side adjacent to *A*. The hypotenuse plays no role in tangent, so eliminate any choice that contains a 3. You're left with Choices (A), (B), and (E).

ANSWERS 501–600

The side length opposite angle A is 2 units, so 2 needs to be in the numerator; eliminate Choice (E).

Don't bother to apply the Pythagorean theorem to find the other side length. The remaining answer choices give you either $\sqrt{13}$ or $\sqrt{5}$. The adjacent side must be fewer units than the hypotenuse, so Choice (B) can't be right. $\sqrt{13}$ is greater than $\sqrt{9}$, so $\sqrt{13}$ is greater than 3.

The answer has to be Choice (A).

If you want to be sure, apply the Pythagorean theorem:

$$a^2 + b^2 = c^2$$
$$2^2 + b^2 = 3^2$$
$$4 + b^2 = 9$$
$$b^2 = 5$$
$$b = \sqrt{5}$$

---

594. **B.** $\frac{4}{5} < \frac{5}{6} < \frac{9}{7} < \frac{7}{3}$

The fractions with numerators greater than their denominators are greater than 1, and those with greater denominators are less than 1. So $\frac{9}{7}$ & $\frac{7}{3}$ have to be greater than $\frac{4}{5}$ & $\frac{5}{6}$. Eliminate Choices (C) and (D). There is a greater range between the denominator and numerator in $\frac{7}{3}$ than there is in $\frac{9}{7}$, so $\frac{7}{3}$ has to be listed after $\frac{9}{7}$. Eliminate Choice (E).

When you put $\frac{4}{5}$ & $\frac{5}{6}$ over a common denominator, you see that $\frac{5}{6}$ is slightly greater than $\frac{4}{5}$:

$$\frac{4}{5} = \frac{24}{30}$$
$$\frac{5}{6} = \frac{25}{30}$$

Therefore, Choice (B) is correct.

ANSWERS 501–600

---

595. **C. It contains 1 positive value and 1 negative value.**

The variable in the equation is squared; therefore, it likely has two solutions, 1 positive and 1 negative. To be sure you can solve the equation. Because the expression is equal to 1, the exponent is equal to 0 because any number to 0 power is equal to 1. Set the exponent equal to 0 and solve:

$$b^2 - 4 = 0$$
$$b^2 = 4$$
$$b = \pm 2$$

Chapter 3

596. D. spreading animosity

The narrator first grinds his teeth at petitioners in the beginning of the third paragraph where he describes that he likes to make people unhappy. He references doing so again later in the same paragraph as a way of making himself unhappy when he's feeling shameful. Choice (D) applies to both situations. In the first he's showing animosity (or hostility) to others; in the second, he's aiming hostility at himself.

Choices (A) and (B) relate only slightly to the first reference and not at all to the second. Choice (C) relates slightly to the second situation but not to the first.

597. B. profound pessimism.

The overall tone of the passage is gloomy, so Choice (A) is completely out of the picture. Choice (D) may tempt you because the narrator seems angry, but the rest of the answer doesn't fit. *Conviviality* means "warmth and friendliness," which are opposite characteristics to the narrator's overall deep cynicism. Although the narrator says he amused himself with the petitioners, this characterization is limited to his statement in the fourth paragraph and doesn't express his general tone throughout the passage. Eliminate Choice (C) and pick Choice (B). The narrator finds little joy in his life, from the beginning descriptions of illness and unattractiveness to his final declaration of old age at forty.

598. D. may have an unhealthy heart.

This one may be a little tricky because the narrator seems utterly confused and contradicts himself throughout the passage. Unless you read very closely, you might assume that the narrator couldn't have stated that he both acted out of spite but could never be spiteful. But he makes references to acting out of spite on several occasions, such as in line 10 and line 58. However, he also declares he could never be spiteful in line 75. Eliminate both Choices (A) and (B) because both are true.

The narrator mentions his ailing liver in several instances and states with certainty that it's bad in the last lines of the first paragraph, so Choice (C) is out. That leaves you with Choice (D), which is correct because he never specifically refers to the condition of his heart.

599. C. he is superstitious despite rational evidence to the contrary.

The narrator states that he respects medicine and doctors, so eliminate Choice (A) because it contradicts information in the passage. Choice (D) is wrong because the narrator claims he is well-educated and blames his reluctance to seek medical advice on his spite rather than his lack of education. Choices (B) and (C) seem similar, but you can eliminate Choice (B) because the passage never indicates that the narrator attended a university, which makes that answer unjustified. The best answer is Choice (C). The narrator claims he is superstitious even though he has enough education (or rational thought) to lack superstition.

600. B. he may display signs of aggression.

The narrator mentions the doll and tea as gestures that may appease his initial mouth foaming, but he doesn't suggest that he foams because he anticipates getting these gifts. Eliminate Choice (A). Choice (D) is out, too. The act indicates an emotion that needs to be appeased. It doesn't make sense to appease amusement.

Nothing in the paragraph suggests that the narrator is literally foaming at the mouth, so Choice (C) is unjustified. But the reference conjures the image of a rabid dog, which relates well to the sign of aggression in Choice (B).

601. A. cast doubt on previous statements about the narrator's character to lead to an ultimate conclusion about narrator's inability to control his character.

As usual, you can best answer this reading question by eliminating wrong answers to reveal the correct choice. Dismissing Choice (D) is pretty easy. Even though the narrator seems to soften a bit in the fourth paragraph, you still can't classify him as a generally kind and moral man. In fact, the entire passage suggests that being truly moral is impossible.

Read Choices (B) and (C) carefully. Both contain elements that make them relatively easy to eliminate. Choice (B) is wrong because it contains *first*. In the third paragraph, the narrator indicates that he isn't really spiteful and talks about the shame he feels. So, though the fourth paragraph reveals the narrator to be a liar and be shameful, it isn't the first paragraph to make these revelations. Choice (C) may seem pretty good at first glance. The paragraph mentions the opposite elements swarming within the narrator, but the paragraph never *identifies* what the very many opposite elements are.

Choices (B) and (C) don't work, so the answer must be Choice (A). Check it to make sure it's justifiable. The fourth paragraph does call into question the narrator's prior statements about his spitefulness. This questioning leads to the final paragraph where the narrator doubts not only his ability to be spiteful but his ability to be anything at all, which justifies the statement in Choice (A) that the narrator questions his ability to control his character.

602. **C. compensate for other transgressions.**

The narrator uses the phrase "find a recompense" when he notes that, despite his unpleasantness in dealing with people in his government job, at least he didn't take bribes. So his not taking bribes sort of made up, or compensated, for his other mean actions. Choice (C) is the clearest explanation of the phrase.

Choice (B) is the opposite of the narrator's meaning; by not taking bribes, he was turning away the possibility of monetary gain. The narrator makes no mention of issuing a punishment, so Choice (A) is unjustified.

The narrator's reference to being witty is actually a comment on his reasons for writing the statement, but he doesn't claim that not taking bribes amuses him, so Choice (D) is wrong.

603. **D. He does not consult a doctor because he wants his liver condition to worsen.**

The narrator contemplates the reasons he avoids consulting a doctor in the first paragraph. He states that he respects doctors and medicine, so Choice (B) isn't correct. In the last lines of the paragraph, he says that not consulting a doctor hurts himself and no one else, so Choice (A)'s inclusion of *others* makes it wrong. Choice (C) is off the mark because, although the narrator seems to think his problem is a bad liver, he expressly states that he doesn't know for sure what ails him.

Choice (D) provides the most accurate reason. At the end of the paragraph, the narrator claims he doesn't go to the doctor out of spite; he wants his bad liver to get worse.

604. **B. Between 1800 and 1900**

Scan the passage for time references. In the final paragraph, the narrator refers to himself as "a man in the 19th century," which is the hundred years between 1800 and 1900. Choice (B) is best justified from information in the passage.

605. A. The petitioners were primarily frightened and weak, which made the narrator look on them with contempt.

The narrator talks about petitioners in the third paragraph, where he characterizes them as a mostly timid bunch. He then contemptuously connects their timidity to their position as petitioners who have to come to him for help. Choice (A) summarizes the narrator's generalizations about petitioners pretty well. Choice (B) reflects the narrator's comments about one officer in particular and not petitioners in general, so it's clearly wrong. Choice (C) may tempt you — the narrator says he wants to make the petitioners unhappy — but then says he *almost* succeeds, which suggests he really didn't achieve his goal. Choice (D) is out; although the narrator states in the second paragraph that he didn't take bribes, that statement alone doesn't provide enough information to justify that *most* petitioners offered him bribes. Choice (A) reflects the narrator's generalization about petitioners most accurately.

606. A. informational.

The author of this passage provides an overview of personality disorders and how they affect one's ability to take ownership of actions as applied to a criminal justice context. She gives information rather than argues a point, and her tone is relatively neutral rather than negative. Therefore, Choices (B) and (C) are out. The author doesn't provide instructions for action, so Choice (A) is a better option than Choice (D).

607. C. adults are more likely to respond to punishment and modify their behavior than are children.

The author mentions Choices (A) and (B) in the third paragraph. In the final paragraph, she notes that punishment is not, in fact, the best way to discourage recidivism. That leaves only Choice (C). Though she does touch on how punishments help teach kids proper behavior, she fails to make a comparison between how children and adults respond to punishment. Thus, the answer is Choice (C)

608. B. Intimidation

When you discover that the information to answer this question lies in the first paragraph, you're golden. The passage clearly states that those with personality disorders and those without both have to work to control their impulses and notes that negotiation, compromise and fair play help people achieve what they want, but that bullying, intimidating and abusing others do not. Thus, the answer is Choice (B).

609. **D. A combination of treatment and punishment stimulates behavioral change in all offenders.**

The author discusses in the third paragraph that children are likely to modify behavior even when they don't understand why what they did was a misdeed, so eliminate Choice (B). She also clearly agrees with Choice (C). In the first paragraph, she says that people with personality disorders "face the same challenges in the same way as the rest of us." She would also more than likely agree with Choice (A) based on her statement in the final paragraph that "punishment is not the most effective way to reduce recidivism overall." That leaves Choice (D). In the final paragraph, the author plainly states that not *all* offenders with personality issues or disorders are treatable.

610. **B. those with personality problems and disorders exhibit behavior that is considered normal, but just barely.**

By saying that people with personality problems would be placed "at the far end of a continuum," the author implies that they fall within the parameters of what is considered normal; however, they would be at "the far end," meaning they just barely fit into the category. So Choice (B) is best.

611. **C. a caring society.**

Quickly eliminate Choice (A). Nowhere in the passage is prison overcrowding mentioned.

The second paragraph discusses excuses for antisocial behavior. Nowhere does the paragraph suggest that those with mental handicaps experience punishment more adversely, so Choice (B) is out. The paragraph doesn't mention whether those with mental handicaps learn from punishment, and in the third paragraph, and the author suggests that those with some disorders may actually learn from punishment. So Choice (D) isn't the best answer.

You can justify Choice (C) with the author's statement in the second paragraph that severely mentally handicapped people are unlikely to be held accountable for their actions in a "caring society."

612. **D. are better helped by treatment in a forensic mental health setting.**

The author mentions Choices (A), (B), and (C) as reasonable excuses for antisocial behavior at the beginning of the second paragraph. She discusses the option of treatment in the final paragraph as a way of dealing with crimes committed by those with disorders but not as an excuse for antisocial behavior.

613. **B. Diminish the consequences of**

Replace *mitigate* in the passage with each of the answer choices. The one that makes the most sense when paired with *excuse* and the reasoning provided in the rest of the sentence is Choice (B). A disorder would diminish the consequences of antisocial behavior because the perpetrators aren't aware significance of their behaviors.

614. **B. The punishment issued will likely encourage a change in behavior.**

In the third paragraph, the author notes that the effectiveness of punishment depends on two separate conditions: first, that the offender sees the connection between the punishment and his or her offense and second, that the punishment will likely enact change in the offender's behavior. Choice (D) states an opposite condition, so you can easily eliminate that option. Choice (A) contains an element that the passage doesn't justify. The offender must see a connection between the punishment and the action but not necessarily recognize that the punishment is inevitable. Choice (C) sounds close to the two stated conditions, but inclusion of *fully* to describe the realization and the specific resolution to never commit another crime are too specific to be supported by the passage. The best answer is Choice (B), which restates the second condition.

615. **C. Dementia**

In the second paragraph, the author notes that intellectual disability and dementia are two conditions that may hinder a person's understanding of the consequences of his or her actions. Of the conditions in the answer choices, the one that appears in the relevant part of the passage is Choice (C).

Antisocial behavior itself isn't considered a disorder. The author describes the disorder as antisocial personality disorder. So Choice (B) isn't justified.

616. **C. imagined scenes and emotions that are typically forgotten upon awaking.**

Oatley begins his discussion of dreams in the first paragraph, so start your search there. This paragraph presents three definitions of dream: the two common meanings — Choices (A) and (D) — and the new way, Choice (B). That leaves Choice (B), which is the exception because Oatley associates dreams with the images people remember when they awake.

617. **C. demonstrate that Shakespeare changed the focus of his plays in a way that incorporated elements of dreams.**

Eliminate incorrect answers. Choice (A) more closely summarizes passage A's third paragraph. Although Oatley mentions two plays in the second paragraph, that isn't his primary purpose for including it. Choice (B) is a representation of the purpose of the first paragraph, so you can eliminate that option. Choice (D) contradicts information in the paragraph, which explains that Shakespeare's later works moved beyond dramatizations of history, so Choice (D) is out, too. Choice (C) is best; the second paragraph builds on the information about dreams in the first paragraph to show that Shakespeare began incorporating dream aspects in later plays.

618. **B. *Henry VI, Part I***

In the middle of the second paragraph, Oatley states that Shakespeare's plays moved beyond dramatizations of history as in the three *Henry VI* plays. The answer that is most likely one of the three *Henry VI* plays is Choice (B).

619. **C. give the reader a look at the world through another dimension.**

Adding a "dream view" to Shakespeare's works may indeed have made them more entertaining, but Choice (A) is not the explanation Oatley provides, so you can eliminate it. Choice (B) is also unlikely; Oatley doesn't suggest that Shakespeare's works involving dream views are comedies. Though referencing dreams may have released Shakespeare's creative juices, the reason Oatley gives for the inclusion of a dream view is to offer the reader an extra view, or dimension, of the world, which aligns with Choice (C).

620. **D. fundamentally**

Replace *intrinsically* in the passage with the answer options. The sentence that contains the word shows that comedy is about how people interact and become connected, so the best answer is Choice (D): Comedy is fundamentally or essentially a social genre. Choices (A) and (B) don't relate to the concept of connectedness at all. Choice (C) focuses on the common meaning of comedy; however, the rest of the sentence doesn't mention humor, so the passage doesn't back up Choice (D).

621. A. Warwickshire

Check passage B for what the author states about *The Taming of the Shrew*. In the second paragraph, Callahan says that this play pays homage to Shakespeare's roots in rural Warwickshire. Choice (A) is the best answer.

Choices (B), (C), and (D) are incorrect. Venice appears in the passage only when referencing Shakespeare's *The Merchant of Venice* and not with any link to his early life. The author does mention Shakespeare's day-to-day life in Stratford and London in the passage, but it's in reference to *A Comedy of Errors* rather than *The Taming of the Shrew*.

622. D. aspects of ordinary life mixed with an alternative dream view, unlike anything from day-to-day life in Stratford.

Focus on the content in passage B and eliminate answers it lists as influences. It mentions Shakespeare's sisters and day-to-day life in Stratford, so Choice (A) is out. The end of the passage discusses the influences of court entertainers, so eliminate Choice (B). You can also cross off Choice (C). Callahan references the contributions of John Florio to *Love's Labour's Lost* and the fact that *A Midsummer Night's Dream* contains elements of Shakespeare's female sovereign, who you can logically assume was the Queen of England. The answer that doesn't fit is Choice (D). Oakely mentions Shakespeare's inclusion of dream elements, but Callahan doesn't.

623. C. Human connections between couples or within communities

Passage B begins with a statement of what the comedies all have in common: the exploration of how men and women go about the business of interacting with one another as pairs or a community. The answer that best summarizes this statement is Choice (C). If you picked Choice (A), you may have read the statement too quickly. It isn't about business but rather the business of interaction. Callahan mentions inclusion family influences but not in all of the comedies, so Choice (B) is wrong. Choice (D) seems to be a common trait until you read the last sentence, which reveals *The Merchant of Venice* as an exception to the general influences of Shakespeare's daily life.

624. B. Both discuss Shakespeare's motivations behind creating some of his most notable works.

Eliminate Choice (A) because it's true of only passage A. Similarly, Choice (D) is out because it's true of only Passage B. Neither passage provides information about Shakespeare's early life, so throw out Choice (C). The best answer is Choice (B). Passage A describes Shakespeare's incorporation of dream views, and passage B provides insight into the elements of Shakespeare's experiences that make their way into his plays.

625. **B. The "little western flower" in *A Midsummer Night's Dream***

Eliminate Choices (A) and (D). The "two eyes, one beside the other," is a reference to the actual physical state of human vision rather than an image from a Shakespearean play, and the historical events are in the *Henry VI* plays rather than *The Taming of the Shrew*.

Of the two remaining choices, the image of the "little western flower" is a better representation of the "flora and fauna" of Shakespeare's native place (lines 71–72) than is Titania, the Fairy Queen. So Choice (B) is best.

626. **C. The passage lays a foundation of general facts that leads to more specific information about one element of that foundation and then more specific detail about one type of that element.**

You can easily eliminate Choice (D). The passage contains fact, not opinions. Similarly, Choice (B) is wrong because the passage presents a series of facts rather than a theory. Choice (A) starts out okay, but when you read to the end, you realize that it has to be wrong. The passage ends with specific detail rather than a general conclusion. So Choice (C) has to be correct. The passage starts with information about the basic components of life, gives more details about cells and the tissues they create, and then provides much more detail about a particular type of tissue — epithelium.

627. **B. a single layer**

When the authors delve into the riveting discussion about epithelial tissues in the third paragraph, they note that the tissues are classified into one of two primary categories: simple, or those composed of a single layer, or stratified, meaning they have many layers. Choice (B) is the answer.

628. **C. impulse control.**

The authors discuss the functions commonly associated with life in the first paragraph. Among them are reproduction, food breakdown (metabolism), and contraction. Eliminate Choices (A), (B), and (D). Impulse control is mentioned in the second paragraph in reference to cell parts.

629. **A. Liver, pancreas, and intestines**

The passage defines a system as a group of organs that participate in a common enterprise. It provides an example of the digestive system made up of the stomach, liver, pancreas, and intestines. So the answer is Choice (A). Choice (B) lists cell parts, and Choice (C) lists cells and groups of cells. Choice (D) refers to elements discussed in the third paragraph about types of tissues.

630. A. They are organized a bit like the cells of a honeycomb.

The epithelial cells found in the upper respiratory tract are described in the sixth paragraph under the classification of columnar epithelial cells, so Choice (D) is wrong. The passage says that columnar types of cells are arranged like the cells of a honeycomb, which means Choice (A) is correct.

Choice (B) is wrong because the passage classifies these cells as pseudostratified; they give the appearance of having more than one layer, but they aren't multilayered.

631. D. nervous.

In the third paragraph, the authors breakdown the four main types of tissue into a nice, neat little list. The fourth on the list is nervous tissues, which the passage states conduct impulses from one part of the body to another. Choice (D) is the clear answer.

632. C. tissue

The second paragraph rattles off the three main parts of a cell. Included are cytoplasm, membrane, and nucleus. Tissue appears in the same paragraph, but tissues are made up of cells rather than the other way around. The exception is Choice (C).

633. D. They specialize in secreting or excreting.

The passage doesn't mention the pituitary and adrenal glands, so you don't have enough information to say that the cells are their *sole* components. Eliminate Choice (A). Choice (B) is true of stratified columnar epithelium, not glandular epithelial cells, so go ahead and cross off that option. Choice (C) is true of transitional epithelium, not glandular epithelial cells; you can knock that one out of the running, too. Glandular epithelial cells specialize in excretion or secretion, as the authors note in the passage's final paragraph. Choice (D) is correct.

634. B. Along the surface of the muscles that pump the blood into the heart

Check out the fifth paragraph for information on simple squamous epithelium. The paragraph states that simple squamous epithelium is found where a smooth surface is required to reduce friction and lists body cavity linings and blood vessels as locations. Choice (A) is therefore out because the inner layers of a large muscle aren't a smooth surface area. The remaining answers concern linings or surface areas, however, so you need to do a little digging to narrow the field.

In the last two paragraphs, the passage specifically associates stratified (not simple) epithelium with the lining of the first part of the digestive tract and the lining of the pharynx and salivary glands, so Choices (C) and (D) must be wrong. Although the passage doesn't specifically state that simple squamous epithelium line the surface of the muscles that pump blood to the heart, it says that they line blood vessels, so Choice (B) is most justifiable answer.

635. **C. Calluses**

The discussion of dead cells appears toward the end of the seventh paragraph. The keratinized (or cornified) cells form calluses, Choice (C). Eliminate Choices (A) and (B) because they relate to the types of tissues that make up the dead cells, but they aren't the result of their becoming thick with friction. The passage doesn't mention warts, so eliminate Choice (D).

636. **D. Wolf stays at the mountain cottage for a few days then leaves; Walt sees Wolf outside a train window; Wolf stays with Walt and Madge for at least a week; they meet Wolf on a hiking trail.**

When the ACT asks for a chronological ordering, it wants the actual order of events rather than the order in which they appear in the passage. Therefore, Choices (A) and (B) are wrong. Even though the trail greeting happened first in the passage, it didn't occur first chronologically. When Wolf showed up at Walt and Madge's home, he wouldn't let them touch him, but he allows them to pat and rub him on the hike. The hike was clearly not the couple's first encounter with Wolf.

By the same reasoning, you can also eliminate Choice (C). The wolf rejected affection when he first drifted to the cottage, so he wasn't seeking affection. The passage also suggests that Walt gave Wolf the collar soon after they returned from the train trip because they hadn't won Wolf over yet. Events on the trail suggest that Wolf and the couple have a strong relationship. Choice (D) is the most logical listing of events from first to most recent.

637. **D. an unidentified commentator**

The man who called to the wolf is the same person as Walt, and because the passage refers to Walt in the third person, the passage isn't told from his point of view. Eliminate Choices (A) and (B). The narrator is omniscient, but the story isn't told in first person, so you can eliminate Choice (C). The story is told from the point of view of one who is observing and commenting on events, but the storyteller isn't identified. You could assume it's the author, but that isn't an option. The best answer is Choice (D).

638. B. north of the mountain cottage.

When describing the train trip in lines 61–64, the author says that Irvine was called to the northern part of the state and was on the train "near to the line between California and Oregon." The address Walt places on the dog's color indicates Walt lives in Sonoma County, California, so it must have been the northern part of California he was traveling to. Therefore, although he traveled near the line between California and Oregon, he likely didn't cross it and go into Oregon. Eliminate Choice (A). Because the dog had traveled 200 miles when Walt spotted him from the train, the train was at least 200 miles from his home, so Walt wasn't riding near his hometown in Sonoma County. Nor was he likely in Mendocino County, which the passage says is 100 (not 200) miles to the north.

Therefore, the most justifiable answer has to be Choice (B). Walt traveled from his mountain cottage, so the train ride had to have been somewhere north of there.

639. B. was happy to see Walt and Madge.

Usually at least one answer choice is clearly incorrect. Nothing in the paragraph suggests that the wolf wanted to harm the couple, so eliminate Choice (C).

The paragraph doesn't describe the couple's appearance, so Choice (A) doesn't make much sense. Between Choices (B) and (D), Choice (B) is more justifiable. Information in the subsequent paragraph describes behavior (ear flattened and head anticipates a snuggle) that suggests he welcomes the couple's company. There are no indicators that the wolf felt superior to them.

640. D. steep.

Try the answer choices in place of *precipitous* in the sentence. The word in the question is an adjective used to describe *descent*. In the context of the lines, the descent isn't hasty, so eliminate Choice (A).

Although precipitous sounds similar to *precipitation*, nothing in the description before the line reference indicates that the ground was wet. Eliminate Choice (B).

Choice (C) could logically describe the path the couple was descending, but information in the rest of the sentence suggests that the descent provoked an avalanche of pebbles, so it wasn't likely *less* rocky. The most logical answer is Choice (D). Because a descent relates to elevation, it makes sense that the trail had become less steep.

641. C. the animal's colors revealed that he was not a timber-wolf.

"The lie was given to his wolf-hood" means that though the animal looked like a wolf, his coloring and marks revealed that he wasn't a wolf. Choice (C) is the answer that clarifies the author's meaning.

The *hood* in wolf-hood refers to the suffix definition of *hood,* which refers to a characteristic or state of being rather than a head covering. So eliminate Choice (B). If the animal's wolf-hood is a lie, the animal isn't a wolf. Eliminate Choice (D).

You can easily dismiss Choice (A) because although the passage states that wolves are never brown, it doesn't specify their usual colors.

642. A. he continued to reject the couple's demonstrations of affection.

The author clearly points out in the eighth paragraph that Wolf never barked, so eliminate Choice (B). Wolf traveled at least 200 miles following the train and 100 miles to Mendocino County, so Choice (C) is indicated and therefore wrong.

Although the author makes a big deal about the dog's lack of wolf coloring, he clearly states that he was built like a wolf in the beginning of the fourth paragraph. Eliminate Choice (D).

It took a while to win Wolf over, but by the time Walt and Madge are with him on the trail, he is allowing them to rub him affectionately. Choice (A) is the exception.

643. C. Walt's resolve to provide care for the dog.

The last paragraph describes Walt's actions to make sure he can find Wolf when he runs away. His actions don't prevent Wolf from running away (so Choice (B) is out), but they facilitate Wolf's return to them so that they can continue to care for him. Choice (C) seems good.

You may be tempted to pick Choice (D) because the paragraph opens with a statement that Walt Irvine liked problems, but the paragraph doesn't continue to talk his general like for problems. It concerns the problem of winning over Wolf in particular.

The answer isn't Choice (A). Although the paragraph describes the dog's wanderlust, it doesn't imply that he was wandering to get away from Walt and Madge. Earlier in the passage, Wolf traveled over 200 miles to catch up with Walt. The main point of the paragraph is best summarized by Choice (C).

644. B. The effort it took to love the dog made the dog's presence that much more valuable.

Skim through the answer choices to see whether any can be easily eliminated. The author describes winning the dog's love as something that required considerable effort, so saying that loving the dog was easy because he showed deep affection is completely unwarranted. Choice (A) is out. Likewise, eliminate Choice (C) because it was a long time before the dog returned the couple's love. Choice (D) suggests that the couple never wins the dog's affection, but events on the trail at the beginning of the passages refute this implication.

The best answer is Choice (B). Walt and Madge loved the dog so deeply because they worked so hard to earn his returned affection.

645. A. guarded.

The passage uses *circumspect* to describe the couple's attempts to show affection to the dog when he first came into their lives and had to be chained. The sentence that contains the word begins with *but*, which indicates that the idea it conveys opposes their efforts to love the dog. The sentence that follows the line reference provides the reason for their circumspect shows of affection: The dog was distant and snarled at them. Snarling wouldn't cause their affection to be tender, so eliminate Choice (D). The paragraph doesn't suggest that they quit showing affection for the dog, so Choice (C) is wrong. Choice (B) makes little sense. *Speculative* means "theoretical"; the couple showed actual rather than hypothetical love for the dog. The best answer is Choice (A). If the dog snarls at their attempts at affection, they likely presented them cautiously.

646. B. homes.

The answer can be found in the first paragraph of the passage, when the authors make their case for why women are such an important part of the modern marketplace. They note that women are responsible for the decisions surrounding the purchasing of "91 percent of homes, 60 percent of automobiles, and 51 percent of consumer electronics."

647. D. most women outlive men.

The authors preface their statement about 80 to 90 percent of women taking charge of family finances with "since women outlive men by an average of five years," so you know your answer has to be Choice (D). Though Choice (A) seems like a good explanation for the statistic in the question, the authors don't say that women will make more than men in the future.

648. **D. men on average donate less to political causes than women do.**

The authors state that "While men may still earn more money, women give as much to charity," yet they do so differently." Choices (A) and (C) summarize this statement, so eliminate them. The authors' inclusion of Margaret Mead's quotes about women's powerful influence in politics substantiates Choice (B), so eliminate that answer.

Choice (D) is the exception; the authors state that women give as much as men do, not that they give more.

649. **C. more time to relax.**

In the second-to-last paragraph, the authors rave about this period in a woman's life. They cite new assets and freedom among its benefits. Later in the same paragraph, they describe the benefits of reconnecting with the soul. They never mention more time to relax, so Choice (C) is the exception.

650. **A. Women should find ways to immerse themselves in politics.**

Quotes from Marie C. Wilson equate more political involvement from women with meaningful change, so Choice (A) is the answer. If you selected Choice (B), you confused quotes from Marie C. Wilson with those of Vi Nichols Chason. Choice (C) relates to comments made by Brenda Pejovich. Choice (D) was a point made by Margaret Mead rather than the founder and president of the White House Project.

651. **C. the third decade of the twenty-first century.**

In the first paragraph, the authors clearly state that 54 percent of America's boomers will be women by the year 2030, which is the third decade of the 21st century. Choice (C) is the clear answer.

652. **A. demonstrate the need for women to take immediate action.**

Much of the passage is arguably dedicated to urging women to take action, particularly on a political level. The paragraph emphasizes "how important taking action is," which is paraphrased in Choice (A). The paragraph really doesn't compare boomers with younger generations, so you eliminate Choice (B). Choice (D) appears in the prior paragraph. The reference to give a happy ending to a sad song isn't a literal suggestion to write songs. It serves as encouragement to take positive action.

653. B. Margaret Mead

The anthropologist Margaret Mead is the woman who can take credit for urging women to engage in pursuits that leave them with a greater sense of meaning, joy and balance. This fact is evident in the second-to-last-paragraph. Choices (A) and (D) refer to women who urged other females to contribute financially as well as with their time, and Choice (C) was only mentioned briefly during the section about the song "Hey Jude." Choice (B) is the correct answer.

654. D. women make nearly half of all consumer electronics purchasing decisions.

You can find Choice (A) toward the end of the second paragraph and Choice (B) in the first line of the second-to-last paragraph. Look for Choices (C) and (D) in the beginning of the passage where the authors make their case for just how influential women are when it comes to making purchasing decisions. The passage states that women make about 60 percent of car purchasing decisions, but it also says they make "51 percent" of decisions involving consumer electronics purchases. Because "51 percent" is more than half, and not "nearly half," Choice (D) has to be the answer.

655. A. customary

Answer this question by simply substituting the answer choices for *unprecedented* in the passage. The one that doesn't make sense is Choice (A).

656. B. both were painted within the same century.

The third paragraph clearly states that the two paintings were significant commissions, so it's easy to eliminate Choice (A). The same paragraph indicates that both were painted for churches in Florence, so Choice (D) isn't the exception. In the first paragraph, the author mentions that no painting can become outmoded, so these two paintings can't become outdated. Eliminate Choice (C). If the two paintings were painted about a hundred years apart, they weren't likely to be painted in the same century. Choice (B) is correct.

657. C. encourage them to look upon the central figure with awe and reverence.

The key to answering this question correctly is to notice that it deals with the purpose of the use of architectural elements. Search the fourth and last paragraphs, where the author describes the painting in detail.

Choice (D) is easy to exclude. Though the author mentions the age of paintings in the first paragraph, he isn't concerned with determining time by elements in a painting. The invitation to join in the sorrow comes from the gesture of one the mourners, who isn't an architectural feature. So Choice (A) is out. In the last paragraph, the author indicates that the light and colors convey the reality of the scene. Choice (B) isn't achieved through the use of architectural elements.

The best answer is Choice (C). In the fourth paragraph, the author shows that by dropping the floor and enhancing the ceiling coffers, the artist places the viewer in a position of looking up at the figure of Christ to inspire respect and reverence.

658. **C. 6**

A close reading of the passage reveals the answer to this question. In the fourth paragraph, the author describes the "the wounded and lifeless body of Christ (the first figure), two figures below who are mourning him (figures two and three), two that kneel in front praying (figures four and five) and God the Father behind the Christ (figure six). No other figures are mentioned or alluded to, so you can't assume Choice (D).

659. **B. works of art do not become obsolete as new works are created.**

You can easily eliminate Choice (D). The author states that art can't be evaluated in the same way as modern science. Choice (A) is out. The first paragraph isn't about determining the actual date artworks were created. Although the author suggests that studying art history is valuable to understanding works of art, the reference doesn't deal directly with the statement that art can't be dated. The author's statement makes the point that art's relevance doesn't progress as new works are created, so Choice (B) is best.

660. **A. The representation of a barrel vault**

The passage mentions all answers as techniques Massacio used in the Trinity, but the only one that the author indicates is original is Choice (A). She expressly states that the representation of the barrel vault was imagined for the first time in the painting and then describes that the technique makes the painting seem to be part of the actual wall it's hanging on. This sense would certainly make viewer feel like they are part of the scene.

661. B. Christ is the focal point of the painting.

The author doesn't talk about the popularity of the Christ as a subject in art, so eliminate Choice (A). Though the passage mentions the importance of the rational light, the reference isn't offered as support for the claim presented in the question. Choice (D) is out.

You may have a harder time choosing between Choices (B) and (C). Focus on the words that immediately follow the statement. They mention God behind Christ's body but only to emphasize that Christ dominates the figure. God is in fact holding Christ from behind, but this fact isn't what the author uses to support her claim that Christ is victorious. Choice (B) is best.

662. B. the figures are representative of real people with real emotions.

When the author notes in the last paragraph that all of the figures in Masaccio's Trinity were naturalistically formed, she implies that they are representative of real people with real emotions, which is Choice (B). The author follows the reference to naturalistically formed figures with descriptions of how the figures behave and feel rather than explanations of how the painter created them, so Choice (B) is your best bet. All of the remaining answer choices involve the act of painting itself.

663. A. dignified.

The word describes both the figures and the drama; both are important, so Choice (B) must be wrong. The sentence preceding the word says that the figures struggle, so they are unlikely to be flawless or infallible. Eliminate Choice (D). You may be tempted by Choice (C). Often, nobility is associated with royalty, but the author doesn't suggest that the scene is royal. A better description of the scene is Choice (A), dignified, a word that defines both the gravity and the humanity of the depiction.

664. B. 100 years

Find the reference by searching for the quoted phrase in the first part of the passage where it discusses the history of art and the irrelevance of time. The author follows the reference with ". . . one hundred years is not much." Choice (B) is correct.

665. D. explain how the artist distinguishes the key figure in the painting.

Choice (A) is a better explanation for the passage's final paragraph, which discusses how light, shading, and color are used in various ways. Although the third paragraph notes that the two paintings are different, the fourth paragraph doesn't indicate how they are different. Choice (B) is out. Eliminate Choice (C), too, because although the paragraph does discuss the other figures in the passage, it makes clear they are secondary to Christ. Most of the discussion involves how the rest of the painting accentuates the central figure of Christ, so Choice (D) is the strongest option.

666. D. describe in detail the eruption of Mt. Toba and its effects.

When you skim through the paragraphs, you see that although the passage begins with a discussion of supervolcanoes in general, it quickly becomes a description of the Mt. Toba eruption. The rest of the passage is about Mt. Toba's eruption and its effects. Therefore, Choices (A) and (B) are too general because they concern all supervolcanoes rather than just Mt. Toba. Choice (C) is too specific. The passage compares Mt. Toba with other eruptions, but that's not the primary focus. Choice (D) is the clearest representation of the passage's purpose throughout.

667. C. no precise measurements exist of its projected material.

First, take a look at your answer options to see whether you can easily eliminate any. Consider Choice (A). Nothing is surprising about a highly studied volcano's being a catastrophic threat. In fact, the threat would explain why Mt. Toba is the most studied volcano. Likewise, both Choices (B) and (D) state facts about Mt. Toba (likely from all that studying it receives), but they don't make assertions that would necessarily be considered surprising, so they probably aren't right, either. Look at Choice (C). You can reasonably assume that if a supervolcano were studied so closely, precise measurements of its projected material would have been performed at some point or other. Thus, Choice (C) is the surprise and correct answer.

668. B. a volcanic winter.

At the beginning of the sixth paragraph, the authors note that both scientists believed Mt. Toba's eruption could trigger a "volcanic winter." Choice (B) is correct.

Be careful to avoid making assumptions based on your own knowledge. Choices (A) and (C) may sound somewhat reasonable given the subject matter, but they aren't assertions attributed specifically to the two scientists, so you can eliminate both choices from contention. If you picked Choice (D), you likely confused "global cooling," which, according to the two scientists, is a possible side effect of a Mt. Toba eruption, with global warming.

669. **A. relatively insignificant.**

The authors note in the third paragraph of the passage that, when compared with the YTT eruption, the eruption of Mr. Toba was minimal. *Minimal* in this context is synonymous with *relatively insignificant,* so Choice (A) is the best answer. You should be able to easily eliminate Choice (C) because the word *minimal* wouldn't suggest more significance. Choices (B) and (D) have to be wrong because the comparison in the passage suggests that the two eruptions were different.

670. **C. evidence of Toba tephra in the earth's surface across the entire planet.**

The authors dedicate the entire fifth paragraph of the passage to giving examples of evidence of the magnitude of the YTT eruption. In the paragraph, they reference Choices (A), (B), and (D); the only answer choice NOT included was Choice (C). The paragraph says the ash covered a wide area but doesn't extend this area across the entire planet.

671. **B. 5 years**

In the fourth paragraph, the authors discuss the expelled material of the YTT eruption and explain why research surrounding the eruption should be accepted cautiously. They note that there is an error margin of about five years, which is Choice (B).

672. **C. unchanging**

The authors describe the reservoirs as *remaining* stagnant and compare them to others that accumulated magma and became more active. Therefore, the most logical substitute is Choice (C). Compared to the other reservoirs, these didn't become more active or larger.

The paragraph doesn't mention temperature in the comparison, so Choices (B) and (D) aren't warranted. Choice (A) is an antonym.

673. **D. Common Era**

In the very first line of the passage, the authors state, "Supervolcanoes, those rare geological events, pose the most catastrophic threat to life on this planet. No super-eruption of Mt. Toba's magnitude has occurred during the Common Era (CE)." So your answer is Choice (D).

674. A. point out the magnitude of a Toba eruption.

If you picked Choice (B), you likely confused the answer choice with the passage's content, which actually says, "long winters and shorter summers." Choice (C) references the content in the sixth paragraph, so you can eliminate it as well. Regarding Choice (D), the passage implies that the two scientists mentioned in the paragraph, Self and Rampino, were in agreement in their theories regarding the Toba eruption, so it isn't accurate to say they had differing opinions. The best answer available is Choice (A).

675. C. 80,000 and 75,000 years ago

The answer to this question is revealed in the first line of the passage's final paragraph, when the authors clearly state, "Evidence from the Vostok ice core from Antarctica indicates that the global drop in temperatures of 7.2°F (4°C) occurred between 80,000 and 75,000 years ago." Hopefully, you recognized the word "Vostok" from your reading and were able to find the part of the passage that refers to it (there's only one) and discusses the 7-degree temperature drop pretty easily. Choice (C) is your only viable option.

676. B. considered the amount of the ticket unreasonable.

Exorbitant means "overpriced" or "very expensive," so Choice (B) is the most obvious answer. Even if you didn't know the definition of *exorbitant*, you could eliminate Choices (A) and (D). The passage doesn't mention what the posted speed limit was, and the narrator never suggests that the traveler didn't deserve the ticket. Choice (C) may have tempted you because speeding tickets are rarely anticipated, but *exorbitant* doesn't mean "unexpected."

You're supposed to choose the best answer out of the four options. To know which is the best, use that secret weapon known as *POE*, or the process of elimination. By eliminating answers you know can't be right, you help isolate the answer that fits best.

677. A. she did not expect him to become overwhelmed by excitement.

The narrator's indication that the traveler's boss is always a pessimist leads you to believe that she doesn't expect him to provide an overly positive reaction to her news, but that's really all you know. You can't assume a lack of specific expectations like a raise offer or party, so eliminate Choices (B) and (C). Just because someone's a pessimist doesn't mean he's prone to breakdowns; Choice (D) is a bit too extreme. The most general and least extreme option is Choice (A).

678. **B. thoughtful.**

The question very kindly directs you specifically to the last paragraph, where the traveler reflects on her decision to move. Her thoughts about the success she has experienced because of her move indicate satisfaction that her boss's earlier prediction that she would fail hadn't come true. Therefore, the best answer of the four is Choice (B); she uses the paragraph to thoughtfully consider the effects of her move. Choices (A) and (C) are way too extreme for the tone and content of the last paragraph. She feels successful rather than frustrated or bitter. You may have had a little more difficulty eliminating Choice (D), though. There is a hint of sarcasm in the last paragraph when she feels "a small amount of satisfaction" that the boss who told her that the grass is always greener ended up mowing lawns, but this reference is just one part of the entire paragraph and suggests a little irony rather than full-blown sarcasm.

679. **B. a valuable learning experience that had both negative and positive aspects.**

You can probably cross out Choices (A) and (D) because they contain disputable words. A "complete" failure means that no part of her move was successful. Unless the passage comes right out and says that there was nothing good about the move, you know Choice (A) has to be wrong. The word that should warn you away from Choice (D) is *solely,* which is another way of saying *only.* Boredom may have been one reason that the traveler wanted to move, but it wasn't the sole reason. That leaves you with Choices (B) and (C). Although the traveler experienced a few setbacks in her travels, you can't say that the trip was mostly hazardous. She did make it to her destination, after all. Process of elimination (POE) leads you to Choice (B), the most generic, and therefore best, summary of the traveler's experience.

680. **C. irony.**

Irony means "using humor to suggest the opposite of something's literal meaning." It's ironic (and a little amusing) that the manager used the "grass is always greener" cliché to suggest that the traveler wouldn't make it away from home when the manager then ended up in the position of literally keeping the grass green. Although the manager may have had a feeling of resentment, which is Choice (A), that feeling doesn't relate the cliché to his new profession. If you picked Choice (B), redundancy, you'd have to think the manager had had a lawn-mowing career in the past, and Choice (D), predestination, implies that the boss was somehow able to foresee his future career, an idea that nothing in the passage supports.

681. C. driving a manual transmission.

If doing so helps you focus, you can rephrase this question to "Which of the following wasn't the traveler concerned about?" Now just eliminate her concerns. The first paragraph suggests that she was worried about leaving her home and family for the first time, so you can cross out Choice (D). Although the passage doesn't come right out and say that she was worried about staying by herself in a hotel room, she does list it as one of her "firsts" at line 39, which tells you that it was an unfamiliar experience. You may not want to eliminate Choice (B) right away, but it's probably wrong. The next paragraph describes her uneasiness when she sees the sign about not stopping for hitchhikers in the prison area. That sounds like a concern! Nowhere in the passage is there any mention of whether she drives a manual or automatic transmission, so you can confidently pick Choice (C) as the best answer.

682. C. the traveler's new life in a new area of the country will not be as great as she thinks it will.

The common phrase "the grass is always greener" has nothing to do with the actual appearance (or aesthetic) of the landscape, so you can toss out Choice (A). Choice (B) is probably wrong, too; the manager uses the phrase in reference to the traveler's life, not his. Though the manager may think that the traveler won't be as happy with her next job, that thought doesn't relate well to the common understanding of the phrase "the grass is always greener." Choice (D) contains a red flag in the word *never.*

683. D. She had a roommate who prepared different foods from the ones she was used to.

The information you need to answer this question comes from the tenth paragraph. Cross out Choice (A) because, although you may think it would be a good idea for the traveler to get a new bed to replace the faulty air mattress, the passage never says that she actually makes that wise purchase. Choice (C) confuses physical hiccups with the kind that mean "glitches." The traveler wasn't really afflicted with hiccups.

You may be tempted to choose Choice (B). The passage does say that she can't find a few things, but the narrator refers to these items as things she was "certain she had packed," which implies that she had left them at home rather than misplaced them in the new abode. Choice (D) works best. Because the narrator says that the traveler's roommate had "odd culinary" habits, you can assume that her roommate created dishes that she wasn't very familiar with.

684. **A. It indicates that, although the journey and transitional period were not without hardship, the traveler was able to overcome the obstacles that stood in her way and eventually feel comfortable with her move.**

Although Choices (B) and (C) may have a little truth to them, the key is the phrasing of the question. The right answer has to reflect the purpose of the whole paragraph. Choice (D) misstates the real theme of the paragraph. The point isn't that there's no place like home. If that were true, the traveler would have ended up back in her small hometown. Choice (A) provides an excellent summary of the point of the paragraph and fits with the theme of the whole passage.

685. **D. negative.**

The traveler refers to her manager as a pessimist; that's all you need to choose Choice (D) because *negative* is a synonym for *pessimistic.* She certainly doesn't think he's an optimist; that's the opposite of a pessimist. You may get the impression that the manager becomes insecure because he was wrong about the traveler's success, but that assumption doesn't have enough support from the passage. The traveler definitely doesn't think the manager is passive. His rude comments wouldn't come from a passive person, so you can eliminate Choice (B), too.

686. **A. his mentor, Socrates, also avoided politics.**

Toward the beginning of the third paragraph, the author notes that when it comes to politics, Socrates "preferred to stay out of such worldly affairs." He then goes on to suggest that it was this decision to maintain neutrality that may have influenced Plato to come to the same conclusion. Socrates never overtly asked Plato to avoid politics, and nothing suggests that he preferred to devote his time to religion, so you can go ahead and eliminate Choices (B) and (C). Finally, the author does indeed note that Plato's family was antidemocratic, and although this could presumably have been a factor in his decision to avoid politics, the passage doesn't connect his family's views to his decision. Stick with Choice (A).

687. **C. a small group of people have all the control.**

The author uses the term *oligarchy* when referencing the ruling of the Thirty Tyrants — implying that there were 30 rulers, and not a single person, a family, or an entire society. Thus, the answer is Choice (C), a small group of people have all the control.

688. **A. he ultimately did pursue a political role after the fall of the Thirty Tyrants.**

The author notes several times that Socrates wasn't at all interested in politics and that he never participated in political affairs. Therefore, Choice (A) isn't true and imust be the exception. Choices (B), (C), and (D) are all stated in the final two paragraphs of the passage.

689. **B. virtue**

In Proffitt's description of the new Athenian government in the third paragraph, he notes that the new rulers were a group of men who were highly conservative and religious. Because the group was all about democracy, as noted in several instances throughout the passage, Choice (A) and Choice (C) can't be right. Choice (B) is a better answer than Choice (D); Proffitt states that the Athenian government saw virtue and nobility as "decidedly undemocratic."

690. **D. smooth talker**

In the second paragraph of the second passage, Allen notes that the literal meaning of *sophist* is "wise man," but the term came to connote someone who "fast-talks his way out of moral, intellectual or practical quandaries. . . ." Thus, you can eliminate Choices (B) and (C) and select Choice (D). Despite what you may hear during an election, a politician is necessarily a fast talker.

691. **C. monogamy.**

The author describes Socrates' idea of a utopia in the final paragraph of the passage. She notes that Socrates believes a utopia should be "led by philosopher-kings and queens and protected by a class of guardian-soldiers, including both men and women, who hold their property in common, have egalitarian gender relations, and enjoy open marriages." Not only does Choice (C) fail to appear in his description, but it also contradicts the idea of open marriages. Therefore, Choice (C) is exception.

ANSWERS 601–700

692. **B. 16.**

In the second paragraph of Passage B, the author discusses how Socrates began to teach Plato's brother, Glaucon, in 408 to 407 BCE, when Plato would have been about 16. The author then goes on to note that it is believed that Socrates began teaching Glaucon as a favor to Plato, suggesting Plato and Socrates already had an established relationship at this point. The justifiable answer is Choice (B).

693. **D. Socrates and Plato likely had a mentor/mentee relationship.**

A good portion of Passage A discusses the relationship between Plato and Socrates, and in Passage B, Allen states that Plato "began to follow Socrates formally." Therefore, the most justifiable answer is Choice (D). Choice (A) is likely something Proffitt would agree with, but there really isn't anything in Passage B to suggest the same. Similarly, Choices (B) and (C) can be attributed to Allen but not to Proffitt.

694. **A. The first passage concentrates on Socrates and Plato's political involvement, or lack thereof, and the second focuses more on the relationship between the two men.**

Choice (B) isn't accurate; Passage A arguably focuses more on Socrates than Plato. Choice (C) isn't a particularly truthful statement, either; Passage B discusses that Socrates was viewed as a *sophist*, which Allen didn't intend as a compliment. You can eliminate Choice (D) because neither author pays much attention to determining the approximate age of Socrates during their discussion (though some attention is given to *Plato's* age, particularly in Passage B). Only Choice (A) offers an accurate summary of the content of each passage.

695. **B. similar in that both authors present their subjects in a way that is primarily informative and scholarly.**

Choice (B) is your best bet; the tone used by the authors of both passages is one that would likely be found in a textbook. Neither passage looks upon the past with longing, so Choice (A) makes little sense. Allen's passage doesn't make its points by presenting a personal story, so Choice (C) is out. Choice (D) is inaccurate; Proffitt is neutral about Socartes and Allen is more critical of him than approving.

696. **A. popular culture often plays a greater role than historical fact in shaping our impressions of the appearances of ancient Egyptians.**

Pick an answer that summarizes the main idea of the passage rather than focuses on one specific concept. Overall, the passage is about how hard it is to know what ancient Egyptians looked like because they have been misrepresented in popular culture. That's what Choice (A) says.

The other three choices are either untrue or address supporting ideas. Choices (B) and (C) deal only with pictures. In addition to pictures, the passage mentions other forms of depiction that contribute to the confusion about the appearance of ancient Egyptians. The use of skeletal remains is mentioned briefly in the last paragraph, so you know it isn't the main idea of the passage. Additionally, Choice (D) makes a generalization about determining the appearance of all ancient peoples and therefore loses the focus on ancient Egyptians

697. **C. give the reader an example of how popular culture often dictates the common perception of ancient Egypt more than scholarly reconsiderations of ancient data.**

The descriptions of the *Antony and Cleopatra* films crops up in the first paragraph right after the author states that the way popular culture portrays ancient Egyptians reveals the way impressions of their appearance changes over time. The discussion must be there to provide support for that statement. The discussion concludes with the author's statement that the changes in Cleopatra's appearance over time in the various films didn't happen because of revelations from scholarly data. Choice (C) is the answer that conveys both of these ideas.

Choice (B) is too general. It doesn't refer to the specific topic of the appearance of ancient Egyptians. Choice (D) is wrong. The passage doesn't say that the perception of ancient Egyptians' appearance is likely to continue changing. The passage wouldn't contain an example to call attention to a fact that it doesn't discuss. Eliminate Choice (A). The author doesn't talk about the uncertainty surrounding the appearance of ancient Egyptians until the next paragraph. It doesn't make sense that the purpose of an example in the first paragraph would be to support an idea that crops up in the second paragraph.

698. **B. uniform appearance.**

The clue to the meaning of *homogeneity* is in the sentence that follows. It says that Egyptian society was made up of a bunch of diverse people from different cultures and with different physical features. If the homogeneity is deceptive, then homogeneity must mean the opposite of diversity. Eliminate Choice (C). Choice (D) means about the same thing as diversity, so you can cross it out, too. Choice (A) is closer, but the passage is about how the appearance of ancient Egyptians has been depicted, not their community. The best answer is Choice (B). The sameness or uniformity of the ancient Egyptians is deceptive.

699. **A. were inadequate and inconclusive.**

The passage says that the comparisons were limited, filled with uncertainties, and unreliable. *Inadequate* and *inconclusive* have similar meanings to *limited* and *unreliable.* Choice (A) seems like a pretty darn good paraphrase of the passage.

Choice (B) deals with the Hollywood portrayals of ancient Egyptians, which is covered in the beginning of the passage and not touched on again in the section about skeletal remains or anywhere else. Eliminate Choice (C) because the passage suggests that the skeletal remains provided little information about ancient Egyptians. The phrase *solid proof* should raise a red flag about the validity of Choice (D), especially because the passage says the remains studies are unreliable.

700. **D. that the perception of who was considered Egyptian was subject to change based upon the intended audience.**

The passage discusses Hekanefer in the third paragraph. The Hekanefer example comes right after the sentence in lines 66–68 that says that the perception of who was Egyptian depended on the audience, which is almost exactly what Choice (D) says.

Eliminate Choice (A) because the passage covers the physical differences between Nubians and Syrians before it mentions Hekanefer. The author makes no connection to Hollywood when he presents the Hekanefer example, so cross out Choice (B). You know Choice (C) can't be right. The author doesn't mention skeletal remains until later after the paragraph on Hekanefer.

701. **C. lacking.**

You can likely figure out that Choice (C), *lacking*, is best answer without even looking at the passage. It's the only answer choice that has a different meaning from the others. It's a simple case of noticing that one of the things isn't like the others! Choices (A), (B), and (D) each generally convey a sense of being overloaded. Choice (C) means "absence."

To make sure you're right, substitute each of the answer choices for *fraught* in the sentence to see which one doesn't make sense. Something lacking uncertainties would be reliable rather than unreliable. Choice (C) contains the word that doesn't belong.

702. **A. It explains how ancient Egyptian art shaped ideas regarding the common physical traits of foreigners, regardless of historical accuracy.**

Eliminate answers that you know don't work. You can cast Choice (B) aside because paragraph three suggests that those ancient portraits of Egyptians were created with similar, noticeable characteristics, and the paragraph about Hollywood's portrayal of Egyptians highlights the different ways modern culture has characterized the appearance of ancient Egyptians. Choice (C) more accurately describes the function of the second paragraph than the third. Discount Choice (D). The reason that portrayals of the same prince differ wasn't to distinguish him from commoners but to either emphasize his foreignness or his Egyptian heritage, depending on the circumstances.

The paragraph is about the way that ancient Egyptian portraits used specific features to distinguish foreigners from Egyptians without regard to physical accuracy. The best answer is Choice (A).

703. **D. Members of ancient Egyptian society, regardless of their origins, have typically been portrayed stereotypically.**

The author makes it clear that neither popular culture nor ancient portraiture have been particularly concerned with accuracy. It's not reasonable to conclude that he thinks one is more or less accurate than the other. They're both inaccurate. Cross out Choice (A). For a similar reason, eliminate Choice (C). The author suggests that both Nubians and Syrians were portrayed stereotypically. Choice (B) directly contradicts the first sentence of the last paragraph. The best answer is Choice (D). The author describes that ancient Egyptians have been depicted stereotypically by popular culture and ancient portraiture alike and summarized this assertion in the last paragraph.

704. **A. that the common perception of the way ancient Egyptians look is based more on cultural interpretations than historical accuracy.**

Choice (A) is the best option. Your clue lies in the first sentence of paragraph three, where the author says that the pictures of ancient Egyptian weren't intended to be accurate. Choice (B) may be true, but it's not the reason that the author mentioned the different ways that Nubians and Syrians were painted. He wanted to show that depictions of Nubians and Syrians were stereotypical to distinguish foreigners. Though the author's description would indeed help you differentiate between Nubians and Syrians in ancient art if you ever found yourself needing that information, the purpose of the description wasn't to help you improve your college art history grade. Eliminate Choice (D) because the author indicates that braided hair applies to a general representations of Nubian descent. He doesn't comment on social status.

705. A. the depiction of Egyptians remained generally the same regardless of the varying cultural differences of the newcomers.

Based on information in the last paragraph, you can quickly eliminate Choice (D). The author implies that even observing skeletal remains hasn't shed any light on what ancient Egyptians actually look like. Therefore, Egyptian depictions haven't become more accurate. Choice (C) requires you to read information into the passage that isn't there. The author says that Hollywood's depiction of Egyptians isn't accurate, so it certainly hasn't captured the characteristics of the new people who populated Egypt.

Choice (B) may have been harder for you to eliminate. In the third paragraph, the author says that ancient Egyptians portrayed Nubians and Syrians differently to distinguish foreigners. His point in the last paragraph, however, is that all Egyptians, regardless of where they came from, were depicted similarly. The different depictions of the Nubians and Syrians talks about in the previous paragraph must have been for one of those specific reasons to make an explicit difference that the author mentions in lines 83–84. Choice (B) is definitely not a better answer than Choice (A). Choice (A) summarizes that author's point in the last paragraph that the different backgrounds of newcomers didn't change the stereotypical depictions of the Egyptians.

706. B. Continental plates

A close read of the content reveals the answer to this question. Though all four answers are discussed in the passage, the information on terranes is found in the second paragraph, where the author says, "The continental plates involved in these collisions were North America, Siberia, Baltica/Europe, and Africa and are also called *terranes.*" The answer is Choice (B).

707. D. scholarly.

The author takes a pretty straightforward approach. His clear intent is to give the reader information about geologic formation in a particular area in Europe. The tone isn't negative, so Choice (A) isn't warranted. The author isn't emotional enough to justify Choice (B). Nor is he presenting an opinion that he'd like to convince the reader to adopt. Therefore, Choices (B) and (C) are suspect. The best answer is Choice (D). *Scholarly* refers to a presentation of information based on formal study or research, which fits the tone of this passage well.

708. **A. mountain chains in Neo-Europe.**

Because most mountains could arguably be described as "arc-shaped" and "winding," you must read the passage carefully. It may help to search the passage for the answers because they contain capitalized words that may be easier to spot than then terms in the question. The answer appears at the end of the passage in the author's description of the Neo-Europe mountain chains. The answer is Choice (A).

709. **C. collisions between continental blocks.**

Both Choices (C) and (D) are mentioned in the passages. In the first paragraph, the author attributes the origins of almost all of Europe's mountains to the movement of plates, which he further explains as the collision of continental blocks. Sediments are explained later in the passage in the description of the Russian Platform as part of just the later phase of mountain-building. Therefore, Choice (C) is a better representation of the formation of nearly all mountain chains.

The passage doesn't mention icebergs or volcanic activity, so you can easily eliminate Choices (A) and (B).

710. **D. 3 billion**

Often questions with numbers for answers are the easiest to answer because numbers are easy to spot as you skim through the passage. The author devotes the entire fourth paragraph to the Baltic Shield, so that's a good place to start your search. Sure enough, the author there dates the Baltic Shield at being somewhere between 3 billion and 3.5 billion years old. The answer is Choice (D). If you picked Choice (A), you read the answers too quickly and didn't distinguish between *million* and *billion*.

711. **A. the number of continental collisions that occurred during the geological evolution of Europe.**

In the fourth paragraph, the passage places the White Sea north of Kola, so Choice (C) is out. The same paragraph describes shape of the Baltic Shield, which is classified as Eo-Europe. Therefore, it establishes Choice (D).

The sixth paragraph describes the plate movements that later fragmented an Early Palaeozoic chain as "the North Sea from the Permian onwards and the opening up of the North Atlantic starting in the Jurassic." So Choice (B) is established.

That leaves Choice (A). The passage states in the second paragraph that a number of collisions occurred, but it doesn't establish what that number is.

712. D. did not experience further major plate movements.

Eliminate Choice (B). The Russian Platform is in Eo-Europe, and the passage states it contains evidence of previously eroded mountain chains. Choice (C) is true of Paleo-Europe rather than Eo-Europe, so it's wrong.

Between Choices (A) and (D), Choice (D) is more justifiable. The passage states that the Eo-European structure is large, but that doesn't mean it is the largest in the region. The third paragraph states that the Eo-European welded block "experienced no further orogenies after the Precambrian." Orogenies are collisions between continental plates. So the passage makes the case that Eo-Europe didn't experience a plate collision after the initial impact that created it.

713. B. The eras when the continents that formed these subdivisions' geological structures welded together

The second paragraph of the passages says that the designations of Eo-, Palaeo, Meso-, and Neo- are "based on the relative ages of these orogenies." *Orogenies* refers to the collision of continents, and *era* refers to age. The only answer that mentions age of orogenies is Choice (B).

714. C. on the earth's surface.

Because the italicized word contains the prefix *sub*, which means *under*, you may be tempted to pick Choice (B) or (D). Choice (A) may sound good because *aerial* could relate to the atmosphere. But read the word in context. Note that the Russian Platform became subaerial after the sea retreated, which implies that it was then visible on the earth's surface, Choice (C).

715. D. it is part of Neo-Europe.

Choice (A) is directly expressed at the beginning of the fifth paragraph, and Choices (B) and (C) are mentioned later in that same paragraph. Although the fifth paragraph says that the Russian Platform is composed of Neoproterozoic sediments, the third paragraph clearly states that the Russian Platform is distinguished in Eo-Europe. Choice (D) is the exception.

716. B. Mr. Casaubon justified his actions to himself in a way that didn't make him seem jealous or vindictive.

The first sentence of the passage actually implies that Mr. Casaubon himself was jealous and vindictive, even though he tried out of a sense of honor to find "other reasons for his conduct than those of jealousy and vindictiveness." You can eliminate Choice (A). The passage doesn't associate jealousy and vindictiveness with Dorothea, so Choice (D) can't be right. Of the two remaining answers, Choice (B) is the better. The sentence doesn't say that others pointed out Casaubon's jealousy and vindictiveness. It suggests that Casaubon tried to justify his jealousy and vindictiveness by covering them up.

717. **B. leave her vulnerable to fortune-hunters.**

In reference to Dorothea, lines 11–13 say that "occasions might arise in which such possession might expose her to the more danger." The next few sentences talk about how men might prey upon her, allowing you to deduce that having money would turn Dorothea into a target for fortune-hunting men. Choice (B) is correct.

Choice (A) is way out of the ballpark. Nothing in the passage talks about Casaubon's having had a previous marriage or children. The paragraph provides Casaubon's explanation of why doesn't think it's a good idea to leave Dorothea his money. Therefore, you can eliminate Choices (C) and (D) based on their first words. He doesn't think leaving her his money is right or fair. Instead Casaubon argues to himself that his responsibility, in fact, is to keep his fortune from Dorothea in order to keep her safe. (Whether Dorothea would appreciate this kind of protection is another matter.)

718. **A. He has never directly expressed any animosity toward Mr. Casaubon.**

The phrase ". . . an animosity which he has constantly vented in ridicule, of which I am as well-assured as if I had heard it. . . ." in lines 19–21 is as amusing as something from a piece of 19th-century literature can be. If you read the words carefully, you see that Casaubon has, in fact, not heard the man express any animosity at all. The sentence implies that this so-called animosity is all in Casaubon's head. The answer that expresses this irony is Choice (A).

Choice (B) doesn't make sense because Casaubon is uneasy about what the man is capable of doing but not about any wrongs Casaubon thinks he may have done the man.

Read the question carefully. It asks for what you can infer about the mysterious man's animosity, not the man himself. Therefore, even if you could support Choice (C) or (D) with information in the passage (and you can't), they still couldn't be right because they're assumptions you'd make about the man rather than his animosity. Double-check the answer you've chosen by rereading the question to make sure your answer actually relates to question.

719. B. has convinced himself that frustrating the other man is his responsibility.

Phrases such as "such a marriage would be fatal to Dorothea" and "it is my duty to hinder to the utmost the fulfillment of his designs," Mr. Casaubon makes it clear that he believes — or at least wants to believe — that the responsibility to foil the other man's intentions to protect Dorothea is his. Choice (B) is the clear answer.

Choices (A), (C), and (D) presuppose that the man is an actual person and not a figment of Casaubon's active imagination conjured up to help him justify leaving Dorothea out of his will. The passage isn't clear about whether the man Casaubon's ranting about actually exists. So you can eliminate answer choices that require the man to be real for them to be true.

720. C. Mr. Casaubon is under the impression that he may die soon.

Eliminate answers that the passage doesn't justify. There's nothing in the lines that links Lydgate to the mysterious man in the second paragraph. Choice (A) is unwarranted. Choice (D) requires you to make assumptions that go way beyond the information in the passage. Casaubon doesn't appear to fear Dorothea anywhere in the passage. You're left to ponder Choices (B) and (C).

The lines mention illness and Casaubon's arrangements, but they don't suggest that thinking about the arrangements has caused Casaubon to feel ill. You can't make a case for Choice (B), so Choice (C) must be the right answer.

At first, you may think that Choice (C) goes beyond the scope of the passage, but when you examine the passage more deeply, you see that Choice (C) is the best answer. The fact that Casaubon is trying to justify that he has made arrangements to not leave his wife his money at his death means that he's thinking about his will. The entire second paragraph concerns his worry over what will happen when he dies. You may think he's just overly concerned with death, but lines 50–52 suggest that he has reason to be concerned. It appears that Casaubon has called Lydgate, who the passage suggests is a doctor, to get his opinion on the calculation of the "probabilities of his own life" based on the nature of Casaubon's illness. It seems that Casaubon is ill and he's called on Lydgate to find out how long he has to live.

721. C. appeared older than other men his age.

Lydgate utters the statement after he observes Casaubon's "signs of premature age." He thinks that Casaubon looks older than his age and older than some men of his age. The best answer is Choice (C). You'd have to read too much into the statement to choose any of the other answers.

722. B. discomfort

Lydgate was "conscious of an energetic frame in its prime," meaning that he knew what an energetic frame in its prime was, probably from personal experience because he seems to easily overtake Casaubon. Lydgate contrasted his vitality with the weakness of the man coming toward him. The passage says that Lydgate felt compassion, and you get the sense that he's aware of the unfairness of the situation and is most likely uncomfortable about it. The best answer is Choice (B).

Choice (C) is the trap answer. Yes, Lydgate felt pity, but pity for Mr. Casaubon, not for himself. And if you picked Choice (D), you went for the big, hard word on the principle of "if I don't know it, it must be the right answer" (everyone has those feelings of insecurity; you're not alone). Usually, the most difficult word is merely a trap answer. Unless you can absolutely, positively eliminate the rest of the answers, don't choose a word you can't define. By the way, *ebullience* means "enthusiasm."

723. B. contrast the beauty of the surroundings with the unattractiveness and frailty of Mr. Casaubon.

The paragraph primarily describes how weak Mr. Casaubon is, contrasting that condition with both Lydgate's vitality and the beauty of the surroundings. Choice (B) is the best answer.

Choice (C) is the trap answer. The paragraph talks about a *dirge*, which is a hymn sung at a funeral. If you knew that, you may have thought the purpose of this description was to predict a death. However, that may be going too far. If you have a choice between a moderate answer, such as contrasting *fit* versus *unfit*, and a dramatic answer — predicting death! — go for the more moderate of the two.

724. D. offered to end an awkward silence.

Eliminate Choice (C) immediately. Very rarely is an overly negative answer correct on the ACT. In this case, Lydgate is filled with compassion at seeing Mr. Casaubon and would be unlikely to be malicious. Choices (A) and (B) are possibilities, but Choice (D) is better because it's more directly related to the author's statement that Lydgate was "filling up a pause." You fill up a pause by saying something when the silence becomes awkward.

The best answer to a Reading Test question is the one that is best justified by the passage. To make sure your answer hits the mark, use your finger to point to place in the passage that supports it.

725. A. change from contempt toward the man at the beginning of the passage to pity for him at the end.

The first half of the passage portrays Mr. Casaubon negatively, discussing how petty, jealous, and vindictive he is. The last half of the passage elicits a feeling of compassion for a prematurely old man. So the reader goes from thinking negatively about him to feeling a little sorry for him, Choice (A).

Choice (B) is exactly wrong. You probably became more tolerant of Mr. Casaubon when you learned about his problems. Choice (C) is unlikely. Although Lydgate shows up toward the end of the passage, the end still focuses on Mr. Casaubon. Choice (D) goes too far. The reader may feel sorry for Mr. Casaubon but is even less likely than before to understand why Dorothea married him (the man is not only nasty but also unattractive and prematurely old).

726. A. describe how surveys of culture differ from another fundamental type of sociological methodology.

The main idea frequently appears in the last paragraph. The last paragraph summarizes the fundamental differences between surveys of culture and surveys of population, so examining the differences must be the main idea. The first paragraph tells you that surveying populations has been a fundamental methodology in sociology. Combine the ideas in the first and final paragraphs to come up with Choice (A).

Choice (C) starts off okay, but the second part of the answer isn't right. The author isn't trying to prove that surveys of culture are better than surveys of population. His point is that they're better for finding out ethnographic information than surveys of population are.

The correct answer to a main theme question takes into consideration the passage as a whole. You can eliminate answers that only deal with a specific element of the passage. For example, the passage tells you why surveys of culture rely on fewer respondents than other surveys, but that's not the passage's only focus. Therefore, you can eliminate Choices (B) and (D) because they're too specific to be main ideas.

727. B. As few as six individuals can provide enough information to indicate shared norms within a given society.

The passage discusses the findings of Romney, et al., in the second paragraph. The main gist of that paragraph is that you only need to survey a sampling of people to get information about cultural beliefs. Don't let that word *normative* throw you. As the passage indicates in lines 17–18, it just means "shared by everyone," so normative features are features that most people in the culture share.

The last line of the second paragraph says, "Romney, Weller, and Batchelder's mathematical-statistical analysis of ethnographic data gathering demonstrated that as few as a half-dozen expert respondents can provide a clear picture of some types of shared norms." This is just a fancy way of saying that you can get information about shared cultural beliefs from surveys just a few people. So the author references Romney and friends to solidify the main point of the paragraph. Choice (B) summarizes the point nicely.

Choice (A) suggests that you need to survey more people to get good information, so it's wrong. The author mentions Choice (C) in his discussion of the best respondents for culture surveys but not in the context of Romney, Weller, and Batchelder's contribution. Choice (D) relates to information in the third paragraph, so it's not right.

728. **D. not particularly relevant.**

The best definition for *tangential* in this context is "not particularly relevant," Choice (D). You know this because of the way the author transitions from the first sentence of the paragraph to the sentence that contains the word. The first sentence mentions that occasionally some complain that surveys of culture use too few respondents. The next sentence begins with a contrasting word *however*. That tells you that the author intends to dispute the complaint. The author counters the complaint by saying that the criticism is tangential for ethnographic (or cultural) data gathering. The passage's point is that cultural surveys don't need a bunch of respondents. You can reasonably infer that the author thinks that the point of the complaint or criticism is irrelevant.

Choice (A) has the opposite meaning, so you can eliminate it. There's nothing in the passage to suggest that the author thinks the criticism is old-fashioned, so Choice (B) is out. If you're not sure about Choice (C), plug *inconclusive* in the sentence in place of *tangential*. You'll see that it makes no sense in the context. The sentence would then say that the criticism is "inconclusive for ethnographic data gathering."

729. **C. Cultural survey respondents are selected from areas where the culture is being regenerated, whereas population survey respondents are chosen from within a political unit.**

Skim the first sentences of each paragraph to find that the question pertains to information in paragraph 6. Once there, eliminate answers that aren't differences. Choice (A) is wrong because respondents to surveys of culture, not populations, are graded on expertise. Choice (B) may tempt you. It's true that surveys of culture rely on a much smaller numbers of respondents, but the author doesn't specifically say that culturally surveys require only 5 respondents. Eliminate Choice (B) because it's too specific. Like Choice (A), Choice (D) mixes up the two surveys. The passage says that cultural surveys seek similarity and population surveys seek diversity. Choice (C) paraphrases the information in the third fundamental difference listed in paragraph 6, which makes it the best answer.

730. A. To define the quintessential elements of a particular culture

Skim the passage for the word *ethnography.* In the middle of paragraph 4, the author notes, "The aim in ethnography is not to describe a population of individuals but, instead, to describe a culture that is being reproduced within the same group." In the next sentence, he says that surveyors get that information by choosing respondents whose answers are quintessential for their culture. If cultural (or ethnographic) surveyors seek quintessential responses, the goal of the survey must be to define the quintessential elements or a particular culture. The best answer is Choice (A).

Choice (B) is clearly wrong. The author says that ethnography isn't designed to describe a population of individuals. Evaluating Choice (C) is a little trickier. It's true that ethnography requires fewer responses, but getting the fewest number of responses possible isn't its *goal.* Just because an answer choice presents a truth doesn't mean it answers the question.

The first part of Choice (D) sounds like a goal of ethnography, but the answer goes on to apply that to people within in geographical boundaries. Population surveys seek responses from a geographical group. Cultural (or ethnographic) surveys seek responses from people within a particular culture.

731. D. Surveys of culture sometimes rely on information gathered from too small of a respondent group, and respondents are not always selected randomly from general populations.

The reference indicates that some criticize surveys of culture because they rely on responses from just a few respondents. The best answer is Choice (D). Choice (B) is a characteristic of surveys of culture, but it's not the characteristic that's been criticized. Choice (A) is a characteristic of surveys of population.

Choice (C) starts off fine, but the second part of the answer mentions a characteristic of population surveys rather than surveys of culture. Be sure to read the entire answer choice before you select it.

732. C. The more homogenous the beliefs of the respondents, the smaller the number of respondents necessary to obtain an accurate view of the culture.

The answer appears in paragraph 4, where the author states, ". . . the more normative the respondents' beliefs and sentiments, the fewer of them are needed to obtain an accurate view of the culture." Choice (C) paraphrases this idea using *homogenous* instead of *normative.* As long as you know that the two terms are synonyms, answering this question is easy.

If you picked Choice (B), you thought that because it's true that normative beliefs require fewer responses, dissenting beliefs require more responses. You can't make that leap of logic without more support from the information in the passage, especially when the perfectly wonderful response in Choice (C) is available.

733. **C. Sampling a population within political boundaries**

How nice! The question directs you to the exact place in the passage where you're likely to find the answer. Choice (C) is the best answer because it's a paraphrase of "sampling individuals in a political unit," which is the inefficiency the author mentions. Choices (A), (B), and (D) refer to desirable components of surveys of culture, so you can eliminate them.

734. **D. provide support for the theory that the best respondents for cultural surveys are those from the behavior settings that reproduce the culture.**

The author provides two examples that support his idea that "best respondents for a culture survey are person who reproduce the culture." The first example is of the researcher who studies middle-class culture. The second is of the researcher who studies black community life. Therefore, the black community life example is there to show that the best respondents are those who live in the settings that reproduce the culture, Choice (D).

735. **A. deciding factor**

The context of the sentence tells you that "proficiency in the target culture" is an important factor in choosing survey of culture respondents. You know that because *whereas* shows a contrasting idea, and respondent "goodness" (or proficiency) isn't important for population surveys. When you plug in the answer choices, you find that Choices (B) and (D) send an opposite message. Choice (C) conveys a similar meaning to the original thought, but *reason* doesn't fit with "in choosing." The answer that best replaces *desideratum* to show the importance of proficiency in the target culture is Choice (A).

736. **C. they all have bases in truth.**

You can knock Choices (A) and (D) out of contention pretty easily; the authors make both statements in the second sentence of the first paragraph. The authors also note that myths were "more than mere stories" in the second paragraph, so eliminate Choice (B). By process of elimination the answer is Choice (C).

737. A. Greek myths are a major component of global culture and therefore easily recognizable.

Because the authors don't explicitly state what they mean by the statement, you must infer the meaning based on the passage. The authors don't discuss characters' names in much detail, so you can likely eliminate Choice (C). Eliminate Choice (B) for a similar reason; the passage doesn't even mention Roman mythology. The passage specifically states that definitions, guidance, or codes of practice aren't necessary, so you've got to get rid of Choice (D). That leaves Choice (A). The authors lead up to their statement with a discussion of the history behind distinguishing myth and declare in the second paragraph that myth is a product of the modern history of ideas from the end of the Enlightenment onward and an objective product of ancient Greece. The best justified answer is Choice (A).

738. B. a writer of tragedies.

Both Choices (B) and (D) are proper definitions of the term *tragedian*, but only Choice (B) makes sense given the context. The authors use the term to describe Homer, who they say acts as a tragedian in his role as a creator of epics. A creator of epics in more related to a writer than an actor. Choice (C) may seem enticing because this section of the passage does discuss Homer's extensive knowledge of myths. However, because it goes on to say that Homer "bent the mythology he had inherited to develop his own economical but panoramic epics," the term must be specific to creating tragedies, Choice (B).

739. B. An epithet

Toward the end of the Passage B's second paragraph, when discussing how to determine the origins of the *Odyssey*, Roisman notes usefulness of examining the "many repetitive descriptive words or phrases," and then adds "epithets" in parenthesis. It can't be spelled out much more clearly than that, so you can safely eliminate all remaining answers and confidently select Choice (B).

740. D. the definitive site of the Troy of the Trojan War.

Find what you need to answer this question in the third paragraph of Passage B, where the author discusses the discovery of the site of Troy. You might note that the question uses the term "exposed," while the passage says ". . . revealed the existence of." The author goes on to clearly note the discoveries of the nine cities and the variety of subsettlements, so you can eliminate Choices (A) and (B). Later in the paragraph, the author states that some interpret findings at the sites to be indications of much larger sites and human destruction (which could be evidence of the Trojan War), so Choice (C) is likely out. Check Choice (D) to be sure. The passage indicates that identifying which site is Troy has been the "bone of scholarly contention," which means there's debate over the definitive site. So you know the answer that wasn't exposed must be Choice (D).

741. **D. disagreement exists on whether the *Illiad* and the *Odyssey* originated in oral traditions.**

Begin your search for this answer in the passage where the author begins discussing why so many scholars are intrigued by Homer. The author explains that the controversy involves several different questions in the first paragraph, among them both Choices (B) and (C), so you can eliminate them. In the next paragraph, the author suggests that though many scholars are positive Homer was an actual figure, some doubts may remain. Check Choice (D). The passage clearly states that the works themselves reveal their oral origins, so that issue isn't part of the controversy, and Choice (D) is the exception.

742. **C. The use of hexameter**

Though there is little question that Homer relied on myths in crafting his famous works, this is not something the author notes as a reason modern scholars believed he wrote the *Iliad* and the *Odyssey.* Go ahead and eliminate Choice (D). Apollodoro's Library isn't even mentioned in Passage B, so you know Choice (B) can't be right. Choice (A) refers to the controversy surrounding Homer's identity and works, so it wouldn't be something scholars would use to back up their beliefs that he did, in fact author, the *Iliad* and the *Odyssey.* Stick with Choice (C), which that passage says is the special rhythm in the works that aids in oral recitation.

743. **A. The *Iliad* and the *Odyssey* are the result of a recalcitrant manipulation of traditional Greek myths.**

The question regards a conclusion you can draw from combining the two passages. You can eliminate Choice (B) because information on the oral tradition is only available from Passage B. Choice (C) is a concept expressly stated in Passage A, so it's incorrect. Choice (D) is wrong because it provides a false statement. Passage B states that Homer's epic reflect realities that project more on Homer's era than on the era of the actual events.

The best answer is Choice (A). Passage A tells you that Homer created his epics by bending myth in a wayward manner, which is paraphrased as a recalcitrant manipulation. Passage B provides the information you need to know that Homer's epics included the *Iliad* and the *Odyssey.* Therefore, you need information from both passages to come up with the statement in Choice (A).

744. C. Troy

Both passages discuss Homer, the ancient Greeks and mythical times, but only the second passage mentions Troy. Thus, Choice (C) is correct.

745. B. he likely lived near the mound of Hissarlik in Asia Minor around 1200.

Choice (A) is noted in the final paragraph of Passage A, where the author discusses Homer's epics. Passage B provides information about the questions surrounding Homer's identity, so eliminate Choice (C). You learn that Choice (D) is true from the introductory sentence of Passage B. The only remaining option is Choice (B). Roisman mentions the mound of Hissarlik to provide more information about possible historical details on Troy but doesn't imply that Homer himself was associated with the location. In fact, Passage B indicates that much is unknown about the details of Homer's life.

746. A. explain why he considers Pluto to be the "picked-on planet" and how its relative size and distance to other planets in the solar system has been misrepresented.

Of the options provided, Choice (A) best describes the author's main points. You may discover this truth better by eliminating the other choices.

Although the passage has a tongue-in-cheek tone, it's not argumentative. Choices (B) and (C) imply that the author feels strongly one way or the other about whether Pluto retains its planet classification. Though the author refers to Pluto as "the picked-on planet," he doesn't offer much in terms of his personal feelings on the matter. The passage covers the information in Choice (D), but it's just one subtopic of a larger big picture that's better summarized by Choice (A).

747. C. Various scale models throughout the nation failed to include Pluto in their models of the solar system.

The author mentions Choices (A), (B), and (D) in the first several paragraphs of the passage. You're looking for the answer he doesn't mention, so you can eliminate all three. The author does describe solar system models around the country and world, but he makes no mention of Choice (C), the failure to include Pluto. On the contrary, when discussing Stockholm's depiction of the solar system, he not only mentions Pluto's inclusion but also describes it in some detail. Choice (C) is the answer the author doesn't state.

748. A. offer a clearer sense of scale than the standard schoolroom poster depiction does.

The most obvious clue that Choice (A) is the best answer lies in the first sentence of the fourth paragraph, which discusses various scale models around the world. The author begins his discussion by saying that he's providing "a better sense of scale."

You can eliminate Choice (B) because, though one city might have made a larger replica of the solar system than another, all were done to scale. Choice (C) is wrong. The author talks about the International Economic Union several paragraphs later in the passage and doesn't link the organization to large-scale solar system models. The models in the various cities include Pluto, so Choice (D) doesn't make sense

749. D. standing.

This question's easy when you substitute the answers for *repute* in the sentence. *Repute* is the base of the word *reputation*. Because Chief is employed at a well-known university, his astronomical endeavors must carry some clout. Therefore, he's likely an astronomer of some *standing*, Choice (D). Choices (A) and (C) don't convey any meaning. That Chief is an astronomer of some *degree* or some *opinion* tells you nothing about his reputation. Choice (B) is completely wrong. *Ignominy* means "shame or dishonor."

750. A. names that were used to identify a Pluto-like world that has been discovered in recent years along the solar system's rim.

At the end of paragraph 9, the author talks about worlds that have been found on the solar system's rim. One in particular was bigger than Pluto, and this was known at different times as Xena and Eris. The answer is Choice (A).

If you picked Choice (C), you skimmed over the word *planets* in the answer choice. The answer refers to Eris as a world, and the two names refer to just one body.

751. B. Its asteroid belt is likely more famous than its sun.

The passage says that Boston's model sun measures 11 feet, the model in Washington D.C. has a 5-inch sun, and the sun in the Mount Vernon Tourist Society's model measures 5 feet. Because all the models are to scale, the relative size of their suns designate the relative size of the models. Therefore, the Tourist Society's model is larger than the one along the National Mall and smaller than the one in Boston. Cross out Choices (A) and (C).

The Tourist Society's Pluto is as small as a piece of gravel, but the passage doesn't say it's made up of a piece of gravel. Choice (D) is out. So Choice (B) must be the answer. The asteroid belt is designated by a sign that has been photographed in a "fair number of pictures" and placed on the Internet. Because the photographers don't know that the sign is part of the solar system model, it's unlikely that as many pictures of the solar system and its sun have made it to the World Wide Web.

752. **D. demonstrate the massive nature of the solar system.**

Paragraph 2 says that Chief and others erected the plaques to show "how big and empty the solar system is." The best paraphrase is Choice (D).

Choice (A) suggests that the other full-scale models were erected before Chief's, and the passage doesn't specify when the models were built. Because Chief built his model to clarify the misconceptions perpetrated by the standard side-by-side solar system model, Choice (B) can't be right. You can cross out Choice (C) because the author says that Chief's model was erected "just for fun." That tells you that the Tourist Society's main goal was not as serious as promoting celestial theories.

753. **B. Ceres and Xena**

In the second to last of the passage's main paragraphs, the author talks about the committee that settled the question of what bodies should be added to the list of planets. He mentions that Eris, Charon (Pluto's largest moon), and Ceres as bodies that were up for consideration. The preceding paragraph tells you that Eris was also named Xena. Therefore, the correct answer is Choice (B), Ceres and Xena.

754. **D. present a necessary transition to the subsequent paragraph by showing how the locations of the planets are normally represented.**

Choice (A) is unlikely. Without the fourth paragraph, the fifth paragraph wouldn't make sense. The fourth paragraph shows how school posters misrepresent the scale of the solar system so that you understand why there's a need for a "better sense of scale." Choice (B) is wrong. Pluto put-downs crop up later in the passage. The fourth paragraph provides an illustration of Pluto's "pea" size, but the main idea of the paragraph is to show that schoolroom posters don't give an accurate representation of the distance between the planets. Therefore, Choice (C) isn't quite right. Choice (D) mentions the transition function of paragraph 4 and its focus on the distance between planets, which make it the best answer.

755. A. as scientific study of the solar system continues, the official planet count is subject to change.

The passage suggests that new astronomical discoveries will continue to appear. Because previous discoveries resulted in changes to the planet count, it's likely that change could occur. Choice (A) is the best option because it leaves room for future changes to be made to the planetary count, something discussed in detail throughout the passage. Choice (D) can't be right because it's too specific. The author gives no specific indication of when or even whether Pluto will be classified as a planet again. Choice (C) is out of contention because the committee's proposal to add Charon to the planetary count was "hooted down" by the IAU. You know that Charon is Pluto's largest moon, but you don't know its size in relation to Pluto. Just because it was up for planetary consideration doesn't mean that it's larger than Pluto. Cross out Choice (B).

756. C. came bearing urgent news that couldn't wait until dawn.

There is nothing in the passages that lets you know who wrote the letter or what's in it. You can cross out Choices (A) and (B). The groom acknowledges the narrator and gives him the letter, which suggests that he was indeed at the correct home. Choice (D) can't be right. The visitor rang the bell and knocked incessantly, so the matter must have been urgent. That the visitor arrived in the middle of the night implies that the matter couldn't wait until the morning. The best answer is Choice (C).

757. B. Loud knocks at his door.

The narrator wavers between a dreamlike state and one of consciousness, and all of his references to the disruptions in Eden are sounds. Thoughts and letter contents aren't sounds, so Choices (A) and (C) are probably wrong. The sound that's awakening the narrator may sound like boat paddles, but there's nothing in the passage to tell you that he hears actual paddles from an actual boat on an actual sea. The most logical cause for the interruption is the knocks on the door that sound like boat paddles, which is confirmed by the narrator's reference in the next paragraph to "somebody knocking and ringing at someone's street door." Choice (B) is the most sensible answer.

758. C. The narrator was well known to the policeman who stood outside his door.

Approach this question by eliminating the answer choices that you can support with information in the passage. You know the gentleman's visit was urgent, so you can cross out Choice (A). Because the author repeatedly uses the word *again* to describe the scene in the second paragraph, you can reasonably assume that narrator has pictured the scene before.

Eliminate Choice (B). The narrator says he was "pretty well accustomed" to the sounds outside his room on Jermyn Street, which means he'd probably lived there awhile. Choice (D) is out. By process of elimination, Choice (C) is the best answer. There's nothing in the passage that implies that the narrator and the policemen knew each other.

759. C. It offers a glimpse into the semiconscious mind of the narrator as he wavers somewhere between the dream described in the beginning of the passage and the real life occurrence toward the end.

The question asks you for the primary purpose of the third paragraph. Eliminate choices that are incorrect or too specific. Although the narrator mentions Eden in the paragraph, he doesn't describe what paradise is like for him. Cross out Choice (A). The narrator laments that there is no perfect rest, but there's nothing in the passage to suggest that this means he is characteristically pessimistic. Choice (B) probably isn't right. Paragraph 4, not paragraph 3, relates the point where the narrator wakes up. So Choice (D) is out. The paragraph describes the process of the narrator's consciousness as he is awakened. Choice (C) is the best answer.

760. A. should not ignore the late-night knocking in the same manner as he usually ignored noises at night in the neighborhood.

You can cross out Choice (D). The first line of the last paragraph indicates that the narrator didn't know who was knocking until he opened the door to find the groom. Choice (C) is also wrong. *Intelligence* in the quote refers to the information the knocker had rather than the level of his intelligence. That leaves you with Choices (B) and (A). Choice (B) is too strong. Though the narrator detects that the knocking indicates important news, he doesn't say that he's worried that the news is ominous or warning of evil. The quotation suggests that there was something different about the knocking that required the narrator to pay attention to it instead of ignoring it as he usually ignored the neighbor's noises. Choice (A) is the best answer.

761. D. The boat ride provided the narrator and the young girl with a temporary escape from their problems.

Call on your trusty friend POE (process of elimination) to answer this one. The lines refer to the July sunlight, so the scene didn't occur in the spring. Cross out Choice (A). The narrator says that the girl sat still, so it's unlikely that she was steering the boat. Eliminate Choice (B). You're down to Choices (C) and (D). The passage doesn't reveal anything about whether the dream describes the couple's first meeting, so you can't say whether Choice (C) is true. Check out Choice (D) to see whether it's a better answer. The author says that the scene provided them with the ability to forget the "great world with its disturbing trouble." Choice (D) is definitely true, so it's a better answer than Choice (C).

762. **A. Dangers exist even in Eden.**

Choices (B) and (C) contain the debatable word *only*. It's a pretty good bet, therefore, that neither of them is correct. In fact, the author says that no place offers perfect rest, including Eden. Cross out Choices (B) and (C). There's no indication that the author thinks he'll see the young girl in Eden. Choice (D) has to be wrong. The best answer is Choice (A). The narrator implies that Eden contains dangers when he states that "even in Eden the snake rears its head."

763. **B. was a method of transportation.**

The same sentence that mentions brougham also describes the condition of the horses. It's reasonable to conclude that the brougham has something to do with the horses who had been running quickly and therefore something to do with the way the visitor got to the narrator's house. Choice (B) is the most logical answer.

If you picked Choice (A), (C), or (D), you read too much into the passage. Make sure you can point to the place in the passage that justifies your answer before you mark it on your answer sheet.

764. **D. numerous.**

The author uses myriad in the same sentence that describes how the environment helped him and the young girl escape the troubles of the world. It's unlikely that loud or unpleasant noises would produce this calming effect. Eliminate Choices (A) and (C). The noises came from nature, so they wouldn't be artificial. Cross out Choice (B). If the noises come from "both without and within" the area, there must be a lot of them. Choice (D) makes the most sense.

765. **B. was discontented with her home life.**

The passage doesn't indicate that the narrator had romantic feelings toward the young girl. You can't assume he loved her based on their boat ride or their conversation about her lonely life. Choice (A) is wrong. He describes the loveliness of the environment but doesn't describe the features of the girl. You can't infer Choice (D). Choice (D) indicates the narrator's romantic feelings toward the young girl, which is never stated or implied in the selection. Choice (C) is unlikely. The author states at lines 40–41 that it's in dreams that "existences merge and renew themselves." This statement suggests that the incidences in his dream truly did exist and that the dream brings their memory back to him. That leaves you with Choice (B). The author says girl was lonely in her new life and that she spoke with an "undertone of sadness." These references indicate that she wasn't contented. Choice (B) is the best answer of the four.

Reading questions ask you for the best answer. Choose the one that's the most reasonable of all of the options. Sometimes that means the best answer isn't one you'd create if you were writing the questions.

766. **B. When the creative potential of the human brain is maximized, there is essentially no limit to the types of innovative and evolutionary developments we can expect to see as time progresses.**

Main theme questions deal with the whole passage. Cross out answers that address only one aspect of the author's message. Choice (C) deals with just the information and technology explosion, which was discussed in only one paragraph. Choice (A) focuses only on the author's comparison of humans to other species. Eliminate Choices (A) and (C). Choice (D) contradicts the author's positive enthusiasm, so it can't be right. The best answer is Choice (B). It summarizes the author's position and duplicates her use of first person (we) to make her points.

A good rule of thumb in trying to determine a passage's main theme is to check out the final paragraph. Often authors (like this one) summarize or restate their main points there.

767. **A. highlight the advancements the human brain has been able to make in just a small fraction of time.**

Cross out Choice (B) because it suggests that the human being and the turtle share something that other species don't. The passage says that turtles are different from humans, not similar. Choice (D) implies that the turtle has made has made lifestyle improvements that can be compared to the improvement humans have made, but the passage directly states that the turtle "has yet to make an innovative lifestyle improvement."

Choice (C) may entice you, but watch out for the debatable word *only*. Plus, the purpose of the turtle example isn't to prove that no other animal in the world can create. The passage is about the human brain. The author compares the multitude of human discoveries to the lack of turtle-based discoveries to show that the human brain is capable of producing great change in a relatively short period of time. The best answer is Choice (A).

768. **D. That human beings can learn to activate different parts of the brain through conscious effort and practice**

The author discusses neuroscience research in the seventh paragraph. Choice (D) nicely paraphrases the information in that paragraph and is the right answer.

Choices (A) and (B) are developments that the human brain has accomplished but not because of neuroscience research. The author says the opposite of Choice (C) in paragraph seven, so it can't be right.

769. A. creativity has many definitions.

Choice (B) contains a debatable word, *impossible*. It's unlikely that the author thinks that it's impossible to define creativity, especially because she provides a definition for creativity in the rest of the paragraph. Choice (D) contradicts the definition of *nebulous*, which means "cloudy or unclear."

Were you tempted by Choice (C) because it had some of the same language as the passage? The paragraph talks about the types of definitions philosophers and writers have come up with, but it doesn't say those definitions are unclear. Just because an answer contains some of the same words as the passage doesn't mean it's right.

The reason that a definition of creativity is nebulous is because it has many definitions. The passage says that philosophers and writers have suggested "a number" of them. The best answer is Choice (A).

770. D. Changes in the way people travel

The ninth paragraph talks about the effects of the information and technology explosion. The author mentions changes in business, personal relationships, parenting, and education, but she doesn't specifically cite different travel methods as a result of the explosion. The correct answer is Choice (D).

771. B. The invention of a new way to preserve foods that does not require refrigeration

The author's definition of creativity required originality and practicality. You already know how the author feels about the creativity of toddlers' scribbles. So, even if you think your two-year-old sister's crayon marks are genius, you have to eliminate Choice (A). Choice (C) is original but not useful. Why would you want to spend more time making toast? Choice (D) is practical because it provides aesthetic enjoyment, but if it's an exact replica, it's not new. The best answer is Choice (B). It's new and it provides a practical service to those who don't have access to refrigerators.

772. A. A person can assimilate old customs in a way that functions in future environments.

The author emphasizes that creativity makes one more adaptable to change. Choices (B), (C), and (D) contradict this adaptability and focus on ways that people may avoid change. The best answer is Choice (A). It paraphrases the idea stated in lines 65–67 that creativity allows people to adapt old traditions for the future.

773. B. provide real-life examples of just how limitless the capabilities of the creative brain are.

Eliminate answers that don't take into consideration all three paragraphs. Choice (A) summarizes the purpose of only paragraph two. Choices (C) and (D) summarize paragraphs three and four but not two. Choice (B) is the only option that appropriately summarizes all three paragraphs.

774. B. guided.

You can eliminate Choice (D) because it has a negative connotation and the rest of the sentence talks about the positive aspects of the brain. Likewise, cross out Choice (A) because it doesn't make sense that your brain would shield or protect you from amazing developments.

If you picked Choice (C), you probably tried to relate fields to shepherds. But *field* means to deal with or tackle, like when the press secretary fields difficult questions from the media. The best answer is Choice (B). Your brain guides you through amazing developments like shepherds direct their sheep.

775. D. The Einsteins and Mozarts of the world were able to maximize their intellectual potential because they were born with an inherent sense of creativity uncommon in the human race.

The author is most likely to disagree with Choice (D). In paragraph seven, the author directly refutes the assumption that the Mozarts and Einsteins of the world have an inherent sense of creativity uncommon in the human race. Instead, the author implies that such creativity may be honed by virtually anyone through practice and conscious effort. The author plainly states Choices (A), (B), and (C) in the passage, and they along with her main message.

776. B. Poetic subject matter does not have to be joyful for a poem to be enjoyable.

The prevailing sentiment throughout the passage is that reading material does not have to be happy in order to make the reader feel pleasure or enjoyment — or in other words, Choice (B). The author more or less disputes Choices (A) and (C) when discussing the fact that reflecting on the happy times of the past can actually make a reader feel dissatisfied with his or her current situation or status, so you can cross those out. Finally, pretty much the entire passage focuses on how reading makes a reader "feel," so Choice (D) is way off, too. Stick with Choice (B).

777. B. A cycle of popular poems by the bard Ossian

You can easily eliminate Choices (A) and (C). The second paragraph of passage A specifically includes the Coleridge and Scott poems in the list of works that contain images of medieval architecture.

Focus on the remaining two answers. In the same paragraph, Stafford states that the settings for Gothic narratives were ruined castles and abbeys. The first paragraph mentions that Ossian was despondent and refers to "Ossian gloom," but the passage doesn't specifically reference medieval architectural imagery in connect with Ossian. Therefore, Choice (B) is a clearer exception to the reliance on medieval architecture than Choice (D) is.

778. C. accept more gratefully their current circumstances.

In the passage's first paragraph, Stafford states, "While a bad memory might prompt gratitude for current well-being, thoughts of happier times now gone were likely to produce more melancholy reflections." Choice (A) is out; happy memories are the ones that produce melancholy.

Choice (B) suggests that bad memories reflect negatively on current situations, so it can't be right. Nowhere does the author discuss prior mistakes, so Choice (D) requires making unjustified assumptions. Choice (C) best paraphrases the author's statement about the effects of reflecting on bad memories.

779. D. Hume

In the first paragraph, Stafford attributes the described sentiment to "some Enlightenment thinkers" but not *all.* Eliminate Choice (B). In the same sentence, she specifically mentions David Hume as one of the Enlightenment thinkers, so Choice (D) is the clear answer.

Though you may be able to assume from the passage that Byron and Macpherson were Enlightenment thinkers, Stafford doesn't specifically include them in her reference to some Enlightenment thinkers.

780. D. epitomize

Consider the italicized word in context. The passage discusses hands and how they have come to serve as symbols for the ideas and concepts of modernist poetry. Substitute each answer for *emblematize* in the passage. Perhaps the automatic and weak hands could publicize the idea that the author has lost independence. Choice (A) may work in this context, but consider the other options.

Choice (B) is meant to attract you because *delegate* appears earlier in the paragraph. But the image of the hands isn't exactly handing over authority to the idea of lost independence. You may not know the meaning of *exacerbate,* but don't use that as a reason to choose it. The word means "to make a bad problem even worse," but the image of the hands doesn't actually worsen the loss of independence. Choice (C) isn't appropriate.

To *epitomize* is to represent. The hands could definitely represent the idea that that the author has lost independence — much more than they *publicize* or "make public" the idea. Between Choices (A) and (D), Choice (D) is closer to the original meaning.

781. B. produces a new prose style that he dotes upon.

Because the question regards what Eliot asserts, look first for direct quotes from Eliot. You find one in final paragraph of passage B. Eliot says that the "typewriter makes for lucidity," so get rid of Choice (A). Remember you're eliminating all answers but the exception.

Eliot's statement that he is "not sure that it encourages subtlety" suggests that the typewriter isn't subtle, so eliminate Choice (C). In that same quote, Eliot describes his sentences as "short staccato" on the typewriter as opposed to the long sentences he used to love. Therefore, the device certainly can be said to encourage brevity.

Although the quote suggests that the typewriter produces a new prose style for Eliot, it doesn't say he dotes upon this style. That reference was to the prior long sentences he crafted. Choice (B) is the least justified by the passage and therefore the correct answer.

782. A. an entity's ability to act and exist in a given environment.

You can likely eliminate Choice (D) because, although it's a suggested topic of the passage, it isn't a viable definition of agency. Choices (A), (B) and (C) provide definitions of agency, but you have to narrow the field to the one that makes the most sense given the context.

The passage has nothing to do with government, so you can also knock Choice (C) out of contention. To choose between Choices (A) and (B), consider the first line of Whitworth's second paragraph, where he describes agency: ". . . While in some cases the subject appears to have delegated its work to disembodied hands, in others the hands have escaped altogether." So agency has something to do with having control over a particular subject, which sound much more like Choice (A) than the organization referred to in Choice (B).

783. **C. detachment and loss of control over creativity.**

First, eliminate Choice (B). Its two adjectives relate to Stafford's passage on romantic poetry and are opposite rather than complementary. Choice (D) is also suspect. Whitworth uses a reference to Eliot's typing to provide an example of the second aspect, but handwriting and typing aren't the two main aspects of modernist poetry.

You must scan the entire passage to choose between Choices (A) and (C). Whitworth first mentions the two aspects in lines 67–68. He goes on to explain that the first aspect is impersonality, which he further describes as detachment. Both choices work regarding the first aspect.

In the second paragraph he describes the second aspect as a loss of agency, which he explains with references to the automatic and the achievement of something unintended. These references suggest a loss of control over the creative process but not a lack of creativity altogether. Eliot's lines indicate not that creativity ceases to exist but that some factor other than the complete mindfulness of the writer accomplishes this result. Therefore, Choice (C) provides a better description of the second aspect than does Choice (A).

784. **A. after the works of romantic poets.**

Eliminate Choices (B) and (C) immediately because Joyce and Eliot appear in the passage about modernist poetry. These two choices refer to the romantic period. Because they were modernist poets, they must have written in modernist period, so Choice (D) must be wrong.

Process of elimination tells you Choice (A) is correct. The passage justifies this answer by suggesting that the romantic period occurred some time around the late eighteenth century in lines 5 and 22 and that the modernist period occurred in the twentieth century in lines 86–87.

785. **B. Both describe the ways in which a certain classifications of writers executed their craft and suggest reasons for these manners of writing.**

Choices (A) and (C) are easy to eliminate; only passage B discusses the writer's hand and provides quotes — that is, direct statements — from a poet. Stafford and Whitworth describe the styles of the periods they analyze, but they don't suggest ways the style could be made better, so Choice (D) isn't a justifiable answer.

The only answer that applies to both passages is Choice (B). Both authors provide a description of the poetic styles of their respective periods. Stafford talks about how romantic period poets included particular imagery to "create an otherworldly atmosphere" and convey the sense that joy can arise from ruin. Whitworth describes the detachment inherent in modernist poetry and reveals a possible source in the sense of "loss of agency" common to many people of the time.

786. A. discussing the impacts of light energy and photosynthesis on warm-season and cool-season grasses.

As is typical for science passages, the authors are mainly concerned with putting out some information, not arguing a position, so you can eliminate Choice (B) based on its first word.

You know that the passage discusses light energy, photosynthesis, and turf grass. On closer inspection, you find that the authors are primarily concerned with educating people so that they know the difference between warm-season and cool-season turf grass and so that they understand the factors that damage grass. The only answer that encompasses all of these ideas is Choice (A). Choices (C) and (D) deal with specific parts of the passage rather than the passage as a whole. Plus, Choice (C) doesn't deal with light energy (and the passage doesn't mention anything about the research being recent), and Choice (D) neglects photosynthesis.

787. B. has a high rate of canopy photosynthesis.

The final paragraph states that "plants with greater leaf area also have higher rates of canopy photosynthesis." So a plant with "very large green leaves" has a higher rate of canopy photosynthesis. That's all there is to it. The answer is Choice (B).

Choices (A), (C), and (D) contradict the information implied in the last paragraph that larger leaves are likely to contain more chlorophyll and have increased rates of photosynthesis.

788. C. They are lower in the green and blue regions than the red.

The authors talk about incandescent lights in the sixth paragraph where they discuss the wavelengths of artificial lights. Choice (B) is wrong; the passage mentions a diurnal pattern only once in the passage, in relation to photosynthetic rates. Choice (A) contradicts the authors' statement that incandescent lights are poor in the blue region. Choice (D) gives a higher percentage of output in the infrared region that the passage provides (75 percent versus 50 percent). The best answer is Choice (C). If incandescent lights are "poor in the blue region, moderate in the green region, and high in the red," they're lower in green and blue than in the red.

789. D. Die back

Going with a definition of the word that you already knew probably wasn't a big issue in this question, because *senesce* isn't a word that normally graces everyday conversation. Read the sentence that contains the word and the ideas around it. The passage talks about senesce occurring in plants that are exposed to light below the light compensation point. This means that the grass isn't getting enough light to carry on the photosynthesis necessary to simply sustain the current height. This indicates that the definition of *senesce* is "to wither" or "to shrink." Go through the answer choices and find the one that best matches your definition.

Eliminate Choices (A) and (B) because the passage indicates that in senescence no growth occurs at all, fast or slow. Choice (C) doesn't have anything to do with shrinking or withering. Choice (D) is the best answer because it's the only one that conveys the idea of withering.

790. **B. Warm-season grasses can handle the higher light levels of summer, while cool-season grasses can grow during under the lower light conditions of winter.**

This specific information question asks you to identify an important difference between cool-season and warm-season grasses. The second paragraph discusses the two kinds of turf grasses. Warm-season grasses do better in the summer because they can withstand higher light intensities. Cool-season grasses don't die back as much in the winter because they can survive on a lower amount of light energy.

Eliminate Choice (C) because the passage says that all plants that photosynthesize do so during the day. Choice (D) is also incorrect because the third paragraph indicates that all green plants use the same light levels. That leaves you with Choices (A) and (B). Both address the important difference in light level tolerance between the two types of grasses, but Choice (A) states that cool-season grasses can withstand higher light intensities, and the opposite is true. Choice (B) is the answer that properly states the actual difference between the two grasses.

791. **D. Both overwatering and underwatering a lawn can inhibit photosynthesis and damage grass.**

The question asks you to make an inference regarding the discussion of oxidative damage. In the first paragraph, you read that oxidative damage occurs not simply because of high light intensity but also because more light energy arrives than photosynthesis can use. Anything that hinders photosynthesis can contribute to oxidative damage.

Choose an answer that you can logically deduce from the information in the passage without making wild assumptions. Choice (A) isn't the right answer because light intensity is greatest at noon, not at sunrise and sunset. And because overwatering can impede photosynthesis and damage grass, Choice (B) is out. Choice (C) is wrong because light intensity alone doesn't damage grass; temperature change, drought, and excessive water can also inhibit photosynthesis. Because the passage lists these preventable impediments to photosynthesis, you can logically reason that homeowners can do something to prevent oxidative damage to their lawns (like watering them), which makes Choice (D) the best answer.

792. its rate depends only on the amount of light energy.

To answer this exception question, return to the text and eliminate the answer choices that fit the description. In this case, eliminate the choices that are mentioned in the passage as being true of photosynthesis. You can locate the information in Choices (B) and (C) in the third paragraph, so cross them off. Choice (D) comes from the first paragraph, and you can cut it, too. You're left with Choice (A), which isn't found in the passage and actually contradicts information in the passage.

793. A. Active only during the daytime

It's better to determine a definition in a reading question by looking at its context rather than by relying on your knowledge of the word itself. Look for clues in the sentence that contains *diurnal* and the ones around it. The authors say that the *diurnal* pattern is followed on "clear, sunny days," which means the pattern isn't as certain as every other day or twice a day. Cross out Choices (B) and (C). Choice (D), "back and forth," suggests that photosynthetic rates start out low, then peak, then return to their original low state. The authors dispute this idea when they say that photosynthetic rates decrease to their lowest levels by sunset. If the rates decrease by sunset, they must be active only during the daytime. Choice (A) is right.

If you have a background in biology (or etymology — the study of words) you may immediately recognize the prefix *di*, which means "two." This may have led you to mistakenly think that Choice (B) is the right answer.

Always check vocabulary-in-context answers by inserting your choice into the passage. Sometimes the words mean something different from their common definition, and the only way you'll know what they mean in the passage is by reading them within the context of the sentence and surrounding ideas.

794. C. very high light intensities.

The authors discuss mechanisms for protection after they mention the effects of very high light intensities. The answer has to be Choice (C).

Choice (A) defines oxidative damage, not protective mechanisms. Choice (B) clearly isn't the best answer. The entire process of photosynthesis is based on the conversion of solar energy to chemical energy, implying that plants in no way have to protect themselves from chemical energy. The authors state in the final paragraph that chlorophyll actually increases photosynthetic rates, so Choice (D)'s not something that needs to be protected against.

795. **B. sulfur is a constituent of proteins that help along the process.**

The passage discusses "nutrient availability" in the second to last paragraph. As you read the paragraph carefully, you can sift through the various nutrients mentioned to come up with the correct answer. It's not Choice (A). Nitrogen and magnesium, not nitrogen and sulfur, are important for photosynthesis. Choice (C) is out. Chlorine is required for oxygen evolution, so it doesn't reduce that evolution. The passage says that potassium promotes stomatal opening rather than the detrimental stomatal closure. The only answer that reveals a true benefit of nutrient availability in photosynthesis is Choice (B). Sulfur is a constituent of some proteins that act as intermediates in photosynthesis.

Chapter 4

796. **A. 10 hours**

Check Figure 1. For each day represented, the bars indicate that the mice spent just short of half the day engaged in activity. The answer that is closest to a bit less than half of 24 hours is Choice (A).

797. **C. the mice experienced only darkness**

The text states that Experiment 2 was conducted in the same way as Experiment 2 but for the hours of light and darkness, so you can eliminate Choice (A).

When you compare Figure 1 and Figure 3, you see that the amount of mouse activity is actually higher in Experiment 2, so Choice (B) is incorrect.

The top of the graph for Experiment 2 shows that all 24 hours of the experiment were conducted in darkness. In contrast, Figure 1 shows that during Experiment 1 the mice received 12 hours of light and 12 hours of darkness.

798. **B. Peak melatonin levels in mice closely coincide with the onset of periods on inactivity.**

To answer this question, you must pay close attention to all the information presented in the figures. In Figure 3, the bars of activity are similar in length during periods of darkness to those during the light periods as indicated in Figure 1. So Choice (A) is incorrect. You can also eliminate Choice (C). According to Figure 2, in Experiment 2, when there was no light, the mice still produced the same amount of melatonin as they did during the light periods in Experiment 1. When you compare Figure 2 to the activity levels indicated in the other two figures, you see that peak melatonin levels occurred right around the same time that mice ceased activity for the day. Therefore, you can eliminate Choice (D). Choice (B) is best.

799. D. Hour 0

This question requires you to recognize the pattern between light cycle and melatonin production: During a light/dark cycle, onset of darkness and peak melatonin levels are very close. The new experiment reverses Experiment 1's light/dark cycle. Because darkness starts around hour 0 in the third experiment, so should peak melatonin.

800. B. Repeat Experiment 2 but with 24 hours of daily light exposure.

Because this is a question asking for the *best* answer, it may be easiest to find the correct response using process of elimination. First, examine the scientist's hypothesis in the passage (exposure to light and dark regulate circadian rhythms by altering the production of a hormone called melatonin). Fewer subjects would provide less information, so eliminate Choice (A). The hypothesis doesn't concern oxygen levels, so Choice (C) isn't relevant. Rule out Choice (D) because it merely duplicates the procedure in Experiment 1. This leaves Choice (B), which is best because exposing the mice to 24 hours of light would show whether experiencing constant light has an effect similar to experiencing constant darkness.

801. A. Before bedtime

Comparing Figure 2 to the other figures reveals that peak melatonin is associated with inactivity. Therefore, if humans wanted to use melatonin to sleep better, they should take it before they plan to be inactive. The best answer is Choice (A).

802. A.

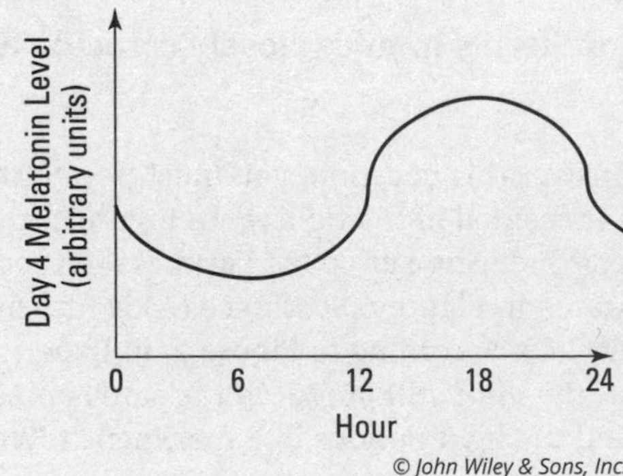

ANSWERS 801–900

The passage information indicates that melatonin seems to peak right around the onset of inactivity. The onset of inactivity on Day 4 of Experiment 2 is around hour 18; therefore, the graph that has peak melatonin around hour 18 is the correct answer.

803. **C. 3**

The passage states that for one cycle, 1 Acetyl-CoA is used with 1 Oxaloacetate. For every 2 Acetyl CoA, 6 NADH are produced. Therefore, for every 1 turn of the cycle (1 Acetyl-CoA), 3 NADH are produced.

804. **A. Number of Glucose molecules applied**

The independent variable is the variable under the direct control of the experimenter. Because the scientist controlled the number of glucose molecules applied to the cell, Choice (A) is the answer. The other answers provide variables that are dependent on experimental procedure.

805. **D. 30**

According to the Table 2, one Glucose molecule yields 6 NADH, 2 $FADH_2$, and 2 GTP. Apply that data to the information in Table 1: $(6\times2.5)+(2\times1.5)+(2\times1)=15+3+2$, or 20 ATP. The question doesn't ask for ATP, so eliminate Choice (C) and keep calculating.

To produce 600 ATP, the cell will need 30 Glucose: $\frac{600}{20}=30$.

806. **B. 2**

To answer this question, you have to pay attention to the number of carbons in each part of the cycle. Citrate has 6 carbons, and Oxaloacetate has 4. Therefore, 2 carbons must have been lost between the two. Because CO_2 has 1 carbon, 2 molecules of CO_2 must have been created.

807. **C. It decreases because less Citrate is produced.**

Figure 1 shows that the reaction between Oxaloacetate and Acetyl-CoA forms Citrate. If this reaction is inhibited, less Citrate forms, so eliminate Choice (A). The lack of Citrate results in the inability for it to be converted back to Oxaloacetate to make NADH, which decreases NADH production. So you can eliminate Choices (B) and (D). Choice (C) is the only answer with the correct result.

808. D. Acetyl-CoA

You may be tempted to pick Choice (B) for this question. It's true that NADH is converted into the most ATP, so its removal would be significant. But you're asked for the *most* significant effect. If Acetyl-CoA is removed from the equation, the cycle stops completely. Therefore, the best answer must be Choice (D).

809. B.

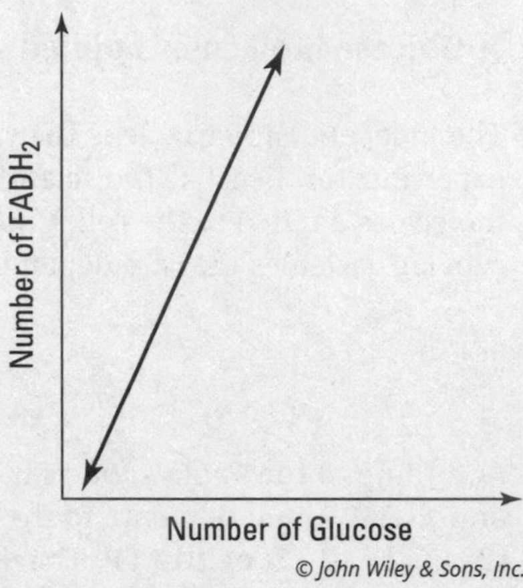

According to the experimental results, for each Glucose added, 2 FAD_2 are created. Therefore, the graph should have a positive slope. The relationship is also unchanging, so the slope should be linear, rather than exponential. This leaves only answer B.

810. C. Material and surface type

Material and surface type are the independent variables because they are the aspects of the experiment directly under the control of the experimenter. Vehicle weight is not varied during this test. Stopping distance is a dependent variable because it *depends* on factors such as material type. F_{stop} is not being tested directly during the study, so it is neither a dependent nor independent variable.

811. B. Material B

Material B had the shortest stopping distance according to the experimental results. On this material, the car stopped in 44 feet, as opposed to 51 feet, 56 feet, and 62 feet for the materials in Choices (A), (C), and (D), respectively.

812. **A. 2,000-pound vehicle using material A on dry concrete**

Look back to the equation in the passage. You can immediately eliminate Choices (C) and (D) because the materials tested are the same as those in Choices (A) and (B), but the vehicle weighs less. The equation demonstrates that vehicles with a greater weight will have a greater stopping force. Between materials A and D, A has a higher coefficient of kinetic friction, so it will generate more stopping force. Choice (A) provides the combination of the heavier vehicle and material with the higher coefficient of kinetic friction.

813. **D. As $\mu_{kinetic}$ decreases, stopping distance increases.**

Choose any one of the surface types to reveal the correct relationship. Compare Table 1 to Table 2. As you examine corresponding columns in both tables, you observe that each time $\mu_{kinetic}$ decreases, the corresponding stopping distance increases.

814. **C. 0.55**

On Table 1 under the "dirt" column, material D stopped in 77 feet, which is close to the value of the new material. The $\mu_{kinetic}$ for material D on dirt is 0.56, so Choice (C) is the closest answer.

815. **C. not change the stopping force because $\mu_{kinetic}$ is not dependent on tire width**

According to the information in the passage, $\mu_{kinetic}$ is *only* dependent on the surface type, so eliminate Choices (A) and (B), which indicate that $\mu_{kinetic}$ is also dependent on tire width. Choice (D) is wrong because the passage states that vehicle weight is a factor in determining $\mu_{kinetic}$. Choice (C) is best. Based on the equation, if $\mu_{kinetic}$ and weight are unchanged, stopping force should also stay the same.

816. **A. μ_{static} is greater than $\mu_{kinetic}$.**

The question states that ABS keep tires from sliding, meaning that they keep the tires and surface in contact without motion. It also tells you that when objects have contact without motion, you use μ_{static} instead of $\mu_{kinetic}$ to determine stopping distance. Because an ABS decreases the length a car slides during stopping (a decrease in stopping distance), the force stopping the car must increase. The question doesn't mention whether the vehicle weight changes: therefore, according to the equation, the coefficient of friction must be greater when the wheels aren't sliding, Choice (A). Eliminate Choices (C) and (D) because an ABS will have no effect on the values of the coefficients themselves; it changes only the coefficient you use, static or kinetic.

817. B. 12.7 m/s

On Table 1, focus on the first entry in the last column for velocity and the first row for point A to find the velocity of water at point A when the pump is set to low. The entry for this condition is 12.7 m/s. Be careful with Choice (C); it provides the correct value but is expressed in incorrect units.

818. C. The water's density remains the same.

Looking at the density data on Table 1 reveals that density does not change no matter the condition. The density is always $20\text{kg}/\text{m}^3$, so the answer is Choice (C).

819. D. less than 1.4 m/s

This question is asking you to understand the relationship between pipe diameter and water velocity. Table 1 shows that as the water moves from point A to point B to point C, velocity decreases no matter which setting the pump is on. At the same time, the diameter of the pipe increases. Therefore, if a larger section of pipe is added to the end, velocity should be slower, and the only logical answer is a value less than 1.4 m/s, Choice (D).

820. C. Double pipe diameter.

The question requires you to evaluate several patterns within the data. Narrow your focus by eliminating answers. Water temperature and pipe length are not mentioned in this passage, so Choices (A) and (B) can't be correct.

Pipe diameter does seem to have an effect on water pressure. Moving from point A to B doubles pipe diameter and decreases pressure from 470kPa to 125kPa. Switching the pump to low decreases pressure from 470kPa to 193kPa. Because doubling the pipe diameter has a greater effect, Choice (C) is the correct answer.

821. B. approximately doubles

Check out the difference between the low and high columns under the velocity header on Table 1. When the pump is switched to high no matter the position in the pipe, velocity roughly doubles (12.7m/s becomes 25.5m/s, 3.2m/s becomes 6.4m/s, and so on).

822. **C. Pump setting: high; pipe diameter: small**

According to Table 1, the highest water velocity occurs at point A, where the pipe is smallest, and when the pump is set to high. Therefore, the correct answer is Choice (C).

823. **D. Polyvinyl chloride**

To find the pipe material that can withstand the pressure of the pipe system, you must select the type of pipe that has a maximum pressure rating greater than or equal to the maximum pressure of the system. The maximum pressure of the system is 470.5 kPa (at point A with high pressure). The only type of pipe that has a max pressure rating greater than 470.7 kPa is polyvinyl chloride, Choice (D).

824. **A. Deposition**

Water vapor (gas) is becoming ice (solid). According to Table 1, the process of transitioning from gas to solid is called *deposition.*

825. **C. Gas or liquid**

Look at the graph for *a* in Figure 1 to find information about water's state. The temperature of water is on the *x*-axis (horizontal axis). At 100 degrees, water is a gas when pressure is below 1 atm. When pressure is above 1 atm at 100 degrees, water is a liquid. Therefore, the answer is Choice (C).

826. **B. Water: solid; CO_2: gas**

Check the graph for *a* for water information and the graph for *b* for information about CO_2. The points on the graph indicate the transition from one state to another. At –10°C (a little to the left of the marked 0° point) and at 1 atm pressure, water is a solid. For CO_2, it may be little harder to see where –10°C falls on the *x*-axis. However, you know that –10°C falls between –56.4°C and 31.1°C (which are marked clearly on the graph). At 1 atm and anywhere between those marked points, CO_2 is a gas.

827. D. Slowly decrease the temperature at high pressures

To determine how to transition to solid CO_2 from liquid CO_2, look at the graph for *b* in Figure 1. Pressure must remain high to keep the liquid CO_2 from turning into a gas instead of a solid. So eliminate Choices (A) and (C) based on pressure. For the liquid to become solid, the temperature must decrease. According to Figure 1, when temperature is increased (a move to the right), the liquid CO_2 becomes a gas. Choice (D) reflects that temperature decrease.

828. C. 100°C

Use the graph for *a* in Figure 1 to determine that at 1 atm pressure, water is a liquid between 0°C and 100°C. The points on the graph indicate the transition from one state to another. Above 100°C, it becomes water vapor (gas). Therefore, the answer is 100 degrees Celsius.

829. A. Cooking at higher pressures (2 atm) increases the maximum temperature of liquid water, which reduces cooking time.

To tackle this question, you must understand the relationship between pressure and temperature. According to the graph for *a* in Figure 1, as the pressure increases with liquid water, its maximum temperature (before it becomes water vapor) increases. Based on this information, you can eliminate all answers except Choice (A). Because cooking temperature is increased, cooking time reduces.

830. D. –78.5°C

Check out the graph for *b* in Figure 1 to determine information about CO_2. The points on the graph indicate the transition from one state to another. At 1 atm, when CO_2 is undergoing sublimation (transition from solid to gas), the CO_2 will have a temperature of –78.5°C.

831. B. Sun compass theory

The only theory that describes a reliance on the sun is the sun compass theory. The magnetic compass theory relies on the Earth's magnetic field, while the geographic features theory relies on large physical landmarks.

832. D. north to south

According to the passage, in the early fall, the butterflies leave their habitats in Canada and the United States and migrate south to Mexico. Therefore, the correct answer is Choice (D).

833. C. Sun compass: The butterflies use the sun to orient themselves. Magnetic compass: The butterflies use magnets to orient themselves.

Answering this question requires reading carefully. Choice (A) is incorrect. The butterflies don't always fly toward the sun according to the sun compass theory. The sun compass theory states that the butterflies use the sun to *orient* themselves. Choice (B) is incorrect because the butterflies use not only mountains to orient themselves but also rivers and lakes. Choice (D) is incorrect; the butterflies don't use the sun in the magnetic compass theory. Therefore, Choice (C) is correct.

834. D. West

According to the magnetic compass theory, the butterflies use magnetic fields to navigate. In this experiment, the scientist blocks the Earth's magnetic field and introduces an artificial one. In the chamber, the artificial magnetic North Pole is oriented toward the actual west. It may help to sketch a quick compass to visualize the problem:

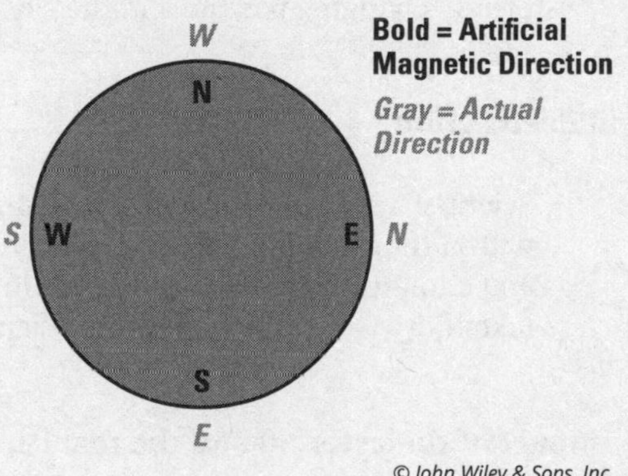

Because the experiment takes place during the early spring, you know that the butterflies want to head north (like heading back from Mexico to the United States). The butterflies are oriented by the artificial magnetic field that is emanating from the west, so the butterflies will fly west.

835. A. Magnetic compass theory and geographic features theory

On a cloudy day, butterflies would not be able to use the sun's position in the sky to orient themselves. Furthermore, clouds would have little to no effect on the Earth's magnetic field or the location of large geographic features. Therefore, this piece of evidence supports the sun compass theory and casts doubt on the magnetic compass and geographic features theories.

836. B. Butterflies consistently change direction when encountering a large river.

The geographic features theory states that butterflies use large geographic landmarks to navigate to central Mexico. These features include large mountain ranges, rivers, lakes, and oceans. If butterflies consistently change direction at a certain large river, this would be evidence for the geographic features theory.

837. B. Sun compass theory only

The sun compass theory states that the position of the sun varies with time of day and season. If butterflies were forced to migrate earlier in the season, the sun would no longer be where the butterflies expect it to be. Global warming may have a slight effect on rivers due to fluctuating water levels, which could affect the geographical features theory. But this change would likely be a smaller effect than that of the sun's completely changing positions in the sky.

838. A. Rapid destruction

Scientist 1 states that the asteroid impact immediately killed "anything within thousands of miles," which indicates Choice (A). Increased CO_2 and climate change are mentioned in both theories, and food chain instability is mentioned by only Scientist 2.

839. C. The impact of the asteroid and the resulting explosion burned or buried most evidence of life.

Choice (A) is incorrect; no evidence is presented that life was nonexistent around the crater. Choice (B) is wrong because Scientist 1 makes no mention of volcanic activity. Scientist 1 also makes no mention of a "slow die-off," so Choice (D) is out. Choice (C) is the most plausible. Scientist 1 describes the magnitude of the impact.

840. D. Iridium is only common in meteors.

Choice (A) suggests that iridium levels are normal and not attributable to any particular phenomenon. Choices (B) and (D) are more consistent with Scientist 2's theory that associates K-T extinction with volcanoes and the Deccan Plateau.

If iridium was common only in meteors (and not common in the Earth's crust), the idea that a large asteroid hit the Earth around the time of the K-T extinction is better supported. Choice (D) is best.

841. A. Climate change

Both scientists describe the increase of CO_2 levels in the atmosphere and how that increase contributed to the K-T extinction and changes in climate.

842. B. Food chain instability was present before the Chicxulub crater appeared.

Practice the process of elimination. Choice (A) is incorrect; a larger asteroid impact would not by itself support the ideas of the volcanic activity presented by Scientist 2. Choice (C) is incorrect because increased CO_2 from lava supports only Scientist 2. Choice (D) sounds plausible but widespread climate change ultimately could be used to support either theory independently and does not necessarily support the events of both theories occurring at once. Choice (B) is best because food chain instability supports Scientist 2's volcanic theory, and the appearance of the Chicxulub crater relates to Scientist 1's impact theory.

843. C. Many fossils show evidence of starvation.

If Scientist 2 is correct, there must have been widespread starvation due to food chain instability. Therefore, the fossils should show signs of starvation, and Choice (C) is right.

Choice (A) relates to Scientist 1's theory. Choice (B) is wrong because plankton and marine life would not be the *only* fossils present. And Choice (D) doesn't take into account that fossils could exist that were affected by the volcanic activity but not necessarily covered by lava flows.

844. D. increased atmospheric CO_2

Both theories describe a rise in atmospheric CO_2. Therefore, any surviving life would have to adapt to these new conditions. There is no mention of sea levels or increased food in either theory, and widespread lava applies only to the volcanic theory.

845. **D. 4**

Table 2 contains data about the results of closing switches. Table 2 shows that when switch 4 is closed in the bottom row of the table, 144 J/s of power is generated, which is greater than occurs with any other switch closure.

846. **B. As current increases, power increases.**

According to Table 2, there is a direct relationship between power output and current. As current increases from 6 to 12 amps, power increases from 72 to 144 J/s. Therefore, Choice (B) is correct.

847. **D. Voltage produced by the battery**

According to Table 2, current and power output vary with each switch closure, so eliminate Choices (A) and (C). Figure 1 and Table 1 indicate that resistance changes depending on which switch is closed, so Choice (B) must be wrong. Therefore, voltage of the battery must be the variable that remains unchanged. The passage verifies that the battery produces a steady 12 volts.

848. **B. 2 ohms**

You know from Figure 1 that closing Switch 1 or Switch 2 results in the same current and power output, so each circuit likely has the same resistance. Closing Switch 3 results in flow through R3, which Table 1 tells you has a resistance of 2 ohms. So Switch 1 likely results in a resistance of 2 ohms, too.

You can also use Figure 1 to verify that finding by noticing that closing Switch 1 results in flow through R1 and R2. According to Table 1, each of these resistors has 1 ohm of resistance. Therefore, the circuit that results from closing Switch 1 would have the resistance that results from flowing through both R1 and R2, or 2 ohms.

849. **C. R3 and R4**

The student's circuit flows through two resistors. Judging from Table 1 and Table 2, power output is minimized when resistance is maximized. Therefore, the student should choose the resistors that have the most resistance. R3 and R4 would accomplish this goal with an overall resistance of 6 ohms.

850. D. Current and power

Current and power are the variables that depend on the variable being directly controlled by the experimenter (resistance).

851. D. decreases, current increases.

Based on the resistors used in each circuit, you can see that circuits generated by closing Switch 1 and Switch 2 have the same resistance and the same current. The circuit resulting from closing Switch 3 has the most resistance and the least current. That from closing Switch 4 falls between the other two in terms of resistance and current. Therefore, as resistance increases, current decreases.

852. D. D

From the passage, you know that V_{max} is the maximum possible reaction rate for an enzyme-catalyzed reaction, so check out the last column of Table 1. Drug version D results in the highest rate, 21 mol/s.

853. B. B

From the passage, you know that enzyme affinity can be estimated using the K_m value, and that a lower K_m correlates to a higher affinity for the substrate (in this case, carbohydrates). Therefore, according to the table, drug B has the lowest affinity because it has the highest K_m.

854. D. D

You know that K_m is the concentration of substrate at which the reaction reaches $\frac{V_{max}}{2}$. Therefore, the lower the K_m, the smaller amount of substrate needed to reach a higher reaction rate. Because the concentration of carbohydrates is usually low, you want to select the enzyme (drug) that has the lowest K_m. According to Table 1, the drug with the lowest K_m is D.

855. C. increases K_m

Compare the two lines on the graph provided in the question. Maximum reaction rate (the highest vertical point on the line) is the same for both lines. This observation rules out Choices (A) and (B). However, the point on the *x*-axis (substrate concentration) at which the line reaches $\frac{1}{2}$ of the maximum reaction rate has moved to the right. This means that K_m has increased.

856. **A. an increase in reaction rate**

Figure 1 shows that as more substrate is added (moving to the right along the *x*-axis), reaction rate (along the *y*-axis) increases, which justifies Choice (A). V_{max} is a function of the type of enzyme involved and not how much substrate is added, so Choice (B) is out. Neither does K_m change with substrate concentration, so eliminate Choice (C). Reaction energy is not indicated on Figure 1, so Choice (D) can't be right.

857. **C. increased K_m and decreased V_{max}**

Given the information in the question, it appears that people with PKU have a less effective form of the enzyme. An enzyme's effectiveness is measured by how fast it can catalyze a reaction (V_{max}) and how much substrate it needs to do it effectively (K_m). Therefore, a non-effective enzyme would have a low V_{max} and a higher K_m.

858. **C. Lenses A and C**

You know from information in the passage that concave lenses are diverging lenses with a negative focal length. According to Table 1, lenses A and C are diverging and have negative focal lengths.

859. **B. As focal length increases, power decreases.**

To answer this question, look at the equation for power. Power is inversely related to focal length, so as one increases, the other must decrease. Because the question asks about absolute values, you can ignore negative numbers. The only answer that contains an inverse relationship is Choice (B).

860. **A. Lens A**

The lens that refracts light at the shortest angle must have the shortest focal length. This question is asking only about converging lenses. The converging lens with the shortest focal length is A.

861. **D. Lenses C and A**

Because focal length and power are inversely related, to minimize focal length, you have to maximize power. Eliminate answers that contain negative values, Choices (B) and (D). The combination of lenses that adds to the highest power is C and A (13.3 diopter).

862. A. The lens is too strong, and the focal point is in front of the retina.

If the focal length of the eye's lens is too short, the focal point falls in front of the retina. Eliminate Choices (C) and (D). A shorter focal length means that a lens must be stronger rather than weaker in power. Therefore, Choice (A) is correct.

863. C. Convex

You can eliminate Choices (A) and (B) because they refer to the same lens. Because a hyperopic eye has a focal length that is too long, the focal point falls behind the retina. This means that the focal length must be made shorter. The only way to decrease focal length is to choose a convex (converging) lens.

864. B. 2

Because the TLC test separates the chemicals in the test solution by their polarity, the number of chemicals of different polarities is equal to the number of different stains on the developed test strip. Because there are two stains present in test solution 1, there are two chemicals of different polarity present.

865. C. draw the test solution up the glass strip

Read the text to answer this question about experimental procedure. According to the passage, the purpose of the solvent is to draw the test solution up the glass strip.

866. B. less than nonpolar chemicals because they interact more with the polar substrate

According to the passage, the TLC strip separates the chemicals in the test solution by polarity. It does this by using a polar substance on the test strip, stating that polar chemicals interact more with this substance and thus travel less. Therefore, Choice (B) is correct.

867. D. 18 centimeters

The most nonpolar chemical is the one that will travel the farthest. The farthest stain in solution 4 traveled 18 centimeters.

868. **B. 0.25**

Find the values for stain 1 on the table. Use the formula in the passage to figure out the answer:

$$R_f = \frac{\text{distance of stain}}{\text{distance of solvent}}$$

$$R_f = \frac{5}{20}$$

$$R_f = 0.25$$

869. **A. 1**

The passage states that the most polar chemical is the one that travels the shortest distance. Overall the shortest distance traveled by any stain was 3 centimeters in test solution 1.

870. **C. nonpolar test solution; slow moving solvent**

Evaluate the formula to answer this question.

$$R_f = \frac{\text{distance of stain}}{\text{distance of solvent}}$$

To maximize R_f value, you want a large travel distance of a stain (which corresponds to a nonpolar chemical in test solution) and a small distance of solvent (which corresponds to one that is slow moving). The combination of nonpolar solution and slow moving solvent is in Choice (C).

871. **C. was born to a mother who was infected with *C. trachomatis* during pregnancy**

The environmental hypothesis explains that unborn children exposed to periods of infection are more likely to develop schizophrenia, and therefore Choice (C) is correct. Choices (A) and (B) apply to the genetic hypothesis, so you can eliminate them right away. Choice (D) is not mentioned by either hypothesis.

872. **B. Schizophrenic parents have a higher incidence of abusive parenting methods than do parents who do not have the disease.**

The environmental hypothesis purports that environmental elements are mostly to blame for the development of schizophrenia, which makes Choice (A) automatically incorrect. Choices (C) and (D) are not specific to children of parents who have schizophrenia. This leaves Choice (B) as the best answer.

873. **D. the types of anatomical changes in the brain that cause the disease**

According to the passage, there are some consistent brain changes that can be described in schizophrenia; therefore, Choice (D) is the best answer. The theories clash on how the disease is transmitted, so Choice (A) is out. Only the environmental hypothesis deals with cannabis use, and only the genetic hypothesis explains the role of the dysregulin gene.

874. **C. $\frac{1}{2}$**

This question requires you to apply a bit of genetics from freshman biology class. Perform a simple genetic cross.

The father has the genotype "dd" where d is the mutation allele. The mother is only a carrier, so she has the "Dd" phenotype, where D is the unmutated allele. Therefore, $\frac{1}{2}$ of their children would have the Dd genotype, and $\frac{1}{2}$ would have the dd genotype and display the dysbindin mutation.

875. **B. Schizophrenia occurs most often in those who experienced a childhood trauma and have mutations in the neuregulin gene.**

Choice (B) explains that both environmental (childhood trauma) and genetics (mutated neuregulin gene) contribute to the development of the disease. Age isn't mentioned by both hypotheses. Choice (C) is related to the environmental hypothesis only, and Choice (D) applies only to the genetic hypothesis.

876. **D. Environmental: Malnutrition *in utero* is linked to schizophrenia. Genetic: Dysbindin mutations are heritable factors in schizophrenia.**

Choice (D) is the best answer. Malnutrition *in utero* is described by the environmental hypothesis, while dysbindin mutation is explained in the genetic hypothesis.

Choices (A) and (B) are suspect because enlarged lateral ventricles are listed as general traits of schizophrenia rather than a cause. Likewise, eliminate Choice (C) because the environmental hypothesis observes a correlation between cannabis use and schizophrenia but doesn't specifically state how it affects D_2 receptors.

877. **A. Current**

You may have been tempted to answer Choice (B) because determining glucose concentration is the purpose of the test. However, according to the passage, the test strip only directly measures voltage. The glucometer uses this voltage and a calibration curve to determine the glucose concentration later.

878. **C. increases, current increases.**

The positive slope of the line on Figure 1 indicates that as the concentration of glucose increases so does current.

879. **D. Lactose**

The glucose test is dependent on the number of electrons flowing across the electrode in the test strip. According to the table in the question, glucose donates two electrons. The molecule that will most influence the test is the one that has the greatest difference from two electrons. The table indicates this to be lactose, which can donate six electrons.

880. **B. 45–60 μA**

Read along the *x*-axis on Figure 1 until your reach about 80 mg/dl. At that point, the corresponding *y*-axis value is about 45 μA. At 100 mg/dl, the corresponding value is 60 μA, so the best answer is Choice (B).

881. **B. Decreased pH causes glucose to donate more electrons to glucose oxidase, resulting in a higher current and a higher reading.**

An increased blood glucose reading corresponds to increased electron flow, or current, across the test strip electrode. Therefore, glucose must be donating more electrons to glucose oxidase (and consequently to ferricyanide). More electrons result in higher current and higher glucose reading.

882. **A. Glucose is oxidized; glucose oxidase is reduced and oxidized.**

Based on the passage, you know that glucose loses electrons. Additionally, glucose oxidase gains and then loses electrons to ferricyanide. Therefore, glucose is oxidized, while glucose oxidase is reduced and then oxidized.

883. **C. Distance travelled**

In both experiments, the dependent variable (the variable being measured) was the distance travelled by the tennis ball.

884. **D. 45°**

To answer this question, you must look at Experiment 1 because it's the one that varies the launch angle. According to Figure 2, the maximum distance was achieved from a 45° launch angle.

885. B. 45° launch angle and increasing launch velocity from 10 m/s to 15 m/s

This question requires you to integrate the results of both experiments. Choice (A) and (B) regard information in Figure 3, and Choices (C) and (D) regard Figure 2.

Choice (A) results in an increase in distance from 2.5 meters to 10 meters, which is a 7.5-meter increase.

Choice (B) results in an increase from 10 meters to 22.5 meters, which is a 12.5-meter increase.

Choice (C) results in an increase from about 14 meters to about 19 meters, which is about a 5-meter increase.

Choice (D) results in an increase from about 8 meters to about 11 meters, which is a 4-meter increase.

Choice (B) results in the greatest distance increase.

886. B. less distance travelled for each velocity tested

Experiment 2 was originally carried out at a 45° launch angle. You know from Experiment 1 that decreasing the launch angle decreases the distance travelled. From this information, you can logically deduce that the distance travelled will be less for each velocity tested.

887. D. About 22 meters

Because gravity has the same effect on objects regardless of mass, you should expect about the same results for this new experiment. Based on the results of Experiment 2, at a launch angle of 45° and a launch velocity of 15 m/s, this ball should still travel about 22 meters.

888. C. Launch angle

The independent variable (the aspect of the experiment under the direct control of the experimenter) in Experiment 1 is the launch angle of the ball.

889. A. Maximum distances are achieved at a 45° launch angle with maximum launch velocity.

From Figure 2, you know that the maximum distances are achieved at 45°. From Figure 3, you know that maximum distances are achieved with the highest launch velocity. Therefore, Choice (A) is the most plausible conclusion.

890. D. Temperature

The variable under the direct control of the experimenter (the independent variable) in Experiment 1 is the temperature of the greenhouses. All of the other options are dependent variables.

891. D. plant height decreased and plant survival decreased

Look at the two tables for Experiment 1. The strains of wheat in the warmer greenhouse are consistently shorter, have less mass, and lower survival rates than the plants in the cooler greenhouse.

892. C. strain C

Focus on the results of Experiment 2, which deals with water pH. Between Table 3 and Table 4, plant strain C lost 0.10 m in height, 0.10 kg in mass, and 10% of its survival rate. However, both strains A and B lost 0.20 m, 0.20 kg, and 20%. survival Therefore, plant strain C is the hardiest of the bunch.

893. B.

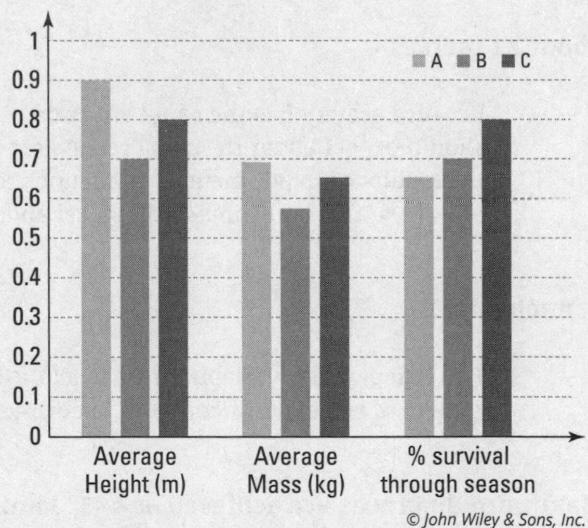

The data for the second greenhouse in Experiment 1 includes plant height, plant mass, and survival rate for all three strains. The only answer that accurately plots all three of these measures is Choice (B).

894. **A. More-acidic water and warmer temperatures will have a negative impact on wheat harvests.**

This question requires you to know the relationship between pH and acidity. Lower pH means higher acidity. Looking all four tables, you can see that increased temperature and lower pH had negative effects across the board for the plants. Reduced plant mass and survival will definitely negatively impact wheat harvests. Eliminate Choice (C) because the experiments only regarded wheat plants, and therefore their results aren't necessarily applicable to all crops.

895. **C. Strain C**

Don't be distracted by the unnecessary information included in the question. The amount of rain and lack of pests and insects are irrelevant to the results of the experiment. However, temperature and pH are relevant. Because the temperature is predicted to be 80° and a temperature of 80° would be relevant to both Table 1 and 2, it is most helpful to check the pH data in Experiment 2. In Experiment 2, plant strain C had the highest survival rate for the 4.2 pH condition.

896. **C. Experiment 2 *e. coli* plates contained an antibiotic; in Experiment 1 the plates did not.**

According to the passage text, only the dishes in Experiment 2 contain the *ampicillin* antibiotic. *E. coli* in both experiments were transformed with the plasmid and had plasmids containing GFP. The growth period was the same for both experiments.

897. **D. Presence of plasmid in bacteria**

The variable under the control of the experimenter (the independent variable) in Experiment 1 was the presence of the plasmid in the bacteria. Plate 1 bacteria had the plasmid, but plate 2 bacteria did not.

898. **B. signal successful transformation of the bacteria**

As explained in the passage, the GFP gene is a "reporter" gene whose job is to show that the plasmid has been successfully incorporated into the bacterial genome. Because the GFP gene and the antibiotic gene are on the same plasmid, only bacteria that show GFP will have the antibiotic resistance. GFP is different than the growth medium and the gene thought to confer resistance, so Choices (A) and (C) can't be right. Choice (D) isn't mentioned at all.

899. **D. 3 and 4**

This question asks for the dish combination that would most appropriately show that the plasmid confers antibiotic resistance. Ideally, all variables being compared between the two plates would be the same except for the presence of the plasmid in question. So eliminate Choices (A) and (B) because they contain one dish from each experiment.

Additionally, because you are trying to show antibiotic resistance, the plates must contain the antibiotic in question, so the scientist can be sure that it's the plasmid (and not some other variable) that is making the *e. coli* resistant to ampicillin. Because dishes 3 and 4 are the ones that have the ampicillin and have all other variables in common except the plasmid, comparing 3 and 4 is the best way to prove the role of the plasmid in resistance.

900. **B. 50%**

Bacteria on dishes 1 and 2 grew to about 35 cm^2 in area. Dish 3 bacteria only grew to 17.5 cm^2. If each dish initially had the same amount of bacteria, and all were resistant to the antibiotic, you could assume that they would grow to about the same extent. Because dish 3 (which had bacteria with the plasmid as well as ampicillin) only grew to about 50% of its theoretical potential (based on dishes 1 and 2), it is valid to conclude that only about 50% of the bacteria on dish 3 successfully received the plasmid.

901. **C. raising one's intake of protein.**

Eliminate answers that don't apply to the opinions of both scientists. Neither of the scientists claim that a low-carbohydrate diet lowers one's metabolism. So Choice (A) is wrong. Scientist 2 states that the diet increases fat burning, but Scientist 1 doesn't mention fat burning. Choice (B) is likely not the best answer. Only Scientist 1 states that low-carb diets lead to a risk for heart disease, so cross out Choice (D). The best answer is Choice (C). Both scientists mention that low-carb diets involve more consumption of protein.

902. **D. Short-term weight loss is a likely result.**

Look for the answer that includes parts of the opinions of both scientists. Eliminate answers that only Scientist 1 would agree with. Scientist 2 doesn't think that low-carb diets are dangerous, so it isn't likely that she would agree with either Choice (A) or Choice (C). Scientist 1 doesn't talk about nutritional supplements, so you don't have enough information to pick Choice (B). Scientist 2 says that low-carb diets are designed for short-term effectiveness. Scientist 1 concedes at the end of his statement that short-term weight loss may occur. So the best answer is Choice (D).

903. **A. The health benefits of weight loss are not sufficient to overcome the risks associated with a low-carbohydrate diet.**

Rely on good old process of elimination to handle this question. Scientist 1 says that people who suffer from gout or kidney disease have an increased health concerns on a low-carb diet, but he doesn't say that most people who start the diet have gout or kidney disease. Cross out Choice (B). Choice (C) is Scientist 2's claim, so it's not right. Scientist 1's argument is more concerned with heart disease and other disease risks than obesity. Eliminate Choice (D) and pick Choice (A). Scientist 1 seems to admit that low-carb diets lead to some weight loss, but he's not sold on them. Therefore, he must think that the health risks associated with low-carb diets can't be overcome by its weight-loss benefit.

904. **B. Protein consumption does not fuel the body.**

If it's true that people on a low-carb diet don't get fuel from the food they consume and the foods that they consume are proteins, it must be true that proteins don't provide fuel. Choice (B) is the best answer. Choice (A) is out because people on low-carb diets restrict glucose. Choice (C) can't be right because Scientist 2 doesn't talk about heart disease. The conclusion in Choice (D) goes way beyond anything stated or implied by Scientist 2's opinion.

905. **D. A recent study has shown that eating protein makes a person feel fuller faster than eating carbohydrates, which means that people who consume primarily protein tend to eat significantly less than those who eat less protein.**

The gist of Scientist 1's argument is that low-carb diets are dangerous because they encourage a high-protein diet that creates a higher risk for disease. You're looking for the statement that would provide evidence *against* Scientist 1. You know Choice (A) is wrong because it supports Scientist 1's contention that low-carb diets are dangerous. Similarly, a study showing the health benefits of carbohydrates would more likely go along with Scientist 1's opinion rather than go against it. You're down to Choices (C) and (D). The fact that a eating a variety of foods is healthy doesn't run contrary to the idea that eating a high-protein diet is dangerous. Choice (D) is better than Choice (C). If it's true that a high-protein diet leads to less overall food consumption, it's likely that people on low-carb diets aren't eating the unlimited amounts of bacon, eggs, and butter that Scientist 1 claims lead to disease.

906. C. By observing proper precautions, most people can receive health benefits from eating a low-carbohydrate diet.

Now you get to concentrate on Scientist 2. She essentially says the low-carb diets are effective and can be balanced with supplements. Find the answer that provides the best summary of her opinion without making assumptions about issues she doesn't talk about. The answer that summarizes Scientist 2's opinion the best is Choice (C).

She doesn't talk specifically about kidney or heart disease, so Choices (A) and (D) are out. She doesn't base her opinion on studies or make a case for unrestricted meat consumption, so Choice (B) isn't as good an answer as Choice (C).

907. A. Sugar cookie

The first paragraph says that the body burns glucose as fuel. It associates glucose with refined carbohydrates and gives sugar, flour, and corn syrup as examples. The answer choice that contains sugar is Choice (A), the sugar cookie. So it's the one that would the body would burn for fuel instead of going to its fat stores. The other three choices are examples of meats and other foods that Scientist 1 implies are eaten on a low-carb diet, and the goal of a low-carb diet is to burn fat for fuel.

908. B. Brian

To answer this question, apply the information in Table 1 to the data in Table 2. According to Table 1, the healthy BMI range is 18.5 to 24.9. The person in Table 2 whose BMI falls within this range is Brian, Choice (B).

909. D. Obese

You could answer this question by plugging the numbers into the formula and solving for BMI, but you don't need to waste your time. Look at Table 2 to see whether it contains an individual with similar height and weight. Tawny's height is within 0.02 meters of the height in the question, and her weight is about 2 kilograms less. Therefore, you know that the individual in the question must have a higher BMI than Tawny. Because Tawny's BMI is in the obese category, a BMI higher than Tawny's falls in the obese category, Choice (D).

910. C. 1.45; 38.6

You don't have to take up precious time calculating the BMI for each answer choice. The underweight category is the one with the lowest BMI. So pick the answer that appears to have the lowest ratio of weight to height. You know that Choices (A) and (B) can't be right. Choice (A) is similar to Julia's measurements, and the measurements for Choice (B) are greater than Julia's in both areas. That leaves you with the individuals in Choices (C) and (D). Both individuals have essentially the same height, but Choice (D) has a greater weight. Therefore, Choice (C) has to have a lower BMI than Choice (D).

911. **B. healthy.**

Using Table 1, you know that Julia's BMI is in the lower range of the overweight scores. If she lost weight, her BMI would go down. She definitely won't be obese. Cross out Choice (D). A 10 percent weight loss is likely significant enough to lower her BMI to the point where she's out of the overweight category, but not so significant that she'd be classified as underweight. The best answer is likely Choice (B).

If you want to make sure, you can perform the calculation. It will take a little while because you can't use your calculator on the science test. Ten percent of Julia's body weight is 7.73 kilograms. If she lost that, her weight would be around 69.50 kilograms. Her height squared is about 3 square meters, and 3 goes into 69.50 around 23 times. Her BMI will be approximately 23, which is clearly in the healthy range.

912. **A. height decreases.**

The formula in the passage shows a direct relationship between BMI and weight and an inverse relationship between BMI and height. Eliminate answers that contradict those two relationships.

Choice (B) indicates an inverse relationship between BMI and weight, so it can't be right. Choices (C) and (D) require a direct relationship between BMI and height, so they're wrong. The best answer is Choice (A), which correctly conveys that as height decreases BMI increases.

913. **D. age.**

The correct answer has to be based on information in the passage. The passage says that the BMI information assumes average body type, but doesn't define what that means (you certainly can't assume it means waist circumference). It also assumes that individuals are over 20 years old, so, the BMI information in Table 1 may not apply to children under 20 years old. According to the information, the factor that could affect accurate BMI results is age, Choice (D).

914. **C. lights in the laboratory were turned off and the sun set.**

According to Figure 1, during the first few hours, the organism was taking CO^2 out of the air and was releasing O^2. The only process that does this is photosynthesis. Something happened at 6:00 p.m. to halt the initial process. The passage tells you that photosynthesis uses light energy, so the absence of light will certainly stop photosynthesis. The answer that shows that something happened to stop the light energy is Choice (C).

There's not enough information in the passage to tell you that the organism died or fell asleep. Nor can you assume that the container leaked. Choices (A), (B), and (D) require you to make assumptions that can't be substantiated by the information in the passage.

If you can't point to a place in the science passage that justifies an answer choice, the answer's most likely incorrect.

915. **C. slime molds, sponge, fish, mushroom, spider**

The passage states that no animals or protists engage in photosynthesis. The complete list of animals and protists in the table contains all organisms except the moss and rose. That list is provided in Choice (C).

916. **D. All listed organisms likely require O^2.**

Be careful with this question. The passage states that animals and protists don't engage in photosynthesis, but it doesn't state that plants don't engage in ACR. In fact, the first sentence states that most organisms perform ACR. Therefore, you can't say that any of the listed of the listed organisms do not require O^2. The best answer is that all likely need oxygen.

917. **B. It can perform photosynthesis and ACR.**

Think about this question carefully. Because the organism performs photosynthesis, you can eliminate Choices (C) and (D). All you need to figure out is whether it's likely that the organism performs ACR. At 6:00 p.m., the container has high levels of O^2 and low levels of CO^2. These levels reversed by 6:00 a.m., which indicates that the organism likely took in the O^2 and gave off CO^2. That's indicative of ACR. If the organism couldn't perform ACR, the levels of the gases would likely have stayed the same from 6:00 p.m. to 6:00 a.m. The best answer is Choice (B).

918. A. primary producer

To answer this question correctly, you have to home in on information in the first paragraph. The passage tells you that plants are primary producers, animals are consumers, and protists can be decomposers. You can deduce that the organism in the container must be a plant because it performs photosynthesis and only plants can do that. The organism must be a primary producer, Choice (A).

919. A. moss

You know that the organism is a plant. The only plants listed on the table are mosses and roses. Rose isn't an option, so the answer must be moss, Choice (A).

920. B. The CO^2 levels would increase a little and the O^2 levels would decrease a little.

The question asks you what would happen if the organism had no light source. Without light, the organism couldn't perform photosynthesis. If the organism can't perform photosynthesis, you can eliminate Choices (C) and (D). Choice (C) describes what happens in photosynthesis, and Choice (D) duplicates the previous experiment in which photosynthesis occurred.

Here's where it gets tricky. Would the levels of the gases stay the same the whole time or would O^2 levels increase a little and CO^2 levels decrease a bit? Before you hastily pick Choice (A) and move on, consider what happened in the original experiment when the lights went off at 6:00 p.m. The O^2 levels decreases and the CO^2 levels increased. In the absence of photosynthesis, the organism likely engaged in ACR. According to Figure 1, the container begins with a little bit of O^2. It's reasonable to conclude that in the absence of light, the organism would take in this little bit of O^2 and give off a little bit of CO^2. The best answer is Choice (B).

921. D. Dish 4

The dish without any antibiotic, Dish 4, is the control. It's there to make sure that whatever happened in the dishes with the antibiotic wouldn't have happened anyway. Choice (D) is the right answer.

922. A. The medium is necessary to encourage bacteria growth.

Because the point of the experiments is to observe the effect of the antibiotics on bacteria growth, the high-nutrient medium must be present to encourage the bacteria to grow in the first place. Eliminate Choices (C) and (D) because the amount of antibiotic isn't affected by the experimental process. Choice (B) is wrong because a medium that inhibited bacteria growth would counteract the effects of the antibiotics and interfere with the experiment results.

923. B. a dish with bacteria and a paper disk that has not been soaked in any substance.

The student wanted to see how bacteria grow in the presence of different antibiotics versus how they grow under regular circumstances. Dishes with a third antibiotic or bleach would be extensions of the current experiment because they would introduce new experimental variables that weren't present before, so Choices (A) and (C) are out. A dish without bacteria wouldn't introduce any new experimental variables. It would eliminate the very thing the student wanted to study, so Choice (D) is also wrong.

A dish with a plain paper circle would be a good control because it isolates and removes the experimental variable even better than Dish 4. The student could make sure that the presence of paper (instead of the antibiotic *on* the paper) doesn't somehow affect bacterial growth. Pick Choice (B).

924. C. Specific bacteria in the culture are immune to either penicillin or erythromycin but not both simultaneously.

The question asks for the best explanation of the results of both experiments, which means that the statements in all four choices could be consistent with the results and you need to find the one that is the best overall explanation for what happened.

According to the results, the growth in Dishes 1 and 2 looked pretty much the same as the control group, so you could conclude from them that erythromycin and penicillin didn't affect the total amount of bacterial growth. That is, the culture contains bacteria that seem to be immune to these antibiotics. Putting the antibiotics together in Dish 3, however, definitely stopped bacterial growth, so the antibiotics weren't completely ineffective. Cross out Choice (B).

The best explanation is that the culture must contain at least two kinds of bacteria: one immune to penicillin and one immune to erythromycin. In Dish 1, the bacteria immune to penicillin grew like crazy and filled the whole dish. In Dish 2, the bacteria immune to erythromycin was able to take over. In Dish 3, however, both kinds of bacteria were stopped, so the area around the paper circles was clear of bacteria. These results were confirmed with Dishes 5 and 6, in which the bacteria that was immune to one antibiotic was overcome by the other. If the antibiotics affected different kinds of bacteria, they didn't have the same effect. Choice (A) is wrong. The phenomenon is best explained by Choice (C).

There's nothing in the experiment to suggest that the first two dishes were contaminated. So Choice (D) can't be right.

---

925. **B. The results of Experiment 2 provide further proof for a conclusion reached by Experiment 1.**

Eliminate the answers you know are wrong. The results of Experiment 1 support the results of Experiment 2. Therefore, Choices (A) and (C) are clearly wrong. That leaves you with Choices (B) and (D).

Beware of answer choices that contain debatable words like *completely*. The two experiments aren't completely different. And if one part of the answer is wrong, the entire answer is wrong. The best answer is Choice (B).

---

926. **C. Neither the bacteria in Dish 1 nor the bacteria in Petri Dish 2 at the end of Experiment 1 are *Staphylococci*.**

The answer choices concern only the bacteria in Dishes 1, 2, and 3, so, do a quick review of the bacteria that remain in the first three dishes after the first experiment.

Dish 1 has bacteria that weren't killed by erythromycin. According to the question, meningitis is immune to erythromycin. So Dish 1 could contain meningitis bacteria at the end and probably doesn't have the bacteria that cause infections of the prostate gland. Eliminate Choice (A).

Dish 2 has bacteria that weren't killed by penicillin. The question implies that bacteria that cause prostate gland infections are immune to penicillin. So Dish 2 could contain those kinds of bacteria and probably doesn't have meningitis bacteria. Choice (B) isn't reasonable.

In Dish 3, erythromycin and penicillin effectively wiped out the bacteria. Cross out Choice (D) because Dish 3 didn't contain much, if any, bacteria at the end of the experiment.

Because both erythromycin and penicillin are effective against *Staphylococci*, those kinds of bacteria probably weren't present in either Dish 1 or Dish 2 at the end of the experiment. The best answer is Choice (C).

927. A. The level of effectiveness of either antibiotic depends on the particular type of bacteria to be controlled.

Be reasonable and choose the answer that doesn't require you to assume too much. Choice (D) has to be wrong because the two antibiotics together did a good job of controlling the bacteria. Nothing in the experiments showed that one did a better job of controlling bacteria than the other, so you can't make a case for Choice (B).

Watch out for the debatable word *always* in Choice (C). The two antibiotics worked better together to control the particular bacteria in these experiments, but that doesn't mean that they'll *always* work better together against other bacteria. The best answer is the safe answer, Choice (A). Notice how wishy-washy it is. An antibiotic's effectiveness depends on the type of bacteria it's supposed to control.

928. A. The scientist wanted to observe the rodents' behavior during the hours when their predators were less present.

The scientist wasn't concerned with observing predator behavior, so you can cross out Choices (C) and (D) immediately. The passage states that the predators are primarily nocturnal, so daylight observations would be made when the predators are less present than they would be at night. The most reasonable answer is Choice (A).

929. D. It was easier for the rodents to find the food in the grassy area.

Study 1 indicates that rodents prefer to eat in the grassy area, so Choice (B) is definitely wrong.

The question asks for the best conclusion for Study 1. Eliminate answer choices that require you to make assumptions that go beyond the information available from Study 1.

Choice (A) *could* be an accurate description of what happened in Study 1. However, the passage doesn't say anything about territorial behavior, so you can't point to anything in Study 1 to justify Choice (A). Check the other answers to see whether there's a better choice.

The passage says that the researcher cleared out all the other animals before putting in the rodent species, so there couldn't have been any competitors. Cross out Choice (C). Choice (D) presents a hypothesis that's consistent with the results in the bar graph without bringing in anything that's beyond the scope of foraging behavior. Therefore, it's a better answer than Choice (A). Choice (D) is the best hypothesis of the options provided.

930. C. Fewer rodents foraged in the grassy area because they felt safe there.

The only difference between Study 2 and Study 1 was the addition of the model hawk, so the correct answer probably has something to do with the hawk. The rodents didn't seek shelter from the sun in Study 1, so it's not reasonable to conclude that they were suddenly seeking shelter in Study 2. Cross out Choice (B). You can't make reasonable assumptions about the rodents' hunger level. They likely need to eat every day. Eliminate Choice (A).

Choices (C) and (D) have something to do with the hawk, but only Choice (C) relates the presence of the hawk to other information in the passage. The passage doesn't tell you that rodents like to leave food for other animals, so Choice (D)'s too far-fetched. The best answer is Choice (C). The passage tells you that the hawk is a predator, so it makes sense that the rodents would forage in the place where they felt less exposed to the hawk.

931. B. Rodents can find food more easily if there is more of it available.

The question asks for the most reasonable conclusion of the four. Look for the one you can justify best. Narrow your options by eliminating any answer choices you know can't be right.

You know from Study 2 that rodents forage in the bushes when predators are around, so running out of food can't be the only reason rodents forage there. Even though the first part of the answer is true, you have to eliminate Choice (C) based on the last part.

Consider Choice (D). Actually, you could make a better case for the opposite conclusion. Because there was less food in the grassy area, the rodents may have had to be more efficient than when they foraged in the bushes. Regardless, the passage doesn't discuss efficiency, so Choice (D) is not the most reasonable answer.

Choice (A) may sound reasonable, but it regards the quantity of food the rodents ate rather than the amount of time they spent foraging. You may be able to make a case that if they foraged longer in the bushes, the rodents ate more food there, but Choice (B) is better.

It deals with the subject of the study, finding food, and when you compare the results of Study 3 to Study 1, you see that the only difference between the two studies is that there was more food in the busy area in Study 3. The rodents increased their foraging time in the busy area when there was more food there. So they must have been able to find more food when there was more of it.

932. **D. The rodents will spend more time foraging in the bushy area than they spent in the bushy area in Study 1.**

Choices (B) and (C) are too all encompassing to be correct. Saying that *no* rodents will forage in either area is unjustifiable. You know that the rodents' predators come out at night. Study 2 presented the rodents with a predator. Therefore, it makes sense that the rodents' foraging behavior in hours with no daylight would be similar to their behavior in Study 2. The results of Study 2 showed that the rodents spent more time in the bushy area than they did in Study 1. Choice (D) is the best answer. Choice (A) isn't right because the studies don't tell you enough about foraging behavior for you to predict the exact amount of increase in time the rodents will spend in the bushy area.

933. **B. Food placement**

The independent variable is the variable that's controlled by the scientist rather than the conditions of the experiment. You can cross out Choice (D) because air temperature wasn't a variable at all. The presence of a predator was controlled by the scientist, but it was only part of Study 2. Eliminate Choice (C) because the question asked for the independent variable in all three studies. The scientist didn't control where the rodents foraged for food. That was the dependent variable. The answer has to be Choice (B). The scientist controlled where the food was placed in all three studies.

934. **C. No, because the study has too many independent variables to provide the scientist with accurate information about the effects of specific predators.**

Focus on the scientist's goal for this additional study. She wants to know how *specific* predators affect rodent foraging behavior. The way to isolate the behaviors associated with specific predators is to introduce the predators one at a time. Therefore, Choice (A) has to be wrong. Choice (B) would work if the scientist's goal was to see how rodents react when they see a predator in the air and one on the ground, but that's not her goal. The scientist was able to observe the effects of a predator using a model in Study 2, so Choice (D) isn't warranted. The best answer is Choice (C). Introducing two independent variables (two different predators) won't provide accurate information about how the rodents react to one specific predator. You may have thought that because the scientist already had data about hawks from Study 2, she could isolate the reaction rodents had to the bobcat. But the rodents may react differently to a bobcat when a hawk's present than they would to a bobcat when it's alone.

935. **C. 8 seconds.**

Check the figure. Find the line for Fluid A. Draw a vertical line from the point midway between 25°C and 100°C on the x-axis to estimate the data for 75°C. The point where your line intersects the line for Fluid A is closest to 8 seconds as defined on the y-axis. Choices (A) and (B) correspond with the times for Fluid B and C, respectively.

936. **D. at some temperatures some fluids have the same viscosity, and at other temperatures they do not.**

You can easily eliminate Choice (C). It's obvious from Figure 1 that the three liquids don't have the same viscosity at every temperature. If they did, their lines on the graph would lie on top of each other. There's a point on the graph where Fluid A and Fluid B have the same viscosity, but it's at a lower temperature rather than a higher temperature, so Choice (B) is wrong. At some temperatures Fluid A is less viscous than Fluid B, but at most temperatures Fluid B is less viscous than Fluid A. So Choice (A) is wrong. That leaves you with the safe bet, Choice (D). Some fluids have the same viscosity at a certain temperature (A and B at about 10 degrees), but at other temperatures the two liquid don't.

937. **A. For all fluids, there is an inverse relationship between temperature and viscosity.**

At higher temperatures all of the liquids had a lower viscosity. Therefore, there is an inverse relationship between temperature and viscosity. Choice (A) is the right answer. If there were a positive relationship between temperature and viscosity, one would go up when the other went up or vice versa. If the relationship were static, the three lines on the graph would be horizontal.

938. **C. Fluid C is either machine oil or olive oil.**

The higher the viscosity of the oil, the higher its line is on the graph. So motor oil's line is higher on the graph than olive oil's. Fluid C is the least viscous of the three fluids so it can't be motor oil. If it were, its line on the graph would have to be above at least one other line. That tells you that Fluid C has to be either machine oil or olive oil. Choice (C) is the answer.

You don't know anything about the relative viscosity of machine oil, so you can't make the statement in Choice (B). Fluid B's line is above Fluid C's, so it's possible that Fluid B is motor oil. Choice (D) isn't right. You may have been attracted to Choice (A). Fluid A could be motor oil because its viscosity is generally less than the other two fluids. However, Fluid B could be motor oil and Fluid C olive oil. In that case Fluid A would be machine oil. Therefore, you can't say that Fluid A is most likely motor oil.

939. D. The number of seconds it would take for the ball to drop to the bottom of Fluid C at 25°C would be about 4.

The graph of Fluid A show that it takes 6 seconds for the ball to drop at 100 degrees, so Choice (A) is wrong. You can't tell what the number of seconds will be for Fluid B at 125 degrees because 125 degrees isn't on the graph, and it looks like it takes about 4 seconds for the ball to drop in Fluid B at 100 degrees. Choice (B) can't be right. The graph shows that at 80 degrees the metal ball drops in Fluid B at around 6 seconds. Cross out Choice (C). The answer must be Choice (D). The temperature on the Fluid C line that intersects 4 seconds is around 25 degrees.

940. C.

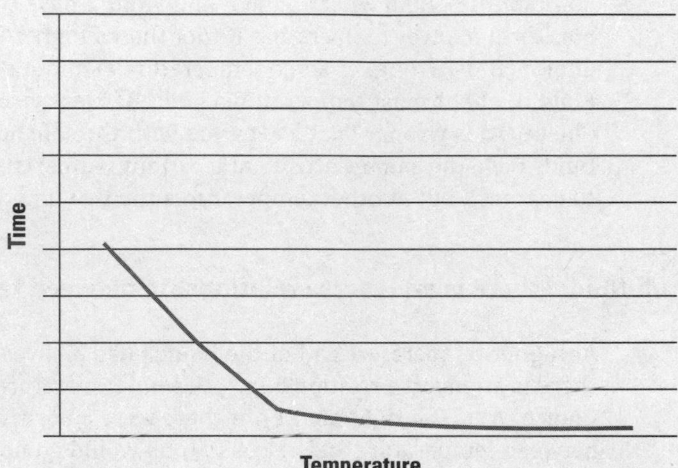

The graph of the viscosity of Fluid C in Figure 1 appears to maintain a consistent pattern. At 100 degrees, it takes just one second for the metal ball to move through the fluid. You know that the line will never reach 0 seconds. It will always take some time for the metal ball to move through the fluid. Therefore, as temperatures increase, the amount of time the metal has to move through the fluid can only decrease by fractions of a second. It's reasonable to conclude that the line will level out somewhat just above 0 and continue regardless of how high the student increase the temperature of the fluid. The graph that illustrates this concept best is in Choice (C).

Choices (B) and (D) don't follow the original pattern of the graph of Fluid C, so they have to be wrong. Choice (A) shows the line at the 0 second mark, which implies that at a certain temperature the metal ball will travel through the fluid so quickly that it will take no time at all. That's not possible.

941. **B. In the second experiment the student conducted, the H_2O was a solid**

The student record no data for the second experiment, H_2O at 0 degrees. The metal ball must have been unable to travel through the fluid at this temperature. A reasonable explanation for this data could be that the fluid was not a fluid. Instead, it was a solid, ice. The best answer is Choice (B).

You can't make a case for Choice (A). If there's no data for the viscosity of H_2O at 0 degrees, you can't compare its viscosity to that of other fluids. Choice (C) is wrong. From 25 to 100 degrees the time it took for the metal ball to move through H_2O decreased by 0.4 seconds. Its graph on the chart in Figure 1 would be practically horizontal.

Did Choice (D) fool you? The student couldn't measure H_2O viscosity at 0 degrees, but he was able to record viscosity data for 25 and 100 degrees. Therefore, it's not impossible to measure the viscosity of H_2O. Read the answer choice very carefully before you select.

942. **C. 4 seconds**

Table 1 shows the speed of the skier in one-second intervals from 0 to 5 seconds. If you relate this table to the slope shown in Figure 1, you have a better understanding of what the table displays. Initially, the skier moves more slowly at a speed of only 2 m/s. Then she gains speed and gets up to 7 m/s, which makes sense when you look at Figure 1 because she's going down a hill. Then the skier goes uphill for a bit, so her speed decreases to 3 m/s. Finally, she goes down another slope, and her speed reaches 10 m/s. This is her maximum speed. According to Table 1, this maximum speed occurred at a time of 4 seconds, which is Choice (C).

943. **C. 3 and 4 seconds.**

Check out Figure 2. Eliminate Choices (B) and (D) because the kinetic energy line *decreases* between 2 and 3 seconds and 4 and 5 seconds. If you picked Choice (D), you were looking at the line for potential energy instead of kinetic energy. The rise in energy between 3 and 4 seconds is much steeper than that for between 1 and 2 seconds, so Choice (C) is the correct answer.

944. **D. The skier experiences greater kinetic energy at greater speeds and less kinetic energy at lower speeds.**

Use time data from the table and Figure 2 to answer this question. The table shows that the skier's greatest speed occurs at 4 seconds. The figure shows the skier's lowest potential energy at 4 seconds. So Choice (A) can't be true; the greatest potential energy isn't associated with the skier's greatest speed. The skier's lowest speed was at 5 seconds, but the table shows the skier's kinetic energy at 5 seconds to be lowest rather than greatest, so Choice (B) can't be right.

When you consider all speeds represented on the table along with the rise and fall of kinetic energy on Figure 2, you see that there is a direct relationship between speed and kinetic energy. When the skier speeds up, kinetic energy increases. A relationship exists between the two, so Choice (C) is wrong and Choice (D) is correct.

945. **A. increases only**

Figure 2 indicates that kinetic energy and potential energy have an inverse relationship. As kinetic energy increases, potential energy decreases. Similarly, when kinetic energy decreases, potential energy increases. The question asks what happens to kinetic energy as potential energy decreases. The inverse is that kinetic energy increases, Choice (A). Choice (D) is wrong because, although kinetic energy increases and decreases in the figure, it only increases when potential energy decreases.

946. **B. The skier is traveling uphill.**

This question asks you to evaluate a specific time interval. Figure 2 tells you what happened to the energy levels of the skier between 2 and 3 seconds. The kinetic energy of the skier decreased and the potential energy of the skier increased. A decrease in kinetic energy means a decrease in speed, and an increase in potential energy means that the skier's height in relation to Earth increased. This information jives with the skier's travelling uphill, which makes Choice (B) the right answer.

Choice (A) is incorrect because it conveys the wrong relationship between kinetic energy and potential energy. For Choice (C) to be right, Figure 2 would have to show that potential energy remained constant between 2 and 3 seconds. Choice (D) is incorrect because kinetic energy between 2 and 3 seconds is not at 0.

947. **B. speed.**

The information about and the formula for kinetic energy provided in the second paragraph tells you that kinetic energy relates to the speed and mass of an object. Mass isn't an option, so speed must be the answer. Pick Choice (B).

The height of an object doesn't directly affect its kinetic energy; it affects the potential energy. Time and distance aren't directly related to kinetic energy. You know this because Figure 2 shows you that kinetic energy increased and decreased while time and distance were only increasing.

948. D. Ride a chair lift back to the top of the mountain

If the skier wants to increase her potential energy, she needs to somehow increase her height in relation to Earth. The only choice that significantly increases the height of the skier is Choice (D). A chair lift ride would put her back on the top of the mountain with all of the potential energy she had at the beginning of the first run. The other three choices would likely serve to increase her speed, which would increase kinetic energy but not necessarily potential energy.

949. A. the most symptoms.

The bottom row of Table 1 shows the symptoms of those who were exposed to a radiation dose of greater than 30 Gy. For that dosage range, all 100 people experienced nausea, headache, and fever. This is the most severe of any of the dosage ranges. With no other dosage did everyone in the group experience all three symptoms. This means that the correct answer is Choice (A). Choice (D) can't be correct because there was no variation. Everyone in the group experienced all three symptoms.

950. C. increased then decreased.

Look for the headache trend over time for the dosage range of 1 to 2 Gy. This is the lowest curve on the graph. It begins at around 0, increases to around 14, and then decreases to around 5. This means that the number of headaches first increased then decreased, exactly what Choice (C) says.

951. A. 1 to 2 Gy

You know that the person is experiencing a headache but not a fever after being exposed to radiation. Check out Table 1 to see which dosage range had the most people who experienced a headache but not a fever. The table shows that the only dosage range where the number of headaches is larger than the number of fevers is the 1-to-2-Gy range. For all other dosage ranges, there were more instances of fever than headaches. Therefore, the correct answer is Choice (A).

952. D. Nausea

In this question you're looking for symptoms based on a dosage rather than a dosage based on symptoms. You know that the dose was 2 to 6 Gy, so you have to look at the second row of data. For this dosage range, there were 74 cases of nausea, 52 cases of headache, and 64 cases of fever. This means that the most common symptom for this dosage range was nausea. Therefore, someone with a dosage of 2 to 6 Gy is most likely to experience nausea. Choice (D) is the correct answer. Choice (A), no symptoms, is not correct because for each symptom, the majority of people in this dosage range were affected.

953. **B. more symptoms because higher doses of radiation exposure result in more cases of headaches, nausea, and fever.**

Both sets of data show an increasing number of symptoms with an increase in radiation dosage. This trend is nicely summarized in Choice (B). Choice (A) can't be right because it's the opposite of the observed trends. Choice (C) isn't correct because the number of headache and fever symptoms at the highest levels of radiation were the same. And you know Choice (D) is incorrect because the data shows more fevers than headaches at higher dosages and the same number of both at the highest dosages.

954. **B. Between 4 and 6**

Given the four answer possibilities, the best answer has to be Choice (B). On Figure 1, the steepest slope along the line for 6 to 8 Gy is between 4 and 6 hours.

955. **C. 2 to 6 Gy and 1 to 2 Gy**

All levels of radiation exposure on Figure 1 show the number of headache incidents increasing and leveling off over time except for exposures of 2 to 6 Gy and 1 to 2 Gy where the incidents decreased after about 14 hours after exposure.

956. **B. The Moon is younger than the Earth.**

This question asks about Scientist 1, so you have to look through those paragraphs to find your answer. The question is essentially asking for the age of the Moon. If you look at the second sentence of Scientist 1's theory, you see that it says "the Moon is younger than the Earth." Choice (B) is the right answer.

957. **A. A large collision caused the Moon to form.**

Examine Scientist 2 for this one, and keep in mind that you're looking for the statement that doesn't support the theory. If you have a basic understanding of what each theory says, you'll notice right away that Choice (A) contains the key idea of Scientist 1 and isn't consistent with Scientist 2. Choice (B) is consistent with both theories, so it's not right. Choices (C) and (D) are mentioned as part of Scientist 2, so you can cross them out, too.

958. **C. Evidence that the oldest craters on the Moon are much younger than the geologic age of the Earth**

You're looking for a statement that violates Scientist 2's theory. Each of these answers is a possible discovery that could be made about the formation of the Moon that would lead to more insight into which theory is more plausible. You have to evaluate each statement to see if it would help or hurt Scientist 2's theory. The one that hurts it is the right answer.

Choice (A), a discovery of large impacts on the Earth's surface, would support Scientist 1, but doesn't necessarily contradict Scientist 2. The Moon and Earth could have formed at the same time, and then at some later point, large impacts could have occurred on the Earth's surface. Choice (B), which suggests that the Moon and Earth are composed of similar material, can support either theory. Choice (C) says that the oldest craters on the Moon are much younger than the Earth. That suggests that the Moon is younger than the Earth. This conflicts with Scientist 2, who says that the Moon and Earth were formed at the same time. Choice (C) is the correct answer. Choice (D) does not necessarily refute Scientist 2. The theory says that the cloud of dust and gas from which the Moon and Earth were formed was not entirely homogeneous, so the Earth could have more iron than the Moon.

959. **D. Scientist 1: Impact of a large body. Scientist 2: Cloud of gas and dust.**

Knowing the main ideas of the two theories is the key to answering this question. There are three explanations used in various combinations to form the four possible choices. The idea of a cloud of gas and dust is one of the main concepts necessary in Scientist 2. The impact of a large body is the key to Scientist 1. Choice (D) must be the correct answer.

You know right away that Choices (B) and (C) are incorrect. The idea that the Earth spun too fast and split to form the Earth and Moon is not presented in either theory. Eliminate Choice (A) because it matches each explanation with the wrong theory.

960. **A. The Moon is composed of material similar to the Earth's crust and mantle.**

Scientist 1 says that the Moon is composed of pieces of the Earth's crust and mantle, as well as the outer parts of the giant impacting body. Choice (A) makes sense. Choice (B), while true, doesn't specifically relate to Scientist 1. The Moon could be covered in craters or not, and Scientist 1's theory could still be valid. Choice (C) states that the Moon's orbit is perfectly circular. This untrue statement is irrelevant because it has nothing to do with Scientist 1's theory. Eliminate Choice (D) because it's related to Scientist 2.

961. **B. The Moon and the Earth are composed of some common matter.**

You're looking for the statement that works with both theories. Keep in mind the concepts behind each individual theory. Cross out Choice (A) because it isn't consistent with Scientist 2. According to that theory, the Moon and the Earth are the same age. Eliminate Choice (C) because Scientist 2 talks about the Moon's atmosphere. Choice (D) can't be true. Scientist 1 says that most of the Earth's core wasn't ejected during the impact and that the Moon may be mostly made of material from the Earth's mantle. That suggests that the Earth's core is denser than the Moon's. That leaves you with Choice (B), which is supported by both theories. Scientist 1 says that the Moon is composed of some of the Earth's mantle and crust, and Scientist 2 says that the Moon and Earth are composed of the same original matter.

962. **D. Some of the matter that makes up the Moon was once part of the Earth.**

Answer this question more quickly by eliminating choices that could be consistent with Scientist 2. That means you can cross out Choices (A), (B), and (C). Choice (A) is consistent with both theories. Both mention that gravitational forces played a part in the Moon's formation. Choice (B), while true, isn't discussed in the explanation of either theory. You therefore have no reason to believe that it conflicts with Scientist 2. Choice (C) is discussed by Scientist 2, so you know it's consistent. Only Choice (D) is inconsistent with Scientist 2's theory. According to that theory, the Moon and Earth are made of their own materials, though the original matter that composes them came from a common cloud of dust and gas.

963. **C. 28 GPM**

You need to look at Figure 2 to see what the flow rate was when a pipe diameter of 1.5 inches was used. Look at the curve and find the corresponding point for a diameter of 1.5 inches. Then follow this point across to the left and see what the corresponding flow rate would be. You can see that it is between 20 and 30 GPM and is much closer to 30. You can then look at the choices and see that the only one that corresponds is Choice (C), 28 GPM. None of the other three choices is in the right range.

964. **A. increased.**

This question asks you for the relationship between velocity and flow rate, as shown in Study 2. To answer it, you need to look at Figure 3. Velocity increases from left to right, and flow rate increases from bottom to top. As you can see, the data line goes from left to right, bottom to top, indicating that both flow rate and velocity are increasing. This shows you that as velocity is increased, flow rate is also increased. Choice (A) is the correct answer. Choice (D) is wrong because the flow rate was in fact measured for every data point in each study.

965. B. Pipe diameter was held constant.

Because you're asked to find what's not true, eliminate answers that are true. First, you have to be comfortable with the parameters of Study 1. Both studies measure flow rate, which clearly changes according to the graphs. Cross out Choice (C) right away because it's a true statement. In Study 1, velocity was held constant, so Choice (A) is also true. In Study 1, pipe diameter was varied and had an effect on flow rate. That means that Choice (D) is true. Thus, Choice (B) is false and therefore the correct answer.

966. D. greater than 50 GPM.

Because the velocity is 5 ft/s, check out Figure 2, where the velocity was held constant at 5 ft/s. The plotted data points only go up to a diameter of 2 inches, where the measured flow of water was about 50 GPM. The figure shows as the diameter increased, the flow rate also increases. Because the diameter of 3 inches is larger than 2 inches, the flow rate will be greater than 50 GPM. Choice (D) is correct. Make sure you're looking for a diameter of 3 inches. If you mistakenly use Figure 3 and look for a velocity of 3 ft/s, you'll end up thinking that the flow rate is less than 10 GPM and choose the incorrect Choice (A).

967. B. 1-inch diameter, 4 ft/s velocity

For this question, you can either look at each figure to determine what conditions would result in a flow rate of 10 GPM or consider each answer choice to see what the flow rate would be for each. From Figure 2, you can see that a flow rate of 10 GPM would occur with a pipe diameter of about 0.9 inches and a velocity of 5 ft/s. This doesn't correspond to any of the possible choices. Figure 3 shows that a flow rate of 10 GPM would occur with a velocity of about 4 ft/s and a pipe diameter of 1 inch. This matches Choice (B), which is the correct answer. If you evaluate each choice individually you see that Choice (A) results in a flow rate of about 3 GPM, Choice (C) results in a flow rate of about 28 GPM, and Choice (D) isn't a measured point in either figure.

968. **A. 5 GPM**

Figure 3 reveals the answer to this question. As the water velocity increases from 2 ft/s to 4 ft/s, the flow rate increases from 5 GPM to 10 GPM. 10 GPM − 5 GPM = 5 GPM. The flow rate increases 5 GPM.

If you picked Choice (B), you read the question too quickly. The question asks for how much the flow rate increases, not what the resulting flow rate will be.

969. **D. Diameter because a 100 percent in diameter results in an approximate 300 percent increase in flow rate.**

You can eliminate Choices (B) and (C) because their statements are untrue based on the graphs in the passage. Of the remaining answers, Choice (D) has to be correct because increasing diameter by 100 percent results in a greater flow rate than does increasing velocity by 100 percent.

970. **C. incomplete dominance.**

Read the text carefully. The second paragraph says that alleles may be dominant and recessive or they may have incomplete dominance, where the combination of the two different alleles produces a different phenotype from the phenotypes produced by combinations of two similar alleles. You know that the combination of the two different alleles (*Hh*) produces a different phenotype (medium height) than those of each allele (*H* is tall, and *h* is short). Therefore, their relationship must be one of incomplete dominance, Choice (C).

971. **D. medium.**

Like animal II, animal I is *Hh*. Therefore, it must have the same phenotype as animal II, which Figure 2 tells you is medium height. The text tells you that this animal's trait for height is incompletely dominant, and it defines incomplete dominance as having a phenotype that isn't like the phenotype of either of the individual genes. Therefore, *Hh* can't be tall, and it can't be short. Neither Choice (A) nor Choice (B) can be right. You don't know the exact genotype of animal IV, so you can't say that Choice (C) *must* be true.

972. **C. 50 percent**

Animal IV can be either *Hh* or *hh*. Animal II is *Hh*. Therefore, there's a 50% chance that animal IV will have the same phenotype (or genotype, for that matter) as animal II.

973. A. *Hh* only.

You can eliminate Choices (C) and (D) because they are phenotypes rather than genotypes. If a tall animal (*HH*) mated with a short animal such as animal III (*hh*), the genotype of all of their offspring would be *Hh*. Every child would get one *H* from the tall parent and one *h* from the short parent.

974. D. all tall and medium animals of the type have curly hair.

The only thing you know is that animals with an *H* allele also express the trait of curly hair. You know nothing about the alleles for curly hair. You don't know whether they're dominant and recessive or have incomplete dominance. You can't assume that because the *H* allele has incomplete dominance, the allele for curly hair also has incomplete dominance. Cross out Choices (A) and (B). You also don't know whether there's association between curly hair and the *h* allele. Just because it's associated with the *H* allele doesn't mean that curly hair can't also be associated with the *h* allele. Choice (C) isn't right. The remaining answer, Choice (D), is correct. All tall and medium animals of this type are *HH* or *Hh*, which means they carry the *H* allele. Because they have the *H* allele, they must have curly hair.

975. A. 0 percent

Animal III has the genotype of *hh* and therefore doesn't carry the tall gene. If animal III mates with another animal with no tall gene, there is a 0 percent chance their offspring will be tall.

976. D. 6

All offspring of animals with the genotypes *hh* and *HH* will have the genotype *Hh*. Therefore, all six will have a different genotype from their parents.

977. C. Volume

From reading the text that explains what was done in Experiment 1, you know that "the student kept the volume of the chamber constant." This means that Choice (C) must be the correct answer. Even if you didn't notice that sentence in the text, you could figure out what that volume was held constant by looking over the data in Table 1. Table 1 shows three columns of data: temperature, pressure, and volume. By looking down the columns, you notice that temperature and pressure are both changing. Volume, however, remains constant at 0.5m^3 throughout the experiment.

978. **B. 0.88.**

The question tells you that the temperature is 25°C. Table 2 records data for this temperature, so use this table to answer the question. The pressure you're looking for, 14.4 kPa, lies between two of the other data points shown in the table: 12.4 kPa, and 16.5 kPa. The volumes corresponding to these pressures are 1.00 and 0.75. Because 14.4 kPa is about halfway between 12.4 kPa and 16.5 kPa, you know that the volume in m^3 is about halfway between 1.00 and 0.75. The only choice that's between these two values is Choice (B).

979. **A. Temperature of 25°C Volume of 0.50 m^3**

This question requires you to look at data from both experiments. There are a couple of ways to figure it out. One way is to look at Experiment 1 and recognize that the volume was held constant at 0.50 m^3 throughout, and then look at Experiment 2 and see that temperature was held constant at 25°C. This combination appears in Choice (A). You can check your answer by making sure that the combination of 25°C and 0.50 m^3 is present in both data tables. Voila! It is.

Another way to arrive at the correct answer is to see which pressure measurement appears in both tables. Then check out the volume and temperature that corresponds with that pressure measurement. A pressure of 24.8 kPa was recorded in both experiments with the temperature and volume readings that appear in Choice (A).

980. **D. Temperature was held constant and volume was varied.**

To figure out the procedure used in Experiment 2, you can either look at the text or look at Table 2. The text tells you that the student kept the temperature of the chamber constant and changed the volume by moving a piston. This information leads you to Choice (D). You can also look at Table 2 and see that temperature was held constant throughout and pressure and volume changed. The only choice that says temperature was held constant is Choice (D).

981. **C. type.**

Skim the text to gain a good understanding of how the experiments were conducted. The main purpose of the experiments was to determine how varying temperature and volume would change the pressure of the gas. You can eliminate Choices (A) and (B) because the student has already tested them. Gas pressure is the dependent variable, so it doesn't make sense to vary the pressure and pick Choice (D). The best answer is Choice (C). Gas type wasn't a variable examined in the other experiments. Therefore, if the student wanted to examine something new and different from these experiments, the best choice would be to vary the gas type.

982. **B. As the volume of the gas was decreased, the pressure increased.**

This question asks you to recognize the overall trends observed in the data tables. Table 1 shows you that increasing temperature caused pressure to also increase. Table 2 shows that decreasing the volume caused an increase in pressure. The only choice that reflects this correlation is Choice (B). Choices (A), (C), and (D) state the correlation backward, saying that pressure increased when it actually decreased and vice versa.

983. **C. temperature remained constant.**

The question is about what is true for Experiment 2. Eliminate Choices (A) and (B) because it's not true that temperature varied or volume stayed the same in Experiment 2. It's true that pressure varied in Experiment 2, but that fact is also true for Experiment 1, so Choice (D) is not a difference between the two experiments. Choice (C) is the best answer.

984. **D. Block Material, Weight Mass, Block Length**

Each study changed a different aspect of the experiment in order to reveal a certain trend about deformation in the blocks. You can quickly identify what the student varied in each study by looking at the table for each study. The first study varied the block material and recorded a different deformation for each material. You can eliminate Choices (B) and (C) because they don't show block material as the variable for Study 1. The second study kept the block material constant and instead changed the mass of the weight placed on top of the block. Choice (A) can't be right because is shows block length as the variable for Study 2. Choice (D) has to be the answer.

985. **A. Steel**

The results of Study 1 are recorded in Table 1. A larger number indicates more deformation, and a smaller number indicates less deformation. The block that has the smallest number in Table 1 is the steel block. Each of the other blocks experienced a greater amount of deformation.

986. **D. 45 centimeters**

This question wants you to relate the deformation to the mass of the block used and then use that information to make a prediction. You don't have to be a fortune teller. Just look at Table 3 to find out where a deformation of 0.474 μm would fall. The table displays measurements of 0.533 μm and 0.427 μm, and the measurement you're looking for falls between these values. A deformation of 0.533 μm corresponds to a block length of

40 centimeters, while a deformation of 0.427 μm corresponds to a block length of 50 centimeters. This lets you know that the block length will be somewhere between 40 centimeters and 50 centimeters. The only choice that falls within this range is 45 centimeters, which is the value you see in Choice (D).

---

987. **B. Rubber**

When you first looked at Study 2, did you notice that the material used is not directly stated? To determine which material was used, you must look at Table 1 to see which material experienced a deformation that matches those shown in Table 2.

The text before Study 2 tells you that one of the blocks from Study 1 was used, so you know that there should a correlation between one of the materials in Study 1 and the data in Study 2. In Study 1, the only mass used is 50 kilograms, so focus your attention on the last row in Table 2. The deformation shown there is 24.525 μm. Then check Table 1 for this amount of deformation. The rubber block had the same deformation value, so Choice (B) is correct.

---

988. **C. A larger block experiences less deformation.**

This question requires you to draw a conclusion based on the outcomes of the various studies. Study 2 reveals that increasing the weight caused more deformation in the block while decreasing the weight caused less deformation in the block. Choices (A) and (B) contradict the outcomes of Study 2, so they can't be right. Study 3 shows you that a larger block had less deformation and a smaller block had more deformation. Therefore, Choice (D) must be wrong.

---

989. **A. A 20-centimeter rubber block**

Study 1 reveals that rubber blocks experienced more deformation than steel blocks. Eliminate Choices (C) and (D). Study 3 suggests that larger blocks experience less deformation than smaller ones. The answer with the smaller rubber block is Choice (A).

---

990. **B. L1 – L2**

The passage states that *d* represents deformation, and deformation is the difference between the original and compressed lengths. The original length is L1 and the compressed length is L2, so the equation is L1 – L2.

991. **B. 8°**

Focus on the part of the table when Material 1 is air, Material 2 is diamond, and θ_1 is 20 degrees. If you move your finger along that specific line of the table, you see that the corresponding angle of refraction (θ_2) is 8 degrees.

Make sure you're looking at the proper line of the table. If you use incorrect materials or the wrong angle of incidence, you could get the wrong answer. All the possible answers are numbers that appear in the table, but only Choice (B) is the angle that the question is asking for.

992. **A. increases.**

You can't figure out this trend by looking at any one of the three material combinations because the trend holds true throughout the table. For any Material 1 and Material 2, a smaller angle of incidence (θ_1) results in the smallest angle of refraction (θ_2), and the largest angle of incidence results in the largest angle of refraction. For example, if you look at the combination of air and water, you can see that when θ_1 is 10 degrees, θ_2 is only 8 degrees. When θ_1 is increased to 30 degrees, θ_2 increases to 23 degrees.

993. **C. 24°**

To answer this question, check out the bottom portion of the table when the examined materials are glass and water. It would be nice to see an angle of refraction (θ_2) of 30 degrees, but it's not there. Therefore, you have to look at the range of values possible for θ_1 and select the value that fits within that range. The values closest to a θ_2 of 30 degrees are 25 degrees and 38 degrees, which correspond to θ_1 of 20 degrees and 30 degrees. This information tells you that the θ_1 you're looking for is between 20 degrees and 30 degrees. The only answer that fits this description is Choice (C), 24 degrees.

994. **B. is larger than the angle of incidence (θ_1).**

The information you need to answer this question is in the bottom portion of the table where Material 1 ($n_1 = 1.6$) is glass and Material 2 ($n_2 = 1.3$) is water. This material combination fulfills the conditions of the question, a material with a higher index of refraction to a material with a lower index of refraction. Then look for how the angle of incidence (θ_1) compares to the angle of refraction (θ_2). You can see that for all three of the given angles of incidence, the angle of refraction is larger. This information allows you to draw the conclusion that the angle of refraction (θ_2) is larger than the angle of incidence (θ_1) when the laser is travelling a material with a higher index of refraction to a material with a lower index of refraction

995. **D. A greater difference between n_1 and n_2 results in a greater difference between θ_1 and θ_2.**

For this question, you need to look at how the difference between n_1 and n_2 relates to the difference between θ_1 and θ_2. When you examine air and water, you can see that n_1 and n_2 are 1.0 and 1.3. The difference between them is 0.3. The corresponding differences for air and water in θ_1 and θ_2 are 2 degrees (10 – 8 = 2), 5 degrees (20 – 15 = 5), and 7 degrees (30 – 23 = 7).

Compare these results to a case where the difference between n_1 and n_2 is greater. Check out the differences in θ_1 and θ_2 for air and diamond. The difference between n_1 and n_2 is 1.4, (2.4 – 1.0 = 1.4), which is greater than the difference between air and water. Now look at the difference in θ_1 and θ_2, and see that the differences are 8 degrees (10 – 4 = 8), 12 degrees (20 – 8 = 12), and 18 degrees (30 – 12 = 18). These differences in θ_1 and θ_2 for air and diamond are larger than the differences in θ_1 and θ_2 that you see for air and water. This allows you to come to the conclusion that a greater difference between n_1 and n_2 results in a greater difference between θ_1 and θ_2, which is exactly what Choice (D) says.

996. **A.** $\mathbf{(1.6)\sin 30^\circ = (1.3)\sin 38^\circ}$

Apply the Snell's law formula, $n_1\sin(\theta_1) = n_2\sin(\theta_2)$, to the information in the table. Focus on the last row where you see the values for glass and water. The n_1 for glass is 1.6, so eliminate Choices (B) and (D) because they show an n_1 of 1.0. Then focus on the θ_2 for water that corresponds with a θ_1 of 30 degrees. The table shows that a θ_1 of 30 degrees corresponds to a θ_2 of 38 degrees rather than 25 degrees. The answer has to be Choice (A).

Chapter 5

997.

Student Essay

When it comes to the question of whether high school students should be able to be in possession of cellphones on school grounds, strong opinions abound. Some think it's a great idea, while others wholeheartedly oppose it. Some people feel that students don't need cellphones in class because they got along just fine without them before they were invented. Well, students didn't have computers or calculators for hundreds of years either, but that's not a particularly good reason for banning their usage.

On the other hand, cellphones at schools do lead to many problems, with the fact that they make it easier for students to cheat ranking among the most troublesome. It's not always overt, either. Some students can make it look as if they're ruffling in a bag for, say, lip balm or a spare pen, but in reality they're checking their phone in such a way that a teacher will probably not spot them. This all begs the question as to what is more important — student safety, or students learning and testing in an honorable manner?

In my opinion, the two options really cannot be reasonably ranked in order of importance, and therefore a compromise of sorts really is the best possible solution. If students still have access to their phones outside of test times, the safety issue would, for the most part, be put to bed. Students would still be able to maintain possession of their phones on school grounds, enabling them to not only use them for safety, but for logistics (maybe they have to coordinate sports schedules and rides with siblings, etc.), too. They would not, however, have direct access to the phones during test times, however, and they therefore couldn't be tempted to cheat. Finally, if the teachers were to store all phones at the front of the classroom prior to test-taking, they would presumably still be accessible for students in the event that an intruder, shooter, or other threatening presence descended upon the school.

Explanation and Score

Ideas and Analysis: 3: The bulk of this essay centers on the idea that there really is no single solution to the issue of whether cellphones should be allowed in schools, because a black-and-white answer requires prioritizing either safety or educational honesty over the other. Recognizing this, the author proposes a solution that falls more into a gray area, not unlike the argument made in Perspective 3. The author does, however, come up with new ideas and points to support the general idea expressed by Perspective 3, which is why the essay would likely earn a 3 in terms of ideas and analysis.

Development and Support: 4: The essay author makes a number of key points to back up his opinion that cellphone use in schools should be restricted at appropriate times, though not completely banned. He makes some important points, such as the fact that if teachers collected phones at the start of class and kept them up front, they would still arguably be available to students in the event that an intruder entered the school. The author also makes a strong argument against banning cellphones in school outright by noting that they have become a part of modern academic life, much like computers and calculators. Just because they weren't always needed, the author notes, doesn't mean they are not beneficial to modern-day students.

Organization: 3: The essay author buries the lede slightly by reiterating other common perspectives before really thoroughly dissecting his own. However, he does refer to each popular argument before proposing a new one that merges both and then appropriately acknowledging the earlier perspectives in accordance with how they relate to his own.

Language Use and Conventions: 4: The language used in this essay is clear and concise, and the author's word choices are appropriate given the subject matter. Sentence structure is clear and largely conversational, which is appropriate given that the issue at hand is one affecting teenagers.

998.

Student Essay

I can't help but ask: Is this really an issue that warrants the creation of a formal policy? Most teachers can't help but "listen in" on student conversations, whether they mean to do so or not. There are laws that exist to prevent egregious invasions of privacy, such as, say, tapping a student's cellphones, but any other, non-illegal forms of "listening in" should really be considered fair game in the school building and anywhere else. After all, schools are, by nature, public settings, as are, say, grocery stores. How many people visit the grocery store to have private conversations they don't want anyone overhearing? My point is, if students are assuming the school building is an ideal place to engage in private conversation, they should know better. Simple common sense ought to dictate otherwise. Some who argue that "listening in" is an invasion of privacy go so far as to equate "listening in" with having video cameras installed in bathroom stalls. This is laughable. One is indeed an egregious invasion of privacy, while the other really just involves teachers being aware of their surroundings, which they are expected to be, anyway.

Rather than issue a formal policy change, school administrators should simply encourage teachers to remain vigilant in the classrooms and speak up when they suspect bullying is taking place or that someone may be considering a violent act against a fellow student or students. While you really cannot be too careful in this day and age when it comes to student safety, students need to be reasonable about just how much privacy they should expect to receive while on school grounds — and this is perhaps even more true when it comes to the public school setting.

In closing, I do not believe this is the type of issue that warrants a formal, controversial change to school policy that may invoke even more ire and cause further division among students and faculty. Simply asking teachers to open their eyes and ears and report suspicious behavior or threats should encourage the same results of a formal policy, but without creating unnecessary strife and animosity between teachers and students.

Explanation and Score

Ideas and Analysis: 4: The main idea of this essay is that teachers should not have to be guided by a formal policy to maintain awareness about what goes on around them. This is a clear thesis that takes into account several perspectives (whether listening in is an invasion of privacy, whether doing so would help reduce bullying, etc.) while still offering up a solid solution of the author's own.

Development and Support: 4: The author supports her theory that simply asking teachers to be more vigilant and aware would likely have the same effect as a new policy, and with far less controversy, throughout the essay. She counters, for example, the argument about listening in being a large invasion of privacy by noting that privacy really should not be assumed in a school setting anyway. She also acknowledges the importance of teachers' remaining aware of the conversations had around the school building by noting that they should still do so as a matter of common sense while maintaining that there does not need to be a formal policy insisting upon it.

Organization: 4: This essay is well organized; it begins by expressing the author's sentiment that the issue at hand is really not one that warrants formal policy changes, and then it goes on to offer support for the main assertion in the subsequent paragraphs. At the end, the author reiterates her main point, bringing the argument successfully full circle.

Language Use and Conventions: 4: The author uses appropriate, easy-to-understand language to support her key points without sounding elementary or juvenile. The author's sentence structure is also varied and appropriate for an audience of students as well as educators.

999.

Student Essay

After a close consideration of the issue, I agree that the issue at hand is indeed controversial. Treating pregnant women with drugs that haven't been specifically tested on this population is undeniably risky, but so is running drug tests and trials on pregnant women without knowing how the drugs will affect the mother or the unborn child.

Since it does appear that pregnant women have become "human guinea pigs" anyway, why not conduct formal testing on these women who are choosing to take the risk anyway? Doing so would, at the very least, provide important information future generations of pregnant women can then use to make their own informed decisions about the safety and effectiveness of morning sickness drugs. Ultimately, many of these women are faced with an unpleasant choice: Take a risky prescription drug that would at least allow them to eat and provide their baby with nourishment, or forgo the drug and struggle to give the child the nutrients it needs to grow and thrive. I'm willing to guess that many of those women who elect to take the drug would be more than willing to take part in a clinical evaluation if it meant helping save other babies and mothers from similar problems moving forward.

Some people who oppose using drugs for off-label purposes argue that physicians who prescribe drugs for off-label use should be dealt with harshly. This sentiment fails to take into account that these drugs do help thousands of patients each year, and that many pregnant women wholeheartedly rely on them in order to hold food down and get enough nourishment to provide for their growing babies. There's also a chance that if prescription anti-nausea medications went away entirely, more women would turn to illicit drugs such as marijuana in an effort to achieve the same anti-nausea effects. Because so little evidence exists about pregnant women who use marijuana, no one can really say at this time just how dangerous choosing to do so could prove to be.

In closing, anti-nausea drugs are already being tested on pregnant women — just not in a controlled, clinical setting. Since some women believe that the pros of using these medications ultimately outweigh the cons, then why not have these women participate in formal trials and tests so we can at least help millions of pregnant women and pregnant women-to-be in the future?

Explanation and Score

Ideas and Analysis: 4: The author appropriately references the perspectives given when analyzing the issue at hand. Although the author's main idea is not largely different than that offered in Perspective 3, he does introduce some new and important ideas of his own to add strength to the existing argument.

Development and Support: 4: The essay author's overall sentiments do not stray too sharply from those made in Perspective 3. The author adds credence to the arguments that perspective makes, however, in noting that some expectant mothers may choose other potentially dangerous solutions to morning sickness, such as marijuana usage, as opposed to prescription drugs and that no one really knows how those options would affect the population in question. The author also offers reasoning for why some women are willing to risk taking these anti-nausea medications when he notes that failing to do so could mean a growing fetus does not receive the nutrients it needs to grow and thrive.

Organization: 5: The essay author first acknowledges the controversy surrounding the issue of pregnant women taking anti-nausea drugs for off-label purposes and then delves into his theory that, because these women are essentially serving as test subjects anyway, why not conduct a formal trial that could help future generations? He again references other perspectives before reiterating his own and effectively closing the essay.

Language Use and Conventions: 5: The language used in this essay is mature and concise, and it maintains a consistent tone throughout the essay. The author also expands upon terminology used in some of the other perspectives provided ("human guinea pigs," "off-label drugs," etc.) and explains the terms further and more clearly than is done in the perspectives.

1000.

Student Essay

The issue of whether transgendered individuals should be allowed to use whatever public restroom they feel is right has indeed increasingly become a hot-button issue, with everyone from celebrities to political hopefuls weighing in on how they feel about it. Like most hot-button issues, however, it isn't a black-and-white one, and that is why finding a "correct" answer is particularly difficult. One common argument suggests that transgendered people should simply use whichever bathroom corresponds with their anatomy. For the sake of argument, however, let's say someone born a woman has yet to undergo gender reassignment surgery but otherwise lives as a man. According to this sentiment, this person should still join the girls in the women's restroom — even though the urinals aren't there, and this person may or may not be dressed in women's attire. My point is, there is a lot to consider, and it seems silly to base a policy simply on whether someone has or has not had a particular part of their body removed or modified.

Some say that transgendered individuals ought to have the right to use whichever bathroom they choose based on how they choose to identify. In my opinion, this opens doors for problems, many of which have nothing to do with the actual transgendered population. I feel this opens up a loophole for child predators and the like, who could arguably say that their presence in a child of the opposite sex's restroom is a matter of choice and freedom — the same freedom that transgendered individuals are granted.

I know that all kinds of laws currently apply to businesses that reach certain sizes, dictating everything from how employers must pay their employees overtime to whether someone can be discriminated against because of his or her age. Since so many guidelines already exist for businesses that grow to a particular size, why not make one of those laws dictate how big a company must be before it needs to offer a unisex bathroom? Meanwhile, smaller businesses that cannot afford multiple bathrooms can offer restrooms intended for use by all people, regardless of one's gender or how he or she chooses to identify. I feel this is the most well-thought-out solution to the problem at hand, and it would also likely make far fewer waves within the community at large than trying to place all transgendered individuals into tight little categories.

Explanation and Score

Ideas and Analysis: 5: The author uses ideas and existing knowledge she has to build upon and offer credence to the sentiments offered in Perspective 3. For example, the author notes that businesses of certain sizes are already required to abide by many laws and that some ideas offered open up to the door to child predators. The author also closely examines the arguments made by the first and second perspectives and refutes and supports them appropriately.

Development and Support: 5: The author adequately backs up her assertions about the transgendered bathroom issue while introducing new information that supports his or her claims. For example, the author acknowledges the problems in letting people use whichever bathroom corresponds with how they choose to identify, and she also references some potential issues that could arise if transgendered individuals were simply made to use the bathroom that corresponds with their anatomy before reiterating her own proposed solution.

Organization: 5: All in all, this essay has a strong structure and is well organized. The author begins by acknowledging the controversial issue and then uses personal thoughts (for example, how some "solutions" may make it easier for pedophiles to find prey) to refute some other proposed solutions to the problem. The author then introduces a possible solution to the problem and uses personal knowledge about laws that pertain to businesses to offer a sensible, attainable solution to the problem.

Language Use and Conventions: 5: The author uses strong, formal language without making to too advanced for high school students. She also approaches the controversial issue in a tactful manner, using appropriate, nonoffensive terms.

1001.

Student Essay

Fast food industry workers have made a lot of noise in recent years, with much of the chatter focusing on the federal minimum wage, which is what many workers in the industry typically earn as a starting salary. Many feel those who work within the industry deserve a salary of at least $15 an hour, while others argue that this is more than many well-educated individuals with degrees are able to make on an hourly basis. In my opinion, fast food workers who work full-time, meaning they put in enough hours to secure benefits, should indeed receive raises. However, a raise to $15 is too excessive. A more reasonable figure might be $9.50 or $10 an hour. The massive jump from the current minimum wage to $15 an hour is simply too much for many people to swallow, and I feel the true supporters of raising fast food workers' salaries would be better poised for a successful campaign if they scaled back the shock value a bit and didn't shoot for such a drastic spike. I also believe those in the industry who work part-time should not necessarily automatically receive the increased salary, as they are more likely to be young and inexperienced workers.

This solution is ideal because it puts more money back in the pockets of hard-working, but possibly less fortunate, Americans. It would also appease those who recommend raising fast food workers' wages, albeit to a lesser degree. Finally, it also lets some of the responsibility fall back on the government, because it would only apply to those who work full 40-hour-or-more work weeks. It would still be up to the government to boost the salary for part-time fast food workers when it feels the time is right. Those who dedicate 40 hours a week to these positions, however, would receive the money necessary to support their families while at the same time bringing more knowledge and experience to the industry.

Explanation and Score

Ideas and Analysis: 4: The author clearly considered each perspective offered before creating a new idea that combines some of the key points already made. The author's primary point centers on a new idea: that those who devote most of their lives to a fast food job — meaning those who are employed full-time — should indeed receive at least a living wage, while offering some ideas of what this wage should probably be. The author also notes that his proposed solution would help enhance the industry in additional ways, such as by "bringing more knowledge and experience to the industry."

Development and Support: 4: The author effectively backs up the points made throughout the essay while noting where the points made in other perspectives need support or additional guidance. For example, he notes that fast food workers do indeed probably deserve a raise but that they'd be more likely to succeed in their efforts if they asked for a more reasonable wage hike, such as one to $9.50 or $10 an hour. He also adds support to his own perspectives by adding information about how salary should be commensurate with the cost of living and how this solution still leaves some of the power to the government — referencing one of the points made in Perspective 3.

Organization: 5: The essay is well-organized and introduces the issue at hand only briefly before delving into the author's own feelings on the topic. It supports or refutes points made in other perspectives before repeating a proposed solution and offering details to back it up. The author then closes the essay with a summary of how his proposed solution would enhance the industry as a whole, bringing the argument full circle and adding credence to the points made.

Language Use and Conventions: 5: The author maintains a mature and consistent tone throughout the essay. Though the language used is adult and appropriate, it is not so complex that younger readers would have trouble understanding the points and arguments made.

Index

C

D

E

F

G

H

I

K

L

M

N

O

P

Q

R

S

T

V

W

About the Authors

Lisa Zimmer Hatch, MA, and **Scott A. Hatch, JD,** have been preparing teens and adults to excel on standardized tests, gain admission to colleges of their choice, and secure challenging and lucrative professional careers since 1987. For virtually 30 years, they have administered their award-winning standardized test-preparation and professional career courses for live college lectures, online forums, and other formats through more than 300 universities worldwide.

Lisa and Scott have taught students internationally through live lectures, online forums, DVDs, and independent study opportunities. They have written the curriculum for all formats, and their books have been translated for international markets. Together they have authored numerous law and standardized test-prep texts, including *ACT For Dummies*, *GMAT For Dummies*, *LSAT For Dummies*, *SAT II U.S. History For Dummies*, *SAT II Biology For Dummies*, *Catholic High School Entrance Exams For Dummies*, and *Paralegal Career For Dummies* (Wiley).

Lisa is currently an independent educational consultant and the president of College Primers, where she applies her expertise to guiding high school and college students through the testing, admissions, and financial aid processes. She dedicates herself to helping students gain admission to the colleges or programs that best fit their goals, personalities, and finances. She graduated with honors in English from the University of Puget Sound and received a master's degree in humanities with a literature emphasis from California State University. She has completed the UCLA College Counseling Certificate Program and is a member of Higher Education Consultants Association (HECA).

Scott received his undergraduate degree from the University of Colorado and his Juris Doctor from Southwestern University School of Law. He is listed in *Who's Who in California* and *Who's Who Among Students in American Colleges and Universities* and was named one of the Outstanding Young Men of America by the United States Junior Chamber (Jaycees). He was also a contributing editor to the *Judicial Profiler* and *Colorado Law Annotated* and has served as editor of several national award-winning publications. His current books include *A Legal Guide to Probate and Estate Planning* and *A Legal Guide to Family Law*, which are the inaugural texts in B & B Publication's Learn the Law series.

Authors' Acknowledgments

This book wouldn't be possible without the contributions of Will Dewispelaere, Julia Brabant, Zachary Hatch, Zoe Hatch, and Hank Zimmer, who provided practice test material and helpful input. We also acknowledge the input of the thousands of students who've completed our test-preparation courses and tutorials over the last 30 years. The classroom and online contributions offered by these eager learners have provided us with lots of information about what areas require the greatest amount of preparation.

Our project organization and attempts at wit were greatly facilitated by the editing professionals at Wiley. Our thanks go out to Tim Gallan and Lindsay Lefevere for their patience and guidance throughout the process and to Megan Knoll for her attention to detail and helpful suggestions during the editing process.

Finally, we wish to thank our literary agent, Margo Maley Hutchinson, at Waterside Productions in Cardiff for her support and assistance and for introducing us to the innovative *For Dummies* series.

We thrive on feedback from our students and encourage our readers to email their comments and critiques to `info@hatchedu.com`.

Dedication

We dedicate *1,001 ACT Practice Questions For Dummies* to our incredibly talented and supportive children and grandchildren. We're very blessed to have them in our lives.

Publisher's Acknowledgments

Executive Editor: Lindsay Sandman Lefevere

Project Editor: Tim Gallan

Copy Editor: Megan Knoll

Technical Reviewer: Cindy Kaplan

Art Coordinator: Alicia B. South

Production Editor: Siddique Shaik

Cover Image: JoeLena/iStockphoto

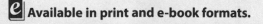

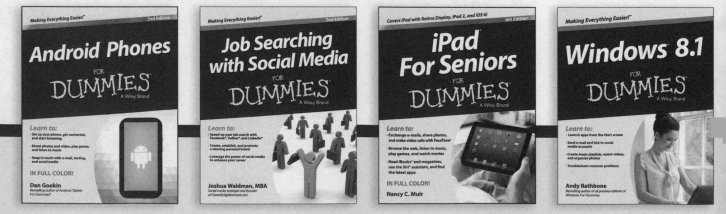

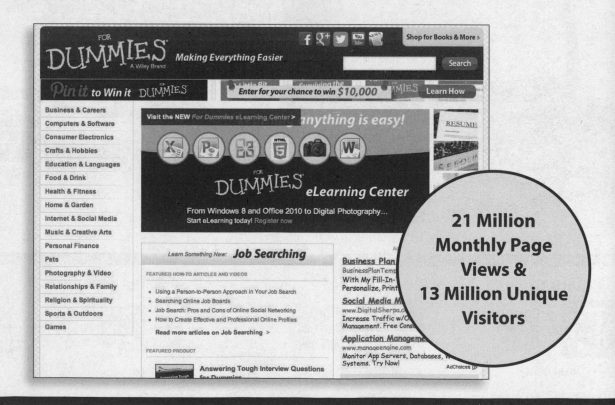